Biographical Directory of American Colonial and Revolutionary Governors 1607-1789

Biographical Directory of American Colonial and Revolutionary Governors 1607-1789

by

John W. Raimo

MECKLER BOOKS
A Division of Microform Review
520 Riverside Ave.
Westport, CT 06880

Library of Congress Cataloging in Publication Data

Raimo, John, 1946-
Biographical directory of American colonial and Revolutionary governors, 1607-1789.

Bibliography: p.
Includes index.
1. Governors—United States—Biography.
2. United States—Politics and government—Colonial period, ca. 1600-1775. 3. United States—Politics and government—Revolution, 1775-1783.
4. United States—Politics and government—1783-1789. I. Title.
E187.5.R34 973'.09'92 [B] 80-13279
ISBN 0-930466-07-1

ISBN 0-930466-07-1

Meckler Books, *A Division of Microform Review Inc.*
520 Riverside Avenue
Westport, Conn. 06880
Printed in United States of America

CONTENTS

For Susan

ACKNOWLEDGEMENT

A number of major libraries on both sides of the Atlantic graciously provided me access to rare historical and genealogical material during my work on this volume. The Alexander Library at Rutgers University, the Boston Public Library, the British Library in London, and the New York Public Library (especially its Local History and Genealogy Division) were all admirably helpful in this regard. I would also like to thank John Walsh, the editor-in-chief at Meckler Books, for his typically intelligent reading of the text, and for his useful advice on format. Finally, besides displaying an exceptional patience in awaiting the finished typescript, the publisher Alan Meckler generously financed several research trips needed to bring this project to a conclusion.

John W. Raimo

INTRODUCTION

Any reference work which seeks to give brief biographical sketches of the men who served as governors between 1607 and 1789 must begin by considering what criteria ought to be used to define that term.[1] In this volume the word governor has been interpreted, broadly speaking, to include anyone who held effective executive power in those British colonies which in 1776 became the first thirteen states. Thus, deputy, lieutenant and acting governors appear here, provided that they served in place of chief executives who were deceased, resident in Great Britain, or *en route* to an assignment. Also mentioned are presidents of the various Committees and Councils of Safety during the American Revolution, men who sometimes possessed significant authority, albeit among only a segment of the population.

There are, however, several circumstances where it seemed advisable to exclude individuals who technically presided as acting governor. Often, a resident chief executive would leave his colony for periods ranging from several days to a number of months, placing in charge of the administration an official who was empowered to govern in his absence. These substitutes, generally presidents of the Council, were limited to only routine duties, and rarely had any important impact on events during their brief tenure.[2] Similarly, although they also theoretically acted as "chief executive" while the meetings were in session, the heads of the various provincial conventions and congresses which sat between 1774 and 1777 are not mentioned here, since their ability to formulate policy on their own account was nominal.[3]

Users of this volume should also remember that there are a number of ways to determine the beginning of a royal governor's term in office. As Charles Andrews has noted,[4] five different dates might conceivably be given, covering the period between the granting of the appointment in England and the actual proclamation of the formal commission in the colony. As a rule, the present study has assumed that a royal governor's administration commenced when he began to perform his executive functions in America. (Biographies of governors who served in more than one colony appear in each colony, under the first term of office).

Several other points ought to be mentioned in closing. First, dates given in these biographies are only in New Style *after* 1752, when the Gregorian calendar was adopted in England. Throughout the work, however, each year starts with January 1 instead of March 25, thereby making an Old Style reference to a date such as February 20, 1644/5 read February 20, 1645. Second, suggested items for further reading are divided into two separate sections. Virtually every biography contains references to published (and often unpublished) sources which pertain either to that individual or to his ancestry. These citations are supplemented by other bibliographies, preceding each colony and at the end of this introduction, suggesting works of a more general nature. Finally, it should be noted that the information on family background contained here, while the result of extensive research in a wide range of genealogical studies and colonial records, is only as accurate as the documentation on which it is based. Specialists in early American history have always realized that the reliability of vital statistics varies greatly from colony to colony, and that genealogy is a field which presents more than the usual number of scholarly pitfalls. Nevertheless, it is hoped that the data included in this volume, especially by illustrating the importance of family ties in areas such as political advancement, will stimulate new explorations along these lines.

John W. Raimo

1. Two useful lists of colonial governors appear in David Hawke, *The Colonial Experience* (Indianapolis, 1966), pp. 686-98, and Charles M. Andrews, "List of the Commissions and Instructions Issued to the Governors . . . 1609 to 1784," American Historical Association *Report* for 1911, I (1913), 393-528. The present work is based on these along with other, more specialized lists published in various state directories and scholarly journals.

2. There are occasional exceptions to this rule. For example, James Habersham (Georgia, 1771-73), Giles Brent (Maryland, 1643-44) and Spencer Phips (Massachusetts Bay, 1749-53 and 1756-57) are all included here, because each of these acting governors administered his colony's affairs while its commissioned chief executive remained abroad for more than one year.

3. For the names of these men and the dates of the meetings called under their supervision, the reader should consult Roy Glashan, *American Governors and Gubernatorial Elections, 1775-1978* (Westport, Conn., 1979).

4. Andrews, *ibid.*, p. 396.

BIBLIOGRAPHY

Alden, John Richard, *The South in the Revolution, 1763-1789* (Baton Rouge, 1957).

Andrews, Charles M., "List of the Commissions and Instructions Issued to the Governors . . . 1609 to 1784," American Historical Association, *Annual Report for the Year 1911*, I (Washington, D.C., 1913), 393-528.

Biographical Directory of the American Congress, 1774-1971 (Washington, D.C., 1971).

Burke, Sir Bernard, *A Genealogical History of the Dormant, Abeyant, Forfeited, and Extinct Peerages of the British Empire* (London, 1883).

Burke, John, *A Genealogical and Heraldic History of the Commoners of Great Britain and Ireland* . . ., 4 vols. (London, 1833-38).

Burke's Genealogical and Heraldic History of the Peerage, Baronetage and Knightage, 105th ed. (London, 1970).

Burns, J. F., *Controversies between Royal Governors and Their Assemblies in the Northern American Colonies* (Boston, 1923).

Crane, Verner W., *The Southern Frontier, 1670-1732* (Durham, N.C., 1928).

Craven, Wesley Frank, *The Southern Colonies in the Seventeenth Century, 1607-1689* (Baton Rouge, 1949).

Dexter, Franklin Bowditch, *Biographical Sketches of the Graduates of Yale College . . .[1701-1815]*, 6 vols. (New York, 1885-1912).

Doyle, J. A., *English Colonies in America*, 5 vols. (New York, 1889-1907).

Dunbar, Louise B., "The Royal Governors in the Middle and Southern Colonies on the Eve of the Revolution: A Study in Imperial Personnel," in Richard B. Morris, ed., *The Era of the American Revolution: Studies Inscribed to Evarts Boutell Greene* (New York, 1939).

Fennelly, Catherine M., "Royal Governors, 1770-1775," unpub. Ph.D. diss., Yale University, 1946.

Greene, Evarts B., *The Provincial Governor in the English Colonies of North America* (New York, 1898).

Greene, Jack P., *The Quest for Power: The Lower Houses of Assembly in the Southern Royal Colonies, 1689-1776* (Chapel Hill, 1963).

Heitman, Francis B., *Historical Register of Officers of the Continental Army* (Washington, D.C., 1914)..

Hinshaw, William Wade, *Encyclopedia of American Quaker Genealogy*, vol. II [New Jersey and Pennsylvania] (comp. by Thomas Worth Marshall) (Ann Arbor, 1938).

Kaye, Percy Lewis, *The Colonial Executive Prior to the Restoration*, in *Johns Hopkins University Studies in Historical and Political Science*, XVIII (1900), 255-338.

Kimball, Gertrude S., ed., *Correspondence of William Pitt, when Secretary of State, with Colonial Governors and Military and Naval Commissioners in America*, 2 vols. (New York, 1906).

Labaree, Leonard W., "The Early Careers of the Royal Governors," in *Essays in Colonial History Presented to Charles McLean Andrews by His Students* (New York and London, 1931).

———. *Royal Government in America* (New Haven, 1930).

———. "The Royal Governors of New England," *Publications of the Colonial Society of Massachusetts*, vol. XXXII (1936), 120-31.

———. ed., *Royal Instructions to the British Colonial Governors, 1670-1776*, 2 vols. (New York and London, 1935).

Lovejoy, David S., *The Glorious Revolution in America* (New York, 1972).

McAnear, Beverley, *The Income of the Colonial Governors of British North America* (New York, 1967).

MacKenzie, George Norbury, ed., *Colonial Families of the United States of America*, 7 vols. (reprint: Baltimore, 1966).

Macmillan, Margaret B., *The War Governors in the American Revolution* (New York, 1943).

Nevins, Allan, *The American States during and after the Revolution, 1775-1789* (New York, 1924).

Savage, James, *A Genealogical Dictionary of the First Settlers of New England . . .*, 4 vols. (Boston, 1860-62).

Sibley, J. L., and C. K. Shipton, *Biographical Sketches of Graduates of Harvard University [1642-1760]*, 14 vols. (Cambridge and Boston, 1873-1968).

Waters, Henry F., *Genealogical Gleanings in England*, 2 vols. (Baltimore, 1969) [originally published in the *New England Historical and Genealogical Register* from July 1883 to January 1899].

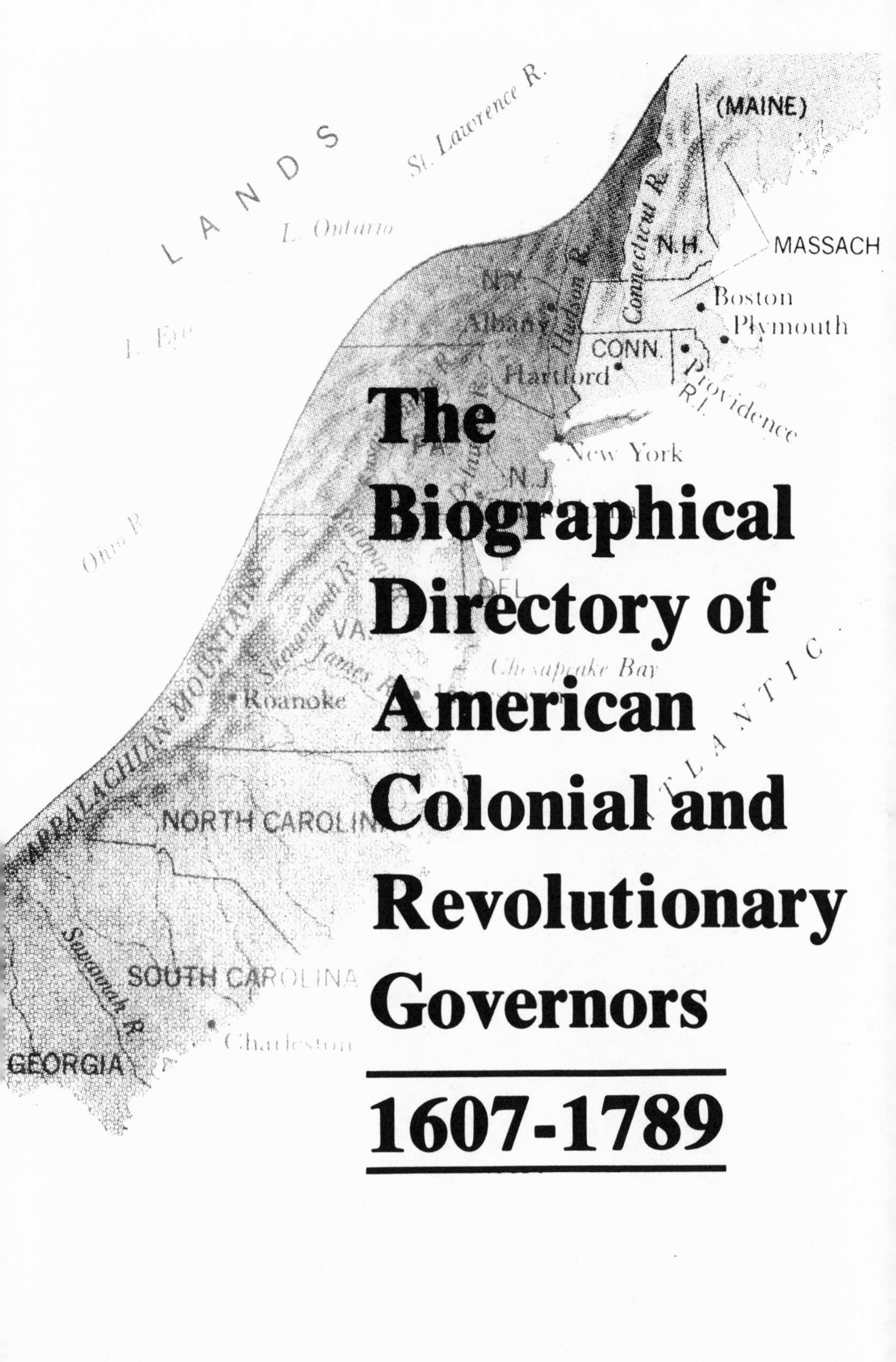

The Biographical Directory of American Colonial and Revolutionary Governors

1607-1789

CONNECTICUT

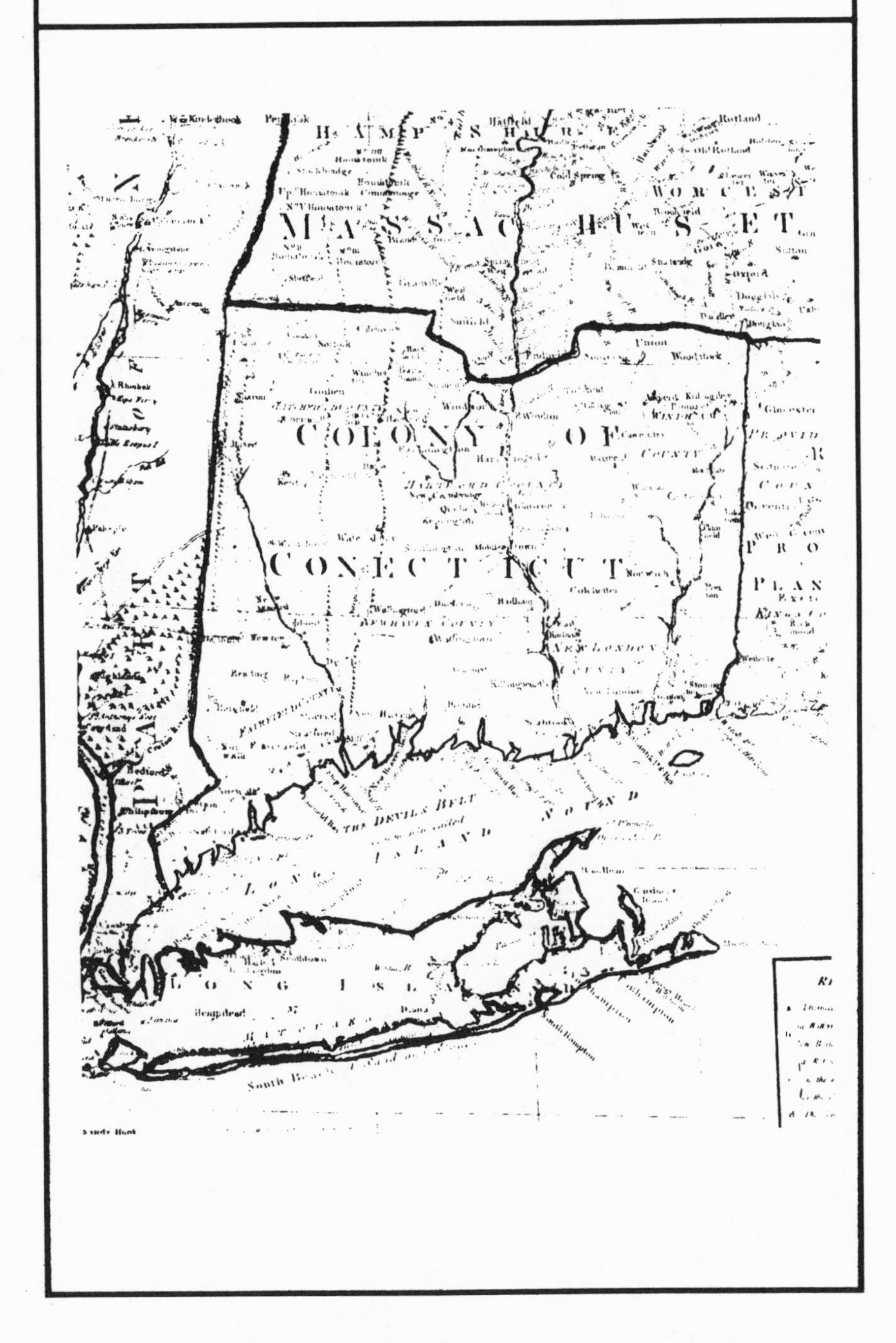

Chronology

1639-1640	John Haynes
1640-1641	Edward Hopkins
1641-1642	John Haynes
1642-1643	George Wyllys
1643-1644	John Haynes
1644-1645	Edward Hopkins
1645-1646	John Haynes
1646-1647	Edward Hopkins
1647-1648	John Haynes
1648-1649	Edward Hopkins
1649-1650	John Haynes
1650-1651	Edward Hopkins
1651-1652	John Haynes
1652-1653	Edward Hopkins
1653-1654	John Haynes
1654-1655	Edward Hopkins (*absent for this term*)
1655-1656	Thomas Welles
1656-1657	John Webster
1657-1658	John Winthrop, Jr.
1658-1659	Thomas Welles
1659-1676	John Winthrop, Jr.
1676-1683	William Leete
1683-1687	Robert Treat
1687-1689	Sir Edmund Andros
1689-1698	Robert Treat
1698-1707	Fitz-John Winthrop
1707-1724	Gurdon Saltonstall
1724-1741	Joseph Talcott
1741-1750	Jonathan Law
1750-1754	Roger Wolcott
1754-1766	Thomas Fitch
1766-1769	William Pitkin
1769-1784	Jonathan Trumbull
1784-1786	Matthew Griswold
1786-1796	Samuel Huntington

BIBLIOGRAPHY

Bushman, Richard L., *From Puritan to Yankee: Character and the Social Order in Connecticut, 1690-1765* (Cambridge, Mass., 1967).

Dinkin, Robert J., "The Nomination of Governor and Assistants in Colonial Connecticut," Connecticut Historical Society, *Bulletin*, 36 (July 1971), 92-96.

Goodwin, Nathaniel, *Genealogical Notes, or Contributions to the Family History of Some of the First Settlers of Connecticut and Massachusetts* (Hartford, 1856).

Hinman, R. R., ed., *Letters from the English Kings and Queens . . . to the Governors of Connecticut* (Hartford, 1836).

Hoadly, C. J., and L. W. Labaree, eds., *Public Records of the State of Connecticut [1776-1803]*, 11 vols. (Hartford, 1894-   ).

———. and J. H. Trumbull, eds., *The Public Records of the Colony of Connecticut, 1636-1776*, 15 vols. (Hartford, 1850-90).

Jones, Mary Jeanne Anderson, *Congregational Commonwealth: Connecticut, 1636-1662* (Middletown, Conn., 1968).

Norton, F. C., *The Governors of Connecticut* (Hartford, 1905).

Taylor, Robert J., *Colonial Connecticut: A History* (New York, 1979).

Trumbull, Benjamin, *A Complete History of Connecticut, Civil and Ecclesiastical . . .* (Hartford, 1797).

Zeichner, Oscar, *Connecticut's Years of Controversy, 1750-1776* (Chapel Hill, 1949).

CONNECTICUT

HAYNES, John, 1639-1640, 1641-1642, 1643-1644, 1645-1646, 1647-1648, 1649-1650, 1651-1652, 1653-1654
Massachusetts, 1635-1636

Born in April 1594, probably in Essex, England, the son of John and Mary (Mitchell) Haynes. A Congregationalist. Brother of Emanuel, Elizabeth, Mary, Margaret, Martha, Deborah, Sarah, Philadelphia, Anne and Priscilla. Married to Mary Thornton, by whom he had Robert, Hezekiah and Mary; remarried, apparently after the death of his first wife, to Mabel Harlakenden; father of John, Roger, Joseph, Ruth and Mabel by his second wife.

Immigrated to Massachusetts Bay in 1633 aboard the *Griffin*, arriving in September of that year. Chosen as an Assistant of the colony in May of 1634, and a year later, in May 1635, elected Governor of Massachusetts. Again became an assistant, following his replacement as chief executive by Henry Vane in May 1636. Moved to Connecticut in May 1637, and soon became a member of that colony's General Corte [Court]. Elected in April 1639 as Connecticut's first Governor under its "Fundamental Orders." Because of the stipulation that a chief executive could not serve two consecutive terms, reelected every alternate year through 1653; usually served as Deputy Governor when he was ineligible for the governorship.

During Haynes' brief tenure as governor of Massachusetts Bay, the colony endured considerable hardship, as its young economy was unable to keep pace with the wave of new emigrants from England. Indeed, by the end of 1635 a "great scarcity of Bread" had made it difficult for the towns in Massachusetts to feed their population. A short time later, however, the migration of settlers like Haynes to the Connecticut River Valley temporarily reduced this rapid rate of growth.

In Connecticut Haynes quickly won the prestige which he had enjoyed in the Bay Colony and, despite the requirement barring him from serving consecutive gubernatorial terms, he became one of its leading political figures. As governor, Haynes worked for the establishment of an alliance which would defend New England from attacks by both Indians and non-English settlers. The New England Confederation, established in 1643, was the culmination of these efforts, and Haynes took an active role in that body's deliberations on several subsequent occasions. Haynes also had a part in the prosecution of alleged witches living under his jurisdiction. In 1651, for example, he and two other Connecticut magistrates visited Stratford, where they judged a woman, Goody Bassett, guilty of witchcraft.

Haynes died in office early in January 1654, while Deputy Governor Edward Hopkins was residing in England. This crisis led the General Court to pass an amendment to the Fundamental Orders, permitting a majority of the magistrates to summon a Court in the absence of any higher authority.

Bibliography: "Will of Governor Haynes," *New England Historical and Genealogical Register*, XVI (April 1862), 167-69; "Papers Relating to the Haines Family," *New England Historical and Genealogical Register*, XXIV (October 1870), 422-24; "Material Relating to the Essex Family of Haynes," *New England Historical and Genealogical Register*, XLIX (July 1895), 304-10; Charles E. Cuningham, "John Haynes of Connecticut," *New England Quarterly*, XII (December 1939), 654-80. *DAB*, *DNB*.

HOPKINS, Edward, 1640-1641, 1644-1645, 1646-1647, 1648-1649, 1650-1651, 1652-1653

Born in 1600 in Shrewsbury, Salop, England, apparently the son of Edward (or Edmund) and Katherine (Lello) Hopkins. A Congregationalist. Brother of Henry, Matthew, Abigail, Margaret, Patience and Judith. Married to Ann Yale; most probably had no children.

Became a prominent London merchant as a young man, specializing in the Turkish trade. Immigrated to New England in 1637 and, after a brief stay in Boston, settled in the newly-established town of Hartford, Connecticut. Elected an Assistant of the colony in 1639, a position to which he was reelected in 1641, 1642, 1655 and 1656 (the last two times *in absentia*); served as Secretary of Connecticut in 1639 and 1640. Chosen Governor in April 1640, and reelected to that office in 1644, 1646, 1648, 1650, 1652 and 1654, although the colony was actually administered during his last term by Thomas Welles; also chosen Deputy Governor of the colony in 1643, 1645, 1647, 1649, 1651 and 1653.

Along with John Haynes, Hopkins was one of the two most respected political leaders in Connecticut during the 1640's and early 1650's. As governor, he was chiefly concerned with defending his colony against outside attack, an aim which was furthered by the establishment of the New England Confederation in 1643. Nevertheless, lack of cooperation between its members sometimes made the Confederation an ineffective deterrent, and relations with Indians and non-English settlers remained a major source of tension throughout Hopkins' tenure. In 1646, for example, the River Indians planned to murder Hopkins and several other Connecticut magistrates in retaliation for the colony's decision to protect Uncas, the Mohegan chief who was an ally of the colony. Although the plot failed, further instances of hostility from neighboring Indians, often apparently encouraged by the Dutch, continued to trouble Connecticut during these years.

Perhaps attracted to England by the opportunity to participate in the Commonwealth government, Hopkins left America in either 1652 or 1653. In December of 1652 he received an appointment as Navy Commissioner from Oliver Cromwell. By November of 1655 Hopkins had been named Commissioner of the Admiralty, and in 1656 he sat in the second Parliament held under the Protectorate as a representative of Dartmouth, Devonshire. Hopkins also inherited the offices of Warden of the Fleet and Keeper of the Palace of Westminster from his brother Henry, who probably died in early 1655. Hopkins himself died in London in March 1657, including in his will generous endowments for the promotion of education in New England.

Bibliography: Information on Hopkins and his family appears in the *New England Historical and Genealogical Register*, XXXVIII (July 1884), 315-16. *DAB, DNB*.

WYLLYS, George, 1642-1643

Born in 1589 or 1590 in Fenny Compton, Warwickshire, England, the son of Richard and Hester (Chambre) Willis. A Congregationalist. Married on November 2, 1609 to Bridget Young, by whom he was the father of George, Hester and Amy; within two years of his first wife's death in 1629, remarried to Mary (Smith) Bisbey; father by his second wife of Samuel. Belonged to the English gentry.

Immigrated to New England, probably in the early 1630's, and was serving as a member of the Massachusetts General Court by the spring of 1634; settled at Hartford, Connecticut in 1638. Elected as an Assistant of the Connecticut General Court in April 1639, and served until 1641. Chosen Deputy Governor of the colony in April 1641, and in April 1642 became Governor of Connecticut.

While he only served as chief executive for one year, Wyllys's period in office witnessed several significant developments. Perhaps the most troublesome was the persistent rumor that Miantonomo, sachem of the Narragansetts, planned to form an alliance of Indian tribes in the area, with the intention of destroying the English settlers. The plot, if it ever existed, never did result in warfare. Still, Connecticut's leaders had made extensive military preparations, and they were persuaded not to strike the first blow only after Massachusetts suggested that such an action would be premature. Politically, Wyllys's brief administration was marked by the important decision of the General Court to enact a penal code in December 1642, a code which included twelve capital offenses. Towards the end of the governor's term, the General

Court also took a step in the direction of greater inter-colonial cooperation, when it appointed John Haynes and Edward Hopkins as its commissioners to a meeting in Boston that eventually approved the Articles of Confederation between Massachusetts Bay, New Haven and Connecticut. (Plymouth Colony joined the alliance four months later.)

Following his gubernatorial service, Wyllys again became an assistant, a position which he held until his death in Hartford, Connecticut on March 9, 1645.

Bibliography: [''By a Descendant''], ''The First Wife of Governor Willys of Connecticut, and Her Family,'' *New England Historical and Genealogical Register*, LIII (April 1899), 217-24; Albert C. Bates, ed., *The Wyllys Papers: Correspondence and Documents Chiefly of Descendants of Gov. George Wyllys of Connecticut, 1590-1796* (in Connecticut Historical Society, *Collections*, XXI, Hartford, 1924); George Dudley Seymour, *Captain Nathan Hale . . . [and] . . . Major John Palsgrave Wyllys . . . A Digressive History . . .* (New Haven, 1933).

WELLES, Thomas, 1654-1656, 1658-1659

Born *circa* 1590 in England, the son of Robert and Alice Welles. A Congregationalist. Brother of Robert and perhaps others. Married soon after July 5, 1615 to Alice Tomes, by whom he was the father of John, Thomas, Samuel, Mary, Ann and Sarah; after the death of his first wife, remarried in about 1646 to Elizabeth (Deming) Foote; no children by his second wife.

Immigrated to New England, probably in late 1635, and had settled in Boston, Massachusetts by June 1636. Moved to Hartford, Connecticut a short time later, where he lived until he moved to Wethersfield following his second marriage. Named an Assistant of the Connecticut General Court in 1637, an office which he held until his death. Chosen Treasurer of Connecticut in 1639, and served for two years; also acted as treasurer from 1648 to 1652. Served as Secretary of the colony from April 1640 to 1648. Became a Commissioner of the United Colonies in 1649 and again in 1659, filling that office on each occasion for a term of one year. Elected Deputy Governor of Connecticut on a yearly basis in 1654 (when he also served as chief executive in the absence of Governor Hopkins), 1656, 1657 and 1659; elected Governor in 1655 and 1658.

During the 1650's Welles was perhaps the most prominent political figure in Connecticut, especially after the death of John Haynes in January 1654 and the departure of Edward Hopkins for England a short time earlier. Welles' years as chief executive were most noteworthy for the divisions which disrupted several of the colony's Congregational churches. Indeed, in the 1650's a schism had split the church in the governor's own home town of Wethersfield. Although the General Court was unsuccessful in its attempt to restore peace, the matter had resolved itself by the end of Welles' second period in office, when dissenting members from the affected congregations united to establish their own church in Hadley, Massachusetts, further up the Connecticut River.

Following his service as chief executive, Welles was reelected deputy governor in the spring of 1659, but he did not live to complete the term. He died in Wethersfield, Connecticut on January 14, 1660, and was probably buried in that community.

Bibliography: Lemuel A. Welles, "The English Ancestry of Gov. Thomas Welles of Connecticut," *New England Historical and Genealogical Register*, LXXX (July 1926), 279-305; Edwin Stanley Welles, *The Life and Public Services of Thomas Welles, Fourth Governor of Connecticut* (Wethersfield, Conn., 1940).*DNB*.

WEBSTER, John, 1656-1657

Names of parents and date and place of birth unknown, although he was apparently a native of Warwickshire, England. A Congregationalist. Married while in England to a woman named Agnes; father of Matthew, William, Thomas, Robert, Anne, Elizabeth and Mary.

Immigrated to New England, probably in the early 1630's; moved from Newtown (now Cambridge), Massachusetts in 1636, and took up residence in what is now Hartford, Connecticut. Became a member of the Connecticut General Court in 1637, and in 1638 was also chosen as a Deputy Commissioner. Served as an Assistant of the colony from 1639 until 1655, when he was named Deputy Governor; elected Governor of Connecticut in the spring of 1656.

In the 1650's Connecticut's Hartford and Wethersfield churches were affected by disputes over questions of church order, including a dispute over the eligibility requirements for infant baptism. Although a council met in Hartford to seek a solution to these differences in June 1656, the Hartford minister and his church refused to abide by the council's recommendations, and religious dissension persisted in the troubled colony.

Despite the fact that he had been named Connecticut's First Assistant following his year as governor, Webster in 1659 joined with those members of the Hartford church who had decided to unite with other dissidents and establish a new congregation in Hadley, Massachusetts. After he settled in Hadley, Webster was in May 1660 "commissioned with magistratticall power for the year ensuing" by the Massachusetts General Court, but he died on April 5, 1661, before his term had expired.

Bibliography: George E. Foster, *Pedigree of Jesse W. Foster, in Lines of Foster, Coggin, Farley, Phelps, Burritt, Curtiss, Lord, Smith, Webster, and Allied Families* (Ithaca, N.Y., 1897); A. W. Webster, *Genealogy of One*

Branch of the Webster Family, 1600 to 1900 (New Haven, *c*. 1900); William Holcomb Webster and Rev. Melville Reuben Webster, *History and Genealogy of the Gov. John Webster Family of Connecticut* . . . (Rochester, N.Y., 1915).

WINTHROP, John, Jr., 1657-1658, 1659-1676

Born on February 12, 1606 in Groton, Suffolk, England, the eldest son of Massachusetts Governor John and Mary (Forth) Winthrop. A Congregationalist. Brother of Henry, Forth, Mary, Anne (died in infancy) and Anne (who also died in infancy). Married on February 8, 1631 to Martha Fones, by whom he was the father of one daughter who died in infancy; after his first wife's death in the late summer of 1634, remarried in 1635 to Elizabeth Reade; father of Elizabeth, Fitz-John (governor of Connecticut from 1698 to 1707), Lucy, Wait-Still, Mary (died young?), Martha, Margaret and Anne by his second wife.

Attended the Free Grammar School of Bury St. Edmunds; later studied at Trinity College, Dublin, and in February 1625 was made a barrister by London's Inner Temple. Named Secretary to Captain Best of the Royal Navy in May 1627, and participated in the unsuccessful effort to relieve La Rochelle. Toured the Mediterranean for over a year during 1628 and 1629, and in August 1631 sailed for America, arriving in Boston in November of that year. Elected an Assistant of Massachusetts Bay in 1632, a position he held, though often *in absentia*, for eighteen years; also became one of the first settlers of Ipswich, Massachusetts in the summer of 1633. Left for England in October 1634, and was commissioned "governor of the river Connecticut" in July 1635, but this colonization scheme was never implemented in an effective manner following his return to America in October 1635. Resided in Ipswich (and later Salem), Massachusetts between 1636 and 1641; named Lieutenant Colonel of the Essex militia in the late 1630's. Developed an interest in various manufacturing projects in the 1640's; from 1641 to 1643 resided in England and Europe, where he sought to promote his proposals for the economic development of New England. Authorized in 1644 to establish iron works in Massachusetts and in the Pequot Country (later part of Connecticut), and for the next few years journeyed frequently between the two places. Elected an Assistant of Connecticut in May 1651 and, following a year's residence in New Haven Colony between 1656 and 1657, returned to Connecticut after being elected Governor of that colony in May 1657.

With the exception of 1658-59, when he served as Deputy Governor, Winthrop remained chief executive of Connecticut until 1676. During his long tenure the colony won perhaps its most notable political victory, when in 1662

Charles II granted Connecticut a charter that was especially generous in its provisions for self-rule. The popular Winthrop resided in England himself from 1661 to 1663, and the charter's liberal guarantees, along with its inclusion of the formerly distinct New Haven Colony within Connecticut's boundaries, were largely due to his skillful diplomacy at the Restoration Court. Elected to the Royal Society in January 1662 for his contributions to science, Winthrop returned to Connecticut the next year at the peak of his popularity. Until his death the grateful colony, despite his periodic requests to be relieved of the office, continued to choose Winthrop as chief executive. In 1675 he was still at the helm of the Connecticut government during the early stages of King Philip's War. His efforts to defend the colony impaired his health, however, and on April 5, 1676 Winthrop died in Boston, Massachusetts.

Bibliography: "The Winthrop Papers," Massachusetts Historical Society, *Collections*, especially 4th ser., vols. VI and VII (Boston, 1863, 1865) and 5th ser., vols. I and VIII (Boston, 1871, 1882); Thomas Franklin Waters, *A Sketch of the Life of John Winthrop the Younger, Founder of Ipswich, Massachusetts, in 1663* (Ipswich?, 1899); F. J. Kingsbury, "John Winthrop, Jr.," American Antiquarian Society, *Proceedings*, n.s., vol. XII (1899), 295-306; Walter R. Steiner, "Governor John Winthrop, Jr., of Connecticut, as a Physician," *Connecticut Magazine*, XI (1907), 25-42; Lawrence Shaw Mayo, *The Winthrop Family in America* (Boston, 1948); Richard S. Dunn, "John Winthrop, Jr., and the Narragansett Country," *William and Mary Quarterly*, 3rd ser., vol. XIII (January 1956), 68-86; Richard S. Dunn, "John Winthrop, Jr., Connecticut Expansionist: The Failure of His Designs on Long Island, 1663-1675," *New England Quarterly*, XXIX (March 1956), 3-26; Richard S. Dunn, *Puritans and Yankees: The Winthrop Dynasty of New England, 1630-1717* (Princeton, 1962); Robert C. Black, III, *The Younger John Winthrop* (New York, 1966); Malcolm Freiberg, "The Winthrops and Their Papers," Massachusetts Historical Society, *Proceedings*, LXXX (1968), 55-70; Ronald S. Wilkinson, "John Winthrop, Jr. and the Origins of American Chemistry," unpub. Ph.D. diss., Michigan State University, 1969. *DAB, DNB*.

LEETE, William, 1676-1683

New Haven, 1660-1664

Born *circa* 1613 in Dodington, Huntingdonshire, England, the son of John and Anna (Shute) Leete. A Congregationalist. Married to Anna Payne, by whom he was the father of John, Andrew, William, Abigail, Caleb, Graciana, Peregrine (died young), Joshua (died young) and Anne; after his first wife's death in 1668, remarried in 1671 to Sarah, the widow of Henry Rutherford;

following the death of his second wife in February 1674, married a third time to Mary, the widow of both Governor Francis Newman of New Haven Colony and the Reverend Nicholas Street; no children by his second and third wives.

Studied law in England, and worked for a time as Registrar in the Bishop's Court at Cambridge. Immigrated to America in May 1639; became one of the founders of the town of Guilford shortly after his arrival. Served as Town Clerk of Guilford from 1639 to 1662, and also represented Guilford in the Assembly after it came under the jurisdiction of the New Haven Colony. Selected as a Magistrate (Assistant) for New Haven in 1651, a position he held until his election as Deputy Governor in May 1658. Served as deputy governor until late 1660, when he replaced the deceased Governor Francis Newman. Chosen governor on an annual basis until 1664; resigned as chief executive of New Haven late in 1664, just before the final absorption of the colony by Connecticut. Elected an Assistant for Connecticut a short time later, and served in that capacity until he was named Deputy Governor in 1669. Succeeded the deceased John Winthrop, Jr. as Governor of Connecticut in the spring of 1676, an office he held until his own death.

Leete's tenure as governor of New Haven was troubled by increasing pressure from Connecticut, aimed at forcing the smaller colony to give up its autonomy. In 1662 any hopes that New Haven may have had for retaining its existence as a separate political unit were dealt a major blow, when Governor Winthrop of Connecticut secured a charter which included New Haven within his jurisdiction. Earlier, during the first part of his administration, Leete's efforts to counter this threat had been hampered by the presence in his colony of colonels Whalley and Goffe, two men who were wanted by Charles II for their part in the execution of his father. Although Leete probably did not personally protect the two regicides, his failure to prosecute them more vigorously aroused the displeasure of authorities in England.

More than eleven years after he had stepped down as the last governor of New Haven, Leete, in a moment of historical irony, was chosen to replace the man whose diplomacy had ended New Haven's history as a distinct colony. As chief executive of Connecticut, Leete's first responsibility was to bring King Philip's War to a successful conclusion. Within a few months that aim had been achieved, and for the next seven years he was largely concerned with refuting the charges of Edward Randolph, the Crown official who criticized Connecticut and the other New England colonies for their disregard of England's acts of trade and navigation. Leete died in office on April 16, 1683 in Hartford, Connecticut; he was buried in the cemetery of that town's First Church.

Bibliography: Bernard C. Steiner, "Governor William Leete and the Absorption of New Haven Colony by Connecticut," in American Historical Association, *Annual Report for 1891* (Washington, D.C., 1892), pp. 207-22; Joseph Leete, *The Family of Leete*, 2nd ed. (London, 1906). *DAB*.

TREAT, Robert, 1683-1687, 1689-1698

Born *circa* 1622 in Pitminster, Somerset, England, the second son of Richard and Alice (Gaylard) Treat [or Trott]. A Congregationalist. Brother of Richard, James, Honor, Joanna, Sarah, Susanna and Catherine. Married *circa* 1647 to Jane Tapp, by whom he was the father of Samuel, John, Mary, Robert, Sarah, Hannah, Joseph and Abigail; after his first wife's death in 1703, remarried on October 24, 1705 to Elizabeth (Powell) Hollingsworth Bryan; no children by his second wife.

Immigrated with his parents to America, probably late in the 1630's; later became one of the early settlers of the town of Milford in New Haven Colony. Was serving as a Deputy in the New Haven General Court by 1653, representing Milford; also named Lieutenant and Chief Military Officer of Milford in 1654. Selected as a Magistrate of New Haven Colony in 1659, a position which he held until he declined to serve in May 1664. Following the formal merger of New Haven with Connecticut in 1665, acted briefly as a member of the Connecticut General Assembly, but soon moved to Newark in East Jersey; served as a Deputy in the East Jersey Assembly from 1667 to 1672; also held office as Magistrate and Recorder of Newark. Returned to Connecticut early in the 1670's, and became an Assistant of that colony in 1673. From 1675 to 1676 played a major military role during King Philip's War, serving as Commander-in-Chief of the Connecticut forces deployed against the Indians. Elected Deputy Governor of Connecticut in May 1676, a position he retained until he succeeded the deceased Governor William Leete in April 1683.

Except for the period between November 1687 and the spring of 1689, when Sir Edmund Andros governed the colony as part of the Dominion of New England, Treat served as chief executive of Connecticut from 1683 to 1698. A political moderate, Treat agreed to serve as a member of Andros' Council during the eighteen months of Dominion rule, but he also wished to avoid unnecessary encroachment by Crown officials. Consequently, after the demise of Andros, Treat advocated resumption of government under Connecticut's old charter, a charter which had never been legally invalidated. The impressive victory by Treat in the gubernatorial election of May 1689 was a major triumph over both the conservative Gershom Bulkeley, who claimed that the overthrow of Andros had been illegitimate, and the popular James Fitch, who attacked Treat's complicity with the Dominion government.

Following his tenure as chief executive, the aged Treat continued to serve as deputy governor until 1708. He died on July 12, 1710.

Bibliography: John Harvey Treat, *The Treat Family* (Salem, Mass., 1893); George W. Solley, "Major Robert Treat," Pocumtuck Valley Memorial Association, *Proceedings*, V (1912), 62-78; George Hare Ford, "Robert Treat, Founder, Farmer, Soldier, Statesman, Governor," New Haven Colony Historical Society, *Papers*, VIII (April 1914), 163-80; Charles A. Scully, *Robert Treat, 1622-1710* (Philadelphia, 1959). *DAB*.

ANDROS, Sir Edmund, 1687-1689

New York, 1674-1677, 1678-1681; East Jersey, 1680-1681, 1688-1689; Massachusetts, 1686-1689; New Hampshire, 1686-1689; Plymouth Colony, 1686-1689; Rhode Island, 1686-1689; West Jersey, 1688-1689; Virginia, 1692-1698; Maryland, 1693, 1694

Born on December 6, 1637 on the Island of Guernsey, the son of Amice and Elizabeth (Stone) Andros. Married to a woman who was related to the Earl of Craven.

Served as Major of a regiment of foot soldiers which in 1666 sailed from England to defend the West Indies against the Dutch. Named a Landgrave of Carolina in 1672; received a commission from the Duke of York in July 1674 to govern the colony of New York, and acted in that capacity, except for an absence in England between November 1677 and August 1678, until January 1681; also exercised control over East Jersey from 1680 until his recall early in the following year. Knighted in about 1681, became Gentleman of the Privy Chamber to Charles II in 1683, and was appointed Lieutenant Colonel of the Princess of Denmark's regiment of horse soldiers in 1685. Commissioned Royal Governor of the Dominion of New England in June 1686, and established his authority in Massachusetts Bay, Maine, New Hampshire, Plymouth and Rhode Island (including the King's Province) in December of that year; Connecticut in November of 1687; and the Jerseys and New York in August 1688 (although Francis Nicholson presided as Andros' substitute in the latter colony). Arrested and sent to England following the overthrow of the Dominion in the spring of 1689, but later received a commission as Royal Governor of Virginia, and served as that colony's chief executive from September 1692 to December 1698; also acted briefly as Governor of Maryland in 1693 and 1694, in the absence of any other executive authority.

Andros' first tenure in New York was marked by several important achievements, especially the improvement of the colony's defenses and the settlement of some boundary difficulties with Connecticut. Nevertheless, even at this stage he had begun to display an inclination to behave in an arbitrary fashion. Perhaps the clearest illustration of this tendency was the high-handed manner in which Andros superseded the authority of Governor Philip Carteret in the Jerseys, provoking Carteret to complain that Andros aimed at "usurping the government" of his colony. This insensitivity to local politics became even more noticeable after Andros assumed control of the Dominion of New England. Following a troubled tenure of less than two and one-half years, he was deposed in the spring of 1689, shortly after news of the Glorious Revolution in England reached Boston.

Although Andros was exonerated of the charges brought against his Dominion government and took over as Virginia's chief executive in 1692, he soon encountered resistance from local leaders like Commissary James Blair, who bitterly informed one London official that Andros "never did any considerable service to the King, nor the people" during his colonial career. Finally, late in 1698, Andros departed for England. He served as Lieutenant Governor of Guernsey from 1704 to 1706, and died in London in February 1714.

Bibliography: "Commission to Sir Edmund Andros," Massachusetts Historical Society, *Collections*, 3rd ser., vol. VII (Boston, 1838), 138-49; W. H. Whitmore, ed., *Andros Tracts: Being a Collection of Pamphlets and Official Papers ... of the Andros Government and the Establishment of the Second Charter of Massachusetts*, 3 vols. (New York, 1868-74) (Publications of the Prince Society, vols. V-VII); Robert N. Toppan, ed., "Andros Records," American Antiquarian Society, *Proceedings*, n.s., vol. XIII (1899-1900), 237-68, 463-99; J.H. Tuttle, ed., "Land Warrants under Andros," Colonial Society of Massachusetts, *Publications*, XXI (1919), 292-361; Albert C. Bates, "Expedition of Sir Edmund Andros to Connecticut in 1687," AAS, *Proceedings*, n.s., vol. 48 (October 1938), 276-99; Jeanne G. Bloom, "Sir Edmund Andros: A Study in Seventeenth-Century Colonial Administration," unpub. Ph.D. diss., Yale University, 1962; Robert C. Ritchie, "London Merchants, the New York Market, and the Recall of Sir Edmund Andros," *New York History*, LVII (January 1976), 5-29. *DAB*, *DNB*.

WINTHROP, John (Fitz-John), 1698-1707

Born on March 14, 1638 in Ipswich, Massachusetts, the son of John Winthrop, Jr. and Elizabeth (Reade) Winthrop. A Congregationalist. Brother of Elizabeth, Lucy, Wait-Still, Mary (died young?), Martha, Margaret and Anne. Apparently entered a common-law marriage with Elizabeth Tongue in the 1670's, by whom he was the father of Mary.

Tutored for a year by Thomas Dudley to prepare him for Harvard College, but never received a degree. Sailed for England in 1657, where he joined Cromwell's Army; eventually attained the rank of Captain. Returned to America in April 1663 and settled in New London, Connecticut. Served as a Deputy in the Connecticut General Assembly in 1671 and 1678; also took part in various military campaigns during the 1670's. Lived in Boston, Massachusetts on a part-time basis after 1676, and became a member of the Council under Joseph Dudley's provisional government in 1686; continued to serve on the Council during the administration of Sir Edmund Andros, although his attendance at Council meetings during this period was sporadic, due to his decision to reside in Connecticut for most of the year. Passively accepted the overthrow of Andros in the spring of 1689; chosen as an Assistant for Connecticut in May 1689 and from May 1693 to May 1697, but never served in that capacity. Acted as Major

General and Commander of a military force which unsuccessfully attempted to capture Montreal in 1690. Sailed for London in the autumn of 1693 and eventually won royal confirmation of Connecticut's charter, a diplomatic triumph which greatly enhanced his stature following his return to that colony early in 1698. Chosen Governor of Connecticut in May 1698, and reelected annually until May of 1707.

Winthrop's tenure as chief executive of Connecticut commenced on an optimistic note, when in 1698 the colony's Assembly broadened his authority to act between legislative sessions. By 1700, however, the governor's efforts to revamp the political and judicial structure of Connecticut had begun to encounter serious criticism from men like James Fitch, who opposed any changes which might threaten the power of his democratic faction. The outbreak of war with France in 1702 also damaged Winthrop's popularity, as neighboring governors, especially Joseph Dudley of Massachusetts, repeatedly charged Connecticut with failing to contribute its quota of military assistance. Although by 1707 opposition both in and outside of Connecticut had become less vociferous, Winthrop was unable to enjoy the politically tranquil atmosphere for long. He died in Boston on November 27 of that year, while still in office.

Bibliography: Robert C. Winthrop, *A Short Account of the Winthrop Family* (Cambridge, 1887); J. C. Frost, *Ancestors of Henry Rogers Winthrop and His Wife Alice Woodward Babcock* (New York?, 1927); Lawrence Shaw Mayo, *The Winthrop Family in America* (Boston, 1948); Richard S. Dunn, *Puritans and Yankees: The Winthrop Family of New England, 1630-1717* (Princeton, 1962). The papers of Fitz-John Winthrop, covering primarily his years as governor of Connecticut, are printed in the Massachusetts Historical Society, *Collections*, 6th ser., vol. III (Boston, 1889)—but see also *Collections*, 5th ser., vol. VIII (Boston, 1882) for letters of an earlier date.

SALTONSTALL, Gurdon, 1707-1724

Born on March 27, 1666 in Haverhill, Massachusetts, the eldest son of Nathaniel and Elizabeth (Ward) Saltonstall. A Congregationalist. Brother of Elizabeth, Richard, Nathaniel and John (died young). Married to Jerusha Richards, by whom he was the father of Elizabeth, Mary, Sarah, Jerusha (died in infancy), and Gurdon (died in infancy); after the death of his first wife in July 1697, remarried to Elizabeth Rosewell, by whom he had Rosewell, Katherine, Nathaniel, Gurdon and Richard (died in infancy); married a third time, following the death of his second wife in September 1710, to Mary (Whittingham) Clarke; no children by his third wife.

Graduated from Harvard College in 1684, and in 1691 was selected minister of the Congregational Church in New London, Connecticut. Became a close friend and confidant of Fitz-John Winthrop, who governed Connecticut from 1698 to 1707. In December 1707, three weeks after the death of Winthrop, received (and later accepted) an offer from the Connecticut General Assembly to take office as Acting Governor. Chosen Governor in his own right the following May, and reelected on an annual basis until his death.

Despite his clerical background and his relative inexperience in political matters, Saltonstall proved to be an effective chief executive. His prowess as a tactician was perhaps best demonstrated in 1719, when he defeated a movement led by Timothy Woodbridge and Thomas Buckingham, two ministers who tried to deny the governor reelection after he supported New Haven as the permanent site of Yale College. Still, religion and church government were always the dominant themes of Saltonstall's administration. In 1708 a synod meeting at Saybrook recommended, among other proposals, a closer union of the Congregational churches in Connecticut, the effect of which was to move the colony's major religious group toward a more Presbyterian form of organization. Saltonstall strongly endorsed this "Saybrook Platform," and at the time of his death from apoplexy on September 20, 1724, the provisions which it contained had become an enduring part of Connecticut Congregationalism.

Bibliography: Eliphalet Adams, *A Funeral Discourse Occasioned by the Much Lamented Death of the Honorable Gurdon Saltonstall* ... (New London, 1724); Cotton Mather, *Decus ac Tutamen. A Brief Essay ... in Commemoration of ... Gurdon Saltonstall* (New London, 1724); "Gov. Saltonstall's Warrant for Calling in the Indians," *New England Historical and Genealogical Register*, XXV (January 1871), 78-81; S. Leroy Blake, "Gurdon Saltonstall, Scholar, Preacher, Statesman," *Records and Papers of the New London County Historical Society*, vol. I, pt. V (1894), 3-28; Leverett Saltonstall, *Ancestry and Descendants of Sir Richard Saltonstall* ... (Cambridge, 1897). *DAB*.

TALCOTT, Joseph, 1724-1741

Born in November 1669 in Hartford, Connecticut, the son of Lieutenant Colonel John and Helena (Wakeman) Talcott. A Congregationalist. Brother of John (died young), John, Elizabeth, Samuel, Mary, Hannah, Dorothy and Helena. Married in 1693 to Abigail Clarke, by whom he had John, Joseph and Nathan; after the death of his first wife in 1705, remarried in June 1706 to Eunice (Howell) Wakeman; father of Abigail, Eunice, Matthew, Samuel, Jerusha and Helen by his second wife.

Played an active part in Connecticut's military affairs throughout most of his career, rising to the rank of Major by 1710. Also served in a judicial capacity on a number of occasions; became Justice of the Peace for Hartford County in May 1705; named Judge of the Hartford County Court and Judge of the Court of Probate in May 1714; promoted to Judge of the Connecticut Superior Court in May 1721. First elected as a Deputy from Hartford to the Connecticut General Assembly in October 1708; chosen as Speaker of the Lower House in 1710. Served as an Assistant in the legislature's Upper House from 1711 to October 1723, when he was named Deputy Governor. Chosen by the Assembly in October 1724 to succeed the deceased Governor Gurdon Saltonstall; elected Governor in his own right in May 1725, and reelected annually until his death.

Talcott's tenure as chief executive of Connecticut, which was exceeded in length only by that of John Winthrop, Jr., was marked by disputes over both monetary policy and religious revivalism. By the early 1730's Connecticut merchants were seeking ways of establishing direct commercial ties with Europe, ties which would eliminate the need to employ agents from neighboring colonies. In 1732 the New London Society for Trade and Commerce was created in order to accomplish this aim. However, the bills of credit issued to finance the ventures of the Society were attacked by those who feared the effects of cheap paper money, and Talcott was forced to suspend its charter. Almost a decade later Connecticut became the stage for religious excitement, as George Whitefield, the young English revivalist, visited the colony during a tour of New England in 1740. Although Talcott welcomed Whitefield's activities, the aged governor died on October 11, 1741,* just as the divisiveness caused by the Great Awakening was becoming a seriously disruptive force in Connecticut's religious life.

Bibliography: S. V. Talcott, comp., *Talcott Pedigree in England and America from 1558 to 1876* (Albany, 1876); Mary Kingsbury Talcott, ed., *The Talcott Papers: Correspondence and Documents (Chiefly Official) During Joseph Talcott's Governorship of the Colony of Connecticut, 1724-1741* (in Connecticut Historical Society, *Collections*, IV and V, Hartford, 1892-96). *DAB*.

*The *DAB* erroneously gives the date of Talcott's death as November 11, 1741.

LAW, Jonathan, 1741-1750

Born on August 6, 1674 in Milford, Connecticut, the only son of Jonathan and Sarah (Clark) Law. A Congregationalist. Married on December 20, 1698 to Ann Eliot, by whom he was the father of Jahleel (died young), Sarah (died young) and Ann; following the death of his first wife, remarried four times—on February 14, 1705 to Abigail Arnold, by whom he had Jonathan; on August 1, 1706 to Abigail Andrew, by whom he was the father of Jahleel, Abigail, Samuel and Richard (died young); in 1726 to Mrs. Sarah Burr; and in 1730 to Eunice (Hall) Andrew, by whom he was the father of Sarah (died young), Richard, John and Sarai.

Studied at Harvard College, graduating from that institution in 1695; awarded an A.M. from Harvard in 1729. Admitted to the Connecticut bar in 1708 and pursued a judicial career, becoming Justice of the Peace and of the Quorum in 1709; later named Judge of the New Haven County Court and Assistant Judge of the Connecticut Superior Court. First elected Deputy to the Connecticut General Assembly in 1706, representing Milford; continued to serve as deputy, with several intervals, until 1717, and occasionally acted as Clerk or as Speaker of the Lower House. Chosen as an Assistant of the colony in 1717; retained that position until 1724. Named Deputy Governor of Connecticut in October 1724 and Chief Judge of the Superior Court in May 1725, offices which he held until he succeeded the deceased Governor JosephTalcott in October 1741; reelected to the governorship annually until his death.

One of the most popular political figures in eighteenth-century Connecticut, Law presided over the colony's affairs during a period marked by the War of the Austrian Succession, and his effective leadership contributed to the successful campaign to capture Louisbourg from the French in 1745. In the realm of internal politics, Law's administration witnessed the emergence of factionalism stemming from the Great Awakening of the early 1740's. Although that religious revival had for the most part run its course in New England by late 1742, it left a legacy of religious controversy between its "Old Light" opponents and "New Light" defenders. These religious disputes eventually spilled over into the political arena, and by the time of Law's death on November 6, 1750, the growing influence of the New Lights had made Connecticut, and especially its Assembly, a scene of frequent party conflict.

Bibliography: Ezra Stiles, *Oratio Funebris pro Exequiis Celebrandis Viri Perillustris Jonathan Law . . .* (New London, 1751); "Hon. Jonathan Law, Governor of Connecticut," *New England Historical and Genealogical Register*, I (April 1847), 188-90; Albert C. Bates, ed., *The Law Papers: Correspondence and Documents During Jonathan Law's Governorship of the Colony of Connecticut, 1741-1750* (in Connecticut Historical Society, *Collections*, XI, XIII and XV, Hartford, 1907-14); Ernest Law, "Jonathan Law, Governor of Connecticut, 1742-51 [*sic*]," Pennsylvania Society of Colonial Governors, *Transactions*, I (1916), 103-11. *DAB*.

WOLCOTT, Roger, 1750-1754

Born on January 4, 1679 in Windsor, Connecticut, the youngest son of Simon and Martha (Pitkin) Wolcott. A Congregationalist. Brother of Elizabeth, Martha, Simon, Joanna, Henry, Christopher, Mary (died young), and William. Married on December 3, 1702 to Sarah Drake, by whom he was the father of Roger, Elizabeth, Alexander (died young), Samuel (died young), Alexander, Sarah, Hepzibah, Josiah, Erastus and Epaphras (twins who died young), Erastus, Ursula, Oliver, Mary Ann and one other.

Apprenticed to a clothier at the age of fifteen, and later established a business on his own. Chosen as a Selectman for Windsor in 1707; acted as a Deputy from Windsor to the Connecticut General Assembly from 1709 to 1714, and served as Clerk of the Lower House in 1710 and 1711. Named Justice of the Peace in 1710; advanced through the judicial ranks to become Judge of the Hartford County Court in 1721, Judge of the Connecticut Superior Court in 1732, and Chief Justice of the Connecticut Superior Court in 1741. Also played a major role in the colony's military affairs; in 1745, with the rank of Major General, acted as second in command during the assault on Louisbourg. Elected an Assistant of Connecticut in 1714 and, except for 1718 and 1719, was reelected annually until he took office as Deputy Governor in October 1741. Chosen by the Assembly to succeed the deceased Governor Jonathan Law late in 1750, and won reelection on an annual basis until May of 1754, when he lost the gubernatorial race to Thomas Fitch.

Wolcott's relatively brief tenure as chief executive was marked by the continuing struggle between the colony's Old and New Light factions. Originating during the Great Awakening of the early 1740's, Old Lights had opposed that religious revival, while their New Light counterparts supported the Awakening as an authentic work of God. Since religion and politics were inevitably associated with each other in Connecticut, the dispute between these two groups had a major impact on public affairs, and by the early 1750's many of the colony's leading politicians had identified themselves with one or the other faction. Indeed, Wolcott's defeat by Fitch in the May 1754 election was thought by many observers to be a victory for the more conservative, or Old Light party.

After his loss to Fitch, Wolcott attempted to regain the governor's chair in 1755, but he was defeated in a close contest. He then retired to private life, occupying himself in part with the writing of letters on the subject of church history and government. Wolcott died on May 17, 1767.

Bibliography: Joseph Perry, *The Character of Moses Illustrated and Improved*... (Hartford, n.d.); Roger Wolcott, "Journal of Roger Wolcott at the Siege of Louisbourg," Connecticut Historical Society, *Collections*, I (Hartford, 1860), 131-62; Samuel Wolcott, *Memorial of Henry Wolcott ... and of*

Some of His Descendants (New York, 1881); Albert C. Bates, ed., *The Wolcott Papers: Correspondence and Documents During Roger Wolcott's Governorship of the Colony of Connecticut, 1750-1754 with Some of Earlier Date* (in Connecticut Historical Society, *Collections*, XVI, Hartford, 1916); Doris E. Cook, "Roger Wolcott's Long Tidal River," Connecticut Historical Society, *Bulletin*, 32 (January 1967), 16-20; Ellsworth S. Grant, "From Governor to Governor in Three Generations," Connecticut Historical Society, *Bulletin*, 39 (July 1974), 65-77. *DAB*.

FITCH, Thomas, 1754-1766

Born *circa* 1700 in Norwalk, Connecticut, the son of Thomas Fitch, Jr. and his wife Sarah. A Congregationalist. Married on September 4, 1724 to Hannah Hall, by whom he was the father of Thomas, Jonathan, Ebenezer, Hannah (died young), Mary, Timothy, Hezekiah, Elizabeth, Esther and Giles (died young).

Studied at Yale College, graduating from that institution in 1721. Elected to the Connecticut General Assembly in 1726, and served as a Deputy from Norwalk until 1730, with the exception of one year. Widely respected for his legal knowledge; played a major role in the revision of Connecticut's statutes in the 1740's. Chosen as an Assistant of the colony in 1734, 1735, and from 1740 to 1750, when he was named Deputy Governor of Connecticut by the Assembly. Continued to serve as deputy governor (and as Chief Justice of the Superior Court) until he defeated Roger Wolcott in the gubernatorial election of May 1754.

Fitch's victory over Wolcott was without precedent in Connecticut history, since it represented the first time in which an incumbent governor actively seeking reelection had been rejected by the voters. Perhaps the most damaging factor contributing to Wolcott's defeat was the widespread suspicion that he had neglected to prevent the theft of cargo aboard a Spanish ship which had docked in New London harbor. Whatever the reasons behind Fitch's triumph, the new governor was popular enough to retain his office for the next twelve years. His long tenure witnessed both the renewal of fighting between Great Britain and France during the Seven Years' War, and the beginning of widespread unrest over Britain's colonial policy. While Fitch provided competent leadership during the war years, he encountered serious difficulties with his fellow colonists in the early 1760's when the major issue became British methods of taxation. Fitch helped in the drafting of arguments against the projected stamp tax in 1764; however, after its passage he felt legally bound to assist in its enforcement. In May 1766 his failure to realize the strength of opposition to the Stamp Act cost him the governor's chair. Ironically, news of the Stamp Act's repeal reached Connecticut one week after the gubernatorial contest of 1766, but Fitch had permanently lost his stature in politics, although he did serve as a Deputy from Norwalk in 1772. Fitch died on July 18, 1774.

Bibliography: Moses Dickinson, *A Sermon, Delivered at the Funeral of the Honorable Thomas Fitch, Esq.* . . . (New Haven, 1774); Albert C. Bates, ed., *The Fitch Papers: Correspondence and Documents During Thomas Fitch's Governorship of the Colony of Connecticut, 1754-1766* (in Connecticut Historical Society, *Collections*, XVII and XVIII, Hartford, 1918-20); John B. Hawkins, "Thomas Fitch, Esq., Governor of the Colony of Connecticut, 1754-1766," unpub. M.A. thesis, Central Connecticut State College, 1970. *DAB*.

PITKIN, William, 1766-1769

Born on April 30, 1694 in Hartford, Connecticut, the eldest son of William and Elizabeth (Stanley) Pitkin. A Congregationalist. Brother of Elizabeth (died young), Elizabeth, Martha, Joseph, Sarah (died young), Thomas, Sarah, John (died young), John and Jerusha. Married on May 7, 1724 to Mary Woodbridge, by whom he was the father of William, Timothy, George, Epaphras and Ashbel.

Along with his brother Joseph, operated the family's fulling mills as a young man. First elected as a Deputy to the Connecticut General Assembly in May 1728, representing Hartford, and served in that capacity until May of 1734; also acted as Speaker of the Lower House on a number of occasions. Played a major role in his colony's military affairs, rising to the rank of Colonel by 1739. Received various judicial appointments, including Judge of the Hartford County Court in May 1735 and Judge of the Connecticut Superior Court in October 1741. Became an Assistant of the Colony in May 1734, a position he held until May 1754, when he was chosen Deputy Governor of Connecticut and Chief Justice of the Superior Court. Continued to serve as both deputy governor and chief justice until he defeated Thomas Fitch in the gubernatorial election of May 1766.

Pitkin's victory over Fitch in 1766 was chiefly the result of the incumbent governor's decision to swear to uphold the Stamp Act in Connecticut. Pitkin, on the other hand, became a leader of the colony's radical party, despite his endorsement as chief executive of an Assembly petition which assured the King and his ministers that Connecticut was content with the "indissoluble Union . . . between Great Britain and her Colonies." A better indication of Pitkin's position appears in his private correspondence with William Samuel Johnson, Connecticut's agent in England, in which he suggested that severe policies by Great Britain could ultimately lead to a rupture of the bond connecting the mother country with her North American colonies. By 1767 grievances over British measures, especially those restricting trade with the foreign West Indies, had helped to crystallize radical sentiment in Connecticut, enabling Pitkin to remain in office until his death in East Hartford on October 1, 1769.

Bibliography: Eliphalet Williams, *The Ruler's Duty and Honor, . . . A Sermon Occasioned by the . . . Death of the Hon. William Pitkin . . .* (Hartford, 1770); Albert P. Pitkin, *Pitkin Family of America. A Genealogy of the Descendants of William Pitkin, from 1659 to 1886* (Hartford, 1887); Albert C. Bates, ed., *The Pitkin Papers: Correspondence and Documents During William Pitkin's Governorship of the Colony of Connecticut, 1766-1769. With Some of Earlier Date* (in Connecticut Historical Society, *Collections*, XIX, Hartford, 1921). *DAB*.

TRUMBULL, Jonathan, 1769-1784

Born on October 12, 1710 in Lebanon, Connecticut, the second son of Joseph and Hannah (Higley) Trumble. (Jonathan changed the spelling of his name to Trumbull in 1766.) A Congregationalist. Brother of Joseph, John, David, Mary, Abigail, Hannah (died young) and Hannah. Married on December 9, 1735 to Faith Robinson, by whom he was the father of Joseph, Jonathan, Faith, Mary, David and John.

Studied at Harvard College, graduating from that institution in 1727. Served for a time as a minister, but in the early 1730's, after the death of his older brother, joined his father's commercial business; expanded his trading interests until he suffered a serious setback in 1766. First elected as a Deputy from Lebanon to the Connecticut General Assembly in May 1733, and acted as a member of that body on various occasions until 1754; also served as Clerk of the Lower House in 1738 and as Speaker in 1739, 1752 and 1754. Named to fill a number of judicial offices, including Judge of the Quorum in 1744, Judge of the Windham County Court in 1746, and Judge of the Windham Probate Court in 1747. Became an Assistant of the colony in 1740, a position he retained, except for several years in the early 1750's, until his election as Deputy Governor of Connecticut and Chief Justice of the colony's Superior Court in May 1766. Selected by the Assembly to fill the unexpired term of the deceased governor, William Pitkin, in October 1769, and reelected as chief executive until his retirement in May 1784.

Trumbull's long tenure as governor of Connecticut covered much of the era of revolutionary unrest which culminated in the outbreak of war with Great Britain in 1775, and lasted until after that war had ended in victory for the American forces. Throughout this long and significant period, Trumbull remained a firm defender of the colonial cause. He made perhaps his most important contribution by supplying much of the *matériel* needed by Washington's Continental Army. Still, despite his efforts on Washington's behalf, Trumbull was at times accused of dealing with the enemy, an allegation which in the early 1780's seriously damaged his standing within Connecticut. Although he was later cleared of these charges, the aged governor had tired of political controversy by 1783, and in May of the following year he declined to run for reelection. Trumbull then retired to private life until his death in Lebanon, Connecticut on August 17, 1785.

Bibliography: Samuel Peters, "History of Jonathan Trumbull, the Present Rebel Governor of Connecticut, from his Birth, early in this Century to the Present Day," *The Political Magazine*, II (January 1781), 6-10; Zebulon Ely, *The Death of Moses the Servant of the Lord; a Sermon Preached at the Funeral Solemnity of His Excellency Jonathan Trumbull* (Hartford, 1786); I. W. Stuart, *Life of Jonathan Trumbull, Sen., Governor of Connecticut* (Boston, 1859); "The Trumbull Papers," Massachusetts Historical Society, *Collections*, 5th ser., vols. IX and X (Boston, 1885, 1888) and 7th ser., vols. II and III (Boston, 1902): J. H. Lea, *Contributions to a Trumbull Genealogy* (Boston, 1895); *A Genealogical Chart of Some of the Descendants of John Trumbull* (n.d.); Jonathan Trumbull, *Jonathan Trumbull, Governor of Connecticut, 1769-1784* (Boston, 1919); Glenn Weaver, *Jonathan Trumbull, Connecticut's Merchant Magistrate (1710-1785)* (Hartford, 1956); David M. Roth, "Jonathan Trumbull, 1710-1785: Connecticut's Puritan Patriot," unpub. Ph.D. diss., Clark University, 1971. *DAB*.

GRISWOLD, Matthew, 1784-1786

Born on March 25, 1714 in Lyme, Connecticut, the eldest son of John and Hannah (Lee) Griswold. A Congregationalist. Brother of Phoebe, Thomas, Hannah, Lucia, Sarah, Clarissa (died in infancy), Clarissa, Deborah, John (died in infancy) and Lydia. Married on November 10, 1743 to Ursula Wolcott, by whom he was the father of John, Matthew, Roger (governor of Connecticut from 1811 to 1812), Ursula (died in infancy), Hannah (died young), Marian and Ursula.

Studied law as a young man, and admitted to the Connecticut bar in 1743; later, in 1779, awarded an honorary LL.D. by Yale College. First represented Lyme as a Deputy to the Connecticut General Assembly in May 1751; also served as a member of that body from October 1754 until 1759. Chosen to the legislature's Upper House (Council) in 1759, and played an important role in the colonial agitation against British policy during the 1760's. Named a Judge of Connecticut's Superior Court in 1766; became both Chief Justice of the Superior Court and Deputy Governor of Connecticut in 1769, and retained those offices until 1784, when he was chosen by the legislature (after receiving only a plurality of the popular vote) to replace Jonathan Trumbull as Governor; also served during the Revolution as a member of Trumbull's Council of Safety.

Griswold's brief tenure was marked by controversy over the powers which the national government should have under the Articles of Confederation. To Griswold, a stronger central authority appeared to be the answer to many of the new nation's economic woes, and during his administration he endorsed the idea of granting to Congress the critical ability to levy an impost tax. Later, after he had left the governor's office, Griswold presided over his state's convention which in January 1788 ratified the Federal Constitution. He then retired to private life until his death in Lyme, Connecticut on April 28, 1799; he was buried in the Duck River Burying Ground in Lyme.

Bibliography: Edward Elbridge Salisbury, "The Griswold Family of Connecticut," *Magazine of American History*, XI (February-April 1884), 120-55, 218-38, 310-34; Glenn E. Griswold, comp., *The Griswold Family: England-America*, 4 vols. (Cleveland, Ohio and Burlington, Vt., 1935-62?). *DAB*.

HUNTINGTON, Samuel, 1786-1796

Born on July 3, 1731 in Windham, Connecticut, the son of Nathaniel, a farmer and clothier, and Mehetable (Thurston) Huntington. Five brothers, including Joseph. Married in 1761 to Martha Devotion; no children, but adopted Samuel and Francis, his brother Joseph's offspring.

Received little formal education; as a young man, studied law independently, and called to the bar in about 1758. Represented Norwich in the Connecticut General Assembly in 1764; also acted as an Assistant in the legislature's Upper House for many years. Occupied various legal and judicial offices, including King's Attorney for Connecticut (1765-1774), Justice of the Peace for New London County (1765-1775), and Judge of the Connecticut Superior Court (1774-1784); named Chief Justice of the Superior Court in 1784. Represented Connecticut in the Continental Congress from 1776 to 1784, except for several leaves of absence, and served as President of that body from September 1779 to July 1781; signed the Declaration of Independence in 1776. Acted as Lieutenant Governor of Connecticut from 1785 to 1786. Defeated the incumbent Matthew Griswold in the gubernatorial election of April 1786, polling 1,701 votes to Griswold's 1,049, with 2,854 scattered ballots; named chief executive by the Connecticut Legislature, the body authorized to decide elections in which no candidate received an absolute majority of the votes cast.

Huntington's career as governor encompassed a decade which included heated discussion over the virtues and defects of the Federal Constitution that had been drafted in Philadelphia in 1787. Recognizing that a stronger central government would be advantageous to Connecticut, Huntington endorsed that document, and his approval was a major factor in the state's decision to ratify in January 1788 by a vote of 128 to 40. By 1789 Huntington's popularity in Connecticut was so great that he received two "favorite son" votes in the first presidential election held under the new Constitution. The remainder of Huntington's gubernatorial service was devoted in large part to the improvement of Connecticut's educational facilities, an aim which he continued to support until his death in Norwich on January 5, 1796.

Bibliography: Joseph Strong, *A Sermon Delivered at the Funeral of His Excellency Samuel Huntington* . . . (Hartford, 1796); E. B. Huntington, *A Genealogical Memoir of the Huntington Family in this Country* . . . (Stamford, Conn., 1863); Susan D. Huntington, "Samuel Huntington," *Connecticut Magazine*, VI (May-June 1900), 247-53; [Huntington Family Association], *The Huntington Family in America* (Hartford, 1915); Albert E. Van Dusen, "Samuel Huntington: A Leader of Revolutionary Connecticut," Connecticut Historical Society, *Bulletin*, 19 (April 1954), 38-62; Michael F. Salvin, "Samuel Huntington in the Continental Congress," unpub. M.A. thesis, Southern Connecticut State College, 1971. *DAB*.

DELAWARE

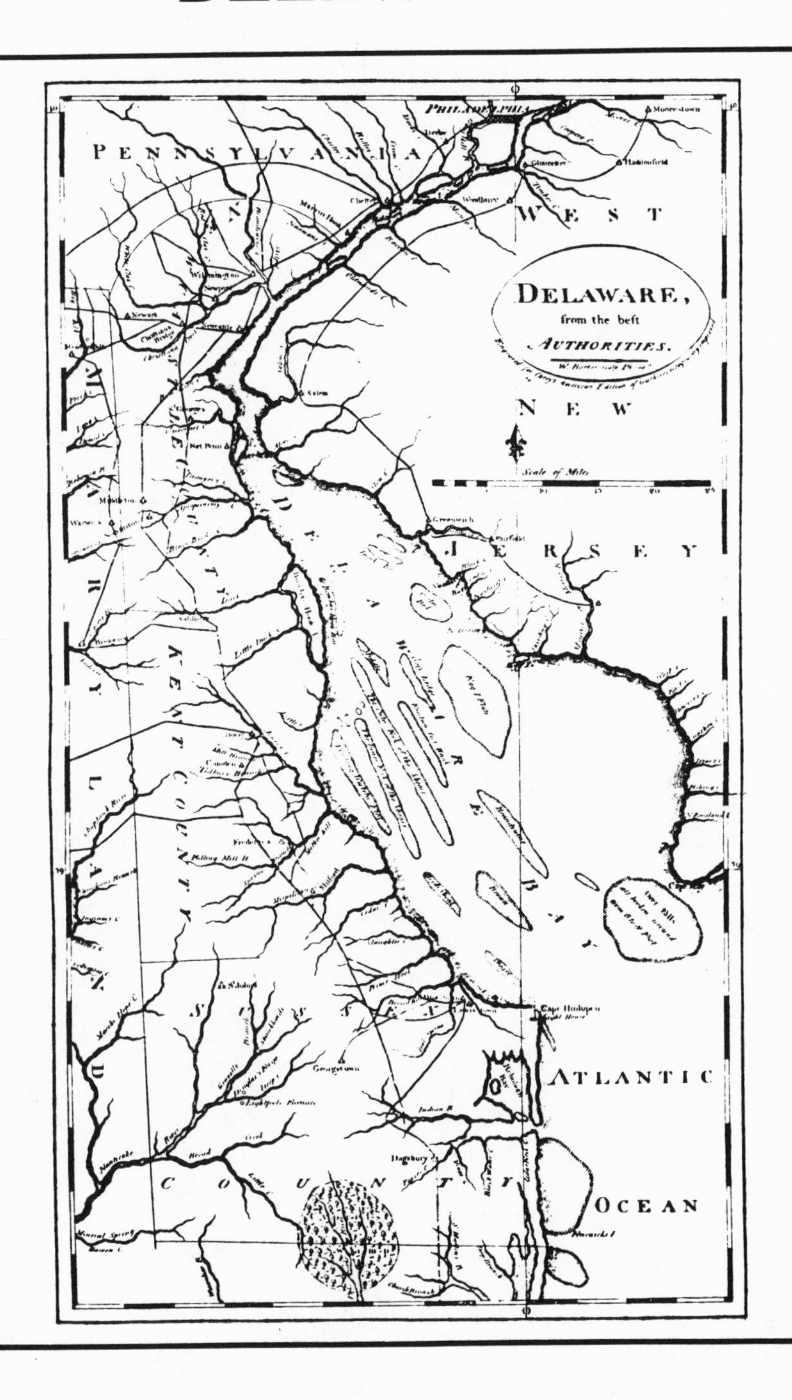

PHILADELPHIA
PENNSYLVANIA
Moorestown
Gloucester
Haddonfield
Woodbury
WEST
DELAWARE,
from the best
AUTHORITIES.
NEW
Scale of Miles
Wilmington
Newark
Salem
Greenwich
JERSEY
KENT COUNTY
Milford
Georgetown
Cape Henlopen
ATLANTIC
OCEAN
Dagsbury
COUNTY

Chronology

1775-1777	John McKinly
1777	Thomas McKean
1777-1778	George Read
1778-1781	Caesar Rodney
1781-1782	John Dickinson
1782-1783	John Cook
1783-1786	Nicholas Van Dyke
1786-1789	Thomas Collins
1789	Jehu Davis

BIBLIOGRAPHY

Delaware Archives, 5 vols. (Wilmington, 1911).

Governor's Register, State of Delaware: Appointments and Other Transactions by Executives of the State from 1674 to 1851, vol. I (Wilmington, 1926).

Munroe, John A., *Colonial Delaware: A History* (New York, 1978).

———. *Federalist Delaware, 1775-1815* (New Brunswick, N. J., 1954).

Scharf, J. Thomas, *et al.*, *History of Delaware, 1609-1888*, 2 vols. (Philadelphia, 1888).

Valinger, Leon de, Jr., comp., *Calendar of Kent County, Delaware Probate Records, 1680-1800* (Dover, Del., 1944).

DELAWARE

McKINLY, John, 1775-1777

Born on February 24, 1721 in the north of Ireland; names of parents unknown. A Presbyterian. Married sometime between 1761 and 1766 to Jane Richardson. Immigrated to Wilmington in the Lower Counties (later Delaware), where he practiced medicine.

Became a member of the Lower Counties militia, and in 1756 received a commission as Major of a regiment in New Castle County. Elected Sheriff in 1757, 1758 and 1759; also chosen as Chief Burgess of the borough of Wilmington in 1759, a position to which he was re-elected eleven times. Elected to the Assembly of the Lower Counties in October 1771, and in October 1773 was chosen by that body to its five-member Committee of Correspondence. Chaired the New Castle County committee which in 1774 approved measures to counter British policy; served in March 1775 as a member of the Assembly committee which wrote the instructions for Delaware's delegates to the Second Continental Congress. Also named Colonel of a regiment of New Castle County militia in March 1775. Elected President of the Council of Safety which first met at Dover in September 1775, and was, at about the same time, promoted to Brigadier General of the three battalions of troops organized in New Castle County. Elected to Delaware's first State Legislature in October 1776, and became Speaker of the Lower House. Chosen President of the Council of Safety which acted as an interim executive from late 1776 to February 1777, when the General Assembly named him as the new state's first President and Commander-in-Chief.

McKinly served as president of the Delaware Council of Safety during a period of transition, when the final ties connecting the former "Lower Counties" with the Penn proprietary were being broken and replaced by local control. After independence was declared in 1776, Delaware began to organize a government which would also be distinct from Pennsylvania, with whom the state had shared the same chief executive for virtually the entire colonial period. McKinly's experience and reputation for moderation made him a logical choice to head the new administration and, despite some opposition from Delaware's radicals, he was elected to a three-year term. Within seven months, however, McKinly was captured by British troops who had taken Wilmington after the Battle of Brandywine Creek, and for the next year he remained in British custody.

After his release by the British, McKinly returned to Wilmington in September 1778, where he retired from the political arena and resumed his medical practice. He was one of the founders of Delaware's first medical society in 1789, and acted as a trustee of Wilmington's First Presbyterian Church for some years. McKinly died on August 31, 1796.

Bibliography: G. S. Rowe, "The Travail of John McKinly, First President of Delaware," *Delaware History*, XVII (Spring-Summer 1976), 21-36. *DAB*.

McKEAN, Thomas, 1777

Born on March 19, 1734 in New London Township, Chester County, Pennsylvania, the second son of William, a farmer and tavern keeper, and Letitia (Finney) McKean. Brother of Robert, Dorothea and William. Married on July 21, 1763 to Mary Borden, by whom he was the father of two sons, including Joseph, and four daughters; following the death of his first wife in 1773, remarried on September 3, 1774 to Sarah Armitage; father of five children by his second wife.

Attended New London Academy; also received private tuition from the Reverend Francis Alison; studied law in New Castle with David Finney, his cousin, and admitted to the bar in 1754; continued his legal training at London's Middle Temple in 1758. Named Deputy Attorney General for Sussex County in 1756, and became Clerk of the Lower Counties Assembly in 1757. Elected to the Assembly in 1762, a position he held until 1779; served as Speaker in 1772 and 1773. Presided as Justice of the Court of Common Pleas in the 1760's; appointed Collector of the port of New Castle in 1771. Attended the Stamp Act Congress in 1765, and later became a prominent leader of the revolutionary movement. Served as a member of the Continental Congress from 1774 to 1783, except for the period between December 1776 and January 1778, and acted as President of that body from July to November of 1781; also signed the Declaration of Independence some months after its promulgation. Took part in the drafting of Delaware's first state constitution in August and September of 1776, and in July 1777 was named Pennsylvania's Chief Justice, an office he retained until 1799. As Speaker of the Assembly, acted as President of Delaware from September to October of 1777, between the capture of President John McKinly by British troops and the return to Delaware of George Read, the state's vice president. Attended the Pennsylvania convention which ratified the Federal Constitution in December 1787. Elected Governor of Pennsylvania in 1799, and served as chief executive of that commonwealth from December 1799 to December 1808, winning re-election in 1802 and 1805.

McKean's brief tenure in Delaware was merely that of a caretaker given the task of keeping the state's administrative machinery running until Vice President Read could be summoned from Congress. By 1799, however, he was ready to seek office in his own right, after breaking with the Federalists in a dispute over that party's approach to foreign policy. Running as a Republican, McKean defeated James Ross of Pittsburgh in what was the first of three successful campaigns for the governorship. During his years as Pennsylvania's chief executive, the commonwealth was wracked by political dissension—initially created by the bitter rivalry between Federalists and Republicans, and later by a split within the Republican camp. Indeed, in 1805 McKean was forced to form an alliance consisting of his own Republican faction and the commonwealth's fading Federalist Party, in order to defeat Simon Snyder, his gubernatorial opponent and the Republican Speaker of the Assembly.

Following his period in office, McKean retired from public life, although he continued to write and take an interest in political affairs. McKean died in Philadelphia, Pennsylvania on June 24, 1817.

Bibliography: Roberdeau Buchanan, *Genealogy of the McKean Family, with a Biography of the Hon. Thomas McKean* (Philadelphia, 1890); "Governor M'Kean's Papers," *Pennsylvania Archives*, 4th ser., vol. IV (Harrisburg, 1900), 435-654; James Hedley Peeling, "The Public Life of Thomas McKean, 1734-1817," unpub. Ph.D. diss., University of Chicago, 1929; James Hedley Peeling, "Governor McKean and the Pennsylvania Jacobins (1799-1808)," *Pennsylvania Magazine of History and Biography*, LIV (October 1930), 320-54; John M. Coleman, "Thomas McKean and the Origin of an Independent Judiciary," *Pennsylvania History*, XXXIV (April 1967), 111-30; Gail S. Rowe, "A Valuable Acquisition in Congress: Thomas McKean, Delegate from Delaware to the Continental Congress, 1774-1783," *Pennsylvania History*, XXXVIII (July 1971), 225-64; Gail S. Rowe, "Thomas McKean and the Coming of the Revolution," *Pennsylvania Magazine of History and Biography*, XCVI (January 1972), 3-47; Gail S. Rowe, "The Legal Career of Thomas McKean, 1750-1775," *Delaware History*, XVI (April 1974), 22-46; John M. Coleman, *Thomas McKean, Forgotten Leader of the Revolution* (Rockaway, N.J., 1975); Gail S. Rowe, *Thomas McKean: The Shaping of an American Republicanism* (Boulder, Colorado, 1978). See also the Thomas McKean Mss. in the Historical Society of Pennsylvania, Philadelphia, especially his "Autobiographical Sketch." *DAB*.

READ, George, 1777-1778

Born on September 18, 1733 near North East, Cecil County, Maryland, the son of John, a prominent landowner, and Mary (Howell) Read. Brother of Thomas, James, William and perhaps others. Married on January 11, 1763 to Gertrude (Ross) Till; father of one daughter and four sons, including John. Received early education in Chester, Pennsylvania and at the academy of Reverend Francis Alison in New London, Pennsylvania; also received legal training from John Moland, a Philadelphia attorney. Admitted to the bar in Philadelphia in 1753, but soon moved his practice to New Castle in the Lower Counties (Delaware).

Appointed Attorney General for the Lower Counties in April 1763, a position he held until October 1774. Elected to the Assembly of the Lower Counties in October 1765, representing New Castle County, and remained a member of that body until the end of the colonial period. Also represented Delaware in the First and Second Continental Congresses; refused to vote for independence on July 2, 1776, but later signed the Declaration after the decision to separate from Great Britain had been made. Played an important role in the deliberation which produced Delaware's Constitution of 1776. Elected that same year to the Delaware Legislative Council; later became the Council's Speaker and consequently Vice President of the state. Elected to the Continental Congress by Delaware's first State Legislature; after the capture of President John McKinly in September 1777, was summoned from Congress to assume the post of Acting President, and arrived in Wilmington in October 1777.

Read's brief tenure was spent in an effort to strengthen the state's defensive posture, an effort made more necessary by the British occupation of Philadelphia. Despite his complaint to General Washington that the Delaware Legislature was "not disposed to unite and give aid to the executive authority," Read did help to make the Patriot cause more popular in a state which still had a strong contingent of British sympathizers.

Although Read turned over the president's office in March 1778 to Caesar Rodney, he continued for a time to serve in the Delaware Legislature. In December 1782 he was elected by Congress as a Judge of the Court of Appeals with jurisdiction over admiralty cases, and in 1784 he served on a commission appointed to settle the dispute over land claims between New York and Massachusetts. He was again a member of the Delaware Council from 1782 to 1788, and represented Delaware both at the Annapolis Convention of 1786 and the Philadelphia Constitutional Convention of 1787, where he emerged as a leading spokesman for the rights of the smaller states. When the new Federal Constitution went into effect, Read was appointed United States Senator from Delaware, and in 1790 he was re-elected to a full six-year term. In September

1793, however, he relinquished his Senate seat to accept an appointment as Delaware's Chief Justice, an office he filled until his death on September 21, 1798.

Bibliography: W. T. Read, *Life and Correspondence of George Read, A Signer of the Declaration of Independence* (Philadelphia, 1870); Daniel T. Boughner, Jr., "George Read and the Founding of the Delaware State: 1781-1798," unpub. Ph.D. diss., Catholic University of America, 1970. *DAB*.

RODNEY, Caesar, 1778-1781

Born on October 7, 1728 near Dover, Delaware, the eldest child of Caesar and Elizabeth (Crawford) Rodney. Brother of seven, including Thomas. Never married. Became the ward of Nicholas Ridgely, a Kent County political figure, after the death of his father in 1745.

Commissioned High Sheriff of Kent County in 1775, and re-appointed in 1756 and 1757; also served at various times as Kent County Register of Wills, Recorder of Deeds, Clerk of the Orphans' Court, Clerk of the Peace, and Justice of the Peace. Elected in 1758 as a delegate from Kent County to the Assembly of the Lower Counties; with the exception of the Assembly which met in 1771, served as a member from 1761 to 1776, and chosen as that body's Speaker in 1769, 1773, 1774 and 1775. Represented Kent County at the Stamp Act Congress which convened in New York in October 1765, and took an active role in the colonial protest against British policy throughout the 1760's and early 1770's, culminating with his election in 1774 and 1775 as a delegate from the Lower Counties to the First and Second Continental Congresses. Also named Third Justice of the Supreme Court for the Three Lower Counties in 1769, and became Second Justice of that court in 1773. With the approach of full-scale fighting between colonial and British troops, appointed to key militia positions, including Colonel of the "Upper" Regiment of Kent County militia, Brigadier General of the Kent County militia, and Brigadier General of the Western Battalion of Sussex County. Presided over the important Assembly session which in June 1776 repudiated the Crown's authority over the Lower Counties; returned to Philadelphia several weeks later to cast his vote in favor of independence, and signed the Declaration. Became Chairman of the Kent County branch of the Council of Safety in November 1776, Judge of the Delaware Admiralty in spring 1777, Major General of the Delaware militia by September of 1777, and a member of the Continental Congress in December 1777 (but did not take his seat). Elected to a three-year term as President of Delaware in the spring of 1778, and served for seven months longer than his appointed term, until November of 1781.

Rodney presided over the state of Delaware throughout much of the Revolution, and he played a vital role in procuring supplies and men for the Continental Army. Despite the deterioration of his health from cancer, and the apathy of those who were disillusioned by the war, Rodney proved to be an effective administrator. Had not the Constitution of 1776 prohibited his re-election, Rodney might have served even longer as the state's chief executive.

Although he was elected to the Upper House of the Delaware Legislature in the autumn of 1783 and became that body's Speaker, Rodney was already critically ill, and he died on June 26, 1784. He was buried at his family farm, but in 1888, he was re-interred in the cemetery of Christ Episcopal Church in Dover, Delaware.

Bibliography: G. H. Ryden, ed., *Letters To and From Caesar Rodney, 1756-1784* (Philadelphia, 1933); Leon de Valinger, Jr., ed., "Rodney Letters," *Delaware History*, I (July 1946), 99-110, and vol. III (September 1948), 105-15; Harold B. Hancock, ed., "Letters to and from Caesar Rodney," *Delaware History*, XII (April-October 1966), 54-76, 147-68. *DAB*.

DICKINSON, John, 1781-1782
Pennsylvania, 1782-1785

Born on November 8, 1732 in Maryland, the second son of Samuel, a planter and lawyer, and Mary (Cadwalader) Dickinson. Brother of a number of siblings, including Philemon. Married on July 19, 1770 to Mary Norris. Received early education at home, and in 1750 studied law in the office of John Moland, a Philadelphia attorney; continued his legal training at London's Middle Temple from 1753 to 1757, when he returned to Philadelphia to practice law.

Elected to the Assembly of the Lower Counties (Delaware) in October 1760, and became Speaker of that body. In the 1760's, argued in the Pennsylvania Assembly the case for proprietary rule; along with George Bryan, chosen in 1764 as a representative from Philadelphia in the Assembly, replacing Benjamin Franklin and Joseph Galloway; reelected in 1770. Named as a delegate from Pennsylvania to the Stamp Act Congress held in New York in October 1765. During the 1760's and early 1770's, emerged as a moderate spokesman for colonial grievances, and authored several influential works, including *The Late Regulations Respecting the British Colonies . . .Considered* (1765) and *Letters from a Farmer in Pennsylvania to the Inhabitants of the British Colonies* (1768). Became Chairman of the Philadelphia Committee of Correspondence in May 1774; represented Pennsylvania at the First Continental Congress, but withdrew in October 1774 after serving only a short time. Appointed Chairman of the Pennsylvania Committee of Safety and Defense in

June 1775 and served for several days, until his replacement by Benjamin Franklin; also named Colonel of the first battalion of troops raised in Philadelphia. Continued to recommend moderation at the Second Continental Congress in 1775, and voted against the Declaration of Independence, although he took up arms in support of the Patriot cause after separation from Great Britain had become a fact. Chaired the committee that drafted the Articles of Confederation in 1776, but otherwise played a minor political role during the first year of independence, losing his seat as a congressional representative from Pennsylvania, resigning from the Pennsylvania Assembly, and declining to represent Delaware in Congress. Served as Brigadier General of the Pennsylvania militia in 1777. Accepted election as a congressman from Delaware in 1779, resigning in the autumn of that year. Elected President of the Supreme Executive Council of Delaware in 1781, and held that office until 1782; in November of 1782, became President of Pennsylvania's Supreme Executive Council.

Dickinson's election as Delaware's chief executive was the result of his middle of the road reputation, a quality favored by those conservatives who had re-established their political dominance of the state by 1781. When Dickinson was chosen as president of Pennsylvania in the autumn of 1782, he left the government of Delaware in the hands of John Cook, the speaker of the Council, and left for Philadelphia. For the next three years he grappled with Pennsylvania's persistent financial problems, but his task was made more complicated by internal political dissension. Although Dickinson's victory over General James Potter in 1782 had marked the emergence of the moderate Anti-Constitutionalist Party as an important political force in the commonwealth, the radical Constitutionalists remained in control of the Council, and were strong enough in 1783 and 1784 to block legislation in the Assembly. Consequently, Dickinson had little opportunity to further any program for political reform or economic recovery, and Pennsylvania remained in turmoil until Benjamin Franklin replaced him in October of 1785.

Following his service as president of Delaware and Pennsylvania, Dickinson become a delegate from Delaware to the Philadelphia Constitutional Convention of 1787, and used his skills as a writer to urge the adoption of the Federal Constitution. While he retained his interest in public affairs, he held no further political office until his death in Wilmington, Delaware on February 14, 1808.

Bibliography: Charles J. Stillé, *Life and Times of John Dickinson, 1732-1808* (Philadelphia, 1891) (published as vol. XIII of the Historical Society of Pennsylvania, *Memoirs*); Paul Leicester Ford, ed., *The Writings of John Dickinson* (Philadelphia, 1895); John H. Powell, "John Dickinson, Penman of the American Revolution," unpub. Ph.D. diss., University of Iowa, 1938; John H. Powell, "John Dickinson, President of the Delaware State, 1781-1782," *Delaware History*, I (January-July 1946), 1-54, 111-34; H. Trevor

Colbourn, "John Dickinson, Historical Revolutionary," *Pennsylvania Magazine of History and Biography*, LXXXIII (July 1959), 271-92; John H. Powell, "John Dickinson as President of Pennsylvania," *Pennsylvania History*, XXVIII (July 1961), 254-67; David L. Jacobson, "John Dickinson's Fight against Royal Government, 1764," *William and Mary Quarterly*, 3rd ser., vol. XIX (January 1962), 64-85; David L. Jacobson, *John Dickinson and the Revolution in Pennsylvania, 1764-1776* (Berkeley, Calif., 1965); Stanley K. Johannesen, "Constitution and Empire in the Life and Thought of John Dickinson," unpub. Ph.D. diss., University of Missouri-Columbia, 1973; Milton E. Flower, "John Dickinson: Delawarean," *Delaware History*, XVII (Spring-Summer 1976), 12-20. *DAB*.

COOK, John, 1782-1783

Born in 1730 in Kent County, Delaware; names of parents unknown. An Episcopalian. Brother of at least one sister, who was the wife of Thomas Collins, president of Delaware from 1786 to 1789. Married to a woman named Elizabeth, by whom he was the father of Michael, Robert, Margaret, Elizabeth and Sarah.

Worked for a number of years as a farmer and tanner. Appointed Sheriff of Kent County in October 1772. As a delegate from Kent County, shared in the deliberations which produced the Delaware Constitution of 1776, and served as a member of the first Legislative Assembly chosen under that instrument. Named Third Justice of the Kent County Supreme Court in July 1777, the same month in which he was appointed to the Court of Capital Cases Offenses in New Castle County. As Vice President and Speaker of the Legislative Council, became President of Delaware in November 1782, although John Dickinson did not formally resign the presidency until January 1783.

While Cook's brief tenure was marked by the return of Delaware troops from the South, where they had participated in the final stages of the Revolution, the consequences of the war continued to have a major impact on the state. On January 31, 1783, for example, Cook issued a proclamation which forbade "illicit Intercourse" between vessels from Delaware and British ships, unless such activities were supervised by the state's militia. The day after he signed this order, Cook relinquished his position as chief executive to the newly-elected Nicholas Van Dyke. Cook died between October 27, 1789, the date of his will, and January 4, 1790, when that will was proved.

VAN DYKE, Nicholas, 1783-1786

Born on September 25, 1738 in New Castle, Delaware, the son of Nicholas and Lytie (Dirks) Van Dyke. Married to Elizabeth Nixon, by whom he had Nicholas, Ann and perhaps others; after his first wife's death, remarried to Charlotte Standley. Studied law, and was authorized to practice before the Supreme Court in Philadelphia in 1765; after a short time, returned to New Castle and resumed his legal career.

Became a moderate Whig during the 1770's, and served on several committees formed to protest British policy. Named to the New Castle Council of Safety in 1776; that same year played an important role in the drafting of Delaware's state constitution. Chosen as a member of the Upper House (or Council) of the Delaware Legislature in the first election held under the new constitution, and in 1779 served as that body's Speaker. Also assigned the rank of Major in the New Castle County militia. Elected to the Continental Congress in February 1777 and remained a member until 1782, although he did not attend regularly and took little part in the Congress's deliberations. Elected President of Delaware in February 1783, and held that office until October of 1786.

Van Dyke succeeded to the presidency of Delaware at a time when commerce and finance had not yet fully recovered from the effects of the Revolutionary War, and much of his effort was directed toward helping Delaware to achieve economic stability. Van Dyke's task was made considerably easier by the Delaware Legislature which, by refusing to issue large amounts of paper currency, avoided a policy that had nearly wrecked Pennsylvania's economy.

Following his period as Delaware's chief executive, Van Dyke returned briefly to the Delaware Council. He died in New Castle County, Delaware on February 19, 1789, and was buried in New Castle's Immanuel Churchyard.

Bibliography: William B. Aitken, *Distinguished Families in America Descended from Wilhelmus Beekman and Jan Thomasse Van Dyke* (New York, 1912). *DAB*.

COLLINS, Thomas, 1786-1789

Born in 1732 in England; names of parents unknown. Married to a sister of John Cook, who acted as president of Delaware from 1782 to 1783; father of William, Mary, Elizabeth and Sarah.

Named High Sheriff of Kent County in 1764, and served in that capacity for some time; later became a member of the Lower Counties Assembly, and represented Kent County on various committees which during the 1770's considered ways of expressing opposition to British policy. Elected Lieutenant Colonel of the "Upper" Regiment of the Kent County militia in May 1775; commanded militia forces until the end of the Revolution, rising to the rank of Brigadier General in June 1778. Participated in the Delaware Constitutional Convention of 1776, and named to the first Legislative Council chosen under that instrument; also appointed to the Delaware Council of Safety in 1776. Commissioned Chief Justice of the Kent County Court of Common Pleas in June 1782. Elected President of Delaware in October of 1786, a position he held until his death.

Although Collins' elevation to the presidency had been uncontested, his tenure was soon disrupted by serious political turmoil. In Sussex County, for example, armed men apparently roamed the countryside in an effort to influence voters during a disputed electoral contest in 1787. Nevertheless, nearly all Delawareans believed that the state's economy would profit considerably from a stronger national union. The popularity of this view was demonstrated at the Dover convention which met in December 1787, where within four days Delaware became the first state to ratify the Federal Constitution. Less than sixteen months later, on March 29, 1789, President Collins died in Kent County, Delaware, while still in office.

DAVIS, Jehu, 1789

Date of birth and names of parents unknown; born in Kent County, Delaware. An Episcopalian. Married to a woman named Rhoda.

Was serving as a member of the Delaware House of Representatives by October of 1777, and won re-election on a number of occasions. Also was acting as Justice of the Peace for Kent County by March of 1785. Chosen Speaker of the House of Representatives in 1788, and in that capacity served as Acting President of Delaware from March to May of 1789, between the death of Thomas Collins and the inauguration of Joshua Clayton.

Davis's brief administration lasted only long enough for the General Assembly to convene in order to choose a successor to the deceased Collins. Late in May 1789 the legislators selected Joshua Clayton as a replacement, and on the thirtieth of that month, Davis relinquished the presidency. During Davis's two-month tenure, Delawareans witnessed the arrival of George Washington in Wilmington, *en route* to New York and his inauguration as president of the United States. Washington's appearance caused considerable excitement; as one eyewitness later recounted, the sight of the revolutionary hero in his chariot encouraged the crowd to respond with "enthusiastic cheers."

Early in 1790, following his service as chief executive, Davis received an appointment as Fourth Justice of the Kent County Court of Common Pleas and Orphans' Court. He was also renamed Justice of the Peace for Kent County in September 1793, and became Commissioner of the Kent County Land Office in February of 1794. Davis died on May 11, 1802.

GEORGIA

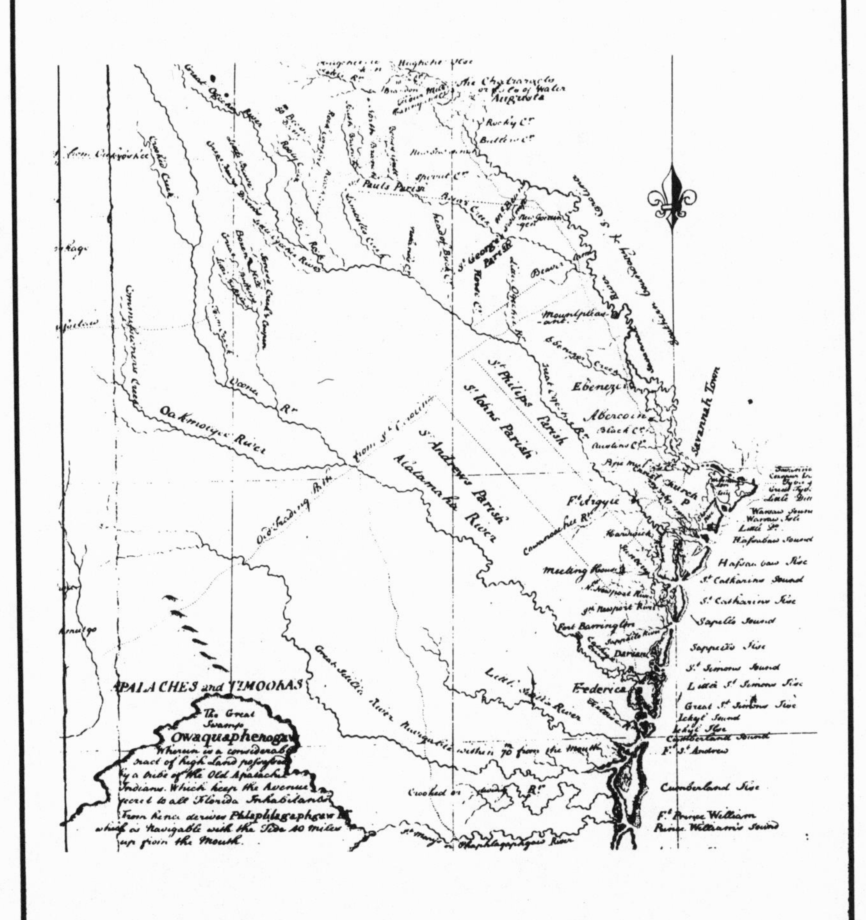
Augusta
Rocky Cr.
Pauls Parish
St. Georges Parish
Ebenezer
Abercorn
Savannah Town
St. Philips Parish
St. Johns Parish
St. Andrews Parish
Alatamaha River
Oakmoigee River
Ft. Argyle
Meeting House
Fort Barrington
Darian
Frederica
APALACHES and TIMOOKAS
The Great Swamp Owaquaphenoga
Wherein is a considerable tract of high land possessed by a tribe of the Old Apalachian Indians. Which keep the Avenue secret to all Florida Inhabitants
From hence derives Phlaphlagaphgaw R. which is navigable with the Tide 40 miles up from the Mouth.
Warsaw Sound
Hafsabaw Sound
St. Catharins Sound
St. Catharins Isle
Sapello Sound
Sappelo Isle
St. Simons Sound
Great St. Simons Isle
Jekyl Sound
Cumberland Sound
Ft. St. Andrew
Cumberland Isle
Ft. Prince William
Prince William's Sound

Chronology

1733-1743	James Edward Oglethorpe
1743-1751	William Stephens
1751-1752	Henry Parker
1752-1754	Patrick Graham
1754-1757	John Reynolds
1757-1760	Henry Ellis
1760-1771	Sir James Wright
1771-1773	James Habersham
1773-1776	Sir James Wright
1775	William Ewen
1775-1776	George Walton
1776	William Ewen
1776-1777	Archibald Bulloch
1777	Button Gwinnett
1777-1778	John Adam Treutlen
1778-1779	John Houstoun
1779	John Wereat
1779-1780	George Walton
1779-1782	Sir James Wright
1780	Richard Howley
1780	Stephen Heard
1780-1781	Myrick Davies
1781-1782	Nathan Brownson
1782-1783	John Martin
1783-1784	Lyman Hall
1784-1785	John Houstoun
1786-1787	Edward Telfair
1787-1788	George Mathews
1788-1789	George Handley
1789	George Walton

BIBLIOGRAPHY

Abbot, W. W., *The Royal Governors of Georgia, 1754-1775* (Chapel Hill, 1959).

Candler, A. D., ed., *Colonial Records of the State of Georgia (1732-1782)*, 26 vols. (Atlanta, 1904-16).

———. ed., *Revolutionary Records of Georgia (1769-84)*, 3 vols. (Atlanta, 1908).

Coleman, Kenneth, *Colonial Georgia: A History* (New York, 1976).

Coulter, E. Merton, *Georgia: A Short History*, rev. ed. (Chapel Hill, 1960).

———. and Albert B. Saye, *A List of the Early Settlers of Georgia* (Athens, Ga., 1949).

Davis, Harold E., *The Fledgling Province: Social and Cultural Life in Colonial Georgia, 1733-1776* (Chapel Hill, 1976).

Flippin, Percy S., "The Royal Government in Georgia, 1752-1776," *Georgia Historical Quarterly*, VIII (1924), 1-37, 81-120, 243-91; IX (1925), 187-245; X (1926), 1-25, 251-76; XII (1928), 326-52; XIII (1929), 128-53.

Hawes, Lilla Mills, ed., "The Proceedings and Minutes of the Governor and Council of Georgia, October 4, 1774 through November 7, 1775 and September 6, 1779 through September 20, 1780," *Georgia Historical Quarterly*, XXXIV (September-December 1950), 203-26, 288-312; XXXV (March-September 1951), 31-59, 126-51, 196-221.

———. ed., "Some Papers of the Governor and Council of Georgia, 1780-1781," *Georgia Historical Quarterly*, XLVI (September-December 1962), 280-96, 395-417.

Jones, Charles C., *The History of Georgia*, 2 vols. (Boston, 1883).

Knight, Lucian Lamar, *Georgia's Landmarks, Memorials and Legends*, 2 vols. (Atlanta, 1913-14).

McCain, James R., "The Executive in Proprietary Georgia," unpub. Ph.D. diss., Columbia University, 1914.

Stevens, William Bacon, *A History of Georgia, from its First Discovery by Europeans to the Adoption of the Present Constitution in MDCCXCVIII [1798]*, 2 vols. (New York, 1847; Philadelphia, 1859).

Waring, T. P., "The Beginning of Georgia Under Her Presidents," *Georgia Historical Quarterly*, XXIV (March 1940), 43-55.

White, George, *Historical Collections of Georgia* . . . (New York, 1855).

GEORGIA

OGLETHORPE, James Edward, 1733-1743

Born on December 22, 1696 in London, England, the son of Sir Theophilus and Lady Eleanor (Wall) Oglethorpe. Brother of Lewis, Theophilus, Anne Henrietta, Eleanor, James (died in infancy), Sutton (died in infancy), Louisa Mary and Frances Charlotte. Married on September 15, 1744 to Elizabeth Wright; no children.

Studied at Eton; matriculated at Corpus Christi College, Oxford in 1714. Held various army commissions from 1710 to 1715; fought in Europe against the Turks under Prince Eugene of Savoy in 1717. Engaged in Jacobite conspiracies until 1719, when he returned to England and succeeded an elder brother as incumbent of ''Westbrook,'' the family estate in Surrey. Author of *The Sailor's Advocate* (1728), a condemnation of the policy of impressment, and *A New and Accurate Account of the Provinces of South-Carolina and Georgia* (1732), a prospectus for colonization. Member of Parliament for Haslemere from 1722 to 1743. Served in 1729 and 1730 as Chairman of a committee appointed to investigate Britain's penal system.

After successfully petitioning with twenty other Trustees for a charter to establish ''the Colony of Georgia in America,'' Oglethorpe, in the capacity of Resident Trustee, left England with the first group of emigrants and arrived off Charlestown, South Carolina on January 13, 1733. Assisted by Colonel (later Governor) William Bull, Sr. of South Carolina, Oglethorpe laid out the town of Savannah in February 1733. Over the next few years, the colony set up its first administrative structure and built military fortifications to protect the new settlements from attacks by Indians and the Spanish. Yet, as Georgia developed, the original purposes of Oglethorpe and the other Trustees began to give way to the practical requirements for colonizing a sparsely settled wilderness. Although the colony was at first envisioned primarily as a refuge for Britain's ''unfortunate poor,'' the Trustees soon began to encourage the emigration of non-English settlers, especially religious sectarians such as the Salzburgers and Moravians. Similarly, Oglethorpe's early intention to prohibit Negro slavery and the importation of rum proved unrealistic. Intemperance became a problem almost immediately, and while some efforts were made to enforce the ban on slavery, the Trustees finally voted to repeal the colony's prohibition in 1750, seven years after Oglethorpe's departure.

After Oglethorpe's return to England in September 1743, he acted as one of the leaders of the Jacobite conspiracy of 1745. When the plot to bring the young claimant, Prince Charles Edward Stuart, to the throne failed, Oglethorpe was brought before a court martial, but was later acquitted. He was promoted to Lieutenant General in 1746 and General in 1765, and in his final years was connected with London's literary circle. Oglethorpe died at "Cranham Hall" in Essex, England on June 30, 1785. Oglethorpe County, Georgia, created in 1793, was named in his honor.

Bibliography: Robert Wright, *A Memoir of General James Oglethorpe* (London, 1867); Henry Bruce, *Life of General Oglethorpe* (New York, 1890); Harriet C. Cooper, *James Oglethorpe, the Founder of Georgia* (New York, 1904); Leslie F. Church, *Oglethorpe: A Study of Philanthropy in England and Georgia* (London, 1932); Amos A. Ettinger, *James Edward Oglethorpe: Imperial Idealist* (Oxford, 1936); B. Phinizy Spalding, "James Oglethorpe: A Biographical Survey," *Georgia Historical Quarterly*, LVI (Fall 1972), 332-48; Mills Lane, ed., *General Oglethorpe's Georgia: Colonial Letters, 1733-1743*, 2 vols. (Savannah, 1975); B. Phinizy Spalding, *Oglethorpe's American Career* (Chicago and London, 1977). *DAB*, *DNB*.

STEPHENS, William, 1743-1751

Born on January 28, 1671 in Bowcombe, Isle of Wight, the son of Sir William, lieutenant governor of the Isle of Wight, and Lady Elizabeth Stephens. Married in 1696 to Mary Newdigate; father of seven sons, including Thomas, and two daughters. Studied at Winchester; received a B.A. from King's College, Cambridge in 1684 and an M.A. in 1688; admitted to the Middle Temple in London. Member of Parliament for Newport, Isle of Wight, and Barton, near Cowes, for about thirty years (prior to 1727). Served as an officer in the Isle of Wight militia; promoted to Colonel prior to 1706. Appointed Commissioner for Victualling the Force in 1712.

After some financial difficulties, left Parliament and worked for the York Building Company in Scotland. Engaged in the timber trade until about 1735. Arrived in South Carolina in 1736 to supervise a survey of four baronies for Colonel Samuel Horsey. Met James Oglethorpe there and, a year later, was appointed "Secretary for the Affairs of the Trust within the Province of Georgia"; served in that capacity until 1743. Author of a published journal, which in its present form covers the years 1737 to 1745. Appointed Indian

Commissioner in 1741, sharing that office with Oglethorpe. Chosen President of the county of Savannah in October 1741; became President of the entire colony of Georgia in April 1743.

When William Stephens became President of Georgia, he assumed control of a colony which had already undergone many of its early growing pains. Still, as its population and wealth steadily increased, Georgia's administration by a president and four assistants under the supervision of Trustees resident in England was felt to be inadequate, and on March 19, 1750 the Trustees relented somewhat by ordering the election of an Assembly to "propose, debate, and represent" suggestions for the colony's welfare. That same year, the Trustees approved an act repealing Georgia's prohibition of slavery, another decision which would have a major impact on the colony's future development. Buttressed by a slave labor system, the cultivation of rice would become during the royal period Georgia's largest agricultural activity.

Stephens left the president's office in poor health in the spring of 1751, and died at "Bewlie," his plantation at the mouth of the Vernon River, in August of 1753.

Bibliography: [William Stephens], *A State of the Province of Georgia* (London, 1742); Thomas Stephens, *The Castle-Builders: or the History of William Stephens* (London, 1759); E. Merton Coulter, ed., *The Journal of William Stephens, 1741-1745*, 2 vols. (Athens, Ga., 1958-59). *DNB*.

PARKER, Henry, 1751-1752

Date and place of birth, and names of parents unknown. Presumably the brother of William, one of Georgia's early settlers. Married to a woman named Anne (who survived him); father of Henry, John Savile, Henry William and Anne.

Immigrated to Georgia in June 1733, arriving in August of that year. Appointed Constable in 1733; became Third Bailiff in 1734 and First Bailiff in 1738. Served as First Assistant under President Stephens; named Vice President in March of 1750, an office which was created to assist the ailing Stephens with his duties. Also chosen as sole Indian Commissioner for Georgia in July 1750. Became President of Georgia in the spring of 1751, after Stephens retired for reasons of health.

As he prepared to assume the presidency of the colony, Parker was accused in an anonymous letter of secretly being a Roman Catholic. This allegation, probably based only on the fact that his mother had converted to Catholicism, was quickly denied by Parker, who signed a statement affirming his belief that "there is not any Transubstantiation in the Sacrament of the Lord's Supper, or in the elements of Bread and Wine." The new chief executive then proceeded to re-organize both Georgia's militia and its judicial system, changes which contributed to a resurgence of immigration into the area. Towards the end of Parker's tenure, royal officials in London began final negotiations with the Georgia Trustees, who had decided to surrender their charter to the Crown. Parker died in office in July 1752, shortly after the conclusion of an agreement which transformed Georgia into a royal colony.

Bibliography: Robert S. Roddenbery, Jr., *Ancestors and Descendants of Cader Atkins Parker, 1810-1886* (Adel, Ga., 1959).

GRAHAM, Patrick, 1752-1754

Date and place of birth, and names of parents unknown. Brother of David, Thomas, Mary and perhaps others. Married on March 6, 1740 to Ann Cuthbert, by whom he was the father of at least one daughter who died in infancy.

Acted as an apothecary and surgeon during the early years of the Georgia colony, and eventually became a planter and prominent resident of Savannah. Named an Assistant of the colony in 1745; appointed Agent in charge of distributing presents to the Indians in 1750. Succeeded the deceased Henry Parker as President of Georgia in the summer of 1752, and held that position until October 1754.

Graham's tenure represents a transitional period in the history of Georgia. Although the colony's Trustees had surrendered their charter to the Crown in June 1752, it was over two years before Governor John Reynolds arrived with his royal commission. During this interval Graham and his Board of Assistants sought to prepare Georgians for a government which owed its ultimate allegiance to the English Board of Trade. Despite the many misgivings expressed before the Crown acquired the colony, Graham's skillful leadership helped to eliminate virtually all signs of local discontent soon after royal rule had become a fact. In November of 1752, for example, the residents of Savannah enthusiastically expressed their gratitude "for His Majesties most gracious and Paternal Regard for them."

Following his replacement by Reynolds, Graham became a member of the Governor's Council. He died on May 30, 1755, and was buried two days later.

Bibliography: An abstract of Graham's will appears in National Society of Colonial Dames of America in the State of Georgia, *Abstracts of Colonial Wills of the State of Georgia, 1733-1777* (Atlanta, 1962), p. 64.

REYNOLDS, John, 1754-1757

Born *circa* 1713 in England; names of parents unknown. Married, and the father of several children. Entered the Royal Navy in 1728; promoted to Lieutenant in October 1736. Served on various ships on the Home Station, in the West Indies, and on the southern American Station. Commissioned as the first Royal Governor of Georgia in August 1754, and in October of that year assumed control of its government.

John Reynold's arrival in Georgia coincided with the first clashes of what would soon develop into a full-scale battle between Great Britain and France for control of North America. Unfortunately, Reynolds quickly showed himself to be a poor administrator, and instead of adopting practical means for improving the colony's precarious defensive posture or collecting taxes, he spent most of his time engaged in squabbles with the Council, which he accused of lacking respect for his executive authority. Supported by William Little, a long-time friend and his private secretary and political henchman, Reynolds treated the Council and eventually the Commons with disdain. After some disaffected Georgians sent an emissary to England with a critical report of the governor's activities, Reynold's behavior became even more high-handed, as he removed and suspended unsympathetic officials—until his own replacement by Henry Ellis in February of 1757.

Following his service as governor, Reynolds resumed his naval career, though he saw little action during the Seven Years' War. He was promoted to Rear Admiral on March 31, 1775 and to Vice-Admiral on January 29, 1778, soon after which he suffered a paralytic stroke. He never fully recovered from this illness, and died in London on February 3, 1788, slightly more than four months after his promotion to Admiral.

Bibliography: Albert B. Saye, ed., "Commission and Instructions of Governor John Reynolds, August 6, 1754," *Georgia Historical Quarterly*, XXX (June 1946), 125-62; Kenneth Coleman and Milton Ready, eds., *Original Papers of Governors Reynolds, Ellis, Wright, and Others, 1757-1763*, in *Colonial Records of the State of Georgia*, vol. 28, pt. 1 (Athens, Ga., 1976); Kenneth Coleman and Milton Ready, eds., *Original Papers of Governor John Reynolds, 1754-1756*, in *Colonial Records of the State of Georgia*, vol. 27 (Athens, Ga., 1977). *DAB*, *DNB*.

ELLIS, Henry, 1757-1760

Born on August 29, 1721 in Ireland, the second son of Francis, of County Monaghan, and Joan (Maxwell) Ellis. Never married. Ran away from home as a youth and went to sea; later reconciled with his father and inherited a large estate upon his father's death. Studied law at the Middle Temple in London. Travelled to Africa and the West Indies; participated in a search for a northwest passage in the Hudson Bay region in 1746-47, serving as the expedition's hydrographer, surveyor and mineralogist. Elected to the Royal Society in 1749. Author of *Voyage to Hudson's Bay, . . . for Discovering a North West Passage* (1748); *Considerations on the Great Advantages which would arise of the North-West Passage* (1750); and various papers on the earth's climate. Took over the government of Georgia in February 1757, and commissioned Royal Governor in July of 1758.

The three and one-half years spent by Henry Ellis as governor of Georgia provided a sharp contrast to the divisiveness which characterized his predecessor's tenure. Unlike John Reynolds, Ellis had an instinct for politics, made even more remarkable by his lack of previous experience in that field. After discouraging some members of the Assembly who were still supporters of Reynolds, Ellis had no further trouble with his legislature, and was able to concentrate on implementing his program to improve defense measures, increase the colony's population, and bring greater wealth into Georgia. Although his short term as governor made it impossible for Ellis to take more than the first steps towards these three goals, he was particularly successful in the area of defense; his administration saw to the construction of a palisade around Savannah, a log fort north of Augusta, and three forts south of Savannah, while at the same time it improved relations with the Creek Indians.

After Ellis's departure from Georgia on November 2, 1760, he was named Governor of Nova Scotia. He never took up the appointment, however, and his duties from 1761 to 1763 were performed by a deputy. Later, Ellis travelled throughout Europe and continued his maritime researches. He died in Naples, Italy on January 21, 1806.

Bibliography: William W. Abbot, "Henry Ellis," in Horace Montgomery, ed., *Georgians in Profile: Historical Essays in Honor of Ellis Merton Coulter* (Athens, Ga., 1958), 17-39; Kenneth Coleman and Milton Ready, eds., *Original Papers of Governors Reynolds, Ellis, Wright, and Others, 1757-1763*, in *Colonial Records of the State of Georgia*, vol. 28, pt. 1 (Athens, Ga., 1976). *DAB*, *DNB*.

WRIGHT, Sir James, 1760-1771, 1773-1776, 1779-1782

Born *circa* 1716 in London, England, the son of Robert, chief justice of South Carolina from 1731 to 1739, and Isabella (Wright) Pitts Wright. Married in 1740 to Sarah Maidman, by whom he was the father of three sons, including James and Alexander, and six daughters.

While still a child, immigrated with his parents to South Carolina. Held various jobs in the South Carolina courts, and began practice as an attorney as early as 1734; later studied law at Gray's Inn in London and called to the bar. Became Acting Attorney General of South Carolina in 1742, and assumed that office in his own right five years later, serving until 1757. Resided in London as Provincial Agent for South Carolina from 1757 to 1760. Appointed Lieutenant Governor of Georgia in May 1760, and sworn in during that October; commissioned Royal Governor in May 1761. Created Baronet in December 1772.

Governor Wright's long tenure covered the crucial period leading to the Revolution, and his success in governing the colony fluctuated with the rise and fall of the revolutionary movement. A good administrator, Wright enjoyed a cordial relationship with his Council and Commons House in the early 1760's, but his defense of the Stamp Act in 1765 and his reference to the Sons of Liberty as "Sons of Licentiousness" damaged his political reputation considerably. His authority deteriorated further when the Townshend Acts of 1767 and the Intolerable Acts of 1774 produced more popular discontent in the colony, and early in 1776, his power base gone, he left Georgia. Although he returned as governor in July 1779 and sought to re-establish royal authority, his control was not always effective, especially in the Georgia up-country, and he was forced to depart for the final time in 1782.

After the Revolution Wright was chosen to head the Board of Agents which considered the claims of American Loyalists; he himself received a sizable settlement to compensate for lost personal property estimated to be worth in excess of £80,000 at the beginning of the war. Wright died in London on November 20, 1785, and was buried in Westminster Abbey. Wrightsborough, in Columbia County, Georgia, was named in his honor.

Bibliography: "Letters from Sir James Wright," in Georgia Historical Society, *Collections*, vol. III (1873), 157-375; William Harden, "Sir James Wright: Governor of Georgia by Royal Commission, 1760-1782," *Georgia Historical Quarterly*, II (March 1918), 22-36; Kenneth Coleman, "James Wright," in Horace Montgomery, ed., *Georgians in Profile: Historical Essays in Honor of Ellis Merton Coulter* (Athens, Ga., 1958), 40-60; Robert G. Mitchell, cont., "Sir James Wright Looks at the American Revolution," *Georgia Historical Quarterly*, LIII (December 1969), 509-18; Kenneth Coleman and Milton Ready, eds., *Original Papers of Governors Reynolds, Ellis, Wright, and Others, 1757-1763*, in *Colonial Records of the State of Georgia*, vol. 28, pt. 1 (Athens, Ga., 1976). *DAB, DNB*.

HABERSHAM, James, 1771-1773

Born in January 1713 in Beverley, Yorkshire, England, the son of James and Elizabeth Habersham. An Anglican, and a friend of the evangelist George Whitefield. Brother of James (died in infancy), Elizabeth, Edward, George (died in infancy), Margaret (died in infancy), Joseph and Margaret. Married on December 26, 1740 to Mary Bolton, and the father of three surviving sons—James, Joseph and John.

Immigrated to Georgia in January 1738, arriving in May of that year. Opened a school for destitute children; joined Whitefield in the founding of the Bethesda Orphanage, and later took charge of the institution for several years. Became a merchant and organized the firm of Harris and Habersham; acquired large farming interests, particularly rice plantations which made extensive use of slave labor. Appointed Secretary of the province in 1750, and served in that capacity throughout most of the royal period; also acted as Councillor, becoming Senior Councillor in 1762. Served as Acting Governor of Georgia during the absence of Royal Governor James Wright, who resided in England from 1771 to 1773.

Habersham's period as acting governor was marked by the continuation of a political controversy over whether the governor had the right to reject a speaker elected by the Lower House. Acting on instructions from the absent Governor Wright, Habersham several times vetoed the election of Noble W. Jones in April 1772, in order to assert the chief executive's power in that area. Although the Lower House eventually selected Archibald Bulloch, a choice which Habersham approved, the refusal of the Lower House to remove from its journal a minute recording its third attempt to elect Jones caused the acting governor to dissolve that body. Habersham later made peace with the new Lower House, which met in December 1772 and elected William Young, after Jones declined the speakership to prevent a further dissolution.

Following his service as acting governor, Habersham's heavy business and political commitments caused his health to deteriorate, and he died in New Brunswick, New Jersey on August 28, 1775, while on a trip which he hoped would help him to recover. He was buried in Savannah, Georgia.

Bibliography: J. G. B. Bulloch, *A History and Genealogy of the Habersham Family*... (Columbia, S.C., 1901); *Historical Collections of the Joseph Habersham Chapter, D.A.R.*, vol. I (1902); *The Letters of the Hon. James Habersham, 1756-1775*, in Georgia Historical Society, *Collections*, vol. VI (1904); C. Ashley Ellefson, "James Habersham and Georgia Loyalism, 1764-1775," *Georgia Historical Quarterly*, XLIV (December 1960), 359-80; Wallace C. Smith, "Georgia Gentlemen: The Habershams of Eighteenth-Century Savannah," unpub. Ph.D. diss., University of North Carolina at Chapel Hill, 1971. *DAB*.

EWEN, William, 1775, 1776

Born *circa* 1720 in England; names of parents unknown. An Anglican. Brother of Richard and perhaps others. Married to Margaret Waldhauer.

Immigrated to Georgia in October 1734, arriving in December of that year. Worked in the Trustees' stores and as a potter; later established a store of his own, and eventually became a prosperous planter. Chosen to represent Abercorn and Goshen districts in Georgia's first Assembly, which convened in January 1751; also represented Ebenezer in the Georgia Commons House of Assembly from 1757 to 1772. Emerged as a leader of opposition to British policy during the early 1770's, and became a member of the Georgia Sons of Liberty. Elected President of a parochial Council of Safety in June 1775, which at first was authorized to act only in Christ's Church Parish; confirmed as president the following month, after Georgia's Second Provincial Congress, and served in that capacity until December of 1775. Also acted as *pro tempore* head of the Council of Safety between February and March of 1776.

Although his service on the Council of Safety lasted somewhat less than a year, Ewen presided over that body during the critical months when the authority of Royal Governor Sir James Wright began to deteriorate dramatically. By September 1775 Wright himself conceded that his power had virtually gone, as the colony's Assembly ceased to meet, and its justices convened only in those scattered areas that remained loyal to British rule. Toward the end of Ewen's tenure, confrontations between Whigs and Tories emphasized the desperate weakness of Georgia's royal government. Finally, in February 1776, Wright and several members of his Council boarded H.M.S. *Scarborough* at Cockspur Island, off the Georgia coast, and left Ewen and his supporters in full control of the province.

While Ewen continued to assist the Patriot cause following his tenure as Council of Safety president, he died in 1777; his will was proved on June 20 of that year.

Bibliography: An abstract of Ewen's will appears in National Society of Colonial Dames of America in the State of Georgia, *Abstracts of Colonial Wills of the State of Georgia*, 1733-1777 (Atlanta, 1962), pp. 46-47.

WALTON, George, 1775-1776, 1779-1780, 1789

Born *circa* 1749 near Farmville, Prince Edward County, Virginia, the son of Robert and Martha (Hughes) Walton. Brother of John, among others. Married in 1775 to Dorothy Camber, by whom he was the father of two sons, including Thomas Camber.

Raised by an uncle after his parents' death, and apprenticed to a carpenter as a young man; attended a local school for a brief period, but was largely self-educated. Studied law, and admitted to the bar in 1774. Became involved in the revolutionary movement in Georgia; attended the Second Provincial Congress which met in July 1775, and became its Secretary. Elected President of Georgia's Council of Safety, acting in that capacity from December 1775 to January 1776. Named to represent Georgia at the Continental Congress in February 1776 and, with the exception of several intervals, continued as a member of that body until September 1781; signed the Declaration of Independence in 1776. Captured by the British during the siege of Savannah late in 1778, and remained in their custody until his release as part of a prisoner exchange in September 1779. Served as Governor of Georgia from November 1779 to January 1780. Named Chief Justice of Georgia in 1783, a position he held until 1789. Attended the Georgia convention which met in 1788 to discuss the adoption of a new state constitution. Served as a Presidential Elector in 1789. Elected to another term as Governor of Georgia, and served from January to November of 1789.

Walton's first two periods as chief executive gave him little opportunity to administer the new state without opposition. In July 1779, for example, Royal Governor Sir James Wright returned under the protection of British arms to Savannah, where until 1782 he endeavored to re-establish his authority. Meanwhile, Georgia's Whigs were themselves at odds, as a faction led by John Wereat contested Walton's election late in 1779. By 1789, however, the return of peace had brought an end to much of this sort of political discord, enabling Georgia's leaders to ratify a new state constitution during Walton's final administration.

Following his final gubernatorial term, Walton briefly left public life, but he was soon lured out of retirement by an appointment as Judge of the Georgia Superior Court, an office which he held intermittently until his death. In 1795 he was designated to serve as a temporary substitute for James Jackson in the United States Senate, and from December of 1795 until April 1796 he remained a rather inconspicuous member of that body. Walton died at "College Hill," his Georgia estate, on February 2, 1801. Although he was first buried in the Rosney Cemetery, he was re-interred in 1848 beneath a monument in Augusta erected to commemorate Georgia's signers of the Declaration of Independence.

Bibliography: Lucian Lamar Knight, "Genealogy of the Knight, Walton, Woodson, Lamar, Daniel, Benning, Cobb, Jackson, Grant, and Other Georgia Families" (193_?), typescript volume in Local History and Genealogy Division, New York Public Library; L. B. Andrus, "1933 Memoranda . . . in *re* Walton Families," mimeograph copy in the Library of Congress, Washington, D.C.; Edward J. Cashin, Jr., "George Walton and the Forged Letter," *Georgia Historical Quarterly*, LXII (Summer 1978), 133-45. *DAB*.

BULLOCH, Archibald, 1776-1777

Born *circa* 1730 in Charlestown, South Carolina, the son of James, a Scottish clergyman and Carolina planter, and Jean (Stobo) Bulloch. Brother of Jane and Christian. Married on October 9, 1764 to Mary De Veaux, by whom he was the father of James, Archibald, Jane and William.

Moved with his parents to a plantation on the Savannah River; later studied law and became a planter. Elected to the Georgia Commons House of Assembly in 1768, and served until 1772; presided as Speaker of the Commons House from 1771 to 1772; again named Speaker in April 1772, but the dissolution of the Commons House by Acting Governor James Habersham prevented him from filling the office. Appointed in January 1775 as a delegate to the Second Continental Congress in Philadelphia, but never attended. Served as member and President of the Second Provincial Congress which met in Georgia in July 1775, and sent by that body as a delegate to Congress. Led a group of militiamen and Creek Indians in an attack on a British and Tory base on Tybee Island in March 1776. Appointed President of Georgia soon after the state's first temporary constitution, the "Rules and Regulations of 1776," went into effect in the spring of that year.

Bulloch's position as president carried with it little real power, since Georgia's Provincial Congress continued to make most of the major decisions during the first months after independence. Indeed, what scant executive authority he possessed was shared with a Council of Safety. Perhaps the most important political development of Bulloch's brief tenure was the adoption of a new and more detailed state constitution on February 5, 1777, only a few weeks before his death in office. Like its predecessor, this constitution placed most of the power in the Legislature, a one-house body known as the House of Assembly, whose members were to be elected annually by the voters.

Bibliography: J. G. B. Bulloch, *A Biographical Sketch of Hon. Archibald Bulloch, President of Georgia, 1776-77* (n.p., 190_?); Emma Hamilton Bulloch, "Archibald Bulloch: A Southern Statesman," *Journal of American History*, II (1908), 225-34; J. G. B. Bulloch, *A History and Genealogy of the Families of Bulloch and Stobo, and of Irvine of Cults* (Washington, D.C., 1911). *DAB*.

GWINNETT, Button, 1777

Born *circa* 1735 in Down Hatherby, Gloucestershire, England, the son of Samuel, an Anglican clergyman, and Anne (Emes) Gwinnett. A Congregationalist. The second son of a family numbering at least seven. Married on April 19, 1757 to Ann Bourne; father of Amelia, Ann and Elizabeth Ann.

Engaged in Anglo-American trade; settled in about 1765 in Savannah, Georgia; worked as a merchant for a short time and then established himself as a planter by purchasing St. Catherine's Island, off the Georgia coast.

Served as Justice of the Peace and local Pilotage Commissioner in 1768-69; member of the Georgia Commons House of Assembly from 1769 to 1771, representing St. John's Parish (now Liberty County). Elected by the Georgia Council of Safety as a dėlegate to the Philadelphia Continental Congress in January 1776, and signed the Declaration of Independence. Returned to Savannah in August 1776; elected Speaker of the Georgia Assembly in October 1776, and re-elected as a delegate to the Continental Congress. Contributed to the drafting of Georgia's Constitution in early 1777. Succeeded Archibald Bulloch as President of the state in March 1777, shortly after Bulloch's death.

Gwinnett's tenure as acting president of Georgia produced almost immediate controversy, which led to his defeat nearly two months later by John A. Treutlen, formerly a member of the Gwinnett political faction. While acting president, Gwinnett had also served as Commander-in-Chief of the state militia, and his military involvement came under legislative scrutiny after the failure of a Georgia expedition against British troops entrenched in East Florida. Gwinnett was eventually cleared of negligence in the matter, but his main political antagonist, General Lachlan McIntosh, was dissatisfied and attacked Gwinnett's credibility. As a result, the two men fought a duel on the outskirts of Savannah, in which Gwinnett was mortally wounded. He died three days later, on May 19, 1777; he is thought to have been buried in Colonial Park Cemetery, Savannah. Gwinnett County, Georgia, established in 1818, was named in his honor.

Bibliography: Charles C. Jones, Jr., "Button Gwinnett," *Magazine of American History*, XII (November 1884), 425-32; William M. Clemens, *Button Gwinnett, Man of Mystery . . . A Brief Biographical Review* (Pompton Lakes, N.J., 1921); Walter G. Charlton, "Button Gwinnett," *Georgia Historical Quarterly*, VIII (June 1924), 146-58; Charles F. Jenkins, *Button Gwinnett* (New York, 1926). *DAB*.

TREUTLEN, John Adam, 1777-1778

A Salzburger, born in 1726 in Austria; names of parents unknown. Married to a woman named Ann Margaret. Employed as a schoolmaster during Georgia's early years as a colony; left the teaching profession by 1766 to begin a business career. Acted as a member of the Georgia Commons House of Assembly in the early 1770's, but decided to support the Patriot cause in the Revolution. Represented St. Matthew's Parish at Georgia's Second Provincial Congress, which convened in July 1775. Served as Governor of Georgia from May 1777 to January 1778.

During Treutlen's brief administration, controversy between South Carolina and Georgia overshadowed the revolutionary struggle between Whigs and Tories. Led by William Henry Drayton and John Smith, South Carolina sought to persuade Georgia to give up its role as an independent state, and to accept annexation by its more populous neighbor to the north. In response to this propaganda, Treutlen issued a proclamation in July 1777, which offered a reward of £100 for the apprehension of Drayton and anyone else involved in the scheme. Drayton replied by ridiculing Georgia's leaders, noting that to "procure something like law and order" many Georgians might choose British rule, rather than remain under the authority of a "burlesque Government."

In January of 1778 a new Assembly which met in Savannah selected John Houstoun to replace Treutlen as chief executive. Four years later Treutlen died, the victim, according to one account, of a murder plot devised by Tories in Orangeburg, South Carolina.

HOUSTOUN, John, 1778-1779, 1784-1785

Born on August 31, 1744 near present-day Waynesboro, Georgia, the son of Sir Patrick Houstoun, a member of Georgia's colonial Council, and his wife, the former Priscilla Dunbar. Brother of Patrick, George, James, William and Ann Priscilla. Married to Hannah Bryan; no children.

Studied law, and began a practice in Savannah. Chosen by the First Provincial Congress, which met in January 1775, to serve as a delegate to the Second Continental Congress in Philadelphia, but did not attend. Participated in efforts which resulted in the creation of a Council of Safety in June 1775 and a Second Provincial Congress in July of that year; again selected by the Provincial Congress as delegate, and on this occasion attended the Continental Congress. Elected Governor of Georgia in January 1778, serving until January 1779;* again served from January 1784 to January 1785.

Houstoun's first period as governor occurred during a critical year of the Revolutionary War, and in his capacity as Commander-in-Chief of the state militia, he took charge in April 1778 when Georgia's troops prepared to join in an assault on St. Augustine in Florida. The expedition began in turmoil, however, as Houstoun and General Robert Howe, the commander of a force of Continentals, quarreled over who would command the operation. After a brief foray to the south which failed to bring about any contact with the enemy, Howe returned north and Houstoun, whose men were now accompanied only by a group of South Carolina militia under Colonel Andrew Williamson, returned to Savannah to protect his weakened army. Later that year Houstoun's renewed failure to co-operate with Howe contributed to the occupation of Savannah by a British force from New York, an occupation which continued until July of 1782. Houstoun returned as governor in 1784 after the war had ended, but while peace had been restored the competition between Georgia's inland and lowland sections was becoming more prominent. With the population of the western part of the state growing at a faster rate than that of the east, concessions to inland interests soon became necessary, such as the later decision to establish the new state university in Athens rather than in the more eastern towns of Augusta or Savannah.

Subsequent to his service as governor, Houstoun occupied a number of other offices, primarily in the judicial sphere. He was Georgia's Chief Justice in 1786, a Justice for Chatham County in 1787, and Judge of the Superior Court of the Eastern Circuit from 1791 to 1793. He was also chosen as a member of the first Board of Trustees of the proposed state university in 1785, and a Commissioner to settle the boundary dispute with South Carolina in 1787; he served as Mayor of Savannah in 1789 and 1790. Houstoun died at "White Bluff," near Savannah, on July 20, 1796. Houston County, Georgia, created in 1821, was named in his honor.

Bibliography: J. G. B. Bulloch, *A History and Genealogy of the Families of Bayard, Houstoun of Georgia, and the Descent of the Bolton Family*... (Washington, D.C., 1919); Edith Duncan Johnston, *The Houstouns of Georgia* (Athens, Ga., 1950). *DAB*.

*Georgia's Whig faction was virtually without leadership between January and August of 1779, following the British capture of Savannah. During this period William Glascock and Seth J. Cuthbert made sporadic efforts to provide leadership for the state's Whigs.

WEREAT, John, 1779

Born *circa* 1730, a native of England's West Country. Married to Hannah Wilkinson. Arrived in Savannah early in 1759, where he entered a partnership with William Handley, a merchant. Despite some business setbacks, acquired considerable wealth by the eve of the Revolution. Participated in each of the provincial congresses which met in Georgia between 1775 and 1777, at first representing St. Andrew's Parish and later the town and district of Savannah. Elected to the Georgia Council of Safety in February 1776, but soon relinquished that position to serve as the new state's Continental Agent. Also became involved in the factionalism which afflicted the Whigs in Georgia during the Revolution, aligning himself with the supporters of General Lachlan McIntosh. Chosen President of the "Supreme Executive Council" in August 1779, a body which exercised authority in Wilkes and Richmond counties.

Wereat's elevation to the presidency of the Supreme Executive Council represented one response to Georgia's desperate military situation. With

British forces in control of Savannah, the conservative Whig faction to which Wereat belonged had no choice but to establish its political base in the Georgia up-country. Although this government was not sanctioned by the Georgia Constitution of 1777, Wereat and his followers promised to arrange for the election of a House of Assembly as soon as circumstances permitted. However, opposition from the state's radical Whigs, along with military reverses and a lack of funds, so restricted Wereat's ability to govern that in late 1779 the Supreme Executive Council reluctantly gave way to a new Whig government led by George Walton.

Wereat then took a seat in the Georgia House of Assembly which met in Augusta early in 1780. While he was taken prisoner later that year and sent to Charlestown, South Carolina, Wereat won his release from the British in the summer of 1781, and from 1782 to 1793 he served as Georgia's State Auditor. Wereat died on January 27, 1799.

Bibliography: George R. Lamplugh, " 'To Check and Discourage the Wicked and Designing': John Wereat and the Revolution in Georgia," *Georgia Historical Quarterly*, LXI (Winter 1977), 295-307.

HOWLEY, Richard, 1780

Born *circa* 1740, probably in St. John's Parish (now Liberty County), Georgia. Married, and the father of at least one daughter. Studied law, and began a practice in St. John's Parish. Served as a member and President of the Supreme Executive Council of Georgia in December 1779, and chosen as Governor of the state early in January of 1780.

Howley's election resolved a factional dispute among Georgia's Whigs, in which both a "Supreme Executive Council" and another group led by George Walton claimed authority, though neither possessed effective power over the entire state so long as British forces held Savannah and coastal Georgia. Consequently, while Howley's accession signified the return of constitutional state government, his authority was at best limited to the piedmont.

Soon after his selection as chief executive, Howley was named as a delegate from Georgia to the Continental Congress, and sometime in the winter of 1780 he left for Philadelphia.* *En route* to that city he carried Georgia's state archives to New Bern, North Carolina, where he deposited them for safekeeping. While Howley did return to Georgia in May of 1780 to resume his administration, the danger of capture by British troops soon forced him to flee the state and to delegate what authority he still held to Stephen Heard, the president of the Council.

As a member of Congress, Howley wrote, with George Walton and William Few, a pamphlet entitled *Observations upon the Effects of Certain Late*

Political Suggestions by the Delegates of Georgia (1781). The pamphlet rejected a proposal that a compromise peace might be arranged granting independence to all the rebellious colonies except South Carolina and Georgia which, since they were then largely under British control anyway, could be offered to Great Britain as an inducement to end the war.

At the end of the Revolution, Howley returned to Georgia and served as that state's Chief Justice from 1782 to 1783. He died in Savannah in December 1784. *DAB*.

*During Howley's initial attendance at Congress, George Wells, Humphrey Wells and Stephen Heard all wielded limited executive authority in those areas not under British control.

HEARD, Stephen, 1780

Born in 1740 in Virginia, the son of John and Bridget (Carroll) Heard. Brother of five. Married to a Miss Germany; following the death of his first wife during the Revolution, remarried to Elizabeth Darden; father of a large number of children.

Fought in the French and Indian War, and later immigrated to Wilkes County, Georgia. Elected to Georgia's Supreme Executive Council in January 1780, and as President of that body, succeeded Richard Howley as the Whig faction's chief executive in May of 1780.

When the Council finally persuaded Richard Howley to leave for Philadelphia and the Continental Congress, his departure from the state made Heard, as Council president, the new leader of Georgia's Whigs. Despite his official title, however, Heard's authority was severely circumscribed by recent British gains. Indeed, only Wilkes County and part of Richmond County remained untouched by the recently revitalized royal government based in Savannah. During Heard's brief tenure military considerations occupied most of his time, since in mid-1780 guerrilla warfare in the Georgia back-country exploded with a violence unsurpassed by anything that had occurred up to that point in the Revolution. When Heard relinquished his office in August of 1780 to Myrick Davies, the new president of the Executive Council, the Whigs were engaged in a desperate holding action, designed to frustrate British efforts to dominate the entire state.

Heard later held several public positions, including Chief Justice of the Inferior Court, before his death in Elbert County, Georgia in 1810. Heard County, established in 1830, was named in his honor.

Bibliography: A. Evans Wynn, *Southern Lineages: Records of Thirteen Families* (Atlanta, 1940); Harold Heard, *Early Records of Heards* (Amarillo, Texas, n.d.).

DAVIES, Myrick, 1780-1781

Date and place of birth, and names of parents unknown, but referred to in the Charlestown *Royal Gazette* for October 24, 1781 as an "old miller from Briar Creek." Named to Georgia's Supreme Executive Council in July 1779. As President of the Council, succeeded Stephen Heard as leader of the Whig faction in the state, after Heard departed for North Carolina in August of 1780.

During Davies' period at the head of Georgia's Whig government, guerrilla warfare continued to ravage the back-country. In September of 1780 an unsuccessful Whig assault on Tory troops who held Augusta led to a renewed effort by the Tories to subdue the entire state. While this new offensive never achieved its goal, the Whig military position remained precarious until 1781. In April of that year Whig militia under the command of Colonel Elijah Clarke and General Andrew Williamson again laid siege to Augusta, and two months later the town capitulated. By August Whig partisans in the Georgia back-country were strong enough to call an Assembly, which attracted delegates from virtually every county in the state. At that meeting Dr. Nathan Brownson was elected governor, enabling Davies to relinquish his office.

Although he returned to his seat on the Council following his tenure as chief executive, Davies only lived until late 1781, when he was killed by a group of Loyalists under the command of a Captain Brantley.

BROWNSON, Nathan, 1781-1782

Born on May 14, 1742 in Woodbury, Connecticut, the fifth son of Timothy and Abigail (Jenner) Brownson. Married to Elizabeth (Donnom) Martin, by whom he may have been the father of one or two children before her death in April 1775; apparently remarried a short time later to another woman with the same first name; father of two sons by his second wife, at least one of whom died young.

Studied at Yale College, and received an A.B. from that institution in 1761. Probably began to practice medicine in his native town, but later moved to Georgia, where he became both a planter and physician in St. John's Parish (present-day Liberty County). Represented St. John's at the Georgia Provincial Congress which met in July 1775; also served intermittently as a delegate from Georgia to the Continental Congress between late 1776 or early 1777 and October 1777. Named Deputy Purchaser of Hospitals by Congress in March 1781, a position he held until his election as Governor by the Georgia Legislature in August of that year; continued to serve as chief executive until January 1782.

Brownson's tenure lasted for only five months, but it represented a transitional period in the state's early history. Although Patriot forces in Georgia had been greatly disorganized since the return of Royal Governor Sir James Wright to Savannah in 1779, the British Army's strategic position had eroded significantly by the summer of 1781, a development which enabled Brownson and his Assembly to take strong measures against residents who had fled the state. By threatening to tax heavily the property of absentee Georgians who did not return and assist the effort to expel the enemy, Brownson's government did much to rally the support of those who only a few months earlier had acquiesced in the British occupation of Savannah.

After his brief gubernatorial career, Brownson remained in public life. In June of 1782 he was appointed head of the hospital facilities operated in the South by the Continental Congress, and several years later he became a Trustee of the future University of Georgia. In 1788 he participated in the state convention which ratified the Federal Constitution, experience which he used to good advantage when he attended the Georgia Constitutional Convention the following year. Brownson also served in the Georgia House of Representatives, acting as Speaker of that body on two occasions, and presided over the State Senate in 1791. He died on his plantation in Liberty County, Georgia on October 18, 1796.

Bibliography: An abstract of the will of Brownson's wife appears in National Society of Colonial Dames of America in the State of Georgia, *Abstracts of Colonial Wills of the State of Georgia, 1733-1777* (Atlanta, 1962), p. 19.

MARTIN, John, 1782-1783

Born *circa* 1730 in Rhode Island; names of parents unknown. Named Naval Officer for the port of Sunbury in 1762, and later became a leader of Georgia's opposition to British colonial policy. Represented the town and district of Savannah in the Second Provincial Congress which met in July 1775; also served on the Georgia Council of Safety until his appointment as First Lieutenant of the colony's Seventh Company; promoted to Captain in July 1776, and by 1781 had risen to the rank of Lieutenant Colonel. Elected Governor by the Georgia Legislature in January 1782, a position he retained until January of the following year.

Martin took office at a time when the British were rapidly losing their hold over the Georgia low-country, and by the spring of 1782 Continental forces under the command of Brigadier General Anthony Wayne had begun to threaten the enemy troops who still occupied Savannah. In July the British finally evacuated the town, thereby placing Martin's government in control of the entire state. Despite this victory, however, Georgia's economy continued to experience severe disruptions as a result of the long war, a problem which intensified Whig hostility toward those residents of the state who had supported the British cause. To appease this anger, the legislature implemented laws which established various penalties, ranging from minor restrictions to confiscation of land and banishment, as a means of punishing Georgia's Loyalist faction.

After his gubernatorial tenure, Martin became a member of a board of commissioners appointed to negotiate a treaty with the Cherokee Indians, and a short time later he was chosen State Treasurer. Martin died in January 1786, while on a trip to the west where he hoped to recover his health.

Bibliography: "Official Letters of Governor John Martin, 1782-1783," *Georgia Historical Quarterly*, I (December 1917), 281-335; J. Montgomery Seaver, *Martin Family Records* (Philadelphia, n.d.).

HALL, Lyman, 1783-1784

Born on April 12, 1724 in Wallingford, Connecticut, the son of John and Mary (Street) Hall. A Congregationalist, and for a time a Congregational minister. Married on May 20, 1752 to Abigail Burr, who died on July 8, 1753; remarried to Mary Osborn, probably in 1754; father of a son, John, by his second marriage. Graduated from Yale in 1747, and later studied theology with an uncle, the Reverend Samuel Hall. Ordained in 1749 by the Fairfield [Connecticut] West Consociation; dismissed by the Consociation in 1751, but reinstated after expressing repentance. Soon resigned from the ministry, studied medicine with a local doctor, and established a practice in Wallingford. Migrated to Dorchester, South Carolina in the 1750's; eventually founded, with some transplanted New England Congregationalists, the town of Sunbury in St. John's Parish (now Liberty County), Georgia. Following the destruction of his Georgia estate in 1778, moved to the North until the end of the Revolution; returned to Georgia in 1782, and practiced medicine in Savannah.

Attended the revolutionary convention held in Savannah in the summer of 1774; sent by St. John's Parish as its "delegate" to the Continental Congress, and admitted by Congress as a non-voting member in May 1775. Later officially appointed as part of the newly-selected Georgia delegation and served, with several intervals, until 1777. Signer of the Declaration of Independence. Elected from St. John's Parish to the State Legislature in January 1783, and chosen by that body as Governor.

Hall's tenure as chief executive of Georgia was marked by both controversy and positive achievement. Taking office shortly after the British had evacuated Savannah, Hall presided over a state which still bore the scars of its occupation by hostile troops. Hall retaliated by making some questionable purchases of confiscated Loyalist lands, and by rejecting a legislative decision which readmitted banished Loyalists to the state. On the other hand, he recommended in July 1783 that available land be used as an endowment for a state university, a recommendation which led to the issuance of a charter in 1785 and the eventual opening of Franklin College (later the University of Georgia) in 1801.

When his term as governor ended in January 1784, Hall returned to Savannah, serving for a time as a Judge of the Inferior Court of Chatham County and as a Trustee of the proposed state university. In 1790 he moved from Savannah and purchased "Shell Bluff," a plantation in Burke County. Hall died at "Shell Bluff" on October 19, 1790, and was buried there; he was later re-interred at the Signer's Monument in Augusta, Georgia. Hall County, Georgia, established in 1818, was named in his honor.

Bibliography: Rev. David B. Hall, *The Halls of New England* (Albany, N.Y., 1883); T. P. Hall, *Genealogical Notes: Relating to the Families of Hon. Lyman Hall of Ga., Hon. Samuel Holden Parsons Hall, of Binghampton, N.Y., and Hon. Nathan Kelsey Hall, of Buffalo, N.Y.* (Albany, N.Y., 1886); Charles C. Jones, Jr., "Dr. Lyman Hall, Governor of Georgia, 1783," *Magazine of American History*, XXV (January 1891), 35-46. *DAB*.

ELBERT, Samuel, 1785-1786

Born *circa* 1740 in Prince William Parish, South Carolina, the son of a Baptist clergyman. Orphaned in his early years. Married to Elizabeth Rae; father of six children. Migrated to Georgia, and became a merchant and a trader to the West Indies.

Member of the Georgia Commons House of Assembly from 1769 to 1771. Joined the Sons of Liberty; was serving as Captain of a Savannah grenadier company in February 1773. Served on Georgia's first Council of Safety in June 1775, and appointed to several Council committees charged with the defense of Georgia. Delegate to the Provincial Congress held in Savannah in July 1775. Joined the Continental Army, and appointed Lieutenant Colonel by the Georgia Provincial Congress in January 1776; promoted to Colonel in July of that year. Commanded Continental forces during an unsuccessful assault on East Florida in spring 1777; assumed command of all Continental troops in Georgia after his return to Savannah. Captured three British vessels in April 1778; fought a losing battle at Briar Creek in March 1779, and was captured by the British; exchanged in June 1781, and commanded a brigade at Yorktown. Brevetted Brigadier General in November 1783, and later became Major General of the Georgia militia. Chosen to the commission which negotiated with the Creeks and Cherokees in 1783. Declined election to the Continental Congress in 1784, but in January 1785 was inaugurated as Governor of Georgia.

Elbert's period as governor occurred during a year when Georgia was still recovering from the economic distress and unsettled conditions brought about by the prolonged war. He sought to discourage squatters who were residing on Georgia soil without legal title, and tried to make peace with restive Indians on the state's northern frontier. Also under Elbert, legislation was passed which attempted to systematize the taxation of land in the state.

Following his term as governor, Elbert served as Sheriff of Chatham County. He was Vice-President of the Society of the Cincinnati, and Grand Master of Georgia's Masonic order. Elbert died in Savannah on November 1, 1788. Elbert County, Georgia, founded in 1790, was named in his honor.

Bibliography: Charles C. Jones, Jr., *The Life and Service of the Honorable Major Gen. Samuel Elbert of Georgia* (Cambridge, 1887). Elbert's order book for 1776-78, and his letter book covering the period from January to November 1785, are both printed in Georgia Historical Society, *Collections*, vol. V, pt. 2 (1902). *DAB*.

TELFAIR, Edward, 1786-1787, 1789-1793

Born *circa* 1735 at "Town Head," the Telfair estate in Kirkcudbrightshire, Scotland; names of parents unknown. Brother of William. Married on May 18, 1774 to Sally Gibbons, by whom he was the father of Josiah, Thomas, Alexander, Mary, Sarah and Margaret.

Educated at a grammar school in Kirckcudbright, and later engaged in commerce. Immigrated to America around 1758 as an agent for a mercantile house; settled in Savannah, Georgia about 1766. Served in the Georgia Commons House of Assembly in 1768, representing Augusta. Became one of the leaders of Georgia's revolutionary movement during the 1770's, attending its provincial congresses; served as a member of the Georgia Council of Safety in 1775 and 1776. Represented Georgia in the Continental Congress from July 1778 to January 1783, except for a leave of absence between November 1778 and May 1780; also sat in Congress from 1784 to 1785, and from 1788 to 1789. Presided as Justice and Assistant Justice for Burke County at different times between 1781 and 1784. Elected to the Georgia Legislature in 1783 and again in 1785. Chosen by the Legislature as Governor of the state, taking office in January 1786 and serving until January of the following year; again named chief executive in 1789, while acting as a member of the Legislature from Richmond County, and occupied that office from November 1789 to November 1793. Attended the Georgia convention which ratified the Federal Constitution in January 1788.

During his initial term as governor, Telfair took vigorous action against the Creek Indians, who had carried out isolated attacks on settlers in the spring of 1786. By November of that year Georgia's commissioners had arranged a treaty which required the Creeks to turn over five of their own people as hostages, in order to guarantee the tribe's "good faith and sincere intentions." Nevertheless, the pact did not endure for more than a few months, since the Creeks remained under the influence of Alexander McGillivray, a part-Indian who had persuaded the Creeks to fight on the British side during the Revolution.

Telfair's second period in the governor's chair was likewise concerned with Indian affairs, especially when Georgia and the federal government wrangled over the question of jurisdiction. Telfair also played a major role in the distribution of Georgia's public lands, a sphere in which he appears to have been guilty of signing illegal warrants for his friends.

Following his second gubernatorial term, Telfair retired to Augusta, Georgia. He died in Savannah on September 19, 1807, and was buried in his family vault in the old Colonial Cemetery; he was later re-interred in Bonaventure Cemetery.

Bibliography: "Some Official Letters of Governor Edward Telfair," *Georgia Historical Quarterly*, I (June 1917), 141-54; E. Merton Coulter, "Edward Telfair," *Georgia Historical Quarterly*, XX (June 1936), 99-124. *DAB*.

MATHEWS, George, 1787-1788, 1793-1796

Born on August 30, 1739 in Augusta County, Virginia, the son of John and Betsy Ann (Archer) Mathews. Brother of ten. Married in 1762 to Anne Polly Paul; following the death of his first wife, remarried in 1790 to Mrs. Margaret Reed, whom he divorced in 1797; married for a third time in the summer of 1804 to Mrs. Mary Carpenter; father of Charles, George, John, William, Ann, Jane, Margaret and Rebecca, all by his first wife.

Self-educated. Commanded a company of volunteers deployed against the Indians in 1757, and fought the Indians again at Point Pleasant in October 1774. Saw extensive military action during the Revolution, participating in campaigns which included the battles of Brandywine Creek and Germantown. Wounded and captured by the British in the latter engagement, but released in December 1781, following a prisoner exchange. Later named Brigadier General of the Georgia militia. Returned to Georgia after the war, where he was elected Governor by the State Legislature; served as chief executive from January 1787 to January 1788. Chosen to represent Georgia in the First United States Congress, and occupied that position from March 1789 to March 1791. Again named Governor by the Georgia Legislature in 1793, an office he held from November of that year until January 1796.

Both of Mathews' terms as governor were concerned with Indian affairs, but his second administration was especially noteworthy for the scandal surrounding the Yazoo land fraud. Late in 1794 four companies offered to purchase approximately thirty-five million acres of land for a price totalling only $500,000. Although Mathews asked for some revisions before approving the sale, he did eventually sign a bill authorizing the transaction. By the time he left office in January of 1796, the uproar over this questionable speculation had not yet subsided, and in April 1798 President John Adams was forced to withdraw Mathews' nomination as governor of the newly-created Mississippi Territory, largely because of criticism over his role in the Yazoo affair.

Toward the end of his life, Mathews participated in various intrigues aimed at acquiring the Floridas from Spain. These efforts culminated in 1812 with a military operation under Mathews' direction, which seized various portions of East Florida in the name of the United States. Secretary of State James Monroe repudiated the ex-governor's course of action, however, and on August 30, 1812 Mathews died in Augusta, Georgia, embittered by Monroe's lack of support.

Bibliography: R. Walton Moore, "General George Mathews," *Sons of the Revolution in the State of Virginia Magazine*, II (1923), 3-11; Isaac J. Cox, "The Border Missions of General George Mathews," *Mississippi Valley Historical Review*, XII (December 1925), 309-33; Paul Kruse, "A Secret Agent in East Florida: General George Mathews and the Patriot War," *Journal of Southern History*, XVIII (May 1952), 193-217; G. Melvin Herndon, "George Mathews, Frontier Patriot," *Virginia Magazine of History and Biography*, LXXVII (July 1969), 307-28. *DAB*.

HANDLEY, George, 1788-1789

Born on February 9, 1752 near Sheffield, Yorkshire, England, the son of Thomas Handley. Married toward the end of the Revolution to Sarah Howe, the niece of Samuel Elbert (who served as governor of Georgia from 1785 to 1786); father of Thomas.

Arrived in Savannah in May 1775; acted as an officer in the Continental Army, becoming a Captain in October 1776 and eventually attaining the rank of Lieutenant Colonel. Captured at Augusta in 1779, and transported to Charlestown, South Carolina as a prisoner of war. Chosen Sheriff of Richmond County, Georgia following the Revolution; also elected regularly to the State Legislature, and in 1787 served as Georgia's Inspector General. Named Governor by the State Legislature in January 1788, after James Jackson declined the office, and acted in that capacity until January of 1789.

The major political development during Handley's period as chief executive was the organization of a state constitutional convention in November 1788. Meeting in Augusta, the delegates drafted a document which in some ways mirrored the Federal Constitution which Georgia had ratified ten months earlier, especially in its guarantee of a stronger role for the executive branch. While this constitution did not go into effect until almost a year later, after a group of amendments had been considered, the final product bore a close resemblance to the draft written under Handley's governorship. During his administration Handley also provided a strong impetus for land speculation, as he approved grants for considerably more than the 1,000 acre limit permitted by state law.

Following his gubernatorial tenure, Handley was named Collector of the port of Brunswick by President Washington in August 1789. He continued to hold that position until his death at "Rae's Hall," Georgia on September 17, 1793.

MARYLAND

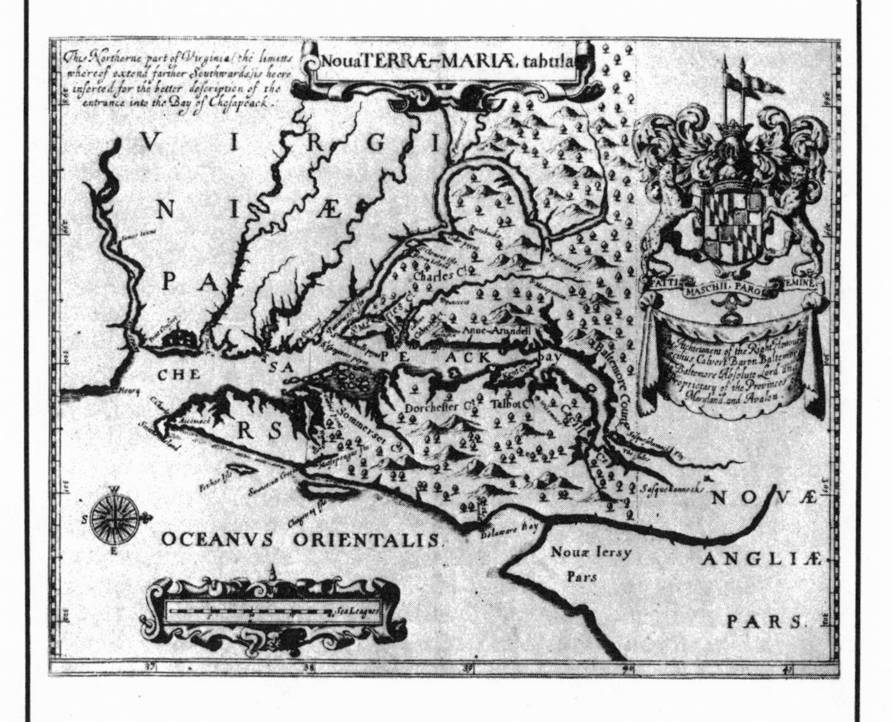
Noua TERRÆ-MARIÆ tabula
This Northerne part of Virginia, the limitts whereof extend farther Southwards, is heere inserted for the better description of the entrance into the Bay of Chesapeack.
V I R G I N I Æ P A R S
CHE SA PEACK bay
Charles Co.
Anne-Arundell
Dorchester Co.
Talbot Co.
Sommerset
Baltemore County
NOVÆ ANGLIÆ PARS
OCEANVS ORIENTALIS
Delaware bay
Nouæ Iersy Pars
Sea Leagues

Chronology

1634-1643	Leonard Calvert
1643-1644	Giles Brent
1644-1645	Leonard Calvert
1645	Richard Ingle
1646	Edward Hill
1646-1647	Leonard Calvert
1647-1649	Thomas Greene
1649-1652	William Stone
1652	*A group of commissioners appointed by the English Parliament governed for several months.*
1652-1654	William Stone
1654-1658	*A group of commissioners appointed by the Parliamentary commissioners governed.*
1658-1660	Josias Fendall
1660-1661	Philip Calvert
1661-1669	Charles Calvert, 3rd Lord Baltimore
1669-1670	*A group of deputy governors administered during Charles Calvert's absence in England.*
1670-1676	Charles Calvert, 3rd Lord Baltimore
1676	Jesse Wharton
1676-1679	Thomas Notley
1679-1684	Charles Calvert, 3rd Lord Baltimore
1684-1688	*A council of deputy governors administered.*
1688-1689	William Joseph
1689-1690	John Coode
1690-1692	Nehemiah Blakiston
1692-1693	Lionel Copley
1693	Sir Edmund Andros
1693-1694	Nicholas Greenberry
1694	Sir Edmund Andros
1694	Sir Thomas Lawrence
1694-1698	Francis Nicholson
1698-1702	Nathaniel Blakiston
1702-1794	Thomas Tench
1704-1709	John Seymour
1709-1714	Edward Lloyd
1714-1720	John Hart
1720	Thomas Brooke

1720-1727	Capt. Charles Calvert
1727-1731	Benedict Leonard Calvert
1731-1732	Samuel Ogle
1732-1733	Charles Calvert, 5th Lord Baltimore
1733-1742	Samuel Ogle
1742-1747	Thomas Bladen
1747-1752	Samuel Ogle
1752-1753	Benjamin Tasker
1753-1769	Horatio Sharpe
1769-1776	Robert Eden
1775-1777	Daniel of St. Thomas Jenifer
1777-1779	Thomas Johnson
1779-1782	Thomas Sim Lee
1782-1785	William Paca
1785-1788	William Smallwood
1788-1791	John Eager Howard

BIBLIOGRAPHY

Browne, W. H., *et al.*, eds., *Archives of Maryland*, 71 vols. to date (Baltimore, 1883-).

Buchholz, Heinrich E., *Governors of Maryland: From the Revolution to the Year 1908* (Baltimore, 1908).

Carr, Lois Green, and David William Jordan, *Maryland's Revolution of Government, 1689-1692* (Ithaca, N.Y. and London, 1974).

Hall, Clayton Colman, *Narratives of Early Maryland, 1633-1684* (New York, 1910).

High, James H., "A Facet of Sovereignty: The Proprietary Governor and the Maryland Charter," *Maryland Historical Magazine*, LV (June 1960), 67-81.

Land, Aubrey C., *et al.*, eds., *Law, Society, and Politics in Early Maryland* (Baltimore and London, 1974).

Richardson, Hester Dorsey, *Side-Lights on Maryland History, with Sketches of Early Maryland Families* (Cambridge, Md., 1967: reprint of material first published between 1903 and 1913).

Scharf, J. Thomas, *History of Maryland from the Earliest Period to the Present Day*, 3 vols. (Baltimore, 1879).

Skaggs, David Curtis, *Roots of Maryland Democracy, 1753-1776* (Westport, Conn., 1973).

Steiner, Bernard C., *Beginnings of Maryland, 1631-1639*, in *Johns Hopkins University Studies in Historical and Political Science*, XXI (1903), 353-464.

———. "A List of Those Who Governed Maryland Before It Was Made a Royal Province," *Pennsylvania Magazine of History and Biography*, XXII (1898), 98-101.

———. *Maryland During the English Civil Wars*, in *Johns Hopkins University Studies in Historical and Political Science*, XXIV (1906), 751-813, and XXV (1907), 151-268.

———. *Maryland Under the Commonwealth: A Chronicle of the Years 1649-1658*, in *Johns Hopkins University Studies in Historical and Political Science*, XXIX (1911), 1-178.

———. "The Protestant Revolution in Maryland," American Historical Association, *Annual Report for the Year 1897* (Washington, D.C., 1898), 279-353.

Walsh, Richard, and William Lloyd Fox, eds., *Maryland: A History, 1632-1974* (Baltimore, 1974).

MARYLAND

CALVERT, Leonard, 1634-1643, 1644-1645, 1646-1647

Born in 1606 in England, the second son of George Calvert, first Baron Baltimore, and his wife, the former Anne Mynne. A Roman Catholic. Brother of Cecilius, George, Francis, Henry, John, Anne, Dorothy, Elizabeth, Grace and Helen. Married to Anne Brent; father of William and Anne.

Travelled to Newfoundland with his father in 1628, and participated in the capture as privateers of some French vessels. Named Lieutenant Governor of Maryland by his brother Cecilius, second Lord Baltimore, in November 1633; arrived in the colony to assume his new position in March of 1634.

Leonard Calvert's appointment as lieutenant governor was made necessary by his brother's inability to administer the province in person, since he was needed in England to defend the proprietary interest. During his years in office, Leonard Calvert presided over the young colony's early political development. In February of 1635 the first Maryland Assembly met and, although Cecilius Calvert later rejected the laws passed by this body, contending that only he could initiate legislation, the colonists did manage to win the right of initiative by the end of 1638. Calvert's period as chief executive was also marked by his efforts to assert the authority of Maryland in the face of outside threats, especially the challenge posed by William Claiborne, who refused to accept either the proprietor's regulations regarding trade or his claim to possess legal title to Kent Island. The intractable stance of both Claiborne and Calvert resulted in several skirmishes between their respective supporters, and it was not until the mercantile firm of William Cloberry and Company replaced Claiborne as factor for the colony that the controversy came to an end.

Leonard Calvert was absent from the province between April 1643 and September 1644, and shortly after his return he was confronted by an insurrection backed by Maryland's Protestant community, an insurrection which ended with the usurpation of the government by Richard Ingle in February 1645. Calvert was forced to flee to Virginia, but by July 1646 he had regained enough support within his troubled colony to appoint Captain Edward Hill as interim governor. Several months later Calvert left Virginia and successfully re-established his personal rule over Maryland. He died on June 9, 1647, while still in office.

Bibliography: John G. Morris, *The Lords Baltimore* (Baltimore, 1874); *The Calvert Papers*, 3 vols. (Baltimore, 1889-99); John Bailey Calvert Nicklin, "The Calvert Family," *Maryland Historical Magazine*, XVI (March-December 1921). *DAB, DNB*.

BRENT, Giles, 1643-1644

Born *circa* 1602 in England, the third son of Richard Brent, Lord of Admington and Stoke, and his wife, the former Elizabeth Reed. A Roman Catholic. Brother of Fulke, Richard, William, Edward, George, Margaret, Mary, Catherine, Elizabeth, Eleanor, Jane and Anne. Married, probably in 1644, to the elder daughter of the Tayac, or Emperor, of the Piscataway tribe; father of at least one child, Giles, who lived to maturity.

Immigrated to America in November 1638, and eventually settled on Kent Island, off the coast of Maryland. Sworn in as both a member of the Maryland Council and Treasurer of the province in March 1639. Also named Captain of the military band of St. Mary's in May of that year. Succeeded William Brainthwait as Commander of Kent Island in February 1640, although Brainthwait was reinstated a few months later; again appointed commander of the "isle and county of Kent" in December 1642. Chosen as a Burgess in September of 1640, representing Kent in the Maryland Assembly, and became one of the leaders of the "popular party" which often opposed the policies of Lieutenant Governor Calvert. Named Judge of all causes in Kent in January 1642. Appointed in April 1643 as "Lieutenant General, Chancellor, Admiral, Chief, Captain, Magistrate and Commander" of Maryland, to serve in the absence of Lieutenant Governor Leonard Calvert; remained acting governor until Calvert's return from England in September 1644.

Brent's tenure was marked by growing uneasiness within the colony following the opening of hostilities in August 1642 between the supporters of Charles I and the adherents of the English Parliament. By early 1644 opposition to the Crown in Maryland had become more conspicuous, and in January of that year Brent issued a warrant calling for the arrest of Captain Richard Ingle on grounds of high treason. Ingle, who was charged with denying the legitimacy of Charles' kingship, managed to escape his captors, however, and finally left for England after promising to return to the colony within a year.

When Lieutenant Governor Calvert arrived in Maryland in September 1644, Brent became a member of the Council. The subsequent usurpation of Maryland's government by Ingle in February 1645 resulted in the seizure of much of Brent's property and his transportation to London as a prisoner, although he was set free soon after landing there. Brent later returned to America and resumed his seat on the Maryland Council for several years. He also lived in Virginia for some time before his death in *c*. 1671-72.

Bibliography: Chester Horton Brent, *The Descendants of Colonel Giles Brent, Captain George Brent and Robert Brent, Gentleman, Immigrants to Maryland and Virginia* (Rutland, Vt., 1946); George Mason Graham Stafford, comp., *General George Mason Graham of Tyrone Plantation, and His People* (New Orleans, 1947); Bruce E. Steiner, "The Catholic Brents of Colonial Virginia: An Instance of Practical Toleration," *Virginia Magazine of History and Biography*, 70 (October 1962), 387-409. Also see the genealogy of the Brent family by W. B. Chilton in the *Virginia Magazine of History and Biography*, XII (July 1904-April 1905) through XXII (January-October 1914).

INGLE, Richard, 1645

Born in 1609, a native of Redriff, Surrey, England. Appeared in America for the first time in *c*. 1631-32; employed as a tobacco trader. Returned to the colonies in March of 1642, and became involved in Maryland's internal affairs during periodic visits over the next few years. Accused of rejecting the legitimacy of the kingship of Charles I and charged with high treason in January 1644, an indictment which he managed to evade. Sailed for England, but returned in February 1645; supported by a crew which indulged in various acts of piracy, seized control of Maryland, and caused Lieutenant Governor Leonard Calvert to flee to Virginia.

Ingle's usurpation of the colony's government introduced a period of unrest, later referred to as the "plundering year." Although he claimed that his actions had been motivated solely by a desire to insure Maryland's loyalty to the English Parliament, Ingle actually used his power for personal profit. The wealthy Thomas Copley, a defender of proprietary rule, later claimed that he had lost £2,000 as a result of Ingle's depredations.

During the summer of 1645 (in all probability), while Maryland entered a period of political anarchy, Ingle sailed for England to engage in a long and bitter series of legal disputes. Over the next few years he continued to represent himself as the rightful governor of Maryland on grounds of his devotion to the Commonwealth cause, but his protestations ultimately failed to persuade the Council of State. Ingle died late in 1653, about the time he filed a petition asking for a settlement of prize money in order to support himself during an illness.

Bibliography: Edward Ingle, *Capt. Richard Ingle, the Maryland Pirate and Rebel, 1642-1653* (Baltimore, 1884) [no. 19 of the Fund Publications of the Maryland Historical Society]; Henry F. Thompson, "Richard Ingle in Maryland," *Maryland Historical Magazine*, I (June 1906), 125-40. *DAB*.

HILL, Edward, 1646

Date and place of birth, and names of parents unknown, but may have been the son of the Edward Hill who was buried in Elizabeth City County, Virginia in May 1624. Married; father of Edward and perhaps others.

Served as a member of the Virginia House of Burgesses at various times between 1639 and 1645, and acted as Speaker of that body in 1644. Moved to Maryland in the mid-1640's, where he was named Acting Governor by the Maryland Council, an appointment which was confirmed in a commission dated July 1646 and signed by Leonard Calvert; served as chief executive until Calvert's restoration in the autumn of 1646.

While Hill was established as head of the Maryland government in a commission bearing Calvert's name, that document may have been issued without the exiled governor's knowledge. Whatever the circumstances surrounding his accession, Hill did manage to restore some order to the politically troubled colony. He even called an Assembly which passed new legislation, although these laws were later disallowed by Lord Baltimore, who argued that certain of them were "very prejudicial to our rights and royal jurisdictions."

Shortly after his brief period as chief executive, Hill returned to Virginia, and resumed his place in the House of Burgesses. For the next several years he demanded the unpaid salary which he claimed Calvert had "covenanted unto him . . . for his service in the office of Governor." Indeed, Hill contended that the administration of Maryland should have reverted to him following Calvert's death in June 1647, until further instructions arrived from the proprietor in England. Hill did have some support in Maryland, mostly among the colony's Protestant community, but his efforts to regain the governorship eventually proved unsuccessful. In 1654 Hill became a member of the Virginia Council, and in 1656 he commanded a combined force of colonists and friendly Indians which suffered a major defeat from hostile Indians near the present city of Richmond. Hill died in about 1663.

GREENE, Thomas, 1647-1649

Date and place of birth, and names of parents unknown. A Roman Catholic. Brother of Robert and perhaps others. First married in England to Ann Cox; later remarried to Winifred Seybourne; father of Thomas, Leonard, Robert and Francis, the last two definitely by his second wife.

Immigrated to Maryland in 1633 aboard the *Ark*, and elected as a Burgess in September 1640, representing St. Mary's in the Assembly; again represented St. Mary's in the Assembly of 1642. Named to the Maryland Council in the autumn of 1644, following Leonard Calvert's return from England, and continued to serve on the Council until 1647. Succeeded the deceased Calvert as Deputy Governor of Maryland in June 1647, acting in that capacity until his replacement by William Stone, probably early in 1649.

Less than two weeks after assuming office, Greene was faced by a challenge from Captain Edward Hill, who declared that the colony's administration ought to be left in his hands "till his Lordship's [i.e., Lord Baltimore's] pleasure be further known." Although Leonard Calvert had personally appointed Greene as his successor, Hill contended that the Maryland Council had selected him in 1646, and he threatened to exploit the discontented Protestant element within Maryland in order to secure the governorship. Greene responded firmly, however, and pointedly refused to yield to any "boasting threats and other vain persuasions," unless Baltimore himself should confirm Hill's claim. Greene's term was also marked by the rather tumultuous Assembly of 1648, in which the deputy governor emerged as virtually the only defender of the proprietary interest.

Following his replacement by William Stone, Greene was reappointed to the Maryland Council. During Stone's temporary absence from the colony in November 1649, Greene imprudently proclaimed Charles II to be the legitimate ruler of England, an action which ultimately led to the formation of a Parliamentary commission that stripped Stone of his authority for several months. Greene died before January 20, 1652, the date on which a Maryland court considered the distribution of his estate.

Bibliography: Harry Wright Newman, *The Maryland Semmes and Kindred Families: A Genealogical History of Marmaduke Semme(s), Gent., and His Descendants, Including the Allied Families of Greene, Simpson, Boarman, Matthews, Thompson, Middleton, and Neale* (Baltimore, 1956).

STONE, William, 1649-1652, 1652-1654

Born in 1603 or 1604 in England, the nephew of Thomas Stone, a London merchant. An Anglican, but with Nonconformist sympathies. Brother of Catherine, John, Richard, Matthew and Andrew. Married to Verlinda Cotton, by whom he was the father of Elizabeth, Thomas, Richard, John, Matthew, Mary and Catherine.

Arrived in Virginia, probably in the early 1630's, and by 1633 had become a Justice in Accomack County. Was serving as Sheriff of Northampton County in 1646. Moved to Maryland in about 1648, and in August of that year received a proprietary commission as Lieutenant Governor of the colony; apparently took office early in 1649.

Shortly after assuming the lieutenant governorship, Stone presided over an especially active session of the Maryland Assembly. In all, the Assembly passed sixteen laws which were sent to Lord Baltimore for his approval, but clearly the most significant of these was an act providing for religious toleration. Based in large part on the ideas of Baltimore himself, the act stipulated that no individual "professing to believe in Jesus Christ shall . . . be any ways troubled, molested or discountenanced" in the practice of his religion. Despite severe penalties for such offenses as blasphemy or denial of the Trinity, the law represents a major stage in the evolution of religious freedom.

The remainder of Stone's administration was considerably less fruitful, as his right to govern was resolutely challenged by the proprietor's Puritan opponents. With the aid of a Parliamentary commission, the Puritans even managed to deprive Stone of his office in March of 1652. While he was restored to power by June of that year, Stone was permanently removed from office in 1654 and replaced by a board of ten commissioners, who governed the colony for over three years in the name of Parliament.

Following his overthrow Stone fought an unsuccessful battle against the Commonwealth's Puritan supporters in the spring of 1655. Nevertheless, he returned to become a member of the Council after Governor Josias Fendall again established the authority of Lord Baltimore in 1658. Stone died *circa* 1660 at his estate in Charles County.

Bibliography: Edward A. Stone, "Stone Data for Maryland and Virginia," *"Old Northwest" Genealogical Quarterly*, IV (1901), 124-25; Harry Wright Newman, *The Stones of Poynton Manor: A Genealogical History of Captain William Stone* (Washington, D.C.?, 1937). *DAB, DNB*.

FENDALL, Josias, 1658-1660

Born *circa* 1620 in England; names of parents unknown. Brother of Samuel. Married to a woman named Mary, who survived him; father of at least one daughter.

In 1655 participated in an unsuccessful effort by former Lieutenant Governor William Stone to depose the commissioners who were administering Maryland in the name of Parliament. Named by Lord Baltimore to be Lieutenant Governor of Maryland in July 1656, and formally accepted the government from the board of commissioners in March 1658.

Soon after consolidating his authority, Fendall began a series of disagreements with Lord Baltimore, disagreements which culminated in March of 1660 with an attempt by Fendall and the Assembly to overthrow the proprietary and establish instead a government which apparently would have derived its sole power from the Maryland House of Burgesses. The projected *coup* was quickly defeated, and Fendall narrowly escaped with his life when the proprietor's request for a sentence of death was altered to one which stipulated only that the disgraced ex-governor should be disenfranchised and barred from office for life.

After a period of retirement Fendall returned to public attention late in the 1670's, when he was named as a representative from Charles County to the Maryland Assembly. Fearing the ability of Fendall to foment disorder, the governor and his Council responded by threatening to declare the seat vacant, and the county's freemen eventually yielded. The remainder of Fendall's life was spent in what amounted to political exile, as he became involved with the growing anti-proprietary party which included men like John Coode. In 1681 Fendall was banished from Maryland for "mutinous and seditious" behavior, and by the next year he had established residence in neighboring Virginia. Fendall probably died in 1687.

Bibliography: Nannie Ball Nimmo and William B. Marye, "Light on the Family of Gov. Josias Fendall," *Maryland Historical Magazine*, XXXVIII (September 1943), 277-86. *DAB*.

CALVERT, Philip, 1660-1661

Born in 1626 in England, the son of George Calvert, first Lord Baltimore, and his second wife, Anne. A Roman Catholic. Half-brother of eleven, including Cecilius Calvert (later second Lord Baltimore). Married *circa* 1658 to Anne Wolseley; following his first wife's death, remarried in 1681 to Jane Sewall; apparently died without issue.

Commissioned Secretary of Maryland in November 1656, an office which he held until 1660; served on the provincial Council from 1656 to 1682. Commissioned Lieutenant Governor of Maryland in June 1660, and acted as chief executive between the autumn of 1660 and November 1661.

Calvert's brief gubernatorial tenure occurred at a crucial time in the colony's history, just after the suppression of an anti-proprietary rebellion led by Josias Fendall. Under the circumstances, Calvert quickly proclaimed his right to head Maryland's government, warning Fendall's supporters in November of 1660 that they would "answere the Contrary at their perills." A year later, when Calvert relinquished his authority to Charles, the son of the second Lord Baltimore, the danger of further plots against proprietary rule had diminished considerably.

Following his career as chief executive, Philip Calvert took office as Chancellor of the province, a position he retained until his death in 1682. He also served as a member of the four-man group which administered Maryland between May 1669 and November 1670, during Charles Calvert's visit to England.

Bibliography: *The Calvert Papers*, 3 vols. (Baltimore, 1889-99); John Bailey Calvert Nicklin, "The Calvert Family," *Maryland Historical Magazine*, XVI (March-December 1921).

CALVERT, Charles (3rd Lord Baltimore), 1661-1669, 1670-1676, 1679-1684

Born on August 27, 1637 in England, the son of Cecilius Calvert, second Lord Baltimore, and his wife Anne, the daughter of Sir Thomas Arundell. A Roman Catholic. Brother of Anne (died young?), Mary, George (died young) and Elizabeth. Married four times: in 1656 to Mary Darnall; in 1666 to Jane (Lowe) Sewall; on December 6, 1701 to Mary (Banks) Thorpe; and in 1712 to Margaret Charleton. Father, all by his second wife, of Cecil, Clare, Anne and Benedict Leonard (later fourth Lord Baltimore); also may have been the father of the Charles Calvert who served as governor of Maryland from 1720 to 1727.

Commissioned Governor of Maryland in September 1661, and assumed office that November. Succeeded his deceased father as Proprietor of the colony in November 1675, becoming third Lord Baltimore.

Except for two intervals when he visited England, Calvert presided over Maryland's affairs from 1661 to 1684. During his long tenure the province experienced recurrent conflicts between its Catholic and Protestant residents, conflicts which on several occasions threatened to disrupt the government. In 1681, for example, an anti-proprietary movement led by Josias Fendall and John Coode, bolstered by rumors of an imminent English civil war, encouraged Protestants in Maryland to oppose the Catholic regime by refusing to pay taxes. Although Calvert brought the two ringleaders to trial in November of 1681, the grievances which they had voiced led to open rebellion against the proprietary in 1689, five years after Calvert had left the province in the hands of a council of deputy governors.

Following his departure from Maryland, Calvert spent much of his time attempting to frustrate periodic efforts to deprive his family of their rights in the province. Despite the English Crown's decision to place Maryland under its own control in 1691, Calvert did manage to preserve title to the land and rents which the Lords Baltimore had traditionally enjoyed. Calvert died on February 21, 1715, three months before the administration of the province was returned to his grandson, the fifth Lord Baltimore, whose acceptance of Protestantism had facilitated restoration of the proprietorship.

Bibliography: John G. Morris, *The Lords Baltimore* (Baltimore, 1874); *The Calvert Papers*, 3 vols. (Baltimore, 1889-99); Clayton Colman Hall, *The Lords Baltimore and the Maryland Palatinate* (Baltimore, 1904); John Bailey Calvert Nicklin, "The Calvert Family," *Maryland Historical Magazine*, XVI (March-December 1921). *DAB*.

WHARTON, Jesse, 1676

Date and place of birth, and names of parents unknown. A Roman Catholic. Married to Elizabeth Sewall, the daughter of Henry Sewall and stepdaughter of Governor Charles Calvert, third Lord Baltimore; father of Henry and perhaps others.

Practiced medicine for a number of years. Emigrated from Barbados to Maryland, and served as a member of the provincial Council from 1672 to 1676. Named Deputy Governor of Maryland in June 1676, an office which he held until his death late in July.

Wharton's appointment by Governor Calvert carried with it the authority to act as chief executive during Calvert's absence from the province, despite the fact that the governor's infant son Cecil nominally headed the administration. Within two months of his commission, however, Wharton died, and was succeeded by Thomas Notley. During his brief tenure defensive measures occupied much of Wharton's time, as he endeavored to prevent the rebellion which had just broken out in neighboring Virginia from spreading into Maryland. Less than two weeks before his death, a nervous Wharton issued a Council proclamation which disarmed certain residents of Maryland who had been given weapons several months earlier; at the same time, the Council ordered Captain John Allen to be on guard against "any men in Armes" who had not received permission to enter the province.

Bibliography: Rev. S. M. Rankin, *The Rankin and Wharton Families and Their Genealogy* (Greensboro, N.C., 1931?).

NOTLEY, Thomas, 1676-1679

Date and place of birth, and names of parents unknown. May have converted to Catholicism. Apparently never married.

Employed as a merchant for some time, and eventually acquired a considerable fortune. Emigrated from Barbados to Maryland in about 1663, where he soon won the favor of Governor Charles Calvert; elected to the Maryland Assembly in September of 1663, and became Speaker of that body in October 1671. Served as Deputy Governor of Maryland between late July of 1676 and early 1679, during the absence in England of Governor Charles Calvert.

Although Bacon's Rebellion in Virginia had been suppressed by 1677, the possibility of further outbreaks continued to attract Notley's attention. In 1678, for example, he kept Josias Fendall, the old anti-proprietary agitator, from occupying an Assembly seat to which he had been elected. Still, the Assembly which met in that year did pass some legislation designed to appease dissident groups in Maryland. The lawmakers voted that judges would no longer be permitted to exercise discretion in applying English law, and provided that election procedures would henceforth be determined by act of the Assembly rather than proprietary proclamation. These and other acts were quickly contested by Governor Charles Calvert following his return to Maryland early in 1679, but in the controversy which resulted he was deprived of the support of Notley, whose will was proved in April of that year.

JOSEPH, William, 1688-1689

Little information available concerning family and professional background, but was living in London at the time of his appointment as President of the Maryland Council by Lord Baltimore in July 1688. A Roman Catholic. Served as chief executive of Maryland between October 1688 and August 1689.

Joseph's inexpert handling of grievances voiced by Maryland's Lower House, due in large part to his lack of familiarity with the issues considered important by residents of that province, was a major factor contributing to Coode's Rebellion in 1689. In the autumn of 1688 Joseph indicated how insensitive he could be, when he lectured the Assembly on the virtues of rule by divine right and insisted that the burgesses take an oath of fidelity to the proprietor. Although Joseph's tactlessness had seriously undermined his authority by early 1689, he unwisely chose to prorogue an Assembly planned for that April, rather than hear the complaints expressed by the burgesses. At this juncture John Coode, whose previous career suggests a consistent distrust of proprietary rule, took advantage of the growing opposition by organizing a movement which in the summer of 1689 overthrew the government in Maryland and deposed Joseph. Several months later, in October of 1689, Joseph fled to Virginia, where he hid on a plantation owned by another member of the now defunct proprietary Council. Coode then unsuccessfully attempted to extradite Joseph. In February 1690, Coode was still complaining to Nathaniel Bacon, the acting governor of Virginia, that Joseph remained "unconfined and at large." The date of Joseph's death is unknown.

COODE, John, 1689-1690

Born in 1648 in Cornwall, England, the second son of John and Grace (Robins) Coode. Married by the autumn of 1674 to Susanna (Gerard) Slye, by whom he was the father of three sons, including John and William, and three daughters, including Winnifred.

Matriculated at Exeter College, Oxford, and later ordained a deacon in the Anglican Church. Immigrated to Maryland by the spring of 1672, and took his seat in the Assembly in 1676, representing St. Mary's County; soon became involved in efforts to defend the colony's frontier from Indian attack. Joined the anti-proprietary party in Maryland, associating with men like former Governor Josias Fendall; accused of "mutinous and seditious" behavior in 1681, but acquitted in November of that year. Served as Captain of a militia band organized by Maryland's "Protestant Association," and early in August of 1689 took control of the government.

Coode defended his decision to seize power by claiming that he merely intended to protect the colony from "Tyranny and Popery," in much the same way that the recent Glorious Revolution in England had preserved that country from Stuart "oppression." As a further justification, Coode claimed that Maryland's Catholics were conspiring with neighboring Indians to annihilate Protestants in the colony. The persuasiveness of these arguments to Maryland's residents enabled Coode to consolidate his military authority by late August of 1689. Indeed, in April of the following year he was already being described by the Lords of Trade in London as the head of a government administered on behalf of the Crown.

In August 1690 Coode sailed for England to defend his actions in overthrowing the proprietary. Partly as a result of his testimony before the Lords of Trade, Maryland was annexed to the Crown, although Lord Baltimore, the former proprietor, was permitted to retain his financial interest in the colony. Nevertheless, the temptation to indulge in other political intrigues proved irresistible for Coode, and on at least one occasion during the 1690's he was forced to flee to Virginia to escape a grand jury indictment. While he finally received a pardon in 1701, Coode's public career was virtually over. He died *circa* March of 1709.

Bibliography: Edwin W. Beitzell, "Thomas Gerard and His Sons-in-Law," *Maryland Historical Magazine*, XLVI (September 1951), 189-206; Rev. Columba J. Devlin, "John Coode and the Maryland Revolution of 1689," unpub. M.A. thesis, Catholic University, 1952; Gene Perkins Thornton, "The Life and Opinions of Captain John Coode, Gentleman," unpub. M.A. thesis, Columbia University, 1953; David W. Jordan, "John Coode, Perennial Rebel," *Maryland Historical Magazine*, LXX (Spring 1975), 1-28. *DAB*.

BLAKISTON, Nehemiah, 1690-1692

Born in England, a younger son of John and Susan (Chambers) Blakiston. Brother of John (died young), John, Joseph (died young), Rebecca and Elizabeth (died in infancy). Married on May 6, 1669 to Elizabeth Gerard, by whom he was the father of John, Susanna, Rebecca and Mary.

Immigrated to Maryland in 1668, where he practiced law. Named Collector of Customs for North Potomac River in 1685, but came into increasing conflict with the colony's proprietary government. Gradually assumed a more prominent role in Maryland politics following the Revolution of 1689 and, as head of the "Grand Committee," became *de facto* Governor after the departure of John Coode for England in August 1690.

With Coode absent, Blakiston was given an excellent opportunity to enhance his political stature during the uncertain months which preceded Lionel Copley's arrival in the spring of 1692 as the colony's first royal governor. In the midst of the bitter factionalism that remained as a legacy of Coode's revolt against the proprietary, Blakiston skillfully accumulated several key official positions, including that of Chief Justice of the re-established Provincial Court. Indeed, his power was so considerable that Copley made Blakiston his most trusted advisor on the Governor's Council, and bestowed on him the additional offices of Chancellor and Commissary General. This apparent complicity between Copley and Blakiston especially angered Edward Randolph, the colonial surveyor general of customs, who in reports to the Lords of Trade severely criticized the behavior of the "silly Animals" surrounding Copley.

Copley's sudden death in September 1693 encouraged Blakiston to attempt to regain control of the government, but his efforts were unsuccessful. In October of 1693 Blakiston himself died, leaving behind a confusing financial tangle which made little distinction between his public and personal accounts.

Bibliography: Christopher Johnston, "The Blakiston Family," *Maryland Historical Magazine*, II (March-June 1907), 54-64, 172-79; Edwin W. Beitzell, "Thomas Gerard and His Sons-in-Law," *Maryland Historical Magazine*, XLVI (September 1951), 189-206; Hayes Baker-Crothers, "Nathaniel Blakiston," typescript biography in files of American Council of Learned Societies, Manuscript Division, Library of Congress, Washington, D.C.; "The Blakiston Family of Durham and of Maryland, 1341-1909," typescript genealogy in Local History and Genealogy Division, New York Public Library.

COPLEY, Lionel, 1692-1693

Born in 1648 in England; names of parents unknown. A Protestant. Married in 1675 to Anne Boteler, by whom he was the father of Lionel, John and Ann.

Settled in Wadsworth, Yorkshire, England, and in 1676 received a commission as Captain of royal foot-guards. Successfully executed a plan to depose the Catholic governor of the fortress of Hull during the English Revolution of 1688, and was made Lieutenant Governor of the fortress and promoted to Colonel for his part in that action. Commissioned as Maryland's first Royal Governor in June 1691, but did not arrive in the province to assume office until late March or early April of 1692.

Copley landed in Maryland several years after a movement led by John Coode had resulted in the overthrow of the colony's proprietary government, and the new chief executive immediately set about to lessen the factionalism which endured as an aftermath of the rebellion. Although Protestant opposition to Lord Baltimore, the Catholic proprietor, had been a major cause of the sequence of events leading to the establishment of royal control, Copley was careful to avoid measures which might be deemed unduly harsh towards the province's Catholic residents. Consequently, while he persuaded the Assembly to pass an act which would have made the Church of England the established religion in Maryland, Copley also permitted Catholics to worship unmolested. Encouraged by the governor's conciliatory approach, the Maryland Assembly passed a series of laws which virtually reorganized the provincial government along more representative lines. Despite the fact that the legitimacy of these reforms remained doubtful until they were approved by the King, they did represent an effort by the Assembly to answer many of the objections to the colony's legal code which had been raised by Coode and his followers. Soon after this encouraging start to his administration, however, Copley died in office in September 1693.

Bibliography: Annie Leakin Sioussat, "Lionel Copley, First Royal Governor of Maryland," *Maryland Historical Magazine*, XVII (June 1922), 163-77. *DAB*.

ANDROS, Sir Edmund, 1693, 1694

New York, 1674-1677, 1678-1681; East Jersey, 1680-1681, 1688-1689; Massachusetts, 1686-1689; New Hampshire, 1686-1689; Plymouth Colony, 1686-1689; Rhode Island, 1686-1689; Connecticut, 1687-1689; West Jersey, 1688-1689; Virginia, 1692-1698

Born on December 6, 1637 on the Island of Guernsey, the son of Amice and Elizabeth (Stone) Andros. Married to a woman who was related to the Earl of Craven.

Served as Major of a regiment of foot soldiers which in 1666 sailed from England to defend the West Indies against the Dutch. Named a Landgrave of Carolina in 1672; received a commission from the Duke of York in July 1674 to govern the colony of New York, and acted in that capacity, except for an absence in England between November 1677 and August 1678, until January 1681; also exercised control over East Jersey from 1680 until his recall early in the following year. Knighted in about 1681, became Gentleman of the Privy Chamber to Charles II in 1683, and was appointed Lieutenant Colonel of the Princess of Denmark's regiment of horse soldiers in 1685. Commissioned Royal Governor of the Dominion of New England in June 1686, and established his authority in Massachusetts Bay, Maine, New Hampshire, Plymouth and Rhode Island (including the King's Province) in December of that year; Connecticut in November of 1687; and the Jerseys and New York in August 1688 (although Francis Nicholson presided as Andros' substitute in the latter colony). Arrested and sent to England following the overthrow of the Dominion in the spring of 1689, but later received a commission as Royal Governor of Virginia, and served as that colony's chief executive from September 1692 to December 1698; also acted briefly as Governor of Maryland in 1693 and 1694, in the absence of any other executive authority.

Andros' first tenure in New York was marked by several important achievements, especially the improvement of the colony's defenses and the settlement of some boundary difficulties with Connecticut. Nevertheless, even at this stage he had begun to display an inclination to behave in an arbitrary fashion. Perhaps the clearest illustration of this tendency was the high-handed manner in which Andros superseded the authority of Governor Philip Carteret in the Jerseys, provoking Carteret to complain that Andros aimed at "usurping the government" of his colony. This insensitivity to local politics became even more noticeable after Andros assumed control of the Dominion of New England. Following a troubled tenure of less than two and one-half years, he was deposed in the spring of 1689, shortly after news of the Glorious Revolution in England reached Boston.

Although Andros was exonerated of the charges brought against his Dominion government and took over as Virginia's chief executive in 1692, he soon encountered resistance from local leaders like Commissary James Blair, who bitterly informed one London official that Andros "never did any considerable service to the King, nor the people" during his colonial career. Finally, late in 1698, Andros departed for England. He served as Lieutenant Governor of Guernsey from 1704 to 1706, and died in London in February 1714.

Bibliography: "Commission to Sir Edmund Andros," Massachusetts Historical Society, *Collections*, 3rd ser., vol. VII (Boston, 1838), 138-49; W. H. Whitmore, ed., *Andros Tracts: Being a Collection of Pamphlets and Official Papers ... of the Andros Government and the Establishment of the Second Charter of Massachusetts*, 3 vols. (New York, 1868-74) (Publications of the Prince Society, vols. V-VII); Robert N. Toppan, ed., "Andros Records," American Antiquarian Society, *Proceedings*, n.s., vol. XIII (1899-1900), 237-68, 463-99; J.H. Tuttle, ed., "Land Warrants under Andros," Colonial Society of Massachusetts, *Publications*, XXI (1919), 292-361; Albert C. Bates, "Expedition of Sir Edmund Andros to Connecticut in 1687," AAS, *Proceedings*, n.s., vol. 48 (October 1938), 276-99; Jeanne G. Bloom, "Sir Edmund Andros: A Study in Seventeenth-Century Colonial Administration," unpub. Ph.D. diss., Yale University, 1962; Robert C. Ritchie, "London Merchants, the New York Market, and the Recall of Sir Edmund Andros," *New York History*, LVII (January 1976), 5-29. *DAB*, *DNB*.

GREENBERRY, Nicholas, 1693-1694

Born in 1627 in England; names of parents unknown. Married to a woman named Anne, by whom he was the father of Charles, Katherine, Ann and Elizabeth.

Immigrated to Maryland in 1674; became a Justice of Anne Arundel County in 1686. After what appears to have been a period of hesitation, joined the "Protestant Association" which overthrew Maryland's proprietary government in 1689. Named to the Association's "Grand Committee" in April of 1690, and acted as a member of the Provincial Court following its re-establishment in 1691. Appointed to the first Council called by Royal Governor Lionel Copley; after Copley's death, chosen as President of the Council by Sir Edmund Andros, and in that capacity served as Maryland's chief executive between October 1693 and May 1694.

Greenberry's brief tenure was marked by considerable political intrigue, as Maryland's leaders awaited the arrival of Francis Nicholson, the newly-appointed royal governor. While Nicholson had received his commission in February 1694, he did not appear in the colony for almost six months, and during this *interregnum* Sir Edmund Andros, the governor of neighboring Virginia, played a pivotal role in Maryland politics. In May of 1694 Andros, despite his previous support for Greenberry, decided that Sir Thomas Lawrence was the province's legal acting governor, in view of the fact that Lawrence's earlier suspension from office by the deceased Copley had been overturned by the Lords of Trade.

After his replacement as chief executive in the spring of 1694, Greenberry continued to play a prominent role in Maryland's affairs, acting as a member of the Council, Chancellor, Judge of the Admiralty Court, and Militia Colonel. He died in December 1697.

Bibliography: Henry Ridgely Evans, *Founders of the Colonial Families of Ridgely, Dorsey and Greenberry of Maryland* (Washington, D.C., 1935).

LAWRENCE, Sir Thomas, 1694

Born *circa* 1645, the son of Sir John Lawrence of Chelsea, Middlesex, England and his wife, the former Mary Hampson. Brother of Martha. Married in 1674 to Anne English, by whom he was the father of John, Margaret and Cecilia.

Matriculated at Oxford University in 1661, receiving an A.B. degree in 1665 and an A.M. in 1668. Inherited his father's title in 1664. Little information is available concerning his activities during the period prior to 1691, the year in which he was named Secretary of Maryland by the Lords of Trade.

Arrived in Maryland late in 1692, where a quarrel with Royal Governor Lionel Copley, which had begun before the two men left England, led to suspension in March 1693 from his positions as secretary, member of the Council, and Judge of the Provincial Court; reinstated to these offices in September 1693 by the Lords of Trade. As President of the Council, acted as chief executive of the province between May and July of 1694.

Despite his earlier differences with Governor Copley, Lawrence soon won the favor of Sir Edmund Andros, who had established his authority in Maryland following Copley's death in September 1693. Indeed, Andros promptly appointed Lawrence to the Council, but later excused him from serving after Lawrence complained that he was "very sick and indisposed in body." By the spring of 1694, however, both Lawrence's health and political prospects had improved, the latter as a result of news that the Lords of Trade had officially overturned his suspension by Copley. Andros then named Lawrence acting chief executive, a position he held until the arrival of Francis Nicholson, the newly-appointed royal governor. During his two-month tenure, Lawrence handled little other than routine administrative matters, and in July of 1694 he relinquished his gubernatorial duties, although he continued to serve as secretary, councillor, and judge when he was not representing Maryland's interests in London. Lawrence died in Chelsea, Middlesex, England on April 25, 1714.

Bibliography: Schuyler Lawrence, "Lawrence of Chelsea, Middlesex, and of Delafore [Delaford], Ivor, Bucks., 1500-1750: Baronets, 1628-1714," (1936) manuscript volume in Local History and Genealogy Division, New York Public Library.

NICHOLSON, Francis, 1694-1698

New York, 1688-1689; Virginia, 1690-1692, 1698-1705; South Carolina, 1721-1725

Born on November 12, 1655 at "Downholme Park," near Richmond, in Yorkshire, England, probably the son of Thomas Nicholson. Never married.

Became a protegé of Lord St. John of Basing, acting for a time as page to his wife. Entered the English Army in January 1678, and in 1686 was appointed Captain of a company of foot soldiers accompanying Sir Edmund Andros to New England. Named to the Council organized under the Dominion of New England, and eventually commissioned Lieutenant Governor; served as Andros' deputy in New York from 1688 to 1689. Sailed for England after the fall of the Dominion, but soon received a commission as Lieutenant Governor of Virginia, a position which he held from June of 1690 to September 1692; again served as Virginia's chief executive, with the rank of Royal Governor, from December 1698 to August 1705. Also presided as Governor of Maryland from July 1694 to December 1698, of Nova Scotia for several weeks in 1713, and of South Carolina from May 1721 to the spring of 1725.

Nicholson's remarkable instinct for political survival enabled him to serve as resident chief executive of five different colonies during a period encompassing some thirty-seven years. Throughout his long professional career, he often experienced opposition from local officials, opposition which became especially virulent during his second tenure in Virginia. In that colony a bitter quarrel with Commissary James Blair and other members of the Virginia Council finally brought about his recall in 1705. Nevertheless, despite the hostility which he sometimes provoked, Nicholson's record as a colonial administrator was not without a number of significant achievements. In Maryland, for example, his strong interest in education led him to aid in the establishment of King William's School (later St. John's College), while several years earlier he had supported Commissary Blair's efforts in Virginia to found the College of William and Mary.

By the 1720's ill health and concern in London over his policy regarding paper currency in South Carolina had reduced Nicholson's political effectiveness, and in the spring of 1725 he sailed for England on a leave of absence. He died in London on March 5, 1728, leaving the bulk of his estate to the Society for the Propagation of the Gospel in Foreign Parts, an organization in which, as a staunch Anglican, he had always taken an active role.

Bibliography: [Unsigned], "Instructions to Francis Nicholson," *Virginia Magazine of History and Biography*, IV (1896), 49-54; [unsigned], "Papers Relating to the Administration of Governor Nicholson . . .," *Virginia Magazine of History and Biography*, VII (1899-1900), 153-72, 275-86, 386-401, vol. VIII (1900-01), 46-58, 126-46, 260-73, 366-85, vol. IX (1901-02), 18-33, 152-62, 251-62; Charles William Sommerville, "Early Career of Governor Francis Nicholson," *Maryland Historical Magazine*, IV (June-September 1909), 101-14, 201-20; Louis B. Wright, "William Byrd's Opposition to Governor Francis Nicholson," *Journal of Southern History*, XI (February 1945), 68-79; Samuel Clyde McCullough, "The Fight to Depose Governor Nicholson," *Journal of Southern History*, XII (August 1946), 403-22; Fairfax Downey, "The Governor Goes A-Wooing: The Swashbuckling Courtship of Nicholson of Virginia, 1699-1705," *Virginia Magazine of History and Biography*, LV (January 1947), 6-19; Ruth M. Winton, "Governor Francis Nicholson's Relations with the Society for the Propagation of the Gospel in Foreign Parts, 1701-1727," *Historical Magazine of the Protestant Episcopal Church*, XVII (September 1948), 274-96; Bruce T. McCully, "From the North Riding to Morocco: The Early Years of Governor Francis Nicholson, 1655-1686," *William and Mary Quarterly*, 3rd ser., vol. XIX (October 1962), 534-56; Gary B. Nash, "Governor Francis Nicholson and the New Castle Expedition of 1696," *Delaware History*, XI (April 1965), 229-39; Stephen S. Webb, "The Strange Career of Francis Nicholson," *William and Mary Quarterly*, 3rd ser., vol. XXIII (October 1966), 513-48. *DAB, DNB*.

BLAKISTON, Nathaniel, 1698-1702

Date and place of birth unknown; son of John and Phoebe (Johnson) Blakiston. Brother of William (died in infancy), Robert, Jane (died young), Sarah (died young) and Margaret. Married, and the father of Nathaniel and Rachel.

Affiliated with the Merchant Adventurers Company of London before his appointment as Royal Governor of Maryland in October 1698; arrived in the colony in December of that year, and took the oath of office the following January.

Blakiston's tenure as chief executive was relatively uneventful, except for the approval of an act by the Assembly in March 1702 which proclaimed the Church of England to be the colony's established religion. The Blakiston administration was also marked by a generally harmonious relationship between the governor and the Assembly. Nevertheless, Blakiston seems not to have enjoyed his position, and he soon asked to be relieved of his responsibilities. The Crown granted this petition in June 1701, although Blakiston did not turn over the government to Thomas Tench, president of the Maryland Council, until June of 1702.

After his resignation as governor, Blakiston served as Maryland's agent in London, an office which he held until 1721. Blakiston also acted for a time as agent for Virginia, and in 1718 he was still serving in that capacity. The date of Blakiston's death is unknown.

Bibliography: Christopher Johnston, "The Blakiston Family," *Maryland Historical Magazine*, II (March-June 1907), 54-64, 172-79; Hayes Baker-Crothers, "Nathaniel Blakiston," typescript biography in files of American Council of Learned Societies, Manuscript Division, Library of Congress, Washington, D.C.; "The Blakiston Family of Durham and of Maryland, 1341-1909," typescript genealogy in Local History and Genealogy Division, New York Public Library.

TENCH, Thomas, 1702-1704

Date and place of birth, and names of parents unknown, but may have been the son of John Tench of Nantwich, Cheshire, an ancestry which would make him the same Thomas Tench who in 1673 matriculated at Brasenose College, Oxford at the age of eighteen. Married *circa* 1684 to Margaret, the widow of Nathan Smith; following the death of his first wife in 1694, remarried to another woman named Margaret; may have been the father of a child or children who died young, but left no direct heirs at the time of his death.

Employed for a number of years as a London merchant, and transported at least eighty-one settlers to Maryland between 1675 and 1684. Immigrated to

Maryland himself in 1684, settling in Anne Arundel County. Appointed Justice of the Peace in 1685, and eventually became a supporter of the "Protestant Association" which overthrew the proprietary government in 1689. Named Justice of the Quorum for the re-established Provincial Court in 1691; appointed to the Maryland Council under Lionel Copley, the colony's first royal governor, and remained a member of that body almost continuously between 1692 and 1708. As President of the Council, served as Acting Governor of Maryland between the departure of Nathaniel Blakiston in June 1702 and the arrival of John Seymour in April 1704.

Although Seymour received his commission as royal governor in February of 1703, a combination of circumstances prevented him from assuming office for fourteen months. Nevertheless, during Seymour's lengthy absence Tench enjoyed a rather tranquil administration, except for a controversy concerning legislation which proclaimed the Church of England to be Maryland's established religion. In January 1703 authorities in London confirmed an act of establishment which had been approved by the Maryland Assembly the previous March, thereby provoking new opposition from non-Anglican religious groups in the colony.

Following his period as acting governor, Tench returned to his seat on the Council, a position he retained until his death in 1708.

SEYMOUR, John, 1704-1709

Born in England, the son of Sir Edward and Lady Letitia (Popham) Seymour; date of birth unknown. A Protestant. Brother of Popham, Francis, Charles, Henry, Alexander and Anne. Married to Hester, the daughter of Sir John Newton, by whom he was the father of two sons, including Berkley, and one daughter.

Served for about thirty years in the British military. Commissioned Royal Governor of Maryland in February 1703 and, after a series of delays, arrived in that province in April of 1704.

During the first months of his administration, Seymour enjoyed a cordial relationship with his Council and Assembly, and by September of 1704 he had inspired Maryland's lawmakers to undertake an extensive revision of the colony's legal code. The new legislation included an act which offered incentives for importing rum, sugar, slaves and other commodities, and laws which provided for matters such as the improvement of Maryland roads and the prompt punishment of convicted criminals. Because Catholicism existed in the province only on sufferance after the Baltimore family had been forced to yield their proprietary rights to the Crown, Seymour also supported legislation which would deter the "growth of Popery." Towards the end of his period as governor, Seymour began to encounter some difficulties with the Maryland

Assembly, particularly when he issued a charter to the city of Annapolis in 1708. The Assembly strongly opposed the governor's action, since the charter would have entitled Annapolis to two delegates in the Assembly and given the city authority to collect tolls and taxes within its boundaries. Shortly after this dispute was settled by a compromise, Seymour died while in office on July 30, 1709. He was buried at St. Anne's Parish in Annapolis, Maryland.

Bibliography: A. Audrey Locke, *The Seymour Family: History and Romance* (London, 1911); Charles B. Clark, "The Career of John Seymour, Governor of Maryland," *Maryland Historical Magazine*, XLVIII (June 1953), 134-59.

LLOYD, Edward, 1709-1714

Born in February 1670 in Maryland, the son of Philemon and Henrietta Maria (Neale) Bennett Lloyd. Brother of Philemon, James, Anna Maria, Margaret, Henrietta Maria and Alice. Married on February 1, 1703 to Sarah Covington, by whom he was the father of Edward (died young), Philemon, Edward, Rebecca Covington, James and Richard.

Acted as a Justice in Talbot County from 1694 to 1697; served as a member of the Maryland Assembly, representing Talbot County, from 1698 to 1701. Appointed to the Maryland Council in November 1701 and, in his capacity as President of that body, succeeded the deceased governor John Seymour in July 1709; continued to serve as chief executive until May 1714. Also commissioned Major General of the provincial militia in July 1707.

Lloyd's administration represented an important stage in the political evolution of colonial Maryland. While officials in London attempted to find a satisfactory replacement for Seymour, Lloyd and the Council conducted Maryland's government in a way which was less responsive to the royal prerogative than it was to pressure applied by local interests. This approach caused Robert Quary, the one member of the Council who remained a staunch defender of the "Queen's Instructions," to recommend late in 1709 that the Lords of Trade arrange for the immediate appointment of a new royal governor, since most of the Upper House seemed to be "wholly in the interest of the Assembly." Still, despite Quary's warning, it was not until May of 1714, over four years later, that John Hart arrived in Maryland with a commission to govern the province. Following his replacement by Hart, Lloyd remained a Council member until his death on March 20, 1719.

Bibliography: Christopher Johnston, "Lloyd Family," *Maryland Historical Magazine*, VII (December 1912), 420-30; Oswald Tilghman, "Lloyd Family," *Maryland Historical Magazine*, VIII (March 1913), 85-87; J. Donnell Tilghman, "Wye House," *Maryland Historical Magazine*, XLVIII (June 1953), 89-108.

HART, John, 1714-1720

Date of birth unknown, but apparently the son of Merrick and Lettice (Vesey) Hart of Crobert, County Craven, Ireland, and the nephew of John Vesey, Archbishop of Tuam. An Anglican.

Served in the British Army, where he advanced to the rank of Captain. Commissioned Royal Governor of Maryland early in 1714, assuming office the following May; reappointed Lieutenant Governor in 1715, after the restoration of proprietary rule, and continued to hold that position until his return to England in about May of 1720.

Hart's administration was frequently disrupted by religious disputes between Catholic and Protestant factions in the province. Although Benedict Leonard Calvert, the fourth Lord Baltimore, had converted to Anglicanism in order to convince the Crown of his loyalty, Protestants in Maryland still believed Catholicism to be a serious danger, especially after they learned that some Catholic prisoners captured during an unsuccessful attempt to overthrow the House of Hanover were on their way to the province. With Hart's encouragement, the Maryland Assembly responded to these fears in the summer of 1716 by approving legislation which barred anyone from public office, unless he renounced the supremacy of the Pope, rejected the claims of the Catholic Pretender to the British throne, and swore allegiance to George I. In 1718 restrictions against Catholics who refused to take these oaths were redefined in a way which deprived them even of their right to vote in provincial elections. Meanwhile, however, the fifth Lord Baltimore and his guardian, Lord Guilford, had decided to recall Hart, and in the spring of 1720, after some procrastination, Hart left the government of Maryland in the hands of Thomas Brooke.

Following his gubernatorial career in Maryland, Hart was commissioned Royal Governor of the Leeward Islands in May 1721, an office he held until his return to England in 1727. The date of Hart's death is unknown.

Bibliography: Bernard C. Steiner, "The Restoration of the Proprietary of Maryland and the Legislation against the Roman Catholics during the Governorship of Capt. John Hart, 1714-1720," in American Historical Association, *Annual Report . . . for the Year 1899*, I (Washington, D.C., 1900), 229-307.

BROOKE, Thomas, 1720

Born *circa* 1659 in Maryland, the eldest son of Thomas and Eleanor (Hatton) Brooke. Member of a Catholic family, but converted to Anglicanism. Brother of Robert, Ignatius, Matthew, Clement, Mary and Eleanor. First married to a woman named Anne, by whom he was the father of Thomas, Eleanor, Sarah and Priscilla; remarried before January 4, 1699 to Barbara Dent, by whom he had Nathaniel, John, Benjamin, Baker, Thomas, Jane, Rebecca, Mary, Elizabeth and Lucy.

Named to the Council under Lionel Copley, Maryland's first royal governor, and held that position from 1692 until his dismissal for non-attendance in 1707; restored to the Council in 1716, and served until 1724. Occupied various other public offices in Maryland, including Justice of the Provincial Court, Deputy Secretary, and Commissary General. In his capacity as President of the Council, served as Acting Governor of Maryland between the departure of John Hart in about May of 1720 and the arrival of Charles Calvert late in the summer of that year.

Brooke's brief tenure was rather uneventful politically, since the Maryland Assembly did not meet between April and October of 1720. Nevertheless, the transfer of power from the departing Hart to Brooke was not without controversy. Before he left for England, some of Hart's opponents apparently circulated a rumor that the colony's proprietors had issued a private commission to Brooke, allowing him to assume control of the government before Hart had actually embarked. In October of 1720 the proprietors rebuked Brooke's overzealous supporters for these "hasty proceedings," and warned them against any future "Malicious reports and Insinuations."

Following his brief period as chief executive, Brook resumed his seat on the Council for several years. He died, according to family records, on January 7, 1731, a date which appears plausible in view of the fact that his will was proved on January 25 of that year.

Bibliography: Thomas Willing Balch, *The Brooke Family of Whitchurch, Hampshire, England* (Philadelphia, 1899); Christopher Johnston, "Brooke Family," *Maryland Historical Magazine*, I (March-December 1906), 66-73, 184-88, 284-89, 376-78; Ellon Brooke Culver Bowen, "The Brooke Family," *Maryland Historical Magazine*, XXIX (June 1934), 152-69.

CALVERT, Charles, 1720-1727

Born *circa* 1680 in England; ancestry uncertain, but related in some way to the Calvert family which held proprietary title to Maryland. Married on November 21, 1722 to Rebecca Gerard, by whom he was the father of Charles (died young), Anne (died young?) and Elizabeth.

May have been the Captain Charles Calvert who was serving with His Majesty's Footguards in 1718. Appointed Governor of Maryland in May 1720, and arrived in the province late that summer to take office.

Although Calvert pledged to reconcile the desires of Maryland's residents with the need to defend proprietary interests, his administration soon experienced severe political turmoil. The Assembly which met following the elections of 1722 proved to be especially recalcitrant, as its members hotly contested a Council attempt to veto a bill banning the shipment of "trash" tobacco. To be sure, many of the other issues which separated the governor and his Council from the Lower House were relatively trivial in nature, but these petty disagreements symbolized a basic difference between the two groups. Under the leadership of men like the elder Daniel Dulany and Thomas Bordley, the Assembly sought to establish its claim to represent the people "for whom all Laws are made," while Calvert and the Council remained determined to uphold the proprietary prerogative.

In July 1727 Charles Calvert was replaced by Benedict Leonard Calvert, the younger brother of Maryland's Lord Proprietor. The former governor then became both Commissary General and a member of the Maryland Council. Charles Calvert died on February 2, 1734.

Bibliography: *The Calvert Papers*, 3 vols. (Baltimore, 1889-99); John Bailey Calvert Nicklin, "The Calvert Family," *Maryland Historical Magazine*, XVI (March-December 1921).

CALVERT, Benedict Leonard, 1727-1731

Born on September 20, 1700 at "Ditchley," his uncle's English estate, the second son of Benedict Leonard Calvert, fourth Lord Baltimore, and his wife Charlotte, the daughter of Edward Henry Lee, Earl of Litchfield. A Roman Catholic at birth, but converted to Protestantism as a young man. Brother of Charles, fifth Lord Baltimore (who served as governor of Maryland from 1732 to 1733), Charlotte, Jane, Edward Henry, Cecil, Barbara (died young) and Anne. Never married.

Studied briefly at a Catholic school in France and the Weston School in England; also matriculated at Christ Church College, Oxford, attending that institution intermittently for several years. Commissioned Lieutenant Governor of Maryland in March 1727, and assumed that position the following July.

Soon after Calvert arrived in the province, he and Commissary Charles Calvert, his relative and predecessor as chief executive, quarreled over the remuneration due their respective offices. Other difficulties soon disrupted his administration, including a chronic boundary dispute with Pennsylvania and disturbances among tobacco planters in Prince George's County. Especially troublesome to Calvert was a controversy over the adoption of English statutes in Maryland, an issue which led the elder Daniel Dulany to publish a tract on the subject. In the end, Calvert's repeated failure to get along with Dulany and other members of the Maryland Legislature convinced his brother, the fifth Lord Baltimore, to send Samuel Ogle as a replacement in 1731.

After his departure from office in December 1731, Calvert remained in Annapolis until the spring of 1732. Although his health was by then seriously impaired, he boarded ship for England, but died at sea on June 1, 1732.

Bibliography: *The Calvert Papers*, 3 vols. (Baltimore, 1889-99); [unsigned], "Benedict Leonard Calvert, the Younger," *Maryland Historical Magazine*, I (September 1906), 274-77; Bernard C. Steiner, "Benedict Leonard Calvert, Esq., Governor of Maryland, 1727-1731," *Maryland Historical Magazine*, III (September-December 1908), 191-227, 283-342; John Bailey Calvert Nicklin, "The Calvert Family," *Maryland Historical Magazine*, XVI (March-December 1921).

OGLE, Samuel, 1731-1732, 1733-1742, 1747-1752

Born *circa* 1702 in Northumberland County, England, the son of Samuel Ogle of Bousden, a member of Parliament for Berwick-on-Tweed, and Ursula (Markham) Altham Ogle. Brother of Thomas and perhaps others. Married in 1741 to Anne Tasker; father of Anne (died young), Samuel (died young), Benjamin (who served as governor of Maryland from 1798 to 1801), Mary and Mellora. Acquired through his marriage "Belair," a large estate in Prince George's County.

While in England served with the British Army, and by the time of his departure for America in 1731, had advanced to the rank of Captain of Cavalry. After his arrival in Annapolis in December 1731, assumed office as Lieutenant Governor of Maryland, a position he held until December of 1732. Also served as lieutenant governor from July 1733 to August 1742, and from March 1747 until his death.

Ogle's three terms as Maryland's chief executive comprised fifteen years of service to the colony. Despite the customary disputes between the governor and the General Assembly, Ogle seems to have won over many of his opponents during this period, largely through a judicious distribution of the political offices under his control. The importance of tobacco to Maryland's economy inevitably meant that issues related to that crop would occupy a major portion of Ogle's attention. As lieutenant governor he was required to deal with mob violence aimed at the destruction of tobacco plants (as a "remedy" for overproduction), and the hostile reaction to the tobacco duty bill which he backed in 1739. Ogle likewise contended with the perennial problem of securing a tobacco inspection bill which would require growers to adhere to a consistent standard of quality, and during the latter years of his administration, he managed to obtain inspection legislation which both protected the industry and permitted a successful emission of paper currency. Ogle also defended Maryland's interests during a "border war" with Pennsylvania in 1736-37, a skirmish resulting from a boundary dispute between the two colonies. While still in office, Ogle died in Annapolis, Maryland on May 3, 1752.

Bibliography: H. A. Ogle, *Ogle and Bothal* (Newcastle-upon-Tyne, England, 1902). *DAB*.

CALVERT, Charles (5th Lord Baltimore), 1732-1733

Born on September 29, 1699 in England, the eldest son of Benedict Leonard Calvert, fourth Lord Baltimore, and Charlotte, the daughter of Edward Henry Lee, Earl of Litchfield. Brother of Benedict Leonard (governor of Maryland from 1727 to 1731), Charlotte, Jane, Edward Henry, Cecil, Barbara (died young) and Anne. Married on July 20, 1730 to Mary Janssen, by whom he was the father of Frederick (later sixth Lord Baltimore), Frances Dorothy (died young), Louisa, Charles (died in infancy) and Caroline; also fathered Benedict Calvert, an illegitimate son.

Educated in London, and placed under the guardianship of Francis, Lord Guilford, after the death of the fourth Lord Baltimore in 1715. Became Gentleman of the Bed Chamber to Frederick, Prince of Wales, in June 1731, and in December of that year was elected a Fellow of the Royal Society.

Although he was more significant in his role as Maryland's Lord Proprietor from 1715 to 1751, Lord Baltimore also served as resident Governor of the province from December 1732 to July 1733, when he dealt with the long-standing Maryland-Pennsylvania boundary dispute. Writing to Pennsylvania's Governor Patrick Gordon in February 1733, Baltimore expressed his disappointment with what he claimed was a reluctance on the part of that colony to settle the issue. Gordon replied in a letter which denied Baltimore's allegation, suggesting that the terms of an agreement which had been worked out earlier were not understood in the same way by the respective commissioners appointed to adjudicate the matter. Frustrated by this *impasse*, Baltimore turned Maryland's governorship over to Samuel Ogle in July 1733, and left the colony with the boundary controversy still unresolved.

After his return to England Baltimore was chosen in 1734 as a member of Parliament, representing St. Germans in Cornwall; he was also elected to Parliament from the county of Surrey in 1741 and 1747. From 1741 to 1745 Baltimore served as Junior Lord of the Admiralty, and in April 1747 he became

Cofferer to the Prince of Wales and Surveyor General of the Duchy Lands in Cornwall. Baltimore died on April 24, 1751, leaving his proprietary interest in Maryland to Frederick, his only surviving legitimate son.

Bibliography: John G. Morris, *The Lords Baltimore* (Baltimore, 1874); *The Calvert Papers*, 3 vols. (Baltimore, 1889-99); Clayton Colman Hall, *The Lords Baltimore and the Maryland Palatinate* (Baltimore, 1904); John Bailey Calvert Nicklin, "The Calvert Family," *Maryland Historical Magazine*, XVI (March-December 1921).

BLADEN, Thomas, 1742-1747

Born in 1698 in Annapolis, Maryland, the son of William and Anne (Van Swearingen) Bladen. Brother of Anne, who married Benjamin Tasker, Maryland's acting governor from 1752 to 1753. Married in the 1730's to Barbara Janssen, the eldest sister of Mary, wife of the fifth Lord Baltimore; father of Harriot and Barbara. Educated in England. Sailed from America to England about 1732, and returned ten years later as Lieutenant Governor of Maryland, assuming that office from Samuel Ogle in August 1742.

After a lengthy dispute with his own Assembly over whether he had the right to appoint commissioners to negotiate a treaty with the chiefs of the Six Nations, Bladen proceeded to make the appointments on his own authority, and in June 1744 the colonies of Virginia, Pennsylvania and Maryland concluded an agreement which ended any Indian claim to Maryland's settlements. Bladen's tenure was also marked by the beginning of King George's War between Great Britain and France. Although neither side in that conflict devoted much effort to military operations in America, Bladen was required in early 1745 to make plans to repel an expected attack by the Shawanese Indians, who sided with the French. Later, in June 1746, the Assembly voted funds to raise troops for a projected attack on French Canada, to be carried out in cooperation with other British and colonial forces, but this venture was subsequently abandoned.

Bladen was replaced by former Lieutenant Governor Ogle in March 1747. In June of that year he departed for London, and while residing in England, served in 1751 as executor under the will of Charles, fifth Lord Baltimore. Bladen also represented several constituencies in Parliament before his death in England in 1780.

Bibliography: Christopher Johnston, "The Bladen Family," *Maryland Historical Magazine*, V (September 1910), 297-99.

TASKER, Benjamin, 1752-1753

Born in 1690, the son of Captain Thomas Tasker, who settled in Calvert County, Maryland in 1682 and became treasurer of the province. Brother of Thomas (died young), John and Elizabeth. Married in 1711 to Anne Bladen, by whom he was the father of William (died young), Benjamin (died in infancy), Bladen (died young), Benjamin, Bladen (died young), Rebecca, Elizabeth, Anne (who married Lieutenant Governor Samuel Ogle in 1741), Bladen (died young) and Frances.

Interested in horses and horsebreeding, and a founder of Maryland's Jockey Club. One of the founders of the Baltimore Ironworks Company in 1731, and a participant in a Maryland land speculation scheme in the 1740's. Acted as a Justice for Anne Arundel County from 1714 to 1717, and served as High Sheriff of that county between 1717 and 1718. Held a variety of other offices during his political career, including Justice of the Provincial Court and Mayor of Annapolis. Named to the Maryland Council in 1722, serving as President of that body for many years; in that capacity, presided as Acting Governor between the death of Samuel Ogle in May 1752 and the arrival of the new lieutenant governor, Horatio Sharpe, in August of 1753.

Tasker's brief administration was essentially that of a caretaker, until Sharpe landed in the colony with his proprietary instructions. Nevertheless, Tasker presided over several significant events in Maryland history, including the opening in 1752 of the first theater to be established in America.

After his period as chief executive, Tasker returned to his seat on the Council. In 1754 he served as one of Maryland's delegates at the congress which met in Albany, New York and adopted a "Plan of Union" based on a proposal put forth by Benjamin Franklin. Tasker also became one of the Maryland commissioners appointed in 1760 to supervise a survey of the boundary between Pennsylvania and Maryland. He died on June 19, 1768, and was buried in St. Anne's Churchyard in Annapolis, Maryland.

Bibliography: Christopher Johnston, "The Tasker Family," *Maryland Historical Magazine*, IV (June 1909), 191-92.

SHARPE, Horatio, 1753-1769

Born on November 15, 1718 near Hull in Yorkshire, England, a member of a distinguished family. Brother of Gregory (a master of the Temple and a prominent scholar), John, Joshua, Philip, William and a number of sisters. Never married.

Commissioned as Captain of Marines in 1745; later promoted to Lieutenant Colonel of Foot in the West Indies. Appointed Lieutenant Governor of Maryland, and arrived in the province in August of 1753 to assume that office.

Sharpe's long tenure of almost sixteen years encompassed a period which opened with Great Britain on the brink of war with France, and ended with America in a state of considerable unrest over British colonial policy. During the first months of the French and Indian War, Sharpe also served as Commander-in-Chief of troops raised "to defend the frontiers of Virginia and the neighboring colonies, and to repel the unjustifiable invasion and encroachments of the French, on the river Ohio." Although General James Braddock replaced him as commander in 1755, Sharpe continued to take a keen interest in military affairs throughout the remainder of the conflict, in spite of strong opposition from the Maryland Assembly. In his other dealings with the Legislature, Sharpe tried with varying success to carry out proprietary instructions without ignoring colonial needs and interests. Nevertheless, the Stamp Act and other instances of controversial British legislation complicated the final years of his administration. Sharpe's exaggerated reference to the Assembly as a body composed of "flaming Patriots or rather inflaming Demagogues" suggests how heated his relationship with Maryland's lawmakers could become. Finally, in June 1769, Sharpe was replaced by Robert Eden, whose appointment was in large part the result of his marriage to Caroline Calvert, the sister of the Maryland proprietor. Sharpe then retired to "Whitehall," his country estate near Annapolis. In 1773 he returned to England, where he remained until his death on November 9, 1790.

Bibliography: Lady [Matilda Ridout] Edgar, *A Colonial Governor in Maryland: Horatio Sharpe and His Times, 1753-1773* (London, 1912); "Correspondence of Governor Sharpe [Oct. 19, 1763-June 20, 1768]," *Maryland Historical Magazine*, XII (December 1917), 370-83; Paul H. Giddens, "The Public Career of Horatio Sharpe, Governor of Maryland, 1753-1769," unpub. Ph.D. diss., University of Iowa, 1930; Paul H. Giddens, "Governor Horatio Sharpe and His Maryland Government," *Maryland Historical Magazine*, XXXII (June 1937), 156-74; James H. High, "Reluctant Loyalist: Governor Horatio Sharpe of Maryland, 1753-1769," unpub. Ph.D. diss., University of California at Los Angeles, 1951; James H. High, "Testing an Eighteenth-Century Personality," *Social Studies*, XLIX (February 1958), 55-59; Aubrey C. Land, ed., "The Familiar Letters of Governor Horatio Sharpe," *Maryland Historical Magazine*, LXI (September 1966), 189-209; James Haw, "The Patronage Follies: Bennet Allen, John Morton Jordan, and the Fall of Horatio Sharpe," *Maryland Historical Magazine*, LXXI (Summer 1976), 134-50. For many of Sharpe's papers, ranging in date from 1753 to 1771, see William H. Brown *et al.*, eds., *Archives of Maryland*, vols. VI, IX, XIV and XXXI (Baltimore, 1888-1911). *DAB*.

EDEN, Robert, 1769-1776

Born on September 14, 1741 in Durham, England, the son of Robert, a member of Parliament for Durham, and Mary (Davison) Eden. Brother of ten, including John, William (later Lord Auckland), Thomas, Morton (later Lord Henley) and Catharine. Married on April 26, 1765 to Caroline Calvert, who was the sister of the sixth Lord Baltimore, Maryland's proprietor; father of Frederick Morton, William Thomas and Catherine.

Commissioned at the age of fifteen as a Lieutenant Fireworker in the Royal Regiment of Artillery; during the Seven Years' War became Ensign, and later Lieutenant and Captain, while serving with the Coldstream Guards in Germany. Commissioned Lieutenant Governor of Maryland in 1768, and arrived in the province to assume that office in June of 1769.

Although he was personally one of Maryland's most popular lieutenant governors, Eden was soon confronted by colonial hostility over the Townshend Acts, and shortly after his arrival he prorogued the Maryland General Assembly until November 1769 rather than run the risk of a legislative protest. When the Assembly did meet, however, it went ahead and endorsed non-importation of British goods as a means of demonstrating opposition to the new tax laws. Less than a year later Eden was again faced by recalcitrant legislators, as the Assembly demanded a reduction in clerical incomes and fees paid to proprietary officials. As a result a stalemate developed between the "court party" in the Council and the Assembly, which lasted for over three years. While the issue was finally settled by a compromise, popular leaders in Maryland like Thomas Johnson and William Paca made use of the controversy to enhance their own position at the expense of proprietary power. By the summer of 1775, when the Maryland Council of Safety was established, Eden's executive authority had already been severely eroded, and in June 1776 he retreated to the British warship *Fowey* at the request of the province's Patriot faction.

Several weeks later Eden left for England, where in September 1776 he was created a Baronet. He returned to Maryland after the Revolution had ended in order to assert his claim to some property, and died in Annapolis, Maryland on September 2, 1784.

Bibliography: Bernard C. Steiner, *Life and Administration of Sir Robert Eden*, in *Johns Hopkins University Studies in Historical and Political Science*, vol. XVI, nos. 7-9 (Baltimore, 1898); "Correspondence of Governor Eden [1769-1777]," *Maryland Historical Magazine*, II (1907), 1-13, 97-110, 227-44, 293-309; Rosamond R. Beirne, "Portrait of a Colonial Governor: Robert Eden," *Maryland Historical Magazine*, XLV (September-December 1950), 153-75, 294-311. *DAB*.

JENIFER, Daniel of St. Thomas, 1775-1777

Born in 1723 in Charles County, Maryland, the son of Dr. Daniel Jenifer and his wife, the daughter of Samuel and Elizabeth Hanson. Brother of Daniel and perhaps others. Never married. Enjoyed considerable wealth and lived at "Stepney," a large estate in Charles County.

Served as Agent and Receiver General for Maryland's last two lord proprietors. Became Justice of the Peace for Charles County as a young man, and later held that office for Maryland's Western Circuit. Served as a member of the commission appointed to settle a boundary dispute between Pennsylvania and Delaware in 1760. Named to the Maryland Provincial Court in 1766, and served on the Governor's Council from 1773 until the beginning of the Revolutionary War. Decided to back the Patriot cause, and in August of 1775 became President of the Maryland Council of Safety.

As head of the Council of Safety, Jenifer in effect acted as chief executive for Maryland's Patriot faction between the demise of royal authority in the colony and the inauguration of Thomas Johnson as the first governor of the state. Along with Maryland's decision to support the Declaration of Independence, the most significant political development during these months was the drafting and adoption of the Maryland Constitution of 1776. By comparison with most of the other state constitutions written during that year, Maryland's instrument of government was notably conservative, as evidenced by its careful distinction between an indirectly-elected Senate and a popularly-elected House of Delegates, as well as the relatively high property qualifications which it required of prospective legislators.

After his service on the Council of Safety ended in March 1777, Jenifer became President of the Maryland Senate. From 1778 to 1782 he also represented Maryland in the Continental Congress, where he supported the idea of a stronger national government. Jenifer served his native state in several other capacities during the 1780's, including that of Intendant of Maryland Revenues (or State Treasurer). In 1787 he acted as a delegate from Maryland at the Philadelphia Constitutional Convention, but although he signed the completed document, he played only a minor role in that body's deliberations. Jenifer died in Annapolis, Maryland on November 16, 1790.

Bibliography: S. Sydney Bradford, ed., "Four Daniel of St. Thomas Jenifer Letters," *Maryland Historical Magazine*, LVI (September 1961), 291-95. *DAB*.

JOHNSON, Thomas, 1777-1779

Born on November 4, 1732 in Calvert County, Maryland, the son of Thomas and Dorcas (Sedgwick) Johnson. An Episcopalian. Brother of Thomas (died in infancy), Benjamin, Mary, Rebecca, James, Elizabeth, Joshua, John, Baker and Roger. Married on February 16, 1766 to Ann Jennings, by whom he was the father of Thomas, Ann, Rebecca, Dorcas and Joshua. Received early education at home, clerked for a time, and later studied law under Stephen Bordley; established a law practice in Annapolis.

First became a member of the Maryland Provincial Assembly in 1762, representing Anne Arundel County. Served on various legislative committees in the 1760's and early 1770's which voiced opposition to British policy. Named as a delegate from Maryland to the First and Second Continental Congresses and served in Congress until early 1777. In the summer of 1775 played a major part in the drafting of the "Association of the Freemen of Maryland," a document that outlined the rights of Maryland's residents; voted for the "Declaration of the Delegates of Maryland" in July 1776, which proclaimed Maryland's separation from England. Also participated in the convention which devised the Maryland Constitution of 1776. Elected First Brigadier General of the Frederick County militia in 1776, and helped to raise and equip troops. Chosen by the State Legislature as Maryland's first Governor in February 1777, assuming office in March of that year; re-elected without opposition in November 1777 and November 1778.

As chief executive of Maryland during the critical years of the Revolution, Johnson spent much of his time preparing the state for war. His period in office was also troubled by disputes within the State Legislature, as the Senate and Assembly wrangled over such issues as whether local civil officers were eligible for appointment to the legislature, the amount of salary to be paid to legislators, and the best means of punishing Maryland's Tories, who were viewed by many as a military threat to the state administration.

After stepping down as governor in November 1779, Johnson became a member of the lower house of the Maryland Legislature, where he served in 1780 and early 1781; he also sat in the State Legislature in 1786 and 1787, and in 1788 worked at the Maryland Constitutional Convention to secure that state's ratification of the Federal Constitution. Johnson was Chief Judge of the Maryland General Court from April 1790 to October 1791, and in November 1791 he was confirmed as an Associate Justice of the United States Supreme Court, although failing health forced him to resign the position early in 1793. Johnson served for several years as a member of the Board of Commissioners which considered proposals for the new "Federal City" (later Washington, D.C.), but in 1794 his infirmities caused him to relinquish that office as well, and he spent the remainder of his life in almost complete retirement. Johnson died at "Rose Hill" in Frederick County, Maryland on October 26, 1819, and was buried in Mount Olivet Cemetery in Frederick.

Bibliography: Lawrence Buckley Thomas, *Genealogical Notes: Containing the Pedigree of the Thomas Family, of Maryland, and of the Following Connected Families: Snowden, Buckley, Lawrence, Chew, Ellicott, Hopkins, Johnson, Rutherfurd, Fairfax, Schieffelin, Tyson and Others* (Baltimore, 1877); Edward S. Delaplaine, *Thomas Johnson, Maryland and the Constitution* [Baltimore?, 1925]; Edward S. Delaplaine, *The Life of Thomas Johnson* . . . (New York, 1927). *DAB*.

LEE, Thomas Sim, 1779-1782, 1792-1794

Born on October 29, 1745 near Upper Marlboro, Maryland, the son of Thomas and Christiana (Sim) Lee. A Roman Catholic. Married on October 27, 1771 to Mary Digges, by whom he was the father of four sons and six daughters.

Privately educated. Named to the Maryland Council in 1777, an office which he held until his selection as Governor by the State Legislature in 1779; served as chief executive from November 1779 to November 1782, winning re-election in 1780 and 1781. Represented Maryland in the Continental Congress in 1783 and 1784, and participated in the state convention which in April 1788 ratified the Federal Constitution. Again elected Governor of Maryland in 1792, and served in that capacity from April 1792 until November 1794; also chosen as a Presidential Elector in 1792.

Lee's first tenure as chief executive was largely concerned with devising measures to further the revolutionary war effort. In that area, the governor endorsed one of the more successful techniques for encouraging recruits to join the Continental Army, when he supported a legislative proposal to grant a bounty of fifty acres of land to all men who agreed to enlist. While Maryland was no longer at odds with Great Britain during Lee's second period in office, it did face the possibility of internal revolution, after the "Whiskey Rebellion," which had originated in Pennsylvania, began to affect various parts of the state. Under the governor's firm leadership, however, state militia were quickly dispatched to quell this outbreak of farmers who had objected to the imposition of federal taxes on distillers of alcoholic beverages.

Following his gubernatorial career, Lee was elected to the United States Senate and, in 1798, to another term as chief executive. Nevertheless, he declined both positions, and remained a private citizen until his death at "Needwood," his estate in Frederick County, Maryland, on November 9, 1819.

Bibliography: Edward C. Mead, ed., *Genealogical History of the Lee Family of Virginia and Maryland*... (New York, 1868); E. J. Lee, *Lee of Virginia, 1642-1892* (Philadelphia, 1895); Helen Lee Peabody, ed., "Revolutionary Mail Bag: Governor Thomas Sim Lee's Correspondence, 1779-1782," *Maryland Historical Magazine*, XLIX (March-December 1954), 1-20, 122-42, 223-37, 314-31, vol. L (March-June 1955), 34-46, 93-108. *DAB*.

PACA, William, 1782-1785

Born on October 31, 1740 near Abingdon, Harford County, Maryland, the second son of John and Elizabeth (Smith) Paca. An Episcopalian. Married on May 26, 1763 to Mary Chew, by whom he had five children, though probably only one, John Philemon, reached maturity; after his first wife's death in 1774, remarried to a woman named Levina; married a third time in 1777 to Anne Harrison. Studied at the College of Philadelphia, receiving an M.A. in 1759; later received legal training in the Annapolis office of Stephen Bordley, and by 1761 was permitted to practice before the Mayor's Court; also studied law in London, and admitted to the bar of the Maryland Provincial Court in 1764.

Elected to the Maryland Legislature in 1768, and soon emerged as a leading opponent of Britain's colonial policy. Became a member of the Maryland Committee of Correspondence in 1773; chosen to represent Maryland at the First and Second Continental Congresses, attending sessions from 1774 to 1779. As a member of Congress, signed the Declaration of Independence in July 1776. Served as a member of the Maryland Council of Safety during the early stages of the Revolution, and in 1776 participated in the deliberations which produced the State Constitution of that year. Chosen as a member of Maryland's first State Senate; became Chief Justice of the Maryland General Court in 1778; and in 1780 was selected by the Continental Congress as Chief Justice of the Court of Appeals in admiralty and prize cases. Elected Governor of Maryland in November 1782, and re-elected without opposition in 1783 and 1784.

Paca's service as a post-war chief executive was largely occupied by his attempts to hasten Maryland's social and economic recovery from a long and costly war. Legislative controversy was also a characteristic of these years. The session which began in November 1784 was an especially heated one, as the legislators argued over issues ranging from a proposed state college on Maryland's western shore to a bill which would levy duties on exports shipped in foreign vessels. Just before Paca left office, Maryland's Senate and House of Delegates grew particularly vexed with each other over the question of paper money, a question that became the major source of political discord during the administration of his successor.

Ineligible for re-election, Paca left the governor's office in November 1785. He later served as Vice President of the Maryland Society of the Cincinnati, and attended the Maryland Constitutional Convention of 1788, where he voted for ratification of the Federal Constitution. Paca was named as a Federal District Judge in 1789, a position he filled until his death on October 13, 1799 at "Wye Hall," on Wye Island in Maryland.

Bibliography: " . . . Wye Hall. The Rise and Decadence of a Noted Family of Maryland. The Tragedy of the Pacas," *The Times* [Philadelphia], April 27, 1879; Albert Silverman, "William Paca, Signer, Governor, Jurist," *Maryland Historical Magazine*, XXXVII (March 1942), 1-25. *DAB*.

SMALLWOOD, William, 1785-1788

Born in 1732 in Charles County, Maryland, the son of Bayne, a planter, merchant and member of the Maryland Assembly, and Priscilla (Heabard) Smallwood. An Episcopalian. Brother of Lucy Heabard, Elizabeth, Margaret, Heabard, Priscilla and Eleanor. Never married. Thought to have been educated in England.

Served in the military during the French and Indian War. Entered the Maryland Assembly in 1761, representing Charles County, and participated in the colonial protest against British policy during the 1760's and early 1770's. Became a member of the "Association of the Freemen of Maryland" in 1775, which advocated armed resistance to attempts at enforcing parliamentary statutes. Named Colonel of a Maryland regiment in January 1776; appointed Brigadier General by the Continental Congress in October 1776, and took part in a number of military campaigns during the Revolutionary War, including the Battle of Camden, where his service earned him a promotion to Major General in September 1780; left the military in November 1783. Elected Governor of Maryland in November 1785, and reelected in 1786 and 1787.

Smallwood's gubernatorial career began on an inauspicious note, as the Maryland Senate engaged in a bitter dispute with the state's House of Delegates over the question of paper money. Despite considerable pressure from popular leaders like Samuel Chase, the Senate eventually prevailed when it resisted House demands for the emission of paper currency. Another feature of the Smallwood administration was the Annapolis Convention of 1786, which served as a prelude to the Constitutional Convention held the next year in Philadelphia. Although the Federal Constitution drafted at the Philadelphia meeting soon aroused strong feelings on both sides, the Maryland Convention called to consider that document voted in favor of ratification in April 1788, rejecting the anti-constitutionalist position adopted by Smallwood himself.

Following his period as governor, Smallwood appears to have taken little part in politics. He died at Mattawoman in Charles County, Maryland on February 14, 1792, and was buried at "Smallwood's Retreat" in Charles County.

Bibliography: Arthur L. Keith, "General William Smallwood," *Maryland Historical Magazine*, XIX (September 1924), 304-06; Arthur L. Keith, "Smallwood Family of Charles County," *Maryland Historical Magazine*, XXII (June 1927), 139-86. *DAB*.

HOWARD, John Eager, 1788-1791

Born on June 4, 1752 near Baltimore, Maryland, the son of Cornelius, a wealthy planter, and Ruth (Eager) Howard. A Roman Catholic. Brother of George, James, Cornelius, Ruth, Violetta and several others. Married on May 18, 1787 to Margaret ("Peggy") Oswald Chew, by whom he had George (who served as governor of Maryland from 1831 to 1833), Juliana, Sophia, John Eager (died young), John Eager, Benjamin Chew, William, James and Charles.

Privately educated. Served during the Revolution as an officer in the Maryland Line of the Continental Army, eventually rising to the rank of Lieutenant Colonel; later named Brigadier General in 1798, during the "quasi-war" with France. Represented Maryland in the Continental Congress in 1787 and 1788. Selected Governor of Maryland by the State Legislature in November 1788, and served in that capacity until November 1791, after winning re-election in 1789 and 1790.

Although Maryland had ratified the Constitution by the time Howard took office as chief executive, the state continued to be involved in other issues affecting its relationship to the federal government. Perhaps the most significant question yet to be resolved concerned the permanent location of the nation's capital, and Howard, a long-time friend of President Washington, adroitly used his influence to press for a site near Baltimore. Largely as a result of Howard's encouragement, the Maryland General Assembly in December 1791 ceded to the United States the state land which some months earlier had been designated as part of the District of Columbia.

Following his gubernatorial career, Howard served as a Presidential Elector in 1792 and as a State Senator from 1795 to 1796. In November 1796 the Maryland Legislature named him to complete an unexpired term in the United States Senate, and a short time later he was re-elected in his own right. In 1803 Howard returned to private life, but during the War of 1812 he organized a regiment of veteran troops and made himself available to fight, although he saw no action. While he ran as the Federalist Party's vice-presidential candidate in 1816, Howard was easily defeated by the Republican Daniel D. Tompkins. He then retired to his estate near Baltimore, where he died on October 12, 1827.

Bibliography: *A Memoir of the Late Colonel John Eager Howard* (1863), reprinted from the Baltimore *Gazette* of October 15, 1827; Elizabeth Read, "The Howards of Maryland," *Magazine of American History*, III (April 1879), 239-49; Elizabeth Read, "Col. John Eager Howard, of the Second Maryland Regiment, in the Continental Line," *Magazine of American History*, VII (October 1881), 276-82; Henry Ridgely Evans, *Progenitors of the Howards of Maryland* (Washington, D.C., *c.* 1938); Cary Howard, "John Eager Howard: Patriot and Public Servant," *Maryland Historical Magazine*, LXII (September 1967), 300-17. *DAB*.

MASSACHUSETTS

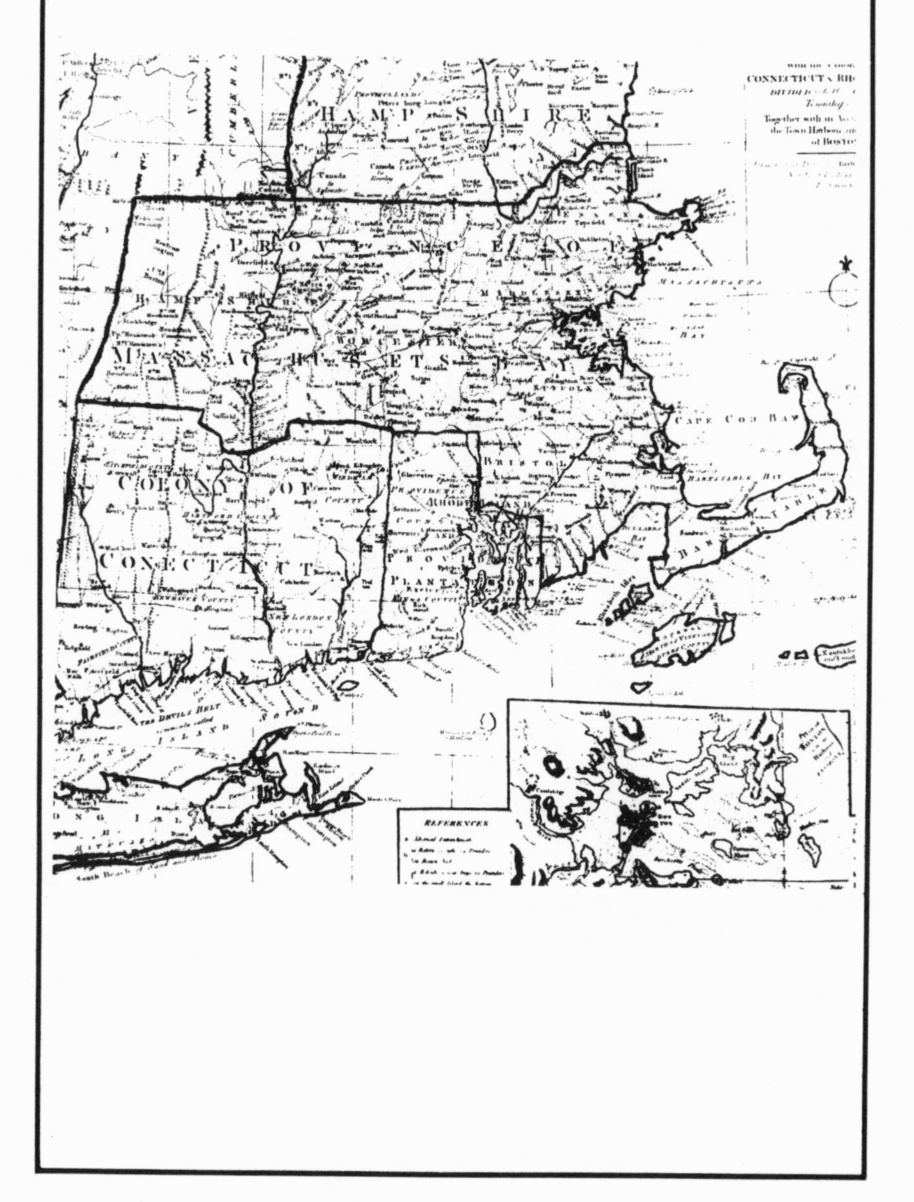

Chronology

1629-1630	John Endecott (or Endicott)
1630-1634	John Winthrop
1634-1635	Thomas Dudley
1635-1636	John Haynes
1636-1637	Sir Henry Vane
1637-1640	John Winthrop
1640-1641	Thomas Dudley
1641-1642	Richard Bellingham
1642-1644	John Winthrop
1644-1645	John Endecott (or Endicott)
1645-1646	Thomas Dudley
1646-1649	John Winthrop
1649-1650	John Endecott (or Endicott)
1650-1651	Thomas Dudley
1651-1654	John Endecott (or Endicott)
1654-1655	Richard Bellingham
1655-1665	John Endecott (or Endicott)
1665-1672	Richard Bellingham
1672-1679	John Leverett
1679-1686	Simon Bradstreet
1686	Joseph Dudley
1686-1689	Sir Edmund Andros
1689-1692	Simon Bradstreet
1692-1694	Sir William Phips
1694-1699	William Stoughton
1699-1700	Richard Coote, Earl of Bellomont
1700-1701	William Stoughton
1701-1702	*Between March 1701 and June 1702, the Massachusetts Council, acting as a body, served as the colony's executive authority.*
1702-1715	Joseph Dudley
1715	*Between February 4 and March 21, 1715, the Massachusetts Council, acting as a body, served as the colony's executive authority.*
1715-1716*	William Tailer
1716-1723	Samuel Shute
1723-1728	William Dummer

1728-1729	William Burnet
1729-1730	William Dummer
1730	William Tailer
1730-1741	Jonathan Belcher
1741-1749	William Shirley
1749-1753	Spencer Phips
1753-1756	William Shirley
1756-1757	Spencer Phips
1757	*Between April 4 and August 3, 1757, the Massachusetts Council, acting as a body, served as the colony's executive authority.*
1757-1760	Thomas Pownall
1760	Thomas Hutchinson
1760-1769	Francis Bernard
1769-1774	Thomas Hutchinson
1774	Thomas Gage
1774-1780	*Massachusetts was governed by a Provincial Congress between October 1774 and July 1775, and by a Council of State between July 1775 and the autumn of 1780.*
1780-1785	John Hancock
1785	Thomas Cushing
1785-1787	James Bowdoin
1787-1793	John Hancock

*Although Elizeus Burgess was commissioned royal governor of Massachusetts Bay in 1715, he resigned the office without ever going to America.

BIBLIOGRAPHY

Bradford, Alden, ed., *Speeches of the Governors of Massachusetts from 1765 to 1775 . . . and Other Public Papers . . .* (Boston, 1818).

Drake, Samuel Adams, *History of Middlesex County, Massachusetts . . .*, 2 vols. (Boston, 1880).

Journal of the House of Representatives of Massachusetts, 1715-1760, 36 vols. (Boston, 1919-64).

Labaree, Benjamin, *Colonial Massachusetts: A History* (New York, 1979).

Lincoln, William, ed., *Journals of Each Provincial Congress of Massachusetts in 1774 and 1775 . . . and Other Documents* (Boston, 1838).

Moore, Jacob Bailey, *Lives of the Governors of New Plymouth, and Massachusetts Bay . . .* (Boston, 1851).

Records of the Court of Assistants of the Colony of Massachusetts Bay, 1630-1692, 3 vols. (Boston, 1901-28).

Shurtleff, Nathaniel B., ed., *Records of the Governor and Company of the Massachusetts Bay in New England [1628-86]*, 5 vols. (Boston, 1853-54).

Spencer, Henry R., *Constitutional Conflict in Provincial Massachusetts: A Study of Some Phases of the Opposition between the Massachusetts Governor and General Court in the Early Eighteenth Century* (Columbus, Ohio, 1905).

Warden, G. B., *Boston, 1689-1776* (Boston, 1970).

MASSACHUSETTS

ENDECOTT [or Endicott], John, 1629-1630, 1644-1645, 1649-1650, 1651-1654, 1655-1665

Born *circa* 1589, probably in Devonshire, England, the son of Thomas and Alice (Westlake?) Endecott. A Congregationalist. Married before leaving England to Anne Gower, who died shortly after her arrival in America; remarried on August 18, 1630 to Elizabeth (Cogan) Gibson, by whom he was the father of John and Zerrubbabel.

May have fought with English troops against the Spaniards in the Low Countries, and earned the rank of Captain. Arrived in New England in September 1628, leading a vanguard of colonists who settled at Naumkeag (now Salem) and prepared the way for the larger group of emigrants to follow. Named resident Governor of the colony by the leaders of the Massachusetts Bay Company in April 1629, and exercised that office until June of 1630, when he was succeeded by John Winthrop, the newly-arrived chief executive; also served as governor of Massachusetts from May 1644 to May 1645, May 1649 to May 1650, May 1651 to May 1654, and May 1655 until his death. Appointed Sergeant-Major-General in 1645; acted as an Assistant of Massachusetts in 1630-35, 1636-41 and 1645-49, and as Deputy Governor in 1641-44, 1650-51 and 1654-55.

Despite his grim and humorless personality, Endecott was widely respected by his fellow colonists in Massachusetts Bay, and from his arrival in America until his death he held high office almost continuously. During his first period as chief executive, Endecott's stern manner proved rather appropriate, as he established a foothold in New England for the thousands of Puritan settlers who would leave home in the 1630's. However, a less laudable effect of his unyielding temperament occurred in his old age. Beginning in 1656, while he was again occupying the governor's chair, Endecott played a prominent part in the persecution of Quaker missionaries who sought to preach their doctrine of the "inner light" in the Bay Colony. Between 1659 and 1661 the repressive policies advocated by Endecott led Massachusetts officials to hang four of these proselytizers, after they had ignored sentences of banishment imposed by the General Court. Until his death on March 15, 1665, Endecott continued to support harsh measures for dealing with Quakerism in New England.

Bibliography: Charles Moses Endicott, *Memoir of John Endecott, First Governor of the Colony of Massachusetts Bay* . . . (Salem, 1847); Stephen Salisbury, *A Memorial of Governor John Endecott* . . . (Worcester, 1874); Sir Roper Lethbridge, *The Devonshire Ancestry and the Early Homes of the Family of John Endecott, Governor of Massachusetts Bay, 1629* . . . [Exeter, 1914]; William Dismore Chapple, "The Public Service of John Endecott in the Massachusetts Bay Colony," *Essex Institute Historical Collections*, LXV (October 1929), 403-47; Lawrence S. Mayo, *John Endecott: A Biography* (Cambridge, 1936). *DAB*.

WINTHROP, John, 1630-1634, 1637-1640, 1642-1644, 1646-1649

Born on January 12, 1588 in Edwardstone, Suffolk, England, the son of Adam and Anne (Browne) Winthrop. A Congregationalist. Brother of Anne (died in infancy), Anne, Jane and Lucy. Married on April 16, 1605 to Mary Forth, by whom he was the father of John, Jr. (governor of Connecticut, 1657-58, 1659-76), Henry, Forth, Mary, Anne (died young) and Anne (died young); after his first wife's death in June 1615, remarried in December of that year to Thomasine Clopton, who died with her infant a year later; married a third time, in April 1618, to Margaret Tyndal; father by his third wife of Stephen, Adam, Deane, Nathaniel (died young?), Samuel, Anne (died young), William (died young?) and Sarah (died young?); after the death of his third wife in June 1647, married a fourth wife, Martha (Rainsborough) Coytmore, by whom he had Joshua, who died at the age of three.

Matriculated at Trinity College, Cambridge in Easter 1603, but left without receiving a degree; admitted to Gray's Inn in 1613, and later established a legal practice in London. Became Lord of the Manor of Groton by 1618, succeeding his father in that position. Continued to practice law in London during the 1620's, although he also became interested in the colonization scheme proposed by the Massachusetts Bay Company. Chosen Governor of the Company, which had decided to transfer its charter to America, in October 1629, but did not actually assume office in Massachusetts until June 1630; remained chief executive until May 1634, and also served in that capacity from May 1637 to May 1640, May 1642 to May 1644, and May 1646 to March 1649. Elected Deputy Governor of Massachusetts for one-year terms in 1636, 1644 and 1645; also acted as a member of the Court of Assistants while not presiding as governor or deputy governor.

Between his arrival at Salem in June 1630 and his death almost nineteen years later, Winthrop was clearly the most prominent figure in Massachusetts Bay, a fact reflected in his frequent election to high office. Nevertheless, even Winthrop faced strong political challenges on several occasions. In May 1634, for example, he lost the gubernatorial contest to Thomas Dudley, after suggesting that the colony's government should for the most part be left to its Court of Assistants. Perhaps the most significant inter-colonial development during Winthrop's period as chief executive occurred in 1643. In that year Massachusetts, Plymouth, Connecticut and New Haven formed a confederation designed primarily to protect the region from incidents like the Pequot War of 1637. Toward the end of his life criticism of Winthrop appears to have diminished somewhat, although the "Remonstrance and humble Petition" of Dr. Robert Child, a Presbyterian who favored toleration, indicates that Winthrop never lacked religious or political opposition. Less than two years after the Child affair ended in victory for Winthrop, the sixty-one year-old governor died on March 26, 1649, while still in office.

Bibliography: "The Winthrop Papers," Massachusetts Historical Society, *Collections*, especially 4th ser., vols. VI and VII (Boston, 1863, 1865) and 5th ser., vol. I (Boston, 1871); Robert C. Winthrop, *Life and Letters of John Winthrop*, 2 vols. (Boston, 1864, 1867); Robert C. Winthrop, *A Pedigree of the Family of Winthrop* (Cambridge, 1874); J.H. Twichell, *John Winthrop* (New York, 1891); J.K. Hosmer, *Winthrop's Journal*, 2 vols. (New York, 1908); G. W. Robinson, ed., *John Winthrop as Attorney: Extracts from the Order Books of the Court of Wards and Liveries, 1627-1629* (Cambridge, 1930); Edgar A. J. Johnson, "Economic Ideas of John Winthrop," *New England Quarterly*, III (April 1930), 235-50; Stanley Gray, "The Political Thought of John Winthrop," *New England Quarterly*, III (October 1930), 681-705; Lawrence Shaw Mayo, *The Winthrop Family in America* (Boston, 1948); Edmund S. Morgan, *The Puritan Dilemma: The Story of John Winthrop* (Boston, 1958); Richard S. Dunn, *Puritans and Yankees: The Winthrop Dynasty of New England, 1630-1717* (Princeton, 1962); Darrett B. Rutman, *Winthrop's Boston, 1630-1649* (Chapel Hill, 1965); Malcolm Freiberg, "The Winthrops and Their Papers," Massachusetts Historical Society, *Proceedings*, LXXX (1968), 55-70; Darrett B. Rutman, *John Winthrop's Decision for America: 1629* (New York, 1975). *DAB, DNB*.

DUDLEY, Thomas, 1634-1635, 1640-1641, 1645-1646, 1650-1651

Born in 1576 in Northampton, England, the son of Captain Roger and Susanna (Thorne) Dudley. A Congregationalist. Brother of Mary. Married on April 25, 1603 to Dorothy Yorke, by whom he was the father of Samuel, Anne (the poet, who later married Governor Simon Bradstreet), Patience, Sarah and Mercy; following the death of his first wife in December 1643, remarried on April 14, 1644 to Catherine (Dighton) Hackburn, by whom he had Deborah, Joseph (later a governor of Massachusetts) and Paul.

Studied at a Latin school as a child, and later employed as a page by the Earl of Northampton. Also worked as a clerk under Judge Nichols, a kinsman. Served as a Captain in the English Army, although he appears not to have engaged in combat. Became steward to the Earl of Lincoln about the time of his first marriage, and served that nobleman for nine years; moved to Boston, Lincolnshire, where he came under the influence of the Reverend John Cotton, but later returned to work for the Earl of Lincoln, until immigrating to Massachusetts Bay aboard the *Arbella* in 1630. Named Deputy Governor of the Massachusetts Bay Company in 1629, before embarking for America, and served in that capacity until 1634; also acted as deputy governor from 1637 to 1640, 1646 to 1650, and 1651 to 1653. Chosen as an Assistant in 1635, 1636, 1641, 1643 and 1644, serving one-year terms on each occasion. Appointed to numerous religious, educational and political bodies throughout his life, including the commission which in 1643 established the New England Confederation. First elected Governor of Massachusetts in May 1634, a position he filled until May of the following year; also served as chief executive from May 1640 to June 1641, May 1645 to May 1646, and May 1650 to May 1651.

While Dudley's long and distinguished career was marked by many notable events, perhaps the most significant development during his years as governor was the emergence of the freemen in Massachusetts Bay as a meaningful political force. Indeed, it was with the selection of Dudley as chief executive over John Winthrop in May 1634 that the freemen began to demonstrate their power to determine the colony's leaders. To be sure, this temporary rebuke to Winthrop by the freemen, who still comprised a small minority of the total population, hardly signifies the triumph of "democracy" in any real sense, but it does represent the emergence of a tradition of accountability which, by the time of Dudley's death on July 31, 1653, had become an important part of Massachusetts politics.

Bibliography: [D. D.], "Governor Thomas Dudley and His Descendants," *New England Historical and Genealogical Register*, X (April-October 1856), 133-42, 337-44; George Adlard, *The Sutton-Dudleys of England and the Dudleys of Massachusetts in New England*... (New York, 1862); Dean Dudley, *History of the Dudley Family* (Wakefield, Mass., 1886-94); Augustine Jones, *The Life and Work of Thomas Dudley, the Second Governor of Massachusetts* (Boston, 1899); George Ellsworth Koues, "Thomas Dudley—1576-1653; Governor of Massachusetts Bay Colony," in *Addresses Delivered before the Society of Colonial Wars in the State of New York, and Year Book for 1911-1912* (New York, 1912), 53-63; Mary Kingsbury Talcott, "The Maternal Ancestry of Governor Thomas Dudley," *New England Historical and Genealogical Register*, LXVI (October 1912), 340-43; William A. Polf, "Puritan Gentlemen: The Dudleys of Massachusetts, 1576-1686," unpub. Ph.D. diss., Syracuse University, 1973. *DAB*.

HAYNES, John, 1635-1636

Connecticut, 1639-1640, 1641-1642, 1643-1644, 1645-1646, 1647-1648 1649-1650, 1651-1652, 1653-1654

Born in April 1594, probably in Essex, England, the son of John and Mary (Mitchell) Haynes. A Congregationalist. Brother of Emanuel, Elizabeth, Mary, Margaret, Martha, Deborah, Sarah, Philadelphia, Anne and Priscilla. Married to Mary Thornton, by whom he had Robert, Hezekiah and Mary; remarried, apparently after the death of his first wife, to Mabel Harlakenden; father of John, Roger, Joseph, Ruth and Mabel by his second wife.

Immigrated to Massachusetts Bay in 1633 aboard the *Griffin*, arriving in September of that year. Chosen as an Assistant of the colony in May of 1634, and a year later, in May 1635, elected Governor of Massachusetts. Again became an assistant, following his replacement as chief executive by Henry Vane in May 1636. Moved to Connecticut in May 1637, and soon became a member of that colony's General Corte [Court]. Elected in April 1639 as Connecticut's first Governor under its "Fundamental Orders." Because of the stipulation that a chief executive could not serve two consecutive terms, reelected every alternate year through 1653; usually served as Deputy Governor when he was ineligible for the governorship.

During Haynes' brief tenure as governor of Massachusetts Bay, the colony endured considerable hardship, as its young economy was unable to keep pace with the wave of new emigrants from England. Indeed, by the end of 1635 a "great scarcity of Bread" had made it difficult for the towns in Massachusetts to feed their population. A short time later, however, the migration of settlers like Haynes to the Connecticut River Valley temporarily reduced this rapid rate of growth.

In Connecticut Haynes quickly won the prestige which he had enjoyed in the Bay Colony and, despite the requirement barring him from serving consecutive gubernatorial terms, he became one of its leading political figures. As governor, Haynes worked for the establishment of an alliance which would defend New England from attacks by both Indians and non-English settlers. The New England Confederation, established in 1643, was the culmination of these efforts, and Haynes took an active role in that body's deliberations on several subsequent occasions. Haynes also had a part in the prosecution of alleged witches living under his jurisdiction. In 1651, for example, he and two other Connecticut magistrates visited Stratford, where they judged a woman, Goody Bassett, guilty of witchcraft.

Haynes died in office early in January 1654, while Deputy Governor Edward Hopkins was residing in England. This crisis led the General Court to pass an amendment to the Fundamental Orders, permitting a majority of the magistrates to summon a Court in the absence of any higher authority.

Bibliography: "Will of Governor Haynes," *New England Historical and Genealogical Register*, XVI (April 1862), 167-69; "Papers Relating to the Haines Family," *New England Historical and Genealogical Register*, XXIV (October 1870), 422-24; "Material Relating to the Essex Family of Haynes," *New England Historical and Genealogical Register*, XLIX (July 1895), 304-10; Charles E. Cuningham, "John Haynes of Connecticut," *New England Quarterly*, XII (December 1939), 654-80. *DAB, DNB*.

VANE, Sir Henry, 1636-1637

Born in 1613, probably in Debden, Essex, England, the son of Sir Henry and Lady Frances (Darcy) Vane. A Puritan. Brother of eleven. Married on July 1, 1640 to Frances Wray, by whom he was the father of thirteen children, including Henry, Christopher, Thomas, Frances, Albinia, Dorothy and Mary.

Attended Westminster School, and later studied briefly at Magdalen Hall, Oxford; continued his education on the Continent, probably at Leyden. Immigrated to New England in 1635, and arrived in Boston in October of that year. Became a member of the Boston church within a few weeks; chosen as a freeman of the colony in March of 1636. Elected Governor of Massachusetts in May 1636, replacing John Haynes.

Although Vane only served as governor of Massachusetts for one year, his period in office was marked by probably the most significant event in that colony's early history. When Anne Hutchinson began to preach the primary importance of the "indwelling spirit" during the conversion process, she set off a quarrel between her adherents and those who attacked her as both religiously unorthodox and politically dangerous. This "Antinomian controversy" soon divided the leaders of the colony, with John Winthrop supporting the anti-Hutchinson position and Vane defending Mrs. Hutchinson's views. As the opponents of Mrs. Hutchinson grew stronger, however, Vane found it impossible to govern effectively. In May 1637 he lost the governorship to Winthrop and, after serving briefly in the General Court, he departed for England to resume his political career on English soil.

By 1639 Vane had secured an appointment as Joint Treasurer of the Navy, and in June of the next year, he was knighted by a grateful Charles I. Nevertheless, Vane's Puritan proclivities resurfaced during the English Civil Wars, when he represented Hull in both the Short and Long Parliaments. Vane also participated in the various councils of state which met during the early years of the Commonwealth. His opposition to the Protectorate government led Vane to retire from public life following the dissolution of the Long Parliament in 1653 and, although for a short time he represented Whitchurch, Hampshire in Parliament during the administration of Richard Cromwell, his political career was nearly at an end. After the restoration of Charles II to the English throne in 1660, Vane was excluded from the Act of Indemnity pardoning former defenders of the Commonwealth. He was later tried for high treason and found guilty, and on June 14, 1662 executed for that crime. Vane was buried in Shipborne Church, Kent. He wrote numerous tracts and speeches, most of which concern religious and political matters.

Bibliography: George Sikes, *Life and Death of Sir Henry Vane, or a Short Narrative of the Main Passages of His Earthly Pilgrimage* (London, 1662); James K. Hosmer, *The Life of Young Sir Henry Vane . . .* (Boston and New York, 1888); William W. Ireland, *The Life of Sir Henry Vane the Younger, with a History of the Events of His Time* (London, 1905); Henry Melville King, *Sir Henry Vane, Jr., Governor of Massachusetts and Friend of Roger Williams and Rhode Island* (Providence, Rhode Island, 1909); John Willcock, *Life of Sir Henry Vane the Younger, Statesman and Mystic (1613-1662)* (London, 1913); George C. Rogers, Jr., "Sir Henry Vane, Jr., Spirit Mystic and Fanatic Democrat," unpub. Ph.D. diss., University of Chicago, 1954; Margaret A. Judson, *The Political Thought of Sir Henry Vane, the Younger* (Philadelphia, 1969); Violet A. Rowe, *Sir Henry Vane the Younger: A Study in Political and Administrative History* (London, 1970); J. H. Adamson and H. F. Folland, *Sir Harry Vane: His Life and Times (1613-1662)* (Boston, 1973). *DAB, DNB*.

BELLINGHAM, Richard, 1641-1642, 1654-1655, 1665-1672

Born *circa* 1592 in Boston, Lincolnshire, England, the son of William and Frances (Amcotts) Bellingham. A Congregationalist. Brother of Susan, Sarah, Judith and William. First married to Elizabeth Backhouse, by whom he was the father of Samuel; remarried in 1641 to Penelope Pelham; father of Hannah, John, James and Grace by his second wife.

Studied law, and served as Recorder of the town of Boston in Lincolnshire from 1625 to 1633. Elected to Parliament, representing Boston, in 1628; in 1629, as a member of the Massachusetts Bay Company, became one of the patentees who received that company's charter. Immigrated to New England in 1634, and in 1635 elected Deputy Governor of Massachusetts Bay, serving until 1636; also acted as deputy governor in 1640-41, 1653-54 and 1655-65. Held other important public offices in the colony, including Assistant (1636-40 and 1642-53) and Treasurer (1637-40). First elected Governor of Massachusetts in June 1641, but lost the position to John Winthrop in the following year; also served as governor from May 1654 to May 1655, and from 1665 until his death.

Bellingham's three periods as chief executive of Massachusetts spanned over thirty years of the colony's history, and throughout that era he epitomized the stern Puritan who scorned outside interference from English authorities. In

1664, for example, a royal commission arrived in Boston to investigate the colony's cooperation with the newly-enacted laws governing trade and navigation. When the obstinate Bellingham denied the commission's authority, he was called to England to explain his behavior. Bellingham ignored the summons, however, and the matter was later dropped after he presented the Royal Navy with a shipload of masts. Bellingham died on December 7, 1672, while still serving as governor.

Bibliography: David King, "William Coddington and Richard Bellingham," *New England Historical and Genealogical Register*, XXVIII (January 1874), 13-16; Charles Hervey Townshend, "Bellingham Sketch," *New England Historical and Genealogical Register*, XXXVI (October 1882), 381-86; E. H. Goss, "About Richard Bellingham," *Magazine of American History*, XIII (March 1885), 262-68. *DAB, DNB*.

LEVERETT, John, 1672-1679

Born in 1616 in Lincolnshire, England, the son of Thomas and Anne (Fisher) Leverett. A Congregationalist. Brother of twelve, although all but Jane and Anne appear to have died young. Married in about 1639 to Hannah Hudson, by whom he was the father of four, all but Hudson dying young; after his first wife's death in July 1646, remarried in 1647 to Sarah Sedgwick; father of about fourteen children by his second wife, though only Elizabeth, Anne, Mary, Hannah, Rebecca and Sarah seem to have reached maturity.

Immigrated to Massachusetts Bay with his parents in 1633, but sailed for England in 1644 to fight with the Parliamentary forces during the Civil Wars. Returned to the Bay Colony by 1648 and held a number of public offices, including member of the General Court from 1651 to 1653 and again from 1663 to 1665; also served as Speaker of that body in 1663 and 1664. Acted as one of the commissioners who in 1652 proclaimed present-day Maine to be within the jurisdiction of Massachusetts; named in 1653 as his colony's Agent in England, and served in that capacity between late 1655 and 1661 or 1662. Became Major General of the Massachusetts military in 1663, a rank he held until 1673. Appointed to the Governor's Council in 1665, remaining a member of that body until his selection as Deputy Governor of Massachusetts in 1671. By virtue of his office as deputy governor, succeeded the deceased Richard Bellingham in December 1672; elected Governor in his own right the following spring, and served until his death on March 16, 1679. Said to have been knighted in 1676, although there is little foundation for the claim.

Leverett's tenure was marked by several developments of major importance in the evolution of Massachusetts Bay. In June 1675 the colony became embroiled in a war with neighboring Indians led by King Philip, and the confrontation severely taxed the military resources of New England's Puritans before they could completely suppress the outbreak in the summer of 1676. Governor Leverett was also forced to deal with the activities of Edward Randolph, the Crown-appointed official who sought to bring Massachusetts into greater conformity with English laws regarding trade and navigation. While Leverett had some success in countering Randolph's moves, his determined adversary continued to criticize the behavior of the Puritan commonwealth during the subsequent administration of Simon Bradstreet, until by 1684 these accusations had culminated in the loss of the Massachusetts charter.

Bibliography: Nathaniel B. Shurtleff, *A Genealogical Memoir of the Family of Elder Thomas Leverett, of Boston* (Boston, 1850); Charles Edward Leverett, *A Memoir, Biographical and Genealogical, of Sir John Leverett, Knt., Governor of Massachusetts, 1673-9 . . . and of the Family Generally* (Boston, 1856); "Was Gov. Leverett a Knight?," *New England Historical and Genealogical Register*, XXXV (July-October 1881), 272-75, 345-56; Arthur D. Kaledin, "The Mind of John Leverett," unpub. Ph.D. diss., Harvard University, 1965. *DAB*.

BRADSTREET, Simon, 1679-1686, 1689-1692

also New Hampshire, 1690-1692

Born in March 1604 in Horbling, Lincolnshire, England, the son of Simon, a non-conformist minister, and Margaret Bradstreet. A Congregationalist. Brother of Samuel, Mercy and John. Married in about 1628 to Anne (Dudley) Bradstreet, the poet; after his first wife's death in September 1672, remarried in June 1676 to Ann (Downing) Gardner; father by his first wife of Samuel, Dorothy, Sarah, Simon, Hannah, Mercy, Dudley and John; no children by his second marriage.

Attended Emmanuel College, Cambridge, receiving an A.B. degree in 1620 and an A.M. in 1624. Sailed for New England aboard the *Arbella* in the spring of 1630. Chosen as an Assistant of Massachusetts Bay before leaving England, and served in that capacity for almost fifty years. Also acted as Secretary of the colony from 1630 to 1636. Represented Massachusetts in the negotiations which led to the formation of the New England Confederation in 1643; later chosen as a Commissioner to the Confederation, an office he filled for thirty-three years. Appointed to a commission which in 1661 left for England to seek confirmation of the Massachusetts charter from the recently-restored Charles II. Served as Deputy Governor of Massachusetts from 1678 to 1679; elected Governor in May 1679.

During his first years as governor, Bradstreet's conciliatory approach to relations with authorities in England became more unpopular, as Massachusetts struggled to retain its charter. When representatives of the Crown like Edward Randolph sought to compel the colony to give up the charter and defenders of the old order responded by becoming more recalcitrant, the hapless Bradstreet was caught in the middle of the confrontation. With the establishment of the Dominion of New England in the spring of 1686, Bradstreet stepped down as governor, rejecting an offer to become one of the councillors for the new government. Shortly after the overthrow of Sir Edmund Andros in April 1689, however, he reluctantly resumed office as chief executive, and presided during the years between the downfall of the Dominion and the arrival in May 1692 of Sir William Phips, Massachusetts' first royal governor. For most of this period Bradstreet also acted as chief executive in New Hampshire, a province whose towns had practiced local self-government between the demise of Andros and 1690. Bradstreet died in Salem, Massachusetts late in March of 1697.

Bibliography: John Dean and Dean Dudley, "Descendants of Gov. Bradstreet," *New England Historical and Genealogical Register*, IX (April 1855), 113-21; Isaac John Greenwood, "Remarks on the Maverick Family, and the Ancestry of Gov. Simon Bradstreet," *New England Historical and Genealogical Register*, XLVIII (April 1894), 168-71; William Andrews Pew, "The Worshipful Simon Bradstreet, Governor of Massachusetts," *Essex Institute Historical Collections*, LXIV (1928), 301-28. *DAB*.

DUDLEY, Joseph, 1686, 1702-1715
also New Hampshire, 1686, 1702-1715; Rhode Island, 1686

Born on September 23, 1647 in Roxbury, Massachusetts, the son of Governor Thomas and Catherine (Dighton) Hackburn Dudley. A Congregationalist, but converted to Anglicanism in the 1690's. Brother of Deborah and Paul; half-brother of Samuel, Anne (the poet, who married Governor Simon Bradstreet), Patience, Sarah and Mercy. Married in 1668 to Rebecca Tyng, by whom he was the father of Thomas, Edward, Joseph, Paul, Samuel, John, Rebecca, Catherine (died in infancy), Ann, William, Daniel, Catherine and Mary.

Attended Harvard College, graduating from that institution in 1665. Served as a member of the Massachusetts General Court, representing Roxbury, from 1673 to 1676. Participated in King Philip's War, after which he was chosen as an Assistant of the colony in almost every year until 1685; also acted as one of the Massachusetts commissioners to the United Colonies from 1677 to 1681. Sailed for England in May 1682, in an unsuccessful attempt to save the Massachusetts charter. Returned to Boston in October 1683, and two years later, in October of 1685, received a royal commission making him President of the Council and chief executive of Massachusetts Bay, New Hampshire and the King's Province (later part of Rhode Island); assumed office in Massachusetts in May 1686, establishing his authority in New Hampshire and the King's Province a short time later; relinquished the governorship to Sir Edmund Andros in December 1686, but remained in office under the Dominion of New England as a member of Andros' Council. Also served for a time as Chief Justice of the Massachusetts Superior Court during the Andros regime. Jailed for ten months following the demise of Andros in the spring of 1689, and eventually transported to England, where he successfully defended his behavior during the Dominion period. Returned to America in 1691 and acted briefly as head of the Council in New York and Chief Justice of that province, although he soon gave up those offices and returned to Massachusetts in 1692. Sailed for England a short time later, remained from 1693 to 1702, and became Deputy Governor of the Isle of Wight during his stay. Awarded a commission as Royal Governor of Massachusetts Bay and New Hampshire in February of 1702, and arrived in America to begin his administration in June of that year.

Although Dudley's first tenure as governor had lasted for only about seven months in 1686, his subsequent support of Sir Edmund Andros during the Dominion period made him especially unpopular in New England, a feeling which was still strong when he appeared in Boston sixteen years later with a new commission to govern. Forced to begin his administration under these inauspicious circumstances, Dudley did little to make himself more acceptable in either Massachusetts or New Hampshire. In Massachusetts, for example, he began by purging old political enemies like Elisha Cooke, who was removed from his position as judge of the Superior Court. Although he apparently modified his arbitrary behavior after 1708, Dudley left a legacy of mistrust and suspicion which plagued the administration of Samuel Shute, his successor as royal governor.

Following his departure from office in 1715, Dudley retired to private life until his death on April 2, 1720. He was buried in Roxbury, Massachusetts.

Bibliography: [D. D.], "Governor Thomas Dudley and His Descendants," *New England Historical and Genealogical Register*, X (April, October 1856), 133-42, 337-44; George Adlard, *The Sutton-Dudleys of England and the Dudleys of Massachusetts in New England*... (New York, 1862); Dean Dudley, *History of the Dudley Family* (Wakefield, Mass., 1886-94); Everett Kimball, *The Public Life of Joseph Dudley* (New York, 1911); Augustine Jones, *Joseph Dudley, Ninth Governor of Massachusetts* (Boston, 1916); Arthur H. Buffinton, "Governor Dudley and the Proposed Treaty of Neutrality, 1705," *Publications of the Colonial Society of Massachusetts*, XXVI (1927), 211-29; William A. Polf, "Puritan Gentlemen: The Dudleys of Massachusetts, 1576-1686," unpub. Ph.D. diss., Syracuse University, 1973. *DAB*.

ANDROS, Sir Edmund, 1686-1689

New York, 1674-1677, 1678-1681; East Jersey, 1680-1681, 1688-1689; New Hampshire, 1686-1689; Plymouth Colony, 1686-1689; Rhode Island, 1686-1689; Connecticut, 1687-1689; West Jersey, 1688-1689; Virginia, 1692-1698; Maryland, 1693, 1694

Born on December 6, 1637 on the Island of Guernsey, the son of Amice and Elizabeth (Stone) Andros. Married to a woman who was related to the Earl of Craven.

Served as Major of a regiment of foot soldiers which in 1666 sailed from England to defend the West Indies against the Dutch. Named a Landgrave of Carolina in 1672; received a commission from the Duke of York in July 1674 to govern the colony of New York, and acted in that capacity, except for an absence in England between November 1677 and August 1678, until January 1681; also exercised control over East Jersey from 1680 until his recall early in the following year. Knighted in about 1681, became Gentleman of the Privy Chamber to Charles II in 1683, and was appointed Lieutenant Colonel of the Princess of Denmark's regiment of horse soldiers in 1685. Commissioned Royal Governor of the Dominion of New England in June 1686, and established his authority in Massachusetts Bay, Maine, New Hampshire, Plymouth and Rhode Island (including the King's Province) in December of that year; Connecticut in November of 1687; and the Jerseys and New York in August 1688 (although Francis Nicholson presided as Andros' substitute in the latter colony). Arrested and sent to England following the overthrow of the Dominion in the spring of 1689, but later received a commission as Royal Governor of Virginia, and served as that colony's chief executive from September 1692 to December 1698; also acted briefly as Governor of Maryland in 1693 and 1694, in the absence of any other executive authority.

Andros' first tenure in New York was marked by several important achievements, especially the improvement of the colony's defenses and the settlement of some boundary difficulties with Connecticut. Nevertheless, even at this stage he had begun to display an inclination to behave in an arbitrary fashion. Perhaps the clearest illustration of this tendency was the high-handed manner in which Andros superseded the authority of Governor Philip Carteret in the Jerseys, provoking Carteret to complain that Andros aimed at "usurping the government" of his colony. This insensitivity to local politics became even more noticeable after Andros assumed control of the Dominion of New England. Following a troubled tenure of less than two and one-half years, he was deposed in the spring of 1689, shortly after news of the Glorious Revolution in England reached Boston.

Although Andros was exonerated of the charges brought against his Dominion government and took over as Virginia's chief executive in 1692, he soon encountered resistance from local leaders like Commissary James Blair, who bitterly informed one London official that Andros "never did any considerable service to the King, nor the people" during his colonial career. Finally, late in 1698, Andros departed for England. He served as Lieutenant Governor of Guernsey from 1704 to 1706, and died in London in February 1714.

Bibliography: "Commission to Sir Edmund Andros," Massachusetts Historical Society, *Collections*, 3rd ser., vol. VII (Boston, 1838), 138-49; W. H. Whitmore, ed., *Andros Tracts: Being a Collection of Pamphlets and Official Papers ... of the Andros Government and the Establishment of the Second Charter of Massachusetts*, 3 vols. (New York, 1868-74) (Publications of the Prince Society, vols. V-VII); Robert N. Toppan, ed., "Andros Records," American Antiquarian Society, *Proceedings*, n.s., vol. XIII (1899-1900), 237-68, 463-99; J.H. Tuttle, ed., "Land Warrants under Andros," Colonial Society of Massachusetts, *Publications*, XXI (1919), 292-361; Albert C. Bates, "Expedition of Sir Edmund Andros to Connecticut in 1687," AAS, *Proceedings*, n.s., vol. 48 (October 1938), 276-99; Jeanne G. Bloom, "Sir Edmund Andros: A Study in Seventeenth-Century Colonial Administration," unpub. Ph.D. diss., Yale University, 1962; Robert C. Ritchie, "London Merchants, the New York Market, and the Recall of Sir Edmund Andros," *New York History*, LVII (January 1976), 5-29. *DAB, DNB*.

PHIPS, Sir William, 1692-1694

Born on February 2, 1651 near the mouth of the Kennebec River in what is now Maine, the son of James and Mary Phips. A Congregationalist. Brother of Mary, Margaret and Ann, among others. Married to Mary (Spencer) Hull; no children, but raised his nephew Spencer Bennett (later Phips) from an early age.

Apprenticed to a Boston ship's carpenter as a young man, and eventually entered that business on his own. Also engaged in various mercantile pursuits. Knighted in June 1687, after commanding an expedition which successfully raised a Spanish treasure ship off the coast of Haiti. Named Provost Marshal-General of New England in August 1687, but spent much of the Dominion period from 1686 to 1689 in England, where he assisted Increase Mather in an attempt to win the restoration of Massachusetts' chartered privileges. Captured Port Royal, Nova Scotia in the spring of 1690; several months later led an assault which completely failed in its efforts to take Montreal and Quebec. Commissioned Royal Governor of Massachusetts in December 1691, and arrived in the colony to assume that office in May of 1692.

Following his appointment as chief executive, Phips faced the difficult task of persuading colonists in Massachusetts that the new royal regime would protect those rights which they had enjoyed under the old charter government. Opposition to him was strong from the beginning, however, and even included the deputy governor, William Stoughton. Phips' term was further complicated by the Salem witchcraft trials, a phenomenon which had become critical by the spring of 1692. Unfortunately, Phips had little skill or experience as a political tactician, and in November of 1694 he was recalled to London to answer charges made against his administration. Phips died in London on February 18, 1695; he was buried in the London church of St. Mary Woolnoth, in Lombard Street.

Bibliography: Francis Bowen, *Life of Sir William Phips* (Boston, 1837); William Goold, "Sir William Phips," Maine Historical Society, *Collections*, vol. IX (1887), 1-72; F. L. Weis, *The Ancestors and Descendants of John Phipps, of Sherborn . . .* (Lincoln, R. I., 1924); H. O. Thayer, *Sir William Phips, Adventurer and Statesman: A Study in Colonial Biography* (Portland, Me., 1927); Viola F. Barnes, "The Rise of William Phips," *New England Quarterly*, I (July 1928), 271-94; Viola F. Barnes, "Phippius Maximus," *New England Quarterly*, I (October 1928), 532-53; Cotton Mather, *The Life of Sir William Phips*, ed. by Mark Van Doren (New York, 1929); C. H. Karraker, "The Treasure Expedition of William Phips to the Bahama Banks," *New England Quarterly*, V (October 1932), 731-52; R. H. George, "Treasure Trove of William Phips," *New England Quarterly*, VI (June 1933), 294-318; Alice Lounsberry, *Sir William Phips: Treasure Fisherman and Governor of the Massachusetts Bay Colony* (New York, 1941); Francis G. Walett, "Sir William Phips: The First Royal Governor of Massachusetts," Bostonian Society, *Proceedings* (1954), 23-36; Philip F. Gura, "Cotton Mather's *Life of Phips*: 'A Vice with the Vizard of Vertue upon It'," *New England Quarterly*, L (September 1977), 440-57. *DAB, DNB*.

STOUGHTON, William, 1694-1699, 1700-1701

Born on September 30, 1631, probably in England, the son of Israel and Elizabeth Stoughton. A Congregationalist. Brother of Israel, John, Hannah and perhaps others. Never married.

Graduated from Harvard College in 1650; later returned to England to study at New College, Oxford, where he received an A.B. in April 1652 and an A.M. in June 1653. Remained in England until 1662, serving for a time as curate at Rumboldswyke in Sussex. Preached at Dorchester, Massachusetts for several years after his return to America, but refused to accept a call as pastor. Elected as an Assistant from 1671 to 1686, except for the period from 1676 to 1679, when he was in England as an Agent for Massachusetts at the court of Charles II; also acted as a Commissioner for the United Colonies from 1674 to 1676 and again from 1680 to 1686. Named Deputy President of the temporary government formed by Joseph Dudley following the accession of Sir Edmund Andros; later served for a time as a member of Andros' Council, although he abandoned his former ally after the revolution of 1689. Appointed Lieutenant Governor of Massachusetts under Sir William Phips, and served in that capacity from May 1692 until late 1694, when he became Acting Governor in the absence of Phips, who had gone to London to defend his administration of the colony. Apart from May 1699 to July 1700, remained at the head of the Massachusetts government until his death in 1701. Also served as Chief Justice of Massachusetts from December 1692 until shortly before his death.

Despite his role as chief justice of the Court of Oyer and Terminer which tried the Salem witches in 1692, Stoughton's credibility and political standing during his subsequent term as acting governor appears not to have been damaged by that incident. Indeed, his adroit handling of the colony's political factions did much to alleviate the strife which had troubled Phips' brief but tumultuous period as royal governor. Stoughton was especially successful in winning the support of the powerful Elisha Cooke, an alliance which the acting governor strengthened by appointing Cooke to the Superior Court. Stoughton died in Dorchester, Massachusetts, while still in office, on July 7, 1701.

Bibliography: [John Ward Dean], "William Stoughton, Lieutenant Governor of Massachusetts," *New England Historical and Genealogical Register*, L (January 1896), 9-12; Ethel (McLaughlin) Turner, *The English Ancestry of Thomas Stoughton, 1588-1661, and His Son Thomas Stoughton, 1624-1684, of Windsor, Conn.; His Brother Israel Stoughton, 1603-1645, and His Nephew William Stoughton, 1631-1701, of Dorchester, Mass.* (Waterloo?, Wis., 1958). *DAB*, *DNB*.

COOTE, Richard, Earl of Bellomont, 1699-1700

New York, 1698-1699, 1700-1701; also New Hampshire, 1699-1700

Born in 1636, the son of Richard and Mary (St. George) Coote. Brother of Charles (died in infancy), Chidley, Thomas, Mary, Catherine, Letitia, Olivia and Elizabeth. Married to Catherine Nanfan, by whom he was the father of Nanfan and Richard.

Succeeded his father as Baron Coote of Coloony, an order of nobility in the Irish peerage, in July 1683; created Earl of Bellomont in November 1689. Became a close friend of William, Prince of Orange, and following the Glorious Revolution received various honors from the new monarchs, including that of Treasurer and Receiver General to the Queen in March 1689. Also served as a member of Parliament for Droitwich from 1688 to 1695. Commissioned Royal Governor of Massachusetts Bay, New Hampshire and New York in June 1697; arrived in New York to begin his administration in April 1698 and, except for an absence from May 1699 to July 1700, when he presided in person as head of the government in Massachusetts and New Hampshire, remained resident chief executive of that colony until his death.

Bellomont landed in New York at a time when factionalism was widespread, largely due to the persistent Leislerian controversy, and the new governor's insensitivity to this volatile political issue did not improve matters. Nevertheless, Bellomont's tenure in New York was not without its achievements. His attempts to discourage commerce with pirates, for example, were fairly successful, as were his techniques for putting New York's administration on a more systematic basis, evidenced by the census carried out under his direction in 1698. In Massachusetts and New Hampshire Bellomont's brief period as resident chief executive was comparatively uneventful, although in New Hampshire he did become embroiled in a dispute involving Samuel Allen, who claimed that he held proprietary title to that province.

By early 1701 Bellomont's health had been seriously impaired by his efforts to preside over three colonies, each with its own set of problems. Finally, on March 5, 1701, the governor succumbed in New York to a particularly severe case of gout.

Bibliography: Frederic De Peyster, *The Life and Administration of Richard, Earl of Bellomont ... 1697 to 1701* (New York, 1879); A. de Vlieger, *Historical and Genealogical Record of the Coote Family* (Lausanne, 1900); Stanley H. Friedelbaum, "Bellomont: Imperial Administrator—Studies in Colonial Administration during the 17th Century," unpub. Ph.D. diss., Columbia University, 1955; Jacob Judd, "Lord Bellomont and Captain Kidd: A Footnote to an Entangled Alliance," *New-York Historical Society Quarterly*, XLVII (January 1963), 66-74; John D. Runcie, "The Problem of Anglo-American Politics in Bellomont's New York," *William and Mary Quarterly*, 3rd ser., vol. XXVI (April 1969), 191-217; John C. Rainbolt, "A 'great and usefull designe': Bellomont's Proposal for New York, 1698-1701," *New-York Historical Society Quarterly*, LIII (October 1969), 333-51; John C. Rainbolt, "The Creation of a Governor and Captain General for the Northern Colonies: The Process of Colonial Policy Formation at the End of the Seventeenth Century," *New-York Historical Society Quarterly*, LVII (April 1973), 101-20. *DAB, DNB*.

TAILER, William, 1715-1716, 1730

Born *circa* 1676 in Massachusetts, the son of William, a prominent Boston merchant, and Rebecca (Stoughton) Tailer. A Congregationalist. Brother of Elizabeth, Stoughton and perhaps others. Married to a daughter of Nathaniel

Byfield; remarried in 1712 to Abigail (Gillam) Dudley; father of William, Gillam, Elizabeth, Abigail, Rebecca and Sarah.

Was serving as Commander of a regiment of foot soldiers in 1710. Commissioned Lieutenant Governor of Massachusetts in April 1711, and assumed the position in the fall of that year; relinquished the lieutenant governorship to William Dummer in 1716, but received a new commission in April 1730, and replaced Dummer the following June. Also named Captain of Castle William. In his capacity as lieutenant governor, served as Acting Governor between March 1715 and the arrival of Governor Samuel Shute in October 1716; also presided as acting chief executive from June to August of 1730, prior to the arrival of Governor Jonathan Belcher.

Tailer's two brief periods as acting governor were of little significance, and he did little more than fulfill the routine duties of the office until he was relieved by his superiors. However, particularly during the administration of Governor Shute, Tailer did serve as an emissary from the Massachusetts General Court to the Indians. In 1719, for example, he accompanied colonels Stoddard and Dudley on a trip to Falmouth in what would eventually become the state of Maine, where the three men sought to persuade the natives to stop harassing white settlers in the area, but without definitive results.

Tailer died in Dorchester, Massachusetts on March 1, 1732, less than two years after he received his second commission as lieutenant governor. His funeral sermon was preached by the Reverend William Cooper of the Brattle Street Church, to whom Tailer was related.

Bibliography: William Cooper, *Man Humbled by Being Compar'd to a Worm. A Sermon Preached at the Publick Lecture in Boston, March 9th, 1731, 2. The Day after the Funeral of the Honourable William Tailer, Esq., Late Lieutenant Governor of the Province of the Massachusetts-Bay in New England*... (Boston, 1732).

SHUTE, Samuel, 1716-1723
also New Hampshire, 1716-1723

Born on January 12, 1662 in England, the son of Benjamin and Patience (Caryl) Shute. A Nonconformist. Brother of John, later Lord Barrington in the Irish peerage.

Studied with Charles Morton, the Puritan schoolmaster, and admitted to London's Middle Temple in November 1683; also admitted to Christ's College,Cambridge in December of that year, although there is no indication that he ever received a degree. Eventually entered the British Army, and by 1712 had advanced to the rank of Lieutenant Colonel of the Third Dragoon Guards. Commissioned Royal Governor of Massachusetts Bay and New Hampshire in

June 1716; arrived in America to take up those appointments in October of 1716.

Shute's administration in both Massachusetts and New Hampshire was marked by considerable political turmoil, as he quarreled with the legislatures in each colony over such matters as his salary, the emission of paper money, timber rights, and defense against neighboring Indians. In New Hampshire Shute's position was further weakened by the machinations of Lieutenant Governor George Vaughan, who claimed that he possessed complete gubernatorial power whenever Shute was absent from that province. Shute finally replaced Vaughan in December 1717; but his problems with other local leaders continued, until in January 1723 he left for England to present his case before the Privy Council.

Although even Jeremiah Dummer, Massachusetts' agent in London, conceded the legitimacy of many of his complaints, the disgruntled governor received little satisfaction from either the colonial legislators or the King, and when George I died in 1727 Shute's commission to govern was permitted to expire. He then received a pensión as a reward for his services, and retired to private life. Shute died on April 15, 1742.

Bibliography: *George Town on Arrowsick Island . . . A Conference of His Excellency the Governour [Shute], with the Sachems and Chief Men of the Eastern Indians* (Boston, 1717) (also printed in Maine Historical Society, *Collections*, III (1853); *Report of the Lords Commissioners for the Plantations upon Gov. Shute's Memorial* . . . (Boston, 1725); "Journal of Gov. Shute from Boston to Portsmouth, October, 1716," New Hampshire Historical Society, *Collections*, IV (1834), 249-51. *DAB, DNB*.

DUMMER, William, 1723-1728, 1729-1730

Born in 1677 in Massachusetts, the son of Jeremiah Dummer, a silversmith, artist and magistrate, and Ann, or Hannah (Atwater) Dummer. A Congregationalist. Brother of eight, including Jeremiah, Jr. and Samuel. Married to Catherine Dudley, a daughter of Governor Joseph Dudley, on April 20, 1714; no children.

Became Lieutenant Governor of Massachusetts following the arrival of Governor Samuel Shute in October 1716; after Shute's departure for England in January 1723, served as Acting Governor until the arrival of Governor William Burnet in July of 1728. Again presided as acting governor between the death of Burnet in September 1729 and the accession of William Tailer as lieutenant governor in June 1730.

Dummer's years as an interim chief executive were concerned chiefly with Indian relations. Shortly before he took over early in 1723, Massachusetts declared war on the ''Eastern Indians'' who, with French encouragement, had carried out a series of raids on outlying settlements in what would later become Maine. During the three-year conflict which followed, North Yarmouth suffered a particularly destructive attack which nearly obliterated the new community. Nevertheless, despite some opposition from the Massachusetts House of Representatives concerning the financing of troops, Dummer pursued the war vigorously, and by the winter of 1725-26 he was able to negotiate a temporary treaty. Along with their disagreement over the Indian war, Dummer and the House disputed such matters as the chief executive's salary, with the acting governor endeavoring to carry out the Crown instruction which maintained that a fixed salary, rather than irregular grants, was the only appropriate means of reimbursement.

Following his replacement as acting governor in June 1730, Dummer spent the remaining years of his life in retirement, until his death on October 10, 1761. In accordance with the provisions of his will, his farm and mansion house were used to endow Dummer Academy in Newbury, an institution which opened for the first time in February 1763 with twenty-eight pupils.

Bibliography: J. L. Chester, ''The Family of Dummer,'' *New England Historical and Genealogical Register*, XXXV (July-October 1881), 254-71, 321-31; Lura Woodside Watkins, ''The Dummer Family and the Byfield Carvings,'' *Essex Institute Historical Collections*, CV (January 1969), 3-28. There is also a long biographical note on Dummer and letters by him in the *New England Historical and Genealogical Register*, XLIV (July 1890), 249-56.

BURNET, William, 1728-1729

New York and New Jersey, 1720-1728; also New Hampshire, 1728-1729

Born in March 1688 at The Hague, the eldest son of Gilbert Burnet, bishop of Salisbury, and his second wife, Mary (Scott) Burnet. Brother of Mary and Gilbert. Married in about May 1712 to a daughter of Dean Stanhope, by whom he was the father of Gilbert; following the death of his first wife, remarried to Anna Maria [or Mary] Van Horne; father of William, Mary and Thomas by his second wife.

Enrolled at Trinity College, Cambridge at the age of thirteen, but left without obtaining a degree; later studied privately, and called to the bar. Commissioned Captain General and Governor-in-Chief of New York and New Jersey in June 1720, and arrived in America to assume office in September of that year. Commissioned Royal Governor of New Hampshire in November 1727, and of Massachusetts Bay in March 1728; left New York in the spring of 1728, following his replacement by the newly-appointed Governor John Montgomerie, and travelled to New England to take up his new positions.

As chief executive of New York, Burnet was confronted by controversy over the extensive fur trade then existing between Albany and Montreal. Contending that such commerce was enhancing New France's stature among Indians in the area, who sold their furs to the English through French *coureurs de bois*, Burnet tried to eliminate the traffic both by means of legislation and by encouraging direct trade between the English and various Indian tribes. Despite some initial success, however, Burnet's policy quickly encountered strong opposition from prominent New York merchants who preferred to conduct their business with the French, and by 1726 it had become apparent that his efforts would fail. In New Jersey Burnet met with similar recalcitrance among leading members of that colony's Assembly, especially over money bills. Nevertheless, after several confrontations with the Assembly, Burnet decided to adopt a more tactful approach, and by the time of his departure in 1728 he had won significant concessions from the legislators.

Although Burnet's tenure in Massachusetts Bay and New Hampshire lasted only a little more than a year, his administration of those colonies was also marked by disputes over financial matters. In particular, the question of the form which the governor's remuneration should take, a recurrent problem during much of the eighteenth century, created tension between Burnet and the Massachusetts Assembly, as Burnet insisted that he be given a permanent salary. On September 7, 1729, however, before the issue could be resolved, Burnet died suddenly in Boston.

Bibliography: William Nelson, *Original Documents Relating to the Life and Administrations of William Burnet*... (Paterson, N.J., 1897). Burnet's will appears in the *New England Historical and Genealogical Register*, XLVII (January 1893), 123-25. *DAB, DNB*.

BELCHER, Jonathan, 1730-1741
also New Hampshire, 1730-1741; New Jersey, 1747-1757

Born on January 8, 1682 in Cambridge, Massachusetts, the son of Andrew and Sarah (Gilbert) Belcher. Brother of Andrew, Sarah, Elizabeth, Mary, Anna, Martha and Deborah (died in infancy). Married on January 8, 1706 to Mary Partridge, by whom he was the father of Andrew, Sarah, Jonathan, William and Thomas; following the death of his first wife on October 6, 1736, remarried on September 9, 1748 to Mary Louisa Emilia Teal; no children by his second wife.

Attended Harvard College, graduating in 1699. Subsequently spent several years in Europe, before returning to Massachusetts and pursuing a mercantile career. First elected to the Massachusetts Council in 1718, and served intermittently as a member of that body until 1728. Sent to England by the Massachusetts House of Representatives to defend, along with Francis Wilks, the House position on the question of the chief executive's salary. Arrived in England early in 1729, and secured a commission as Royal Governor of Massachusetts Bay and New Hampshire in January 1730, shortly after news of Governor Burnet's death reached London; returned to America in August 1730 to begin his new assignment. Dismissed as chief executive of Massachusetts and New Hampshire in May 1741, but later returned to England, where in February 1747 he received a commission to govern New Jersey; occupied that office between his arrival in the province in August 1747 and his death ten years later.

Belcher's tenure in Massachusetts and New Hampshire was troubled by sharp disputes with the assemblies of both colonies over issues like the governor's salary and paper currency. While Belcher managed to resolve some of his disagreements with the legislators, monetary policy remained a source of bitter dissension, especially in Massachusetts. In that province the governor disapproved of the creation of a "land bank," which issued notes backed by mortgages at three percent interest, and the resulting controversy did much to intensify opposition to his administration. Eventually, charges of corruption, including an allegation that he had accepted a bribe to settle a boundary dispute between Massachusetts and New Hampshire, culminated in Belcher's removal by Crown officials.

After he had regained the favor of authorities in England, the indefatigable Belcher assumed the governorship of New Jersey. There he again encountered problems, chiefly concerning the question of land titles. Shortly before his second period as governor began, the College of New Jersey (now Princeton University) was founded, and Belcher, always a supporter of education, bequeathed his personal library to that institution when he died in Elizabethtown, New Jersey on August 31, 1757.

Bibliography: W. H. Whitmore, "Notes on the Belcher Family," *New England Historical and Genealogical Register*, XXVII (July 1873), 239-45; "Belcher Papers, parts 1 and 2," in Massachusetts Historical Society, *Collections*, 6th ser., vols. VI and VII (Boston, 1893-94); Henry Lyttleton Savage, "Jonathan Belcher and 'Our Young College'," *Princeton University Library Chronicle*, XIX (Spring-Summer 1958), 191-96; Michael Clement Batinski, "Jonathan Belcher of Massachusetts, 1682-1741," unpub. Ph.D. diss., Northwestern University, 1970. There is also a microfilm of the Belcher letterbooks from 1723 to 1754, the originals of which are in the Massachusetts Historical Society. *DAB*.

SHIRLEY, William, 1741-1749, 1753-1756

Born on December 2, 1694 in Preston, Sussex, England, the son of William, a London merchant, and Elizabeth (Godman) Shirley. An Anglican. Married before 1720 to Frances Barker, by whom he was the father of nine, including Thomas, William, John and Frances; after the death of his first wife in September 1746, remarried to a Frenchwoman named Julie.

Educated at the Merchant Taylors' School in London, and later attended Pembroke College, Cambridge, receiving an A.B. from that institution in 1715. Also admitted to London's Inner Temple in October 1713, and studied there for some years until he was called to the bar in July 1720. Practiced law in London for eleven years; immigrated to Massachusetts in 1731, possibly as a result of a setback in his financial affairs. Appointed Judge of Admiralty by Governor Belcher in 1733, but soon relinquished that position to become Advocate General. Commissioned Royal Governor of Massachusetts in May 1741, and assumed office in August, following Belcher's departure.

Shortly after taking over as chief executive, Shirley was required to deal with a variety of matters, especially regarding the question of paper money and the need to provide Massachusetts with an adequate means of defense. When war with France broke out in 1744, Shirley's enthusiastic cooperation with other colonial leaders greatly enhanced the British war effort, an effort which was highlighted by the capture of Louisbourg in June 1745. In 1749 Shirley sailed for England on leave, naming Spencer Phips to serve as acting governor in his absence. Four years later, however, he arrived in America just as war with France once more seemed imminent. Appointed Major General in February 1755, Shirley quickly rose to become Commander of Britain's North American forces. Nevertheless, military setbacks eventually caused him to lose considerable prestige, and in October 1756 he returned to England to defend himself against charges of incompetence and possible treason.

In London Shirley successfully justified his conduct during the war, and he was soon promoted to Lieutenant General. In December 1758 he received a commission as Governor of the Bahama Islands, a position which he assumed one year later. Shirley retired from this office in 1768 in favor of his son Thomas; he then sailed for Massachusetts, where he lived at "Shirley Place," his mansion in Roxbury, until his death on March 24, 1771. Shirley was buried in King's Chapel, Boston.

Bibliography: Justin Winsor, "Boston in 1741, and Governor Shirley," *Magazine of American History*, XX (November 1888), 368-71; C. H. Lincoln, ed., *Correspondence of William Shirley . . . 1731-1760*, 2 vols. (New York, 1912); George Arthur Wood, *William Shirley, Governor of Massachusetts, 1741-1756* (New York, 1920); Amelia C. Ford, ed., "William Shirley to Samuel Waldo," *American Historical Review*, XXXVI (January 1931), 350-60; Francis D. Haines, Jr., "Governor Shirley's Use of a Joint Legislative

Committee in Colonial Massachusetts," *Research Studies of the State College of Washington*, XXIII (March 1955), 62-72; John A. Schutz, *William Shirley, King's Governor of Massachusetts* (Chapel Hill, 1961); Daniel Lewis Salay, "The William Johnson-William Shirley Dispute: Origins, Course, and Consequences," unpub. M.A. thesis, Vanderbilt University, 1972. *DAB, DNB*.

PHIPS, Spencer, 1749-1753, 1756-1757

Born on June 6, 1685 in Rowley, Massachusetts, the son of David Bennett, a physician, and Rebecca (Spencer) Bennett, a sister of the wife of Governor Sir William Phips. A Congregationalist. Taken into the family of Governor Phips at an early age, and legally changed his name to Phips in 1716. Married on November 20, 1707 to Elizabeth Hutchinson; father of Spencer, William, David, Sarah, Elizabeth, Rebecca and Mary. Attended Harvard College, and graduated from that institution in 1703.

Named Justice of the Peace for the county of Middlesex in 1713; about the same time became Colonel in a cavalry organization. Elected to the Massachusetts House of Representatives from Cambridge in 1721, and chosen as a Councillor-at-Large shortly after assuming his seat in the House; lost his position on the Council in 1724, but regained it in the following year. Held various judicial positions in the 1720's, including that of Special Justice of the Middlesex Inferior Court. Named Lieutenant Governor of Massachusetts in 1732, during the administration of Governor Jonathan Belcher, and later served in that capacity under Governor William Shirley. While lieutenant governor, appointed Captain of Castle William. Took office as acting governor in September 1749, after Shirley's departure for England, and served until the governor's return in August of 1753; also presided as acting governor from October 1756 until his death.

Phips' periods as chief executive in Massachusetts Bay were largely occupied by negotiations with neighboring Indians. Soon after Shirley sailed for England in 1749, for example, Phips endeavored to conclude a treaty with the Indians in the vicinity of Falmouth, but his efforts were hampered by whites who murdered some of the natives and continued to provoke the survivors. In the realm of Massachusetts politics, Phips enjoyed a fairly harmonious relationship with the colony's General Court; on the other hand, he and the Board of Trade in London were often at odds over what the Board viewed as Phips' lax interpretation of his royal instructions. Phips died on April 4, 1757, while still serving as acting governor.

Bibliography: *Instructions for Treating with the Eastern Indians, Given to the Commissioners Appointed for that Service, in the Year 1752* (Boston, 1865) [includes a brief notice of Phips].

POWNALL, Thomas, 1757-1760

New Jersey, 1757

Born on September 4, 1722 in England, the eldest son of William and Sara (Burniston) Pownall. Brother of John, Richard, Edward and probably a number of sisters. Married in August 1765 to Harriet, the natural daughter of General Charles Churchill and the widow of Sir Everard Fawkener; after the death of his first wife in 1777, remarried on August 2, 1784 to Hannah (Kennett) Astell; no children by either marriage.

Attended grammar school in Lincoln; matriculated at Trinity College, Cambridge in 1740, and graduated from that institution in 1743. Served for a number of years as a Clerk in the Board of Trade, where his brother John occupied a prominent position. Became in 1753 Secretary to Sir Danvers Osborn, the recently-appointed governor of New York. Following Osborn's suicide in October 1753, acted as an unofficial source of information on colonial affairs, reporting to the Board of Trade. Commissioned Lieutenant Governor of New Jersey in May 1755. Returned to England in February 1756 and, after rejecting an offer to serve as governor of Pennsylvania, became "Secretary Extraordinary" to Lord Loudoun, the new commander-in-chief of British forces in North America. Commissioned Royal Governor of Massachusetts Bay in February 1757, and arrived in that province the following August to begin his administration. Also became Acting Governor of New Jersey late in August 1757, after the death of Jonathan Belcher, but soon turned over his authority in that colony to John Reading, New Jersey's senior councillor.

Pownall's tenure in Massachusetts was largely preoccupied with military matters, as Britain's war with France on the North American continent reached a critical stage. During these years Pownall consistently asserted his authority as governor, thereby irritating Lord Loudoun, his former superior, who found truculence on the part of colonial officials to be a handicap in his prosecution of the war. Pownall also offended many members of the conservative faction in Massachusetts, especially when he established ties with the "anti-prerogative" party in the province and sought to win the friendship of popular leaders in the Assembly. By late 1759 the Board of Trade had decided to remove Pownall from the Massachusetts governorship, and in June of 1760 he left for England.

Following his departure from America, Pownall declined the governorship of Jamaica. Although he received a commission as governor of South Carolina in January 1760, he resigned that position without ever having taken office in the colony. Pownall served for a time in the British military during the early 1760's, achieving the rank of Colonel. In 1767 he became a member for Tregony, Cornwall in the House of Commons, a position he held until becoming a member for Minehead, Somerset in 1774. In the summer of 1780 Pownall abandoned politics for private life, where he remained until his death in Bath, England on February 25, 1805. Pownall was the author of *The Administration of the Colonies*, an argument for a more thoughtful and flexible approach to British colonial policy, which first appeared in 1764.

Bibliography: Thomas Pownall, *The Administration of the Colonies* (London, 1764: also later, enlarged editions); Robert Ludlow Fowler, "Governor Thomas Pownall, Colonial Statesman," *Magazine of American History*, XVI (November 1886), 409-32; "Governor Pownall's Reasons for Declining the Government of Pennsylvania," *Pennsylvania Magazine of History and Biography*, XIII (1889), 440-46; Frederick Tuckerman, ed., "Letters to Thomas Pownall," *American Historical Review*, VIII (January 1903), 301-30; C. A. W. Pownall, *Thomas Pownall, M.P., F.R.S., Governor of Massachusetts Bay* . . . (London, 1908); William Otis Sawtelle, "Thomas Pownall, Colonial Governor, and Some of His Activities in the American Colonies," Massachusetts Historical Society, *Proceedings*, LXIII (June 1930), 233-84; John A. Schutz, "Thomas Pownall and His Negro Commonwealth," *Journal of Negro History*, XXX (October 1945), 400-04; John A. Schutz, "Thomas Pownall's Proposed Atlantic Federation," *Hispanic American Historical Review*, XXVI (May 1946), 263-68; John A. Schutz, *Thomas Pownall, British Defender of American Liberty: A Study of Anglo-American Relations in the Eighteenth Century* (Glendale, Calif., 1951); Caroline Robbins, "An Active and Intelligent Antiquary, Governor Thomas Pownall," *Pennsylvania History*, XXVI (January 1959), 1-20. *DAB, DNB*.

HUTCHINSON, Thomas, 1760, 1769-1774

Born on September 9, 1711 in Boston, Massachusetts, the son of Thomas and Sarah (Foster) Hutchinson. A Congregationalist, but Anglican in his sympathies. Brother of Foster (died young), Sarah, Abigail, Hannah, Elisha, Lydia, Foster, and four others who died in infancy. Married on May 16, 1734 to Margaret Sanford, by whom he was the father of Thomas, Elisha, William, Sarah, Margaret, and seven or eight others who died in infancy.

Studied at the North Grammar School, and received an A.B. from Harvard College in 1727. Awarded an M.A. in 1730, also from Harvard. Entered his father's commercial business after graduation. Elected to the Massachusetts House of Representatives in 1737, and served as a member of that body, except for one year, until 1749; acted as Speaker of the House from 1746 to 1748. Became a member of the Massachusetts Council in 1749, an office he held until 1766; also served for a time as President of the Council. Named Judge of

Probate and Justice of Common Pleas for Suffolk County in 1752; became Chief Justice of Massachusetts in 1760. Attended the Albany Congress, which in 1754 considered Benjamin Franklin's Plan of Union. Appointed Lieutenant Governor of Massachusetts in 1758, and served in that capacity until 1771. By virtue of his position as lieutenant governor, presided as Acting Governor from June to August of 1760, between the administrations of Thomas Pownall and Francis Bernard; resumed office as acting chief executive in August 1769, following the departure of Bernard. Commissioned Royal Governor of Massachusetts Bay in November 1770, and began to administer the province in his own right in March of 1771.

As chief executive of Massachusetts during its most tumultuous period before the Revolution, Hutchinson was forced to deal with a situation which his pragmatic approach to politics left him incapable of comprehending. By training and instinct a man who preferred cool reason to emotional rhetoric, Hutchinson could not appreciate the often fierce devotion to principle which culminated in incidents like the Boston Massacre of March 1770 or the Tea Party of December 1773. Within six months after the destruction of the tea, Hutchinson's authority in the province had all but disintegrated, and in June 1774 he left for England to spend the remaining years of his life in exile from his native country.

Hutchinson died in England from the effects of a stroke on June 3, 1780, and was buried in Croydon. He was the author of numerous works on the history of his province, perhaps the most important of which was *The History of the Colony of Massachusetts Bay*, a three-volume work published between 1764 and 1828.

Bibliography: William H. Whitmore, *A Brief Genealogy of the Descendants of William Hutchinson* . . . (Boston, 1865); P. O. Hutchinson, ed., *The Diary and Letters of His Excellency Thomas Hutchinson* . . ., 2 vols. (Boston, 1884-86); James K. Hosmer, *The Life of Thomas Hutchinson* (Boston and New York, 1896); Edmund S. Morgan, "Thomas Hutchinson and the Stamp Act," *New England Quarterly*, XXI (December 1948), 459-92; Malcolm Freiberg, "Prelude to Purgatory: Thomas Hutchinson in Massachusetts Politics, 1760-1770," unpub. Ph. D. diss., Brown University, 1950; Malcolm Freiberg, "Thomas Hutchinson: The First Fifty Years (1711-1761)," *William and Mary Quarterly*, 3rd ser., vol. XV (January 1958), 35-55; Malcolm Freiberg, "How to Become a Colonial Governor: Thomas Hutchinson of Massachusetts," *The Review of Politics*, XXI (October 1959), 646-56; Bernard Bailyn, *The Ordeal of Thomas Hutchinson* (Cambridge, 1974); Philip J. Schwarz, " 'To Conciliate the Jarring Interests': William Smith, Thomas Hutchinson, and the Massachusetts-New York Boundary, 1771-1773," *New-York Historical Society Quarterly*, LIX (October 1975), 299-319. *DAB*, *DNB*.

BERNARD, Sir Francis, 1760-1769

New Jersey, 1758-1760

Born in 1712 in England, the son of the Reverend Francis and Margery (Winlowe) Bernard. No brothers or sisters. Married in 1741 to Amelia Offley, by whom he had eight children.

Entered St. Peter's College, Westminster in 1725, and later studied at Christ Church, Oxford. Admitted to the Middle Temple, London, in 1733, where he prepared for a legal career; called to the bar in 1737. Named Commissioner of Bails in 1740 for an area which included Lincoln, York and Nottingham. Became a friend of the second Viscount Barrington, his wife's cousin. Commissioned Captain General and Governor-in-Chief of New Jersey in February 1758, largely as a result of Barrington's influence, and arrived in June of that year to take up his assignment. Appointed Royal Governor of Massachusetts in January 1760; resigned as New Jersey's chief executive in the summer of 1760 to assume his new position.

Although Bernard's period of service in New Jersey was brief, his energetic leadership quickly left its mark on that province. Realizing that his instructions regarding paper money emissions were too inflexible, Bernard sought to persuade officials in London to modify their policy. The concessions on this issue which Bernard managed to win from home authorities, combined with his vigorous response to Indian attacks during the French and Indian War, greatly enhanced his stature in the eyes of the New Jersey Assembly. Bernard's ability was also highly regarded in England, and early in 1760 he received a commission to govern Massachusetts Bay, a promotion which gave him an opportunity to experience colonial politics on a larger and more complicated scale. While his first years in office were generally successful, the popular outcry during the mid-1760's against such measures as the Sugar and Stamp acts greatly hampered his ability to administer the province effectively. By 1769, when some controversial letters which he had written to English officials were published in Boston, Bernard had lost his hold over the government, and in August of that year he was recalled by his superiors.

In April 1769, shortly before his dismissal as governor of Massachusetts, Bernard became a Baronet. His final years were spent in relative obscurity, although he did secure an appointment as Commissioner of Customs for Ireland. Bernard died in Aylesbury, Buckinghamshire on June 16, 1779.

Bibliography: Francis Bernard, *Letters to the Ministry from Governor Bernard* (London, 1769); Thomas Bernard, *Life of Sir Francis Bernard* ...(London, 1790); Mrs. Napier Higgins, *The Bernards of Abington and Nether Winchendon* (London, 1903); Edward Channing and Archibald C. Coolidge, eds., *The Barrington-Bernard Correspondence ... 1760-1770* (Cambridge, 1912); Charles Penrose, ... *New England in the Year of Grace 1776 – and Sir Francis Bernard, His Outlook on Trade and Navigation*

(Princeton, 1940); Jordan D. Fiore, "Francis Bernard, Colonial Governor," unpub. Ph.D. diss., Boston University, 1950; Jordan D. Fiore, "The Temple-Bernard Affair: A Royal Custom House Scandal in Essex County," *Essex Institute Historical Collections*, XC (January 1954), 58-83; Leslie J. Thomas, "Partisan Politics in Massachusetts during Governor Bernard's Administration, 1760-1770," unpub. Ph.D. diss., University of Wisconsin, 1960; Francis G. Walett, "Governor Bernard's Undoing: An Earlier Hutchinson Letters Affair," *New England Quarterly*, XXXVIII (June 1965), 217-26. *DAB*, *DNB*.

GAGE, Thomas, 1774

Born in 1721 in Firle, Sussex, England, the second son of Thomas, first Viscount Gage, of the Irish peerage, and Viscountess Benedicta [or Beata Maria Theresa] (Hall) Gage. Brother of William and Theresa. Married on December 8, 1758 to Margaret Kemble, by whom he was father of eleven children, including Henry (later third Viscount Gage), John, William Hall, Maria Theresa, Louisa Elizabeth, Harriet, Charlotte Margaret and Emily.

Entered the British Army at an early age, and in January 1741 was commissioned Lieutenant of a regiment eventually known as the 48th Foot. Received a series of promotions over the next decade, until by March 1751 he had become Lieutenant Colonel of the 44th Foot. Accompanied General Edward Braddock to America in 1754, and saw considerable action during the French and Indian War; also served for a short time as Military Governor of Montreal. Promoted to Major General in 1761, and became Commander-in-Chief of British forces in North America two years later, following Lord Amherst's return to England. Sailed for England in February 1773, but returned in fifteen months, after receiving a commission as Captain General and Governor-in-Chief of Massachusetts in April 1774; arrived in the colony to assume his duties as chief executive in May of that year.

Gage's arrival in Massachusetts to replace the departing Thomas Hutchinson symbolized the decision of Parliament to adopt sterner measures for dealing with the revolutionary movement in the Bay Colony. One of the first of these new measures was the Boston Port Act, an order to close the province's major harbor in retaliation for the Tea Party of December 1773. By late 1774, however, this and other oppressive actions had aroused so much hostility in Boston that Gage had virtually no means, other than military, of enforcing his authority. Following the formation of a Provincial Congress in October 1774, Gage was in effect deposed as anything other than a *de jure* chief executive.

In 1775 Gage took a prominent part in the initial military confrontations of the Revolution, including the skirmishes at Lexington and Concord in April and the Battle of Bunker Hill in June. As the war progressed, he sailed for England in October of 1775, thereby conceding that his efforts to enforce his commission were hopeless. After his return to England, Gage continued his military career, and in November 1782 he became a full General. Gage died on April 2, 1787.

Bibliography: Clarence E. Carter, ed., *The Correspondence of General Thomas Gage with the Secretaries of State, 1763-1775*, 2 vols. (New Haven, 1931-33); John R. Alden, *General Gage in America* (Baton Rouge, 1948); Gerard H. Clarfield, "The Short Unhappy Civil Administration of Thomas Gage," *Essex Institute Historical Collections*, CIX (April 1973), 138-51. *DAB, DNB*.

HANCOCK, John, 1780-1785, 1787-1793

Born on January 12, 1737 in Braintree (now Quincy), Massachusetts, the son of Reverend John, a Congregationalist minister, and Mary (Hawke) Thaxter Hancock. Brother of Ebenezer and Mary. Married on August 28, 1775 to Dorothy Quincy; father of Lydia and John, both of whom died while young.

Adopted by his uncle Thomas Hancock, a wealthy merchant, after his father's death in 1744. Attended Boston Latin School; graduated from Harvard College in 1754. Pursued a mercantile career as a young man, and by January 1763 had become a partner in his uncle's firm, Thomas Hancock and Company; took over operation of the business when his uncle died in August 1764. Emerged as a prominent figure during the revolutionary movement in Massachusetts, especially after the seizure for smuggling of his sloop *Liberty* in 1768. Elected to the Massachusetts General Court in May 1766, and held that position until 1774, when the Court reorganized itself into a Provincial Congress; served as President of the Provincial Congress from 1774 to 1775. Represented Massachusetts at the Second Continental Congress in 1775, where he was also elected President, an office which he filled between May 1775 and October 1777; signed the Declaration of Independence in July 1776. Left Congress in 1779, the same year in which he was chosen Speaker of the Massachusetts House. Served as a delegate to the Massachusetts constitutional convention of 1780. Elected Governor of Massachusetts in October 1780, an office to which he was reelected annually until 1784; resigned in January 1785, but later won the annual gubernatorial polls held between the spring of 1787, when he defeated James Bowdoin, and 1793.

During Hancock's first period as chief executive, Massachusetts experienced severe inflation and a growing restiveness among the commonwealth's debtor class. This financial chaos continued even as the Revolution seemed to be ending in victory for the Patriot cause. In the autumn of 1782, for example, the Massachusetts General Court had to adopt extraordinary means, such as duties and excises, to raise money badly needed by the Continental Congress. Indeed, when Hancock resigned for reasons of health early in 1785, one of the less obvious factors leading him to choose that course of action may have been the increasing economic discontent which would soon erupt in Shays's Rebellion.

Although he was named President of the Continental Congress in November 1785, Hancock's painful gout condition kept him from assuming that post, and in June 1786 he finally resigned. By May of 1787, however, he was back in the governor's chair, where he remained until his death. Hancock's second term in office was marked by Massachusetts' ratification of the Federal Constitution in February 1788, with the chief executive himself presiding over the state convention which approved that document. Hancock died in Boston on October 8, 1793, and was buried in the Old Granary Burial Ground.

Bibliography: W. C. Burrage, *John Hancock and His Times* (Boston, 1891); A. E. Brown, *John Hancock, His Book* (1898); "Letters of John Hancock, 1760, 1761," Massachusetts Historical Society, *Proceedings*, XLIII (1910), 193-200 [There are also Hancock letters in vols. XLVIII (1915) and LX (1927) of the MHS *Proceedings*, and in the *Proceedings* of the American Antiquarian Society, n.s., vol. XV (1904)]; Lorenzo Sears, *John Hancock, the Picturesque Patriot* (Boston, 1912); Francis Hurtubis, Jr., "First Inauguration of John Hancock, Governor of the Commonwealth of Massachusetts," Bostonian Society, *Publications*, 2nd ser., vol. I (1916), 39-77; W. T. Baxter, *The House of Hancock* (Cambridge, 1945); O. M. Dickerson, "John Hancock: Notorious Smuggler or Near Victim of British Revenue Racketeers?," *Mississippi Valley Historical Review*, XXXII (March 1946), 517-40; H. S. Allan, *John Hancock, Patriot in Purple* (New York, 1948); William Fowler, "John Hancock: The Paradoxical President," *New England Historical and Genealogical Register*, CXXX (July 1976), 164-78; Donald J. Proctor, "John Hancock: New Soundings on an Old Barrel," *Journal of American History*, LXIV (December 1977), 652-77. *DAB*.

CUSHING, Thomas, 1785

Born on March 24, 1725 in Boston, Massachusetts, the eldest son of Thomas and Mary (Bromfield) Cushing. Brother of Edward, Mary and Elizabeth. Married on October 1, 1747 to Deborah Fletcher, by whom he was the father of Mary and Margaret.

Attended Harvard College, graduating from that institution in 1744; also studied law and was admitted to the bar; awarded an honorary LL.D. by Harvard in 1785. Engaged in commerce for a number of years, and from 1761 to 1774 served as a member of the Massachusetts General Court, representing Boston; acted as Speaker of the House of Representatives almost continuously from 1766 to 1774. Emerged during the 1760's as a prominent leader of the revolutionary movement in Massachusetts; participated in the protest against the Stamp Act in 1765, and signed the non-importation agreement of 1768. Named to the Boston Committee of Correspondence in May 1773; appointed to the Massachusetts Committee of Safety in July 1774, and a short time later became a delegate to the Massachusetts Provincial Congress, a body which served as the colony's *de facto* executive branch from October 1774 to July 1775. Attended the First and Second Continental Congresses in 1774 and 1775. Named annually to the Council, which exercised executive authority in Massachusetts from July 1775 to 1780; acted for a time as President of the Council. Following the adoption of the State Constitution of 1780, elected Lieutenant Governor of Massachusetts, a position which he held until his death; in his capacity as lieutenant governor, served as the commonwealth's Acting Governor from January to May of 1785, between the resignation of John Hancock and the inauguration of James Bowdoin.

Cushing's brief tenure as chief executive was actually part of a maneuver by John Hancock, his political mentor, who early in 1785 had suffered a severe seizure of gout. Hancock had intended his resignation merely to be a temporary expedient, enabling him both to recover his health and to create an atmosphere of sympathy. However, the Massachusetts Legislature, instead of asking him to remain in the chair while Cushing conducted the state's ordinary business, decided to accept Hancock's resignation at face value. For the next few months Cushing campaigned for office against James Bowdoin, and when Bowdoin won the governorship by vote of the Legislature in May 1785, his victory represented the first major defeat for Hancock's party.

Cushing resumed his duties as lieutenant governor following his brief period as chief executive. Shortly before his death in Boston on February 28, 1788, he attended the Massachusetts convention which ratified the Federal Constitution. Cushing was buried in the Old Granary Burial Ground in Boston.

Bibliography: "Letters of Thomas Cushing, from 1767 to 1775," Massachusetts Historical Society, *Collections*, 4th ser., vol. IV (Boston, 1858), 347-66; "Cushing Family," *New England Historical and Genealogical Register*, XIX (January 1865), 39-41; James S. Cushing, *The Genealogy of the Cushing Family* (Montreal, 1905). Also see the selections from the De Berdt correspondence, appearing in the Massachusetts Colonial Society, *Publications*, XIII (1910-11), for other material pertaining to Cushing.

BOWDOIN, James, 1785-1787

Born on August 7, 1726 in Boston, Massachusetts, the son of James, a prosperous merchant, and Hannah (Pordage) Bowdoin. Brother of Samuel (died young), Elizabeth and Judith. Married on September 15, 1748 to Elizabeth Erving, by whom he was the father of James and Elizabeth.

Educated at Harvard College, receiving an A.B. in 1745. Became a prominent merchant and landowner after leaving Harvard. Elected to the Massachusetts House of Representatives in 1753, and served in that capacity for three terms; chosen as a member of the Massachusetts Council in 1757, a position which he held, except for one year, until his election was vetoed by General Thomas Gage in 1774. Became an important figure in the revolutionary movement in the 1760's and early 1770's; named as a delegate to the First Continental Congress in 1774, although his own ill health and that of his wife forced him to decline the office. Appointed in August 1775 to the twenty-eight member Council which acted as Massachusetts' executive authority between July 1775 and 1780; resigned from the Council in 1777, again due to physical infirmity. Elected President of the constitutional convention which first met in September 1779, and played a major role in the drafting of Massachusetts' Constitution of 1780. Chosen as the first President of the American Academy of Arts and Sciences, a position he held until his death. Elected Governor of Massachusetts by the legislature in May 1785, when no candidate polled a majority of the popular vote (3,502 votes were cast for Bowdoin, 2,997 for Thomas Cushing, 1,141 for Benjamin Lincoln, and 298 for Oliver Prescott); reelected in April of the following year, receiving 6,001 votes out of a total of 8,231.

Bowdoin's two one-year terms as chief executive were marked by economic distress and the threat of widespread revolt, as Massachusetts passed through a period of post-war crisis. By the summer of 1786 the new commonwealth's legal system appeared unable to control the problem, and Bowdoin finally found it necessary to call on the militia to prevent armed groups from interfering with foreclosure proceedings in the courts. However, while military action by troops under General Benjamin Lincoln early in 1787 ended this insurrection, known as Shays's Rebellion, Bowdoin's stern treatment of the irate debtors did contribute to his defeat by John Hancock in the gubernatorial contest of that year.

Following his defeat by Hancock, Bowdoin represented Boston at the convention which in January 1788 met to consider the proposed Federal Constitution. His support of that document was a major factor in its eventual acceptance by Massachusetts, where strong anti-federalist sentiment made ratification a closely contested issue, Bowdoin died in Boston on November 6, 1790. Bowdoin College, chartered in 1794, was named in his honor.

Bibliography: Robert C. Winthrop, *Washington, Bowdoin, and Franklin, as Portrayed in Occasional Addresses* (Boston, 1876); Temple Prime, *Some Account of the Bowdoin Family* (New York, 1887); ''Bowdoin and Temple Papers,'' Massachusetts Historical Society, *Collections*, 6th ser., vol. IX and 7th ser., vol. VI (Boston, 1897, 1907); Francis G. Walett, ''James Bowdoin and the Massachusetts Council,'' unpub. Ph.D. diss., Boston University, 1948; Francis G. Walett, ''James Bowdoin, Patriot Propagandist,'' *New England Quarterly*, XXIII (September 1950), 320-38. *DAB*.

NEW HAMPSHIRE

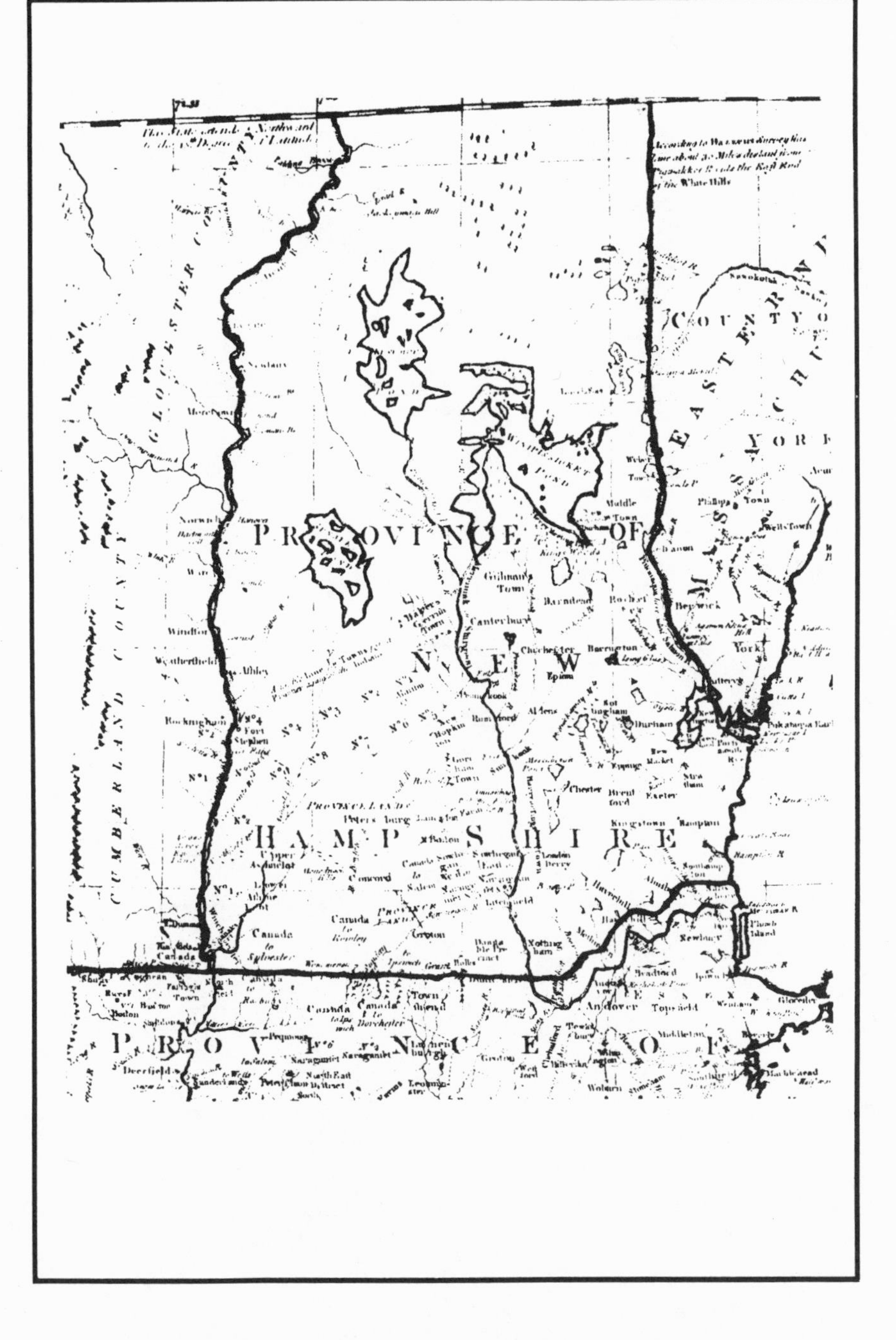

Chronology

1680-1681	John Cutt
1681-1682	Richard Walderne (or Waldron)
1682-1685	Edward Cranfield
1685-1686	Walter Barefoote
1686	Joseph Dudley
1686-1689	Sir Edmund Andros
1689-1690	*In the absence of a chief executive, each town exercised local self-government.*
1690-1692	Simon Bradstreet
1692-1697	John Usher
1697-1698	William Partridge
1698-1699	Samuel Allen
1699-1700	Richard Coote, Earl of Bellomont
1700-1702	William Partridge
1702-1715	Joseph Dudley
1715-1716*	George Vaughan
1716-1723	Samuel Shute
1723-1728	John Wentworth
1728-1729	William Burnet
1729-1730	John Wentworth
1730-1741	Jonathan Belcher
1741	*Between Jonathan Belcher's departure in May 1741 and the arrival of the newly-appointed Governor Benning Wentworth in December of that year, no lieutenant governor was present in the province. Consequently, the New Hampshire Council, acting as a body, normally conducted executive affairs.*
1741-1767	Benning Wentworth
1767-1775	John Wentworth
1775-1776	Matthew Thornton
1776-1785	Meshech Weare
1785-1786	John Langdon
1786-1788	John Sullivan
1788-1789	John Langdon
1789	John Pickering
1789-1790	John Sullivan

1789-1790 John Sullivan

*Although Elizeus Burgess was commissioned royal governor of Massachusetts Bay in 1715, he resigned the office without ever going to America.

BIBLIOGRAPHY

Bouton, Nathaniel, *et al.*, eds., *Documents and Records Relating to the Province [Towns and State] of New Hampshire, 1623-1800*, 40 vols. (Concord, 1867-1943).

Farmer, John, "A List of Counsellors of New-Hampshire, From 1680 to 1837," New Hampshire Historical Society, *Collections*, V (1837), 231-37.

Noyes, Sybil, Charles Thornton Libby and Walter Goodwin Davis, *Genealogical Dictionary of Maine and New Hampshire* (Baltimore, 1972).

Sanborn, Franklin Benjamin, *New Hampshire: An Epitome of Popular Government* (Boston and New York, 1904).

Van Deventer, David E., *The Emergence of Provincial New Hampshire, 1623-1741* (Baltimore and London, 1976).

NEW HAMPSHIRE

CUTT, John, 1680-1681

Born in 1613 in England, the son of John and Bridget (Baker) Sherston Cutt. A Congregationalist. Brother, among others, of Baker, Richard, Walter, Robert and Ann. Married on July 30, 1662 to Hannah Starr, by whom he was the father of John, Elizabeth, Hannah, Mary and Samuel; after his first wife's death in November 1674, remarried by 1677 to a woman named Ursula.

Immigrated to New England before 1646, and became a prominent Portsmouth merchant. Served as Portsmouth Selectman for eleven years between 1657 and 1678; also acted as a Deputy to the Massachusetts General Court in 1670 and 1676. Named President of the New Hampshire Provincial Court in 1680, and in that capacity became the colony's first chief executive.

Between the early 1640's and 1679, the towns which would eventually comprise New Hampshire had been under the political jurisdiction of Massachusetts Bay, but in February 1679 the Lords of Trade in England proposed the creation of a distinct government. After a compromise had been reached with Robert Mason, who claimed proprietary rights in New Hampshire based on his inheritance of land rights from John Mason, the Crown issued the "Cutt Commission," which provided for a separate administration in the colony. Although there was at first some reluctance among the councillors named in the commission, both because of resentment over the concessions made to Mason and a lingering desire to retain the connection with Massachusetts, the new government was finally established early in 1680, with Cutt as chief executive. Until his death in office on March 27, 1681, Cutt continued to grapple with problems arising from the Crown's recognition of proprietary rights assumed by Mason, whom most of New Hampshire's residents rejected as a "pretended claimer to our soil."

Bibliography: "Brief Notices of Some of the Early Councillors of New-Hampshire: John Cutt," New-Hampshire Historical Society, *Collections*, VIII (1866), 308-11; Cecil Hampden Cutts Howard, comp., *Genealogy of the Cutts Family in America* (Albany, N.Y., 1892); Alma J. Herbert, "President John Cutt," *Granite Monthly*, XIV (December 1892), 370-75.

WALDERNE [or WALDRON], Richard, 1681-1682

Born in late 1614 or early 1615 in Warwickshire, England, the son of William and Catherine (Raven) Walderne. Brother of ten, including George and William. Married first to a woman in England, whose name is unknown; remarried later to Ann Scammon; father by his two wives of Timotheus, Paul, Elizabeth, Richard, Anna, Elnathan (died young), Esther, Mary, Eliazer, Elizabeth and Marah.

First travelled to New England to "see the country" in 1635, and remained for two years; after returning to England in 1637, immigrated to New England on a permanent basis in about 1640, settling in Dover, New Hampshire, and eventually became a prominent landowner. Acted as a Dover Selectman for a number of years between 1647 and 1675; had become an Associate of the Dover Court by 1650, and from 1654 to 1679 served almost continuously as a Deputy to the Massachusetts General Court, where he was often chosen as Speaker (1666-1668, 1673-1675 and 1679). Also served in a military capacity on a number of occasions, and had risen to the rank of Major by 1674, just before the outbreak of King Philip's War. Appointed to the New Hampshire Council after the creation of a separate administration for that colony in 1679. Became Acting President of New Hampshire following the death of John Cutt in March of 1681, and served until the arrival of Lieutenant Governor Edward Cranfield in October 1682.

Walderne's brief administration, like that of his predecessor and those of his immediate successors, was chiefly concerned with the controversial claims of Robert Mason. Mason's contention that he possessed proprietary rights in New Hampshire was hotly disputed by Walderne during his term in office. Indeed, after his replacement as chief executive by Cranfield, Walderne's continued resistance to the alleged proprietor played a major part in his dismissal from the Council by the new lieutenant governor. Although he returned to serve on the Council for a brief period, Walderne was later suspended permanently and never again held public office. He died on June 28, 1689, during an Indian attack on Cochecho (now part of Dover), New Hampshire.

Bibliography: "Biographical Notice of Major Richard Waldron," New-Hampshire Historical Society, *Collections*, II (1827), 40-47; "Brief Notices of Some of the Early Councillors of New-Hampshire: Richard Waldron," New-Hampshire Historical Society, *Collections*, VIII (1866), 332-41; George M. Bodge, "Soldiers in King Philip's War: No. XXII, Major Richard Walderne and His Men," *New England Historical and Genealogical Register*, XLII (April-July 1888), 185-97, 285-98; [anonymous], "Major Richard Waldron," *Granite Monthly*, XLIV (March 1912), 79-83. *DAB*.

CRANFIELD, Edward, 1682-1685

Date and place of birth, and names of parents unknown, though he may have been related to the Edward Cranfield who was acting as a member of the Council in Barbados in July 1636. Married, possibly to Elizabeth Parker, and the father of an unknown number of children.

Served for a number of years as an administrator in Barbados and Jamaica. Named Lieutenant Governor of New Hampshire, largely as a result of his friendship with Robert Mason, and arrived in the colony to take up that appointment in October 1682; served as lieutenant governor until the spring of 1685.

Cranfield's administration was from the beginning characterized by opportunism and political turmoil. Shortly after his arrival in New Hampshire, the new lieutenant governor formed an alliance with Mason, who continued to assert his proprietary right to collect quitrents (residence fees). This political understanding, though shaken at first when Cranfield realized the tenacity of the colonists' opposition to Mason, was strengthened by the New Hampshire Assembly's refusal to levy taxes for the governor's salary. An irate Cranfield proceeded to dissolve the Assembly and to purge the Council of anyone who opposed his administration or Mason's claims. He then lent his support to a series of land suits which, under the control of friendly judges, probably decided in favor of Mason in every instance. Meanwhile, however, Cranfield's heavy-handed tactics were brought to the attention of English authorities by Nathaniel Weare, a wealthy farmer-lumberer. In March of 1685 the Lords of Trade concluded that Cranfield was guilty of several serious infractions, and by May of that year he had left the colony, leaving Deputy Governor Walter Barefoote in his place.

Following his period as chief executive, Cranfield appears to have sailed to Barbados and then to England; by May of 1686 he was again in Barbados, serving as a member of that colony's Council. He later returned to England, where he died in November 1700; he was buried in Bath Abbey.

Bibliography: A sketch of Cranfield by Jacob Bailey Moore appears in the *American Quarterly Register*, XV (1843), 163-65.

BAREFOOTE, Walter, 1685-1686

Born about 1636 in England; names of parents unknown. Brother of Sarah and perhaps others. Married to a daughter of Robert Mason; accused in 1676 of abandoning a wife and two children in England.

Worked for a time as a naval Surgeon and Captain. Probably immigrated in the 1650's to Barbados and later to New Hampshire, where he practiced medicine; also indulged in land speculation. Served as Deputy Collector of Customs from 1680 to 1681, during President Cutt's administration; named a member of the New Hampshire Council by Lieutenant Governor Cranfield's commission, and held that office from October 1682 to January 1683. Appointed Deputy Governor of New Hampshire in January 1683, and in that capacity succeeded Cranfield when the lieutenant governor left the colony in the spring of 1685.

Barefoote's brief term in office witnessed a continuation of the political unrest which had troubled the tenure of his predecessor. Ignoring the instructions of the Lords of Trade in England, Barefoote staunchly defended the proprietary claims of Robert Mason, whose daughter he had married. His support of Mason's efforts to collect quitrents based upon earlier executions even caused Barefoote to engage in fisticuffs with the wealthy Thomas Wiggin, after Wiggin had denied Mason's authority. In the fight Barefoote suffered two broken ribs and lost a tooth, but more importantly, his administration suffered a loss of prestige which endured until New Hampshire came under the control of Massachusetts Governor Joseph Dudley's Council in May of 1686.

Following his departure from office, Barefoote was made a New Hampshire Justice. He only served for about two years, however, before his death in late 1688 or early 1689.

Bibliography: "Gov. Barefoote's Will," *New England Historical and Genealogical Register*, XXVI (January 1872), 13-16; Franklin Benjamin Sanborn, *The So-Called Rebellion of 1683: A Curious Chapter of New Hampshire History* (Boston?, 190?) (Cover title is *Edward Gove and Walter Barefoot, 1653-1691*.)

DUDLEY, Joseph, 1686, 1702-1715

also Massachusetts, 1686, 1702-1715; Rhode Island, 1686

Born on September 23, 1647 in Roxbury, Massachusetts, the son of Governor Thomas and Catherine (Dighton) Hackburn Dudley. A Congregationalist, but converted to Anglicanism in the 1690's. Brother of Deborah and Paul; half-brother of Samuel, Anne (the poet, who married Governor Simon Bradstreet), Patience, Sarah and Mercy. Married in 1668 to Rebecca Tyng, by whom he was the father of Thomas, Edward, Joseph, Paul, Samuel, John, Rebecca, Catherine (died in infancy), Ann, William, Daniel, Catherine and Mary.

Attended Harvard College, graduating from that institution in 1665. Served as a member of the Massachusetts General Court, representing Roxbury, from 1673 to 1676. Participated in King Philip's War, after which he was chosen as an Assistant of the colony in almost every year until 1685; also acted as one of the Massachusetts commissioners to the United Colonies from 1677 to 1681.

Sailed for England in May 1682, in an unsuccessful attempt to save the Massachusetts charter. Returned to Boston in October 1683, and two years later, in October of 1685, received a royal commission making him President of the Council and chief executive of Massachusetts Bay, New Hampshire and the King's Province (later part of Rhode Island); assumed office in Massachusetts in May 1686, establishing his authority in New Hampshire and the King's Province a short time later; relinquished the governorship to Sir Edmund Andros in December 1686, but remained in office under the Dominion of New England as a member of Andros' Council. Also served for a time as Chief Justice of the Massachusetts Superior Court during the Andros regime. Jailed for ten months following the demise of Andros in the spring of 1689, and eventually transported to England, where he successfully defended his behavior during the Dominion period. Returned to America in 1691 and acted briefly as head of the Council in New York and Chief Justice of that province, although he soon gave up those offices and returned to Massachusetts in 1692. Sailed for England a short time later, remained from 1693 to 1702, and became Deputy Governor of the Isle of Wight during his stay. Awarded a commission as Royal Governor of Massachusetts Bay and New Hampshire in February of 1702, and arrived in America to begin his administration in June of that year.

Although Dudley's first tenure as governor had lasted for only about seven months in 1686, his subsequent support of Sir Edmund Andros during the Dominion period made him especially unpopular in New England, a feeling which was still strong when he appeared in Boston sixteen years later with a new commission to govern. Forced to begin his administration under these inauspicious circumstances, Dudley did little to make himself more acceptable in either Massachusetts or New Hampshire. In Massachusetts, for example, he began by purging old political enemies like Elisha Cooke, who was removed from his position as judge of the Superior Court. Although he apparently modified his arbitrary behavior after 1708, Dudley left a legacy of mistrust and suspicion which plagued the administration of Samuel Shute, his successor as royal governor.

Following his departure from office in 1715, Dudley retired to private life until his death on April 2, 1720. He was buried in Roxbury, Massachusetts.

Bibliography: [D. D.], "Governor Thomas Dudley and His Descendants," *New England Historical and Genealogical Register*, X (April, October 1856), 133-42, 337-44; George Adlard, *The Sutton-Dudleys of England and the Dudleys of Massachusetts in New England* . . . (New York, 1862); Dean Dudley, *History of the Dudley Family* (Wakefield, Mass., 1886-94); Everett Kimball, *The Public Life of Joseph Dudley* (New York, 1911); Augustine Jones, *Joseph Dudley, Ninth Governor of Massachusetts* (Boston, 1916); Arthur H. Buffinton, "Governor Dudley and the Proposed Treaty of Neutrality, 1705," *Publications of the Colonial Society of Massachusetts*, XXVI (1927), 211-29; William A. Polf, "Puritan Gentlemen: The Dudleys of Massachusetts, 1576-1686," unpub. Ph.D. diss., Syracuse University, 1973. *DAB*.

ANDROS, Sir Edmund, 1686-1689

New York, 1674-1677, 1678-1681; East Jersey, 1680-1681, 1688-1689; Massachusetts, 1686-1689; Plymouth Colony, 1686-1689; Rhode Island, 1686-1689; Connecticut, 1687-1689; West Jersey, 1688-1689; Virginia, 1692-1698; Maryland, 1693, 1694

Born on December 6, 1637 on the Island of Guernsey, the son of Amice and Elizabeth (Stone) Andros. Married to a woman who was related to the Earl of Craven.

Served as Major of a regiment of foot soldiers which in 1666 sailed from England to defend the West Indies against the Dutch. Named a Landgrave of Carolina in 1672; received a commission from the Duke of York in July 1674 to govern the colony of New York, and acted in that capacity, except for an absence in England between November 1677 and August 1678, until January 1681; also exercised control over East Jersey from 1680 until his recall early in the following year. Knighted in about 1681, became Gentleman of the Privy Chamber to Charles II in 1683, and was appointed Lieutenant Colonel of the Princess of Denmark's regiment of horse soldiers in 1685. Commissioned Royal Governor of the Dominion of New England in June 1686, and established his authority in Massachusetts Bay, Maine, New Hampshire, Plymouth and Rhode Island (including the King's Province) in December of that year; Connecticut in November of 1687; and the Jerseys and New York in August 1688 (although Francis Nicholson presided as Andros' substitute in the latter colony). Arrested and sent to England following the overthrow of the Dominion in the spring of 1689, but later received a commission as Royal Governor of Virginia, and served as that colony's chief executive from September 1692 to December 1698; also acted briefly as Governor of Maryland in 1693 and 1694, in the absence of any other executive authority.

Andros' first tenure in New York was marked by several important achievements, especially the improvement of the colony's defenses and the settlement of some boundary difficulties with Connecticut. Nevertheless, even at this stage he had begun to display an inclination to behave in an arbitrary fashion. Perhaps the clearest illustration of this tendency was the high-handed manner in which Andros superseded the authority of Governor Philip Carteret in the Jerseys, provoking Carteret to complain that Andros aimed at "usurping the government" of his colony. This insensitivity to local politics became even more noticeable after Andros assumed control of the Dominion of New England. Following a troubled tenure of less than two and one-half years, he was deposed in the spring of 1689, shortly after news of the Glorious Revolution in England reached Boston.

Although Andros was exonerated of the charges brought against his Dominion government and took over as Virginia's chief executive in 1692, he soon encountered resistance from local leaders like Commissary James Blair, who bitterly informed one London official that Andros "never did any considerable service to the King, nor the people" during his colonial career. Finally, late in 1698, Andros departed for England. He served as Lieutenant Governor of Guernsey from 1704 to 1706, and died in London in February 1714.

Bibliography: "Commission to Sir Edmund Andros," Massachusetts Historical Society, *Collections*, 3rd ser., vol. VII (Boston, 1838), 138-49; W. H. Whitmore, ed., *Andros Tracts: Being a Collection of Pamphlets and Official Papers ... of the Andros Government and the Establishment of the Second Charter of Massachusetts*, 3 vols. (New York, 1868-74) (Publications of the Prince Society, vols. V-VII); Robert N. Toppan, ed., "Andros Records," American Antiquarian Society, *Proceedings*, n.s., vol. XIII (1899-1900), 237-68, 463-99; J.H. Tuttle, ed., "Land Warrants under Andros," Colonial Society of Massachusetts, *Publications*, XXI (1919), 292-361; Albert C. Bates, "Expedition of Sir Edmund Andros to Connecticut in 1687," AAS, *Proceedings*, n.s., vol. 48 (October 1938), 276-99; Jeanne G. Bloom, "Sir Edmund Andros: A Study in Seventeenth-Century Colonial Administration," unpub. Ph.D. diss., Yale University, 1962; Robert C. Ritchie, "London Merchants, the New York Market, and the Recall of Sir Edmund Andros," *New York History*, LVII (January 1976), 5-29. *DAB*, *DNB*.

BRADSTREET, Simon, 1690-1692
also Massachusetts, 1679-1686, 1689-1692

Born in March 1604 in Horbling, Lincolnshire, England, the son of Simon, a non-conformist minister, and Margaret Bradstreet. A Congregationalist. Brother of Samuel, Mercy and John. Married in about 1628 to Anne (Dudley) Bradstreet, the poet; after his first wife's death in September 1672, remarried in June 1676 to Ann (Downing) Gardner; father by his first wife of Samuel, Dorothy, Sarah, Simon, Hannah, Mercy, Dudley and John; no children by his second marriage.

Attended Emmanuel College, Cambridge, receiving an A.B. degree in 1620 and an A.M. in 1624. Sailed for New England aboard the *Arbella* in the spring of 1630. Chosen as an Assistant of Massachusetts Bay before leaving England, and served in that capacity for almost fifty years. Also acted as Secretary of the colony from 1630 to 1636. Represented Massachusetts in the negotiations which led to the formation of the New England Confederation in 1643; later chosen as a Commissioner to the Confederation, an office he filled for thirty-three years. Appointed to a commission which in 1661 left for England to seek confirmation of the Massachusetts charter from the recently-restored Charles II. Served as Deputy Governor of Massachusetts from 1678 to 1679; elected Governor in May 1679.

During his first years as governor, Bradstreet's conciliatory approach to relations with authorities in England became more unpopular, as Massachusetts struggled to retain its charter. When representatives of the Crown like Edward Randolph sought to compel the colony to give up the charter and defenders of the old order responded by becoming more recalcitrant, the hapless Bradstreet was caught in the middle of the confrontation. With the establishment of the Dominion of New England in the spring of 1686, Bradstreet stepped down as governor, rejecting an offer to become one of the councillors for the new government. Shortly after the overthrow of Sir Edmund Andros in April 1689, however, he reluctantly resumed office as chief executive, and presided during the years between the downfall of the Dominion and the arrival in May 1692 of Sir William Phips, Massachusetts' first royal governor. For most of this period Bradstreet also acted as chief executive in New Hampshire, a province whose towns had practiced local self-government between the demise of Andros and 1690. Bradstreet died in Salem, Massachusetts late in March of 1697.

Bibliography: John Dean and Dean Dudley, "Descendants of Gov. Bradstreet," *New England Historical and Genealogical Register*, IX (April 1855), 113-21; Isaac John Greenwood, "Remarks on the Maverick Family, and the Ancestry of Gov. Simon Bradstreet," *New England Historical and Genealogical Register*, XLVIII (April 1894), 168-71; William Andrews Pew, "The Worshipful Simon Bradstreet, Governor of Massachusetts," *Essex Institute Historical Collections*, LXIV (1928), 301-28. *DAB*.

USHER, John, 1692-1697

Born on April 17, 1648 in Massachusetts, the son of Hezekiah, a prominent Boston merchant, and Frances Usher. An Anglican in his religious sympathies. Brother of Hezekiah, Rebecca, John (died young), Elizabeth and Sarah. Married on April 24, 1668 to Elizabeth Lidgett, by whom he was the father of Elizabeth and Jane; after his first wife's death in August 1698, remarried on March 11, 1699 to Elizabeth Allen, the daughter of New Hampshire Governor Samuel Allen; father by his second wife of John, Frances, Hezekiah and Elizabeth.

Employed as a stationer (printer) as a young man, and in 1672 published an edition of the laws of Massachusetts Bay. Travelled to London in the 1670's, representing Massachusetts during that colony's negotiations to purchase the province of Maine from the Gorges heirs. Served as Councillor of Massachusetts under Governor Joseph Dudley in 1686, and as Councillor and Treasurer under the subsequent Andros regime. Became Lieutenant Governor and Commander-in-Chief of New Hampshire in August 1692, serving until December 1697; again acted as Lieutenant Governor from 1702 to 1715.

Usher presided as New Hampshire's chief executive during his first period as lieutenant governor, since Governor Samuel Allen had elected to remain in England. Allen's claim to have a proprietary title to the land as well as political jurisdiction in the colony was the major point of contention during these years, and Usher, a strong defender of the Allen position, endeavored to make New Hampshire's residents amenable to the wishes of his superior. Usher began by seeking to create a court system which would favor the proprietary interest, an effort which was partially successful. By 1696, however, anti-proprietary elements in New Hampshire had gained considerable strength, and had even sent a petition to London calling for Usher's removal. Ironically, the lieutenant governor's demise finally came as a result of a decision made by Allen himself, when William Partridge convinced the supposed proprietor to permit him to replace Usher.

Usher did manage to return as lieutenant governor during the administration of Governor Joseph Dudley, after which he seems to have left public life. He then retired to his estate in Medford, Massachusetts, where he died on September 25, 1726.

Bibliography: "The Usher Family," *New England Historical and Genealogical Register*, XXIII (October 1869), 410-13; Margaret Kinard, ed., "John Usher's Report on the Northern Colonies, 1698," *William and Mary Quarterly*, 3rd ser., vol. VII (January 1950), 95-106. There are also some letters from Usher in the *New England Historical and Genealogical Register*, XXXI (April 1877), 162-65.

PARTRIDGE, William, 1697-1698, 1700-1702

Born *circa* 1654; place of birth and names of parents unknown, although he may have been the son of William Partridge of Salisbury, Massachusetts. Married on December 8, 1680 to Mary Brown; father of Richard, Nehemiah, Mary, William and Elizabeth.

Became a prominent merchant and shipbuilder. Was serving as Treasurer of New Hampshire by 1692, but later dismissed from that position by Lieutenant Governor John Usher. Served as Lieutenant Governor of New Hampshire from 1697 to 1703, and in that capacity acted as the colony's interim chief executive from December 1697 to November 1698, and again from July 1700 to 1702.

Although Partridge's two terms as acting governor were interrupted by the governorships of Samuel Allen and the Earl of Bellomont, the question of the legitimacy of Allen's proprietary title remained the major political issue during each of his periods in office. Before he took up his commission as lieutenant governor in December of 1697, Partridge sought to disassociate himself from the anti-proprietary position, despite his lack of sympathy for Allen's claims. When the Earl of Bellomont superseded Allen as the colony's governor in mid-1699, however, Partridge made his stance clearer, as he worked to win over Bellomont to his point of view. Bellomont's return to New York in July 1700 put Partridge back in the governor's chair on an interim basis, but in June 1702 Joseph Dudley arrived to assume that office. A short time later the Board of Trade in London ordered that John Usher, a staunch supporter of the proprietary position, should replace Partridge as lieutenant governor.

Partridge appears to have retired from public life after his removal from office, although his signature at one point appeared on a petition calling for the removal of Dudley. Partridge died on January 3, 1729.

ALLEN, Samuel, 1698-1699

Born in 1636 in England; name of parents unknown. Married to Elizabeth Dowse; father of Thomas, Elizabeth, Jane, Frances and Ann.

Became a prominent London merchant. Purchased the supposed proprietary title to New Hampshire from the heirs of John Mason early in 1692, and came to that colony in November 1698 to assume office as Governor; served as chief executive until mid-1699, when he was superseded by Governor Richard Coote, Earl of Bellomont.

For six years before Allen arrived to assert his proprietary claim in person, the residents of New Hampshire had been attempting to bring about a reunion of the colony with Massachusetts, in order to guarantee their freedom of land tenure. Soon after Allen's administration began, their worst fears seemed to be confirmed, when the governor approved the introduction of two land suits in the spring of 1699. Several months later, however, the Earl of Bellomont appeared in Portsmouth with a commission which gave him political jurisdiction over New Hampshire, and Allen left office.

Despite Lord Bellomont's contention that Allen's title was defective, the persistent "proprietor" continued to seek satisfaction. Indeed, Bellomont alleged that he had been offered a bribe of £10,000 and a share in New Hampshire if he would support Allen's proprietary title. Finally, early in May of 1705, a New Hampshire meeting offered Allen a compromise which would have granted him certain waste and unimproved lands, along with a cash settlement. Allen died on May 5, 1705, two days after this proposal was made, and before he could give his answer. He was buried in the fort at Newcastle, New Hampshire.

Bibliography: Anonymous, *A Short Narrative of the Claim, Title and Right of the Heirs of the Honourable Samuel Allen, Esq., Deceased, to the Province of New-Hampshire in New-England* (Boston, 1728); Elwin L. Page, "The Case of Samuell Allen of London Esq. Governor of New-Hampshire," *Historical New Hampshire*, XXV (Winter 1970), 47-53.

COOTE, Richard, Earl of Bellomont, 1699-1700

New York, 1698-1699, 1700-1701; also Massachusetts, 1699-1700

Born in 1636, the son of Richard and Mary (St. George) Coote. Brother of Charles (died in infancy), Chidley, Thomas, Mary, Catherine, Letitia, Olivia and Elizabeth. Married to Catherine Nanfan, by whom he was the father of Nanfan and Richard.

Succeeded his father as Baron Coote of Coloony, an order of nobility in the Irish peerage, in July 1683; created Earl of Bellomont in November 1689. Became a close friend of William, Prince of Orange, and following the Glorious Revolution received various honors from the new monarchs, including that of Treasurer and Receiver General to the Queen in March 1689. Also served as a member of Parliament for Droitwich from 1688 to 1695. Commissioned Royal Governor of Massachusetts Bay, New Hampshire and New York in June 1697; arrived in New York to begin his administration in April 1698 and, except for an absence from May 1699 to July 1700, when he presided in person as head of the government in Massachusetts and New Hampshire, remained resident chief executive of that colony until his death.

Bellomont landed in New York at a time when factionalism was widespread, largely due to the persistent Leislerian controversy, and the new governor's insensitivity to this volatile political issue did not improve matters. Nevertheless, Bellomont's tenure in New York was not without its achievements. His attempts to discourage commerce with pirates, for example, were fairly successful, as were his techniques for putting New York's administration on a more systematic basis, evidenced by the census carried out under his direction in 1698. In Massachusetts and New Hampshire Bellomont's brief period as resident chief executive was comparatively uneventful, although in New Hampshire he did become embroiled in a dispute involving Samuel Allen, who claimed that he held proprietary title to that province.

By early 1701 Bellomont's health had been seriously impaired by his efforts to preside over three colonies, each with its own set of problems. Finally, on March 5, 1701, the governor succumbed in New York to a particularly severe case of gout.

Bibliography: Frederic De Peyster, *The Life and Administration of Richard, Earl of Bellomont ... 1697 to 1701* (New York, 1879); A. de Vlieger, *Historical and Genealogical Record of the Coote Family* (Lausanne, 1900); Stanley H. Friedelbaum, "Bellomont: Imperial Administrator—Studies in Colonial Administration during the 17th Century," unpub. Ph.D. diss., Columbia University, 1955; Jacob Judd, "Lord Bellomont and Captain Kidd: A Footnote to an Entangled Alliance," *New-York Historical Society Quarterly*, XLVII (January 1963), 66-74; John D. Runcie, "The Problem of Anglo-American Politics in Bellomont's New York," *William and Mary Quarterly*, 3rd ser., vol. XXVI (April 1969), 191-217; John C. Rainbolt, "A 'great and usefull designe': Bellomont's Proposal for New York, 1698-1701,'' *New-York Historical Society Quarterly*, LIII (October 1969), 333-51; John C. Rainbolt, ''The Creation of a Governor and Captain General for the Northern Colonies: The Process of Colonial Policy Formation at the End of the Seventeenth Century,'' *New-York Historical Society Quarterly*, LVII (April 1973), 101-20. *DAB, DNB*.

VAUGHAN, George, 1715-1716

Born on April 13, 1676 in Portsmouth, New Hampshire, the son of Major William and Margaret (Cutt) Vaughan. A Congregationalist. Brother of Eleanor, Mary, Cutt, Bridget, Margaret, Abigail and Elizabeth. Married on December 8, 1698 to Mary Belcher, by whom he had one child that died in infancy; after the death of his first wife in February 1699, remarried on January 9, 1701 to Elizabeth Eliot; father by his second wife of Sarah, William, Margaret, George (died young), Elizabeth, Abigail, Eliot, Mary, Jane and George (died young). Studied at Harvard College, graduating with the class of 1696.

Became a member of his father's mercantile house in Portsmouth, and eventually established a connection with another firm in Massachusetts. As a young man, named to a number of local political offices in Portsmouth, including Constable, Selectman, Justice of the Peace and Captain (probably of the local militia). Appointed Judge of the Court of Common Pleas in 1707; in that same year became New Hampshire's Agent in England, where he opposed the Mason claims. Returned to New Hampshire in 1709, serving on several committees. Again travelled to England in the spring of 1715, and received a commission as Lieutenant Governor of New Hampshire from Elizeus Burgess, the newly-appointed governor of Massachusetts and New Hampshire.

Burgess eventually decided not to serve as governor in New England, and his resignation gave Vaughan the opportunity to preside as chief executive of New Hampshire from October 1715 until October 1716, when Samuel Shute, Burgess' replacement, arrived in the province. During his brief administration Vaughan and the Assembly clashed over his salary, with the Assembly claiming that it could only grant him the income from a year's imposts and excises. After Shute appeared in New Hampshire, Vaughan became embroiled in another political controversy. Insisting that he held complete gubernatorial authority during Shute's absence from the province, Vaughan ignored the governor's orders on several occasions, and his behavior eventually resulted in his replacement as lieutenant governor in December of 1717.

Following his departure from office, Vaughan devoted himself primarily to private affairs such as land speculation, although he continued his complaints to the Privy Council about the Shute administration. Vaughan died on November 20, 1724, leaving a large estate.

Bibliography: William Goold, "Col. William Vaughan, of Matinicus and Damariscotta," Maine Historical Society, *Collections*, VIII (1881), 291-313; George E. Hodgdon, *Reminiscences and Genealogical Record of the Vaughan Family of New Hampshire* (Rochester, N.Y., 1918).

SHUTE, Samuel, 1716-1723

also Massachusetts, 1716-1723

Born on January 12, 1662 in England, the son of Benjamin and Patience (Caryl) Shute. A Nonconformist. Brother of John, later Lord Barrington in the Irish peerage.

Studied with Charles Morton, the Puritan schoolmaster, and admitted to London's Middle Temple in November 1683; also admitted to Christ's College, Cambridge in December of that year, although there is no indication that he ever received a degree. Eventually entered the British Army, and by 1712 had advanced to the rank of Lieutenant Colonel of the Third Dragoon Guards. Commissioned Royal Governor of Massachusetts Bay and New Hampshire in June 1716; arrived in America to take up those appointments in October of 1716.

Shute's administration in both Massachusetts and New Hampshire was marked by considerable political turmoil, as he quarreled with the legislatures in each colony over such matters as his salary, the emission of paper money, timber rights, and defense against neighboring Indians. In New Hampshire Shute's position was further weakened by the machinations of Lieutenant Governor George Vaughan, who claimed that he possessed complete gubernatorial power whenever Shute was absent from that province. Shute finally replaced Vaughan in December 1717, but his problems with other local leaders continued, until in January 1723 he left for England to present his case before the Privy Council.

Although even Jeremiah Dummer, Massachusetts' agent in London, conceded the legitimacy of many of his complaints, the disgruntled governor received little satisfaction from either the colonial legislators or the King, and when George I died in 1727 Shute's commission to govern was permitted to expire. He then received a pension as a reward for his services, and retired to private life. Shute died on April 15, 1742.

Bibliography: *George Town on Arrowsick Island . . . A Conference of His Excellency the Governour [Shute], with the Sachems and Chief Men of the Eastern Indians* (Boston, 1717) (also printed in Maine Historical Society, *Collections*, III (1853); *Report of the Lords Commissioners for the Plantations upon Gov. Shute's Memorial* . . . (Boston, 1725); "Journal of Gov. Shute from Boston to Portsmouth, October, 1716," New Hampshire Historical Society, *Collections*, IV (1834), 249-51. *DAB, DNB*.

WENTWORTH, John, 1723-1728, 1729-1730

Born on January 16, 1671 in New Hampshire, the son of Samuel and Mary (Benning) Wentworth. Brother of Samuel, Daniel, William (?), Mary, Ebenezer, Dorothy and Benning. Married on October 12, 1693 to Sarah Hunking; father of Benning (governor of New Hampshire from 1741 to 1767), Hunking, Hannah, Sarah, John, William, Mary, Samuel, Mark, Elizabeth, Rebecca, Ebenezer, Daniel and George.

Employed for a time as a mariner, and later as a merchant. Named to the New Hampshire Council in February 1712, and served as a Justice of the Court of Common Pleas from 1713 to 1718. Appointed Lieutenant Governor of New Hampshire in December 1717, a position which he held until his death; in his capacity as lieutenant governor, served as the colony's acting head from January 1723 to July of 1728, between the governorships of Samuel Shute and William Burnet; also presided as chief executive between the death of Burnet in September 1729 and the arrival of Jonathan Belcher in August of 1730.

The first of three Wentworths who served as colonial governor of New Hampshire, John Wentworth assumed office at a time when northern New England was involved in an Indian war. Along with Lieutenant Governor William Dummer of Massachusetts, Wentworth devoted much of his time to raising troops and stores, and by the winter of 1725-26 the Indians had finally agreed to a temporary treaty of peace. Ostensibly to assist the war effort, the New Hampshire General Assembly issued and received over £14,600 in bills of credit during these years, an emission which was endorsed by the lieutenant governor. In a letter to the Board of Trade written in August 1727, Wentworth criticized a royal instruction of 1720 which made legislation providing for bills of credit illegal unless it included a clause suspending enactment until receipt of royal approval. According to Wentworth, New Hampshire's trade had expanded five-fold in the previous ten years, a development which was in large part due to the availability of paper money in the colony. Thus, Wentworth reasoned, the Board should consider adopting a more lenient currency policy.

Wentworth stepped down as acting governor for the final time in August 1730, following the arrival of Governor Jonathan Belcher. He died four months later, on December 12, 1730, while still serving as lieutenant governor.

Bibliography: "Notes on the Wentworth Family," *New England Historical and Genealogical Register*, IV (October 1850), 321-38d; John Wentworth,

The Wentworth Genealogy: English and American (Boston, 1878); Harriet S. Lacy, "The Wentworth Papers, 1717-1940," *Historical New Hampshire*, XXIII (Spring 1968), 25-30. Wentworth's commission as lieutenant governor is printed in New-Hampshire Historical Society, *Collections*, I (1824), 142-43.

BURNET, William, 1728-1729

New York and New Jersey, 1720-1728; also Massachusetts, 1728-1729

Born in March 1688 at The Hague, the eldest son of Gilbert Burnet, bishop of Salisbury, and his second wife, Mary (Scott) Burnet. Brother of Mary and Gilbert. Married in about May 1712 to a daughter of Dean Stanhope, by whom he was the father of Gilbert; following the death of his first wife, remarried to Anna Maria [or Mary] Van Horne; father of William, Mary and Thomas by his second wife.

Enrolled at Trinity College, Cambridge at the age of thirteen, but left without obtaining a degree; later studied privately, and called to the bar. Commissioned Captain General and Governor-in-Chief of New York and New Jersey in June 1720, and arrived in America to assume office in September of that year. Commissioned Royal Governor of New Hampshire in November 1727, and of Massachusetts Bay in March 1728; left New York in the spring of 1728, following his replacement by the newly-appointed Governor John Montgomerie, and travelled to New England to take up his new positions.

As chief executive of New York, Burnet was confronted by controversy over the extensive fur trade then existing between Albany and Montreal. Contending that such commerce was enhancing New France's stature among Indians in the area, who sold their furs to the English through French *coureurs de bois*, Burnet tried to eliminate the traffic both by means of legislation and by encouraging direct trade between the English and various Indian tribes. Despite some initial success, however, Burnet's policy quickly encountered strong opposition from prominent New York merchants who preferred to conduct their business with the French, and by 1726 it had become apparent that his efforts would fail. In New Jersey Burnet met with similar recalcitrance among leading members of that colony's Assembly, especially over money bills. Nevertheless, after several confrontations with the Assembly, Burnet decided to adopt a more tactful approach, and by the time of his departure in 1728 he had won significant concessions from the legislators.

Although Burnet's tenure in Massachusetts Bay and New Hampshire lasted only a little more than a year, his administration of those colonies was also marked by disputes over financial matters. In particular, the question of the form which the governor's remuneration should take, a recurrent problem during much of the eighteenth century, created tension between Burnet and the Massachusetts Assembly, as Burnet insisted that he be given a permanent salary. On September 7, 1729, however, before the issue could be resolved, Burnet died suddenly in Boston.

Bibliography: William Nelson, *Original Documents Relating to the Life and Administrations of William Burnet* . . . (Paterson, N.J., 1897). Burnet's will appears in the *New England Historical and Genealogical Register*, XLVII (January 1893), 123-25. *DAB, DNB*.

BELCHER, Jonathan, 1730-1741

also Massachusetts, 1730-1741; New Jersey, 1747-1757

Born on January 8, 1682 in Cambridge, Massachusetts, the son of Andrew and Sarah (Gilbert) Belcher. Brother of Andrew, Sarah, Elizabeth, Mary, Anna, Martha and Deborah (died in infancy). Married on January 8, 1706 to Mary Partridge, by whom he was the father of Andrew, Sarah, Jonathan, William and Thomas; following the death of his first wife on October 6, 1736, remarried on September 9, 1748 to Mary Louisa Emilia Teal; no children by his second wife.

Attended Harvard College, graduating in 1699. Subsequently spent several years in Europe, before returning to Massachusetts and pursuing a mercantile career. First elected to the Massachusetts Council in 1718, and served intermittently as a member of that body until 1728. Sent to England by the Massachusetts House of Representatives to defend, along with Francis Wilks, the House position on the question of the chief executive's salary. Arrived in England early in 1729, and secured a commission as Royal Governor of Massachusetts Bay and New Hampshire in January 1730, shortly after news of Governor Burnet's death reached London; returned to America in August 1730 to begin his new assignment. Dismissed as chief executive of Massachusetts and New Hampshire in May 1741, but later returned to England, where in February 1747 he received a commission to govern New Jersey; occupied that office between his arrival in the province in August 1747 and his death ten years later.

Belcher's tenure in Massachusetts and New Hampshire was troubled by sharp disputes with the assemblies of both colonies over issues like the governor's salary and paper currency. While Belcher managed to resolve some of his disagreements with the legislators, monetary policy remained a source of bitter dissension, especially in Massachusetts. In that province the governor disapproved of the creation of a "land bank," which issued notes backed by mortgages at three percent interest, and the resulting controversy did much to intensify opposition to his administration. Eventually, charges of corruption, including an allegation that he had accepted a bribe to settle a boundary dispute between Massachusetts and New Hampshire, culminated in Belcher's removal by Crown officials.

After he had regained the favor of authorities in England, the indefatigable Belcher assumed the governorship of New Jersey. There he again encountered problems, chiefly concerning the question of land titles. Shortly before his second period as governor began, the College of New Jersey (now Princeton University) was founded, and Belcher, always a supporter of education, bequeathed his personal library to that institution when he died in Elizabethtown, New Jersey on August 31, 1757.

Bibliography: W. H. Whitmore, "Notes on the Belcher Family," *New England Historical and Genealogical Register*, XXVII (July 1873), 239-45; "Belcher Papers, parts 1 and 2," in Massachusetts Historical Society, *Collections*, 6th ser., vols. VI and VII (Boston, 1893-94); Henry Lyttleton Savage, "Jonathan Belcher and 'Our Young College'," *Princeton University Library Chronicle*, XIX (Spring-Summer 1958), 191-96; Michael Clement Batinski, "Jonathan Belcher of Massachusetts, 1682-1741," unpub. Ph.D. diss., Northwestern University, 1970. There is also a microfilm of the Belcher letterbooks from 1723 to 1754, the originals of which are in the Massachusetts Historical Society. *DAB*.

WENTWORTH, Benning, 1741-1767

Born on July 24, 1696 in Portsmouth, New Hampshire, the eldest son of Lieutenant Governor John and Sarah (Hunking) Wentworth. An Anglican. Brother of Hunking, Hannah, Sarah, John, William, Mary, Samuel, Mark, Elizabeth, Rebecca, Ebenezer, Daniel and George. Married on December 31, 1719 to Abigail Ruck, by whom he was the father of three sons; remarried on March 15, 1760 to Martha Hilton.

Studied at Harvard College, receiving an A.B. from that institution in 1715. Employed as a merchant in Boston shortly after his graduation from Harvard. Later served for a brief period in the New Hampshire Assembly, and in 1734 became a member of the colony's Council. Also travelled to England and Spain on several occasions between 1734 and 1739. Commissioned Royal Governor of New Hampshire in July 1741, and commenced his administration in December of that year.

Wentworth's long tenure as chief executive of New Hampshire began with the colony finally achieving complete political separation from Massachusetts, and ended during the revolutionary movement which culminated in independence from the mother country. During these twenty-five years Wentworth used the powers of his office to advance the political and economic fortunes of the Wentworth family, a pattern of behavior which provoked criticism of his administration. Wentworth also engaged in periodic struggles with the New Hampshire Assembly over many of the same issues that had confronted other royal governors, particularly the questions of a fixed governor's salary, emissions of paper currency, and the extent of the chief executive's authority over political appointments, land grants, and the colonial militia. Although the eventual departure of Wentworth from office was clearly affected by these conflicts, the erosion of his power base in England also had much to do with his demise, since by 1765 home authorities had become greatly concerned over Wentworth's failure to communicate with their government. Ultimately, after some adroit maneuvering by his nephew, John Wentworth, Benning Wentworth was allowed to resign in June 1767. He was then replaced by his nephew, who had received a commission to govern the province in August of 1766.

Benning Wentworth died in Little Harbor, New Hampshire on October 14, 1770; he was buried in the family tomb in the cemetery of Queen's Chapel, St. John's Church, Portsmouth.

Bibliography: "Notes on the Wentworth Family," *New England Historical and Genealogical Register*, IV (October 1850), 321-38d; John Wentworth, *The Wentworth Genealogy: English and American* (Boston, 1878); "Letters of Hugh Hall to Benning Wentworth," *New England Historical and Genealogical Register*, XLII (July 1888), 300-07; John F. Looney, "The King's Representative: Benning Wentworth, Colonial Governor, 1741-1767," unpub. Ph.D. diss., Lehigh University, 1961; Jere R. Daniell, "Politics in New Hampshire under Governor Benning Wentworth, 1741-1767," *William and Mary Quarterly*, 3rd ser., vol. XXIII (January 1966), 76-105; John F. Looney, "Benning Wentworth's Land Grant Policy: A Reappraisal," *Historical New Hampshire*, XXIII (Spring 1968), 3-13; Harriet S. Lacy, "The Wentworth Papers, 1717-1940," *Historical New Hampshire*, XXIII (Spring 1968), 25-30; Allan R. Raymond, "Benning Wentworth's Claims in the New Hampshire-New York Border Controversy: A Case of Twenty-Twenty Hindsight?," *Vermont History*, XLIII (Winter 1975), 20-32. *DAB*.

WENTWORTH, John, 1767-1775

Born on August 9, 1737 in Portsmouth, New Hampshire, the son of Mark Hunking, a prominent merchant, and Elizabeth (Rindge) Wentworth. Brother of Thomas and Anna. Married on November 11, 1769 to Frances (Wentworth) Atkinson, Jr., by whom he was the father of Charles-Mary.

Studied at Harvard College, graduating from that institution in 1755. Worked for his father for a time after leaving Harvard, and in 1763 travelled to

England on business, where he also acted as an Agent for New Hampshire. Received a commission as Royal Governor of New Hampshire in August 1766, along with an appointment as Surveyor-General of His Majesty's Woods in America; returned to America early in 1767 and, after a journey originating in Charleston, South Carolina, arrived in Portsmouth, New Hampshire in June 1767 to begin his tenure as chief executive of that colony.

Although Wentworth was a capable and energetic governor, the growth of revolutionary sentiment in New Hampshire had by the 1770's weakened his position considerably. Whereas the early years of his administration were marked by achievements of major significance, including the granting of a charter to Dartmouth College and the development of New Hampshire's largely unsettled interior, his final period as chief executive was preoccupied by efforts to discourage collaboration between New Hampshire's residents and leaders of the revolutionary movement in other colonies. By 1775, however, Wentworth was no longer in control of the province, and in August of that year he left for Boston, after having sought refuge aboard a British ship anchored off Portsmouth.

Following his enforced departure from New Hampshire, Wentworth spent several years with the British forces, at first in Boston and later in New York. In 1778 he sailed for England, but after the war he returned to Halifax, Nova Scotia, where he again acted as Surveyor of the King's Woods in North America. In May 1792 Wentworth became Lieutenant Governor of Nova Scotia, a position he held until 1808; in April 1795 he was made a Baronet. Wentworth died in Halifax, Nova Scotia on April 8, 1820.

Bibliography: *Two Reports on the Matter of Complaint of Mr. Livius against Gov. Wentworth* (London, 1773); "Notes on the Wentworth Family," *New England Historical and Genealogical Register*, IV (October 1850), 321-38d; John Wentworth, *The Wentworth Genealogy: English and American* (Boston, 1878); "Case of Councillor Peter Livius *vs.* Governor John Wentworth—Testimony for the Defense," New Hampshire Historical Society, *Collections*, IX (1889), 304-63; Lawrence Shaw Mayo, *John Wentworth, Governor of New Hampshire, 1767-1775* (Cambridge, 1921); Harriet S. Lacy, "The Wentworth Papers, 1717-1940," *Historical New Hampshire*, XXIII (Spring 1968), 25-30; Derek H. Watson, "John Wentworth's Description of the American Colonies in 1765," *Historical New Hampshire*, XXVII (Fall 1972), 141-65; Gordon E. Kershaw, "John Wentworth *vs.* Kennebeck Proprietors: The Formation of Royal Mast Policy, 1769-1778," *American Neptune*, XXXIII (April 1973), 95-119. *DAB, DNB*.

THORNTON, Matthew, 1775-1776

Born *circa* 1714 in Ireland, the son of James and Elizabeth (Jenkins) Thornton. A Presbyterian. Brother of James, Andrew and Hannah. Married to Hannah Jack, probably between 1760 and 1762; father of James, Andrew, Mary, Hannah and Matthew.

Arrived in America with his family in 1717 or 1718, settling first in Maine and later in Massachusetts, where he studied medicine with a Dr. Grout. Moved to Londonderry, New Hampshire in 1740, and practiced medicine in that community until 1779. Accompanied a New Hampshire regiment during the expedition to Cape Breton in 1745, serving as a surgeon in the military campaign which culminated with the capture of Louisbourg. Filled numerous public offices on the local and provincial level, and from 1758 to 1762 represented Londonderry in the New Hampshire Assembly. Named Chief Justice of the Court of Common Pleas for Hillsborough County in 1776, a position he held until 1776. Chosen President of New Hampshire's Fourth and Fifth Provincial Congresses, which convened in May and December of 1775; also elected Chairman of the Committee of Safety in 1775, an office which made him the leading executive authority in New Hampshire during the months between the departure of Governor John Wentworth in the summer of 1775 and the selection of Meshech Weare as First Councillor in January 1776.

Although Thornton's term as chairman of the Committee of Safety was relatively brief, he presided over a period which was of major significance in the history of New Hampshire. By late 1775 fighting between colonial and British troops had reached a critical stage, and calls for a final and complete break with the mother country were becoming more insistent. In these circumstances Thornton served as head of a committee which drafted a plan of government for New Hampshire (during the winter of 1775-76), a plan that remained in effect until the end of the war.

After the approval of this constitution, Thornton became Speaker of the newly-created House of Representatives, but he relinquished that office several days later when the House named him Second Councillor. Throughout the remainder of the Revolution Thornton continued to hold high public office. In June 1776 he was sworn in as Second Justice of New Hampshire's Superior Court of Judicature, a position he held until 1782; in September of 1776 Thornton was elected as a delegate from New Hampshire to the Continental Congress. During his brief Congressional service, Thornton in November 1776 affixed his name to the Declaration of Independence, despite the fact that he had not been a member of Congress when the document was originally signed.

Following the war Thornton remained an important figure in the new state's affairs. In the 1780's, for example, he served for several years as a member of the New Hampshire Senate. Indeed, at the time of his death, he was still holding office, albeit nominally, as a Justice of the Peace. Thornton died in Newburyport, Massachusetts on June 24, 1803, and was buried in the graveyard at Thornton's Ferry, his estate in Merrimack, New Hampshire.

Bibliography: William W. Bailey, "Matthew Thornton," *Granite Monthly*, XIV (March 1892), 77-88; Charles Thornton Adams, *Matthew Thornton of New Hampshire, A Patriot of the American Revolution* (Philadelphia, 1903); Charles Thornton Adams, *The Family of James Thornton*... (New York, 1905). Other information about Thornton and his family appears in a paper by C. H. Woodbury, published in the New Hampshire Historical Society, *Proceedings*, III (1902), 76-109. *DAB*.

WEARE, Meshech, 1776-1785

Born on January 16, 1713 in Hampton Falls, New Hampshire, the youngest son of Judge Nathaniel and Mary (Waite) Weare. Brother of Nathan, Mary, Mercy, Sarah, Elizabeth, Abigail, Mehitable and Susanna; half-brother of Daniel, Peter, John, Hannah and Huldah. Married on July 20, 1738 to Elizabeth Shaw, by whom he had two children; after his first wife's death, remarried on December 11, 1746 to Mehitable Wainwright, by whom he was the father of eight children.

Studied at Harvard College, receiving an A.B. in 1735. Apart from several intervals, represented Hampton in the New Hampshire Legislature from 1745 to 1775; also served as Speaker of the Assembly for three years, and as Clerk of that body for eight. Acted as Justice of New Hampshire's Superior Court from 1747 to 1775. Attended the Albany Congress in 1754 which considered Benjamin Franklin's Plan of Union; served for many years as a Colonel in the New Hampshire militia. Chosen First Councillor of New Hampshire under the constitution adopted in January 1776, and in that capacity acted as the new state's chief executive until 1784; also served during the war as Chairman of the New Hampshire Committee of Safety, and from 1776 to 1782 as Chief Justice of the state. Elected President of New Hampshire in June 1784, an office created by the state constitution drafted the previous year, but declined re-election to that position in 1785 due to failing health.

Weare's tenure as chief executive covered nine years which marked the transformation of New Hampshire from a rebellious colony into a state, and throughout this tumultuous period he provided wise and judicious guidance. Although New Hampshire managed to escape invasion during the Revolution, largely due to its relative poverty and strategic insignificance, Weare nevertheless cooperated closely with military leaders like Major General John Sullivan.

Weare also accepted a proposal which in 1782 resolved New Hampshire's boundary dispute with Vermont, a settlement which served as a prelude to the admission of the latter state into the Union in 1791.

Weare died on January 14, 1786, less than one year after leaving the president's office.

Bibliography: Paine Wingate, "Sketch of Hon. Meshech Weare," New Hampshire Historical Society, *Collections*, V (1837), 243-47; W. M. Sargent, *The Weare Family of Hampton, New Hampshire, and North Yarmouth, Maine* (Yarmouth, Me., 1879); Ezra S. Stearns, "Meschech [*sic*] Weare," *Magazine of History*, VI (July 1907), 41-54; Franklin Benjamin Sanborn, "Colonel Weare of Hampton Falls (1713-1786)," Massachusetts Historical Society, *Proceedings*, XLVI (1914), 61-66; Otis G. Hammond, "The Weare Papers," *Granite Monthly*, LI (August 1919), 357-61; Avery J. Butters, "New Hampshire History and the Public Career of Meshech Weare, 1713 to 1786," unpub. Ph.D. diss., Fordham University, 1961. There are also numerous letters to and from Weare in Otis G. Hammond, ed., *Letters and Papers of Major-General John Sullivan, Continental Army*, 2 vols. (Concord, N.H., 1930-31). *DAB*.

LANGDON, John, 1785-1786, 1788-1789, 1805-1809, 1810-1812

Born on June 26, 1741 in Portsmouth, New Hampshire, the son of John, a farmer, and Mary (Hall) Langdon. Brother of Woodbury, Mary, Elizabeth, Abigail and Martha. Married early in February of 1777 to Elizabeth Sherburne, by whom he was the father of Elizabeth and John (died in infancy).

Studied at Hale's Latin Grammar School, and later worked as a clerk for a Portsmouth merchant; began his own commercial career in the 1760's. Became an opponent of British policy during the revolutionary movement, taking part in the protest against the Tea Act in 1773. Elected to the New Hampshire Legislature in 1775, a position he also held in 1777-81, 1786-87 and 1801-05; served as Speaker of that body on a number of occasions. Attended the Second Continental Congress from 1775 to 1776, and in June 1776 was named Naval Agent for any Continental prizes seized in New Hampshire waters; supplied *matériel* for the Continental Army during much of the Revolution, and supervised the construction of several ships. Again attended sessions of Congress from 1783 to 1784, and briefly in 1787; served in the New Hampshire Senate from 1784 to 1785. Participated in the Philadelphia convention which drafted the Federal Constitution in 1787, signed the finished document, and supported its ratification at the New Hampshire Convention of 1788. First elected President of New Hampshire in 1785, an office to which he was chosen on seven other occasions; served as chief executive from June 1785 to June 1786, June 1788 to January 1789, June 1805 to June 1809, and June

1810 to June 1812. Also represented New Hampshire in the United States Senate from March 1789 to March 1801, becoming that body's first President *pro tempore*.

Langdon's years as president of New Hampshire (after 1792, as governor) encompassed more that a quarter of a century of the state's history. During his initial year in office the chief political problem involved the protests of debtors seeking relief from the depressed economic conditions which characterized much of the post-war period. By the 1790's, however, the focus had changed to international affairs, and Senator Langdon, who had earlier displayed some sympathy for the Federalist Party, gradually became an advocate of Jeffersonian principles. This new political credo affected many of his subsequent decisions as chief executive. From 1807 to 1809, for example, Langdon defended Jefferson's tactic of embargo, even though his endorsement of that unpopular policy probably cost him the gubernatorial election of 1809.

Following his final term as governor, Langdon retired from politics to take a more active interest in religion, an interest which led him to become a founder of the New Hampshire Bible Society. Langdon died in Portsmouth on September 18, 1819; he was buried there in the North Burying Ground.

Bibliography: John Langdon Elwyn, "Some Account of John Langdon," *Early State Papers of New Hampshire*, XX (1891), 850-80; Lawrence Shaw Mayo, *John Langdon of New Hampshire* (Concord, N.H., 1937); Harriet S. Lacy, "The Langdon Papers, 1716-1841," *Historical New Hampshire*, XXII (Autumn 1967), 55-65. There is also a sketch of Langdon by William Plumer in *Early State Papers of New Hampshire*, XXI (1892). *DAB*.

SULLIVAN, John, 1786-1788, 1789-1790

Born on February 17, 1740 in Somersworth, New Hampshire, the son of John, a schoolmaster, and Margery (Browne) Sullivan. Brother of Benjamin, Daniel, James (who served as governor of Massachusetts from 1807 to 1808), Ebenezer and Mary. Married in 1760 to Lydia Remick Worster, by whom he was the father of Lydia, John, James, George and two daughters who died in infancy.

Studied law under Samuel Livermore of Portsmouth, and later established his own practice. Named Major of the New Hampshire militia in 1772, and represented that province at the First and Second Continental Congresses. Appointed Brigadier General by the Second Continental Congress in June 1775; promoted to Major General in August 1776. Played a prominent role in many of the major engagements fought between 1776 and 1777, including the battles of Long Island, Trenton, Princeton, Brandywine and Germantown; also commanded the American troops who attempted unsuccessfully to capture

Newport, Rhode Island from the British in 1778. Resigned from the Continental Army in November 1779, citing reasons of health. Served as a delegate from New Hampshire to the Continental Congress between 1780 and 1781. Represented Durham at the New Hampshire Constitutional Convention which met between 1781 and 1783. Served as Attorney General of New Hampshire from 1782 to 1786, became President of the state's branch of the Cincinnati in 1783, and acted as Speaker of the New Hampshire Assembly in 1785 and 1786. Elected President of New Hampshire in 1786, and served in that capacity from June of that year until June 1788, winning reelection in 1787; named to a third term as chief executive in 1789, serving from June 1789 to June 1790.

Sullivan's tenure as president was most noteworthy for the state convention which met in Exeter in February 1788 to consider the proposed Federal Constitution. At the convention Sullivan, who presided over the discussions, gave his support to those who advocated ratification, a step which appears to have persuaded many of the Constitution's critics to vote in favor of that document in June 1788. During the first few months of his administration, Sullivan also confronted the threat of insurrection among the state's poor, some of whom were demanding new emissions of paper money, the redistribution of property, and release from debt. Sullivan promptly responded to this crisis, however, and his firmness, assisted by an economic upturn in 1787, reduced the danger of rebellion.

In September 1789, toward the end of his service as president, Sullivan was appointed United States District Judge for New Hampshire. He held this office until his death in Durham, New Hampshire on January 23, 1795, despite deteriorating health which prevented him from fulfilling the duties of the position for several years.

Bibliography: "Master Sullivan of Berwick—His Ancestors and Descendants," *New England Historical and Genealogical Register*, XIX (October 1865), 289-305; Thomas C. Amory, *The Military Services and Public Life of Major-General John Sullivan* (Boston and Albany, N.Y., 1868); A. Tiffany Norton, *History of Sullivan's Campaign against the Iroquois* (Lima, N.Y., 1879); Frederick Cook, ed., *Journals of the Military Expedition of Major General John Sullivan against the Six Nations of Indians in 1779 . . .* (Auburn, N.Y., 1887); Thomas C. Amory and G. E. Meredith, *Materials for a History of the Family of John Sullivan* (Cambridge, 1893); John Scales, "Master John Sullivan of Somersworth and Berwick and His Family," New Hampshire Historical Society, *Proceedings*, IV (1903), 180-201; Patrick F. McGowan, "The Patriotism of Sullivan," American Irish Historical Society *Journal*, XII (1913), 209-15; Louise W. Murray, ed., *Notes from the Craft Collection in Tioga Point Museum on the Sullivan Expedition* (Athens, Pa., 1929); Otis G. Hammond, ed., *Letters and Papers of Major-General John Sullivan, Continental Army*, 2 vols. (Concord, N.H., 1930-31); Daniel F. Cohalan, "General John Sullivan," American Irish Historical Society *Journal*, XXX (1932),

25-59; Charles P. Whittemore, *A General of the Revolution: John Sullivan of New Hampshire* (New York, 1961); Donald R. McAdams, "The Sullivan Expedition: Success or Failure," *New-York Historical Society Quarterly*, LIV (January 1970), 53-81. *DAB*.

PICKERING, John, 1789

Born on September 22, 1737 in Newington, New Hampshire, the son of Joshua and Mary Deborah (Smithson) Pickering. Married to Abigail Sheafe.

Attended Harvard College, graduating from that institution in 1761; later studied law and began his own practice. Held minor civil offices during the Revolution; participated in New Hampshire's constitutional conventions of 1781-83 and 1791-92. Represented Portsmouth in the New Hampshire Legislature between 1783 and 1787, and took part in the state convention which ratified the Federal Constitution in June 1788. Chosen as a Presidential Elector in 1788 and 1792, and sat briefly in the New Hampshire Senate; served as Acting President of New Hampshire between the resignation of John Langdon in January 1789 and the inauguration of John Sullivan in June of that year.

Pickering's brief administration encouraged him to run for the chief executive's office in his own right, but his bid to win a complete term failed when he was narrowly defeated by Sullivan in the gubernatorial contest of 1789. In August 1790, however, he was named Chief Justice of the state's Superior Court of Judicature, an office which he continued to hold until he became a United States District Court Judge in February 1795. Pickering suffered a nervous breakdown in 1801, causing him to be replaced temporarily by one of the state's Circuit Court judges. In February 1803 Pickering's continued mental instability was discussed in the United States House of Representatives, whose members voted to impeach him on grounds of "loose morals and intemperate habits." Following a token trial, Pickering was officially removed from his position by the Senate in March 1804. He died about a year later, on April 11, 1805.

Bibliography: R. H. Eddy, *Genealogical Data Respecting John Pickering of Portsmouth, New Hampshire and His Descendants* (Boston, 1884) (see also the *Supplement* to this work, also published in Boston in 1884). A paper by Andrew P. Peabody, discussing Pickering and the impeachment charges brought against him, appears in the Massachusetts Historical Society, *Proceedings*, XX (September 1883), 333-38. There is also a short sketch of Pickering by William Plumer in *Early State Papers of New Hampshire*, XXII (1893), 839-43. *DAB*.

NEW HAVEN

Yorkshire Quarter
Suburbs Quarter
Oystershell Field
Mr. Davenport's Quarter
The Governor's Quarter
NEW HAVEN
IN
1641

Chronology

1639-1658	Theophilus Eaton
1658-1660	Francis Newman
1660-1664	William Leete

BIBLIOGRAPHY

Andrews, Charles M., *The Rise and Fall of the New Haven Colony* (New Haven, 1936) (*Publications* of the Tercentenary Commission of the State of Connecticut, vol. XLVIII).

Atwater, Edward E., *History of the Colony of New Haven to its Absorption into Connecticut* (Meriden, Conn., 1902).

Calder, Isabel MacBeath, *The New Haven Colony* (New Haven, 1934).

Dexter, Franklin Bowditch, comp., *Historical Catalogue of the Members of the First Church of Christ in New Haven, Connecticut (Center Church). A.D. 1639-1914* (New Haven, 1914).

Hoadly, Charles J., ed., *Records of the Colony and Plantation of New Haven, from 1638 to 1649* . . . (Hartford, 1857).

———. ed., *Records of the Colony or Jurisdiction of New Haven, from May, 1653, to the Union* (Hartford, 1858).

Osterweis, Rollin G., *Three Centuries of New Haven, 1638-1938* (New Haven and London, 1953).

NEW HAVEN

EATON, Theophilus, 1639-1658

Born in 1590 in Stony Stratford, Buckinghamshire, England, the son of the Reverend Richard Eaton. A Congregationalist. Brother of eight, including Samuel and Nathaniel. Married in England to a woman whose name is unknown, and who died within a few years; father of two children by his first wife, including Mary; remarried, again in England, to Ann (Lloyd) Yale, by whom he had two sons and three daughters, including Samuel, Theophilus and Hannah.

Apprenticed to a merchant in London as a young man, and eventually began trading on his own, especially with the Baltic countries. Appointed Deputy Governor of the East Land Company, a commercial enterprise, and may also have been the Agent of James I at the Danish Court. Became one of the original patentees of the Massachusetts Bay Company, served as one of the Company's English managers, and in 1637 immigrated to New England. Arrived in Boston in June of 1637, and the following spring settled in what is now New Haven. Participated in the town meeting which, in June 1639, drafted the Fundamental Laws of New Haven; elected Magistrate of the new colony in October 1639, and served in that capacity (from 1643, as Governor) until his death. While governor, represented New Haven as a Commissioner of the United Colonies of New England.

The dominant political figure for almost all of New Haven's brief history, Eaton played an influential role in virtually every phase of its life. Early in the 1640's his leadership helped New Haven to organize a government separate from larger neighbors like Massachusetts and Connecticut, but the lack of a viable economic base in the small colony remained a serious weakness throughout his administration. At the same time, jurisdictional disputes between New Haven and both New Netherlands and New Sweden created other problems. Although Eaton attempted to strengthen New Haven by encouraging trade and by supporting defensive alliances like the New England Confederation, his efforts were unable to overcome the colony's difficulties. By the time he died on January 7, 1658, New Haven was already approaching the day when it would lose its cherished autonomy.

Bibliography: Jacob Bailey Moore, "Memoir of Theophilus Eaton, First Governor of the Colony of New Haven," New-York Historical Society, *Collections*, 2nd ser., vol. II (New York, 1849), 467-93; George Dudley Seymour, comp., *Memorials of Theophilus Eaton, First Governor of the New Haven Colony* (New Haven, 1938). *DAB, DNB*.

NEWMAN, Francis, 1658-1660

Born in the early seventeenth century in England; names of parents unknown. Married to a woman named Mary; father of Elizabeth and perhaps others.

Emigrated from London to New England in 1637, and by 1638 had become one of the first settlers of New Haven. Held a variety of local offices before his election in March 1645 as a Deputy to the New Haven General Court; also named Secretary of the colony in 1647, and appears to have served in that capacity until 1658. Appointed to a commission which travelled to New Netherlands in the spring of 1653 to determine that colony's attitude towards the English settlements; also represented New Haven as a Commissioner of the United Colonies for several years during the 1650's. Was serving as a New Haven Magistrate by 1653, and was reelected annually until his selection as Governor in May of 1658.

Although tensions with neighboring Indians continued after Newman succeeded the deceased Theophilus Eaton, the new chief executive did attempt to avoid open warfare with the natives. Politically, this period witnessed the continuation of New Haven's ultimately unsuccessful struggle to establish itself as a separate colony, a struggle which was hindered in part by its lack of a charter. The New Haven economy was especially weak during these years, making it impossible for the colony to shoulder the expense of sending an agent to England to defend itself against absorption by a larger neighbor. While New Haven's chances of remaining a distinct political unit grew less promising, Governor Newman fell ill and died in office on November 18, 1660. *DNB*.

LEETE, William, 1660-1664

Connecticut, 1676-1683

Born *circa* 1613 in Dodington, Huntingdonshire, England, the son of John and Anna (Shute) Leete. A Congregationalist. Married to Anna Payne, by whom he was the father of John, Andrew, William, Abigail, Caleb, Graciana, Peregrine (died young), Joshua (died young) and Anne; after his first wife's death in 1668, remarried in 1671 to Sarah, the widow of Henry Rutherford; following the death of his second wife in February 1674, married a third time to Mary, the widow of both Governor Francis Newman of New Haven Colony and the Reverend Nicholas Street; no children by his second and third wives.

Studied law in England, and worked for a time as Registrar in the Bishop's Court at Cambridge. Immigrated to America in May 1639; became one of the founders of the town of Guilford shortly after his arrival. Served as Town Clerk of Guilford from 1639 to 1662, and also represented Guilford in the Assembly after it came under the jurisdiction of the New Haven Colony. Selected as a Magistrate (Assistant) for New Haven in 1651, a position he held until his election as Deputy Governor in May 1658. Served as deputy governor until late 1660, when he replaced the deceased Governor Francis Newman. Chosen governor on an annual basis until 1664; resigned as chief executive of New Haven late in 1664, just before the final absorption of the colony by Connecticut. Elected an Assistant for Connecticut a short time later, and served in that capacity until he was named Deputy Governor in 1669. Succeeded the deceased John Winthrop, Jr. as Governor of Connecticut in the spring of 1676, an office he held until his own death.

Leete's tenure as governor of New Haven was troubled by increasing pressure from Connecticut, aimed at forcing the smaller colony to give up its autonomy. In 1662 any hopes that New Haven may have had for retaining its existence as a separate political unit were dealt a major blow, when Governor Winthrop of Connecticut secured a charter which included New Haven within his jurisdiction. Earlier, during the first part of his administration, Leete's efforts to counter this threat had been hampered by the presence in his colony of colonels Whalley and Goffe, two men who were wanted by Charles II for their part in the execution of his father. Although Leete probably did not personally protect the two regicides, his failure to prosecute them more vigorously aroused the displeasure of authorities in England.

More than eleven years after he had stepped down as the last governor of New Haven, Leete, in a moment of historical irony, was chosen to replace the man whose diplomacy had ended New Haven's history as a distinct colony. As chief executive of Connecticut, Leete's first responsibility was to bring King Philip's War to a successful conclusion. Within a few months that aim had been achieved, and for the next seven years he was largely concerned with refuting the charges of Edward Randolph, the Crown official who criticized Connecticut and the other New England colonies for their disregard of England's acts of trade and navigation. Leete died in office on April 16, 1683 in Hartford, Connecticut; he was buried in the cemetery of that town's First Church.

Bibliography: Bernard C. Steiner, "Governor William Leete and the Absorption of New Haven Colony by Connecticut," in American Historical Association, *Annual Report for 1891* (Washington, D.C., 1892), pp. 207-22; Joseph Leete, *The Family of Leete*, 2nd ed. (London, 1906). *DAB*.

NEW JERSEY

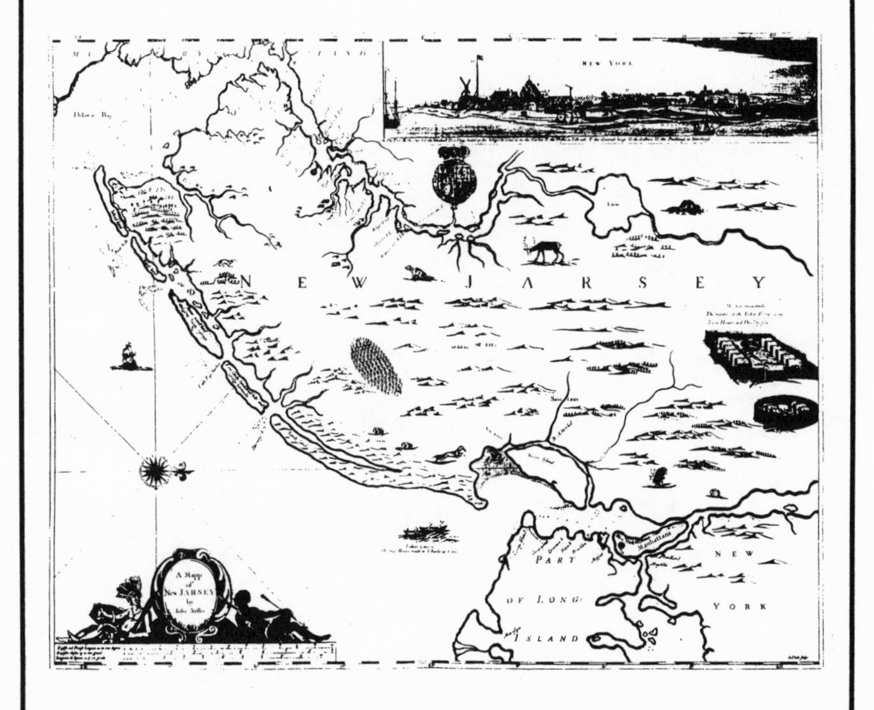
NEW YORK
N E W J A R S E Y
PART
OF LONG
ISLAND
NEW
YORK
Manhattans
A Mapp
of
New JARSEY
by

Chronology

Prior to the establishment of English hegemony in 1664, parts of the territory which would eventually become New Jersey were under both Dutch and Swedish control. The Dutch directors and governors exercising jurisdiction were: Cornelis Jacobsen May (1624-1625), Willem Verhulst (1625-1626), Peter Minuit (1626-1631), Bastiaen Janseen Krol (1632-1633), Wouter Van Twiller (1633-1638), Willem Kiefft (1638-1647) and Peter Stuyvesant (1647-1664). The governors of the colony of New Sweden, which was particularly prominent along the Delaware River until its absorption by the Dutch in 1655, were Peter Minuit (1638), Jost van Bogardt (1640), Peter Hollender Ridder (1640-1643), Johan Björnsson Printz (1643-1653), Johan Papegoja (1653-1654) and Johan Classon Rising (1654-1655).

New Jersey

1664-1665	Richard Nicolls
1665-1672	Philip Carteret
1672-1673	John Berry
1673-1674	*During this period the Dutch occupied New Jersey, thereby superseding the English administration.*
1674-1676	Philip Carteret

East Jersey

1676-1680	Philip Carteret
1680-1681	Sir Edmund Andros
1681-1682	Philip Carteret
1682-1684	Thomas Rudyard
1684-1686	Gawen Lawrie
1686-1687	Lord Neil Campbell
1687-1688	Andrew Hamilton
1688-1689	Sir Edmund Andros
1689-1698	Andrew Hamilton
1698-1699	Jeremiah Basse
1699	Andrew Bowne
1699-1703	Andrew Hamilton

West Jersey

1676-1681	*A Board of commissioners governed West Jersey.*
1681-1684	Samuel Jennings (or Jenings)
1684-1685	Thomas Olive (or Ollive)
1685-1688	John Skene
1688-1689	Sir Edmund Andros
1689-1690 (or 1691)	John Skene
1692-1698	Andrew Hamilton
1698-1699	Jeremiah Basse
1699	Andrew Bowne
1699	Jeremiah Basse
1699-1703	Andrew Hamilton

New Jersey *(reunited)*

1703	Lewis Morris
1703-1708	Edward Hyde, Viscount Cornbury
1708-1709	John Lovelace, 4th Baron Lovelace of Hurley
1709-1710	Richard Ingoldesby
1710	William Pinhorne
1710-1719	Robert Hunter
1719-1720	Lewis Morris
1720-1728	William Burnet
1728-1731	John Montgomerie
1731-1732	Lewis Morris
1732-1736	William Cosby
1736	John Anderson
1736-1738*	John Hamilton
1738-1746	Lewis Morris
1746-1747	John Hamilton
1747	John Reading
1747-1757	Jonathan Belcher
1757	Thomas Pownall
1757-1758	John Reading
1758-1760	Francis Bernard
1760-1761	Thomas Boone
1761-1763	Josiah Hardy
1763-1776	William Franklin
1776-1790	William Livingston

*John West, 1st Earl De La Warr, was commissioned royal governor of New Jersey in 1737, but never assumed that position in the colony.

BIBLIOGRAPHY

Gerlach, Larry R., *Prologue to Independence: New Jersey in the Coming of the American Revolution* (New Brunswick, N.J., 1976).

Journal of the Procedure of the Governor and Council of the Province of East New Jersey from and after the First Day of December Anno Domini 1682 (Jersey City, 1872).

Kull, Irving S., ed., *New Jersey: A History*, 4 vols. (New York, 1930).

Minutes of the Council of Safety of the State of New Jersey, 1777-1778 (Jersey City, 1872).

Minutes of the Provincial Congress and the Council of Safety of the State of New Jersey, 1774-1776 (Trenton, 1879).

Mott, George S., *The First Century of Hunterdon County, State of New Jersey* (Flemington, N.J., 1878).

Pomfret, John E., *Colonial New Jersey: A History* (New York, 1973).

———. *The New Jersey Proprietors and Their Lands, 1664-1776* (Princeton, 1964).

———. *The Province of East New Jersey, 1609-1702: The Rebellious Proprietary* (Princeton, 1962).

———. *The Province of West New Jersey, 1609-1702: A History of the Origins of an American Colony* (Princeton, 1956).

Shourds, Thomas, *History and Genealogy of Fenwick's Colony* (Bridgeton, N.J., 1876).

Whitehead, William A., *Contributions to the Early History of Perth Amboy and Adjoining Country* . . . (New York, 1856).

———. *et al.*, eds., *Archives of the State of New Jersey, 1631-1800*, 30 vols. (Newark, etc., 1880-1906).

Woodward, E. M., and John F. Hageman, *History of Burlington and Mercer Counties, New Jersey, with Biographical Sketches of Their Pioneers and Prominent Men* (Philadelphia, 1883).

NEW JERSEY

NICOLLS, Richard, 1664-1665

also New York, 1664-1668

Born in 1624 in England, the fourth son of Francis, a barrister, and Margaret (Bruce) Nicolls.Brother of William, Edward, Francis, Bruce and perhaps others. Never married.

Became a supporter of the Royalist cause during the English Civil Wars, and in 1643 commanded a troop of horse against Parliamentary forces. Joined the Royalists in exile on the Continent after Cromwell's victory, and served under the Duke of York in the French Army, where he probably acquired the title of Colonel; named Groom of the Bedchamber to the Duke of York following the Restoration of 1660. Appointed in April 1664 as head of a military expedition to New Netherlands, which Charles II hoped to take from the Dutch; accepted the surrender of the Dutch outpost of New Amsterdam late in August 1664, and became the first English Deputy Governor of New York, serving under the Duke of York. Acted as chief executive of New Jersey from September 1664 until August 1665, when Philip Carteret arrived in that colony with his commission to govern.

Although Nicolls had arrived in America as head of a commission assigned to investigate affairs in New England, the arduous task of transforming New Netherlands into an English colony prevented him from devoting much attention to the commission's duties. In New York, however, Nicolls pursued an active administration, highlighted by his drafting and implementation of the "Duke's Laws." This legal code, despite omitting provisions for the elective assembly and town meetings which were customary in New England, did guarantee a degree of religious toleration unknown in most of the colonies to the north. Nicolls' religious policy, intended chiefly as a means of persuading the Dutch inhabitants of New York to accept the new English regime, was accompanied by other concessions, especially the deputy governor's decision to permit some of the local political practices established by the Dutch to remain undisturbed. Still, there were some protests against the Nicolls administration. On Long Island, for example, transplanted New Englanders asserted that the absence of a representative assembly in New York deprived them of a meaningful voice in government.

Nicolls resigned his position in August 1668 and returned to England, where he again served as the Duke of York's Groom of the Bedchamber. When the Third Dutch War broke out in 1672, Nicolls decided to join the English fleet, and was killed at the Battle of Southwold Bay on May 28, 1672. He was buried in Ampthill Church in Bedfordshire.

Bibliography: Edward Holland Nicol, "Biography of Colonel Richard Nicolls, Deputy Governor of New York, etc." *New York Genealogical and Biographical Record*, XV (July 1884), 103-05; Montgomery Schuyler, *Richard Nicolls: First Governor of New York, 1664-1668* (New York, 1933); Kenneth Scott and Charles E. Baker, "Renewals of Governor Nicolls' Treaty of 1665 with the Esopus Indians," *New-York Historical Society Quarterly*, XXXVII (July 1953), 251-72. *DAB, DNB*.

CARTERET, Philip, 1665-1672, 1674-1676 *(as Deputy Governor of New Jersey), 1676-1680, 1681-1682 (as Deputy Governor of East Jersey)*

Born in 1639 on the Island of Jersey, the son of Helier de Carteret and Rachel (La Cloche) Carteret; also a fourth cousin of Sir George Carteret who, with John Lord Berkeley, was awarded the colony of New Jersey by the Duke of York in 1664. Brother of Peter (Governor of Albemarle County from 1670 to 1672). Married to Elizabeth (Smith) Lawrence in April 1681; no children. Commissioned as Deputy Governor of New Jersey in February 1665, and arrived in the colony in August of that year.

Carteret's long tenure as deputy governor encompassed a period of turmoil which was perhaps without precedent in New Jersey's colonial history. During his first years in office, Carteret encouraged immigration, chartered towns, approved land purchases, and organized a general assembly, but by the early 1670's complaints over the collection of quitrents and other issues had made his authority less certain. In 1672 a rebellion took place, in which deputies meeting in Elizabethtown chose Captain James Carteret, the son of Sir George, as "president of the province." In response, Philip Carteret appointed Captain John Berry as acting deputy governor, and in July 1672 departed for England, where he successfully defended his right to office and refuted the charges which had been made against him. In 1673, however, the Dutch took control of New Jersey as part of their conquest of New York, and until 1674 both colonies were governed first by a Council of War and then by the Dutch Governor Anthony Colve. After New Jersey was restored to England, Carteret returned to assert his authority in November 1674. Between 1676, when the colony was partitioned into East and West Jersey, and early 1681, Governor Sir Edmund Andros of New York attempted to extend his jurisdiction over the Jerseys; this led Carteret, in turn, to claim that Andros' activities were aimed at "usurping the government'' of his colony. Although Andros had successfully established his control over East Jersey by 1680, he was soon recalled to England, and Carteret resumed his position as chief executive. He served in that capacity until he relinquished the office to Thomas Rudyard in November 1682. Carteret died a month later, in December 1682.

Bibliography: Catharina Romana Baetjer, *Carteret and Bryant Genealogy* (New York, 1887); Willis Fletcher Johnson, "The Story of the Carterets," New Jersey Historical Society, *Proceedings*, n.s., vol. IX (October 1924), 328-33. *DAB*.

BERRY, John, 1672-1673

Date and place of birth, and names of parents unknown. Married to a woman named Francina, by whom he was the father of Sarah, Richard, Francina, Hannah, John (?) and perhaps others. Came from Barbados to New Jersey in the late 1660's, where he acquired extensive property above the New Barbados land tract, in what was then part of Newark Township; also owned land north of Hoboken, in Bergen Township.

First appointed to the Governor's Council in 1669 by Philip Carteret, and remained a member, with several intervals, until at least 1688. While a member of the Council, chosen in July 1672 as Acting Deputy Governor of New Jersey, to serve during Philip Carteret's absence in England.

Following Carteret's departure, Berry and the Council received a series of instructions from New Jersey's Proprietors, suggesting methods of settling the disputes over land grants and quitrents which had caused considerable turmoil in the colony. In political terms, these instructions reduced the authority of the Assembly, and placed greater power in the hands of the governor and his Council. The governor and Council, for example, were now permitted to make land allotments without consulting the Lower House. Berry and the Council also took steps to punish those colonists who had supported the claims of Captain James Carteret, the illegally-elected "president of the province," with the acting deputy governor ordering that participants in the rebellion should appear before him and submit to his authority. In the summer of 1673, however, Berry was stripped of his office by an unexpected source, when the Dutch took New Jersey in the course of their conquest of New York.

Berry resumed his membership on the Council after New Jersey was restored to English rule in 1674. He was also prominent in a judicial capacity; during the 1670's and 1680's he held office at various times as Justice of the Peace of the Quorum, Justice of the Court of Common Right, and Justice of the Court of Sessions for the County of Bergen. Finally, Berry was empowered to act as William Penn's agent in East Jersey when Penn became one of that colony's twenty-four Proprietors in 1682. Although he was again suggested as a possible appointee to the Council in 1702, Berry apparently was not selected. He died early in 1715.

Bibliography: Thomas Henry Edsall, "Deputy Governor John Berry, of New Jersey, and His Family," *New York Genealogical and Biographical Record*, XV (April 1884), 49-57.

ANDROS, Sir Edmund, 1680-1681, 1688-1689 *(as governor of East Jersey), 1688-1689 (as governor of West Jersey); New York, 1674-1677, 1678-1681; Massachusetts, 1686-1689; New Hampshire, 1686-1689; Plymouth Colony, 1686-1689; Rhode Island, 1686-1689; Connecticut, 1687-1689; Virginia, 1692-1698; Maryland, 1693, 1694*

Born on December 6, 1637 on the Island of Guernsey, the son of Amice and Elizabeth (Stone) Andros. Married to a woman who was related to the Earl of Craven.

Served as Major of a regiment of foot soldiers which in 1666 sailed from England to defend the West Indies against the Dutch. Named a Landgrave of Carolina in 1672; received a commission from the Duke of York in July 1674 to govern the colony of New York, and acted in that capacity, except for an absence in England between November 1677 and August 1678, until January 1681; also exercised control over East Jersey from 1680 until his recall early in the following year. Knighted in about 1681, became Gentleman of the Privy Chamber to Charles II in 1683, and was appointed Lieutenant Colonel of the Princess of Denmark's regiment of horse soldiers in 1685. Commissioned Royal Governor of the Dominion of New England in June 1686, and established his authority in Massachusetts Bay, Maine, New Hampshire, Plymouth and Rhode Island (including the King's Province) in December of that year; Connecticut in November of 1687; and the Jerseys and New York in August 1688 (although Francis Nicholson presided as Andros' substitute in the latter colony). Arrested and sent to England following the overthrow of the Dominion in the spring of 1689, but later received a commission as Royal Governor of Virginia, and served as that colony's chief executive from September 1692 to December 1698; also acted briefly as Governor of Maryland in 1693 and 1694, in the absence of any other executive authority.

Andros' first tenure in New York was marked by several important achievements, especially the improvement of the colony's defenses and the settlement of some boundary difficulties with Connecticut. Nevertheless, even at this stage he had begun to display an inclination to behave in an arbitrary fashion. Perhaps the clearest illustration of this tendency was the high-handed manner in which Andros superseded the authority of Governor Philip Carteret in the

Jerseys, provoking Carteret to complain that Andros aimed at ''usurping the government'' of his colony. This insensitivity to local politics became even more noticeable after Andros assumed control of the Dominion of New England. Following a troubled tenure of less than two and one-half years, he was deposed in the spring of 1689, shortly after news of the Glorious Revolution in England reached Boston.

Although Andros was exonerated of the charges brought against his Dominion government and took over as Virginia's chief executive in 1692, he soon encountered resistance from local leaders like Commissary James Blair, who bitterly informed one London official that Andros ''never did any considerable service to the King, nor the people'' during his colonial career. Finally, late in 1698, Andros departed for England. He served as Lieutenant Governor of Guernsey from 1704 to 1706, and died in London in February 1714.

Bibliography: ''Commission to Sir Edmund Andros,'' Massachusetts Historical Society, *Collections*, 3rd ser., vol. VII (Boston, 1838), 138-49; W. H. Whitmore, ed., *Andros Tracts: Being a Collection of Pamphlets and Official Papers . . . of the Andros Government and the Establishment of the Second Charter of Massachusetts*, 3 vols. (New York, 1868-74) (Publications of the Prince Society, vols. V-VII); Robert N. Toppan, ed., ''Andros Records,'' American Antiquarian Society, *Proceedings*, n.s., vol. XIII (1899-1900), 237-68, 463-99; J.H. Tuttle, ed., ''Land Warrants under Andros,'' Colonial Society of Massachusetts, *Publications*, XXI (1919), 292-361; Albert C. Bates, ''Expedition of Sir Edmund Andros to Connecticut in 1687,'' AAS, *Proceedings*, n.s., vol. 48 (October 1938), 276-99; Jeanne G. Bloom, ''Sir Edmund Andros: A Study in Seventeenth-Century Colonial Administration,'' unpub. Ph.D. diss., Yale University, 1962; Robert C. Ritchie, ''London Merchants, the New York Market, and the Recall of Sir Edmund Andros,'' *New York History*, LVII (January 1976), 5-29. *DAB, DNB*.

JENNINGS [or JENINGS], Samuel, 1681-1684 *(as Deputy Governor of West Jersey)*

Born in England; date of birth and names of parents unknown. A Quaker. Married on November 7, 1672 to Ann Ollive, by whom he was the father of William, Sarah, Joyce, Ann, Elizabeth (died young) and Mercy. Purchased a one-quarter share in the West Jersey proprietary during the early years of the colony, and in 1685 acquired 2,000 acres of land in Salem County. Immigrated to America from Cole's Hill in Buckinghamshire after his appointment by Edward Byllynge as Deputy Governor of West Jersey in the summer of 1680; arrived in the colony in September 1680, but did not assume office as deputy governor until more than a year later, due to local opposition to Byllynge. In the meantime, became in March 1681 a member of the Board of Commissioners which had been assigned the task of governing the province.

Before he was accepted by West Jersey's colonists as their deputy governor, Jennings was required to agree to certain "fundamental propositions," the purpose of which was to guarantee that political power would remain in the hands of the people and their elected representatives. Jennings accepted these terms in November 1681, and over the next eighteen months illustrated his sympathy for the colonists' position by ratifying acts passed by the Assembly without obtaining the approval of Byllynge who, as chief proprietor, was legally entitled to review West Jersey's legislation. By the spring of 1683, however, it was rumored that Byllynge intended to come to West Jersey to administer the colony in person, and in an attempt to forestall the anticipated seizure of the government by the proprietor, the Assembly which met that May elected Jennings as governor. This election, which constituted a usurpation of power by the Assembly, created much controversy, as Byllynge's friends in the province defended his right to govern. In the spring of 1684 Jennings sought a solution to the matter by departing for England, where he hoped to negotiate with Byllynge directly. Thomas Olive, the Speaker of the Assembly, was chosen to act as deputy governor during Jennings' absence.

Following his period as chief executive of West Jersey, Jennings continued to play a prominent role in politics. In September of 1688 he was chosen to the West Jersey Council of Proprietors which dealt with Sir Edmund Andros, the new governor. After residing in Philadelphia early in the 1690's, where he became a member of that province's Council and a Justice of the County Court, Jennings returned to West Jersey and was restored to the Council of Proprietors in 1695. He was frequently elected to the West Jersey Assembly, and in May 1697 and again in December 1699, he was chosen as that body's Speaker. As the leader of a powerful Quaker faction, Jennings opposed Deputy Governor Jeremiah Basse in 1698 and 1699; in 1702 he was appointed to New Jersey's first Council under the royal government which was established in that year. Jennings became Speaker of the New Jersey Assembly in 1707, a position which he used to oppose Lord Cornbury, the colony's royal governor. Jennings died in 1708.

Bibliography: [John Tatham, Thomas Revell and Nathaniel Westland], *The Case Put and Decided by George Fox, George Whitehead, Stephen Crisp, and other of the most Antient & Eminent Quakers between Edward Billing on the one part, and some West-Jersians, headed by Samuell Jenings on the other Part, in an Award* . . . (Philadelphia, 1699); Samuel Jenings, *Truth Rescued from Forgery and Falsehood, Being an Answer to a late Scurrilous piece Entituled The Case Put and Decided &c Which Stole in the World without any known Authors name affixed thereto* . . . (Philadelphia, 1699); William Henry Jennings, *A Genealogical History of the Jennings Families in England and America*, vol. 2 (Columbus, Ohio, 1899).

RUDYARD, Thomas, 1682-1684 *(as Deputy Governor of East Jersey)*

Born *circa* 1642 in North Staffordshire, England, probably the son of Anthony Rudyard of Delacres Abbey. A Quaker, but may have left the Society of Friends shortly after arriving in East Jersey. Brother of Ralph and perhaps others. Married, and the father of Anne, Margaret, Benjamin and apparently a natural son named John. Practiced law in London, numbering William Penn among his clients.

Joined Penn and other noted Quakers on missionary trips to the Continent in 1671 and 1677. Played a prominent role in Quaker activities throughout the 1670's, and in 1676 was appointed, with William Meade, to gather information on Friends who had suffered persecution in Durham and Northumberland; also worked with James Claypoole on a project which reported Quaker developments in Staffordshire and Derbyshire. Became one of the twenty-four Proprietors of East Jersey in 1682; also became a Proprietor of the colony of West Jersey, and a "First Purchaser" of Pennsylvania. Appointed Deputy Governor of East Jersey in September 1682, arriving in the colony to assume office that November.

Rudyard's brief tenure as deputy governor was complicated by his disputes with Samuel Groom, the province's Surveyor General, over the appropriate method of distributing lands in East Jersey. The Rudyard administration was also marked by a growing cleavage between the Governor's Council and the deputies in the Assembly, a development which was becoming a serious source of political unrest. In the summer of 1683 the East Jersey Proprietors, who sided with Groom on the question of land policy and deplored the deputy governor's inability to end the wrangling between the Council and the Assembly, finally decided to replace Rudyard with Gawen Lawrie.

After Lawrie arrived in January 1684 to take over as chief executive, Rudyard remained in East Jersey for almost two years, where he served as Secretary and as Secretary-Register. In November 1685, still disturbed by a recent censure from the Proprietors over his land policy while governor, Rudyard embarked for Barbados, where he died in 1692.

Bibliography: Alfred W. Braithwaite, *Thomas Rudyard: Early Friends' "Oracle of Law"* (London, 1956) (supplement no. 27 to the Friends Historical Society, *Journal*).

OLIVE [or OLLIVE], Thomas, 1684-1685 *(as Deputy Governor of West Jersey)*

Date and place of birth, and names of parents unknown. A Quaker. Married to a woman named Mary, who survived him. Employed as a haberdasher in

Wellingborough, Northamptonshire, before his immigration to America. Owned, together with Dr. Daniel Wills and William Biddle, three proprietary shares in West Jersey.

Served as one of nine commissioners in charge of the expedition which settled in West Jersey in 1677; continued as a member of the Board of Commissioners until 1681, when Samuel Jennings took over as deputy governor of the province. Chosen Speaker of West Jersey's first General Assembly, which met in November 1681; also named to the Governor's Council in May 1682. After the departure of Jennings for England in the spring of 1684, chosen as West Jersey's Deputy Governor, to serve during Jennings' absence.

The most significant political development during Olive's brief administration was the decision in October 1684 by a group of arbitrators in London that Edward Byllynge, West Jersey's Chief Proprietor, had been deprived of the government of the province without his consent, and that the Assembly's election of Samuel Jennings as governor in May 1683 had been "worthy of blame in Jennings and all persons connected therein." While Olive served in the capacity of a caretaker in West Jersey, Jennings remained in England for a number of months after the judgement was announced, endeavoring to overturn the verdict. He was unsuccessful, however, and when John Skene, Byllynge's appointment as the new deputy governor, presented his commission in November 1685, Olive was forced to step down in his favor.

Following his tenure as deputy governor, Olive remained in politics. In September 1688 he was chosen President of the resident Council of Proprietors which was established that month, and in May 1689 he was re-elected to the post. Olive was also a prominent member of the Society of Friends in West Jersey; in 1687, for example, he represented Burlington Quarterly Meeting at the yearly meeting held in Philadelphia. Olive died in 1693.

LAWRIE, Gawen, 1684-1686 *(as Deputy Governor of East Jersey)*

Date of birth and names of parents unknown, though he was from Hertfordshire and apparently of Scottish ancestry. A Quaker until just before his death. Brother of Arthur, Christian and Agnes. Married to a woman named Mary, by whom he was the father of James, Mary and Rebecca. Became a London merchant.

Served from 1675 to 1683 as a Trustee of Edward Byllynge, West Jersey's bankrupt Chief Proprietor; in that capacity, was instrumental in the founding of the Quaker settlement at Burlington, West Jersey in 1677. In 1682 named a Trustee of the East Jersey Proprietary purchased by Arent Sonmans. Commissioned Deputy Governor of East Jersey in July 1683, and arrived in the colony in January 1684, settling in Elizabethtown.

Before his departure for East Jersey, Lawrie was given a detailed set of instructions for governing the colony according to the wishes of its Proprietors, and throughout his period in office he received further directives. Nevertheless, despite this attempt by the Proprietors to exert meaningful control over the East Jersey government, Lawrie often acted on his own initiative. Perhaps the most serious problem faced by the deputy governor during his administration was his difficulty in collecting the quitrents and proceeds from land sales due to the Proprietors. Since Lawrie was also Receiver General for the colony, these matters were his direct responsibility, and he spent much of his time from late 1684 until 1686 in an attempt to negotiate acceptable settlements with East Jersey's towns. As a result of his preoccupation with these issues, no Assembly was convened in the colony until April 1686. Less than six months later the Proprietors, who objected to Lawrie's abuse of their land regulations, his failure to keep them informed of developments in the colony, and his inability to persuade the colonists to accept a legal code called the "Fundamental Constitutions," decided to replace him with Lord Neil Campbell.

After his removal as deputy governor, Lawrie remained a member of the Governor's Council. He died in Elizabethtown, East Jersey in 1687.

Bibliography: "Propositions of Gawen Lawrie for the Settlement of East Jersey, 1682," New Jersey Historical Society, *Proceedings*, n.s., vol. VI (1921), 227-33; John E. Pomfret, "The Apologia of Governor Lawrie of East Jersey, 1686," *William and Mary Quarterly*, 3rd ser., vol. XIV (July 1957), 344-57. Also see Lawrie's "Brief Account of the Severall treaties between the Governour of East New Jersey and the Inhabitants thereof . . . ," in New Jersey Historical Society, *Proceedings*, LXXV (April 1957), 98-111 (edited by John E. Pomfret).

SKENE, John, 1685-1688, 1689-1690 [1691?] (*as Deputy Governor of West Jersey*)

Born *circa* 1649 in Scotland, the son of Alexander, an Aberdeen magistrate, and Lilias (Gillespie) Skene. A Quaker. Brother of Robert (died young), Lilias, Alexander (died young), Cristen, Rachel (died young), Patrick, Anna, Jean and Elizabeth. Married to Helena Fullerton, by whom he had at least one daughter.

Purchased 250 acres of land in West Jersey from Edward Byllynge, the colony's Chief Proprietor, in June 1682; bought another 300 acres in November of that year.

Elected to the West Jersey Assembly in the spring of 1683, and appointed to the Council in May 1683, but "divested of his office," apparently for opposing the choice of Samuel Jennings as deputy governor. Named a Land Commissioner for West Jersey about the same time. Commissioned as Deputy Governor of West Jersey by Edward Byllynge, and assumed office in November of 1685; also purchased a proprietary interest in West Jersey from Thomas Hutchinson of Talbot County, Maryland in September 1686.

Skene's tenure as deputy governor covered approximately five years of West Jersey's proprietary history, interrupted only by Sir Edmund Andros' brief period as chief executive of the colony. One of the most pressing issues faced by Skene was the problem of ascertaining the boundary lines separating West Jersey from both East Jersey and New York, and in June 1686 he met with the deputy governors of these neighboring colonies in an attempt to arrive at a settlement. Although East and West Jersey managed to come to terms early in 1687, confusion over their agreement persisted for decades.

When Andros established royal control over West Jersey in August 1688, Skene relinquished his post as deputy governor. However, he did serve as a Justice of the Burlington Court, and Edward Randolph, Andros' secretary and register, acknowledged Skene's importance in the province by entrusting him with various commissions. In the spring of 1689 the Andros regime ended, after news of the overthrow of James II reached the American colonies, and Skene returned as deputy governor, an office which he seems to have filled until his death in 1690 or 1691. Skene also acted in a judicial capacity following the demise of Andros. In November 1689, for example, he presided as a Judge of both the Quarter Sessions and the Court of Common Pleas which were held that month in Burlington.

Bibliography: William Forbes Skene, ed., *Memorials of the Family of Skene of Skene* (Aberdeen, 1887).

CAMPBELL, Lord Neil, 1686-1687 *(as Deputy Governor of East Jersey)*

Date and place of birth unknown; the son of Archibald Campbell, eighth Earl and first Marquess of Argyll, and Lady Margaret Douglas. Brother of Jane, Mary and Archibald, ninth Earl of Argyll, who was executed in 1685 for participating in Monmouth's rebellion against James II. Married to Lady Vere Ker, the third daughter of the third Earl of Lothian; father of at least two sons, including Archibald, who later became bishop of Aberdeen.

Purchased a quarter share in East Jersey from George Mackenzie, Earl of Cromarty; also became joint owner (with Robert Blackwood) of a half-share purchased from William Dockwra. Ordered to remain in the Edinburgh area because of his suspicious family connections, but received permission to immigrate to East Jersey; arrived in the colony in 1686 with a retinue of fifty-two indentured servants and followers, and in the autumn of that year became East Jersey's Deputy Governor.

Although he could not persuade the Assembly to accept his proposals for raising revenue, Campbell continued to take an active part in the political affairs of East Jersey during his brief period as deputy governor. Perhaps the most significant issue with which he concerned himself was the question of East Jersey's boundaries. Late in 1686 Campbell met with officials from New York and West Jersey, in an effort to resolve disputes with those two neighbors over the territorial limits of East Jersey. A short time later, however, Campbell announced that personal affairs required his immediate departure for Scotland, and in February 1687 he left the colony, after naming Andrew Hamilton as his interim replacement. Campbell never returned to East Jersey; he died in 1693.

Bibliography: Rev. Hely Smith, *The MacCallum More: A History of the Argyll Family from the Earliest Times* (London, 1871).

HAMILTON, Andrew, 1687-1688, 1689-1698, 1699-1703 *(as Deputy Governor of East Jersey), 1692-1698, 1699-1703 (as Deputy Governor of West Jersey), 1701-1703 (as Lieutenant Governor of Pennsylvania and the Lower Counties)*

Date and place of birth, and names of parents unknown. An Anglican. Married three times, his second wife being Anne (Rudyard) Wharton, the daughter of Deputy Governor Thomas Rudyard of East Jersey, and his third spouse a woman named Agnes; father of John (by his first wife) and perhaps others. Became an Edinburgh merchant as a young man.

Acquired a one-twentieth share in East Jersey from Sir John Gordon of Durno in 1683. Appointed in March 1686 by the East Jersey Proprietors to conduct an inquiry into the colony's administration, especially in the areas of quitrent collection and land sales. As a member of the East Jersey Council, chosen early in 1687 to succeed on an interim basis the departing deputy governor, Lord Neil Campbell, and in August 1687 assumed that office in his own right. Served also as Deputy Governor of West Jersey between 1692-98 and 1699-1703, and as Lieutenant Governor of Pennsylvania and the Lower Counties from November 1701 until 1703.

With the exception of two brief interludes—the Andros regime of 1688-89 and the Basse-Bowne administration of 1698-99—Hamilton was East Jersey's deputy governor throughout the remainder of the proprietary period. His early years in East Jersey were disrupted by economic problems and the seizure of the government by Sir Edmund Andros, a combination of circumstances which apparently persuaded Hamilton to leave the colony. He sailed for England in June 1690 and remained there until 1692, leaving East Jersey with no regular government for over two years. When he returned in September of 1692, however, his authority had been enhanced by the decision of both East and

West Jersey's Proprietors to appoint him chief executive, and for the next decade he fought a skillful but ultimately unsuccessful battle to enforce proprietary rule. Hamilton's inability to govern effectively in the Jerseys was due more to the confused circumstances in which he found himself, rather than to any major deficiency on his part. The chronic disputes over land titles and quitrent collections remained unresolved, and when the Proprietors of East and West Jersey finally surrendered their political authority to the Crown in April 1702, the decision was a predictable response to the growing anti-proprietary movement which had complicated the last two years of Hamilton's administration. Hamilton's service in Pennsylvania and the Lower Counties from November 1701 until his death was likewise troubled by political unrest, as Anglican legislators and court officials periodically attempted to obstruct governmental functions in order to dramatize what they perceived to be a need for royal control in Pennsylvania. During his tenure as governor, Hamilton maintained an interest in the postal system of the American colonies, and he acted as Deputy Postmaster General for a number of years before his death in Perth Amboy, New Jersey on April 26, 1703. *DAB*.

BASSE, Jeremiah, 1698-1699, 1699 *(as Deputy Governor of East and West Jersey)*

Date and place of birth, and names of parents unknown. Served as an Anabaptist minister as a young man, although later in life he joined a group of militant Anglicans. Married, and the father of Burchfield, Katherine and Ann.

In 1692 became both Agent for Dr. Daniel Coxe, West Jersey's Chief Proprietor, and Factor for the West Jersey Society, a group of investors which had acquired an interest in that colony. Commissioned Deputy Governor of East and West Jersey in July 1697, but did not assume office until April 1698; appointed about the same time Surveyor General for the West Jersey Society.

Basse's short tenure as governor of East and West Jersey was disrupted from the start by factionalism between proprietary and anti-proprietary forces within the colony. Basse himself contributed to the unrest by tactlessly appointing his friends to the Council in West Jersey, and by antagonizing many of East Jersey's key political leaders, including Lewis Morris, whom he dismissed from the Council. Shortly after Basse returned in July 1699 from a visit to England, where he had gone to represent his interests in a legal case, the colony's proprietors replaced him as chief executive with former Deputy Governor Andrew Hamilton.

Following New Jersey's transformation into a royal colony in 1702, Basse became part of the notorious "Cornbury Ring," and served as Secretary of the province until his removal by Governor Robert Hunter. Under Cornbury,

Basse also acted briefly as New Jersey's Treasurer. He was later elected to the Assembly as a representative from Cape May County in 1716, and in 1719 he was appointed New Jersey's Attorney General by Governor Hunter, with whom he had by then made peace. Basse died in 1725. He was the author of a history of St. Mary's Anglican Church in Burlington, New Jersey. *DAB*.

BOWNE, Andrew, 1699 *(as Acting Governor of East and West Jersey)*

Born in 1638 in Salem, Massachusetts, the son of William and Ann Bowne. Brother of John, James, Philip and several sisters. Married to a woman named Elizabeth, by whom he was the father of Elizabeth and perhaps others.

Became a merchant in New York City. As a resident of New York, chosen as an Admiralty Judge in 1683 and an Alderman in 1685. Moved to East Jersey after acting as an administrator of his uncle's estate, and eventually settled in Middletown, where he served in the Sessions Court. Elected to the Governor's Council in 1692 and, except for a brief interval, remained a member until his death. Chosen Acting Governor of East and West Jersey in May 1699 to replace Jeremiah Basse, who was leaving on a trip to England, and served in that capacity until July 1699.

Almost immediately upon assuming office, Bowne was forced to contend with widespread discontent in the colony over a revenue act passed in March 1699. Although the harried acting governor suggested that he and the Council were prepared to consider any reasonable amendment, the act's opponents, led by men like Lewis Morris, refused to accept a compromise. As a result, the session of the Assembly which convened in mid-May adjourned after only a few days, and Bowne was unable to accomplish anything of importance during the remainder of his short tenure.

After Basse's return in the latter part of July 1699, Bowne resumed his seat on the Council. In 1701 he and Andrew Hamilton, who had replaced Basse as deputy governor late in 1699, engaged in a dispute over a proprietary commission produced by Bowne which authorized him to govern East Jersey. Hamilton rejected the commission, claiming that it contained too few signatures to be valid, and refused to relinquish his office to Bowne. Following the transformation of New Jersey into a royal colony in 1702, Bowne again sat on the Council. He also served for a brief time as a Supreme Court Justice before his death, sometime between May 1707, when his will was dated, and 1708, when it was proved.

Bibliography: Alethia Hunt Weatherby, ''Some Colonial Families: Bowne of New Jersey,'' *American Historical Register*, III (September 1895), 37-42; Miller K. Reading, *William Bowne, of Yorkshire, England, and His Descendants* (Flemington, N.J., 1903).

MORRIS, Lewis, 1703, 1719-1720, 1731-1732, 1738-1746

Born on October 15, 1671 on "Bronck's land" (later part of Bronx County), New York, the son of Richard, a soldier in Cromwell's army and a merchant, and Sarah (Pole) Morris; no brothers nor sisters. Member of the Church of England and vestryman of Trinity Church in New York from 1697 to 1700. Married on November 3, 1691 to Isabella Graham; father of Lewis, Robert Hunter, John, James, Isabella, Sarah, Mary, Euphemia, Anne, Elizabeth, Margaret and Arabella. Raised by an uncle, Lewis Morris, after the death of his father in 1672. Studied under Hugh Coppothwaite, a Quaker tutor, and travelled in Virginia and Jamaica. Settled in "Tintern" (later Tinton), New Jersey in 1691. Became First Lord of the Manor of Morrisania in 1697.

Appointed to the East Jersey Court of Common Right in 1692 and to Governor Andrew Hamilton's Council the following year. Dismissed from the Council by Governor Jeremiah Basse in 1698; reappointed by Governor Hamilton in 1700 and served, with several intervals, until 1733. Elected to the New Jersey Assembly from Perth Amboy in 1699; in 1707 played a major role in formulating the Assembly's complaint to Queen Anne concerning the conduct of the royal governor, Lord Cornbury. Also acted as the London agent of the East Jersey Board of Proprietors in 1701-02. Chosen to represent Westchester in the New York Assembly from 1711 to 1727; elected to the New York Assembly from Eastchester in 1733. Served as Chief Justice of the province of New York from 1715 to 1733. Resided in England in 1735 and 1736 as the representative of factional opposition to New York Governor William Cosby.

Morris's brief periods as interim chief executive of New Jersey spanned three decades, during which the colony struggled to free itself from the influence of New York, whose royal governors also exercised authority over New Jersey from 1703 to 1738. As President of the New Jersey Council and Acting Governor in 1703, 1719-20 and 1731-32, Morris was a proponent of political autonomy for the colony. Ironically, after that autonomy had been achieved with his commission as Governor-in-Chief and Captain General of New Jersey in March 1738, Morris was accused by his opponents of subserviency to the British Crown, and his tenure was marked by considerable hostility between the governor and the Assembly over land and money matters.

Morris died at Kingsbury Farm, near Trenton, New Jersey on May 21, 1746, while still in office. He was buried at Morrisania, in New York.

Bibliography: Robert Davidson, "Memoir of Lewis Morris, Governor of New Jersey from 1738 to 1746," New Jersey Historical Society, *Proceedings*, 1st ser., vol. IV (1849), 19-32; *The Papers of Lewis Morris, Governor of the Province of New Jersey from 1738 to 1746*, in New Jersey Historical Society, *Collections*, IV (Newark, 1852); E. M. W. Lefferts, comp., *Descendants of*

Lewis Morris of Morrisania . . . (New York, 1907?); Charles W. Parker, "Lewis Morris, First Colonial Governor of New Jersey," New Jersey Historical Society, *Proceedings*, n.s., vol. XIII (July 1928), 273-82; Gordon B. Turner, "Governor Lewis Morris and the Colonial Government Conflict," New Jersey Historical Society, *Proceedings*, LXVII (October 1949), 260-304; Maureen McGuire, "Struggle over the Purse: Governor Morris versus the New Jersey Assembly," New Jersey Historical Society, *Proceedings*, LXXXII (July 1964), 200-07; Stanley N. Katz, "A New York Mission to England: The London Letters of Lewis Morris to James Alexander, 1735-1736," *William and Mary Quarterly*, 3rd ser., vol. XXVIII (July 1971), 438-84; Eugene R. Sheridan, "Politics in Colonial America: The Career of Lewis Morris, 1671-1746," unpub. Ph.D. diss., University of Wisconsin, 1972; Carol A. Hyland, "Lewis Morris of New York and New Jersey (1671-1746): A Biography," unpub. Ph.D. diss., State University of New York at Buffalo, 1976; John R. Strassburger, "The Origins and Establishment of the Morris Family in the Society and Politics of New York and New Jersey, 1630-1746," unpub. Ph.D. diss., Princeton University, 1976. *DAB*.

HYDE, Edward (Viscount Cornbury), 1703-1708

also New York, 1702-1708

Born in 1661 in England, the eldest son of Henry Hyde, the second Earl of Clarendon, and his wife, the former Theodosia Capel. An Anglican. Married in 1688 to Katherine O'Brien; father of one son and two daughters.

Served as an officer in the British Army; acted as a member of Parliament for sixteen years. Commissioned Captain General and Governor-in-Chief of New York in September 1701, and arrived in America to take up his position in May of 1702; also commissioned Governor of New Jersey in December 1702, but only assumed office in that province in August of 1703.

In both New York and New Jersey, the Cornbury administration proved to be an almost complete failure, as corruption and venality grew more widespread. The governor himself encouraged the unscrupulous behavior which became the most conspicuous feature of his tenure, especially by approving land grants to his political favorites. Cornbury also displayed a lack of tact in dealing with the religiously heterogeneous population of New York. In 1707, for example, he denied a local preacher's license to Francis Makemie, a prominent Scottish Presbyterian. Makemie eventually stood trial and was vindicated, but the ill will which Cornbury had provoked was less easy to dismiss than the weak case brought against the Scottish minister. Cornbury's reputation was further damaged by his habit of dressing in women's formal attire, a peculiarity which one historian has attributed to the governor's wish to represent his cousin, Queen Anne, in a more vivid manner [*sic*]. Whatever Cornbury's motivation, the colonists in New York and New Jersey responded only with frequent expressions of contempt for their chief executive. Authorities in England finally admitted their error in 1708 when, yielding to protests from irate colonists like Lewis Morris, a leader of the New Jersey Assembly, they removed Cornbury in favor of John, Lord Lovelace.

Following his replacement in December of 1708, Cornbury returned to England, but not until his creditors in New York had delayed his departure by having him arrested for unpaid debts. Upon the death of his father, Cornbury inherited the title of Earl of Clarendon, and in 1711 he was made a member of the Privy Council. He also served as an Envoy Extraordinary to Hanover in 1714, nine years before his death on April 1, 1723.

Bibliography: John Sharp, *A Sermon [on Job xiv. 14] Preached . . . in New York . . . 1706, at the Funeral of . . . Katherine Lady Cornbury . . .* (New York, 1706); Charles Worthen Spencer, "The Cornbury Legend," New York State Historical Association, *Proceedings*, XIII (1914), 309-20; Arthur D. Pierce, "A Governor in Skirts [Cornbury]," New Jersey Historical Society, *Proceedings*, LXXXIII (January 1965), 1-9. *DAB*.

LOVELACE, John (4th Baron Lovelace of Hurley), 1708-1709

also New York, 1708-1709

Born in England, the son of William and Mary (King) Lovelace; date of birth unknown. Married on October 20, 1702 to Charlotte Clayton; father of John (died young), Nevil and Wentworth (died young).

Created fourth Baron Lovelace of Hurley in 1693; became a member of the House of Lords in November of 1693. Named Colonel of a regiment of troops in January 1706. Commissioned Captain General and Governor-in-Chief of New York and New Jersey in May 1708, and arrived to take up his new assignment in December of that year.

Accompanying Lord Lovelace to New York in 1708 was a large group of Palatines, who were seeking refuge from religious persecution in the Rhineland. This encouragement of full-scale emigration, along with Lovelace's willingness to attend sessions of the New Jersey Council on a regular basis, suggests that he intended to carry on an active administration in both colonies. At the same time, there were indications that Lovelace hoped to break up the notorious Cornbury Ring, which had controlled politics in New Jersey during the tenure of his predecessor. In April of 1709, for example, Lovelace appointed Thomas Gordon as New Jersey's chief justice in place of Roger Mompesson, one of the more prominent members of the Cornbury group, who had resigned under fire. Lovelace's sudden death from apoplexy on May 6, 1709, however, put an end to any expectations that he would eliminate the political corruption which had marked Cornbury's years in office. Lovelace was buried in New York.

Bibliography: William Vesey, *A Sermon Preached in Trinity Church in New York, in America, May 12, 1709, at the Funeral of the Right Honourable John Lord Lovelace . . .*, New-York Historical Society, *Collections*, XIII (New York, 1881), 321-38; James Grant Wilson, "Lord Lovelace and the Second Canadian Campaign—1708-1710," American Historical Association, *Annual Report for the Year 1891* (Washington, D.C., 1892), 269-97. *DNB*.

INGOLDESBY, Richard, 1709-1710

also New York, 1691-1692, 1709-1710

Born in England; date of birth and names of parents unknown. Married; father of Mary and probably others.

With the rank of Major, commanded a company of British troops in January 1691, and served as Acting Governor of New York after the suppression of Leisler's Rebellion; eventually obtained the military title of Colonel. As Commander-in-Chief of New York, conducted a conference with the Five Nations of Indians in June 1692. Sailed for England in 1696 and remained until 1704, apparently in an attempt to win the governorship of New York. Returned to New York in March 1704, bringing with him a commission as Lieutenant Governor of both New York and New Jersey. Clashed on several occasions with Governor Cornbury of New York and New Jersey, who in 1706 requested Ingoldesby's removal as lieutenant governor of New York, and his appointment instead to the New Jersey Council. Following the death of Governor John, Lord Lovelace in May 1709, assumed office as chief executive of New York and New Jersey, serving in that capacity until April of 1710.

Ingoldesby's first interim governorship of New York only lasted from July 1691 to August of 1692, between the sudden death of Governor Henry Sloughter and the arrival from England of Governor Benjamin Fletcher. His selection as chief executive by that colony's Council signified the triumph of the anti-Leislerian faction in New York, whom Ingoldesby had helped to achieve power by deploying the troops at his command against Jacob Leisler and his supporters. Almost two decades later Ingoldesby's brief administration in New York and New Jersey was disrupted by confusion over his right to govern both provinces. Although the Board of Trade had prepared a warrant directing his removal as lieutenant governor of New York as early as April of 1706, no ruling had been made at that time affecting his credentials in New Jersey. Indeed, no record even existed to prove that Queen Anne had signed the warrant revoking his New York commission. With Ingoldesby's legal status so unclear, officials in London were forced to reconsider the whole matter, and in October of 1709 the Queen permanently rescinded his New Jersey commission (his commission for New York having been annulled a month earlier). Yielding to this verdict, Ingoldesby gave up his executive authority in April 1710 to Gerardus Beekman and William Pinhorne, respectively presidents of the New York and New Jersey Councils. During his eleven months as chief executive, Ingoldesby took advantage of the position in New Jersey by confirming, with the backing of the old Cornbury Ring, the large New Britain land patent and numerous purchases of Indian land by white settlers. After his dismissal as lieutenant governor he appears to have left America and returned to England, where nothing is known of his subsequent career.

PINHORNE, William, 1710

Born *circa* 1650 in England; names of parents unknown. Married in 1678 to Mary Hailstone, by whom he was the father of at least four children, including John (who married a daughter of New Jersey's Lieutenant Governor Richard Ingoldesby), Elizabeth and Martha.

Arrived in New York not later than 1675, when he first appeared as Attorney of Record in the New York City Mayor's Court. Served as an Alderman in New York City from 1683 to 1684. Became Speaker of the New York Assembly in 1685; elected to the New Jersey Assembly in 1686, but did not attend the session. Appointed in 1691 to the New York Council under Governor Henry Sloughter and served, with one brief interval, until 1698; also acted as Recorder of New York City (1691-92), Justice of the provincial Supreme Court (1691-92, 1693-98), and Judge of the Court of Admiralty (1691-92, 1696-98). Moved to New Jersey in 1692, but in 1693 returned to New York. Suspended from his offices in 1698, after incurring the displeasure of the Leislerian faction in New York; again settled in New Jersey, where he was a member of the Governor's Council from 1699 to 1713, and Second Judge of the New Jersey Supreme Court from 1704 to 1708. Became a prominent member of the Cornbury Ring during the first years of the eighteenth century. In his capacity as President of the New Jersey Council, served as Acting Governor of that province between the resignation of Lieutenant Governor Richard Ingoldesby in April 1710 and the arrival of Governor Robert Hunter in June of that year.

Pinhorne's two months as New Jersey's interim chief executive marked the final period of control of that colony by the corrupt Cornbury Ring. Following the appearance of Governor Robert Hunter in June of 1710, the movement to break up the Ring gained in momentum, and in the spring of 1711 the new royal governor felt secure enough to recommend Pinhorne's dismissal from the New Jersey Council. Two years later Queen Anne finally approved Hunter's request. Until his death in late 1719 or early 1720, Pinhorne remained a political outsider as Hunter, with the assistance of the Board of Trade, removed members of the Ring from office and replaced them with his own supporters.

HUNTER, Robert, 1710-1719

also New York, 1710-1719

Born in Hunterston, Ayrshire, Scotland, the son of James and Margaret (Spalding) Hunter; date of birth unknown. Married to Elizabeth (Orby) Hay; father of Thomas Orby, Katherine, Henrietta and Charlotte.

Entered the British Army as a young man, and fought with the troops of the Duke of Marlborough during the War of the Spanish Succession. Participated in the Battle of Blenheim in 1704, and a short time later rose to the rank of Lieutenant Colonel. Sailed for America in May 1707, after acquiring the lieutenant governorship of Virginia, but was captured by a privateer while at sea and transported to France. Released in an exchange of prisoners and returned to England, where in October of 1709 he was commissioned Captain General and Governor-in-Chief of New York and New Jersey; arrived in New York City in June 1710 to assume his new office.

Compared with the administrations of Cornbury, Lovelace and Ingoldesby, each of which had been tainted by corruption and venality, Hunter's tenure as chief executive represented a political change for the better. In New Jersey the new governor worked to dismantle the corrupt Cornbury Ring, and by the spring of 1711 he was ready to press for the removal of key members of that group from that colony's Council. New York politics also quickly felt the force of Hunter's energetic approach to government. During his early years in office Hunter battled with the New York Assembly over the issue of public credit, a battle which between 1715 and 1717 resulted in a series of compromises which assured the governor of tax revenues on a five-year basis, as long as he agreed to spend the money according to a program designed by the legislature and approved a naturalization bill endorsed by New York's Dutch residents. Guided by his own shrewd political instincts, Hunter's success in New York was aided by his friendship with Chief Justice Lewis Morris, who helped form a party which defended the "governor's interest." Still, by the end of Hunter's administration this group had already begun to encounter resistance from men like the wealthy merchant Peter Schuyler, thereby setting the stage for the factionalism which would influence New York and New Jersey politics for the rest of the colonial period.

In July 1719 Hunter returned to England and exchanged his governorship for the position of Comptroller General of Customs, then held by William Burnet. Hunter also served as Governor of Jamaica from 1727 until his death in March 1734. An occasional author and the friend of prominent literary figures like Jonathan Swift, Hunter's most famous work is the farce *Androboros*, which satirized New York politics.

Bibliography: Richard L. Beyer, "Robert Hunter, Royal Governor of New York," unpub. Ph.D. diss., University of Iowa, 1929; Lawrence H. Leder, ed., "Robert Hunter's *Androboros*," *Bulletin of the New York Public Library*,

LXVIII (March 1964), 153-90; James E. Scanlon, "A Life of Robert Hunter, 1666-1734," unpub. Ph.D. diss., University of Virginia, 1969; Alison G. Olson, "Governor Robert Hunter and the Anglican Church in New York," in Anne Whiteman *et al.*, eds., *Statesmen, Scholars and Merchants: Essays in Eighteenth-Century History Presented to Dame Lucy Sutherland* (Oxford, 1973), 44-64; James E. Scanlon, "British Intrigue and the Governorship of Robert Hunter," *New-York Historical Society Quarterly*, LVII (July 1973), 199-211. *DAB, DNB*.

BURNET, William, 1720-1728

also New York, 1720-1728; Massachusetts and New Hampshire, 1728-1729

Born in March 1688 at The Hague, the eldest son of Gilbert Burnet, bishop of Salisbury, and his second wife, Mary (Scott) Burnet. Brother of Mary and Gilbert. Married in about May 1712 to a daughter of Dean Stanhope, by whom he was the father of Gilbert; following the death of his first wife, remarried to Anna Maria [or Mary] Van Horne; father of William, Mary and Thomas by his second wife.

Enrolled at Trinity College, Cambridge at the age of thirteen, but left without obtaining a degree; later studied privately, and called to the bar. Commissioned Captain General and Governor-in-Chief of New York and New Jersey in June 1720, and arrived in America to assume office in September of that year. Commissioned Royal Governor of New Hampshire in November 1727, and of Massachusetts Bay in March 1728; left New York in the spring of 1728, following his replacement by the newly-appointed Governor John Montgomerie, and travelled to New England to take up his new positions.

As chief executive of New York, Burnet was confronted by controversy over the extensive fur trade then existing between Albany and Montreal. Contending that such commerce was enhancing New France's stature among Indians in the area, who sold their furs to the English through French *coureurs de bois*, Burnet tried to eliminate the traffic both by means of legislation and by encouraging direct trade between the English and various Indian tribes. Despite some initial success, however, Burnet's policy quickly encountered strong opposition from prominent New York merchants who preferred to conduct their business with the French, and by 1726 it had become apparent that his efforts would fail. In New Jersey Burnet met with similar recalcitrance among leading members of that colony's Assembly, especially over money bills. Nevertheless, after several confrontations with the Assembly, Burnet decided to adopt a more tactful approach, and by the time of his departure in 1728 he had won significant concessions from the legislators.

Although Burnet's tenure in Massachusetts Bay and New Hampshire lasted only a little more than a year, his administration of those colonies was also marked by disputes over financial matters. In particular, the question of the form which the governor's remuneration should take, a recurrent problem during much of the eighteenth century, created tension between Burnet and the Massachusetts Assembly, as Burnet insisted that he be given a permanent salary. On September 7, 1729, however, before the issue could be resolved, Burnet died suddenly in Boston.

Bibliography: William Nelson, *Original Documents Relating to the Life and Administrations of William Burnet*... (Paterson, N.J., 1897). Burnet's will appears in the *New England Historical and Genealogical Register*, XLVII (January 1893), 123-25. *DAB, DNB*.

MONTGOMERIE, John, 1728-1731

also New York, 1728-1731

Born in Scotland; date of birth and names of parents unknown. Apparently never married.

Served for a number of years in the British Army, and probably attained the rank of Colonel; also acted as Leicester House Groom of the Bed-Chamber for George II before that monarch's ascension to the British throne. Sat in Parliament; commissioned in October of 1727 as Captain General and Governor-in-Chief of New York and New Jersey, following the transfer of William Burnet to New England; assumed office as chief executive in April 1728, and held that position until his death.

Montgomerie's period as governor was relatively tranquil, largely because a wish to enhance his personal fortune and a distaste for controversy made him unwilling to defy the New Jersey and New York legislatures. Indeed, the political opposition which he encountered in New Jersey from "unmanageable Quakers" seems only to have led him to adopt a more cautious approach in asserting the royal prerogative. In New York members of the legislature—such as Adolph Philipse, the powerful speaker of the colony's Assembly—took advantage of Montgomerie's timidity and strengthened their own positions.

Perhaps the most significant piece of legislation associated with Montgomerie's name was the "Montgomerie Charter" of 1730, which gave New York City a greater degree of political autonomy. Montgomerie died suddenly during the night of June 30, 1731, the victim, according to some authorities, of a smallpox epidemic; he died intestate.

COSBY, William, 1732-1736

also New York, 1732-1736

Born *circa* 1690, probably in Ireland, the son of Alexander and Elizabeth (L'Estrange) Cosby. Brother of Dudley, Henry, Thomas, Loftus, Alexander, Arnold, Anne, Elizabeth, Jane, Dorcas, Isabella, Celia and Dorothy. Married to Grace Montague, the sister of George, Earl of Halifax, and a first cousin of the Duke of Newcastle; father of William, Henry, Elizabeth and Grace.

Entered the British Army in 1704, and had risen to the rank of Colonel by 1717. After his regiment's transfer in 1718 to Minorca in the Balearic Islands, served for about ten years as civil and military Governor, a position which, it was later alleged, he illegally used to improve his own finances. Commissioned in spring of 1732 as Captain General and Governor-in-Chief of New York and New Jersey, and arrived in New York to take up the appointment in August of that year.

Having acquired the governorship of New York and New Jersey through his wife's influential family connections, Cosby felt little need to adopt a conciliatory attitude towards local political leaders. Nevertheless, in New Jersey his abrasive behavior had little impact, since he rarely played an active role in governing that province. Indeed, he met with the New Jersey Assembly on only one occasion, and the colony's lawmakers took advantage of Cosby's absence by enhancing their own authority. New York, however, was more directly affected by the heavy-handed mode of administration practiced by Cosby, especially when the governor informed his Council in November 1732 that he was entitled to one-half of the salary paid to Rip Van Dam during Van Dam's thirteen months as acting governor. The controversy which resulted divided the province politically, and culminated in August of 1733 with Cosby's suspension of Chief Justice Lewis Morris, who had refused to permit the New York Supreme Court to be used as the governor's weapon against Van Dam. About a year later Cosby became involved in an even more celebrated legal decision involving freedom of the press. Declaring the *New-York Weekly Journal* to be a seditious publication, the Governor's Council requested the attorney general to take legal action against the authors of the paper and its printer, John Peter Zenger. In the end Zenger was acquitted of libel, a verdict which represented a triumph for the opponents of the governor, led by former Chief Justice Morris. Cosby died on March 10, 1736, while still in office.

Bibliography: [Cadwallader Colden], "History of Governor William Cosby's Administration and of Lieutenant-Governor George Clarke's Administration through 1737," in *Colden Papers*, vol. IX (New York, 1937) [published in the New-York Historical Society, *Collections* for the year 1935], 281-355; Vincent Buranelli, "Governor Cosby and His Enemies (1732-36),"

New York History, XXXVII (October 1956), 365-87; J. H. Smith and L. Hershkowitz, "Courts of Equity in the Province of New York: The Cosby Controversy, 1732-1736," *American Journal of Legal History*, XVI (January 1972), 1-50. *DAB*.

ANDERSON, John, 1736

Born in 1665 in Scotland, the son of John Anderson. An Angelican. Brother of Reverend James Anderson, and perhaps others. Married to Anna Reid, the daughter of John Reid, who was at one time Surveyor General of New Jersey; father of John, Jr., James, Kenneth, Jonathan, Margaret, Helena, Anna, Elizabeth and Isabella. Commanded the *Unicorn* as part of the Darien colonization scheme of 1699, but settled in New Jersey after abandoning his ship as being no longer seaworthy.

Acted as a Judge in New Jersey's provincial courts, and in 1711 presided as a Justice of the Monmouth County Quarter Sessions. Served as a member of the New Jersey Council from 1713 until his death, although he was suspended from office by Governor William Burnet from 1722 to 1726. In his capacity as senior councillor, became Acting Governor of New Jersey following the death of Governor William Cosby on March 10, 1736.

Anderson's tenure as acting governor ended abruptly when he died on March 28, 1736, only eighteen days after the death of Cosby. During his few weeks in office Anderson had of course little opportunity to achieve anything politically, although he did indicate that he favored a separate governor for New Jersey. On March 18th he joined other members of the Council and Assembly in signing a petition to that effect, which asked the Crown to commission "some person to be their Governour Different and Distinct from the Person that is to be Governour . . . of New York." Ten days later Anderson died in Manalapan, New Jersey following a brief illness. He was interred in the Old Topanemus burial ground near Marlboro, New Jersey.

Bibliography: William N. Mervine, "John Anderson, President of His Majesty's Council of New Jersey, and His Descendants," New Jersey Historical Society, *Proceedings*, 3rd ser., vol. VII (October 1912-January 1913), 75-84, 137-46; "John Anderson, a Scotch Sailorman . . .," in William S. Horner, *New Jersey: This Old Monmouth of Ours* (Freehold, N.J., 1932), 112-15.

HAMILTON, John, 1736-1738, 1746-1747

Date and place of birth unknown; son of Andrew Hamilton, chief executive of the Jerseys and Pennsylvania in the late seventeenth and early eighteenth centuries, and his first wife. An Anglican, who served as vestryman of St. Peter's Church in Perth Amboy from 1730 to 1736, and again from 1742 to 1745. Married to a woman named Elizabeth.

Acted for a time as Deputy Postmaster General of North America. Named to the East Jersey Board of Proprietors following its reorganization in 1725, and eventually chosen as President of that body. Became Second Judge of the New Jersey Supreme Court in September 1734. Served as a member of the New Jersey Council from 1713 until his death; as senior member of the Council, became New Jersey's Acting Governor between the death of John Anderson on March 28, 1736 and the accession of Lewis Morris in August 1738; again served as acting governor after the death of Lewis Morris in May 1746.

Hamilton's first period as acting governor was fairly uneventful, although these years did witness the growth of a movement which would end in the appointment of Lewis Morris as New Jersey's royal governor, marking the final administrative separation of New Jersey from New York. Hamilton's brief second term was less tranquil, however, as disputes over land titles and timber rights led to rioting in several communities. The violence became so severe that at one point the acting governor suggested that the British Parliament should intervene to help bring peace to the colony, but that proposal was rejected by the New Jersey Assembly.

Meanwhile, declining health restricted Hamilton's ability to perform his executive duties, and on June 17, 1747 he died in Perth Amboy, New Jersey, while still in office. He was buried in Perth Amboy.

READING, John, 1747, 1757-1758

Born on June 6, 1686 in Gloucester, West Jersey, the son of John Reading, a member of Governor Robert Hunter's Council from 1713 to 1717, and his wife, Elizabeth. A Presbyterian. Brother of Elsie. Married on November 30, 1720 to Mary Ryerson; father of John, Ann, George, Daniel, Joseph, Elizabeth, Richard, Thomas, Mary, Sarah and Samuel (died young). Educated in England; later in life became a Trustee of the College of New Jersey (now Princeton).

Became a surveyor for settlers in the Burlington area of New Jersey during the 1710's. Served in 1719 as one of the commissioners chosen to decide the boundary line between New Jersey and New York; acted in a similar capacity in 1740, when he helped to establish the boundary between Massachusetts and Rhode Island. Also named to a commission set up in 1728 in order to try pirates in the colonies. Appointed to the New Jersey Council in 1720, remaining a member until 1758. As senior councillor, succeeded the deceased John Hamilton as Acting Governor of New Jersey in June 1747, and served until the accession of Governor Jonathan Belcher in August of that year; after at first objecting to becoming acting governor following the death of Belcher in August 1757, citing reasons of age and health, finally agreed to accept the position, and served in that capacity until the arrival of Governor Francis Bernard in June 1758.

Although Reading's first tenure as acting governor lasted only two months, it was troubled by a continuation of the rioting over land titles which had plagued the administration of his predecessor. A particularly serious disturbance occurred in Perth Amboy in July 1747, causing Reading to ask for the passage of an anti-riot act. During his second period in office, which continued for almost a year, the aged and infirm Reading was unable to exert effective control over the Legislature. Sensing this, the New Jersey Assembly took advantage of the acting governor's incapacity by pressing for a bill which provided for the emission of £30,000 in paper money.

Reading asked leave to resign from the Council shortly after relinquishing the administration of the colony to Governor Bernard. His request was granted, and he retired from public life. Reading died on November 5, 1767; he was buried in Hunterdon County, New Jersey.

Bibliography: Josiah Granville Leach, *Genealogical and Biographical Memorials of the Reading, Howell, Yerkes, Watts, Latham, and Elkins Families* (Philadelphia, 1898); "Copy of Journal of [John] Reading, while surveying Lands in the northern part of New Jersey, April 17th to June 10th, 1715," New Jersey Historical Society, *Proceedings*, 3rd ser., vol. X (January-October 1915), 35-46, 90-110, 128-33.

BELCHER, Jonathan, 1747-1757

Massachusetts and New Hampshire, 1730-1741

Born on January 8, 1682 in Cambridge, Massachusetts, the son of Andrew and Sarah (Gilbert) Belcher. Brother of Andrew, Sarah, Elizabeth, Mary, Anna, Martha and Deborah (died in infancy). Married on January 8, 1706 to Mary Partridge, by whom he was the father of Andrew, Sarah, Jonathan, William and Thomas; following the death of his first wife on October 6, 1736, remarried on September 9, 1748 to Mary Louisa Emilia Teal; no children by his second wife.

Attended Harvard College, graduating in 1699. Subsequently spent several years in Europe, before returning to Massachusetts and pursuing a mercantile career. First elected to the Massachusetts Council in 1718, and served intermittently as a member of that body until 1728. Sent to England by the Massachusetts House of Representatives to defend, along with Francis Wilks, the House position on the question of the chief executive's salary. Arrived in England early in 1729, and secured a commission as Royal Governor of Massachusetts Bay and New Hampshire in January 1730, shortly after news of Governor Burnet's death reached London; returned to America in August 1730 to begin his new assignment. Dismissed as chief executive of Massachusetts and New Hampshire in May 1741, but later returned to England, where in February 1747 he received a commission to govern New Jersey; occupied that office between his arrival in the province in August 1747 and his death ten years later.

Belcher's tenure in Massachusetts and New Hampshire was troubled by sharp disputes with the assemblies of both colonies over issues like the governor's salary and paper currency. While Belcher managed to resolve some of his disagreements with the legislators, monetary policy remained a source of bitter dissension, especially in Massachusetts. In that province the governor disapproved of the creation of a "land bank," which issued notes backed by mortgages at three percent interest, and the resulting controversy did much to intensify opposition to his administration. Eventually, charges of corruption, including an allegation that he had accepted a bribe to settle a boundary dispute between Massachusetts and New Hampshire, culminated in Belcher's removal by Crown officials.

After he had regained the favor of authorities in England, the indefatigable Belcher assumed the governorship of New Jersey. There he again encountered problems, chiefly concerning the question of land titles. Shortly before his second period as governor began, the College of New Jersey (now Princeton University) was founded, and Belcher, always a supporter of education, bequeathed his personal library to that institution when he died in Elizabethtown, New Jersey on August 31, 1757.

Bibliography: W. H. Whitmore, "Notes on the Belcher Family," *New England Historical and Genealogical Register*, XXVII (July 1873), 239-45; "Belcher Papers, parts 1 and 2," in Massachusetts Historical Society, *Collections*, 6th ser., vols. VI and VII (Boston, 1893-94); Henry Lyttleton Savage, "Jonathan Belcher and 'Our Young College'," *Princeton University Library Chronicle*, XIX (Spring-Summer 1958), 191-96; Michael Clement Batinski, "Jonathan Belcher of Massachusetts, 1682-1741," unpub. Ph.D. diss., Northwestern University, 1970. There is also a microfilm of the Belcher letterbooks from 1723 to 1754, the originals of which are in the Massachusetts Historical Society. *DAB*.

POWNALL, Thomas, 1757

Massachusetts 1757-1760

Born on September 4, 1722 in England, the eldest son of William and Sara (Burniston) Pownall. Brother of John, Richard, Edward and probably a number of sisters. Married in August 1765 to Harriet, the natural daughter of General Charles Churchill and the widow of Sir Everard Fawkener; after the death of his first wife in 1777, remarried on August 2, 1784 to Hannah (Kennett) Astell; no children by either marriage.

Attended grammar school in Lincoln; matriculated at Trinity College, Cambridge in 1740, and graduated from that institution in 1743. Served for a number of years as a Clerk in the Board of Trade, where his brother John occupied a prominent position. Became in 1753 Secretary to Sir Danvers Osborn, the recently-appointed governor of New York. Following Osborn's suicide in October 1753, acted as an unofficial source of information on colonial affairs, reporting to the Board of Trade. Commissioned Lieutenant Governor of New Jersey in May 1755. Returned to England in February 1756 and, after rejecting an offer to serve as governor of Pennsylvania, became "Secretary Extraordinary" to Lord Loudoun, the new commander-in-chief of British forces in North America. Commissioned Royal Governor of Massachusetts Bay in February 1757, and arrived in that province the following August to begin his administration. Also became Acting Governor of New Jersey late in August 1757, after the death of Jonathan Belcher, but soon turned over his authority in that colony to John Reading, New Jersey's senior councillor.

Pownall's tenure in Massachusetts was largely preoccupied with military matters, as Britain's war with France on the North American continent reached a critical stage. During these years Pownall consistently asserted his authority as governor, thereby irritating Lord Loudoun, his former superior, who found truculence on the part of colonial officials to be a handicap in his prosecution of the war. Pownall also offended many members of the conservative faction in Massachusetts, especially when he established ties with the "anti-prerogative" party in the province and sought to win the friendship of popular leaders in the Assembly. By late 1759 the Board of Trade had decided to remove Pownall from the Massachusetts governorship, and in June of 1760 he left for England.

Following his departure from America, Pownall declined the governorship of Jamaica. Although he received a commission as governor of South Carolina in January 1760, he resigned that position without ever having taken office in the colony. Pownall served for a time in the British military during the early 1760's, achieving the rank of Colonel. In 1767 he became a member for Tregony, Cornwall in the House of Commons, a position he held until becoming a member for Minehead, Somerset in 1774. In the summer of 1780 Pownall abandoned politics for private life, where he remained until his death in Bath, England on February 25, 1805. Pownall was the author of *The*

Administration of the Colonies, an argument for a more thoughtful and flexible approach to British colonial policy, which first appeared in 1764.

Bibliography: Thomas Pownall, *The Administration of the Colonies* (London, 1764: also later, enlarged editions); Robert Ludlow Fowler, "Governor Thomas Pownall, Colonial Statesman," *Magazine of American History*, XVI (November 1886), 409-32; "Governor Pownall's Reasons for Declining the Government of Pennsylvania," *Pennsylvania Magazine of History and Biography*, XIII (1889), 440-46; Frederick Tuckerman, ed., "Letters to Thomas Pownall," *American Historical Review*, VIII (January 1903), 301-30; C. A. W. Pownall, *Thomas Pownall, M.P., F.R.S., Governor of Massachusetts Bay* . . . (London, 1908); William Otis Sawtelle, "Thomas Pownall, Colonial Governor, and Some of His Activities in the American Colonies," Massachusetts Historical Society, *Proceedings*, LXIII (June 1930), 233-84; John A. Schutz, "Thomas Pownall and His Negro Commonwealth," *Journal of Negro History*, XXX (October 1945), 400-04; John A. Schutz, "Thomas Pownall's Proposed Atlantic Federation," *Hispanic American Historical Review*, XXVI (May 1946), 263-68; John A. Schutz, *Thomas Pownall, British Defender of American Liberty: A Study of Anglo-American Relations in the Eighteenth Century* (Glendale, Calif., 1951); Caroline Robbins, "An Active and Intelligent Antiquary, Governor Thomas Pownall," *Pennsylvania History*, XXVI (January 1959), 1-20. *DAB, DNB*.

BERNARD, Sir Francis, 1758-1760

Massachusetts, 1760-1769

Born in 1712 in England, the son of the Reverend Francis and Margery (Winlowe) Bernard. No brothers or sisters. Married in 1741 to Amelia Offley, by whom he had eight children.

Entered St. Peter's College, Westminster in 1725, and later studied at Christ Church, Oxford. Admitted to the Middle Temple, London, in 1733, where he prepared for a legal career; called to the bar in 1737. Named Commissioner of Bails in 1740 for an area which included Lincoln, York and Nottingham. Became a friend of the second Viscount Barrington, his wife's cousin. Commissioned Captain General and Governor-in-Chief of New Jersey in February 1758, largely as a result of Barrington's influence, and arrived in June of that year to take up his assignment. Appointed Royal Governor of Massachusetts in January 1760; resigned as New Jersey's chief executive in the summer of 1760 to assume his new position.

Although Bernard's period of service in New Jersey was brief, his energetic leadership quickly left its mark on that province. Realizing that his instructions regarding paper money emissions were too inflexible, Bernard sought to persuade officials in London to modify their policy. The concessions on this issue which Bernard managed to win from home authorities, combined with his vigorous response to Indian attacks during the French and Indian War, greatly enhanced his stature in the eyes of the New Jersey Assembly. Bernard's ability was also highly regarded in England, and early in 1760 he received a commission to govern Massachusetts Bay, a promotion which gave him an opportunity to experience colonial politics on a larger and more complicated scale. While his first years in office were generally successful, the popular outcry during the mid-1760's against such measures as the Sugar and Stamp acts greatly hampered his ability to administer the province effectively. By 1769, when some controversial letters which he had written to English officials were published in Boston, Bernard had lost his hold over the government, and in August of that year he was recalled by his superiors.

In April 1769, shortly before his dismissal as governor of Massachusetts, Bernard became a Baronet. His final years were spent in relative obscurity, although he did secure an appointment as Commissioner of Customs for Ireland. Bernard died in Aylesbury, Buckinghamshire on June 16, 1779.

Bibliography: Francis Bernard, *Letters to the Ministry from Governor Bernard* (London, 1769); Thomas Bernard, *Life of Sir Francis Bernard* . . .(London, 1790); Mrs. Napier Higgins, *The Bernards of Abington and Nether Winchendon* (London, 1903); Edward Channing and Archibald C. Coolidge, eds., *The Barrington-Bernard Correspondence . . . 1760-1770* (Cambridge, 1912); Charles Penrose, . . . *New England in the Year of Grace 1776 – and Sir Francis Bernard, His Outlook on Trade and Navigation* (Princeton, 1940); Jordan D. Fiore, "Francis Bernard, Colonial Governor," unpub. Ph.D. diss., Boston University, 1950; Jordan D. Fiore, "The Temple-Bernard Affair: A Royal Custom House Scandal in Essex County," *Essex Institute Historical Collections*, XC (January 1954), 58-83; Leslie J. Thomas, "Partisan Politics in Massachusetts during Governor Bernard's Administration, 1760-1770," unpub. Ph.D. diss., University of Wisconsin, 1960; Francis G. Walett, "Governor Bernard's Undoing: An Earlier Hutchinson Letters Affair," *New England Quarterly*, XXXVIII (June 1965), 217-26. *DAB, DNB*.

BOONE, Thomas, 1760-1761
South Carolina, 1761-1764

Born *circa* 1730 in England, the son of Charles Boone, at one time a member of Parliament, and his wife Elizabeth, the sister of John Garth. Brother of Charles. Married to Sarah Ann (Tattnall) Peronneau; apparently had no children.

Educated at Eton and at Trinity College, Cambridge. Travelled to South Carolina in 1752, where he established his claim to the extensive estate once owned by his uncle Joseph Boone, a leader of the colony's anti-proprietary faction during the early eighteenth century. Returned to England several years later, but in 1758 again sailed for South Carolina. Commissioned Captain General and Governor-in-Chief of New Jersey in January 1760, arriving in that province the following July; left New Jersey in October 1761 in order to accept the governorship of South Carolina, a position he occupied from December 1761 to May 1764.

Boone's brief tenure in New Jersey was rather uneventful, as the Assembly concerned itself chiefly with routine matters, such as the raising of troops needed for the latter stages of the French and Indian War. However, in South Carolina the political harmony which Boone had experienced in New Jersey was replaced by bitter controversy. Despite a warm reception from the Commons House of Assembly, Boone soon became embroiled in a conflict over the naming of Christopher Gadsden to that body, an election whose validity the governor contested in retaliation for the Commons' refusal to consider his proposed amendments to an election act. The *impasse* which resulted eventually disrupted Boone's administration, and in the spring of 1764 the frustrated chief executive decided to return home on a leave of absence.

Once in England Boone defended his actions in South Carolina before the Board of Trade, which nevertheless concluded that he had "been actuated by a degree of passion and resentment inconsistent with good policy." In December 1769 Boone received an appointment as a Commissioner of Customs, an office which he finally resigned in 1805. Boone died at "Lee Place," his paternal home in Kent, on September 25, 1812.

Bibliography: L. B. Namier, "Charles Garth and His Connexions," *English Historical Review*, LIV (July 1939), 443-70; Felix Gilbert, ed., "Letters of Francis Kinloch to Thomas Boone, 1782-1788," *Journal of Southern History*, VIII (February 1942), 87-105.

HARDY, Josiah, 1761-1763

Date and place of birth unknown; son of Vice-Admiral Sir Charles and Lady Elizabeth (Burchett) Hardy. Brother of five, including Sir Charles Hardy, who served as governor of New York from 1755 to 1757 and later became an admiral in the Royal Navy. Married, and the father of an unknown number of children. Appears to have had no previous political experience before his commission as Captain General and Governor-in-Chief of New Jersey in May 1761; arrived in the colony to assume that office in October of 1761.

Only five months after he began his term as New Jersey's royal governor, Hardy provoked his superiors in London, when he appointed Robert Hunter Morris and two other judges to the provincial Supreme Court during "good behavior," rather than "at the King's pleasure." In response to this direct violation of his royal instructions, the Board of Trade petitioned the King for Hardy's removal, suggesting that his recall would be a useful precedent to discourage other governors "from like Acts of Disobedience." By September of 1762 the Crown had agreed with the Board's request, and the Earl of Egremont informed Hardy that he had been replaced by William Franklin, who arrived in New Jersey to take up the appointment in February of 1763. During his brief tenure Hardy managed to displease the home authorities in other ways, especially by his failure to compel the New Jersey Assembly to retire its issue of paper currency according to an approved schedule. In the end, Hardy's dismissal indicated a new determination on the part of the Crown to exert more rigorous control over Britain's American empire.

Following his period as royal governor, Hardy sailed from New York to England in September 1763. In November 1764 he was named Consul at Cadiz and Port St. Mary. Hardy died in 1790.

FRANKLIN, William, 1763-1776

Born *circa* 1730, the son of Benjamin Franklin and, allegedly, Deborah Read, his common-law wife. Married on September 4, 1762 to Elizabeth Downes, who died during the Revolution; may have remarried to an Irish woman after the death of his first wife; father of one natural son, William Temple Franklin.

Pursued a military career as a young man, rising to the rank of Captain. Acted briefly as Postmaster of Philadelphia; also served as Comptroller of the General Post Office in the northern colonies from 1754 to 1756, an appointment he received largely because of his father's influence. Presided between 1751 and 1757 as Clerk of the Pennsylvania Assembly. Accompanied his father on a trip to England in June 1757, entered London's Middle Temple, and later was called to the bar; received also an M.A. from Oxford University in 1762. Commissioned Royal Governor of New Jersey in September 1762, and arrived in that colony to begin his administration in February of the following year.

Although he possessed considerable executive ability, Franklin took over as governor of New Jersey on the eve of its protest against British colonial policy. That circumstance, combined with the rumors surrounding his illegitimate birth, made his tenure a controversial one. Franklin's assignment was especially complicated by the furor in New Jersey over paper money, an issue which until 1774 was perhaps the single most important source of dissension in the colony. While Franklin was usually prepared to back Assembly measures which provided for the emission of paper currency, the repeated disallowance of these bills by the Privy Council in England caused him to lose much of his prestige. As the revolutionary movement progressed, Franklin refused to sanction violent opposition to British rule, and by early 1776 his authority had almost completely disintegrated. Finally, in June 1776, Franklin was deposed by New Jersey's Provincial Congress, which branded him an "enemy to the liberties of this country"—forming an ironic counter to epithets applied at the time to his father.

After his removal as governor, Franklin spent several years under arrest, until in October 1778 he was released in a prisoner exchange. He then served for a time as President of the Board of Associated Loyalists in New York, but in August 1782 he sailed for England, where he subsisted on a pension for the remainder of his life. Franklin died on November 16, 1813.

Bibliography: William A. Whitehead, "A Biographical Sketch of William Franklin, Governor from 1763 to 1776," New Jersey Historical Society, *Proceedings*, 1st ser., vol. III (1848), 137-59; Charles Henry Hart, "Who Was the Mother of Franklin's Son," *Pennsylvania Magazine of History and Biography*, XXXV (July 1911), 308-14; Charles Henry Hart, ed., "Letters from William Franklin to William Strahan," *Pennsylvania Magazine of History and Biography*, XXXV (October 1911), 415-62; Catherine Fennelly, "William Franklin of New Jersey," *William and Mary Quarterly*, 3rd ser., vol. VI (July 1949), 361-82; William H. Mariboe, "The Life of William Franklin, 1730(1)-1813: 'Pro Rege et Patria'," unpub. Ph.D. diss., University of Pennsylvania, 1962; Glenn H. Smith, "William Franklin: Expedient Loyalist," *North Dakota Quarterly*, XLII (Summer 1974), 57-75; Larry R. Gerlach, *William Franklin: New Jersey's Last Royal Governor* (Trenton, N.J. 1975); Willard S. Randall, "William Franklin: The Making of a Conservative," in Robert A. East and Jacob Judd, eds., *The Loyalist Americans: A Focus on Greater New York* (Tarrytown, N.Y., 1975). *DAB*.

LIVINGSTON, William, 1776-1790

Born in November 1723 in Albany, New York, the son of the first Philip Livingston, one of the patroons of New York, and Catharine (Van Brugh) Livingston. A Presbyterian. Brother of Robert, Peter Van Brugh, Peter (died young), John, Philip, Henry, Sarah (died young), Sarah, Alida and Catharine. Married in about 1745 to Susanna French, by whom he was the father of thirteen children, including Henry Brockholst, Susanna and Sarah Van Brugh.

Attended Yale College, graduating from that institution in 1741; later studied law, and was admitted to the bar in 1748; also developed a reputation as a satirist. During the 1750's became a leading opponent of the drive to establish Anglicanism in America, a stance which helped make him spokesman for the "Livingston faction" in New York politics. Retired to his estate near Elizabethtown, New Jersey in the early 1770's, following his faction's defeat by their political rivals, the DeLanceys; emerged from retirement a short time later to become a member of the Essex County Committee of Correspondence and a delegate from New Jersey to the First and Second Continental Congresses. Commissioned Brigadier General of the East Jersey militia in October 1775, and took command of the New Jersey militia in June 1776. Elected Governor of New Jersey after the adoption of the state's first constitution in July 1776; served as chief executive from August 1776 until his death, winning re-election on an annual basis.

While New Jersey's constitution of 1776 did not entrust much authority to the executive branch of government, the need to reach swift decisions during the Revolution meant that in practice Livingston had to exercise greater discretionary powers. Fortunately, through his influence over the Council of Safety and Privy Council, Livingston was provided with two administrative agencies which could act whenever the Legislature proved unable or unwilling to keep the state's machinery functioning efficiently. Livingston's enormous influence as wartime governor of New Jersey continued after peace was restored. Indeed, his prestige as a state leader was an important factor in New Jersey's decision in December 1787 to ratify the Federal Constitution, a document which the governor himself had helped to draft several months earlier. Livingston died in Elizabethtown, New Jersey on July 25, 1790.

Bibliography: Theodore Sedgwick, Jr., *A Memoir of the Life of William Livingston* (New York, 1833); *Selections from the Correspondence of the Executive of New Jersey, from 1776 to 1786* (Newark, 1848); E. B. Livingston, *The Livingstons of Livingston Manor* (New York, 1910); Frank Monaghan, ed., "Unpublished Correspondence of William Livingston and John Jay," New Jersey Historical Society, *Proceedings*, LII (July 1934), 141-62; Harold W. Thatcher, "The Social Philosophy of William Livingston," unpub. Ph. D. diss., University of Chicago, 1935; Harold W. Thatcher, "The Political Ideas of New Jersey's First Governor," New Jersey Historical Society, *Proceedings*, LX (April-July 1942), 81-98, 184-99; Harold W. Thatcher, "The Social and Economic Ideas of New Jersey's First Governor," New Jersey Historical Society, *Proceedings*, LX (October 1942), 225-38, and vol. LXI (January 1943), 31-46; Dorothy R. Dillon, *New York Triumvirate: A Study of the Legal and Political Careers of William Livingston, John Morin Scott [and] William Smith, Jr.* (New York, 1949); Milton M. Klein, "The American Whig: William Livingston of New York," unpub. Ph.D. diss.,

Columbia University, 1954; Milton M. Klein, ''Rise of the New York Bar: The Legal Career of William Livingston,'' *William and Mary Quarterly*, 3rd ser., vol. XV (July 1958), 334-58; David A. Bernstein, ''William Livingston: The Role of the Executive in New Jersey's Revolutionary War,'' *New Jersey in the American Revolution II* (1973), 13-29; Michael Lewis Levine, ''The Transformation of a Radical Whig under Republican Government: William Livingston, Governor of New Jersey, 1776-1790,'' unpub. Ph.D. diss., Rutgers University, 1975; John M. Mulder, ''William Livingston: Propagandist against Episcopacy,'' *Journal of Presbyterian History*, LIV (Spring 1976), 83-104; Carl E. Prince, ed., *The Papers of William Livingston*, vol. I (Trenton, N.J., 1979) [*in progress*]. *DAB*.

NEW YORK

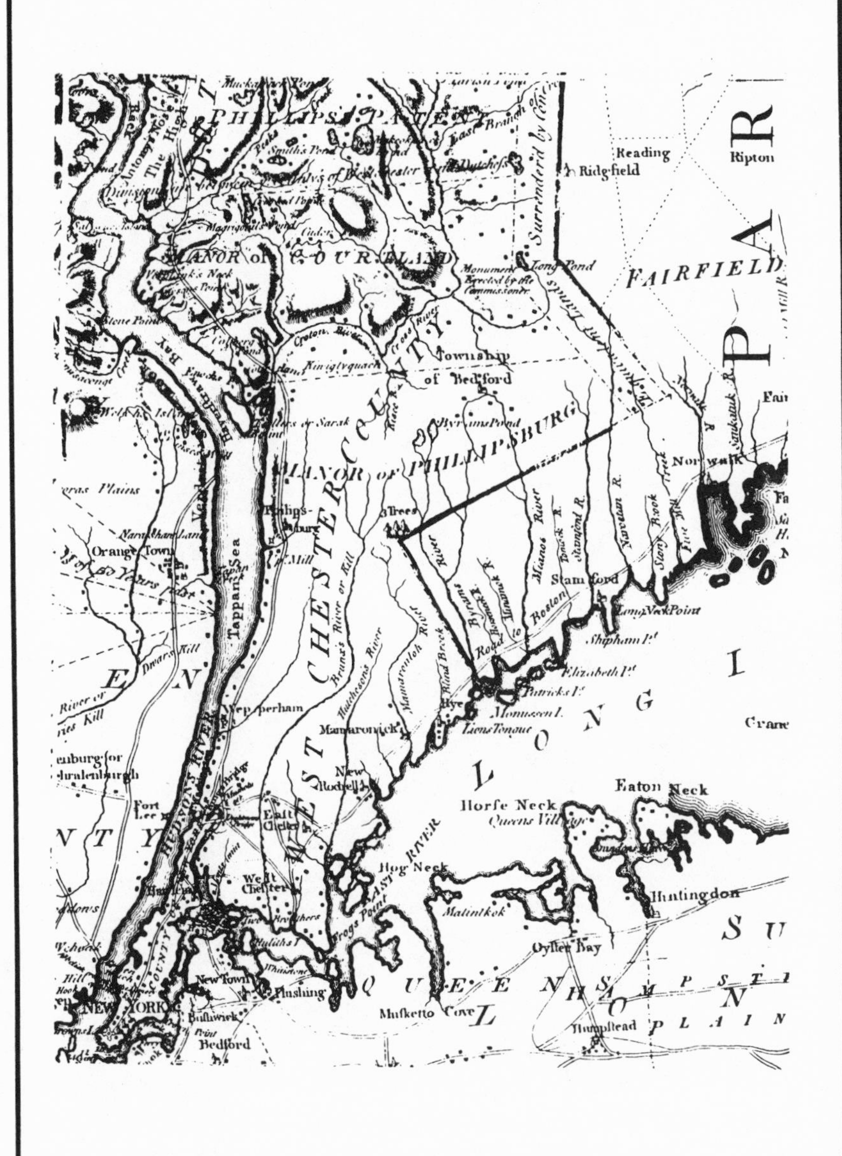

PHILLIPS PATENT
MANOR of CORTLAND
Croton River
Township of Bedford
MANOR of PHILLIPSBURG
WEST CHESTER COUNTY
Reading
Ridgfield
Ripton
FAIRFIELD
Norwalk
Stamford
Long Neck Point
Shipham Pt
Elizabeth Pt
Rye
Mamaroneck
New Rochell
East Chester
West Chester
Orange Town
Tappan Sea
HUDSONS RIVER
Fort Lee
NEW YORK
New Town
Flushing
Bushwick
Bedford
Hog Neck
Horfe Neck
Eaton Neck
Huntingdon
Oyfter Bay
Mufketto Cove
QUEENS
LONG

Chronology

Prior to the establishment of English hegemony in 1664, parts of the territory which would eventually become New York were under Dutch rule. A series of seven directors and governors exercised jurisdiction: Cornelis Jacobsen May (1624-1625), Willem Verhulst (1625-1626), Peter Minuit (1626-1631), Bastiaen Janseen Krol (1632-1633), Wouter Van Twiller (1633-1638), Willem Kiefft (1638-1647) and Peter Stuyvesant (1647-1664).

1664-1668	Richard Nicolls
1668-1673	Francis Lovelace
1673-1674	*During this period the Dutch occupied New York, thereby superseding the English administration.*
1674-1677	(*later Sir*) Edmund Andros
1677-1678	Anthony Brockholls
1678-1681	Sir Edmund Andros
1681-1683	Anthony Brockholls
1683-1688	Thomas Dongan
1688-1689	Francis Nicholson
1689-1691	Jacob Leisler
1691	Henry Sloughter
1691-1692	Richard Ingoldesby
1692-1698	Benjamin Fletcher
1698-1699	Richard Coote, Earl of Bellomont
1699-1700	John Nanfan
1700-1701	Richard Coote, Earl of Bellomont
1701	William Smith
1701-1702	John Nanfan
1702-1708	Edward Hyde, Viscount Cornbury
1708-1709	John Lovelace, 4th Baron Lovelace of Hurley
1709	Peter Schuyler
1709-1710	Richard Ingoldesby
1710	Gerardus Beekman
1710-1719	Robert Hunter
1719-1720	Peter Schuyler
1720-1728	William Burnet
1728-1731	John Montgomerie
1731-1732	Rip Van Dam
1732-1736	William Cosby

1736-1743*	George Clarke
1743-1753	George Clinton
1753	Sir Danvers Osborn
1753-1755	James DeLancey
1755-1757	Sir Charles Hardy
1757-1760	James DeLancey
1760-1761	Cadwallader Colden
1761	Robert Monckton
1761-1762	Cadwallader Colden
1762-1763	Robert Monckton
1763-1765	Cadwallader Colden
1765-1769	Sir Henry Moore
1769-1770	Cadwallader Colden
1770-1771	John Murray, 4th Earl of Dunmore
1771-1774	William Tryon
1774-1775	Cadwallader Colden
1775-1780	William Tryon
1777	Pierre Van Cortlandt
1777-1795	George Clinton
1780-1783	James Robertson
1783	Andrew Elliot

*John West, 1st Earl De La Warr, was commissioned royal governor of New York in 1737, but never assumed that position in the colony.

BIBLIOGRAPHY

Abstract of Wills, vols. I and II [1665-1728], in New-York Historical Society, *Collections*, vols. XXV-XXVI (New York, 1893-94).

Bonomi, Patricia U., *A Factious People: Politics and Society in Colonial New York* (New York, 1971).

Hamlin, Paul M., and Charles E. Baker, *Supreme Court of Judicature of the Province of New York, 1691-1704*, 3 vols. (New York, 1959).

Journal of the Legislative Council of the Colony of New York [1691-1775], 2 vols. (Albany, 1861).

Kammen, Michael, *Colonial New York: A History* (New York, 1975).

Katz, Stanley Nider, *Newcastle's New York: Anglo-American Politics, 1732-1753* (Cambridge, Mass., 1968).

Lincoln, Charles Z., "The Governors of New York," New York State Historical Association, *Proceedings*, IX (1910), 33-98B.

O'Callaghan, E. B., ed., *Documentary History of the State of New York*, 4 vols. (Albany, 1849-51).

———. and Berthold Fernow, eds., *Documents Relative to the Colonial History of the State of New York*, 15 vols. (Albany, 1856-87).

Ovadia, Neil, "Placemen's Progress: The Governors of Provincial New York, 1717-1753," unpub. Ph.D. diss., City University of New York, 1974.

Pelletreau, William S., *Historic Homes and Institutions and Genealogical and Family History of New York*, 4 vols. (New York, 1907).

Scott, Kenneth, comp., *Rivington's New York Newspaper: Excerpts from a Loyalist Press, 1773-1783* (New York, 1973).

Severance, Frank Hayward, "Some English Governors of New York and Their Part in the Development of the Colony," New York State Historical Association, *Proceedings*, XVII (1919), 124-40.

Van Rensselaer, Mrs. Schuyler, *History of the City of New York in the Seventeenth Century*, 2 vols. (New York, 1909).

NEW YORK

NICOLLS, Richard, 1664-1668

also New Jersey, 1664-1665

Born in 1624 in England, the fourth son of Francis, a barrister, and Margaret (Bruce) Nicolls.Brother of William, Edward, Francis, Bruce and perhaps others. Never married.

Became a supporter of the Royalist cause during the English Civil Wars, and in 1643 commanded a troop of horse against Parliamentary forces. Joined the Royalists in exile on the Continent after Cromwell's victory, and served under the Duke of York in the French Army, where he probably acquired the title of Colonel; named Groom of the Bedchamber to the Duke of York following the Restoration of 1660. Appointed in April 1664 as head of a military expedition to New Netherlands, which Charles II hoped to take from the Dutch; accepted the surrender of the Dutch outpost of New Amsterdam late in August 1664, and became the first English Deputy Governor of New York, serving under the Duke of York. Acted as chief executive of New Jersey from September 1664 until August 1665, when Philip Carteret arrived in that colony with his commission to govern.

Although Nicolls had arrived in America as head of a commission assigned to investigate affairs in New England, the arduous task of transforming New Netherlands into an English colony prevented him from devoting much attention to the commission's duties. In New York, however, Nicolls pursued an active administration, highlighted by his drafting and implementation of the "Duke's Laws." This legal code, despite omitting provisions for the elective assembly and town meetings which were customary in New England, did guarantee a degree of religious toleration unknown in most of the colonies to the north. Nicolls' religious policy, intended chiefly as a means of persuading the Dutch inhabitants of New York to accept the new English regime, was accompanied by other concessions, especially the deputy governor's decision to permit some of the local political practices established by the Dutch to remain undisturbed. Still, there were some protests against the Nicolls administration. On Long Island, for example, transplanted New Englanders asserted that the absence of a representative assembly in New York deprived them of a meaningful voice in government.

Nicolls resigned his position in August 1668 and returned to England, where he again served as the Duke of York's Groom of the Bedchamber. When the Third Dutch War broke out in 1672, Nicolls decided to join the English fleet, and was killed at the Battle of Southwold Bay on May 28, 1672. He was buried in Ampthill Church in Bedfordshire.

Bibliography: Edward Holland Nicol, "Biography of Colonel Richard Nicolls, Deputy Governor of New York, etc." *New York Genealogical and Biographical Record*, XV (July 1884), 103-05; Montgomery Schuyler, *Richard Nicolls: First Governor of New York, 1664-1668* (New York, 1933); Kenneth Scott and Charles E. Baker, "Renewals of Governor Nicolls' Treaty of 1665 with the Esopus Indians," *New-York Historical Society Quarterly*, XXXVII (July 1953), 251-72. *DAB, DNB*.

LOVELACE, Francis, 1668-1673

Born *circa* 1621 in England, the third son of Sir William and Lady Anne (Barne) Lovelace. Brother of Anna, Richard (the Cavalier poet), Thomas, Joanna (or Joan), William, Elizabeth and Dudley. Married secretly in about 1659 to Blanche Talbot, by whom he was the father of Edward and John.

Fought with Charles I during the English Civil Wars, acting from 1644 to 1645 as Governor of Carmarthen Castle in Wales; served for a time as a soldier in France. Visited Virginia between 1650 and 1652, and by late 1652 had joined Charles II in exile on the Continent. Returned to England in 1658 to aid the Royalist cause; arrested by the Commonwealth, but freed after that government's collapse. Commissioned in June 1667 as Lieutenant Colonel of a regiment of troops raised by Colonel Sir Walter Vane. Appointed by James, Duke of York, as successor to New York's Deputy Governor Richard Nicolls in April 1667, and arrived in America in March 1668.

Although his predecessor stayed in the colony through the summer of 1668 in order to familiarize Lovelace with his executive duties, the New York deputy-governorship remained a difficult and complicated assignment. External problems included relations with the Indians, a political rebellion in neighboring New Jersey in 1672, and the constant danger of Dutch invasion; internally, the colony needed a firm hand to guide the growth of its young economy and to resolve differences among the many religious groups who lived within its boundaries. In most of these areas the Lovelace administration was fairly successful, and especially in the realm of religion, where the deputy governor implemented the enlightened policy of guaranteeing "liberty of conscience to all, provided they raise not fundamentalls." Politically, however, Lovelace tended to act either unilaterally or in consultation with his English councillors, and his failure to give greater consideration to the wishes of New York's Dutch residents eventually led to his demise. In the summer of 1673, encouraged by four hundred armed burghers, a Dutch fleet invaded New York while Lovelace was absent from the colony. With popular support for the English government so weak, the deputy governor's subordinates surrendered to the fleet following a brief exchange of gunfire.

After he returned to New York Lovelace was arrested while on Long Island, and forced to leave the colony. He then returned to England, where the disappointed Duke of York seized his estate for debt. Lovelace was also imprisoned in the Tower of London for several months. He died on May 10, 1683 (or 1686, depending upon source) in Woodstock, Oxfordshire, England.

Bibliography: A. J. Pearman, "The Kentish Family of Lovelace," *Archaeologia Cantina*, X (1876); Elizabeth Doremus, *Lovelace Chart* (New York, 1900?); E. C. Delavan, "Colonel Francis Lovelace and His Plantation on Staten Island," Natural Science Association of Staten Island, *Proceedings* (March 10, 1900) [reprinted separately in 1902]; Victor H. Paltsits, ed., *Minutes of the Executive Council of the Province of New York: Administration of Francis Lovelace, 1668-1673*, 2 vols. (Albany, 1910); J. Hall Pleasants, "Francis Lovelace, Governor of New York, 1668-1673," *New York Genealogical and Biographical Record*, LI (July 1920), 175-94; Florance Loveless Keeney Robertson, *The Lovelace – Loveless and Allied Families* (Los Angeles?, 1952). *DAB, DNB*.

ANDROS, Sir Edmund, 1674-1677, 1678-1681

East Jersey, 1680-1681, 1688-1689; Massachusetts, 1686-1689; New Hampshire, 1686-1689; Plymouth Colony, 1686-1689; Rhode Island, 1686-1689; Connecticut, 1687-1689; West Jersey, 1688-1689; Virginia, 1692-1698; Maryland, 1693, 1694

Born on December 6, 1637 on the Island of Guernsey, the son of Amice and Elizabeth (Stone) Andros. Married to a woman who was related to the Earl of Craven.

Served as Major of a regiment of foot soldiers which in 1666 sailed from England to defend the West Indies against the Dutch. Named a Landgrave of Carolina in 1672; received a commission from the Duke of York in July 1674 to govern the colony of New York, and acted in that capacity, except for an absence in England between November 1677 and August 1678, until January 1681; also exercised control over East Jersey from 1680 until his recall early in the following year. Knighted in about 1681, became Gentleman of the Privy Chamber to Charles II in 1683, and was appointed Lieutenant Colonel of the Princess of Denmark's regiment of horse soldiers in 1685. Commissioned Royal Governor of the Dominion of New England in June 1686, and established his authority in Massachusetts Bay, Maine, New Hampshire, Plymouth and Rhode Island (including the King's Province) in December of that year; Connecticut in November of 1687; and the Jerseys and New York in August 1688 (although Francis Nicholson presided as Andros' substitute in the latter colony). Arrested and sent to England following the overthrow of the Dominion in the spring of 1689, but later received a commission as Royal Governor of Virginia, and served as that colony's chief executive from September 1692 to December 1698; also acted briefly as Governor of Maryland in 1693 and 1694, in the absence of any other executive authority.

Andros' first tenure in New York was marked by several important achievements, especially the improvement of the colony's defenses and the settlement of some boundary difficulties with Connecticut. Nevertheless, even at this stage he had begun to display an inclination to behave in an arbitrary fashion. Perhaps the clearest illustration of this tendency was the high-handed manner in which Andros superseded the authority of Governor Philip Carteret in the Jerseys, provoking Carteret to complain that Andros aimed at "usurping the government" of his colony. This insensitivity to local politics became even more noticeable after Andros assumed control of the Dominion of New England. Following a troubled tenure of less than two and one-half years, he was deposed in the spring of 1689, shortly after news of the Glorious Revolution in England reached Boston.

Although Andros was exonerated of the charges brought against his Dominion government and took over as Virginia's chief executive in 1692, he soon encountered resistance from local leaders like Commissary James Blair, who bitterly informed one London official that Andros "never did any considerable service to the King, nor the people" during his colonial career. Finally, late in 1698, Andros departed for England. He served as Lieutenant Governor of Guernsey from 1704 to 1706, and died in London in February 1714.

Bibliography: "Commission to Sir Edmund Andros," Massachusetts Historical Society, *Collections*, 3rd ser., vol. VII (Boston, 1838), 138-49; W. H. Whitmore, ed., *Andros Tracts: Being a Collection of Pamphlets and Official Papers . . . of the Andros Government and the Establishment of the Second Charter of Massachusetts*, 3 vols. (New York, 1868-74) (Publications of the Prince Society, vols. V-VII); Robert N. Toppan, ed., "Andros Records," American Antiquarian Society, *Proceedings*, n.s., vol. XIII (1899-1900), 237-68, 463-99; J.H. Tuttle, ed., "Land Warrants under Andros," Colonial Society of Massachusetts, *Publications*, XXI (1919), 292-361; Albert C. Bates, "Expedition of Sir Edmund Andros to Connecticut in 1687," AAS, *Proceedings*, n.s., vol. 48 (October 1938), 276-99; Jeanne G. Bloom, "Sir Edmund Andros: A Study in Seventeenth-Century Colonial Administration," unpub. Ph.D. diss., Yale University, 1962; Robert C. Ritchie, "London Merchants, the New York Market, and the Recall of Sir Edmund Andros," *New York History*, LVII (January 1976), 5-29. *DAB*, *DNB*.

BROCKHOLLS, Anthony, 1677-1678, 1681-1683

Date and place of birth, and names of parents unknown. A Roman Catholic. Married to Susanna Schrich; father of Mary, Henry, Judith, Susanna, and Jennette (or Joanna?).

Commissioned in July 1674 as First Lieutenant of a company of foot under the command of Major Edmund Andros; appointed that same month as successor to Andros, should Andros die or be unable to act as deputy governor of New York. Served as a member of the Deputy Governor's Council after his arrival in New York late in 1674. Acted as chief executive of New York from November 1677 to August 1678, during Andros' absence in England, and again from January 1681 to August 1683, between Andros' recall and the arrival of Governor Thomas Dongan.

Brockholls' years as acting governor were marked by considerable political unrest. Indeed, late in 1681 he reported that the colony's government was "in the greatest confusion and disorder possible." There were several reasons for this disaffection, including the feeling among the settlers on Long Island that their "just liberties" would be better protected if they were under the jurisdiction of Connecticut. At the same time, Brockholls was unable to collect the unpopular customs mandated by the Duke of York, as merchants prevented frightened members of the courts from prosecuting those who evaded the duties.

Brockholls resumed his seat on the Council following the arrival of Governor Dongan in August 1683. He fell from power during the regime of Jacob Leisler, however, and in January 1690 the Leisler government ordered Brockholls' arrest, forcing him to flee from the colony. After Leisler's demise Brockholls settled in New Jersey, *circa* 1696-97. His will was proved in New York on August 29, 1723, shortly after his death.

Bibliography: "Notes and Queries: Henry Brockholst," *New York Genealogical and Biographical Record*, IX (October 1878), 188-89.

DONGAN, Thomas, 1683-1688

Born in 1634 in Castletown, County Kildare, Ireland, a younger son of Sir John and Lady Mary (Talbot) Dongan. A Roman Catholic. Brother of Walter, William, Edward, Robert, Michael, Jerome, James, Bridget, Margaret and Alice. Never married.

Pursued a military career as a young man, and became attached to the Paris entourage of Charles II during the 1650's; served also as an officer in the French Army for many years. Appointed Lieutenant Governor of British-held Tangier, Morocco in the late 1670's, an office which he held until 1680.

Commissioned Lieutenant Governor of New York in September 1682, serving under the Duke of York, and arrived in the province to assume that position in August 1683.

Perhaps the most significant development during Dongan's administration occurred late in October of 1683, shortly after his appearance in New York, when he gave his approval to the "Charter of Libertyes." This document, the product of the first New York Assembly, sought to outline those freedoms which the colonists felt belonged to them by right of their connection with the English Crown. A major concern of the men who drafted the Charter was the need to protect fundamental personal property rights, and the legislators included provisions guaranteeing their right to vote for representatives, trial by jury, and no taxation without representation. Although in May 1686 the Charter was "disallowed . . . Repealed, determined and made void" by James II, Dongan's actions in the matter were creditable, as was his handling of New York's fur trade and its problems with the French and Indians.

Nevertheless, in August 1688 Dongan was replaced as governor of New York by Sir Edmund Andros, who had already extended his authority over Massachusetts Bay, New Hampshire, Rhode Island and Connecticut. When the ultra-Protestant Jacob Leisler replaced Andros as New York's chief executive following the overthrow of the Dominion of New England, Dongan at first remained on Long Island, where his Catholicism made him a conspicuous target of abuse. Dongan finally left America in 1691 and returned to England; in 1698 he succeeded his elder brother to become the second Earl of Limerick. Dongan died on December 14, 1715, and was buried in London, England.

Bibliography: P. F. Dealy, S. J., "[Dongan], The Great Colonial Governor," *Magazine of American History*, VIII (February 1882), 106-11; James W. Gerard, "The Dongan Charter of the City of New York," *Magazine of American History*, XVI (July 1886), 30-49; Franklin M. Danaher, *An Address before the Dongan Club of Albany, New York, July 22, 1889* (Albany, 1889); Edward Channing, "Colonel Thomas Dongan, Governor of New York," American Antiquarian Society, *Proceedings*, n.s., vol. XVIII (October 1907), 336-45; John H. Kennedy, *Thomas Dongan, Governor of New York (1682-1688)* (Washington, D. C., 1930); Thomas P. Phelan, *Thomas Dongan, Colonial Governor of New York, 1683-1688* (New York, 1933); Henry Allain St. Paul, "Governor Thomas Dongan's Expansionist Policy," *Mid-America*, XVII (July-October 1935), 172-84, 236-72; Jesse Merritt, "Thomas Dongan and the Charter of Liberties," *Nassau County Historical Journal*, XIV (Spring 1953), 99-105; Lawrence H. Leder, "Dongan's New York and Fletcher's London: Personality and Politics," *New-York Historical Society Quarterly*, LV (January 1971), 28-37. *DAB*.

NICHOLSON, Francis, 1688-1689

Virginia, 1690-1692, 1698-1705; Maryland, 1694-1698; South Carolina, 1721-1725

Born on November 12, 1655 at "Downholme Park," near Richmond, in Yorkshire, England, probably the son of Thomas Nicholson. Never married.

Became a protegé of Lord St. John of Basing, acting for a time as page to his wife. Entered the English Army in January 1678, and in 1686 was appointed Captain of a company of foot soldiers accompanying Sir Edmund Andros to New England. Named to the Council organized under the Dominion of New England, and eventually commissioned Lieutenant Governor; served as Andros' deputy in New York from 1688 to 1689. Sailed for England after the fall of the Dominion, but soon received a commission as Lieutenant Governor of Virginia, a position which he held from June of 1690 to September 1692; again served as Virginia's chief executive, with the rank of Royal Governor, from December 1698 to August 1705. Also presided as Governor of Maryland from July 1694 to December 1698, of Nova Scotia for several weeks in 1713, and of South Carolina from May 1721 to the spring of 1725.

Nicholson's remarkable instinct for political survival enabled him to serve as resident chief executive of five different colonies during a period encompassing some thirty-seven years. Throughout his long professional career, he often experienced opposition from local officials, opposition which became especially virulent during his second tenure in Virginia. In that colony a bitter quarrel with Commissary James Blair and other members of the Virginia Council finally brought about his recall in 1705. Nevertheless, despite the hostility which he sometimes provoked, Nicholson's record as a colonial administrator was not without a number of significant achievements. In Maryland, for example, his strong interest in education led him to aid in the establishment of King William's School (later St. John's College), while several years earlier he had supported Commissary Blair's efforts in Virginia to found the College of William and Mary.

By the 1720's ill health and concern in London over his policy regarding paper currency in South Carolina had reduced Nicholson's political effectiveness, and in the spring of 1725 he sailed for England on a leave of absence. He died in London on March 5, 1728, leaving the bulk of his estate to the Society for the Propagation of the Gospel in Foreign Parts, an organization in which, as a staunch Anglican, he had always taken an active role.

Bibliography: [Unsigned], "Instructions to Francis Nicholson," *Virginia Magazine of History and Biography*, IV (1896), 49-54; [unsigned], "Papers Relating to the Administration of Governor Nicholson . . .," *Virginia Magazine of History and Biography*, VII (1899-1900), 153-72, 275-86, 386-401, vol. VIII (1900-01), 46-58, 126-46, 260-73, 366-85, vol. IX (1901-02),

18-33, 152-62, 251-62; Charles William Sommerville, "Early Career of Governor Francis Nicholson," *Maryland Historical Magazine*, IV (June-September 1909), 101-14, 201-20; Louis B. Wright, "William Byrd's Opposition to Governor Francis Nicholson," *Journal of Southern History*, XI (February 1945), 68-79; Samuel Clyde McCullough, "The Fight to Depose Governor Nicholson," *Journal of Southern History*, XII (August 1946), 403-22; Fairfax Downey, "The Governor Goes A-Wooing: The Swashbuckling Courtship of Nicholson of Virginia, 1699-1705," *Virginia Magazine of History and Biography*, LV (January 1947), 6-19; Ruth M. Winton, "Governor Francis Nicholson's Relations with the Society for the Propagation of the Gospel in Foreign Parts, 1701-1727," *Historical Magazine of the Protestant Episcopal Church*, XVII (September 1948), 274-96; Bruce T. McCully, "From the North Riding to Morocco: The Early Years of Governor Francis Nicholson, 1655-1686," *William and Mary Quarterly*, 3rd ser., vol. XIX (October 1962), 534-56; Gary B. Nash, "Governor Francis Nicholson and the New Castle Expedition of 1696," *Delaware History*, XI (April 1965), 229-39; Stephen S. Webb, "The Strange Career of Francis Nicholson," *William and Mary Quarterly*, 3rd ser., vol. XXIII (October 1966), 513-48. *DAB, DNB*.

LEISLER, Jacob, 1689-1691

Born in 1640 in Frankfort, Germany, the son of Jacob Victorius Leyssler, a Calvinist minister, and his wife, Susanna. Married on April 11, 1663 to Elsje (Tymens) van der Veen; father of Susanna, Catharina, Jacob, Mary, Johannes (died young), Hester and Francina.

Arrived in New Amsterdam in 1660 as an obscure soldier in the service of the Dutch West India Company; eventually became a wealthy merchant, due in part to his marriage to the socially prominent widow of Pieter van der Veen. Held several minor public offices, including Captain of the Militia and Justice of the Peace, until his sudden emergence in 1689 as the leader of a rebellion aimed at the ouster of Lieutenant Governor Francis Nicholson; assumed the government of New York in June 1689, after the flight of Nicholson from the province.

During the first months of his regime, Leisler worked to secure his political position. In June of 1689 he was modestly proclaimed "Captain of the fort" by a Committee of Safety composed of members of his faction, but several months later that title was altered to "Commander-in-Chief." By December of 1689 Leisler felt secure enough to style himself "Lieutenant Governor," and until early 1691 he was, given the tumultuous nature of New York politics at the time, reasonably successful in ruling the province. During this period a representative Assembly met twice in New York, and by the spring of 1690 the legislators had begun to grapple with such issues as the need to tax all real, personal and "visible" property in order to secure funds to aid in the defense of New York against encroachment by the French and Indians. The Leislerian Assembly also aimed at ending the discriminatory laws regulating the flour trade, laws which protected New York City merchants and millers at the expense of farmers in the Hudson River Valley. Although Leisler saw this policy as an inducement for the common people to support his movement, the animosity which it aroused among the city's wealthy merchants proved to be more significant in the long run.

As early as January 1690 the English king had commissioned Henry Sloughter as governor of New York, and when the dilatory Sloughter finally appeared in the province in March 1691, he had Leisler and his followers seized and imprisoned. Two months later Leisler was convicted of rebellion and murder by a Special Court of Oyer and Terminer. He died by hanging on May 16, 1691, along with Jacob Milborne, one his staunchest supporters.

Bibliography: Charles F. Hoffman, *The Administration of Governor Leisler* (Boston, 1844); Edmund B. O'Callaghan, ed., "Papers Relating to the Administration of Lieut. Gov. Leisler, 1689-1691," *Documentary History of the State of New York*, vol. II (Albany, 1849), 1-438; Edmund B. O'Callaghan, ed., "Documents Relating to the Administration of Leisler," New-York Historical Society, *Collections* (New York, 1868), 241-426; Edwin R. Purple, "Contributions to the History of the Ancient Families of New York City: Leisler," *New York Genealogical and Biographical Record*, VII (October 1876), 145-51; Lawrence H. Leder, ed., "Records of the Trials of Jacob Leisler and His Associates, *New-York Historical Society Quarterly*, XXXVI (October 1952), 431-57; Jerome R. Reich, *Leisler's Rebellion: A Study of Democracy in New York, 1664-1720* (Chicago, 1953); Charles H. McCormick, "Leisler's Rebellion," unpub. Ph.D. diss., American University, 1971. *DAB*.

SLOUGHTER, Henry, 1691

Date, place of birth and names of parents unknown, although he may have been a Protestant refugee from Ireland. Married to a woman named Mary.

Served in the British Army for a number of years, rising to the rank of Colonel. Became an early supporter of William of Orange during the Glorious Revolution of 1688; commissioned in January 1690 as Captain General and Governor-in-Chief of New York, and arrived in the colony to assume that position in March of 1691.

Because of his duties as a commander of troops on the Isle of Wight, Sloughter's departure for New York was delayed for some time, and it was not until fourteen months after he had received his commission that he finally landed in the colony. In an attempt to establish his right to govern before he arrived, Sloughter decided to send his subordinate officer, Major Richard Ingoldesby, as his emissary, but Ingoldesby's appearance in late January 1691 only made matters more complicated. Jacob Leisler, who had seized the New York government following the demise of the Dominion of New England, refused to acknowledge the major's authority, a stance which led to a bitter power struggle between pro- and anti-Leislerian factions. The arrival of Sloughter in New York in mid-March quickly produced new developments, when Leisler procrastinated before turning over his command to the new royal governor. Charged with rebellion and murder by a Court of Oyer and Terminer, Leisler and one of his supporters were executed in May 1691. On July 23, 1691, however, Sloughter himself died in New York, probably of pneumonia, and the provincial Council named Major Ingoldesby as an interim governor.

Bibliography: Charles H. McCormick, "Governor Sloughter's Delay and Leisler's Rebellion, 1689-1691," *New-York Historical Society Quarterly*, LXII (July 1978), 238-52.

INGOLDESBY, Richard, 1691-1692, 1709-1710
also New Jersey, 1709-1710

Born in England; date of birth and names of parents unknown. Married; father of Mary and probably others.

With the rank of Major, commanded a company of British troops in January 1691, and served as Acting Governor of New York after the suppression of Leisler's Rebellion; eventually obtained the military title of Colonel. As Commander-in-Chief of New York, conducted a conference with the Five Nations of Indians in June 1692. Sailed for England in 1696 and remained until 1704, apparently in an attempt to win the governorship of New York. Returned to New York in March 1704, bringing with him a commission as Lieutenant Governor of both New York and New Jersey. Clashed on several occasions with Governor Cornbury of New York and New Jersey, who in 1706 requested Ingoldesby's removal as lieutenant governor of New York, and his appointment instead to the New Jersey Council. Following the death of Governor John, Lord Lovelace in May 1709, assumed office as chief executive of New York and New Jersey, serving in that capacity until April of 1710.

Ingoldesby's first interim governorship of New York only lasted from July 1691 to August of 1692, between the sudden death of Governor Henry Sloughter and the arrival from England of Governor Benjamin Fletcher. His selection as chief executive by that colony's Council signified the triumph of the anti-Leislerian faction in New York, whom Ingoldesby had helped to achieve power by deploying the troops at his command against Jacob Leisler and his supporters. Almost two decades later Ingoldesby's brief administration in New York and New Jersey was disrupted by confusion over his right to govern both provinces. Although the Board of Trade had prepared a warrant directing his removal as lieutenant governor of New York as early as April of 1706, no ruling had been made at that time affecting his credentials in New Jersey. Indeed, no record even existed to prove that Queen Anne had signed the warrant revoking his New York commission. With Ingoldesby's legal status so unclear, officials in London were forced to reconsider the whole matter, and in October of 1709 the Queen permanently rescinded his New Jersey commission (his commission for New York having been annulled a month earlier). Yielding to this verdict, Ingoldesby gave up his executive authority in April 1710 to Gerardus Beekman and William Pinhorne, respectively presidents of the New York and New Jersey Councils. During his eleven months as chief executive, Ingoldesby took advantage of the position in New Jersey by confirming, with the backing of the old Cornbury Ring, the large New Britain land patent and numerous purchases of Indian land by white settlers. After his dismissal as lieutenant governor he appears to have left America and returned to England, where nothing is known of his subsequent career.

FLETCHER, Benjamin, 1692-1698

Pennsylvania, 1693-1695

Born, perhaps in 1640, in England, the son of William and Abigail (Vincent) Fletcher. An Anglican. Married to Elizabeth Hodson, and the father of two daughters and a son, Benjamin.

Served in the Irish Army under the Duke of Ormonde from 1683 to 1685, eventually rising to the rank of Captain. Later became an officer in Princess Anne of Denmark's regiment of foot soldiers, which was stationed in England; fought in Ireland under William III and attracted the notice of several distinguished patrons, who recommended him for the New York governorship. Commissioned Captain General and Governor-in-Chief of New York in March 1692, and landed in the colony to take up the office in August of that year; also commissioned Royal Governor of Pennsylvania in October 1692 (for a two-year period), and began his administration in that province in April of 1693. Named Commander of the militia in the Jerseys, Connecticut and Rhode Island at various times after his first gubernatorial appointment.

Fletcher came to America with a wide-ranging commission, and he quickly sought a means of reducing his responsibilities to manageable proportions. In Pennsylvania he chose to relinquish most of the daily executive duties to William Markham, his lieutenant governor, a policy which enabled him to devote more attention to New York matters. In New York, Fletcher was faced with the bitter division between supporters and opponents of the political cause of Jacob Leisler, the executed rebel governor of New York. During the factionalism which disrupted that colony's politics in the 1690's, Fletcher sided with the anti-Leislerians, but in return for his support he demanded bribes in a variety of forms. This avaricious behavior only exacerbated the spirit of factionalism in New York, as the governor's opponents grew increasingly indignant over his practice of "squeezing money both out of the publick and private purses."

Fletcher was recalled to England following the arrival in April 1698 of his replacement, the Earl of Bellomont, and returned to England to answer charges of delinquent behavior while in office, charges which included the allegation that his administration had condoned piracy. Although he was censured and threatened with prosecution, Fletcher appears to have avoided imprisonment. Nevertheless, he fell into considerable financial distress, and in 1702 he petitioned the authorities for military pay which he needed to avoid ruin. Fletcher died in Ireland in 1703.

Bibliography: Alice Davis, "The Administration of Benjamin Fletcher in New York," New York Historical Association, *Journal*, II (October 1921), 213-50; James S. Leamon, "War, Finance, and Faction in Colonial New York: The Administration of Governor Benjamin Fletcher, 1692-1698," unpub. Ph.D. diss., Brown University, 1961; James S. Leamon, "Governor Fletcher's Recall," *William and Mary Quarterly,* 3rd ser., vol. XX (October 1963), 527-42. *DAB*.

COOTE, Richard, Earl of Bellomont, 1698-1699, 1700-1701
Massachusetts and New Hampshire, 1699-1700

Born in 1636, the son of Richard and Mary (St. George) Coote. Brother of Charles (died in infancy), Chidley, Thomas, Mary, Catherine, Letitia, Olivia and Elizabeth. Married to Catherine Nanfan, by whom he was the father of Nanfan and Richard.

Succeeded his father as Baron Coote of Coloony, an order of nobility in the Irish peerage, in July 1683; created Earl of Bellomont in November 1689. Became a close friend of William, Prince of Orange, and following the Glorious Revolution received various honors from the new monarchs, including that of Treasurer and Receiver General to the Queen in March 1689. Also served as a member of Parliament for Droitwich from 1688 to 1695. Commissioned Royal Governor of Massachusetts Bay, New Hampshire and New York in June 1697; arrived in New York to begin his administration in April 1698 and, except for an absence from May 1699 to July 1700, when he presided in person as head of the government in Massachusetts and New Hampshire, remained resident chief executive of that colony until his death.

Bellomont landed in New York at a time when factionalism was widespread, largely due to the persistent Leislerian controversy, and the new governor's insensitivity to this volatile political issue did not improve matters. Nevertheless, Bellomont's tenure in New York was not without its achievements. His attempts to discourage commerce with pirates, for example, were fairly successful, as were his techniques for putting New York's administration on a more systematic basis, evidenced by the census carried out under his direction in 1698. In Massachusetts and New Hampshire Bellomont's brief period as resident chief executive was comparatively uneventful, although in New Hampshire he did become embroiled in a dispute involving Samuel Allen, who claimed that he held proprietary title to that province.

By early 1701 Bellomont's health had been seriously impaired by his efforts to preside over three colonies, each with its own set of problems. Finally, on March 5, 1701, the governor succumbed in New York to a particularly severe case of gout.

Bibliography: Frederic De Peyster, *The Life and Administration of Richard, Earl of Bellomont ... 1697 to 1701* (New York, 1879); A. de Vlieger, *Historical and Genealogical Record of the Coote Family* (Lausanne, 1900); Stanley H. Friedelbaum, "Bellomont: Imperial Administrator—Studies in Colonial Administration during the 17th Century," unpub. Ph.D. diss., Columbia University, 1955; Jacob Judd, "Lord Bellomont and Captain Kidd: A Footnote to an Entangled Alliance," *New-York Historical Society Quarterly*, XLVII (January 1963), 66-74; John D. Runcie, "The Problem of Anglo-American Politics in Bellomont's New York," *William and Mary Quarterly*, 3rd ser., vol. XXVI (April 1969), 191-217; John C. Rainbolt, "A 'great and usefull designe': Bellomont's Proposal for New York, 1698-1701," *New-York Historical Society Quarterly*, LIII (October 1969), 333-51; John C. Rainbolt, "The Creation of a Governor and Captain General for the Northern Colonies: The Process of Colonial Policy Formation at the End of the Seventeenth Century," *New-York Historical Society Quarterly*, LVII (April 1973), 101-20. *DAB*, *DNB*.

NANFAN, John, 1699-1700, 1701-1702

A native of Birtsmorton, Worcestershire, England; date of birth and names of parents unknown, but the grandson of John Nanfan. Married to Elizabeth, the daughter of William Chester of Barbados.

Pursued a military career as a young man, eventually rising to the rank of Captain. Commissioned Lieutenant Governor of New York in July 1697, and succeeded Acting Governor William Smith as chief executive of the province in May 1701, serving in that capacity until the arrival of Lord Cornbury in May 1702. Acted as New York's interim head from May 1699 to July 1700, during the administration of Lord Bellomont, when that governor was absent in Massachusetts and New Hampshire on Crown business.

Lord Bellomont kept a fairly tight rein on New York affairs during Nanfan's first period as acting governor, and on at least one occasion in 1699, he left his subordinate a detailed set of instructions for administering the colony. The prudence of Bellomont in refusing to give Nanfan greater control became obvious when the lieutenant governor again assumed the governorship in the spring of 1701. Nanfan's allegiance to the Leislerian faction in New York politics provoked the anti-Leislerian cabal to sent petitions to the King, to Parliament, and to Governor-designate Lord Cornbury, all of which were extremely critical of Nanfan's behavior in office. Nanfan responded rashly by attacking a number of his most powerful opponents, including Nicholas Bayard, whom he prosecuted for treason, and Robert Livingston, whom he suspended from the Council.

Following his replacement by Lord Cornbury, Nanfan was arrested in the autumn of 1702 and charged with non-payment of soldiers' subsistence money. His legal woes continued until 1705, when he fled to England "in a miserable and naked condition." Nanfan died intestate in 1706. *DNB*.

SMITH, William, 1701

Born on February 2, 1655 in Higham Ferrars, Northamptonshire, England, the son of William Smith, a justice of the peace. Married on November 26, 1675 to Martha Tunstall; father of Henry, William, Charles, Martha, Jane, Georgiana (or Gloriana) and several others who died young.

Appointed Mayor of Tangier in 1674, and served as chief magistrate of that English military outpost for ten years. Returned home after authorities in England decided to abandon the post; a short time later immigrated to New York, arriving in August 1686. Acted as a member of the court which tried Jacob Leisler and his supporters in the spring of 1691; nominated that May to New York's Supreme Court. Served as Chief Justice of New York, with two intervals, from November 1692 to April 1703; also held office at various times as Judge of the prerogative court for Suffolk County, Judge of the New York Court of Vice-Admiralty, Presiding Judge of a Special Court of Oyer and Terminer, and member of the New York Court of Chancery. Served as Chairman of a committee which in 1699 produced a "scheam" for a province-wide court system, which remained the framework for the New York judiciary throughout the colonial period. Named to the New York Council in 1691, a position which he filled until his death in 1705; in his capacity as President of the Council, served as Acting Governor of New York between the death of Governor Bellomont in March 1701 and the arrival of New York's Lieutenant Governor John Nanfan in May of that year.

Smith's brief period as chief executive was marred by a dispute over the extent of his official powers. This quarrel eventually disrupted both the Council and the Assembly, and resulted in the expulsion of Major Matthew Howell from his Assembly seat. In two months time, however, Lieutenant Governor Nanfan returned from Barbados and established his authority in the province, thus bringing an end to the controversy. Smith then resumed his seat on the Council and his judicial duties. He died at "St. George," his Long Island estate, on February 18, 1705 and was buried nearby.

Bibliography: William S. Pelletreau, *Wills of the Smith Families of New York and Long Island, 1664-1794* (New York, 1898); Rev. Howard Duffield, *The Tangier Smith Manor of St. George* (Baltimore, 1921).

HYDE, Edward (Viscount Cornbury), 1702-1708
also New Jersey, 1703-1708

Born in 1661 in England, the eldest son of Henry Hyde, the second Earl of Clarendon, and his wife, the former Theodosia Capel. An Anglican. Married in 1688 to Katherine O'Brien; father of one son and two daughters.

Served as an officer in the British Army; acted as a member of Parliament for sixteen years. Commissioned Captain General and Governor-in-Chief of New York in September 1701, and arrived in America to take up his position in May of 1702; also commissioned Governor of New Jersey in December 1702, but only assumed office in that province in August of 1703.

In both New York and New Jersey, the Cornbury administration proved to be an almost complete failure, as corruption and venality grew more widespread. The governor himself encouraged the unscrupulous behavior which became the most conspicuous feature of his tenure, especially by approving land grants to his political favorites. Cornbury also displayed a lack of tact in dealing with the religiously heterogeneous population of New York. In 1707, for example, he denied a local preacher's license to Francis Makemie, a prominent Scottish Presbyterian. Makemie eventually stood trial and was vindicated, but the ill will which Cornbury had provoked was less easy to dismiss than the weak case brought against the Scottish minister. Cornbury's reputation was further damaged by his habit of dressing in women's formal attire, a peculiarity which one historian has attributed to the governor's wish to represent his cousin, Queen Anne, in a more vivid manner [*sic*]. Whatever Cornbury's motivation, the colonists in New York and New Jersey responded only with frequent expressions of contempt for their chief executive. Authorities in England finally admitted their error in 1708 when, yielding to protests from irate colonists like Lewis Morris, a leader of the New Jersey Assembly, they removed Cornbury in favor of John, Lord Lovelace.

Following his replacement in December of 1708, Cornbury returned to England, but not until his creditors in New York had delayed his departure by having him arrested for unpaid debts. Upon the death of his father, Cornbury inherited the title of Earl of Clarendon, and in 1711 he was made a member of the Privy Council. He also served as an Envoy Extraordinary to Hanover in 1714, nine years before his death on April 1, 1723.

Bibliography: John Sharp, *A Sermon [on Job xiv. 14] Preached . . . in New York . . . 1706, at the Funeral of . . . Katherine Lady Cornbury . . .* (New York, 1706); Charles Worthen Spencer, "The Cornbury Legend," New York State Historical Association, *Proceedings*, XIII (1914), 309-20; Arthur D. Pierce, "A Governor in Skirts [Cornbury]," New Jersey Historical Society, *Proceedings*, LXXXIII (January 1965), 1-9. *DAB*.

LOVELACE, John (4th Baron Lovelace of Hurley), 1708-1709

also New Jersey, 1708-1709

Born in England, the son of William and Mary (King) Lovelace; date of birth unknown. Married on October 20, 1702 to Charlotte Clayton; father of John (died young), Nevil and Wentworth (died young).

Created fourth Baron Lovelace of Hurley in 1693; became a member of the House of Lords in November of 1693. Named Colonel of a regiment of troops in January 1706. Commissioned Captain General and Governor-in-Chief of New York and New Jersey in May 1708, and arrived to take up his new assignment in December of that year.

Accompanying Lord Lovelace to New York in 1708 was a large group of Palatines, who were seeking refuge from religious persecution in the Rhineland. This encouragement of full-scale emigration, along with Lovelace's willingness to attend sessions of the New Jersey Council on a regular basis, suggests that he intended to carry on an active administration in both colonies. At the same time, there were indications that Lovelace hoped to break up the notorious Cornbury Ring, which had controlled politics in New Jersey during the tenure of his predecessor. In April of 1709, for example, Lovelace appointed Thomas Gordon as New Jersey's chief justice in place of Roger Mompesson, one of the more prominent members of the Cornbury group, who had resigned under fire. Lovelace's sudden death from apoplexy on May 6, 1709, however, put an end to any expectations that he would eliminate the political corruption which had marked Cornbury's years in office. Lovelace was buried in New York.

Bibliography: William Vesey, *A Sermon Preached in Trinity Church in New York, in America, May 12, 1709, at the Funeral of the Right Honourable John Lord Lovelace* . . ., New-York Historical Society, *Collections*, XIII (New York, 1881), 321-38; James Grant Wilson, "Lord Lovelace and the Second Canadian Campaign—1708-1710," American Historical Association, *Annual Report for the Year 1891* (Washington, D.C., 1892), 269-97. *DNB*.

SCHUYLER, Peter, 1709, 1719-1720

Born on September 17, 1657 in Beverwyck (now Albany, New York), the second son of Philip Pieterse and Margarita (Van Slichtenhorst) Schuyler. Brother of Brandt, Geertru, Alida, Arent, Philip, Johannes, Margaret, and two others who died young. Married *circa* 1681 to Engeltie Van Schaick, by whom he had four children, although only one, Margarita, survived past childhood; remarried on September 14, 1691 to Maria Van Rensselaer; father by his second wife of Maria, Geertru, Philip, Jeremias and Peter.

Was serving as a Lieutenant of Cavalry by the age of twenty-seven, and eventually rose to the rank of Colonel. Chosen as the first Mayor of Albany in 1686, a position which he held, with several brief intervals, at least until 1691; also acted as head of the Board of Indian Commissioners. Appointed Judge of the Court of Common Pleas in 1691, and in 1692 became a member of the New York Council. In his capacity as President of the Council, served as Acting Governor of New York for about ten days in spring 1709; again presided from July 1719 to September 1720, between the administrations of Robert Hunter and William Burnet.

Schuyler's periods as chief executive witnessed the continuation of New York's commercial growth, stimulated by the activities of wealthy merchant-politicians such as himself. More ominously, his final tenure was also characterized by the emergence of factionalism as an important aspect of New York politics. Indeed, when Governor William Burnet arrived from England to assume the governorship from Schuyler in 1720, he so feared the Council president's influence as an opposition leader that he arranged for his removal from the Council. Schuyler died a short time later, on February 19, 1724.

Bibliography: Jonathan Pearson, "Contributions to the History of the Ancient Dutch Families of New York and Albany: Schuyler," *New York Genealogical and Biographical Record*, II (October 1871), 190-91; George W. Schuyler, *Colonial New York: Philip Schuyler and His Family*, 2 vols. (New York, 1885); Montgomery Schuyler, *The Schuyler Family* (New York, 1926). *DAB*.

BEEKMAN, Gerardus, 1710

Born in 1653 in New York City, the son of William and Catharine (De Boog) Beekman. Brother of Maria, Henry, Cornelia, Johannes, Jacobus, Wilhelmus, Martin and Catherine. Married on October 25, 1677 to Magdalen Abeel; father of William (died young), Christopher, Adrian, William, Jacobus, Catharine, Gerardus, Johannes, Cornelia, Henry and Maria.

Worked for a number of years as a "doctor of physick." Became a prominent supporter of Jacob Leisler between 1689 and 1691, serving as a representative of King's County on the Committee of Safety and on the Council; also acted as "Major of Horse," Justice of the Peace, and a member of the Court of Oyer and Terminer. Sentenced to death in April 1691, after the fall of the Leisler regime, but was pardoned in 1694 and indemnified in 1699 for the penalties which he had suffered. Named to the Governor's Council in 1702, a position which he held until his death; in his capacity as President of the Council, served as Acting Governor of New York from April to June of 1710.

Following the sudden death of Lord Lovelace in May 1709, Richard Ingoldesby, who took office as chief executive of New Jersey, claimed that his commission as lieutenant governor also gave him authority over New York. In practical terms, however, Ingoldesby was never able to exercise much personal supervision over the latter colony. Although Beekman also endeavored to fill the administrative void in New York for several months, that colony's Assembly actually enjoyed the most significant amount of power during this period. An example of the Assembly's strength was its treatment of New York's fiscal officials, who were all made accountable to the Lower House.

After Robert Hunter came to New York and began to reassert the governor's authority, Beekman returned to the Council, where he remained until his death on October 10, 1723.

Bibliography: James R. Gibson, Jr., "Some Records of the Beekman Family," *New York Genealogical and Biographical Record*, XIX (April 1888), 41-52; Mrs. William B. Beekman, *The Beekman Family* (Baltimore, 1925); Alexander J. Wall, Jr., " 'Her Majesty Does Particularly Recommend'," *New-York Historical Society Quarterly*, XXXI (October 1947), 193-98; Philip L. White, *The Beekmans of New York in Politics and Commerce, 1647-1877* (New York, 1956).

HUNTER, Robert, 1710-1719
also New Jersey, 1710-1719

Born in Hunterston, Ayrshire, Scotland, the son of James and Margaret (Spalding) Hunter; date of birth unknown. Married to Elizabeth (Orby) Hay; father of Thomas Orby, Katherine, Henrietta and Charlotte.

Entered the British Army as a young man, and fought with the troops of the Duke of Marlborough during the War of the Spanish Succession. Participated in the Battle of Blenheim in 1704, and a short time later rose to the rank of Lieutenant Colonel. Sailed for America in May 1707, after acquiring the lieutenant governorship of Virginia, but was captured by a privateer while at sea and transported to France. Released in an exchange of prisoners and returned to England, where in October of 1709 he was commissioned Captain General and Governor-in-Chief of New York and New Jersey; arrived in New York City in June 1710 to assume his new office.

Compared with the administrations of Cornbury, Lovelace and Ingoldesby, each of which had been tainted by corruption and venality, Hunter's tenure as chief executive represented a political change for the better. In New Jersey the new governor worked to dismantle the corrupt Cornbury Ring, and by the spring of 1711 he was ready to press for the removal of key members of that group from that colony's Council. New York politics also quickly felt the force of Hunter's energetic approach to government. During his early years in office Hunter battled with the New York Assembly over the issue of public credit, a battle which between 1715 and 1717 resulted in a series of compromises which assured the governor of tax revenues on a five-year basis, as long as he agreed to spend the money according to a program designed by the legislature and approved a naturalization bill endorsed by New York's Dutch residents. Guided by his own shrewd political instincts, Hunter's success in New York was aided by his friendship with Chief Justice Lewis Morris, who helped form a party which defended the "governor's interest." Still, by the end of Hunter's administration this group had already begun to encounter resistance from men like the wealthy merchant Peter Schuyler, thereby setting the stage for the factionalism which would influence New York and New Jersey politics for the rest of the colonial period.

In July 1719 Hunter returned to England and exchanged his governorship for the position of Comptroller General of Customs, then held by William Burnet. Hunter also served as Governor of Jamaica from 1727 until his death in March 1734. An occasional author and the friend of prominent literary figures like Jonathan Swift, Hunter's most famous work is the farce *Androboros*, which satirized New York politics.

Bibliography: Richard L. Beyer, "Robert Hunter, Royal Governor of New York," unpub. Ph.D. diss., University of Iowa, 1929; Lawrence H. Leder, ed., "Robert Hunter's *Androboros,*" *Bulletin of the New York Public Library*, LXVIII (March 1964), 153-90; James E. Scanlon, "A Life of Robert Hunter, 1666-1734," unpub. Ph.D. diss., University of Virginia, 1969; Alison G. Olson, "Governor Robert Hunter and the Anglican Church in New York," in Anne Whiteman *et al.*, eds., *Statesmen, Scholars and Merchants: Essays in Eighteenth-Century History Presented to Dame Lucy Sutherland* (Oxford, 1973), 44-64; James E. Scanlon, "British Intrigue and the Governorship of Robert Hunter," *New-York Historical Society Quarterly*, LVII (July 1973), 199-211. *DAB, DNB*.

BURNET, William, 1720-1728

also New Jersey, 1720-1728; Massachusetts and New Hampshire, 1728-1729

Born in March 1688 at The Hague, the eldest son of Gilbert Burnet, bishop of Salisbury, and his second wife, Mary (Scott) Burnet. Brother of Mary and Gilbert. Married in about May 1712 to a daughter of Dean Stanhope, by whom he was the father of Gilbert; following the death of his first wife, remarried to Anna Maria [or Mary] Van Horne; father of William, Mary and Thomas by his second wife.

Enrolled at Trinity College, Cambridge at the age of thirteen, but left without obtaining a degree; later studied privately, and called to the bar. Commissioned Captain General and Governor-in-Chief of New York and New Jersey in June 1720, and arrived in America to assume office in September of that year. Commissioned Royal Governor of New Hampshire in November 1727, and of Massachusetts Bay in March 1728; left New York in the spring of 1728, following his replacement by the newly-appointed Governor John Montgomerie, and travelled to New England to take up his new positions.

As chief executive of New York, Burnet was confronted by controversy over the extensive fur trade then existing between Albany and Montreal. Contending that such commerce was enhancing New France's stature among Indians in the area, who sold their furs to the English through French *coureurs de bois*, Burnet tried to eliminate the traffic both by means of legislation and by encouraging direct trade between the English and various Indian tribes. Despite some initial success, however, Burnet's policy quickly encountered strong opposition from prominent New York merchants who preferred to conduct their business with the French, and by 1726 it had become apparent that his efforts would fail. In New Jersey Burnet met with similar recalcitrance among leading members of that colony's Assembly, especially over money bills. Nevertheless, after several confrontations with the Assembly, Burnet decided to adopt a more tactful approach, and by the time of his departure in 1728 he had won significant concessions from the legislators.

Although Burnet's tenure in Massachusetts Bay and New Hampshire lasted only a little more than a year, his administration of those colonies was also marked by disputes over financial matters. In particular, the question of the form which the governor's remuneration should take, a recurrent problem during much of the eighteenth century, created tension between Burnet and the Massachusetts Assembly, as Burnet insisted that he be given a permanent salary. On September 7, 1729, however, before the issue could be resolved, Burnet died suddenly in Boston.

Bibliography: William Nelson, *Original Documents Relating to the Life and Administrations of William Burnet* . . . (Paterson, N.J., 1897). Burnet's will appears in the *New England Historical and Genealogical Register*, XLVII (January 1893), 123-25. *DAB, DNB*.

MONTGOMERIE, John, 1728-1731

also New Jersey, 1728-1731

Born in Scotland; date of birth and names of parents unknown. Apparently never married.

Served for a number of years in the British Army, and probably attained the rank of Colonel; also acted as Leicester House Groom of the Bed-Chamber for George II before that monarch's ascension to the British throne. Sat in Parliament; commissioned in October of 1727 as Captain General and Governor-in-Chief of New York and New Jersey, following the transfer of William Burnet to New England; assumed office as chief executive in April 1728, and held that position until his death.

Montgomerie's period as governor was relatively tranquil, largely because a wish to enhance his personal fortune and a distaste for controversy made him unwilling to defy the New Jersey and New York legislatures. Indeed, the political opposition which he encountered in New Jersey from "unmanageable Quakers" seems only to have led him to adopt a more cautious approach in asserting the royal prerogative. In New York members of the legislature—such as Adolph Philipse, the powerful speaker of the colony's Assembly—took advantage of Montgomerie's timidity and strengthened their own positions.

Perhaps the most significant piece of legislation associated with Montgomerie's name was the "Montgomerie Charter" of 1730, which gave New York City a greater degree of political autonomy. Montgomerie died suddenly during the night of June 30, 1731, the victim, according to some authorities, of a smallpox epidemic; he died intestate.

VAN DAM, Rip, 1731-1732

Born *circa* 1660 in Fort Orange (now Albany, New York), the son of Claas Ripse, a carpenter, and Maria (Bords) van Dam. Brother of four or five. Married in September 1684 to Sara van der Spiegel; father of two sons and three daughters who reached maturity, including Mary.

Engaged in trade and shipbuilding as a young man, and by the age of thirty had established himself as a merchant in New York City. Beginning in 1693, elected for three consecutive years to the New York City Board of Aldermen. Appointed to the Governor's Council in 1703 by Lord Cornbury, and served in that capacity for over thirty years. Following the death of Governor John Montgomerie late in June of 1731, became, as President of the Council, the chief executive of New York.

Van Dam's brief tenure at the helm of New York's government was fairly uneventful, although it did witness the continued growth of the Assembly as a major political force. This period was also characterized by the formation of relatively stable factional alignments in the legislature, which would become more important following the arrival of Governor William Cosby in August 1732.

Soon after his replacement by Cosby, Van Dam became involved in a bitter dispute with the new governor. When Cosby insisted that he was entitled to one-half of the salary collected by Van Dam while he had administered the province, Van Dam refused to accept Cosby's claim. A lengthy legal battle ensued, which eventually brought about the governor's suspension of Chief Justice Lewis Morris in August 1733. In November 1735 Cosby also suspended Van Dam from his seat on the Council and, despite Van Dam's effort to fight the ouster attempt, his public career ended a short time later. Van Dam died on June 10, 1749.

Bibliography: [James Alexander and William Smith], *The Arguments of the Council for the Defendant ... Rip Van Dam ... in the Supreme Court of New-York* (New York, 1733); *The Proceedings of Rip Van Dam, Esq.; in Order for Obtaining Equal Justice of His Excellency William Cosby, Esq.* (New York, 1733); Frederic De Peyster, *Memoir of Rip Van Dam* (New York, 1865). *DAB*.

COSBY, William, 1732-1736
also New Jersey, 1732-1736

Born *circa* 1690, probably in Ireland, the son of Alexander and Elizabeth (L'Estrange) Cosby. Brother of Dudley, Henry, Thomas, Loftus, Alexander, Arnold, Anne, Elizabeth, Jane, Dorcas, Isabella, Celia and Dorothy. Married to Grace Montague, the sister of George, Earl of Halifax, and a first cousin of the Duke of Newcastle; father of William, Henry, Elizabeth and Grace.

Entered the British Army in 1704, and had risen to the rank of Colonel by 1717. After his regiment's transfer in 1718 to Minorca in the Balearic Islands, served for about ten years as civil and military Governor, a position which, it was later alleged, he illegally used to improve his own finances. Commissioned in spring of 1732 as Captain General and Governor-in-Chief of New York and New Jersey, and arrived in New York to take up the appointment in August of that year.

Having acquired the governorship of New York and New Jersey through his wife's influential family connections, Cosby felt little need to adopt a conciliatory attitude towards local political leaders. Nevertheless, in New Jersey his abrasive behavior had little impact, since he rarely played an active role in governing that province. Indeed, he met with the New Jersey Assembly on only one occasion, and the colony's lawmakers took advantage of Cosby's absence by enhancing their own authority. New York, however, was more directly affected by the heavy-handed mode of administration practiced by Cosby, especially when the governor informed his Council in November 1732 that he was entitled to one-half of the salary paid to Rip Van Dam during Van Dam's thirteen months as acting governor. The controversy which resulted divided the province politically, and culminated in August of 1733 with Cosby's suspension of Chief Justice Lewis Morris, who had refused to permit the New York Supreme Court to be used as the governor's weapon against Van Dam. About a year later Cosby became involved in an even more celebrated legal decision involving freedom of the press. Declaring the *New-York Weekly Journal* to be a seditious publication, the Governor's Council requested the attorney general to take legal action against the authors of the paper and its printer, John Peter Zenger. In the end Zenger was acquitted of libel, a verdict which represented a triumph for the opponents of the governor, led by former Chief Justice Morris. Cosby died on March 10, 1736, while still in office.

Bibliography: [Cadwallader Colden], "History of Governor William Cosby's Administration and of Lieutenant-Governor George Clarke's Administration through 1737," in *Colden Papers*, vol. IX (New York, 1937) [published in the New-York Historical Society, *Collections* for the year 1935], 281-355; Vincent Buranelli, "Governor Cosby and His Enemies (1732-36)," *New York History*, XXXVII (October 1956), 365-87; J. H. Smith and L. Hershkowitz, "Courts of Equity in the Province of New York: The Cosby Controversy, 1732-1736," *American Journal of Legal History*, XVI (January 1972), 1-50. *DAB*.

CLARKE, George, 1736-1743

Born in 1676 in Swainswick, Somersetshire, England, the son of George Clarke, Sr. Married in 1705 to Anne Hyde, a daughter of Governor Edward Hyde of North Carolina; father of George, Edward, Robert, Hyde, Elizabeth, Anne, Penelope and Mary.

Articled to an attorney as a young man, and later practiced law in Dublin. Named Secretary of the province of New York, largely because of the influence of his near relation, William Blathwayt, and arrived in New York to take up that appointment in July 1703; retained the office of provincial secretary, along with a variety of positions related to the secretaryship, for thirty-five years. Also appointed New York's Deputy to the Auditor General of the Plantations in 1702, and acted in that capacity for many years. Named to the Governor's Council in 1716, an office which he held until 1736; became one of the commissioners who in 1718 determined the boundary between New York and Connecticut. As President of the Council, succeeded the deceased Governor William Cosby in March 1736; a short time later received a commission as Lieutenant Governor of New York.

Clarke's efforts as chief executive were directed towards reducing the party warfare which had disrupted the administration of his predecessor. Despite his decision in May of 1736 to take the oath of office as Chancellor, a position which Cosby had also assumed in defiance of his enemies, Clarke usually sought to maintain an attitude that transcended factional politics. This policy appears to have been fairly successful, and the decline of factionalism under Clarke made it possible both for the province to improve its economic condition and for the lieutenant governor to acquire large new land grants from the compliant Council.

Following his replacement by George Clinton in September 1743, Clarke retired from public life. Taking with him the considerable fortune which he had amassed during his American career, Clarke returned in 1745 to England, where he purchased a large estate in Cheshire. Clarke died on January 12, 1760, and was buried in Chester Cathedral.

Bibliography: E. B. O'Callaghan, ed., *Voyage of George Clarke, Esq. to America* (Albany, 1867); [Cadwallader Colden], "History of Governor William Cosby's Administration and of Lieutenant-Governor George Clarke's Administration through 1737," in *Colden Papers*, vol. IX (New York, 1937) [published in the New-York Historical Society, *Collections* for the year 1935], 281-355. *DAB*.

CLINTON, George, 1743-1753

Born *circa* 1686 in England, the son of Sir Francis Fiennes Clinton, sixth Earl of Lincoln, and his wife Susan, the daughter of Anthony Penniston. Brother of Henry and Susan. Married to Anne Carle; father of Henry, Mary and Lucy Mary.

Began a naval career in 1707, and by 1716 had risen to the rank of Captain. Appointed in 1731 as the Commander of the naval squadron sent yearly to Newfoundland, a position which included responsibility for the civil administration of that area. Promoted to Commander-in-Chief of the Royal Navy's Mediterranean squadron in 1736, and given the rank of Admiral. Commanded British men-of-war during the late 1730's. Commissioned Captain General and Governor-in-Chief of New York in July 1741, but did not arrive in the province to assume that office until September of 1743.

Clinton's promotions while in the Royal Navy and his subsequent appointment as New York's chief executive were due largely to his family ties with the Duke of Newcastle. It soon became clear, however, that Newcastle's nomination of the inexperienced Clinton for the New York governorship was an unwise decision. Newcastle's error was made especially apparent when Clinton chose to rely on the advice of James DeLancey, New York's powerful chief justice. By the end of 1745 DeLancey's clever political maneuvers had given him almost total control over the Governor's Council and the administration of New York City. Nevertheless, when Clinton and DeLancey quarreled over a relatively minor piece of legislation in 1746, their dispute quickly resulted in the formation of a faction led by the chief justice, who now openly opposed the governor. For the remainder of his period in office Clinton, bolstered by an alliance with Surveyor General Cadwallader Colden, battled the DeLancey group without much success. Although Clinton did manage to regain some of his political power by the end of his administration, his overall failure to defend the royal prerogative against attacks by the New York Assembly finally brought about his replacement by Sir Danvers Osborn in October of 1753.

Following his period as chief executive, Clinton returned to England, where in 1754 he obtained a seat in Parliament through the intercession of the Duke of Newcastle. Clinton continued in Parliament as a member for the borough of Saltash until 1760. He also received his half-pay as an admiral, an award intended to ease his chronic money problems. Clinton died on July 10, 1761.

Bibliography: Charles B. Moore, "Introductory Sketch to the History of the Clinton Family," *New York Genealogical and Biographical Record*, XII (October 1881), 195-98, vol. XIII (January-October 1882), 5-10, 139, 173-80; Serena Moody Bradshaw, "A Study in Incompetency: Governor George Clinton and the New York Opposition, 1743-1754," unpub. Ph.D. diss., Ohio State University, 1977. Letters concerning Clinton's governorship are published in Cadwallader Colden, *The Letters and Papers of Cadwallader Colden . . . 1711- [1775]*, vols. III-IV (New York, 1920-21) [published as part of the New-York Historical Society, *Collections* for the years 1919-20]. *DAB*.

OSBORN, Sir Danvers, 1753

Born on November 17, 1715 in England, the son of John and Sarah (Byng) Osborn. Brother of five, including John. Married on September 25, 1740 to Lady Mary Montagu, the daughter of the first Earl of Halifax; father of George and John.

Acted as Colonel of a Bedford regiment which fought under the Duke of Cumberland during the Rebellion of 1745. Served as a member of Parliament for Bedfordshire from 1747 to 1753. Commissioned Captain General and Governor-in-Chief of New York in August 1753, and arrived in the province in October of that year to take up his new position.

Osborn's selection as chief executive of New York was due primarily to his late wife's relationship to the second Earl of Halifax, who had become president of the Board of Trade in 1748. Unfortunately, Osborn was ill-suited for the office, since his young wife's death in 1743 appears to have reinforced his already melancholy nature. Despite his tumultuous reception by the citizens of New York in the autumn of 1753, Osborn believed, quite correctly, that the provincial Assembly intended to continue its customary aggressive approach to political issues. Unable to accept this opposition, Osborn committed suicide on October 12, 1753, only a few days after assuming the governorship, and was discovered "in the lower part of Mr. Murray's Garden . . . strangled in his Handkerchief." Osborn was succeeded by Lieutenant Governor James DeLancey.

Bibliography: Wayne Andrews, "In Flocks, Like Ill-Boding Ravens, being an Account of the Tragic End of Sir Danvers Osborne, Bart.," *New-York Historical Society Quarterly*, XXXV (October 1951), 405-07.

DeLANCEY, James, 1753-1755, 1757-1760

Born on November 27, 1703 in New York, the son of Stephen and Anne (Van Cortlandt) DeLancey. Brother of Stephen, James (died young), Peter, Susannah, Anne (died young), Etienne, John, Oliver and Anne. Married in about 1729 to Anne Heathcote; father of James, Stephen, Heathcote, Susannah, Maria, Anne, Martha, and John Peter. Educated in England, becoming a fellow commoner at Corpus Christi College, Cambridge; also read law at the Inner Temple in London.

Returned to New York in 1725, admitted to the bar, and in January 1729 became a member of the Governor's Council. Headed the commission which framed the "Montgomerie Charter" of New York City in 1730. Named Second Judge of the provincial Supreme Court in June 1731, and in August 1733 replaced Lewis Morris as Chief Justice, after Morris had refused to yield to the wishes of Governor William Cosby concerning the Van Dam salary case;

held the office of chief justice until his death. Assumed the position of Lieutenant Governor in 1753, when the departing Governor George Clinton finally delivered the commission which he had withheld from DeLancey for six years; in his capacity as lieutenant governor, became chief executive of New York following the suicide of Governor Sir Danvers Osborn in October 1753, and served until the arrival of Governor Sir Charles Hardy in September 1755; also acted as chief executive of the province from July 1757 until his death.

Although he had long been a powerful political figure in New York, DeLancey's emergence as executive head of the province was sudden and unexpected. Nevertheless, when the distraught Sir Danvers Osborn committed suicide only a few days after assuming the governorship, DeLancey made the most of his opportunity. During his first period in office the first skirmishes of the French and Indian War broke out, encouraging DeLancey to host in mid-1754 a conference held at Albany which was attended by commissioners from seven colonies. The delegates to this meeting suggested various ways of combatting encroachments by the French, and devised policies aimed at improving relations with the Indian tribes. While the "Albany Plan" which resulted from the conference was never ratified by the assemblies of all the colonies who had sent representatives, many of the proposals put forth at Albany were later adopted by the Board of Trade in London. DeLancey's second term was also occupied for the most part with military preparations, and his adroit handling of the New York Assembly contributed greatly to the British war effort. Early in 1759, for example, the Assembly approved in less than two weeks a resolution which provided for New York's quota of almost 3,000 men, in compliance with the decision of William Pitt to prosecute the war in North America more vigorously. DeLancey died on July 30, 1760, shortly before the end of hostilities, and was succeeded by Lieutenant Governor Cadwallader Colden.

Bibliography: [Lewis Morris?], *Some Observations on the Charge Given by the Honourable James DeLancey, Esq., Justice of the Province of New-York, to the Grand Jury, the 15th Day of January, 1733* (New York, 1734); Edward Floyd DeLancey, "Memoir of James DeLancey," in *Documentary History of New York*, ed. by E. B. O'Callaghan (Albany, 1851), vol. IV, 1037-59; D. A. Story, *The DeLancey's: A Romance of a Great Family* (London, 1931); Stanley N. Katz, "Between Scylla and Charybdis: James DeLancey and Anglo-American Politics in Early Eighteenth-Century New York," in A. G. Olson and R. M. Brown, eds., *Anglo-American Political Relations, 1675-1775* (New Brunswick, N.J., 1970), 92-108; Leopold S. Launitz-Schurer, Jr., "Whig Loyalists: The DeLanceys of New York," *New-York Historical Society Quarterly*, LVI (July 1972), 179-98. *DAB*.

HARDY, Sir Charles, 1755-1757

Born *circa* 1716 in England, the son of Vice-Admiral Sir Charles and Lady Elizabeth (Burchett) Hardy. Brother of five, including Josiah Hardy, who served as governor of New Jersey from 1761 to 1763. Married in 1749 to Mary Tate; remarried to Catherine Stanyan, by whom he was the father of three sons and two daughters, including Catherine.

Entered the Royal Navy at an early age, and by 1741 had been made Commander of the *Rupert's Prize*. Participated in a number of naval engagements against Spanish and French vessels during the 1740's, especially in 1745, when he commanded the *Jersey* in a battle with the French ship *Saint Esprit*. Commissioned Captain General and Governor-in-Chief of New York in March 1755, and was knighted before his departure for America; arrived in the province in September 1755 to take up his new appointment.

Military preparations for the French and Indian (or Seven Years') War were the chief concern of Hardy's twenty-two months in office. Still, New York remained in a rather weak defensive position, a state of affairs due in part to rivalries among the political and military men responsible for organizing the war effort. In August of 1756, for example, French troops under Montcalm easily attacked and destroyed two English outposts at Oswego. Although the New York governor endeavored to improve the situation by deploying troops for the protection of the frontier, the French held a distinct military advantage until almost a year after Hardy gave up his administration to Lieutenant Governor James DeLancey in July 1757.

Following his period as chief executive, Hardy resumed his naval career on a full time basis. He took part in the final stages of the Seven Years' War, and in October of 1762 was rewarded for his services with a promotion to Vice-Admiral. Hardy became Admiral of the Blue in October 1770; in August of the next year he was also appointed Governor of Greenwich Hospital. Elected to Parliament as a representative for the borough of Portsmouth in 1774, Hardy nevertheless returned to the sea in 1779, when he took command of the Channel fleet. On May 18, 1780, while preparing to continue his command of the fleet, Hardy died of an apoplectic fit in Portsmouth.

Bibliography: W. E. May, "Capt. Charles Hardy on the Carolina Station, 1742-1744," *South Carolina Historical Magazine*, 70 (January 1969), 1-19. *DNB*.

COLDEN, Cadwallader, 1760-1761, 1761-1762, 1763-1765, 1769-1770, 1774-1775

Born on February 17, 1688 in Ireland, the son of Alexander Colden, a Scottish minister. Married on November 11, 1715 to Alice Christie; father of Alexander, David (died young), Elizabeth, Cadwallader, Jane, Alice, Sarah (died young), John, Catharine and David. Received an A.B. degree from the University of Edinburgh in 1705, and studied medicine for a time in London.

Immigrated to Philadelphia in 1710, where he both practiced medicine and worked as a merchant. Moved to New York in 1718, and by 1720 had become Surveyor General of that province. Named to the Council under Governor William Burnet in 1721, a position which he held until his death; also became Lieutenant Governor of New York in 1761. As President of the Council and (from 1761) Lieutenant Governor, served as Acting Governor of New York on five occasions: July 1760 to October 1761, November 1761 to June 1762, June 1763 to November 1765, September 1769 to October 1770, and April 1774 to June 1775.

Although Colden never received a commission as royal governor, the relatively short tenures of New York's chief executives during the 1760's and 1770's provided him with frequent opportunities to serve as an interim head of the province. As a result, Colden's time in office was marked by some of the most significant incidents of the revolutionary movement—incidents like the passage of the Stamp Act in 1765, which so outraged a New York mob that it burned the lieutenant governor in effigy. Colden eventually modified his stand on the Stamp Act when he realized that the law was unenforceable, but he continued to espouse conservative policies in a colony which was becoming more radical politically. Following the outbreak of war in 1775 Colden gave up the New York government for the fifth and final time, and resumed his duties as councillor and lieutenant governor. Colden died at "Spring Hill," his Long Island estate, on September 28, 1776, less than three months after the thirteen colonies declared their independence from England.

Throughout his life Colden demonstrated an impressive knowledge of fields other than politics, including history, philosophy, physics, mathematics and botany. He included among his correspondents some of the leading eighteenth-century men of science, and wrote a number of scientific articles and pamphlets. Colden was also the author of *The History of the Five Indian Nations Depending on the Province of New York*, a study which, though perhaps confused in some respects, is still considered an important source of information on the subject.

Bibliography: Edwin R. Purple, "Notes, Biographical and Genealogical, of the Colden Family, and of Some of its Collateral Branches in America," *New York Genealogical and Biographical Record*, IV (October 1873), 161-83; A.

M. Keys, *Cadwallader Colden: A Representative Eighteenth Century Official* (New York, 1906); Cadwallader Colden, *The Letters and Papers of Cadwallader Colden . . . 1711-[1775]*, 9 vols. (New York, 1918-37) [published as part of the New-York Historical Society, *Collections* for the years 1917-35]; S. B. Rolland, "Cadwallader Colden: Colonial Politician and Imperial Statesman, 1718-1760," unpub. Ph.D. diss., University of Wisconsin, 1952; F. L. Engelman, "Cadwallader Colden and the New York Stamp Act Riots," *William and Mary Quarterly*, 3rd ser., vol. X (October 1953), 560-78; Brooke Hindle, "Cadwallader Colden's Extension of the Newtonian Principles," *William and Mary Quarterly*, 3rd ser., vol. XIII (October 1956), 459-75; Mirian E. Murphy, "Cadwallader Colden, President of the Council, Lieutenant Governor of New York, 1760-1775," unpub. Ph.D. diss., Fordham University, 1957; Brooke Hindle, "A Colonial Governor's Family: The Coldens of Coldengham," *New-York Historical Society Quarterly*, XLV (July 1961), 233-50; John S. Martin, "Social and Intellectual Patterns in the Thought of Cadwallader Colden," unpub. Ph.D. diss., University of Wisconsin, 1965; Carole Shammas, "Cadwallader Colden and the Role of the King's Prerogative," *New-York Historical Society Quarterly*, LIII (April 1969), 103-26; Alfred R. Hoermann, "A Figure of the American Enlightenment: Cadwallader Colden," unpub. Ph.D. diss., University of Toronto, 1970; Allan R. Raymond, "The Political Career of Cadwallader Colden," unpub. Ph.D. diss., Ohio State University, 1971; Alfred R. Hoermann, "A Savant in the Wilderness: Cadwallader Colden of New York," *New-York Historical Society Quarterly*, LXII (October 1978), 271-88. *DAB, DNB*.

MONCKTON, Robert, 1761, 1762-1763

Born on June 24, 1726 in England, the second son of John Monckton, who became Viscount Galway in 1727, and his wife, Lady Elizabeth Manners. Brother of William, second Viscount Galway. Married, and the father of three sons and one daughter.

Entered the British Army at an early age, and rose to the rank of Lieutenant Colonel by 1751; also served for a short time as a member of Parliament for Pontefract in the early 1750's. Went with his regiment to Nova Scotia in 1752, and from August of that year until June of 1753 acted as Commander at Fort Lawrence; named to Nova Scotia's Council in 1753. Served during the early stages of the French and Indian War in a military capacity, which was rewarded in 1755 by an appointment as Lieutenant Governor of Nova Scotia; presided for a brief period in 1758 as Acting Governor of Nova Scotia, during the absence of Governor Charles Lawrence. Continued to play an active role in military operations in the final years of the French and Indian War; became in

1759 second in command of the Quebec expedition, with a temporary rank of Brigadier General. Commissioned Captain General and Governor-in-Chief of New York in May 1761, and arrived in the province to take up the position in October of that year.

Monckton actually spent little time in New York during his administration. In November of 1761 he was made Major General and Commander-in-Chief of a military expedition sent to attack the French outpost of Martinique and, leaving Lieutenant Governor Cadwallader Colden in charge of the province, he departed for the island. While he returned to New York in June of 1762, Monckton did not remain for long. In June 1763 he again turned the chief executive's office over to Colden, and set sail for England.

Following his return Monckton was named Governor of Berwick-on-Tweed in 1765; in 1770 he became a Lieutenant General in the British Army. Although he was offered the chief command in North America in 1773, he declined the appointment, and the next year again took a seat in Parliament as a representative of Pontefract. Beginning shortly after his selection as Governor of Portsmouth in 1778, Monckton served until his death as a parliamentary member for that town. Monckton died on May 21, 1782.

Bibliography: Martha J. Lamb, ''Governor Robert Monckton,'' *Magazine of American History*, XVII (June 1887), 470-73; D. H. Monckton, *A Genealogical History of the Family of Monckton* . . . (London, 1887); ''Monckton's Report of His Expedition Against the French on the St. John in 1758,'' New Brunswick Historical Society, *Collections*, no. 5 (1904). *The Northcliffe Collection* (Ottawa, 1926) contains 400 pages of Monckton's papers. *DAB*, *DNB*.

MOORE, Sir Henry, 1765-1769

Born on February 7, 1713 in Vere, Jamaica, the son of Samuel and Elizabeth (Lowe) Moore. Married to Catharine Maria Long; father of John Henry. Studied at Eton and at the University of Leyden.

Returned to Jamaica after receiving his formal education and acted in succession as a member of the Assembly and the Council; also served for a time as Secretary of the island. Commissioned Lieutenant Governor of Jamaica in February 1756, and later that year became Acting Governor, following the departure of Admiral Sir Charles Knowles; continued as acting governor until 1762, with the exception of a brief interval from April to July 1759. Sailed for England after his Jamaican service, and in January of 1764 was created a Baronet. Commissioned Captain General and Governor-in-Chief of New York in July 1765, and arrived in the province in November of that year to assume his new position.

Moore's arrival in New York coincided with the popular outcry in America caused by the passage of the Stamp Act. New Yorkers were especially vociferous opponents of the proposed duties, and in December of 1765 even the colony's lawyers passed a resolution proclaiming their intention to do business without the stamps. Although news of the Stamp Act's repeal in May of 1766 did eliminate one major grievance, New York was disturbed by other crises during the Moore administration, particularly the controversy arising from the Quartering Act. This act, which stipulated that civil officials were required to provide barracks and supplies for British troops, was repudiated by the New York Assembly, a gesture of defiance which in 1767 led to a parliamentary decision to suspend the Assembly until it complied with the legislation. While this suspension never went into effect, the incident did for a time intensify the feelings of mistrust which divided New York's colonists and the British Parliament. Nevertheless, from 1767 to 1769 political dissension in New York became less frequent, and Moore's death in office on September 11, 1769 occurred during the period of relative calm which prevailed in the colony until 1773. *DAB, DNB*.

MURRAY, John (4th Earl of Dunmore), 1770-1771
Virginia, 1771-1775

Born in 1732, the eldest son of William Murray, third Earl of Dunmore, and his wife, Catherine Nairne. Married on February 21, 1759 to Lady Charlotte Stewart, the daughter of the Earl of Galloway; father of five sons and four daughters, including Virginia. Inherited his father's title and estate in 1756; also held the titles of Viscount Fincastle, and Baron of Blair, of Moulin, and of Tillymont.

Chosen in 1761 as a Peer representing Scotland in the British Parliament; again elected to Parliament in 1768. Commissioned Royal Governor of New York in January 1770 and arrived in the colony in October of that year.

Dunmore's tenure as governor of New York was brief and uneventful. His arrival in the colony coincided with the beginning of a three-year interlude between the protests of the 1760's and the resurgence of opposition in 1773 (which would eventually culminate in revolution). Within a year Dunmore was replaced in New York by William Tryon and sent to Virginia as that colony's Royal Governor. In this new setting he at first enjoyed a period of tranquility, but by 1773 the revolutionary movement in Virginia had gained momentum, and Dunmore faced a House of Burgesses which was becoming more intractable. The governor responded by dissolving the Burgesses in March 1773 and again in May 1774, when that body expressed sympathy with colonial complaints. By the summer of 1774 the already troubled colony found itself at war with the Shawnee and Ottawa Indians who lived along the frontier. Taking an active role in the military operations against the Indians, Dunmore helped to suppress the outbreak, though some critics contended that the war had been due to the governor's aggressive land policy and had been used by him as a means of drawing attention from the colonists' grievances. By the spring of 1775 these grievances had reached such a point that Dunmore no longer felt safe, and in June 1775 he left Virginia and retreated to the British man-of-war *Fowey*, off Yorktown, from which he directed efforts to subdue the rebellion. In July of 1776 he left Virginia for England, where he once again represented Scotland in Parliament.

Dunmore also served as Governor of the Bahamas from 1787 to 1796. He died in Ramsgate, England on March 5, 1809.

Bibliography: Randolph C. Downes, ''Dunmore's War: An Interpretation,'' *Mississippi Valley Historical Review*, XXI (December 1934), 311-30; Percy B. Caley, ''Lord Dunmore and the Pennsylvania-Virginia Boundary Dispute,'' *Western Pennsylvania Historical Magazine*, XXII (1939), 87-100; Percy B. Caley, ''Dunmore: Colonial Governor of New York and Virginia, 1770-1782,'' unpub. Ph.D. diss., University of Pittsburgh, 1939; Benjamin Quarles, ''Lord Dunmore as Liberator,'' *William and Mary Quarterly*, 3rd ser., vol. XV (October 1958), 494-507; Richard O. Curry, ''Lord Dunmore—Tool of Land Jobbers or Realistic Champion of Colonial 'Rights'?: An Inquiry,'' *West Virginia History*, XXIV (April 1963), 289-95; J. Leitch Wright, Jr., ''Lord Dunmore's Loyalist Asylum in the Floridas,'' *Florida Historical Quarterly*, XLIX (April 1971), 370-79. *DAB, DNB*.

TRYON, William, 1771-1774, 1775-1780

North Carolina, 1765-1771

Born in 1729 at ''Norbury Park,'' Surrey, England, the son of Charles and Lady Mary (Shirley) Tryon. Brother of Ann, Mary, Harriot and Sophia. Married in 1757 to Margaret Wake, by whom he had Margaret and a son who died young. Received a commission in 1751 as Lieutenant in the First Regiment of Foot Guards; promoted to Captain (with army rank of Lieutenant Colonel) in 1758. Appointed Lieutenant Governor of North Carolina in 1764, probably through his wife's family connection with Lord Hillsborough. Succeeded the deceased Governor Arthur Dobbs in April 1765, and officially commissioned as Royal Governor the following July.

Tryon's period as governor of North Carolina was dominated by the Regulator movement, an attempt on the part of the western residents of the colony to correct what they perceived to be misgovernment by eastern interests. The central concern of the Regulators was malpractice by local officials, including the charging of excessive taxes and fees. Tryon, though sympathetic to some of their accusations, refused to accept the legitimacy of Regulator violence and took firm steps to end the movement. The governor's efforts culminated in May 1771 with a confrontation on Great Alamance Creek, in which a group of about 2,000 poorly equipped Regulators were routed by 1,400 militia under Tryon's command.

Soon after the Battle of Alamance, Tryon learned that he had been awarded the governorship of New York; in July 1771 he sailed for that colony to take up his new appointment. While Governor of New York he was confronted by the revolutionary movement and, following an absence in England from April 1774 to June 1775, he returned to find the colony in a state of open rebellion. In October 1775 Tryon retreated to a British warship off New York, from which he sought for almost a year to re-establish his authority. When British General Sir William Howe conquered the city of New York in September 1776, Tryon returned, but he was never able to gain effective political control over the entire state, and for the next few years he tried to strengthen the British military position. Tryon was promoted in 1778 to Major General "in America"; he also served as Colonel of the 70th Foot. In 1780 he was succeeded by James Robertson as military and civil governor of New York.

On September 4, 1780 illness forced Tryon to return to England. Despite a promotion to Lieutenant General in 1782 and an appointment as Colonel of the 29th Foot in 1783, his active military service was at an end. Tryon died on January 27, 1788 in London and was buried in Twickenham. Counties in North Carolina and New York were named in his honor, but North Carolina changed the name of its Tryon County in 1779, and New York followed suit in 1784.

Bibliography: Marshall DeLancey Haywood, *Governor William Tryon and His Administration in the Province of North Carolina, 1765-1771* . . . (Raleigh, 1903); Alonzo T. Dill, *Governor Tryon and His Palace* (Chapel Hill, 1955); William S. Powell, ed., "Tryon's 'Book' on North Carolina," *North Carolina Historical Review*, XXXIV (July 1957), 406-15; Solomon Henner, "The Career of William Tryon as Governor of the Province of New York, 1771-1780," unpub. Ed.D. diss., New York University, 1968. W. M. Tryon, ed. and comp., *The Tryon Family in America* (Wheaton, Md., 1969). *DAB, DNB*.

VAN CORTLANDT, Pierre, 1777

Born on January 10, 1721 in New York City, New York, the son of Philip and Catharine (De Peyster) Van Cortlandt. Brother of Stephen, Abraham, Philip, John and Catharine (died young). Married on May 28, 1748 to Joanna Livingston, by whom he was the father of Philip, Catharine, Cornelia, Gertrude (died young), Gilbert, Stephen (died young), Pierre and Ann.

Settled in New York City shortly after his marriage, but in September 1749 moved to his family's manor house near Croton, which he inherited when his father died in September 1748. Served as a member of the New York militia during the French and Indian War. Elected to the New York Assembly in 1768 and, despite an avowed preference for moderation, decided to support the Patriot cause following the break with Great Britain. Commissioned Colonel of the Westchester militia in October 1775, and participated in the Second, Third and Fourth Provincial Congresses held in New York. Acted as a leader of the Committee of Safety in 1776; became President of New York's Council of Safety in May 1777, and served in that capacity until the inauguration of Governor George Clinton in July of that year; also took part in the deliberations which produced the state's first constitution in April 1777.

Although his presidency of the Council of Safety lasted little more than two months, Van Cortlandt's tenure was an extremely active one. Politically, the new state was in the midst of its gubernatorial contest, with George Clinton leading a field of four candidates. New York also experienced serious military reversals during Van Cortlandt's administration, when General Burgoyne invaded the state from Quebec early in June 1777. Throughout the next eight weeks, the British achieved an impressive series of victories, including the capture of Ticonderoga.

Following Clinton's inauguration as New York's first popularly-elected chief executive, Van Cortlandt became Lieutenant Governor, a position he continued to hold until he retired from public life in 1795. Van Cortlandt also served on the Board of Regents of the University of the State of New York from 1784 to 1795. He spent his final years at his estate, devoting considerable attention to religion and the work of the Methodist Church. Van Cortlandt died on May 1, 1814, and was interred in the family cemetery on his estate.

Bibliography: Margherita Arlina Hamm, "Van Cortlandt," in *Famous Families of New York*, vol. II (New York and London, 1902), 185-93; [anonymous], *The Van Cortlandt Manor* (Baltimore, 1920); L. Effingham De Forest, *The Van Cortlandt Family* (New York, 1930); Jacob Judd, ed., *The Revolutionary War Memoir and Selected Correspondence of Philip Van Cortlandt* (Tarrytown, N.Y., 1976); Jacob Judd, ed., *Correspondence of the Van Cortlandt Family of Cortlandt Manor, 1748-1800* (Tarrytown, N.Y., 1977). *DAB*.

CLINTON, George, 1777-1795, 1801-1804

Born on July 26, 1739 in Little Britain, Ulster County (later part of Orange County), New York, the youngest child of Charles and Elizabeth (Denniston) Clinton. Brother of Catharine, James (died young), Mary (died young),

Charles, Alexander and James. Married on October 28, 1769 to Cornelia Tappen, by whom he was the father of Catharine, Cornelia, George Washington, Elizabeth, Martha Washington (died young) and Maria.

Studied law with William Smith, Jr., of New York City, and later began his own legal practice in Ulster County. Elected to the New York Assembly in 1768, a position he retained until the dissolution of that body in 1775. Attended the Second Continental Congress in 1775 and 1776; became Brigadier General of the provincial militia in December 1775. Elected Governor of New York in June 1777, and served in that capacity from July 1777 to July 1795, winning re-election every three years; elected to a seventh term as chief executive in 1801, an office he held from July 1801 to July 1804.

Clinton's victory in 1777 marked the commencement of an era in which he would emerge as one of the state's most prominent political figures. Throughout the Revolution he demonstrated his ability as a wartime governor, especially by helping to organize a punitive expedition against the Six Nations, who had been terrorizing white settlers along the frontier of western New York. By the mid-1780's Clinton's popularity was still high, but his outspoken opposition to the Federal Constitution of 1787 cost him much of his earlier political support. Indeed, the machinations of Alexander Hamilton almost ousted Clinton from office in the gubernatorial contest of 1789. By 1795 the old governor's political standing had become even more perilous, leading him to decline re-election rather than risk almost certain defeat at the polls. In 1801, however, Clinton's Republican sympathies were more popular with the electorate, a development which enabled him to win in an election skillfully engineered by Aaron Burr.

Following his long tenure as governor, Clinton was the successful vice-presidential running mate of Thomas Jefferson in 1804, and in 1808 he was re-elected to the same office on a ticket headed by James Madison. Clinton died in Washington, D.C. on April 20, 1812, while still serving as the nation's Vice-President.

Bibliography: Charles B. Moore, "Introductory Sketch to the History of the Clinton Family," *New York Genealogical and Biographical Record*, XII (October 1881), 195-98, vol. XIII (January-October 1882), 5-10, 139, 173-80; George Clinton, *Public Papers*, 10 vols., ed. by Hugh Hastings and J. A. Holden (New York and Albany, 1899-1914); Benjamin Myer Brink, "Governor George Clinton," *Olde Ulster*, vols. IV and V (1908-09); Gilbert D. B. Hasbrouck, "Governor George Clinton," New-York State Historical Association, *Journal*, I (July 1920), 143-64; Joseph M. Beatty, Jr., "Notes on the English Ancestry of George Clinton, First Governor of New York," *New York Genealogical and Biographical Record*, LI (October 1920), 360-62; Joseph M. Beatty, Jr., "The English Ancestry of the Clintons of New York," *New York Genealogical and Biographical Record*, LXVI (October 1935), 330-35;

Major B. Jenks, "George Clinton and New York State Politics, 1775 to 1801," unpub. Ph.D. diss., Cornell University, 1936; Lynton K. Caldwell, "George Clinton—Democratic Administrator," *New York History,* XXXII (April 1951), 134-56; Ernest W. Spaulding, *His Excellency George Clinton, Critic of the Constitution*, 2nd ed. (New York, 1964). *DAB*.

ROBERTSON, James, 1780-1783

Born *circa* 1720 in Fifeshire, Scotland; names of parents unknown. Married, and the father of at least one daughter.

Entered the British Army at an early age; sailed to America in 1756, where he became Barrack-Master at New York. Promoted to Colonel in 1772, and in 1776 led a brigade of British soldiers at the Battle of Long Island. Later appointed Commandant of British troops in New York. With the military rank of Major General in America, commissioned Governor of New York in May 1779, while on leave in England; assumed that office in March 1780.

Robertson apparently earned little respect from either Patriot or Loyalist factions during his tenure as governor. Judge Thomas Jones, the prominent New York Loyalist, was especially scathing in his criticism of Robertson's personal behavior, complaining that he could be seen "waddling about town with a couple of young tits about twelve years of age under each arm." Even more irritating to many inhabitants of New York was the hypocrisy of the chief executive, evidenced by his proposal in 1782 to expand the powers of the police, "in view of the great depravation of Manners in the City." Robertson's diplomatic skills were also undistinguished. In the autumn of 1780, for example, he acted as a member of the committee named to intercede on behalf of Major John André, the British spy, but was unable to obtain André's release.

By the spring of 1782 the British government had begun to explore ways of ending hostilities in America, and in April of the following year Robertson, who had recently been made a Lieutenant General, sailed from New York for England. Robertson died in London on March 4, 1788. *DNB*.

ELLIOT, Andrew, 1783

Born in November 1728 in Scotland, the son of Sir Gilbert Elliot, second Baronet of Minto, and his wife, the former Helen Stuart. Brother of Gilbert (later third Baronet), Eleanor, Jane and John, among others. Married on October 31, 1754 to Eleanor McCall, who died in May 1756, after giving birth to a daughter named Eleanor; remarried late in 1759 or early in 1760 to Elizabeth Plumsted, by whom he was the father of Elizabeth, Agnes Murray, Gilbert, John, William, Andrew, Mariann, Rebecca and Emma.

Educated at the Dalkeith School, and later attended Edinburgh's High School. Immigrated to Philadelphia in 1746, where he pursued a mercantile career for a number of years; also served in several minor public positions while living in Philadelphia, including a period on the City Council. Visited Scotland in 1763, but returned to America in August 1764, after winning an appointment as Receiver General of His Majesty's Revenue and Collector of Customs for the Port of New York; continued to hold these offices until 1776, when popular resistance to British policy forced him to leave the city. Named "Superintendent of all Imports and Exports to and from the Islands of New York, Long Island, and Staten Island" in July 1777; appointed New York's Superintendent General of Police in May 1778. Chosen Lieutenant Governor of New York by the British in 1780, and served in that capacity until he became Acting Governor in April 1783, following the departure for England of Governor James Robertson.

For almost two decades Elliot had witnessed the growth of opposition to British rule among the residents of New York, and by the time he took office as acting governor, it was obvious that a complete transfer to American control was only months away. Under these circumstances, he attempted during his brief tenure to persuade the Patriot administration of Governor George Clinton to adopt a compassionate policy towards the state's Loyalists. Late in 1783 Elliot finally sailed for England aboard H.M.S. *Amphyon*, several days after British troops had evacuated New York City.

Elliot eventually received a pension from the British government as compensation for his services. Although he never again occupied public office, he did decline an informal offer in 1790 to become Britain's first minister to the United States. Elliot died at "Minto," his family's Scottish estate, on May 25, 1797.

Bibliography: Eugene Devereux, "Andrew Elliot, Lieutenant Governor of the Province of New York," *Pennsylvania Magazine of History and Biography*, XI (1887), 129-50; George F.S. Elliot, *The Border Elliots and the Family of Minto* (Edinburgh, 1897); Robert Ernst, "Andrew Elliot, Forgotten Loyalist of Occupied New York," *New York History*, LVII (July 1976), 285-320.

NORTH CAROLINA

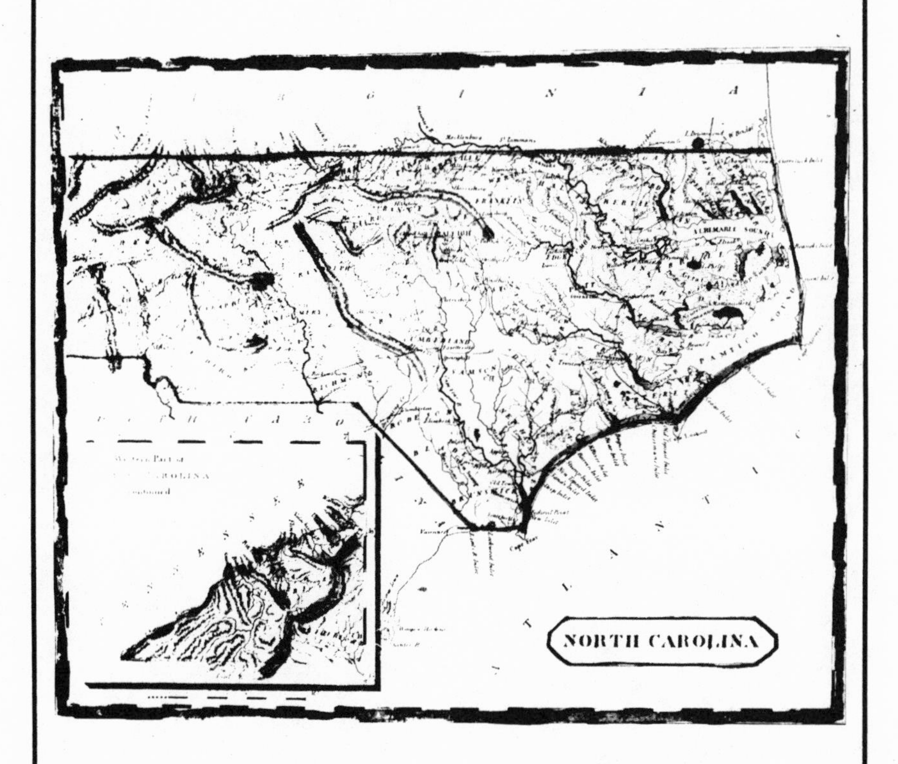

Chronology

North Carolina was Albemarle County until 1690, and northern Carolina until 1712.

Albemarle County

1664-1667	William Drummond
1667-1670	Samuel Stephens
1670-1672	Peter Carteret
1672-1675	John Jenkins
1675-1676	Thomas Eastchurch
1676-1677	John Jenkins
1677	Thomas Miller
1677-1679	*Following Culpeper's Rebellion in late 1677, Albemarle County was apparently without a chief executive until 1679, although there is a possibility that John Jenkins may have served for part of that time.*
1679	John Harvey
1680-1681	John Jenkins
1682-1689	Seth Sothel
1689-1690	John Gibbs

Carolina "north and east of the Cape Fear River"

1690	Philip Ludwell
1690-1694	Thomas Jarvis
1694-1699	Thomas Harvey
1699-1703	Henderson Walker
1703-1705	Robert Daniel
1705-1706	Thomas Cary
1706-1708	William Glover
1708-1711	Thomas Cary
1711-1712	Edward Hyde (*as governor of North Carolina from May 1712*)

North Carolina

1712-1714	Thomas Pollock
1714-1722	Charles Eden
1722	Thomas Pollock
1722-1724	William Reed

1724-1725	George Burrington
1725-1731	Sir Richard Everard
1731-1734	George Burrington
1734	Nathaniel Rice
1734-1752	Gabriel Johnston
1752-1753	Nathaniel Rice
1753-1754	Matthew Rowan
1754-1765	Arthur Dobbs
1765-1771	William Tryon
1771	James Hasell
1771-1775	Josiah Martin
1775-1776	Cornelius Harnett
1776	Samuel Ashe
1776	Willie Jones
1777-1780	Richard Caswell
1780-1781	Abner Nash
1781	Thomas Burke
1781-1782	Alexander Martin
1782	Thomas Burke
1782-1785	Alexander Martin
1785-1787	Richard Caswell
1787-1789	Samuel Johnston

BIBLIOGRAPHY

Butler, Lindley S., "The Governors of Albemarle County, 1663-1689," *North Carolina Historical Review*, XLVI (July 1969), 281-99.

Clark, Walter, ed., *State Records of North Carolina, 1777-1790*, 16 vols. (Winston and Goldsboro, N.C., 1895-1905).

Connor, Robert D. W., *Revolutionary Leaders of North Carolina* (Greensboro, N.C., 1916).

Cooke, Charles S., "The Governor, Council, and Assembly in Royal North Carolina," *James Sprunt Historical Publications*, vol. XII, no. 1 (1912), 7-40.

Crabtree, Beth G., *North Carolina Governors, 1575-1968* (Raleigh, 1968).

Grimes, J. Bryan, comp., *Abstract of North Carolina Wills* (Raleigh, 1910).

Huhta, James K., "Government by Instruction: North Carolina, 1731-1776. A Study of the Influence of the Royal Instructions on the Major Controversies Between the Governors and the Lower House," unpub. Ph.D. diss., University of North Carolina at Chapel Hill, 1965.

Lefler, Hugh T., and Albert Ray Newsome, *North Carolina: The History of a Southern State*, rev. ed. (Chapel Hill, 1963).

———. and William S. Powell, *Colonial North Carolina: A History* (New York, 1973).

Powell, William S., *The Proprietors of Carolina* (Raleigh, 1963).

———. ed., *Ye Countie of Albemarle in Carolina* (Raleigh, 1958).

Price, William S., Jr., "'Men of Good Estates': Wealth Among North Carolina's Royal Councillors," *North Carolina Historical Review*, XLIX (Winter 1972), 72-82.

Raper, Charles S., "North Carolina, a Royal Province, 1729-75: The Executive and Legislature," unpub. Ph.D. diss., Columbia University, 1902.

Robinson, Blackwell P., *The Five Royal Governors of North Carolina, 1729-1775* (Raleigh, 1963).

Salley, Alexander S., Jr., ed., *Narratives of Early Carolina, 1650-1708* (New York, 1911).

Saunders, W. L., ed., *Colonial Records of North Carolina [1662-1776]*, 10 vols. (Raleigh, 1886-90).

Wheeler, John H., *Historical Sketches of North Carolina, from 1584 to 1851*, 2 vols. (Philadelphia, 1851).

———. "The Lives and Characters of the Early Governors of North Carolina," *North Carolina University Magazine*, I (1852), 431-47.

NORTH CAROLINA

DRUMMOND, William, 1664-1667

Born in Scotland; date of birth and names of parents unknown. A Presbyterian. Married to a woman named Sarah, by whom he was the father of at least five children, including John and Sarah.

Settled in James City County, Virginia by 1648, and worked as an attorney in that colony. Also was acting as a Justice in James City County in 1656. Appointed to a three-year term as Governor of Albemarle County in October 1664, and probably assumed that office a short time later, although his commission did not reach the colony until February 1665.

Drummond's period as chief executive was of major significance in the colony's early history. Besides presiding over the formation of a new government, Albemarle's first leader early in his administration helped to resolve a boundary dispute with Virginia. During these years Albemarle County also experienced both trouble with the Tuscarora Indians and a certain amount of economic distress caused by overproduction of tobacco. In October 1666, after the Indian threat had subsided, the colony joined with Virginia and Maryland in enacting a law which forbade the planting of tobacco from February 1667 to February 1668, a measure designed to encourage demand for the crop and increase its market value.

Following his tenure as governor, Drummond returned to Virginia, where he later became a supporter of Nathaniel Bacon. On January 20, 1677, after the defeat of Bacon's Rebellion by forces loyal to Governor William Berkeley, Drummond was executed for his part in the uprising.

Bibliography: Stephen B. Weeks, "William Drummond: The First Governor of North Carolina, 1664-1667," *National Magazine*, XV (April 1892), 616-28; Wilcomb E. Washburn, "The Humble Petition of Sarah Drummond," *William and Mary Quarterly*, 3rd ser., vol. XIII (July 1956), 354-75.

STEPHENS, Samuel, 1667-1670

Born *circa* 1629 in Virginia, the son of Richard and Elizabeth (Peirsey) Stephens. Married in 1652 to Frances Culpeper; no children.

Acquired the military rank of Captain; commissioned in October 1662 by the Virginia Council to serve as "commander of the southern plantation." Named to a three-year term as Governor of Albemarle County by Carolina's Lords Proprietors in October 1667, and took office a short time later.

During Stephens' tenure as governor the colony's land policy was liberalized when the Proprietors approved a petition which they had received from the "Grand Assembly of the County of Albemarle." Like their neighbors in Virginia, settlers in Albemarle were now given the right to take lands on the basis of a fifty-acre headright, with one farthing per acre quitrent. Towards the end of Stephens' administration, however, the colonists received word of a less welcome decision, one which threatened to alter dramatically their form of government. By January 1670 the Fundamental Constitutions of 1669 had reached the colony, a body of law that included provisions for both a feudal nobility and a complex court system. Prior to March 7, 1670, before the impact of the constitutions on Albemarle could be fully assessed, Stephens died while still in office.

CARTERET, Peter, 1670-1672

Born in 1641 on the Island of Jersey, the son of Helier de Carteret and Rachel (La Cloche) Carteret; related as fourth cousin to Sir George Carteret, one of the Lords Proprietors of Carolina. Brother of Philip, who served as governor of New Jersey for most of the period between 1665 and 1682.

Named a Lords Proprietors' Deputy; arrived in Carolina in February 1665, where he served at various times as Secretary, Chief Registrar and Councillor. Also commissioned Lieutenant Colonel of the Albemarle militia in October 1668. Chosen by the Council of Albemarle County to succeed the deceased Governor Samuel Stephens in March 1670.

Carteret's period as governor was disrupted by the growth of factionalism in Albemarle. The anti-proprietary faction, perhaps goaded by the feudalistic trappings of the Fundamental Constitutions, objected to the powers given to the Lords Proprietors and, by proxy, to their deputies in the colony. In response, the proprietary party attempted to enforce their right to govern, a right which they claimed had been conveyed to the Proprietors by the Charter of 1663. These political differences were exacerbated by the continued weakness of the colony economically. In his account of Albemarle, Governor

Carteret noted that disasters like the destructive hurricane which struck Carolina in 1670 were causing the settlers "to growne under the burtyn of poverty."

Discontent in the colony had become so widespread by 1672 that Carteret embarked for England, where he presented the Proprietors with a list of grievances. The Proprietors were not very responsive to this petition, however, and eight years later they even sought to blame Carteret for the colony's condition, asserting that he had left Albemarle's government "in ill order & worse hands." The date of Carteret's death is unknown.

JENKINS, John, 1672-1675, 1676-1677, 1680-1681

Date and place of birth, and names of parents unknown, but may have been the John Jenkins who graduated from Clare College, Cambridge in 1642. Married to a woman named Johanna.

Settled in Albemarle County in about 1658; later served as a member of the Governor's Council, as a Lords Proprietors' Deputy for the Earl of Craven, and as a member of the Assembly. Eventually became both a member of the anti-proprietary faction in Albemarle, and a close associate of Governor Peter Carteret. Commissioned by Carteret as Deputy Governor in May 1672, a commission which was to remain valid until Carteret's return from England or until the Proprietors selected a new chief executive.

Although Jenkins was legally entitled to govern in Albemarle during Carteret's absence, his administration was made ineffective by the growing tension between proprietary and anti-proprietary forces in the colony. Economic conditions also continued to deteriorate during these years, as Parliament levied a tobacco duty and imposed various restrictions on the tobacco trade, thereby endangering Albemarle's major source of revenue. In 1675 these problems culminated in rebellion, when Thomas Eastchurch, the head of the proprietary faction and newly-elected speaker of the Assembly, deposed Jenkins and placed him under arrest. While Jenkins was restored to power early in 1676, by July 1677 he was again out of office. This time his successor was Thomas Miller, who had been named acting governor by Eastchurch after the two men had visited England and presented their case to the Proprietors. The durable Jenkins assumed the governorship a third time in 1680, following the death of John Harvey, and served in that capacity until his own death on December 17, 1681.

EASTCHURCH, Thomas, 1675-1676

Date and place of birth, and names of parents unknown, but may have been the Thomas Eastchurch of Devon who graduated from Queen's College, Oxford in 1628. Married in 1677 to a woman residing in Nevis, West Indies.

Settled in Albemarle County by 1671. Became a leader of the proprietary faction in Albemarle, elected Speaker of the colony's Assembly, and organized the overthrow of Governor John Jenkins in 1675.

Eastchurch's assumption of power, while clearly without legal sanction, was defended on the grounds of Governor Jenkins' alleged failure to collect customs in Albemarle. By early 1676, however, the popular faction which backed Jenkins had ousted Eastchurch from office. Eastchurch then decided to defend his position before the Lords Proprietors and, accompanied by Thomas Miller, he arrived in England in the autumn of 1676. Impressing the Proprietors as a "discreet and worthy man," Eastchurch succeeded in winning a commission as governor in November 1676. The following year he met and married a wealthy woman in the West Indies while *en route* to Carolina, a development which led Eastchurch to appoint Miller as acting governor of Albemarle while he remained in the islands temporarily. Although he attempted to assume power in 1677, the outbreak of Culpeper's Rebellion in Carolina prevented Eastchurch from enforcing his commission, and a short time later, probably in late 1677, he succumbed to a fever in Virginia.

MILLER, Thomas, 1677

Information concerning his family history is scanty, but may have been the Thomas Miller of Albemarle whose will, dated February 1694 and proved July 1694, mentioned sons Thomas, William, Richard and Nathaniel.

Became a leader of Albemarle County's proprietary faction, and a close associate of Thomas Eastchurch. Accompanied Eastchurch to England where, in November 1676, he was named by the Proprietors to be Secretary and Collector of Customs for the colony. Commissioned President of the Council by Eastchurch about six months later, and in July 1677 arrived in Albemarle with authorization to serve as Acting Governor during Eastchurch's absence.

Although the bitter feud between proprietary and anti-proprietary forces in Albemarle had not diminished, Miller was nevertheless able to establish his right to govern soon after landing in the colony. In an effort to restore some semblance of order, Miller set up a civil court, called for elections in the autumn of 1677, and began to collect the required duty on tobacco. At the same time, however, he continued to show open preference for members of the proprietary faction, especially by appointing two of his staunchest supporters to be deputy collectors of customs. In December 1677 popular resentment over Miller's partisan behavior ended in rebellion, when an armed troop led by Valentine Bird and John Culpeper imprisoned the governor and other leaders of the proprietary faction. For more than a year, until the governorship of John Harvey began in 1679, Albemarle County was apparently without a chief executive, although there is a possibility that John Jenkins may have served for part of that time.

Miller eventually escaped his captors in the autumn of 1679. He then sailed for England, where he complained to the Crown about his treatment at the hands of Culpeper and his followers. The date of Miller's death is uncertain, although, as noted above, he may have died between February and July of 1694.

HARVEY, John, 1679

Born in England; date of birth and names of parents unknown. Married to Dorothy Tooke. Immigrated *circa* 1658 to the area which would later become Carolina, and in September 1663 received a land grant in the Albemarle River area. Became one of the leaders of the anti-proprietary faction in Albemarle; appointed to accompany Governor Peter Carteret to England in 1672, but did not sail because of business commitments in Carolina. Appointed President of the Council and Acting Governor of Albemarle County in February 1679, and served in that capacity until his death late in 1679.

Harvey's appointment came in the wake of news that Seth Sothel, the Proprietors' first choice as governor, had been captured by Turkish pirates while *en route* to his assignment. The selection of Harvey as an interim chief executive seems to indicate a conciliatory spirit on the part of the Proprietors, especially in view of his earlier identification with Albemarle's anti-proprietary faction. However, Harvey was also known to enjoy widespread respect in the colony, even among his political rivals, and his untimely death curtailed a real opportunity to restore tranquility to the colony.

Bibliography: "The Harvey Family," *North Carolina Historical and Genealogical Register*, III (July 1903), 476-80.

SOTHEL, Seth, 1682-1689

South Carolina, 1690-1692

Date and place of birth, and names of parents unknown. Married to Anna Willix; no surviving children. Purchased the Earl of Clarendon's proprietary share in Carolina in 1677, thereby becoming a Proprietor of that colony in his own right. Appointed Governor of Albemarle County late in 1678, but captured by Turkish pirates while *en route* to America. Released in July 1681, and by 1682 had arrived in Albemarle.

Selected as chief executive because of his "discreet" and "sober" character, Sothel eventually showed evidence of the damage which over two years in slavery had done to his personality. His first few years in office won the approval of John Archdale, a Quaker and future governor of Carolina; however, Sothel's actions appear to have become increasingly arbitrary. As a result, late in 1689 he was overthrown, after being accused of seizing property and inflicting imprisonment on his enemies without benefit of trial. Sothel finally left Albemarle when the General Assembly banished him for twelve months and barred him from holding public office for life, but by 1690 he had managed to secure the governorship of the southern part of Carolina. There he soon advocated legislation which would improve his own financial position, such as an act regulating the Indian trade which permitted the governor to receive one-third of the export duties and fines collected on furs and skins.

Within a short time, however, news of Sothel's behavior reached the Proprietors, and in the spring of 1692 Philip Ludwell, who had been appointed governor the previous November, arrived in Charles Town. Following a brief and unsuccessful attempt to resist Ludwell's commission, Sothel seems to have left the colony in the autumn of 1692. He died a short time later, possibly in late 1693 or early 1694. *DNB*.

GIBBS, John, 1689-1690

Date and place of birth, and names of parents unknown, but may have been the John Gibbs who was made a "Cacique" in 1682, a title in the order of nobility devised for the colony of Carolina by the philosopher John Locke.

Claiming that he had been elected Governor by the Albemarle Council following the overthrow of Seth Sothel late in 1689, served as *de facto* chief executive until the arrival of the proprietary appointee, Philip Ludwell, in the spring of 1690.

Gibbs's assertion that he was entitled to assume the governorship of Albemarle County after Sothel's departure was accepted by most of the colony's residents before the appearance of Ludwell with a commission and instructions from the Lords Proprietors. When Ludwell arrived in the colony, however, Gibbs refused to yield, calling the new chief executive a "Rascal, imposter & Usurper." With the aid of a group of armed men, Gibbs imprisoned two magistrates from the Currituck Precinct Court in June 1690, and forbade any court in the colony "to sit or act by any Commission but his." A short time later, popular feeling against him forced Gibbs to flee to Virginia. Eventually he sailed to London and defended his position before the Lords Proprietors, but Ludwell's right to govern was confirmed. The date of Gibbs's death is unknown.

LUDWELL, Philip, 1690

South Carolina, 1692-1693

Born *circa* 1640 in Bruton, Somersetshire, England, the son of Thomas and Jane (Cottington) Ludwell. Brother of Thomas, Mary, Margaret, Sarah and Jane. Married before October 1667 to Lucy (Higginson) Burwell Bernard; after his first wife's death in 1675, remarried in the spring of 1680 to Frances (Culpeper) Stephens Berkeley, the widow of previous governors of Albemarle County and of Virginia; father of Philip and Jane, both by his first wife.

After his immigration to Virginia in about 1660, acquired "Rich Neck" and "Green Spring," two estates in James City County. Became deputy to his brother, Thomas Ludwell, who served as secretary of the colony. Appointed to the Virginia Council in March 1675, and soon afterwards acted as Secretary; lost his seat on the Council in 1678, but was later reinstated. Also served as Deputy Surveyor of Customs in the 1680's. Played a major role in the resistance to Francis, Lord Howard of Effingham, who governed Virginia from 1684 to 1689; as a result of his opposition to Howard, was suspended and eventually dismissed from the Council. Elected to the Virginia House of Burgesses in 1688, but forbidden to take his seat. Sent to England that year to present the appeal of the Burgesses against Lord Howard, and while there chosen by Carolina's Lords Proprietors as "Governor of that part of our province . . . that lyes North and East of Cape Fear." Qualified as Governor in May of 1690. Received an expanded commission from the Proprietors in November 1691 which included the southern part of Carolina, and presented his credentials in Charles Town in the spring of 1692.

Since his right to administer the northern section of Carolina was quickly challenged by John Gibbs, Ludwell appointed Thomas Jarvis as acting governor and left for London to defend his claim late in 1690. Following his return to America in 1692, Ludwell encountered other problems in southern Carolina, chiefly over the collection of quitrents and the methods of granting land, and in May 1693 the Proprietors revoked his southern appointment. A short time later Ludwell's northern commission was also recalled by his superiors. He then returned to England, probably in 1695, and died there sometime after 1704 (1723?).

Bibliography: Cassius F. Lee., Jr., "Ludwell Genealogy," *New England Historical and Genealogical Register*, XXXIII (April 1879), 220-22; "Philip Ludwell's Account [of Bacon's Rebellion]," *Virginia Magazine of History and Biography*, I (October 1893), 174-86; "Ludwell Family," *William and Mary Quarterly*, 1st ser., vol. XIX (January 1911), 199-214; "The Ludwells and Other Families," in Cazenove Gardner Lee, Jr., *Lee Chronicle: Studies of the Early Generations of the Lees of Virginia . . .*, comp. and ed. by Dorothy Mills Parker (New York, 1957). *DAB*.

JARVIS, Thomas, 1690-1694

Date and place of birth, and names of parents unknown. Married to a woman named Dorcas. Settled in Albemarle County before 1663. Was serving on the Council of that colony in 1672, and as a member of its Assembly in 1677. Presided as Acting and later Deputy Governor of Carolina north and east of the Cape Fear River from November 1690 to 1694, in place of the absent Governor Philip Ludwell.

Jarvis first became acting chief executive of northern Carolina when Ludwell was forced to visit London, in order to defend his claim to govern against that of John Gibbs. By the spring of 1692 Ludwell was back in America, but with a commission which now included all of Carolina. Consequently, Jarvis continued to serve as chief executive in the north, while Ludwell personally administered the southern portion of the colony. Throughout this period Jarvis's able leadership helped northern Carolina to recover from the divisiveness which had plagued its early history. Significantly, these years were also marked by the beginning of what would soon become a major influx of French Huguenot settlers into the area. The date of Jarvis's death is uncertain, although it apparently occurred sometime in 1694, the year in which he was succeeded as deputy governor by Thomas Harvey.

HARVEY, Thomas, 1694-1699

Born in England, the son of John and Mary Harvey; date of birth unknown. Brother of Richard, Robert and perhaps others. Married on April 13, 1682 to Johanna Jenkins, the widow of Albemarle Governor John Jenkins; after his first wife's death in March 1688, remarried to Sarah Laker, by whom he was the father of John (died young), Thomas and Mary.

Immigrated to Albemarle County as Secretary to Governor Jenkins, and by 1690 was serving on the northern Carolina Council. Acted as Deputy Governor of the region north and east of the Cape Fear River between 1694 and 1699, presiding in place of the absent Governor John Archdale.

Since Archdale spent most of his time as chief executive either in England or in the southern portion of Carolina, Harvey was able to administer his section of the colony with few restrictions. Like Thomas Jarvis, his predecessor as deputy governor, Harvey had considerable experience as a political leader, experience which he needed in a colony whose steady population growth necessitated the creation of Bath County in 1696.

While northern Carolina endured little internal dissension during Harvey's administration, it did face several attempts by Governor Sir Edmund Andros of

Virginia to extend his authority southward. In 1698, for example, Andros notified Harvey that he had received a commission which empowered him to appoint judges to Carolina's Court of Admiralty in case vacancies occurred. Harvey responded to this challenge by notifying Andros that no vacancy existed, thereby sidestepping what he believed to be a "great incroachment upon the powers Granted to the proprietors in their Charter." Harvey died in office on July 3, 1699, following a long illness.

Bibliography: "Copy of a Letter from Deputy Governor Thomas Harvey to Governor Archdale," *North Carolina Historical and Genealogical Register*, III (January 1903), 35-39; "The Harvey Family," *North Carolina Historical and Genealogical Register*, III (July 1903), 476-80.

WALKER, Henderson, 1699-1703

Born *circa* 1659, probably in America; names of parents unknown. An Anglican. Married on April 7, 1686 to Deborah Green, by whom he was the father of Elizabeth; following the death of his first wife, remarried on February 20, 1693 to Ann Lillington; no children by his second wife.

Studied law, and later became Attorney General and Justice of the General Court in Albemarle County. Became a prominent landowner, acquiring grants such as one consisting of 428 acres on the Chowan River, which he received in April 1697. Served for a number of years as a member of the northern Carolina Council; as President of that body, became Acting Governor of Carolina north and east of the Cape Fear River after the death of Deputy Governor Thomas Harvey in July 1699.

Walker's tenure as chief executive was marked by the continued migration of settlers into that section of Carolina near the Virginia border. Indeed, the number of new residents was so great that the acting governor had to deny an allegation that his colony was providing refuge for men seeking to escape Virginia law. While political harmony appears generally to have characterized Walker's years in office, signs of discord began to surface in 1701, when a vestry act was passed in the colony. Since its provisions included a poll tax for the support of Anglican clergymen, the act was opposed by the Quakers and Presbyterians in Carolina, who objected to the additional financial burden which they were being asked to assume. In 1703 an even more prejudicial vestry act became law, this time requiring members of the Assembly to take an oath of allegiance to Queen Anne and pledge that they were communicants of the Church of England. As Quaker opposition to this legislation grew more heated, Walker died near Edenton, Carolina on April 14, 1704, shortly after turning over his position as chief executive to Robert Daniel.

Bibliography: "Governor Walker and the Bay River Indians," *North Carolina Historical and Genealogical Register*, I (October 1900), 597-600; Annie (Walker) Burns Bell, "Walker Family History (which Originated in North Carolina)" (1931), typescript volume in Local History and Genealogy Division, New York Public Library.

DANIEL, Robert, 1703-1705

South Carolina, 1716-1717

Date and place of birth, and names of parents unknown. An Anglican. Emigrated in 1679 from Barbados to Carolina, where he became one of the leaders of the "Goose Creek" political faction. Later named a Landgrave of Carolina. Acquired the military rank of Colonel, and at one time commanded the provincial militia in southern Carolina; played a prominent role in that colony's attack on St. Augustine during the autumn of 1702. Named Deputy Governor of northern Carolina in 1703, when Governor Sir Nathaniel Johnson decided to administer the southern section of Carolina himself and appoint a substitute to preside in the north.

Daniel's tenure as chief executive of Carolina north and east of the Cape Fear River was disrupted by the bitter controversy over the Vestry Act of 1703. That legislation, which denied the colony's large Quaker community the right of affirmation by insisting that all Assembly members take an oath of allegiance to the Queen, became the catalyst which finally resulted in the removal of Daniel from office early in 1705. The former deputy governor appears to have been reluctant to participate in northern Carolina politics after this incident. In October 1708, for example, he was named to the Council under Thomas Cary, but he asked "to be excused from sitting in this House."

Nevertheless, Daniel did not abandon politics completely. He represented Berkeley and Craven counties in the South Carolina Commons House of Assembly in 1706-07, 1708-09 and 1713-15, and in April 1716 he took over as Deputy Governor of that colony, replacing the departing Charles Craven. Daniel's administration in South Carolina, however, was no more tranquil than had been his previous experience in the governor's chair. Along with periodic squabbles with the Lower House, he engaged in a procedural dispute with William Rhett, a surveyor general of customs, who allegedly threatened to "kill the old Rogue" when Daniel interfered with his attempt to seize the Crown's share of cargo from a ship accused of trading with pirates.

Daniel's brief but tumultuous service in South Carolina ended with the arrival of Governor Robert Johnson (*circa* June-October) in 1717. The date of Daniel's death is unknown.

CARY, Thomas, 1705-1706, 1708-1711

Born in 1678, the son of Walter Cary of Chipping Wycombe, Buckinghamshire, England, and a stepson of John Archdale, who served as governor of southern Carolina from 1695 to 1696.

Became a prominent Charles Town merchant following his immigration to Carolina, and eventually acquired the military rank of Colonel. Was serving as Deputy Governor of Carolina north and east of the Cape Fear River by March of 1705.

Although Cary was reputed to be friendly toward religious dissenters in Carolina, his behavior as chief executive at first differed little from that of his predecessor, Robert Daniel. Indeed, his insistence that Quakers in the Assembly take an oath of allegiance to Queen Anne and swear that they were communicants of the Church of England so incensed his political opponents that in 1706 he was replaced by William Glover, president of the northern Carolina Council. Cary refused to abandon his efforts to return to power, however, and in November 1707, he was already acting as a member of the colony's Upper House.

In 1708, after Glover had himself alienated the Quaker faction, Cary decided to endorse their cause, and later that year he and his followers ousted Glover from office. For over two years Cary, as President of the Council, was occupied chiefly by attempts to insure Quaker political dominance, a strategy which in 1711 led him and his supporters to revolt against Edward Hyde, the new head of the troubled colony. By the summer of 1711 Hyde, with the help of Governor Alexander Spotswood of Virginia, had managed to crush the rebellion, forcing Cary to flee to Virginia. He was later captured and sent to England for trial, where he was released due to lack of evidence. Cary died in 1722.

Bibliography: Fairfax Harrison, *The Virginia Carys: An Essay in Genealogy* (New York, 1919).

GLOVER, William, 1706-1708

Born *circa* 1670; place of birth and names of parents unknown. Married to a woman named Catherine, by whom he had Elizabeth and perhaps other children.

Acted as Clerk of the northern Carolina General Court in the 1690's, and was commissioned a Justice of the Court in 1701. In his capacity as President of the northern Carolina Council, served as Acting Governor of that colony from 1706 until late 1708.

After succeeding the deposed Thomas Cary, Glover was at first accepted by both Anglican and Quaker factions in northern Carolina. In 1707 his authority was further bolstered by an order from the Lords Proprietors which confirmed the legitimacy of Cary's removal, and permitted the colony's Quakers to continue in public office despite their scruples against taking oaths. A short time later, however, Glover reversed his position by insisting that all new members of the Council take an oath in order to qualify. As a result, the Quaker contingent in the colony established an alliance with the ousted Cary, and late in 1708 Glover was himself removed as chief executive by Cary's supporters, and forced to flee to Virginia. The date of Glover's death is unknown, although it occurred sometime between July 1711 and October 1712.

HYDE, Edward, 1711-1712

Born *circa* 1650 in England; was possibly related to Edward Hyde, first Earl of Clarendon, as a grandson. An Anglican. Married to a woman named Catherine, who survived him; father of Anne and perhaps others. First chosen by the Lords Proprietors as Deputy Governor of the northern part of Carolina in 1709, but Governor Edward Tynte of Carolina, from whom he was to receive his commission, died before Hyde's arrival in America in August 1710. Selected as a compromise choice for President of the northern Carolina Council early in 1711, in an effort to settle a power struggle in the colony between an Anglican faction led by William Glover and a Quaker-backed faction headed by Thomas Cary.

Once in office, Hyde, as President of the Council and Acting Governor, was faced with an attempted purge of Cary's supporters by the Gloverite-controlled Assembly. The punitive measures passed by the Assembly against Cary and his allies, combined with Hyde's tactless handling of the matter, soon caused a rebellion among Cary's men, and Hyde was forced to request military support from Virginia's Governor Spotswood to suppress the outbreak. Cary himself fled to Virginia and was captured and charged with treason, although his trial in England was eventually dismissed when Hyde neglected to supply evidence against him.

Hyde's brief tenure was also affected by the important decision in December 1710 by Carolina's Lords Proprietors to establish the separate colonies of North and South Carolina. Hyde was chosen as Governor of North Carolina, qualifying for the post on May 9, 1712. During the next few months he encouraged the labors of the Society for the Propagation of the Gospel in his colony. Hyde also endeavored to protect North Carolina from attacks by the Tuscarora Indians; however, he died from yellow fever in September 1712, before he could bring an end to the Indian war. Wickham County, North Carolina was renamed Hyde County in 1712 in his honor. *DAB*.

POLLOCK, Thomas, 1712-1714, 1722

Born on March 6, 1654 in Scotland, the son of Thomas Pollock. Brother of James, Margaret and Helen. Married on June 19, 1690 to Martha (Cullen) West, by whom he was the father of Martha, Thomas, Cullen, George and four children who died in infancy; after his first wife's death in March 1701, remarried to Esther (Sweetman) Harris Wilkinson; no children by his second wife.

Arrived in Carolina in June 1683, where he became a member of the General Court and the Governor's Council. As President of the Council, served as Acting Governor of North Carolina from September 1712 to May 1714, between the administrations of governors Edward Hyde and Charles Eden; again took office as interim chief executive in March 1722, following the death of Eden.

During Pollock's first administration, warfare between whites and the Tuscarora Indians in North Carolina continued to disrupt life in the colony. In March 1713 the Tuscarora suffered their most serious defeat, when a military force consisting of white settlers from North and South Carolina, aided by a large body of friendly Indians, killed almost 1,000 Indian men, women and children. A short time later peace negotiations began, although a definitive treaty was not approved until February of 1715. Pollock's second period as chief executive was considerably more tranquil, but the acting governor died on August 30, 1722, only five months after he had replaced his deceased predecessor.

Bibliography: ''Queries and Answers [*re* Pollock Family],'' *North Carolina Historical and Genealogical Register*, III (January 1903), 156-58; Mrs. John W. Hinsdale, ''Governor Thomas Pollok [*sic*],'' *North Carolina Booklet*, V (April 1906), 219-31.

EDEN, Charles, 1714-1722

Born in 1673, a member of the Eden family of Durham in the north of England. Brother of Anne. Married to Penelope Golland; no children.

Although his appointment as Deputy Governor of North Carolina received the royal approval in May 1713, Eden did not take the oath of office until May 28, 1714. A religious man, he was elected to the vestry of ''the Eastern Parish of Chowan Precinct'' (now St. Paul's Parish) in 1715, while he was chief executive. Three years later the Lords Proprietors bestowed on Eden the title of Landgrave, a rank in the order of nobility under the system of government devised for Carolina by John Locke.

Eden's first few years as governor were generally successful, as he managed to restore peace and political stability following the disruptions brought about by the colony's struggle with the Tuscarora Indians. In February 1715 a peace treaty was signed with the Tuscarora; that same year the North Carolina General Assembly under Eden's direction codified "the ancient standing laws" of the colony. This promising beginning was somewhat tarnished, however, by the revelation that several of Eden's closest associates had probably been cooperating with the pirate Edward Teach (or Thatch), more commonly known as "Blackbeard." In 1718 Blackbeard and his men had moved their base of operations to the coast of Carolina, and it was not until late that year, when the pirate was killed off the North Carolina coast, that piracy began to decline as a threat to coastal shipping. Eden's administration was also marked by the first wave in 1717 of what would later become a torrent of Scotch-Irish immigration to America, although only a handful from this early group actually settled in North Carolina.

Eden died on March 26, 1722, while still in office. He was buried at "Eden House," his estate in Bertie County.

Bibliography: Marshall De Lancey Haywood, "Governor Charles Eden," *North Carolina Booklet*, III (December 1903), 5-24; Rev. Robert Allan Eden, *Some Historical Notes of the Eden Family* (London, 1907). *DAB*.

REED, William, 1722-1724

Date and place of birth, and names of parents unknown. Brother of Joseph and perhaps others. Married to a woman named Christian; after his first wife's death, remarried to a woman named Jane; father of Christian and William.

First appeared in Currituck Precinct, northern Carolina *circa* 1692, and eventually attained the military rank of Colonel. Became a member of the North Carolina Council in 1712; as President of that body, succeeded the deceased Thomas Pollock as Acting Governor in August 1722, a position which he held until the arrival of Governor George Burrington in January of 1724.

Reed's tenure as interim chief executive was characterized by the rapid growth of North Carolina in both size and population. Encouraged by the recent successful administration of Charles Eden, settlers moved to the area in such numbers that between 1722 and 1730 four new counties were established. Indeed, many individuals were prepared to ignore proprietary instructions on landholding whenever the prize seemed tempting enough. In about 1723, for example, colonists began to migrate to the Cape Fear Valley, despite the decision of the Proprietors to close the land office in that region.

Following his period as chief executive, Reed returned to the Governor's Council, serving in that capacity until his death in Pasquotank Precinct, North Carolina on December 11, 1728.

BURRINGTON, George, 1724-1725, 1731-1734

Born *circa* 1680, probably to a family of some prominence living in Devonshire, England. Awarded a commission as Captain in the British Army before arriving in North Carolina as "Governor General and Admiral of the Province."

Although he took the governor's oath of office on January 15, 1724, Burrington's service was interrupted eighteen months later when his altercation with Christopher Gale, North Carolina's chief justice, caused him to be replaced by Sir Richard Everard in July 1725. Nevertheless, Burrington recovered from this political setback and, after the Crown purchased North Carolina from the Proprietors in 1729, he returned in February 1731 as that colony's first Royal Governor. While he did make some improvements to North Carolina's road system, Burrington soon found it difficult to get along with the Lower House and at the same time enforce the Crown's instructions. He clashed with the Lower House over a number of issues, but particularly over the form of currency to be used in paying quitrents. Burrington insisted that quitrents could only be paid in "proclamation money," or coins of various countries valued at a price fixed by royal proclamation; on the other hand, the Lower House asserted that other kinds of payment should be acceptable, such as commodities or provincial currency, and that collection of quitrents ought to be postponed for two years. As the *impasse* continued with Burrington becoming more intransigent, the Board of Trade finally decided to recommend his recall in the summer of 1733. In April of 1734 he was replaced by Nathaniel Rice, the president of the Council, who in turn made way for the new royal governor, Gabriel Johnston, in November 1734.

After his return to England Burrington wrote several works, including *Seasonable Considerations on the Expediency of a War with France* (1743) and *An Answer to Dr. William Brakenridge's Letter Concerning the Number of Inhabitants within the London Bills of Mortality* (1757). Burrington was murdered in St. James's Park, London in February 1759.

Bibliography: Marshall De Lancey Haywood, *Governor George Burrington, With an Account of His Official Administrations in the Colony of North Carolina, 1724-1725, 1731-1734* (Raleigh, 1896); William S. Price, Jr., "A Strange Incident in George Burrington's Royal Governorship," *North Carolina Historical Review*, LI (Spring 1974), 149-58. *DAB*.

EVERARD, Sir Richard, 1725-1731

Born in England, probably in the county of Essex, the son of Sir Hugh and Lady Mary (Brown) Everard; date of birth unknown. Brother of Hugh, Morton, Elizabeth and Frances. Married in December 1705 to Susannah Kidder, by whom he was the father of Richard, Hugh, Susannah and Anne.

Inherited the title of Baronet from his father in 1706. Appointed Deputy Governor of North Carolina by the Lords Proprietors of that province, and assumed office in July of 1725.

The last chief executive of North Carolina under proprietary rule, Everard presided over an area in the midst of rapid territorial expansion. Inevitably, the colony's accelerated growth led to boundary disputes with Virginia, and in 1728 Everard appointed four men to a joint commission, in an effort to make an accurate survey of the line dividing the two neighbors. After the work was completed, leaders in North Carolina were delighted to discover that the boundary as drawn gave them "a very great Quantity of Lands and Number of Families that before had been under Virginia."

In the sphere of internal politics, these years were characterized by factional turbulence, largely instigated by the deposed George Burrington, Everard's predecessor as chief executive. Burrington's persistent opposition was rewarded after the British Crown completed its purchase of North Carolina from the Proprietors in July 1729, when he secured an appointment as the colony's first royal governor. Following his replacement by Burrington in February 1731, Everard moved to Virginia, although he later returned to England and died in London on February 17, 1733.

Bibliography: Marshall De Lancey Haywood, "Sir Richard Everard, Baronet, Governor of the Colony of North Carolina, 1725-1731, and His Descendants in Virginia," *North Carolina Booklet*, XIV (July 1914), 50-61.

RICE, Nathaniel, 1734, 1752-1753

Born probably in England; date of birth and names of parents unknown. Married to Mary Bursey, by whom he was the father of John and perhaps others.

Settled in North Carolina before 1730 and became a leading planter, acquiring an estate which included over 6,200 acres of land and seventeen slaves. Was serving as Secretary of the province by 1731. Remained a member of the North Carolina Council from 1731 to 1753; as President of the Council, served as Acting Governor between April and November of 1734, and again from July 1752 until his death.

Rice's assumption of power in the spring of 1734 represented a final victory over George Burrington, the unpopular royal governor with whom several of the province's most prominent councillors had been feuding for some time. Indeed, at one juncture Burrington alleged that Rice and other members of this opposition faction had attempted to assassinate him, an accusation which forced them to flee to Virginia to avoid a bill of indictment. Rice's second interim governorship was also characterized by political dissension, despite his assurance to the Board of Trade in August 1752 that "the Country enjoys great quietness." During these months a persistent dispute over representation in the Lower House kept the Albemarle and Cape Fear regions at odds with each other. Bishop August Gottlieb Spangenberg, a Moravian leader looking for a suitable tract in North Carolina where his co-religionists could settle, noted in a diary entry for September 12, 1752 that the controversy had "greatly weakened the authority of the Legislature," and seriously interfered with the administration of justice. With this *impasse* still unresolved, Rice died on January 29, 1753.

Bibliography: Elizabeth Moore, *The Rice, Hasell, Hawks, and Carruthers Families of North Carolina* (Bladensburg, Md., 1966).

JOHNSTON, Gabriel, 1734-1752

Born in 1699 in Scotland, a member of the Johnston family of Annandale. Brother of Samuel and Elizabeth. Married to Penelope (Golland) Pheney, who died in 1741; remarried to Frances Butler; father of a daughter, Penelope, by his first wife. Thought to have attended the University of St. Andrews in Scotland as a medical student and later as a student of Oriental languages; held a minor instructorship at St. Andrews, but appears not to have received a degree.

Beginning in 1730, began to write for *The Craftsman*, a literary and political weekly which opposed Prime Minister Sir Robert Walpole. Awarded the post of North Carolina Royal Governor in May 1733, largely due to his acquaintance with the Earl of Wilmington, the Lord of the Treasury who shared an interest in *The Craftsman*.

Soon after his inauguration in November 1734, Johnston took steps to enforce the Crown's orders regarding the collection of quitrents. However, unlike his predecessor, George Burrington, Johnston managed in December 1738 to arrive at a compromise with the Lower House, although the agreement was disallowed in July 1741 by his superiors in London. In 1746 Johnston was confronted by a schism of the colony's Albemarle and Cape Fear regions, resulting from jealousy between the two sections over representation in the Lower House. The Albemarle or northern counties finally withdrew from the

Lower House, and until 1754 conditions remained chaotic in the north. Nevertheless, despite these and other instances of political turmoil, North Carolina did make some progress under Johnston. In 1749 James Davis established a printing press in New Bern, and two years later he founded *The North Carolina Gazette*, a weekly newspaper. Johnston's administration also saw the beginning of a dramatic increase in population, as the governor himself encouraged the immigration of Highland Scots to the colony.

Johnston died on July 17, 1752 in North Carolina, while still in office. Johnston County, North Carolina, established in 1746, was named in his honor.

Bibliography: M. S. R. Cunningham, "Gabriel Johnston, Governor of North Carolina, 1734-1752," unpub. M.A. thesis, University of North Carolina at Chapel Hill, 1945. *DAB*.

ROWAN, Matthew, 1753-1754

A native of County Antrim in Ireland; date of birth and names of parents unknown. Brother of Andrew, Atchison and William. Apparently entered a common-law marriage with Jane Stubbs, by whom he was the father of a son named John.

Became a prominent planter in North Carolina, acquiring an estate which included over 9,000 acres of land and twenty-six slaves; also acted for a time as Surveyor General of the province. Served as a member of the North Carolina Council from 1734 until 1760 and, as head of that body, presided as Acting Governor between the death of Nathaniel Rice in January 1753 and the arrival of Royal Governor Arthur Dobbs in October of 1754.

Despite the continued immigration of settlers to the western area of North Carolina, Rowan faced serious defense problems during his brief administration. The residents of the new counties established in this interior region were particularly vulnerable to raids by hostile Indians, and by late 1753, as England moved closer toward war with France, that danger had increased significantly. In February of the following year Rowan conveyed to the North Carolina Assembly a letter he had received from Governor Robert Dinwiddie of Virginia, warning against possible French-inspired Indian attacks. Recognizing the need to guard the province against this threat, the Lower House appropriated £40,000 for the protection of North Carolina's frontier and for the raising of a military force which would fight in co-operation with Virginian troops.

While his replacement by Dobbs in the autumn of 1754 freed Rowan from his responsibilities as chief executive, he continued to serve on the Governor's Council until his death sometime between April and July of 1760.

DOBBS, Arthur, 1754-1765

Born on April 2, 1689 at Castle Dobbs, County Antrim, Ireland, the son of Richard, a high sheriff of Antrim, and Mary (Stewart) Dobbs. Brother of four, although only Richard survived to maturity. Married in 1719 to Anne (Osburn) Norbury, by whom he was the father of a number of children, including Conway, Edward and Frances; remarried at the age of seventy-three to Justina Davis of North Carolina.

Well educated, although the institutions which he may have attended are unknown. Inherited his father's estate in 1711. In the 1730's received, with London merchant Henry McCulloh, a grant of land in North Carolina in present-day Duplin County; purchased with John Selwyn 400,000 acres of land in North Carolina in 1745. Author of numerous essays and tracts on trade, exploration and science, including *Essay on the Trade and Improvement of Ireland* (1729 and 1731), *An Account of the Countries Adjoining to Hudson's Bay* (1744), and a paper on "Bees, and the mode of taking Wax and Honey" (*Philosophical Transactions*, 1750).

Appointed High Sheriff of Antrim in 1720, and in 1727 elected to the Irish Parliament's House of Commons, representing Carrickfergus. Named Engineer-in-Chief and Surveyor General of Ireland in 1730. Commissioned in February 1753 as the successor to North Carolina Royal Governor Gabriel Johnston, and took office on October 31, 1754.

Soon after Dobbs' arrival in the colony, many of the disputes which had plagued previous North Carolina royal governors had reached a point of disruption for his administration. These quarrels concerned such matters as what constituted a quorum of the Lower House, the issue of paper money, and the perennial question of appropriations, including those for executive and judicial salaries. On the other hand, Dobbs and the Lower House were sometimes able to work effectively, particularly when the colony was in danger of outside attack. Late in 1755, for example, construction was begun on Fort Dobbs, near a branch of the Yadkin River, and throughout most of the French and Indian War, one of the Lower House's first concerns was to provide adequate defense funds. Dobbs himself actively sought a solution to North Carolina's vulnerability to Indian attack; in November 1763 he joined other colonial governors in negotiating a peace with Indian tribes bordering Britain's southern settlements.

Dobbs suffered an apoplectic stroke in 1762, an illness from which he never fully recovered. While still in office, Dobbs died at "Towncreek," his home in Brunswick, North Carolina, on March 28, 1765.

Bibliography: Alfred J. Morrison, "Arthur Dobbs of Castle Dobbs and Carolina," *South Atlantic Quarterly*, XVI (January 1917), 30-38; Desmond Clarke, *Arthur Dobbs, Esquire, 1689-1765* (Chapel Hill, 1957). *DAB, DNB*.

TRYON, William, 1765-1771
New York, 1771-1774, 1775-1780

Born in 1729 at "Norbury Park," Surrey, England, the son of Charles and Lady Mary (Shirley) Tryon. Brother of Ann, Mary, Harriot and Sophia. Married in 1757 to Margaret Wake, by whom he had Margaret and a son who died young. Received a commission in 1751 as Lieutenant in the First Regiment of Foot Guards; promoted to Captain (with army rank of Lieutenant Colonel) in 1758. Appointed Lieutenant Governor of North Carolina in 1764, probably through his wife's family connection with Lord Hillsborough. Succeeded the deceased Governor Arthur Dobbs in April 1765, and officially commissioned as Royal Governor the following July.

Tryon's period as governor of North Carolina was dominated by the Regulator movement, an attempt on the part of the western residents of the colony to correct what they perceived to be misgovernment by eastern interests. The central concern of the Regulators was malpractice by local officials, including the charging of excessive taxes and fees. Tryon, though sympathetic to some of their accusations, refused to accept the legitimacy of Regulator violence and took firm steps to end the movement. The governor's efforts culminated in May 1771 with a confrontation on Great Alamance Creek, in which a group of about 2,000 poorly equipped Regulators were routed by 1,400 militia under Tryon's command.

Soon after the Battle of Alamance, Tryon learned that he had been awarded the governorship of New York; in July 1771 he sailed for that colony to take up his new appointment. While Governor of New York he was confronted by the revolutionary movement and, following an absence in England from April 1774 to June 1775, he returned to find the colony in a state of open rebellion. In October 1775 Tryon retreated to a British warship off New York, from which he sought for almost a year to re-establish his authority. When British General Sir William Howe conquered the city of New York in September 1776, Tryon returned, but he was never able to gain effective political control over the entire state, and for the next few years he tried to strengthen the British military position. Tryon was promoted in 1778 to Major General "in America"; he also served as Colonel of the 70th Foot. In 1780 he was succeeded by James Robertson as military and civil governor of New York.

On September 4, 1780 illness forced Tryon to return to England. Despite a promotion to Lieutenant General in 1782 and an appointment as Colonel of the 29th Foot in 1783, his active military service was at an end. Tryon died on January 27, 1788 in London and was buried in Twickenham. Counties in North Carolina and New York were named in his honor, but North Carolina changed the name of its Tryon County in 1779, and New York followed suit in 1784.

Bibliography: Marshall DeLancey Haywood, *Governor William Tryon and His Administration in the Province of North Carolina, 1765-1771* . . . (Raleigh,

1903); Alonzo T. Dill, *Governor Tryon and His Palace* (Chapel Hill, 1955); William S. Powell, ed., "Tryon's 'Book' on North Carolina," *North Carolina Historical Review*, XXXIV (July 1957), 406-15; Solomon Henner, "The Career of William Tryon as Governor of the Province of New York, 1771-1780," unpub. Ed.D. diss., New York University, 1968. W. M. Tryon, ed. and comp., *The Tryon Family in America* (Wheaton, Md., 1969). *DAB, DNB*.

HASELL, James, 1771

Born in England; date of birth and names of parents unknown. Brother of Frances and possibly others. Married, probably in England, to a woman whose maiden name was perhaps Susan Cooke; later remarried to Susannah Sampson, a widow; married a third time in 1755 to Ann Sophia Von Blade Durlace, widow of Baron Von Rosentine; father of James by his first wife.

Immigrated to the Cape Fear area of North Carolina in about 1734; gained prominence as a planter, accumulating an estate which included over 12,500 acres of land and thirty-nine slaves. Was acting as Chief Justice of North Carolina by 1750, a position which he held for a number of years. Remained a member of the Council from 1752 to 1775 and, as President of that body, served as Acting Governor of the province between the departure of William Tryon in July and the arrival of Josiah Martin in August of 1771.*

When he began his brief interim administration, Hasell took over a province still reeling from Regulator violence against malpractice by local officials, a protest movement which had disrupted the North Carolina back-country for several years. While Governor Tryon's victory at the Battle of Alamance in May 1771 had apparently broken the power of the rebel forces, a sense of apprehension remained, despite Hasell's assurance to the Earl of Hillsborough that the Regulators had been "convinced of their folly."

In August of 1771 Hasell relinquished his executive authority to Josiah Martin, the newly-arrived royal governor, but he continued to serve as a member of Martin's Council. With the outbreak of the Revolution Hasell quietly endorsed the Loyalist position, a stance which resulted in the loss of his estate, although he was permitted to live at home unmolested until his death in February 1785.

Bibliography: Henry Bacon McKoy, *The McKoy Family of North Carolina, and Other Ancestors including Ancrum, Berry, Halling, Hasell [and] Usher* (Greenville, S.C., 1955); Elizabeth Moore, *The Rice, Hasell, Hawks, and Carruthers Families of North Carolina* (Bladensburg, Md., 1966).

*Hasell also presided as chief executive during short absences from the colony of Governor Dobbs in 1763 and Governor Martin in 1774.

MARTIN, Josiah, 1771-1775

Born on April 23, 1737 in Dublin, Ireland, the son of Colonel Samuel and Sarah (Wyke) Martin. Brother of Henry, William Byam and four others who survived infancy. Married in 1761 to his cousin, Elizabeth Martin; father of eight children.

Served as an officer in the British Army from 1757 to 1769, when ill health compelled him to sell his rank of Lieutenant Colonel. Commissioned by the Crown as Royal Governor of North Carolina in January 1771, and inaugurated in August of that year.

Despite a reputation for amiability that had preceded his appointment as Royal Governor, Martin quickly became embroiled with the North Carolina Lower House over several controversial issues. The most significant of these was the "foreign attachments clause," a provision which authorized colonial courts to settle unpaid debts by attaching the property of Britons who had never resided in the colonies. A heated argument erupted in 1773 between Martin, who rejected legislation containing the clause, and the North Carolina Lower House, which endorsed it as a means of collecting debts owed by recalcitrant British merchants. Acting on instructions from the Crown, Martin attempted to establish Courts of Oyer and Terminer, designed to operate without legislative approval, but by early 1774 North Carolina's judicial system had virtually collapsed. In December of 1773 the first North Carolina Committee of Correspondence was set up, and by August 1774 the Patriots were strong enough to convene the colony's First Provincial Congress, which chose delegates to a proposed Continental Congress. A Second Provincial Congress, held in April 1775, endorsed the system of county committees of safety, a tactic that eventually undermined Martin's authority and forced him to flee from office.

After boarding the British sloop H.M.S. *Cruizer* in the Cape Fear River in July 1775, Martin sought to devise a scheme which would quell the rebellion in the southern colonies. He organized a group of Loyalist Scottish Highlanders who met Patriot forces in February 1776, but the Loyalists were defeated. During the remainder of the war, Martin participated in other British campaigns, and he served with particular distinction under Cornwallis in 1780 and 1781. When his health again began to fail, Martin departed from America in the spring of 1781 and returned to England. In his last years he was a key witness before the American Loyalist Claims Commission, and was himself awarded a settlement to compensate for lost property. Martin died in London on April 13, 1786. Martin County, North Carolina, established in 1774, was named in his honor.

Bibliography: Joseph Younger Blanks, Jr., "The Administration of Governor Josiah Martin in North Carolina," unpub. M.A. thesis, University of

North Carolina at Chapel Hill, 1948; Vernon O. Stumpf, "Josiah Martin and His Search for Success: The Road to North Carolina," *North Carolina Historical Review*, LIII (Winter 1976), 55-79; Richard B. Sheridan, "The West Indian Antecedents of Josiah Martin, Last Royal Governor of North Carolina," *North Carolina Historical Review*, LIV (Summer 1977), 253-70. *DAB*.

HARNETT, Cornelius, 1775-1776

Born on April 20, 1723, probably in Chowan County, North Carolina, the son of Cornelius and Mary (Holt) Harnett. Married to a woman named Mary.

Represented Wilmington in the North Carolina Lower House of Assembly from 1754 to 1775. Member in 1764 of an Assembly committee which criticized the Sugar Act and the proposed Stamp Act; chairman of the Cape Fear Sons of Liberty from 1765 to 1766, and led resistance to the Stamp Act; headed a Wilmington committee appointed to enforce a non-importation agreement adopted in 1769 by a special convention of the Assembly.* Served in all but the first of North Carolina's five provincial congresses held from 1774 to 1776. Chaired the committees of safety established in Wilmington and New Hanover counties from 1774 to 1775, and served as President of North Carolina's Provincial Council (and later of the Council of Safety) from September 1775 to August 1776.

As head of the Council, Harnett was in effect North Carolina's chief executive, and he presided during the important transitional period between the departure of Royal Governor Josiah Martin and the Declaration of Independence. Harnett and the Council were especially responsible for preparing North Carolina for war; his efforts in this area later caused Sir Henry Clinton, the British general, to exempt Harnett from an amnesty which he offered to those rebels who would lay down their arms. Harnett's period in office was also marked by the gathering of the Fourth Provincial Congress in Halifax, North Carolina on April 4, 1776. At that Congress, Harnett himself chaired a committee which drafted the "Halifax Resolves," a document empowering North Carolina's delegates to the Continental Congress "to concur with the delegates of the other colonies in declaring Independency."

Following his service as president of the Council, Harnett played an active role in North Carolina's Fifth Provincial Congress, and was a member of the committee which wrote the state's first constitution. When the new state government commenced in January of 1777, Harnett acted as President of the Council of State; in May of that same year, he was chosen as a delegate to the Continental Congress. Taking his seat in July 1777, Harnett served in Congress until his return to North Carolina early in 1780. Soon after the British occupied Wilmington in January 1781, Harnett was captured while attempting to flee, and he died a prisoner on parole *circa* April 28, 1781. Harnett County, North Carolina, formed in 1855, was named in his honor.

Bibliography: R. D. W. Connor, "Cornelius Harnett: The Pride of the Cape Fear," *North Carolina Booklet*, V (January 1906), 171-201; R. D. W. Connor, *Cornelius Harnett: An Essay in North Carolina History* (Raleigh, 1909); John G. Coyle, "Cornelius Harnett," American Irish Historical Society, *Journal*, XXIX (1931), 148-56; David T. Morgan, "Cornelius Harnett: Revolutionary Leader and Delegate to the Continental Congress," *North Carolina Historical Review*, XLIX (July 1972), 229-41. *DAB*.

*The *DAB* also includes Harnett as one of nine members of North Carolina's first Committee of Correspondence, formed in December 1773, but this is not confirmed in Lefler and Powell, *Colonial North Carolina*, which does not mention Harnett among the seven men there named.

ASHE, Samuel, 1776, 1795-1798

Born in 1725 near Beaufort, North Carolina, the son of John Baptista Ashe, speaker of the North Carolina Assembly, and Elizabeth (Swann) Ashe. An Episcopalian. Brother of John and Mary. Married before 1748 to Mary Porter, by whom he was the father of John Baptista, Samuel and Cincinnatus; following the death of his first wife, remarried to Elizabeth Merrick, a widow, by whom he had Thomas.

Raised by his uncle, Samuel Swann, after his father's death in 1734. Educated at Harvard; also studied law. Served for a time as Assistant Attorney for the Crown in the Wilmington District, but by the 1770's had become one of the leaders of the revolutionary movement in North Carolina. Named to the Council of Safety, representing Wilmington, and as President of that body acted as chief executive of North Carolina from August to September of 1776; also served as Governor of North Carolina from November 1795 to December 1798.

Following his one-month tenure as head of North Carolina's revolutionary government, Ashe played a major role in the new state's political and legal development. In late 1776, for example, he served as a member of the committee assigned the task of preparing a constitution for North Carolina, and, after a short period as Speaker of the new State Senate, he was named in 1777 as Presiding Judge of North Carolina's first Supreme Court. By 1795, when he left the judiciary to become chief executive, Ashe was among the most prominent public figures in the state. As governor, Ashe was a strong proponent of the Jeffersonian view on states' rights, a position which was popular enough to win him re-election in 1796 and 1797. One of the major developments of Ashe's administration was the Tennessee land grant scandal, in which the governor intervened after Secretary of State Glasgow was charged with destroying incriminating state records in 1796.

Following his gubernatorial service, Ashe took little part in politics, although he did act as a Presidential Elector in 1804. Ashe died at "Rocky Point," his plantation in New Hanover County, North Carolina, on February 3, 1813.

Bibliography: S. A. Ashe, "Samuel Ashe," in S. A. Ashe, *Biographical History of North Carolina*, VIII (Greensboro, N.C., 1917). *DAB*.

JONES, Willie, 1776

Born *circa* 1741 in Northampton County, North Carolina, the son of Robert (also known as Robin) Jones, an attorney general for North Carolina under the Crown, and Sarah (Cobb) Jones. A freethinker in religion. Brother of Allen Jones, and perhaps others. Married on June 27, 1776 to Mary Montfort, by whom he was the father of Willie, Robert, Patsy and Sallie. Educated in England, studying for a time at Eton, and travelled on the Continent. Returned to North Carolina about 1760 and built his home, "The Grove," in the town of Halifax. Became a successful planter and businessman.

Assisted in Governor William Tryon's fight against the Regulators during the Alamance campaign of 1771. Served as chairman of the Halifax Committee of Safety in 1774. Represented either the borough or the county of Halifax at all but the fourth of North Carolina's five provincial congresses from 1774 to 1776, missing the fourth congress only because of his selection by the Continental Congress as Superintendent of Indian Affairs for the Southern Colonies. Served as President of the North Carolina Council of Safety from September to November 1776.

As the new state's chief executive by virtue of his Council presidency, Jones lent his voice to the appeals of North Carolina's radical Whig faction. During the Fifth Provincial Congress, which opened its deliberations on November 12, 1776, the state's radicals worked for a constitution embodying the principles of a "simple democracy"—a government in which a strong legislature would hold the executive in check, and which would provide religious freedom unaccompanied by an established church. On balance, the radicals in 1776 won most of their demands, and Jones himself continued to play a major role in North Carolina politics for the next twelve years. As a member of the House of Commons, he represented the borough of Halifax in 1777-78 and the county of Halifax in 1779-80. Jones sat from 1780 to 1781 in the Continental Congress; he returned in 1781 to take a place on the North Carolina Council of State, a position he again held in 1787. He was also a state senator in 1782, 1784 and

1788. A strong critic of the proposed Federal Constitution, Jones declined an opportunity to represent North Carolina at the Philadelphia Constitutional Convention, and helped to persuade his state convention to vote against ratification in 1788, although that verdict was overturned a year later. Jones also served on the first Board of Trustees of the University of North Carolina. He died in Raleigh, North Carolina on June 18, 1801, and was buried there. Jones County, North Carolina, created in 1778, was named in his honor.

Bibliography: Cadwallader Jones, *A Genealogical History* (Columbia, S.C., 1900); Blackwell P. Robinson, "Willie Jones of Halifax County," *North Carolina Historical Review*, XVIII (January-April 1941), 1-26, 133-70; William D. Hoyt, Jr., ed., "Letters from Willie Jones to His Son at the University of North Carolina, 1796-1801," *North Carolina Historical Review*, XIX (October 1942), 375-79; Samuel E. Morison, "The Willie Jones-John Paul Jones Tradition," *William and Mary Quarterly*, 3rd ser., vol. XVI (April 1959), 198-206. *DAB*.

CASWELL, Richard, 1777-1780, 1785-1787

Born on August 3, 1729 in Harford County, Maryland, the son of a merchant. Married twice, the second time to Sarah Herritage; father of William, Richard, Winston, and several others. Moved to Raleigh, North Carolina at the age of seventeen, and worked as a surveyor and a lawyer.

Served as Deputy Surveyor of North Carolina and as Clerk of Orange County, North Carolina. Member of the North Carolina Lower House of Assembly from 1754 to 1771, and again from 1773 to 1775; Speaker of the Assembly from 1770 to 1771, and a member of that body's first Committee of Correspondence in December 1773. Commanded a wing of Governor Tryon's army in battle against the Regulators at Great Alamance Creek in 1771. Named in March 1773 as a Judge of Courts of Oyer and Terminer. Member of North Carolina's First Provincial Congress in 1774; delegate to the First and Second Continental Congresses, 1774-76; presided over North Carolina's Fifth Provincial Congress in late 1776, and participated in the drafting of the state's first constitution that same year. Chosen Governor by the North Carolina Legislature seven times, taking office for the first time in January 1777.

Despite being constitutionally restricted from exercising much real power, Caswell as a war governor tried to provide for the welfare of the state militia, and from 1776 to 1777 he also served as Colonel of the state's Partisan Rangers. Again governor at the time of the Federal Constitutional Convention of 1787, he played a major role in North Carolina's deliberations over the nature of its relationship to the national government. Although he was selected as a delegate to the Philadelphia Convention, Caswell refused the appointment, and both during and after his period as chief executive he led a strong but eventually unsuccessful campaign within North Carolina against ratification of the Federal Constitution. Caswell's second period in office was also marked by the continuation of a secessionist movement in western North Carolina, which sought to establish the sovereign "State of Franklin;" nevertheless, firm measures by the governor helped bring a halt to the affair.

Between his first and second periods as chief executive, Caswell was Major General of the state militia, and he commanded militia forces in August 1780 during the crushing defeat of Patriot troops at the Battle of Camden, a setback which damaged his political and military reputation. He recovered quickly, however, and held a variety of state offices before again becoming governor in 1785. While serving as Speaker of the State Assembly, Caswell died on November 10, 1789 in Fayetteville, North Carolina, and was buried in the family cemetery in Lenoir County. Caswell County, North Carolina, formed in 1777, was named in his honor.

Bibliography: C. B. Alexander, "The Training of Richard Caswell," *North Carolina Historical Review*, XXIII (January 1946), 13-31; C. B. Alexander, "Richard Caswell: Versatile Leader of the Revolution," *North Carolina Historical Review*, XXIII (April 1946), 119-41; C. B. Alexander, "Richard Caswell's Military and Later Public Services," *North Carolina Historical Review*, XXIII (July 1946), 287-312. *DAB*.

NASH, Abner, 1780-1781

Born *circa* 1740 at "Templeton Manor" in Amelia (later Prince Edward) County, Virginia, the third son of John and Ann (Owen) Nash. Brother of Francis Nash, who died in 1777 while fighting under Washington at the Battle of Germantown, and six others. Married to Justina (Davis) Dobbs, the widow of former Governor Arthur Dobbs, by whom he had Abner, Margaret and Justina; after the death of his first wife, remarried in 1774 to Mary Jones, by whom he was the father of Frederick, Elizabeth, Maria and Frances. Moved in 1762 from Virginia to Halifax, North Carolina, where he practiced law; settled in New Bern, North Carolina in the early 1770's.

Represented Prince Edward County in the Virginia House of Burgesses in 1761 and 1762. One of the organizers of North Carolina's Sons of Liberty in the 1760's. Member of the North Carolina Lower House, representing Halifax town in 1764 and 1765 and Halifax County from 1770 to 1771. Appointed Major of Brigade by Governor William Tryon in 1768, during the Regulator disturbances. Delegate from New Bern to each of North Carolina's five provincial congresses from 1774 to 1776, and a major participant on the committee which drafted the State Constitution of 1776. Member of the North

Carolina Provincial Council of Safety in 1775 and 1776. Under the new State Constitution, elected to the House of Commons from New Bern in 1777 and from Craven County in 1778; Speaker of the first House of Commons under the state government in April 1777. Elected in 1779 to represent Jones County in the State Senate, and served as Speaker. Chosen Governor of North Carolina in the spring of 1780.

Nash's year as chief executive was disrupted by a major dispute between the governor and his Assembly. The radical legislators, suspicious of Nash's moderate stance on many issues, stripped him of most of his authority and gave it to a "Board of War" in the autumn of 1780. When the governor criticized what he felt was an unconstitutional usurpation of his powers, the Board of War was replaced by a "Council Extraordinary" early in 1781. This Council, while less offensive than the Board of War, was still viewed by Nash as an infringement of his constitutional role. Disgusted with the confusing political situation, Nash withdrew his name from the gubernatorial contest of June 1781.

Although Nash retired from public life a short time after the expiration of his term as governor, he soon returned to the House to represent Jones County in 1782, 1784 and 1785. He was also elected to the Continental Congress in 1782, 1783 and 1785, and in 1786 was chosen as a delegate to, but did not attend, the Annapolis convention of that year. Nash died in New York on December 2, 1786, while attending Congress; he was buried in St. Paul's Churchyard in New York, and later re-interred at "Pembroke," his estate near New Bern, North Carolina.

Bibliography: J. G. de Roulhac Hamilton, *Presentation of Portrait of Governor Abner Nash to the State of North Carolina . . .* (Raleigh, 1909); Frank Nash, "Governor Abner Nash," *North Carolina Booklet*, XXII (1922-23), 3-11. *DAB*.

BURKE, Thomas, 1781, 1782

Born *circa* 1747 in County Galway, Ireland, the son of Ulrick and Letitia (Ould) Burke. Married in 1770 to Mary Freeman, and the father of a daughter named Mary. Attended university, probably in Dublin, before immigration to America. Resided first in Accomack County, Virginia, and later moved to Norfolk; settled in Orange County, North Carolina in 1771 and established "Tyaquin," an estate named after the Irish seat of the Burke family. Practiced medicine and law in Virginia, and admitted to the practice of law in the Superior Court of Orange County in 1772.

Served as delegate from Orange County to all except the first of North Carolina's provincial congresses from 1774 to 1776. Played a major role in the formation of the North Carolina Constitution of 1776. Elected to the Continental Congress in December 1776 and, apart from a period between April and August 1778, represented North Carolina in Congress until June 1781, when he was chosen Governor of the state.

In September 1781 Burke and his Council were captured in Hillsborough, North Carolina during a raid led by David Fanning, the Tory leader. Burke was transferred from North Carolina to a more secure place of incarceration on Sullivan's Island in Charlestown harbor, and in January 1782, two months after his parole to James Island, he escaped his captors. He then returned to North Carolina to complete his term as governor, replacing Alexander Martin, who had served as acting governor during Burke's absence. Burke's activities as chief executive were considerably curtailed by his capture and imprisonment, but while governor he did attempt to systematize the procedures for supplying Patriot troops, and to eliminate the abuses which had sprung up among the state's revenue collectors and impressment officers.

After his tumultuous term expired in the spring of 1782, Burke declined to run for re-election, and he died at "Tyaquin" on December 2, 1783. Burke County, North Carolina, established in 1777, was named in his honor.

Bibliography: J. G. de Roulhac Hamilton, "Governor Thomas Burke," *North Carolina Booklet*, VI (October 1906), 103-22; James E. Smith, Jr., "Thomas Burke, Governor of North Carolina," American Irish Historical Society, *Journal*, XXVIII (1930), 61-64; Jennings B. Sanders, "Thomas Burke in the Continental Congress," *North Carolina Historical Review*, IX (January 1932), 22-37; Elisha P. Douglass, "Thomas Burke, Disillusioned Democrat," *North Carolina Historical Review*, XXVI (April 1949), 150-86; Ruth Franklin Sutton, "Thomas Burke," unpub. M.A. thesis, University of North Carolina at Chapel Hill, 1949; Richard Walser, ed., *The Poems of Governor Thomas Burke of North Carolina* (Raleigh, 1961); John S. Watterson, III, "Dr. Thomas Burke, A Revolutionary Career," unpub. Ph.D. diss., Northwestern University, 1970; John S. Watterson, III, "The Ordeal of Governor Burke," *North Carolina Historical Review*, XLVIII (Spring 1971), 95-117; John Watterson, ed., "Poetic Justice; or, an Ill-fated Epic by Thomas Burke," *North Carolina Historical Review*, LV (Summer 1978), 339-46. *DAB*.

MARTIN, Alexander, 1781-1782, 1782-1785, 1789-1792

Born in 1740 in Hunterdon County, New Jersey, the son of Hugh, a Presbyterian minister, and Jane Martin. Brother of James, Thomas, Samuel, Robert, Martha and Jane. Never married. Received an A.B. degree from the College of New Jersey (later Princeton University) in 1756.

Moved to Salisbury, North Carolina shortly after his graduation from college, and became a merchant. Elected Justice of the Peace in 1764 and Deputy King's Attorney in 1766; also served as a Judge during the 1770's. Member of the North Carolina Lower House of Assembly in 1773-74, representing Guilford County. Participated in North Carolina's Second and Third Provincial Congresses in 1775. As Lieutenant Colonel of the Second North Carolina Continental Regiment, fought against Loyalist forces in the "Snow Campaign" of late 1775, and in the Moore's Creek Campaign of February 1776; promoted to Colonel in 1776, and participated in the defense of Charlestown. After joining Washington's army in 1777, fought at the Battle of Germantown and was charged with cowardice, but was later acquitted. Returned to North Carolina in November 1777, where he was elected to the State Senate, representing Guilford County in 1778-82, 1785 and 1787-88; served as Speaker of that body at every session except those held in 1778-79. Member of the Board of War and the "Council Extraordinary" in 1780-81. Acted as chief executive of North Carolina during the captivity of Governor Thomas Burke in the autumn and winter of 1781-82. Chosen Governor of the state in his own right in April 1782, and re-elected in 1783 and 1784; after a hiatus of almost five years, again served as chief executive from December 1789 to December 1792.

Martin's three periods as governor spanned a decade during which North Carolina wrested its independence from Great Britain and assumed its new identity as part of the United States. Throughout most of his tenure the question of how much authority should be granted to the federal government was widely debated in North Carolina, but Martin, despite his selection as a delegate to the Philadelphia Convention of 1787, was alternately ambivalent and silent on the issue of national vs. states' rights. Although he had been elected to the Continental Congress in December 1786 and appreciated the need to broaden its powers, Martin left the Constitutional Convention in August 1787 without signing the finished document.

In 1792, when he was required to step down as governor after having served the maximum of three consecutive one-year terms, Martin was chosen by North Carolina's Republican Legislature to represent the state in the United States Senate. As his first term came to a close, however, his advocacy of the Alien and Sedition Acts cost him many of his former political friends, and in December of 1798 he failed to win re-election. Towards the end of his life, in 1804 and 1805, Martin represented Rockingham County in the State Senate, where he served briefly as Speaker during the latter year. Martin died at "Danbury," his estate in Rockingham County, on November 10, 1807.

Bibliography: R. M. Douglas, "Alexander Martin," in S. A. Ashe, *Biographical History of North Carolina*, vol. III (Greensboro, N.C., 1906); Francis Nash, *Presentation of Portrait of Governor Alexander Martin to the State of North Carolina* . . . (n.p., 1908); E. W. Yates, "The Public Career of

Alexander Martin,'' unpub. M.A. thesis, University of North Carolina at Chapel Hill, 1943; Richard Walser, ''Alexander Martin, Poet,'' *Early American Literature*, VI (Spring 1971), 55-61; J. A. Leo Lamay, ''A Note on the Canon of Alexander Martin,'' *Early American Literature*, VII (Spring 1972), 92. *DAB*.

JOHNSTON, Samuel, 1787-1789

Born on December 15, 1733 in Dundee, Scotland, the son of Samuel and Helen (Scrymoure) Johnston, and the nephew of Gabriel Johnston (who served as governor of North Carolina from 1734 to 1752). Brother of John, Jane, Penelope, Isabelle, Ann and Hannah. Married to Frances Cathcart; father of Penelope, Gabriel, Fanny, Helen and James Cathcart. Attended school in New Haven, Connecticut, and studied law in Edenton, North Carolina, where he had settled in 1754. Lived after 1765 at ''Hayes,'' his home on Albemarle Sound.

Elected to the North Carolina Lower House of Assembly in 1754, representing Chowan from 1754 to 1760 and again from 1766 to 1775; represented Edenton in the Lower House from 1761 to 1765. While a member of the Assembly, served as Clerk of the Court of Edenton District, and as Deputy Naval Officer of the Port of Edenton; also named to the Assembly's first Committee of Correspondence, created in December 1773. Served as a delegate to North Carolina's first four provincial congresses from 1774 to 1776, and acted as President of the third and fourth congresses. Elected Colonial Treasurer, District Paymaster of Troops, and an at-large member of the Provincial Council of Safety, all in 1775. Chosen to codify the state's laws by the Fifth Provincial Congress, which met in November 1776. Member of the North Carolina Senate in 1779, 1783 and 1784. Elected to the Continental Congress in 1780, and retired from that body in 1782, after having declined an offer the previous year to become president of Congress. Served in 1785 on a commission assigned the task of resolving a boundary dispute between Massachusetts and New York. Chosen Governor of North Carolina in 1787, and twice re-elected.

Johnston's period as chief executive was dominated by the question of whether North Carolina should ratify the proposed Constitution of the United States. Although he served as President of a state convention called in July 1788 to consider the issue, the pro-ratification position adopted by Johnston was not enough to sway the state's anti-federalists. It was not until November of 1789, when the governor presided at a similar convention, that North Carolina gave its assent to the document.

Johnston resigned as governor shortly after the beginning of his third term, in order to become United States Senator from North Carolina; he filed that office until 1793. He was also the University of North Carolina's first Trustee, serving for twelve years, and a North Carolina Superior Court Judge from 1800 to 1803. Johnston died near Edenton, North Carolina on August 18, 1816, and was buried in the family burial ground.

Bibliography: T. Murray Allen, "Samuel Johnston in Revolutionary Times," Trinity College Historical Society, *Papers*, ser. V (1905), 39-49; R. D. W. Connor, "Governor Samuel Johnston of North Carolina," *North Carolina Booklet*, XI (April 1912), 259-85. *DAB, DNB*.

PENNSYLVANIA

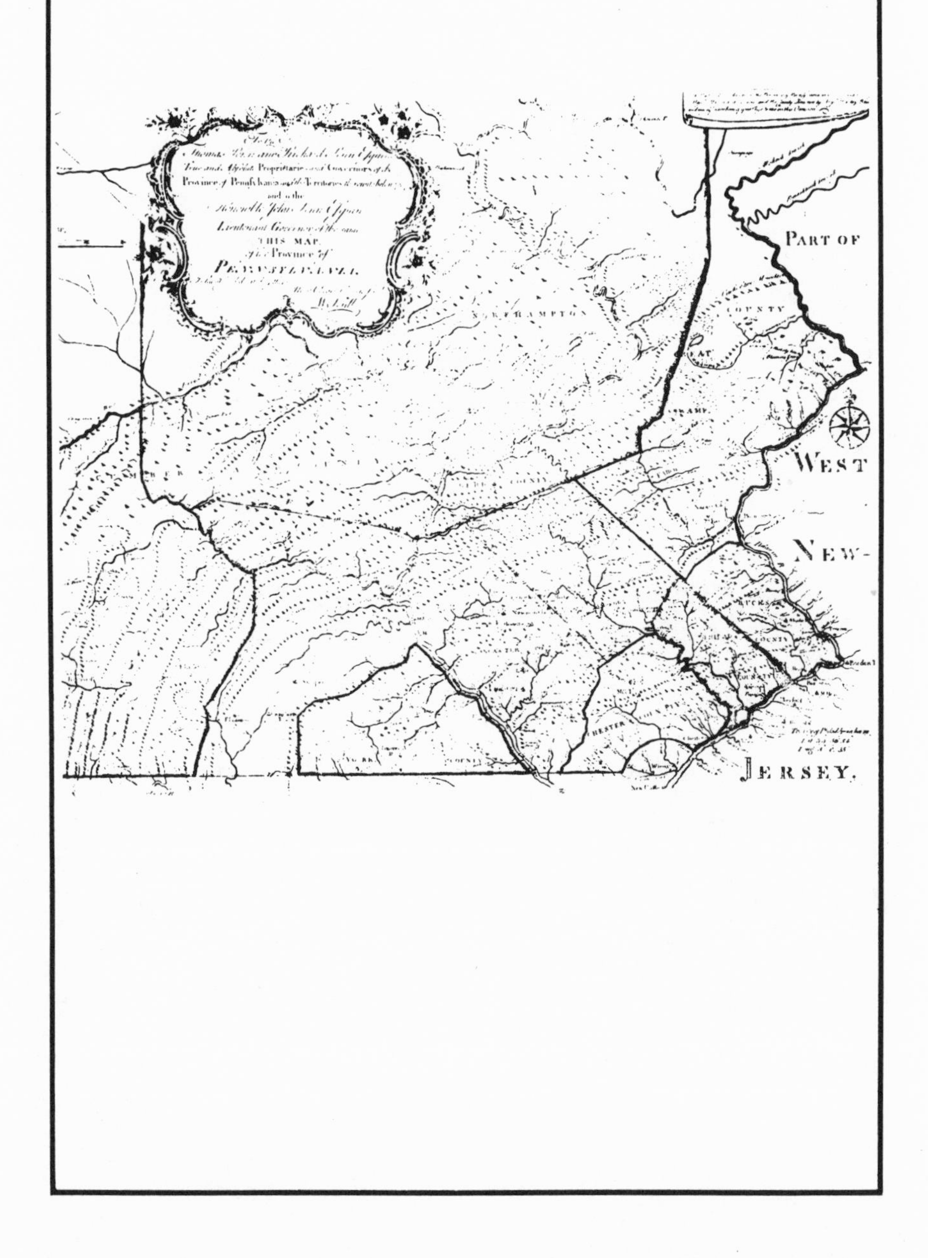

Chronology

Before William Penn received a charter for Pennsylvania from King Charles II in 1681, the Delaware region was administered by officials representing New Sweden (until 1655) and New Netherland (until 1664). Following the English conquest of New Netherland in 1664, various emissaries of the English governor at New York exercised jurisdiction over the area, except for a brief period from 1673 to 1674, when the Dutch reoccupied New York.

Pennsylvania's chief executives also held jurisdiction over the Lower Counties (Delaware) until 1775.

1681-1682	William Markham
1682-1684	William Penn
1684-1688	Thomas Lloyd
1688-1690	John Blackwell
1690-1693	Thomas Lloyd
1693-1695	Benjamin Fletcher
1695-1699	William Markham
1699-1701	William Penn
1701-1703	Andrew Hamilton
1703-1704	Edward Shippen
1704-1709	John Evans
1709-1717	Charles Gookin
1717-1726	Sir William Keith
1726-1736	Patrick Gordon
1736-1738	James Logan
1738-1747	George Thomas
1747-1748	Anthony Palmer
1748-1754	James Hamilton
1754-1756	Robert Hunter Morris
1756-1759	William Denny
1759-1763	James Hamilton
1763-1771	John Penn
1771	James Hamilton
1771-1773	Richard Penn
1773	James Hamilton
1773-1776	John Penn
1776	David Rittenhouse
1776	Samuel Morris, Sr.

1776-1778	Thomas Wharton
1778	George Bryan
1778-1781	Joseph Reed
1781-1782	William Moore
1782-1785	John Dickinson
1785-1788	Benjamin Franklin
1788-1799	Thomas Mifflin

BIBLIOGRAPHY

Armor, W. C., *Lives of the Governors of Pennsylvania* (Philadelphia, 1872).

Bridenbaugh, Carl and Jessica, *Rebels and Gentlemen: Philadelphia in the Age of Franklin* (New York, 1942).

Burt, Struthers, *Philadelphia: Holy Experiment* (Garden City, N.Y., 1945).

Gough, Robert, "Notes on the Pennsylvania Revolutionaries of 1776," *Pennsylvania Magazine of History and Biography*, XCVI (January 1972), 89-103.

Green, Le Roy, *Shelter for His Excellency: The Story of Pennsylvania's Executive Mansion and the One Hundred Governors of the Commonwealth* (Harrisburg, 1951).

Illick, Joseph E., *Colonial Pennsylvania: A History* (New York, 1976).

Keith, Charles P., *Chronicles of Pennsylvania from the English Revolution to the Peace of Aix-la-Chapelle, 1688-1748*, 2 vols. (Philadelphia, 1917).

———. *The Provincial Councillors of Pennsylvania Who Held Office between 1733 and 1776* . . . (Philadelphia, 1883).

Klein, Philip S., and Ari Hoogenboom, *A History of Pennsylvania* (New York, 1973).

Myers, Albert Cook, ed., *Narratives of Early Pennsylvania, West New Jersey and Delaware, 1630-1707* (New York, 1912).

Nash, Gary B., *Quakers and Politics: Pennsylvania, 1681-1726* (Princeton, 1968).

Read, George Edward, ed., *Papers of the Governors, 1681-1785*, in *Pennsylvania Archives*, 4th ser., vols. I-III (Harrisburg, 1900).

Sharpless, Isaac, *Political Leaders of Provincial Pennsylvania* (New York, 1919).

PENNSYLVANIA

MARKHAM, William, 1681-1682, 1695-1699
also Deputy Governor of the Lower Counties (Delaware), March 1691 to April 1693

Born *circa* 1635 in England, probably the son of William Markham of Nottinghamshire, England and his wife, a sister of Admiral Sir William Penn. Member of the Church of England. Married at least twice, the last time to a woman named Johannah; father of Ann.

Believed to have been an English army officer before his immigration to America. Commissioned Deputy Governor of Pennsylvania in April 1681, and assumed office several months later; served until October of 1682, when William Penn arrived to take over personal supervision of the government. Remained a member of the Provincial Council after Penn's arrival, but soon travelled to England on proprietary business. Served as Provincial Secretary from May 1685 to March 1691; Clerk of the Philadelphia County Court from the 1680's until 1690; and Deputy Governor of the Lower Counties from March 1691 to April 1693. Also appointed to the colony's Board of Propriety in 1687. Acted as Deputy Governor of both Pennsylvania and the Lower Counties from April 1693 to December 1699.

A kinsman of William Penn, Markham was the proprietor's choice as the first deputy governor, and was instructed to oversee the establishment of a provincial government in 1681 and 1682. For the next two decades Markham remained a steady defender of proprietary interests, although from April 1693 to March 1695 he technically served as the deputy of New York's Governor Benjamin Fletcher, who was given authority over Pennsylvania when that province temporarily came under Crown control. After Penn resumed his role as proprietor, Markham continued as deputy governor, and soon became involved in a dispute with the Pennsylvania Assembly over a proposal for constitutional reform. The issue was finally settled by compromise, as Markham reluctantly approved the ''Frame of 1696'' in return for the Assembly's passage of a military appropriations bill. The same year Markham and the Assembly joined forces in an effort to undermine the unpopular Navigation Acts, a tactic which incurred the hostility of Edward Randolph, the Crown's

Surveyor General of Customs. Continued efforts on the part of Markham to obstruct enforcement of the acts caused the Privy Council to order his removal from office. Penn eventually complied in December of 1699, when he returned to America and took over the provincial government himself.

Following his service as chief executive, Markham was appointed Pennsylvania's Register General in 1703, but his right to hold that office was disputed. Before the issue was resolved, Markham died in Philadelphia in the spring of 1704.

Bibliography: Sir Clements Markham, *Markham Memorials*, 2 vols. (London, 1913); Frank W. Leach, "William Markham, Deputy Governor of Pennsylvania, 1681-1682," Pennsylvania Society of Colonial Governors, *Publications*, II (1923), 12-32; Gary B. Nash, "The First Decade in Pennsylvania: Letters of William Markham and Thomas Holme to William Penn," *Pennsylvania Magazine of History and Biography*, 90 (July-October 1966), 314-52, 491-516. *DAB*.

PENN, William, 1682-1684, 1699-1701

Born on October 14, 1644 in London, England, the son of Admiral Sir William Penn and Lady Margaret (Jasper) Vanderscure Penn. Brother of Richard (died young) and Margaret. Married on April 4, 1672 to Gulielma Maria Springett, by whom he was the father of Gulielma Maria (died in infancy), William and Margaret (twins who died in infancy), Springett, Letitia, William and Gulielma Maria (died young); following the death of his first wife in February 1694, remarried on March 5, 1696 to Hannah Callowhill, by whom he had John, Thomas, Hannah Margareta (died young), Richard, Dennis (died young), Hannah (died in infancy) and Margaret.

Studied at Christ Church College, Oxford, but expelled from that institution in February 1662; sent to France by his father in July 1662, and spent time at a Huguenot academy in Saumur; also attended Lincoln's Inn for a short period, where he acquired some legal training. Became an adherent of the Society of Friends in 1667, a conversion which led to his imprisonment on several occasions. Wrote extensively on religious and political matters, including *No Cross, No Crown* (1669), one of his most famous works. Travelled on the Continent as a witness to Quaker beliefs during the 1670's. Became a Trustee of West Jersey in February 1675; joined with the proprietors who gained title to East Jersey, although this contract was later called into question. Received a proprietary charter to an extensive tract of land in America in March 1681, as compensation from the King for a debt owed to Penn's father; also acquired the territory of Delaware from the Duke of York. Arrived in his colony, which had been named Pennsylvania in honor of Admiral Penn, in October 1682, and acted as its resident Governor until August 1684; also served personally as chief executive between December 1699 and November 1701.

Penn's efforts to establish a foothold in America were based on the "Frame of Government" which he promulgated in the spring of 1682, and when he arrived in Pennsylvania later that year he immediately set out to further his political and religious ideas. Besides supervising the planning of Philadelphia, the energetic governor travelled widely in both the Pennsylvania interior and in neighboring colonies, where he dealt with such matters as a boundary dispute with Lord Baltimore. Although he sailed for England in August 1684, chiefly to defend his territory against possible *quo warranto* proceedings, Penn was eventually confronted by an even more serious threat. After the Glorious Revolution had swept James II from the British throne, Penn's long friendship with the now-exiled king suggested to some government officials that he might be guilty of treason, and for over two years his proprietary rights in Pennsylvania were declared forfeit. By August of 1694, however, Penn had managed to gain restoration of his charter, and late in 1699 he returned to America. While there he took steps to suppress piracy, encourage cordial relations with neighboring Indians, and implement a new "Frame of Government," which changed the administration of the colony in several important ways. One of the more significant political adjustments involved the creation of separate legislatures for Pennsylvania and Delaware, with each popularly-elected Assembly being given the right to propose, amend and repeal laws, subject to review by an appointed Council.

Following his second tenure at the head of Pennsylvania's government, Penn returned to England. During his final years he was plagued by financial difficulties and the need to adjudicate the frequent disputes between his lieutenant governors and the Pennsylvania Assembly. Penn died on July 30, 1718.

Bibliography: Edward Armstrong, ed., *The Correspondence of William Penn and James Logan . . .*, 2 vols. (Philadelphia, 1879-80); William J. Buck, *William Penn in America* (Philadelphia, 1888); Arthur Pound, *The Penns of Pennsylvania and England* (New York, 1932); William I. Hull, *William Penn: A Topical Biography* (New York, 1937); Catherine O. Peare, *William Penn: A Biography* (Philadelphia, 1957); Joseph E. Illick, *William Penn the Politician: His Relations with the English Government* (Ithaca, 1965); Mary Maples Dunn, *William Penn: Politics and Conscience* (Princeton, 1967); Caroline Robbins, "The Papers of William Penn," *Pennsylvania Magazine of History and Biography*, 93 (January 1969), 3-12; Harry Emerson Wildes, *William Penn* (New York and London, 1974). *DAB, DNB*.

LLOYD, Thomas, 1684-1688, 1690-1693

Born on April 17, 1640 in Dolobran, Montgomeryshire, Wales, the son of Charles and Elizabeth (Stanley) Lloyd. Brother of Charles and perhaps others. Married on November 9, 1665 to Mary Jones; after the death of his first wife, remarried to Patience (Gardiner) Story, possibly in 1684; father of Hannah, Rachel, Mordecai, John, Mary, Thomas, Elizabeth, Margaret, Deborah and Samuel (died young), all by his first wife. Educated at Jesus College, Oxford, where he graduated in January 1662; later studied medicine.

Joined the Society of Friends in Wales and, despite some harassment and internment from 1665 to 1672, was permitted to follow his profession. Immigrated to America in 1683, arriving in Philadelphia in August of that year. Appointed Master of the Rolls in December 1683; named to William Penn's Board of Propriety in 1684, a body having complete supervision over land policy. Also made Keeper of the Seal by Penn in August 1684. Elected to the Provincial Council early in 1684; served as President of the Council, and in that capacity became chief executive of the province between the departure of Penn in August of 1684 and the Council's replacement by a five-man executive commission in February 1688. Member of the commission which governed the province from February to December 1688. Resumed service as chief executive from January 1690 to March 1691, when Pennsylvania and the three lower counties on the Delaware River were temporarily divided; continued as Deputy Governor of Pennsylvania alone until April of 1693.

Between the years 1684 and 1693, Lloyd was a pivotal figure in Pennsylvania politics, and his activities had an important impact on the development of the province. As the representative of an economic elite of prominent merchants, Lloyd soon became disillusioned with the ineffectual proprietary policies of William Penn, and by 1686 he and his followers had begun to assume greater control in such areas as the province's land policy and court system. Lloyd's tenure was also marked by the outbreak of the Keithian controversy. When George Keith arrived in Pennsylvania in 1685 and started to expound a more doctrinal form of Quakerism, he quickly attracted colonists who had been alienated by the overbearing behavior of Lloyd and his wealthy followers. Although Keith himself left the province late in 1693, the religious and political disputes which he had provoked continued to disrupt Pennsylvania for some time.

After Lloyd's replacement by Deputy Governor William Markham in April 1693, members of his Quaker faction, who had been ousted from positions of responsibility, began to engage in obstructionism. Lloyd himself died in Philadelphia about a year later, in 1694.

Bibliography: Charles Perrin Smith, comp., *Lineage of the Lloyd and Carpenter Family* (Camden, N.J., 1870); Mrs. R. H. Lloyd, *The Pedigree of the Lloyds of Dolobran* (priv. print., 1877); Thomas Allen Glenn, *Genealogical Notes Relating to the Families of Lloyd, Pemberton, Hutchinson, Hudson, and Parke . . .* (Philadelphia, 1898); George Q. Horwitz, "Thomas Lloyd, Deputy Governor of Pennsylvania, 1684-1688, 1690-1693," Pennsylvania Society of Colonial Governors, *Publications*, I (1916), 132-38. *DAB*.

BLACKWELL, John, 1688-1690

Born on March 8, 1624 in England, the eldest son of John Blackwell, Sr., a London merchant, and Juliana (Gillian) Blackwell. A Puritan. Brother of nine. Married on June 9, 1647 to Elizabeth Smithsby; after the death of his first wife in March 1669, remarried, probably in 1672, to Frances Lambert; father of seven children by his first marriage, including Sir Lambert Blackwell, and ten children by his second.

Served as an Ensign in the "Maiden Troop" of horse during the early stage of the English Civil Wars; later took part in several important military encounters, including the Battle of Naseby in June 1645, and rose to the rank of Captain. Became a Treasurer of War and a Receiver General for Assessments in the early 1650's under Cromwell; also appointed Justice of the Peace for Middlesex in 1653. Elected as a member of Parliament for Surrey, and played an active role in the Parliament which met from 1656 to 1658. Penalized after the restoration of Charles II, and forbidden to hold any future official positions in England or Wales. Sailed for Boston in December 1684, becoming a Justice of the Peace in Massachusetts in 1686. Commissioned Deputy Governor of Pennsylvania in July 1688 by William Penn, and assumed office in December of that year.

Blackwell's authority as deputy governor was undercut from the beginning by a political faction led by Thomas Lloyd, the president of Pennsylvania's Council. This antagonism was probably heightened by the fact that Blackwell, a prominent Puritan, was thought by many to be an unsuitable and unsympathetic choice to govern the Quaker-dominated colony. Six months into his administration Blackwell complained privately of the "witless zealots" in the legislature who were making his job impossible, and in January 1690 he delivered a speech in which he bid farewell to the Council. Blackwell then left for Boston and later departed America for England, where he died in 1701.

Bibliography: Joseph Dorfman, "Captain John Blackwell: A Bibliographical Note," *Pennsylvania Magazine of History and Biography*, 69 (July 1945), 233-37; Nicholas B. Wainwright, "Governor John Blackwell," *Pennsylvania Magazine of History and Biography*, 74 (October 1950), 457-72; W. F. L. Nuttall, "Governor John Blackwell: His Life in England and Ireland," *Pennsylvania Magazine of History and Biography*, 88 (April 1964), 121-41.

FLETCHER, Benjamin, 1693-1695
New York, 1692-1698

Born, perhaps in 1640, in England, the son of William and Abigail (Vincent) Fletcher. An Anglican. Married to Elizabeth Hodson, and the father of two daughters and a son, Benjamin.

Served in the Irish Army under the Duke of Ormonde from 1683 to 1685, eventually rising to the rank of Captain. Later became an officer in Princess Anne of Denmark's regiment of foot soldiers, which was stationed in England; fought in Ireland under William III and attracted the notice of several distinguished patrons, who recommended him for the New York governorship. Commissioned Captain General and Governor-in-Chief of New York in March 1692, and landed in the colony to take up the office in August of that year; also commissioned Royal Governor of Pennsylvania in October 1692 (for a two-year period), and began his administration in that province in April of 1693. Named Commander of the militia in the Jerseys, Connecticut and Rhode Island at various times after his first gubernatorial appointment.

Fletcher came to America with a wide-ranging commission, and he quickly sought a means of reducing his responsibilities to manageable proportions. In Pennsylvania he chose to relinquish most of the daily executive duties to William Markham, his lieutenant governor, a policy which enabled him to devote more attention to New York matters. In New York, Fletcher was faced with the bitter division between supporters and opponents of the political cause of Jacob Leisler, the executed rebel governor of New York. During the factionalism which disrupted that colony's politics in the 1690's, Fletcher sided with the anti-Leislerians, but in return for his support he demanded bribes in a variety of forms. This avaricious behavior only exacerbated the spirit of factionalism in New York, as the governor's opponents grew increasingly indignant over his practice of "squeezing money both out of the publick and private purses."

Fletcher was recalled to England following the arrival in April 1698 of his replacement, the Earl of Bellomont, and returned to England to answer charges of delinquent behavior while in office, charges which included the allegation that his administration had condoned piracy. Although he was censured and threatened with prosecution, Fletcher appears to have avoided imprisonment. Nevertheless, he fell into considerable financial distress, and in 1702 he petitioned the authorities for military pay which he needed to avoid ruin. Fletcher died in Ireland in 1703.

Bibliography: Alice Davis, "The Administration of Benjamin Fletcher in New York," New York Historical Association, *Journal*, II (October 1921), 213-50; James S. Leamon, "War, Finance, and Faction in Colonial New York:

The Administration of Governor Benjamin Fletcher, 1692-1698,'' unpub. Ph.D. diss., Brown University, 1961; James S. Leamon, ''Governor Fletcher's Recall,'' *William and Mary Quarterly*, 3rd ser., vol. XX (October 1963), 527-42. *DAB*.

HAMILTON, Andrew, 1701-1703 *(as Lieutenant Governor of Pennsylvania and the Lower Counties), 1687-1688, 1689-1698, 1699-1703 (as Deputy Governor of East Jersey), 1692-1698, 1699-1703 (as Deputy Governor of West Jersey)*

Date and place of birth, and names of parents unknown. An Anglican. Married three times, his second wife being Anne (Rudyard) Wharton, the daughter of Deputy Governor Thomas Rudyard of East Jersey, and his third spouse a woman named Agnes; father of John (by his first wife) and perhaps others. Became an Edinburgh merchant as a young man.

Acquired a one-twentieth share in East Jersey from Sir John Gordon of Durno in 1683. Appointed in March 1686 by the East Jersey Proprietors to conduct an inquiry into the colony's administration, especially in the areas of quitrent collection and land sales. As a member of the East Jersey Council, chosen early in 1687 to succeed on an interim basis the departing deputy governor, Lord Neil Campbell, and in August 1687 assumed that office in his own right. Served also as Deputy Governor of West Jersey between 1692-98 and 1699-1703, and as Lieutenant Governor of Pennsylvania and the Lower Counties from November 1701 until 1703.

With the exception of two brief interludes—the Andros regime of 1688-89 and the Basse-Bowne administration of 1698-99—Hamilton was East Jersey's deputy governor throughout the remainder of the proprietary period. His early years in East Jersey were disrupted by economic problems and the seizure of the government by Sir Edmund Andros, a combination of circumstances which apparently persuaded Hamilton to leave the colony. He sailed for England in June 1690 and remained there until 1692, leaving East Jersey with no regular government for over two years. When he returned in September of 1692, however, his authority had been enhanced by the decision of both East and West Jersey's Proprietors to appoint him chief executive, and for the next decade he fought a skillful but ultimately unsuccessful battle to enforce proprietary rule. Hamilton's inability to govern effectively in the Jerseys was due more to the confused circumstances in which he found himself, rather than to any major deficiency on his part. The chronic disputes over land titles and quitrent collections remained unresolved, and when the Proprietors of East and West Jersey finally surrendered their political authority to the Crown in April

1702, the decision was a predictable response to the growing anti-proprietary movement which had complicated the last two years of Hamilton's administration. Hamilton's service in Pennsylvania and the Lower Counties from November 1701 until his death was likewise troubled by political unrest, as Anglican legislators and court officials periodically attempted to obstruct governmental functions in order to dramatize what they perceived to be a need for royal control in Pennsylvania. During his tenure as governor, Hamilton maintained an interest in the postal system of the American colonies, and he acted as Deputy Postmaster General for a number of years before his death in Perth Amboy, New Jersey on April 26, 1703. *DAB*.

SHIPPEN, Edward, 1703-1704

Born on March 5, 1639 in Methley, Yorkshire, England, the son of William and Mary (Nunes) Shippen. Married in 1671 to Elizabeth Lybrand, by whom he was the father of Edward, Joseph, Anne and five other children who died young; following his first wife's death in October 1688, remarried on September 4, 1689 to Rebecca (Howard) Richardson, by whom he had Elizabeth, who died young; married a third time, after the death of his second wife in 1705, to Esther (Wilcox) James on or about August 1, 1706; father of John (died young) and William by his third wife. Immigrated to New England in 1688, where he soon acquired considerable real estate and became a prosperous Boston merchant. Moved to Philadelphia about 1694 and continued his mercantile career.

Elected to Pennsylvania's Provincial Assembly in 1695, and served as that body's Speaker; also a member of the Assembly in 1700-01 and 1705-06. Filled various judicial offices, including Justice of the Peace from 1698 to 1701, and Associate Justice of the Pennsylvania Supreme Court from 1699 to 1703. Served as Philadelphia's first Mayor from 1701 to October of 1703; appointed a Commissioner of Propriety by William Penn in 1701, and served in that capacity until 1712. Elected to the Pennsylvania Provincial Council from 1696 until 1701, and continued to sit on the Council from 1701, when the position was made appointive, until 1712. As President of the Council from 1702 to 1712, served as Acting Governor between April 1703 and February 1704, during the interval between the death of Lieutenant Governor Andrew Hamilton and the arrival of Lieutenant Governor John Evans.

Shippen's tenure as acting governor was too brief to have any significant impact on Pennsylvania's politics. Nevertheless, several developments did take place which hinted at future problems. Despite a brief revival of the West Indian grain trade in the autumn of 1703, that trade had resumed its decline by February 1704, bringing with it serious financial losses for many of Philadelphia's most prominent businessmen. At the same time, England's ongoing war against France increased the danger of French privateering, which in turn discouraged both seagoing trade and immigration into the province.

After Evans' arrival in Pennsylvania, Shippen returned to his post as President of the Council; from 1705 to 1712 he also served as Philadelphia's City Treasurer. He died in Philadelphia on October 2, 1712.

Bibliography: T. W. Balch, *The English Ancestors of the Shippen Family and Edward Shippen of Philadelphia* (Philadelphia, 1904); George Schuyler Bangert, "The New Jersey Shippens," New Jersey Historical Society, *Proceedings*, n.s., vol. I (January 1916), 30-47; Robert H. Davis, "Edward Shippen, Deputy Governor of Pennsylvania, 1703-1704," Pennsylvania Society of Colonial Governors, *Publications*, I (1916), 98-102; Randolph S. Klein, "The Shippen Family: A Generational Study in Colonial and Revolutionary Pennsylvania," unpub. Ph.D. diss., Rutgers University, 1972; Kenneth R. Kimsey, "The Edward Shippen Family: A Search for Stability in Revolutionary Pennsylvania," unpub. Ph.D. diss., University of Arizona, 1973. *DAB*.

EVANS, John, 1704-1709

Born *circa* 1678 in Wales, the son of Thomas Evans, who was a friend of William Penn. An Anglican. Married in 1709 to Rebecca Moore. Named Lieutenant Governor of Pennsylvania and the Lower Counties in 1703, and assumed that office in February of 1704.

Evans was an unfortunate choice as lieutenant governor, since his youth, love of pleasure, and lack of experience made him ill-suited to govern a colony which was in any case notorious for its turbulent politics. Other factors, including an economic slump and the danger of French invasion, made Evans' position even more difficult. Taking advantage of these problems, David Lloyd, the speaker of the Assembly, headed an anti-proprietary movement which had as its goal the transformation of Pennsylvania into a royal colony. Although James Logan and the Council at first sided with Evans in order to protect the proprietorship, even they were angered by Evans' rashness, especially his use of false rumors of an impending French attack in May 1706 to show Philadelphia's Quakers how "naked and defenseless" the city was against military action. In the end Lloyd and his anti-proprietary followers failed to achieve their objective of royal control, but throughout the remainder of Evans' tenure, the Assembly led by Lloyd fought with the lieutenant governor over such issues as military appropriations and the courts. The resulting political *impasse* finally persuaded William Penn to replace Evans, and early in 1709 Charles Gookin arrived in the colony as the new lieutenant governor.

After his removal Evans returned to Wales. He died sometime after July 19, 1743, the date given on his will.

Bibliography: Edward D. Neill, "Memoir of John Evans, Deputy Governor of Pennsylvania," *New England Historical and Genealogical Register*, XXVI (October 1872), 421-25; J. Montgomery Seaver, *Evans Family Records* (Philadelphia, [1929]). *DAB*.

GOOKIN, Charles, 1709-1717

Born *circa* 1662 in Ireland, the son of Thomas and Hester Gookin. An Anglican. Brother of Arnold, Dorothy, Ann, Katherine, Judith, Hester and Elizabeth. Married in 1698 to Mary Wallis, by whom he was the father of Charles.

Served for a time as Captain in Thomas Erle's Royal Regiment, and eventually reached the rank of Colonel. Commissioned Lieutenant Governor of Pennsylvania and the Lower Counties in September 1708, arriving in the province to assume that office early in 1709.

Gookin's military career had given him little opportunity to practice the art of political compromise, and his lack of tact soon antagonized Pennsylvania's Assembly. By 1714 Gookin's relationship with both branches of the legislature had so deteriorated that the powerful James Logan joined other members of the Council in petitioning for his removal. Gookin encountered similar resistance in the Lower Counties, where in 1715 he engaged in a bitter dispute with the Assembly. Although the Assembly members continued to meet in spite of the governor's description of them as an "unlawful Riot," they were so angered by his behavior that they drafted a petition to William Penn, the aged proprietor, asking that he dismiss his intemperate representative.

In November 1716 the Penn family, realizing that Gookin was incapable of administering the province effectively, commissioned Sir William Keith as his replacement, and in May of the following year Keith arrived in Philadelphia to take over the government. The date of Gookin's death is unknown, although he was apparently still living in 1723, when he was rumored to be a candidate for a second term as lieutenant governor.

Bibliography: J. Wingate Thornton, "The Gookin Family," *New England Historical and Genealogical Register*, I (October 1847), 345-52, vol. II (April 1848), 167-74; Richard N. Gookins, comp., *An Historical and Genealogical Sketch of the Gookin Family of England, Ireland, America* (Tacoma, Wash., 1952).

KEITH, Sir William, 1717-1726

Born in 1680, probably within the barony of Inverugie in Scotland, the son of Sir William and Lady Jean Keith, who was the daughter of Smith of Rapness. Married to Ann (Newbury [or Newberry]) Diggs; father of William, Alexander Henry, Jane, Robert, James and perhaps others who died in early childhood. Succeeded to his father's baronetcy about 1720.

As a young man became implicated in a plot to restore the Stuarts to power in Scotland and was subsequently imprisoned, but released in February 1704. Named Surveyor General of Customs for the Southern Colonies in 1714, serving in that capacity for less than two years. Returned to England in search of the lieutenant governorship of Pennsylvania and the Lower Counties; commissioned in November 1716, and sworn in as Lieutenant Governor in May of 1717.

During his first four or five years as lieutenant governor, Keith compiled an impressive record of achievement in Pennsylvania, as he instituted major reforms in the judicial system, including the creation of a Court of Chancery in 1720, and pursued a successful Indian policy. By 1721, however, the province had entered a period of serious economic decline, due in part to the bursting of the "South Sea Bubble," a disastrous investment scheme which bankrupted many in England. Keith responded by backing demands for the emission of large amounts of paper currency, a move which was opposed by wealthy Philadelphia political leaders like James Logan. Eventually, Keith emerged as the head of a coalition which included Philadelphia's lower class. Logan and his conservative supporters, who feared the levelling tendencies of the city's "poorer sort," began to exert pressure on Pennsylvania's proprietors to remove the lieutenant governor, achieving their purpose in the summer of 1726, when Keith was replaced by Patrick Gordon.

After his dismissal Keith was elected to the Pennsylvania Assembly in 1726 and 1727, although he failed in his attempt to unseat David Lloyd as Assembly Speaker. In 1728 Keith returned to England, where for a time he served as an adviser to the Board of Trade. He later fell heavily into debt, and in 1734 was incarcerated in Fleet Street Prison. Keith died in the "Old Bailey" on November 18, 1749, while still a prisoner. He was the author of a *Collection of Papers and Other Tracts Written Occasionally on Various Subjects*, a compilation of his essays on colonial matters published in 1740. Keith may also have had a hand in several propaganda tracts, such as *The Just and Plain Vindication of Sir William Keith*, which defended his actions as lieutenant governor.

Bibliography: "A Biographical Sketch of Sir William Keith," Historical Society of Pennsylvania, *Memoirs*, I (1826), 451-63; [Andrew Hamilton], "Narrative of Sir William Keith's Coming to the Government of Pennsylvania with His Conduct in It," Historical Society of Pennsylvania, *Memoirs*, II (1830), [23]-41; Charles P. Keith, "Sir William Keith," *Pennsylvania Maga-*

zine of History and Biography, XII (1888), 1-33; Charles P. Keith, "The Wife and Children of Sir William Keith," *Pennsylvania Magazine of History and Biography*, LVI (1932), 1-8; Richard S. Rodney, "Delaware Under Governor Keith, 1717-1726," *Delaware History*, III (March 1948), 1-25; Roy N. Lokken, "Sir William Keith's Theory of the British Empire," *The Historian*, XXV (August 1963), 403-18; Thomas Wendel, "The Life and Writings of Sir William Keith, Lieutenant Governor of Pennsylvania and the Three Lower Counties, 1717-1726," unpub. Ph.D. diss., University of Washington, 1964; Thomas Wendel, "The Keith-Lloyd Alliance: Factional and Coalition Politics in Colonial Pennsylvania," *Pennsylvania Magazine of History and Biography*, 92 (July 1968), 289-305. *DAB*.

GORDON, Patrick, 1726-1736

Born *circa* 1664 in Scotland, a descendant of Alexander Gordon, Laird of Strathaven. Married to Isabella Clarke, by whom he was the father of at least six children.

Pursued a career in the British Army, eventually rising to the rank of Major. Nominated by Hannah and Springett Penn to serve as Lieutenant Governor of Pennsylvania and the Lower Counties, a nomination which received the royal approbation in April of 1726; arrived in Philadelphia on June 22 of that year and assumed his new position.

Gordon's appointment as a replacement for the charismatic Sir William Keith was not a decision endorsed by everyone in Pennsylvania, and shortly after he took the oath of office the new chief executive was confronted by an opposition movement led by Keith himself. Despite Gordon's desire to avoid trouble, in view of his professed ignorance of "refined Politicks," he was on at least one occasion forced to proclaim the Riot Act, when a mob set fire to the pillory stand and some market stalls in Philadelphia. In 1728, however, Keith abruptly left Pennsylvania on a voyage to Great Britain, and his absence from the province eliminated one major source of discontent. Gordon's tenure was also marked by controversy between the lieutenant governor and the Pennsylvania Assembly over paper money. Under strong pressure from the legislature, Gordon agreed in 1729 to approve the emission of £30,000 at five percent interest, a sum which was supplemented two years later.

Toward the end of his administration, Gordon's failing health frequently prevented him from attending sessions of the Council and Assembly. He died in office on August 5, 1736, and was succeeded by Senior Councillor James Logan.

Bibliography: J. Montgomery Seaver, *Gordon Family Records* (Philadelphia, 1929).

LOGAN, James, 1736-1738

Born on October 20, 1674 in Lurgan, County Armagh, Ireland, the son of Patrick, a Scottish Quaker schoolmaster, and Isabel (Hume) Logan. Brother of eight, though only William lived past childhood. Married on December 9, 1714 to Sarah Read; father of James, Sarah, Hannah and William. Received early education from his father, and apprenticed for a short time to a Quaker merchant named Edward Webb; later became a schoolmaster in Bristol and engaged in the linen trade.

Appointed Secretary to William Penn in 1699, and in September of that year embarked for Pennsylvania. Served as Secretary of the province and Clerk of the Provincial Council from 1701 to 1717. Also named by Penn in 1701 as Commissioner of Propriety and Receiver General. Appointed a temporary member of the Provincial Council in 1702, and in 1704 given a permanent seat on that body, a position which he held until 1747. Chosen as a member of the Philadelphia Board of Aldermen in 1717, Mayor of Philadelphia in 1722, a Justice of Philadelphia County in the 1720's, and a Judge of the Court of Common Pleas in 1727. Named Chief Justice of the Pennsylvania Supreme Court in 1731, filling that office until 1736. In his capacity as President of the Provincial Council, served as Acting Governor of Pennsylvania and the Lower Counties from August 1736 to June 1738.

Logan's tenure as acting chief executive was marked by some political skirmishing between the Assembly and Council, but the major crisis which he encountered involved a long-standing boundary dispute between Pennsylvania and Maryland. In the summer of 1736 border warfare broke out, as both colonies claimed authority over land and settlers in the Susquehanna region. The fighting and political bickering continued for a year, and peace was not restored until a royal order-in-council demanded that both parties end all "tumults, riots or other outrageous disorders" and stop issuing land grants in the area.

After the arrival in Pennsylvania of Lieutenant Governor George Thomas in June of 1738, Logan returned to his seat on the Council until his retirement in 1747. By 1749 his health had deteriorated greatly, and he died at "Stenton," his estate near Germantown, on October 31, 1751. Logan was a prominent member of the trans-Atlantic scholarly community, and frequently contributed papers on natural science and other subjects to the Royal Society in London.

Bibliography: Wilson Armistead, *Memoirs of James Logan* (London, 1851); Edward Armstrong, ed., *The Correspondence of William Penn and James Logan* . . ., 2 vols. (Philadelphia, 1879-80); Irma Jane Cooper, "The Life and Public Services of James Logan," unpub. Ph.D. diss., Columbia University, 1921; Joseph E. Johnson, "A Statesman of Colonial Pennsylvania: A Study of the Private Life and Public Career of James Logan to the

Year 1726," unpub. Ph.D. diss., Harvard University, 1942; Albright G. Zimmerman, "James Logan, Proprietary Agent," *Pennsylvania Magazine of History and Biography*, LXXVIII (April 1954), 143-76; Frederick B. Tolles, "Quaker Humanist: James Logan as a Classical Scholar," *Pennsylvania Magazine of History and Biography*, LXXIX (October 1955), 415-38; Frederick B. Tolles, "Philadelphia's First Scientist: James Logan," *Isis*, XLVII (1956), 20-30; Everett G. Alderfer, "James Logan: The Political Career of a Colonial Scholar," *Pennsylvania History*, XXIV (January 1957), 34-54; Frederick B. Tolles, *James Logan and the Culture of Provincial America* (Boston and Toronto, 1957); Roy N. Lokken, "Social Thought of James Logan," *William and Mary Quarterly*, 3rd ser., vol. XXVII (January 1970), 68-89. *DAB, DNB*.

THOMAS, George, 1738-1747

Born *circa* 1695 in Antigua, British West Indies, the son of Colonel George and Sarah (Winthrop) Thomas. Married on April 18, 1717 to Elizabeth King; father of two sons and three daughters. Received his early education in Antigua.

Served in the Antigua Assembly from 1716 to 1717 and again from 1721 to 1728, and acted as Speaker of the Assembly in 1727-28. Member of the Leeward Islands' Council from 1728 to 1738. Confirmed as Lieutenant Governor of Pennsylvania and the Lower Counties in February 1738, and arrived in Philadelphia in June of that year.

Thomas's tenure was marked by several serious disputes between the lieutenant governor and the powerful Pennsylvania Assembly. While he succeeded in settling a disagreement over the emission of paper money without too much difficulty, Thomas encountered more resistance when in 1740 he requested funds for use in England's war effort against Spain. Despite his assurance that the money would only be spent on the non-military necessities of Pennsylvania's troops, the Quaker majority in the Assembly claimed that their commitment to pacifism precluded even indirect military appropriations. In May 1741 the frustrated Thomas reported to Proprietor John Penn that the Assembly's power had left the colony's governor a "cypher or no more than nominal." An attempt at compromise in 1743 made the controversy less intense, but throughout the remainder of Thomas's term a large Quaker contingent in the Assembly remained reluctant to approve funds for military purposes. As Benjamin Franklin later recalled, the Quakers used "a variety of evasions to avoid complying, and modes of disguising the compliance when it became unavoidable."

Following his retirement in May of 1747, Thomas sailed for England, although he later returned to America to serve as Governor of the Leeward Islands from 1753 until 1766. He was made a Baronet in September of 1766, and spent his final years in retirement in England, where he owned the manors of "Yapton" and "Ratton" in Sussex. He died in London on December 31, 1774, and was buried in Willingdon, Sussex.

Bibliography: J. Montgomery Seaver, *Thomas Family Records* (Philadelphia, [1929]). *DAB*.

PALMER, Anthony, 1747-1748

Names of parents unknown, but probably born *circa* 1675 in England. Married in Barbados to Thomasine Baker; following his first wife's death in 1745, remarried in August 1748 to Catherine Carter; father of Anthony, William (died young), Francis, John, Thomasine, Ellen (died young), Jane and Elizabeth, all by his first wife.

As a young man travelled to Barbados, becoming a prominent merchant in Bridgetown; continued his mercantile career in Philadelphia after 1707. Named to Pennsylvania's Provincial Council in 1708, and served on the Council until his death. Chosen as a Justice of the Peace in 1718 and a Master in Chancery in 1720. As President of the Council, became Acting Governor of Pennsylvania and the Lower Counties after the resignation of Lieutenant Governor George Thomas in May 1747, and served in that capacity until November of 1748.

Palmer's elevation to the office of acting governor came at a time when the threat of incursions by Spanish and French privateers up the Delaware River posed a real danger to Pennsylvania, and Palmer skillfully won the support of a number of Quaker politicians, including Speaker of the Assembly John Kinsey, who supported military measures for the defense of the province. However, the Quakers in the Assembly still tried to avoid direct complicity in these actions by placing defense decisions in the hands of the executive rather than the legislature. Pennsylvania's Quakers also stopped short of endorsing the taking up of arms. Nevertheless, despite these qualifications, the decision of some Friends in 1748 to support the administration's defense policy indicated a growing split within the Quaker community, a split which would become more significant during the next decade. Palmer's tenure was also noteworthy for the efforts which Pennsylvania made to secure peace with its Indian neighbors, especially the Six Nations.

Following his period as acting governor, Palmer resumed his seat on the Council for a short time. He died in May of 1749. *DNB*.

HAMILTON, James, 1748-1754, 1759-1763, 1771, 1773

Born *circa* 1710, probably in Accomack County, Virginia, the son of Andrew, a prominent Philadelphia lawyer, and Anne (Brown) Preeson Hamilton. Brother of Andrew and Margaret. Never married. Educated in both Philadelphia and England. Inherited his father's large estate in 1741, including "Bush Hill," the family home.

Studied law, and in 1733 appointed Prothonotary of the Pennsylvania Supreme Court. Served in the Pennsylvania Assembly from 1734 to 1739. Elected Mayor of Philadelphia in 1745, and also served on the Provincial Council from 1745 to 1746. Visited England at the end of 1746; returned to America in November of 1748 as Lieutenant Governor of Pennsylvania and the Lower Counties, a position he held until his resignation in October 1754. Continued as a member of the Pennsylvania Council after October 1754, and in November 1759 was again named lieutenant governor, filling that office until October 1763. As President of the Council, served as Acting Governor from May to October of 1771 and from July to August of 1773.

Hamilton's career as Pennsylvania's chief executive spanned a twenty-five year period during which the province moved from a position of relative satisfaction with British rule to one of widespread discontent. When Hamilton first took office in 1748, Benjamin Franklin expressed the popular attitude toward the new lieutenant governor by applauding the appointment of a man who was "benevolent and upright." By the early 1750's, however, Hamilton had begun to encounter some serious opposition from the Pennsylvania Assembly, particularly over the question of paper currency. In February of 1752, for example, the Assembly approved the emission of £40,000 in new paper money, but Hamilton, acting on proprietary instructions, rejected the bill. Even after he gave currency legislation his endorsement a year and a half later, he insisted that the bill could not become law until it had received royal approval. Along with the chronic dispute over paper money, Hamilton's second term was disrupted by Indian attacks in 1753 against Pennsylvania's western settlements, and the Assembly's reluctance to provide funds and troops for defense of the frontier. During his two brief terms as acting governor in the early 1770's popular opinion in Pennsylvania bore little resemblance to Hamilton's conservative devotion to the Crown and the colony's proprietors.

Towards the end of his life, Hamilton gave less attention to public affairs, although he did express disappointment over the colonies' quest for independence. He died on August 14, 1783.

Bibliography: James Andrew Phelps, *The Hamilton Family in America* (New York, 1913). *DAB*.

MORRIS, Robert Hunter, 1754-1756

Born *circa* 1700 at "Morrisania" in New York, the second son of Lewis, a colonial governor of New Jersey, and Isabella (Graham) Morris. Brother of eleven, including Lewis, Sarah and Mary. Never married, but the father of at least three natural children, including Robert and Mary.

Served on the New Jersey Council in the 1730's, and named by his father as that province's Chief Justice shortly after the elder Morris's appointment as governor. Also appointed to the East Jersey Council of Proprietors in 1742. Left for England in 1749 to represent proprietary interests, settle unresolved matters connected with his late father's estate, and testify against a proposal to reunite politically New York and New Jersey. While in England awarded the post of Lieutenant Governor of Pennsylvania and the Lower Counties by John and Thomas Penn, and assumed that office in October of 1754.

Morris's relatively brief tenure was troubled by almost incessant quarreling between the lieutenant governor and the Pennsylvania Assembly. When he attempted to enforce his instructions by insisting, among other requirements, that any paper money emissions could be spent only at the discretion of the proprietors, Morris encountered serious resistance from the legislators. During the succeeding months other disputes developed, particularly over the raising of funds for defense of the province during the French and Indian War. Morris tried to amend a defense appropriations bill by exempting proprietary land holdings from taxation, using the argument that the authority granted by the proprietor's charter justified such a policy. The Assembly reacted violently, and Morris himself was subjected to severe personal criticism. Although compromise legislation was eventually passed as Indian massacres on the frontier became more threatening, the province remained in political turmoil until Morris finally resigned in August 1756.

Following his resignation Morris returned to New Jersey, where for a short time he again served as chief justice. He travelled to England in 1757 and, after a controversy involving another claimant to his court seat had been settled in Morris's favor, he retained his position on the bench until he died in Shrewsbury, New Jersey on January 27, 1764.

Bibliography: E. M. W. Lefferts, comp., *Descendants of Lewis Morris of Morrisania* (New York, 1907?); "Correspondence Relating to the Morris Family," New Jersey Historical Society, *Proceedings*, n.s., vol. VII (January 1922), 41-48; John B. Stoudt, ed., *Letters Addressed to the Honorable Robert Hunter Morris Upon His Appointment as Governor of the Province of Pennsylvania* . . . (Allentown, Pa., 1939); Beverly McAnear, ed., "R. H. Morris: An American in London, 1735-1736," *Pennsylvania Magazine of History and Biography*, LXIV (April-July 1940), 164-217, 356-406; Edmond Dale Daniel, "Robert Hunter Morris and the Rockey Hill Copper Mine," *New Jersey*

History, XCII (Spring 1974), 13-32; John R. Strassburger, "The Origins and Establishment of the Morris Family in the Society and Politics of New York and New Jersey, 1630-1746," unpub. Ph.D. diss., Princeton University, 1976. *DAB*.

DENNY, William, 1756-1759

Born on March 9, 1709 in Hertfordshire, England, the only surviving son of the Reverend Hill and Abigail (Berners) Denny. Married to Mary Hill; no children. Studied at Oriel College, Oxford, and received a B.A. in January 1730; probably continued his education during a "grand tour" of the Continent. One of the founders of the Society of Dilettanti in December 1735, a group dedicated to reviving interest in the arts of the ancients.

Entered the British Army early in the 1740's, and by 1746 had risen to the rank of Captain. Promoted to Lieutenant Colonel before his appointment as Lieutenant Governor of Pennsylvania and the Lower Counties in May 1756; arrived in Philadelphia to assume office in August of that year.

Denny's appearance was anxiously awaited by those who had grown weary of the political discord which had troubled the administration of his predecessor, but the hope for a more harmonious relationship between the lieutenant governor and the Pennsylvania Assembly was quickly shattered. Burdened by a rigid set of proprietary instructions and his own laziness, corruption and ineptitude, Denny soon quarreled with the Assembly over a money bill for defense and a quartering act. The latter issue became especially disruptive, with the lieutenant governor threatening to house troops in private homes if necessary. Over the next two years other disputes developed concerning such matters as a land tax bill and acts for the defense of the province during the French and Indian War. Finally, in November 1759, the incompetent Denny was replaced as chief executive by James Hamilton.

After residing a short time in Pennsylvania, Denny returned to England in the summer of 1760, where from 1761 to 1764 he resumed his interest in the arts and sat on various committees appointed by the Society of Dilettanti. Denny died in England late in 1765.

Bibliography: H. L. L. Denny, "Memoir of His Excellency Colonel William Denny, Lieutenant-Governor of Pennsylvania, etc.," *Pennsylvania Magazine of History and Biography*, XLIV (April 1920), 97-121; Nicholas B. Wainwright, "Governor William Denny in Pennsylvania," *Pennsylvania Magazine of History and Biography*, 81 (April 1957), 170-98; John J. Zimmerman, "Governor Denny and the Quartering Act of 1756," *Pennsylvania Magazine of History and Biography*, 91 (July 1967), 266-81.

PENN, John, 1763-1771, 1773-1776

Born on July 14, 1729 in London, England, the eldest son of Richard and Hannah (Lardner) Penn, and the grandson of William Penn. Member of the Church of England. Brother of Richard, Hannah and William (died young). As a young man, married Mary, the daughter of James Cox of London, but was forced to repudiate the marriage due to the displeasure of the Penn family. Married on May 31, 1766 to Ann Allen; no children. Studied at the University of Geneva from 1747 to 1751.

Resided in Pennsylvania from 1752 to 1755, and served on the Provincial Council. Returned to England, but in 1763 again sailed for America after being commissioned by his father and his uncle, Thomas Penn, as Lieutenant Governor of Pennsylvania and the Lower Counties, an office which he filled from October 1763 to spring 1771, and again from August 1773 to September 1776.

Although the first few months of Penn's administration were marked by a close cooperation between the lieutenant governor and the Provincial Assembly, the march of the "Paxton Boys" on Philadelphia in February 1764 precipitated a split which never completely healed. The "Paxton Boys" protest against inadequate protection of the western frontier from Indian assault became a subject of bitter discussion, with both Penn and the Assembly blaming each other for the problem. During the remainder of his first term, Penn and his supporters were so often attacked by a strong anti-proprietary party led by Benjamin Franklin that the differences between these two provincial factions sometimes overshadowed the larger conflict between the colonies and Great Britain. Soon after he replaced James Hamilton as chief executive in August 1773, Penn's position grew even more untenable. While his role as proprietary governor ended with the final meeting of the Provincial Assembly in September 1776, Penn's effective control had actually ceased several months earlier, when Pennsylvania's Council of Safety emerged as a governing power.

Following his departure from office Penn spent a short time as a prisoner on parole, but he remained moderate in his criticism of the revolutionary movement. In 1779 he was promised a substantial settlement as compensation for the loss of his proprietary interest, and was also permitted to retain many of his holdings in Pennsylvania. Except for some years which he spent abroad, Penn continued to reside in Pennsylvania until he died on February 9, 1795. He was buried in Christ Church, Philadelphia.

Bibliography: Howard M. Jenkins, *The Family of William Penn, Founder of Pennsylvania: Ancestry and Descendants* (Philadelphia and London, 1899); Arthur Pound, *The Penns of Pennsylvania and England* (New York, 1932). *DAB, DNB*.

PENN, Richard, 1771-1773

Born in 1735 in England, the son of Richard and Hannah (Lardner) Penn, and the grandson of William Penn. Brother of John, Hannah and William (died young). Married on May 21, 1772 to Mary Masters, by whom he was the father of William, Hannah, Richard and Rose. Studied for a tim St. John's College, Cambridge, but left without receiving a degree.

Immigrated to Pennsylvania with his older brother John in 1763; remained until 1769, when he returned to England. In 1771 appointed Lieutenant Governor of Pennsylvania and the Lower Counties by John Penn and his uncle, Thomas Penn, and arrived in the province in October of that year to assume office.

Richard Penn's brief tenure was an interlude of tranquility when compared with his brother's politically turbulent administration from 1763 to 1771 and again from 1773 to 1776. Between 1771 and 1773 some Philadelphia merchants complained of a shortage of currency and an economic slump which had left them with a surplus of imported goods, but there was also a welcome increase in the price of agricultural exports. Politically, many of the men who had been vocal opponents of Crown policy in the 1760's grew tired of controversy and, despite intermittent disputes between customs officials and merchants, the province no longer seemed especially receptive to the warnings of agitators like Charles Thomson of Philadelphia.

Although Richard Penn resided in Pennsylvania for a few years after stepping down as chief executive in the summer of 1773, in 1775 he sailed for England where, except for one brief visit to Philadelphia, he lived until his death. He was elected to Parliament as a representative of Appleby in 1784, Haslemere in 1790 and 1802, and Lancaster in 1796. Penn died in Richmond, Surrey, England on May 27, 1811.

Bibliography: Howard M. Jenkins, *The Family of William Penn, Founder of Pennsylvania: Ancestry and Descendants* (Philadelphia and London, 1899); Arthur Pound, *The Penns of Pennsylvania and England* (New York, 1932). *DAB, DNB*.

RITTENHOUSE, David, 1776

Born on April 8, 1732 at Paper Mill Run near Germantown, Pennsylvania, the son of Matthias and Elizabeth (Williams) Rittenhouse. Brother of ten, of whom seven, including Benjamin and Esther, lived to maturity. Married on February 20, 1766 to Eleanor Coulston, by whom he had Elizabeth and Esther; following his first wife's death in February 1771, remarried late in 1772 to Hannah Jacobs, by whom he was the father of one child who died in infancy.

Largely self-educated, displaying at a young age a precocious aptitude for mathematics and mechanics. Became a clockmaker in the early 1750's, a trade he practiced until the Revolution. Also constructed a variety of scientific instruments, including an "orrery," a device which he designed in 1767 to represent the motions of various bodies in the solar system. Elected to the American Philosophical Society in January 1768, in recognition of his achievements; chosen as President of that organization in January 1791. Continued his experiments, especially in the field of astronomy, until 1775, when the outbreak of war with Great Britain diverted some of his energy into the political arena. Appointed Engineer of the Pennsylvania Committee of Safety in October 1775; chosen to complete Benjamin Franklin's unexpired term in the Pennsylvania Assembly in March of the following year. Named to the convention which met in July 1776 to draft a constitution for Pennsylvania. Served intermittently between July 24 and August 6, 1776 as Chairman *pro tempore* of the newly-organized Council of Safety.

As temporary chairman of the Council, Rittenhouse headed a political body charged with exercising "the whole of the executive powers of government, so far as relates to the military defense and safety of the province." He appears to have taken a serious approach to this responsibility, attending the sessions regularly. In recognition of his services, Rittenhouse was chosen as the Council's Vice President on August 6, 1776, in the same election which elevated Thomas Wharton to the presidency of that body.

While he lost his seat in the Assembly late in 1776, Rittenhouse continued to take an active role in politics during the Revolution. In January 1777 he was named Pennsylvania's Treasurer, and that March he became a member of the commonwealth's Board of War. Rittenhouse also served on the new Council of Safety which was formed in 1777, after the government was driven from Philadelphia to Lancaster by British troops.

The postwar years brought with them a renewal of Rittenhouse's scientific investigations, although he never abandoned his political ambitions completely. In April 1792, for example, Washington appointed Rittenhouse Director of the United States Mint, a position he held until his resignation in June 1795. Rittenhouse died on June 26, 1796, two months after he had agreed to run as a presidential elector for Thomas Jefferson.

Bibliography: William Barton, *Memoirs of the Life of David Rittenhouse* (Philadelphia, 1813); Daniel K. Cassel, *A Genea-Biographical History of the Rittenhouse Family*, vol. I (Philadelphia, 1893); Maurice J. Babb, "David Rittenhouse," *Pennsylvania Magazine of History and Biography*, LVI (1932), 193-224; Calvin Kephart, "Rittenhouse Genealogy Debunked," *National Genealogical Society Quarterly*, XXVI (December 1938), 105-10; Edward Ford, *David Rittenhouse, Astronomer-Patriot, 1732-1796* (Philadelphia, 1946); Brooke Hindle, *David Rittenhouse* (Princeton, 1964). *DAB*.

MORRIS, Samuel, Sr., 1776

Born on November 21, 1711 in Philadelphia, Pennsylvania, the son of Anthony and Phoebe (Guest) Morris. Brother of Anthony, James, John, Samuel (died in infancy), Mary, Joseph, Elizabeth, Benjamin (died young), Phoebe (died young), Susanna (died young), Deborah, Benjamin and one other who died in infancy. Married on May 26, 1737 to Hannah Cadwalader, by whom he was the father of Anthony (died young), John, Cadwalader, Anthony (died young), Samuel, Anthony Cadwalader, Phoebe, Martha, Thomas and Benjamin.

Became a member of the Philadelphia bar in September 1751. Commissioned Sheriff of Philadelphia County in March 1752, and served in that capacity until October 1755; again acted as sheriff from 1758 to 1761. Named to the Philadelphia Common Council in October 1755. Acted as a member of the Pennsylvania Council of Safety from July 1776 to March 1777, and served as Chairman *pro tempore* of that body on July 27 and August 1, 1776.

One of Pennsylvania's most prosperous citizens, Morris was an especially significant recruit for the Patriot faction. During his two days as chairman of the Council, the supply of arms for troops in the field was the major issue under discussion. On August 1, for example, the Council requested that the commissary provide Colonel James Moore of Chester County with weapons for his battalion, including "50 Bayonets or Tomhawks" and "30 Hatchets."

Following the election of Thomas Wharton as president of the Council of Safety in August 1776, Morris continued to participate in the Council's deliberations intermittently until September 1777, acting briefly as its Vice President. He was also named to the Board of War in March 1777, the same month in which he became Register of Wills for the City and County of Philadelphia. Morris held the latter post until his death on March 31, 1782. Throughout his life he displayed an interest in education, an interest which was acknowledged when he was named a Trustee of the University of the State of Pennsylvania late in 1779.

Bibliography: Robert C. Moon, *The Morris Family of Philadelphia*, 5 vols. (Philadelphia, 1898-1909).

WHARTON, Thomas, 1776-1778

Born in 1735 in Chester County, Pennsylvania, the son of John, a saddler and coroner of Chester County, and Mary (Dobbins) Wharton. Brother of four. Married on November 4, 1762 to Susannah Lloyd, by whom he had five children; after his first wife's death, remarried on December 7, 1774 to

Elizabeth Fishbourne, who bore him three children. Apprenticed at the age of twenty to Reese Meredith, a Philadelphia merchant, and eventually entered business himself as a partner in the exporting firm of Stocker and Wharton.

Opposed the Stamp Act in 1765, and became a vocal opponent of British policy in the early 1770's. Served as a delegate to the provincial convention which met in July 1774, and was chosen by the Assembly as a member of the provincial Committee of Safety in the summer of 1775. Chosen President of the Pennsylvania Council of Safety in August 1776; after the adoption of a new constitution, inaugurated as President of the Supreme Executive Council in March 1777.

Wharton's tenure as president of the Council of Safety, and later of the Supreme Executive Council, was a critical era in Pennsylvania history, as the new commonwealth set about organizing the machinery of government following its formal separation from Great Britain. Wharton himself tried to pursue a moderate course which would protect Pennsylvania from the activities of disloyal citizens and at the same time avoid the levelling tendencies of the commonwealth's more radical Whigs. The president also played a role in the formulation of Pennsylvania's first constitution in 1776. Although he complained that the radical document contained "many faults" and needed much improvement, he warned that its complete repudiation would be dangerous while the commonwealth remained under the threat of British invasion. In September of 1777 Wharton's fears materialized, as the British Army took Philadelphia, forcing the Pennsylvania government and the Continental Congress to flee further west to Lancaster. About eight months later Wharton died in office on May 22, 1778.

Bibliography: Anne H. Wharton, *Genealogy of the Wharton Family of Philadelphia, 1664 to 1880* (Philadelphia, 1880); Anne H. Wharton, "Thomas Wharton, Junr., First Governor of Pennsylvania Under the Constitution of '76," *Pennsylvania Magazine of History and Biography*, V (1881), 426-39, vol. VI (1882), 91-105. *DAB*.

BRYAN, George, 1778

Born on August 11, 1731 in Dublin, Ireland, the son of Samuel, a merchant, and Sarah (Dennis) Bryan. A Presbyterian. Married on April 21, 1757 to Elizabeth Smith. Immigrated to America in 1752, and began an importing business in partnership with James Wallace; continued the business alone after the dissolution of the partnership in 1755.

Appointed to a commission in 1762 which supervised the use of tonnage dues to make improvements to Philadelphia's harbor; elected to the Provincial Assembly in 1764 as a supporter of proprietary rule. Also named in 1764 as a

Judge of the Orphans' Court and the Court of Common Pleas; again commissioned as a judge in 1770 and 1772. Chosen in September 1765 as a delegate from Pennsylvania to the Stamp Act Congress in New York. Played a major role in the drafting of Pennsylvania's first constitution in 1776, and appointed Naval Officer of the Port of Philadelphia that same year. In March 1777, began his term as Vice President of the commonwealth's Supreme Executive Council, an office which he held until October of 1779. In his capacity as vice president, served as Acting President of Pennsylvania between the death of Thomas Wharton in May 1778 and the inauguration of Joseph Reed in December of that year.

Bryan's brief period as acting president began on an auspicious note, when the British Army's decision to evacuate Philadelphia permitted the return of the commonwealth government and the Continental Congress. Although Bryan tried to discourage violence, some extreme Whigs demanded punishment of those Loyalists who had collaborated with the British during the occupation, and in November of 1778 two men convicted of treason were executed. In the Assembly elections that same month, Bryan and others who supported the Constitution of 1776 saw their legislative strength decline, as the Anti-Constitutionalist Party became a major political force by winning almost one-third of the seats in the Pennsylvania Assembly.

Following his service as acting governor, Bryan was himself elected to the Assembly in October 1779, and chaired several important committees, including the committee which produced an act, probably written by Bryan, authorizing the gradual abolition of slavery in the commonwealth. In April 1780 he became a Judge of the Pennsylvania Supreme Court, a position which he held until his death, and in 1784 he was elected to the commonwealth's Council of Censors. He was a bitter foe of the Federal Constitution, remaining opposed to the document even after its ratification by Pennsylvania in December 1787. Bryan died on January 27, 1791.

Bibliography: Burton Alva Konkle, *George Bryan and the Constitution of Pennsylvania, 1731-1791* (Philadelphia, 1922). *DAB*.

REED, Joseph, 1778-1781

Born on August 27, 1741 in Trenton, New Jersey, the eldest son of Andrew, a prominent merchant, and Theodosia (Bowes) Reed. A Presbyterian. Brother of five, three of whom survived childhood. Married on May 31, 1770 to Esther De Berdt; father of Martha, Joseph, Esther, Theodosia (died young), Dennis De Berdt and George Washington. Received early education at the Academy of Philadelphia, and in 1757 awarded a B.A. from the College of New Jersey (later Princeton University); studied law with Richard Stockton, and began to practice in May 1763; also studied at the Middle Temple in London for two years in the 1760's.

Named Deputy Secretary of New Jersey in 1767 and, after another visit to England, arrived in Philadelphia to practice law. Became a member of Philadelphia's Committee of Correspondence in May 1774, and its Committee of Observation and Inspection in November 1774; served as President of Pennsylvania's Second Provincial Congress in January 1775. Following the outbreak of the Revolution, named Lieutenant Colonel of the Pennsylvania Associated Militia and Military Secretary to George Washington, the Associated Militia's commander-in-chief. Also elected to the Continental Congress and the Pennsylvania Committee of Safety in 1775. Became Adjutant General of the Continental Army with the rank of Colonel in June 1776; served as an adviser for several important campaigns during the early years of the war, especially in New Jersey and Pennsylvania. Again elected to the Continental Congress in 1777, and in December 1778 became President of Pennsylvania's Supreme Executive Council, an office he filled until November of 1781.

During Reed's tenure as the head of Pennsylvania's government, the new commonwealth was troubled more by internal political dissension and economic chaos than it was by the threat of British invasion. Although the strength of his Constitutionalist Party enabled Reed to be reelected in 1779 and 1780, his administration was made less effective by disputes between Constitutionalists and Anti-Constitutionalists, who blamed each other for the inflation which by early 1781 had caused the virtual collapse of Pennsylvania's paper money and legal tender system. In January of that year Reed's financial woes were complicated by the mutiny of troops of the Pennsylvania Line over grievances which included their failure to receive back pay. While Reed's efforts did help to quell the mutiny, he could do little to resolve the commonwealth's economic dilemma before leaving office.

Reed returned to his law practice after his period as chief executive. He was elected to Congress in 1784, but was unable to serve because of poor health. Reed died on March 5, 1785.

Bibliography: Henry Reed, *Life of Joseph Reed*, in Jared Sparks, ed., *The Library of American Biography*, 2nd ser., vol. VIII (Boston, 1846); William B. Reed, *Life and Correspondence of Joseph Reed*, 2 vols. (Philadelphia, 1847); William B. Reed, ed., *Reprint of the Original Letters from Washington to Joseph Reed* (Philadelphia, 1852); William B. Reed, *Life of Esther Reed* (Philadelphia, 1853); Ellsworth Eliot, Jr., *The Patriotism of Joseph Reed* (New Haven, 1943); John F. Roche, "Was Joseph Reed Disloyal?," *William and Mary Quarterly*, 3rd ser., vol. VIII (July 1951), 406-17; John F. Roche, *Joseph Reed: A Moderate in the Revolution* (New York, 1957). *DAB*.

MOORE, William, 1781-1782

Born *circa* 1735 in Philadelphia, Pennsylvania, the son of Robert, a shopkeeper, and Elizabeth Moore. Married on December 13, 1757 to Sarah Lloyd; father of three children, including Elizabeth. Trained for a mercantile career.

Became a moderate opponent of British policy in the 1760's and early 1770's. Decided to endorse the Patriot cause by 1776, and lent his support to the Pennsylvania Constitution of that year. Appointed to the Pennsylvania Council of Safety in December 1776, and in March 1777, named to the Board of War by the commonwealth's Executive Council. Also elected to the Continental Congress in February 1777, but did not serve because of business commitments. Began his term as Vice President of the Supreme Executive Council in November 1779, and in November 1781, succeeded Joseph Reed as President of that body.

Moore's position as president included with it an appointment as Judge of the Pennsylvania High Court of Errors and Appeals, and he used both offices to promote his conciliatory point of view during the period of severe economic dislocation which accompanied the end of the war. Despite his approval of the radical Constitution of 1776, Moore remained at odds with the more extreme members of his party on such matters as paper money, where his approach was closer to the conservative policy of financiers such as Robert Morris. When Moore relinquished the president's office to John Dickinson in November 1782, that transition marked the end of radical control of the commonwealth's executive office, and the emergence of the moderate Anti-Constitutionalist Party as a major force in Pennsylvania politics.

After his tenure as president, Moore continued to take an active interest in programs aimed at solving Pennsylvania's financial problems. He became a member of the Assembly in 1784, and was also a Director of the Bank of Pennsylvania, a member of the St. Tammany Society, and from 1784 to 1789 a Trustee of the University of the State of Pennsylvania. Moore died on July 24, 1793.

Bibliography: Thomas Allen Glenn, *Genealogical Notes Relating to the Families of Lloyd, Pemberton, Hutchinson, Hudson, and Parke* . . . (Philadelphia, 1898). *DAB*.

DICKINSON, John, 1782-1785

Delaware, 1781-1782

Born on November 8, 1732 in Maryland, the second son of Samuel, a planter and lawyer, and Mary (Cadwalader) Dickinson. Brother of a number of siblings, including Philemon. Married on July 19, 1770 to Mary Norris.

Received early education at home, and in 1750 studied law in the office of John Moland, a Philadelphia attorney; continued his legal training at London's Middle Temple from 1753 to 1757, when he returned to Philadelphia to practice law.

Elected to the Assembly of the Lower Counties (Delaware) in October 1760, and became Speaker of that body. In the 1760's, argued in the Pennsylvania Assembly the case for proprietary rule; along with George Bryan, chosen in 1764 as a representative from Philadelphia in the Assembly, replacing Benjamin Franklin and Joseph Galloway; reelected in 1770. Named as a delegate from Pennsylvania to the Stamp Act Congress held in New York in October 1765. During the 1760's and early 1770's, emerged as a moderate spokesman for colonial grievances, and authored several influential works, including *The Late Regulations Respecting the British Colonies . . .Considered* (1765) and *Letters from a Farmer in Pennsylvania to the Inhabitants of the British Colonies* (1768). Became Chairman of the Philadelphia Committee of Correspondence in May 1774; represented Pennsylvania at the First Continental Congress, but withdrew in October 1774 after serving only a short time. Appointed Chairman of the Pennsylvania Committee of Safety and Defense in June 1775 and served for several days, until his replacement by Benjamin Franklin; also named Colonel of the first battalion of troops raised in Philadelphia. Continued to recommend moderation at the Second Continental Congress in 1775, and voted against the Declaration of Independence, although he took up arms in support of the Patriot cause after separation from Great Britain had become a fact. Chaired the committee that drafted the Articles of Confederation in 1776, but otherwise played a minor political role during the first year of independence, losing his seat as a congressional representative from Pennsylvania, resigning from the Pennsylvania Assembly, and declining to represent Delaware in Congress. Served as Brigadier General of the Pennsylvania militia in 1777. Accepted election as a congressman from Delaware in 1779, resigning in the autumn of that year. Elected President of the Supreme Executive Council of Delaware in 1781, and held that office until 1782; in November of 1782, became President of Pennsylvania's Supreme Executive Council.

Dickinson's election as Delaware's chief executive was the result of his middle of the road reputation, a quality favored by those conservatives who had re-established their political dominance of the state by 1781. When Dickinson was chosen as president of Pennsylvania in the autumn of 1782, he left the government of Delaware in the hands of John Cook, the speaker of the Council, and left for Philadelphia. For the next three years he grappled with Pennsylvania's persistent financial problems, but his task was made more complicated by internal political dissension. Although Dickinson's victory over General James Potter in 1782 had marked the emergence of the moderate Anti-Constitutionalist Party as an important political force in the commonwealth, the radical Constitutionalists remained in control of the Council, and were strong enough in 1783 and 1784 to block legislation in the Assembly. Consequently, Dickinson had little opportunity to further any program for political reform or economic recovery, and Pennsylvania remained in turmoil until Benjamin Franklin replaced him in October of 1785.

Following his service as president of Delaware and Pennsylvania, Dickinson become a delegate from Delaware to the Philadelphia Constitutional Convention of 1787, and used his skills as a writer to urge the adoption of the Federal Constitution. While he retained his interest in public affairs, he held no further political office until his death in Wilmington, Delaware on February 14, 1808.

Bibliography: Charles J. Stillé, *Life and Times of John Dickinson, 1732-1808* (Philadelphia, 1891) (published as vol. XIII of the Historical Society of Pennsylvania, *Memoirs*); Paul Leicester Ford, ed., *The Writings of John Dickinson* (Philadelphia, 1895); John H. Powell, "John Dickinson, Penman of the American Revolution," unpub. Ph.D. diss., University of Iowa, 1938; John H. Powell, "John Dickinson, President of the Delaware State, 1781-1782," *Delaware History*, I (January-July 1946), 1-54, 111-34; H. Trevor Colbourn, "John Dickinson, Historical Revolutionary," *Pennsylvania Magazine of History and Biography*, LXXXIII (July 1959), 271-92; John H. Powell, "John Dickinson as President of Pennsylvania," *Pennsylvania History*, XXVIII (July 1961), 254-67; David L. Jacobson, "John Dickinson's Fight against Royal Government, 1764," *William and Mary Quarterly*, 3rd ser., vol. XIX (January 1962), 64-85; David L. Jacobson, *John Dickinson and the Revolution in Pennsylvania, 1764-1776* (Berkeley, Calif., 1965); Stanley K. Johannesen, "Constitution and Empire in the Life and Thought of John Dickinson," unpub. Ph.D. diss., University of Missouri-Columbia, 1973; Milton E. Flower, "John Dickinson: Delawarean," *Delaware History*, XVII (Spring-Summer 1976), 12-20. *DAB*.

FRANKLIN, Benjamin, 1785-1788

Born on January 6, 1706 in Boston, Massachusetts, the son of Josiah and Abiah (Folger) Franklin. Brother of John, Peter, Mary, James, Sarah, Ebenezer (died young), Thomas, Lydia and Jane; half-brother of seven others. Entered what was presumably a common-law marriage with Deborah Read on September 1, 1730, by whom he had Francis Folger (died young) and Sarah; also the father of William (who served as governor of New Jersey from 1763 to 1776), perhaps by this union.

Apprenticed at the age of twelve to James Franklin, his brother, from whom he learned the printing trade. Moved to Philadelphia in 1723, where he cultivated a wide range of interests, including educational reform, publishing, scientific experimentation, and politics. Served as Clerk of the Pennsylvania Assembly from 1736 until 1751, when he was elected as a member of that body; became a leader of the anti-proprietary faction in Pennsylvania politics. Served as Deputy Postmaster from 1737 to 1753, and as Postmaster General for the Colonies from 1753 to 1774. Played a major role in the revolutionary movement during the 1760's and 1770's; appointed Colonial Agent for Pennsylvania in 1764, Georgia in 1768, New Jersey in 1769, and Massachusetts in 1770. Attended the Second Continental Congress in 1775, and emerged as a leading advocate of separation from England. Chosen President of the Pennsylvania Committee of Safety in July 1775, a position he held until his resignation in February 1776. Represented Pennsylvania in the Continental Congress during this period; signed the Declaration of Independence in July 1776. Sailed to France in October 1776, where he acted as a member of the three-man joint commission assigned the task of promoting French assistance to the American war effort; named Minister Plenipotentiary in September 1778. Returned to America in September 1785, and chosen President of Pennsylvania in October of that year; continued to serve as chief executive until the autumn of 1788, winning reelection without opposition in 1786 and 1787.

Although he was already seventy-nine years old at the time of his inauguration as Pennsylvania's president, Franklin continued to participate in national and state politics during the twilight of his illustrious career. Despite frequent ill health, he attended the Federal Convention in 1787, where his conciliatory approach helped promote work on the constitutional proposals under consideration. In December of 1787, partly due to Franklin's enormous prestige, Pennsylvania became the second state to ratify the Constitution. At the same time Franklin sought, with intermittent success, to alleviate the bitter party controversy which characterized Pennsylvania politics during his administration.

Following his tenure as chief executive, the elderly Franklin spent his remaining years in retirement. He died in Philadelphia, Pennsylvania on April 17, 1790.

Bibliography: James Parton, *The Life and Times of Benjamin Franklin*, 2 vols. (Boston, 1864); Carl Van Doren, *Benjamin Franklin* (New York, 1938); Verner W. Crane, *Benjamin Franklin and a Rising People* (Boston, 1954); John J. Zimmerman, "Benjamin Franklin: A Study of Pennsylvania Politics and the Colonial Agency, 1755-1775," unpub. Ph.D. diss., University of Michigan, 1956; Leonard W. Labaree *et al.*, eds., *The Papers of Benjamin Franklin*, 21 vols. [1706-75] (New Haven, 1959-in progress); Leonard W. Labaree, "Benjamin Franklin and the Defense of Pennsylvania, 1754-1757," *Pennsylvania History*, XXIX (January 1962), 7-23; Benjamin Franklin, *Autobiography*, Leonard W. Labaree *et al.*, eds. (New Haven and London, 1964);

William S. Hanna, *Benjamin Franklin and Pennsylvania Politics* (Stanford, 1964); Benjamin H. Newcomb, *Franklin and Galloway: A Political Partnership* (New Haven, 1972); Catherine Drinker Bowen, *The Most Dangerous Man in America: Scenes from the Life of Benjamin Franklin* (Boston and Toronto, 1974); Arthur Bernon Tourtellot, *Benjamin Franklin, The Shaping of Genius: The Boston Years* (Garden City, N.Y., 1977). *DAB*.

MIFFLIN, Thomas, 1788-1799

Born on January 10, 1744 in Philadelphia, Pennsylvania, the son of John, a prosperous merchant, and Elizabeth (Bagnell) Mifflin. Brother of six, although only George and John survived to maturity. Married on March 4, 1767 to Sarah Morris, by whom he was the father of Emily.

Attended a Quaker school as a child; admitted to the College of Philadelphia (now the University of Pennsylvania) at an early age, and graduated from that institution in May 1760. Worked for William Coleman, a wealthy Philadelphia merchant, from 1760 to 1764, when he sailed for Europe. Returned about a year later to start a business partnership with his brother George. Elected to the Pennsylvania Assembly in 1772, and played a conspicuous role in the province's revolutionary movement. Attended the First and Second Continental Congresses in 1774 and 1775. Named Major of a volunteer company in May 1775; received an appointment one month later as Aide-de-Camp to George Washington; selected as Quartermaster General of the Continental Army in August 1775, a position he filled almost continuously until late 1777; awarded the rank of Major General in February 1777, but eventually resigned that commission after becoming involved in a quarrel with Congress over his performance as quartermaster. Also served as a member of the reorganized Board of War from November 1777 to April 1778. Represented the city of Philadelphia (1778-79), Berks County (1780-81) and Philadelphia County (1785-88) in the Pennsylvania Assembly, acting as Assembly Speaker during the last period. Again served in the Continental Congress from 1782 to 1784; chosen as President of Congress in November 1783, and served in that capacity from December 1783 to June 1784. Attended the Federal Convention of 1787, and later gave his support to the Constitution drafted by that body. Elected President of Pennsylvania's Supreme Executive Council in the autumn of 1788, an office to which he was reelected in 1789. In October 1790, following the adoption of the Pennsylvania Constitution of that year, won the commonwealth's first popular gubernatorial contest; served as Governor from December 1790 to December 1799, gaining reelection twice.

During his eleven years as chief executive, Mifflin presided over a commonwealth which often reflected the political changes taking place on the national scene. Like the country itself, Pennsylvania between 1788 and 1799 became more receptive to the political views expounded by Thomas Jefferson, a development which had an important impact on public affairs. In 1794, for example, Mifflin at first tried to avoid calling up the militia to help quell the Whiskey Insurrection in western Pennsylvania, partly because he did not wish to alienate his Jeffersonian supporters. Although he did ultimately comply with the national government's request, this reluctance to enforce a Federalist-sponsored law presaged the bitter party strife which would become a feature of Pennsylvania politics in the early nineteenth century.

Following Mifflin's gubernatorial tenure, he again took a seat in the Legislature, a position which he continued to hold until he died, a bankrupt, on January 20, 1800. Mifflin was buried at state expense in the graveyard of Trinity Lutheran Church in Lancaster, Pennsylvania.

Bibliography: William Rawle, "A Sketch of the Life of Thomas Mifflin," Historical Society of Pennsylvania, *Memoirs*, II (1830), 107-26; John Houston Merrill, *Memoranda Relating to the Mifflin Family* (priv. print., 1890); Martha J. Mifflin, "Thomas Mifflin," Lancaster County Historical Society, *Papers*, III (1899), 173-81; Kenneth R. Rossman, *Thomas Mifflin and the Politics of the American Revolution* (Chapel Hill, 1952). *DAB*.

PLYMOUTH

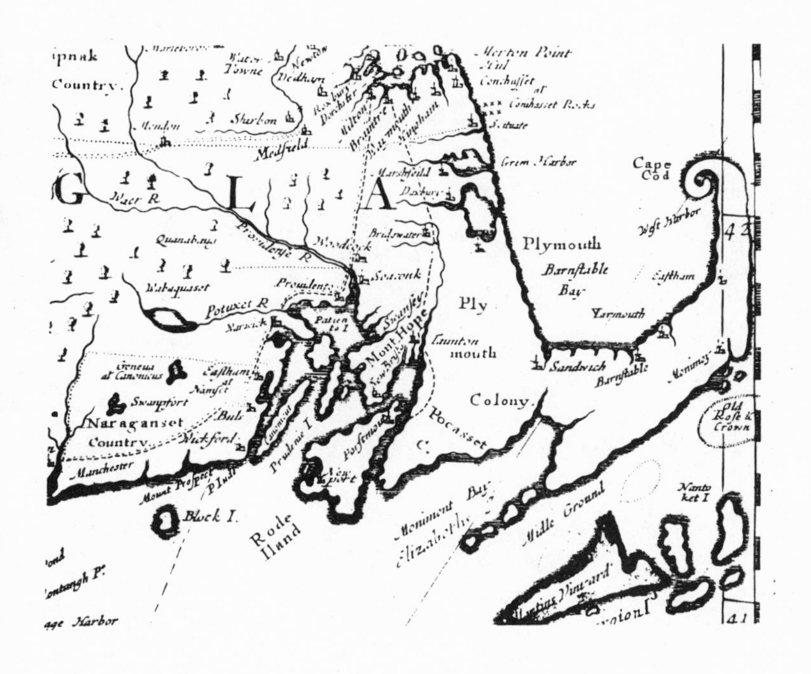

Country
Sharbon
Medfield
Water R
Providence R
Woodcock
Bridgewater
Seacunk
Providence
Potuxet R
Swansey
Mont Hope
Pocasset
Colony
Ply
Plymouth
Barnstable Bay
Cape Cod
West Harbor
Eastham
Yarmouth
Sandwich
Barnstable
Marshfield
Duxbury
Scituate
Merton Point
Conihasset Rocks
Naraganset Country
Swampfort
Manchester
Mount Prospect
Block I.
Rode Iland
Monument Bay
Elizabeth
Midle Ground
Nanto ket I
Old Rose & Crown
42
41

Chronology

1620-1621	John Carver
1621-1633	William Bradford
1633-1634	Edward Winslow
1634-1635	Thomas Prence
1635-1636	William Bradford
1636-1637	Edward Winslow
1637-1638	William Bradford
1638-1639	Thomas Prence
1639-1644	William Bradford
1644-1645	Edward Winslow
1645-1657	William Bradford
1657-1673	Thomas Prence
1673-1680	Josiah Winslow
1680-1686	Thomas Hinckley
1686-1689	Sir Edmund Andros
1689-1692	Thomas Hinckley

BIBLIOGRAPHY

Banks, Charles Edward, *The English Ancestry and Homes of the Pilgrim Fathers* . . . (New York, 1929).

Baylies, Francis, *An Historical Memoir of the Colony of New Plymouth*, 2 vols. (Boston, 1866).

Gill, Crispin, *Mayflower Remembered: A History of the Plymouth Pilgrims* (New York, 1970).

Goodwin, John A., *The Pilgrim Republic: An Historical Review of the Colony of New Plymouth* . . . (Boston, 1888).

Langdon, George D., Jr., *Pilgrim Colony: A History of New Plymouth, 1620-1691* (New Haven and London, 1966).

Moore, Jacob Bailey, *Lives of the Governors of New Plymouth, and Massachusetts Bay* . . . (Boston, 1851).

Morison, Samuel Eliot, *The Story of the "Old Colony" of New Plymouth [1620-1692]* (New York, 1956).

Plymouth Church Records, 1620-1859, 2 vols. (Boston, 1920-23), in *Publications* of the Colonial Society of Massachusetts.

Shurtleff, Nathaniel, and Daniel Pulsifer, eds., *Records of the Colony of New Plymouth* . . . 12 vols. (Boston, 1855-61).

PLYMOUTH

CARVER, John, 1620-1621

Born *circa* 1576 in either Nottinghamshire or Derbyshire, England. An Independent (Separatist). Married to Catherine (White) Leggatt.

Employed as a merchant as a young man, eventually acquiring a considerable fortune. Immigrated to Holland in 1609, and a year or two later joined the Pilgrim community at Leyden. Named Deacon of the Pilgrim Church, an office which established him as one of that sect's leaders. Returned to England in September 1617; participated in the negotiations which resulted in a patent, granted by the Virginia Company in February 1620, that authorized the Pilgrims to set up a colony in America; also helped to persuade certain prosperous merchants to finance the venture. Along with some prospective colonists whom he had organized, left London in July 1620; aboard the *Mayflower*, sailed for America from Plymouth with the first Pilgrim contingent in September of that year. Confirmed as Governor of Plymouth Colony in November 1620, thereby becoming the first head of the government created by the Mayflower Compact.

Apart from learning how to survive in a strange and inhospitable climate, the major problem confronting Carver and the Pilgrims was the need to establish good relations with their Indian neighbors. In March 1621 Carver attempted to resolve this matter by negotiating a peace treaty with Massasoit, sachem of the Wampanoag tribe. That same month the popular governor was confirmed as chief executive for the next year, but, weakened by his first winter in New England, he died in April 1621, probably from the effects of a stroke. *DAB, DNB*.

BRADFORD, William, 1621-1633, 1635-1636, 1637-1638, 1639-1644, 1645-1657

Born in 1590 in Austerfield, Yorkshire, England, the son of William and Alice (Hanson) Bradford. An Independent (Separatist). Brother of Margaret (died in infancy) and Alice. Married on November 30, 1613 to Dorothy May, by whom he was the father of John; after his first wife's death in December 1620, remarried on August 14, 1623 to Alice (Carpenter) Southworth; father of William, Mercy and Joseph by his second wife.

Came under the influence of Yorkshire's Puritan community at an early age, and in 1609 left England for the Low Countries, eventually settling in Leyden. Became a weaver among this group of religious *emigrés*; quickly won the attention of the elders of the congregation, and played a major part in the preparations for moving to America (underway by 1617). Immigrated to New England in 1620, arriving off Cape Cod late in that year. Emerged as one of the leaders of the group which founded Plymouth Colony and, following the death of Governor John Carver in April 1621, became chief executive of the infant settlement. Except for five years, served as governor of Plymouth until his death; chosen as an Assistant of the colony during those years when he was not presiding as chief executive.

Although Bradford's enormous prestige gave him several chances to extend his authority at the expense of the colony, he consistently resisted opportunities for self-aggrandizement. In 1630, for example, a patent which Plymouth received from the Council for New England was granted in his name, thereby offering him a means of establishing himself as sole proprietor. Bradford elected to share the proprietary power with the Pilgrim Fathers, however, and a decade later he persuaded the Fathers to yield the patent to the whole body of freemen. Apart from leading the community through its harsh early years, Bradford's major concern was to put Plymouth on a firm economic footing. This goal was made especially difficult by the large debt which the settlers owed to the English merchants who had subsidized their venture, a debt which in 1631 stood at £5,771. By 1648, Bradford and the other leaders of the colony had managed to free themselves of this financial burden, although they had been required to sell much of their own property in order to do so.

Along with his political and administrative contributions, Bradford was a chronicler of the Pilgrim experience, and his *History of Plimoth Plantation* remains the chief source of information concerning colony life through 1646. Bradford died on May 9, 1657, while still serving as governor.

Bibliography: Guy M. Fessenden, "A Genealogy of the Bradford Family," *New England Historical and Genealogical Register*, IV (January, July 1850), 39-50, 233-45; James Shepard, *Governor William Bradford, and His Son Major William Bradford* (New Britain, Conn., 1900); "Governor Bradford's

Letter Book," *Mayflower Descendant*, V-VII (January 1903-April 1905); Albert H. Plumb, *William Bradford of Plymouth* (Boston, 1920); E. F. Bradford, "Conscious Art in Bradford's History," *New England Quarterly*, I (1928), 133-57; William Bradford Browne, "Ancestry of the Bradfords of Austerfield, Co. York," *New England Historical and Genealogical Register*, LXXXIII (October 1929), 439-64, vol. LXXXIV (January 1930), 5-17; Isidore S. Meyer, "The Hebrew Preface to Bradford's History of the Plymouth Plantation," American Jewish Historical Society, *Publications*, XXXVIII (June 1949), 289-305; Bradford Smith, *Bradford of Plymouth* (Philadelphia, 1951); William Bradford, *Of Plymouth Plantation*, ed. Samuel Eliot Morison (New York, 1952); William Bradford and Edward Winslow, *Mourt's Relation; or, Journal of the Plantation at Plymouth* (New York, 1969: reprint of the 1865 edition of the work first published in London in 1622). *DAB*, *DNB*.

WINSLOW, Edward, 1633-1634, 1636-1637, 1644-1645

Born on October 18, 1595 in Droitwich, Worcestershire, England, the son of Edward, a yeoman farmer, and Magdalen (Ollyver) Winslow. An Independent. Brother of John, Eleanor, Kenelm, Gilbert, Elizabeth, Magdalen and Josiah. Married on May 27, 1618 to Elizabeth Barker; after the death of his first wife in March 1621, remarried on May 12, 1621 to Susanna (Fuller) White; father by his second wife of Josiah, who served as governor of Plymouth Colony from 1673 to 1680, and Elizabeth; also the father, probably by his first wife, of Edward and John, both of whom died at an early age.

Received a good education at King's School in Worcester; apprenticed to a stationer (i.e., printer) in 1613, but did not complete his apprenticeship. In 1617, during a trip to Holland, joined the Separatist congregation of John Robinson in Leyden. Sailed for America in 1620, and arrived in Plymouth in December of that year. Became a leading propagandist for the Pilgrim community, writing such narratives as *A Relation or Journall of the beginning and proceedings of the English Plantation setled at Plimoth in New England* (1622). Chosen as a member of Plymouth Colony's first Board of Assistants in 1624, and filled that office almost every year until 1646. Became active as an explorer and trader, and in 1629 was made the colony's Agent. Elected to three one-year terms as Governor of Plymouth Colony in 1633, 1636 and 1644. Also served as a Plymouth Commissioner to the New England Confederation, established in 1643.

During the second of Winslow's three years as chief executive, Plymouth Colony experienced a political development of major significance. In November of 1636 the colony's General Court passed legislation which for the first time clearly prohibited Plymouth's governor and assistants from enacting legislation. While this decision by the Court merely confirmed customary practice, it set in motion a process which three years later also deprived the governor and assistants of the important right to make land grants.

Following his final term as governor, Winslow returned to England, where he published replies to the charges of Samuel Gorton and John Child against the Massachusetts Bay Company. Among his other works, Winslow wrote *The Glorious Progress of the Gospel among the Indians in New England* (1649), a tract which played a prominent role in the founding that year of the Society for the Propagation of the Gospel in New England. In 1654 Winslow was named by Oliver Cromwell to several commissions dealing with naval affairs, and while accompanying an English fleet returning from Jamaica after its conquest of that island, he contracted a fever from which he died on May 8, 1655. Winslow was buried at sea.

Bibliography: John H. Sheppard, "Genealogy of the Winslow Family," *New England Historical and Genealogical Register*, XVII (April 1863), 159-62; D. P. and F. K. Holton, *Winslow Memorial*, 2 vols. (New York, 1877-88); William C. Winslow, "Governor Edward Winslow: His Part and Place in Plymouth Colony," *New York Genealogical and Biographical Record*, XXVII (July 1896), 121-31; Maria Whitman Bryant, *Genealogy of Edward Winslow of the 'Mayflower' and His Descendants from 1620 to 1865* [New Bedford, Mass., 1915]; W. Sterry-Cooper, *Edward Winslow* (Birmingham, Eng., 1953); William Bradford and Edward Winslow, *Mourt's Relation; or, Journal of the Plantation at Plymouth* (New York, 1969: reprint of the 1865 edition of the work first published in London in 1622). *DAB, DNB*.

PRENCE, Thomas, 1634-1635, 1638-1639, 1657-1673

Born in 1600 in England, the son of Thomas Prence, a carriage-maker of All Hallows, Barking, London. An Independent. Married on August 5, 1624 to Patience Brewster; after his first wife's death in 1634, remarried on April 1, 1635 to Mary Collier; married a third time in 1662 to Mrs. Apphia Freeman, who died before August 1, 1668; married a fourth time before August 1, 1668 to Mrs. Mary Howes; father by his first two wives of Thomas, Rebecca, Sarah, Mercy, Hannah, Jane, Judith, Mary and Elizabeth.

Arrived in North America in November 1621 aboard the *Fortune*. Named Governor of Plymouth Colony in 1634 and again in 1638, perhaps because neither William Bradford nor Edward Winslow wanted the position. Except for his two short periods as chief executive, served as an Assistant of Plymouth Colony from the early 1630's to 1657, when he was again chosen as governor, an office he filled until his death. Also acted at various times as a Commissioner as well as Treasurer of Plymouth Colony.

Prence's early tenure as governor was brief and concerned primarily with land policy, as he and his assistants endeavored to settle disagreements with the colony's freemen over the procedures to be used in making grants to persons or townships. In 1657, however, Prence commenced a period of gubernatorial service to Plymouth Colony that lasted for over fifteen years. During that time in office he was required to deal with a wide variety of issues, ranging from religious dissent to relations with neighboring Indian tribes. Soon after he succeeded the deceased governor, William Bradford, Prence made clear his attitude towards religious radicals; he asked for legislation, which he received from the General Court, aimed at suppressing Quaker proselytizing in Plymouth Colony. Prence's dealings with Indians in the area were equally rigid. Indeed, his rather tactless handling of native concerns probably contributed to the outbreak of King Philip's War several years after his death in office on March 29, 1673. Prence was buried at Plymouth ten days later, on April 8, 1673.

Bibliography: George Ernest Bowman, ed., "Governor Thomas Prence's Will and Inventory, and the Records of His Death," *Mayflower Descendant*, III (October 1901), 203-16; Ella Florence Elliot, "Gov. Thomas Prence's Widow Mary, Formerly the Widow of Thomas Howes, and the Inventory of Her Estate," *Mayflower Descendant*, VI (October 1904), 230-35; Anna C. Kingsbury, comp., *A Historical Sketch of Thomas Prence* (n.p., 1924). *DNB*.

WINSLOW, Josiah, 1673-1680

Born *circa* 1629 in Plymouth, Plymouth Colony, the son of Edward Winslow, the third governor of Plymouth Colony, and Susanna (Fuller) White Winslow. An Independent. Brother of Elizabeth. Married, probably in 1657, to Penelope Pelham; father of Elizabeth, Edward and Isaac. Studied at Harvard College, but never took a degree.

As a young man represented Marshfield in the Plymouth General Court, and commanded the Marshfield militia. Served for a number of years as a Commissioner of the United Colonies, representing Plymouth; also named as chief of the Plymouth Colony military in 1659, and given the rank of Major. First selected as an Assistant of Plymouth Colony in 1657, and re-elected annually until June 1673, when he was chosen to succeed the deceased Thomas Prence as Governor; filled that office until his own death in 1680.

Winslow's period as head of the Plymouth government was marked by several important political developments, but certainly the most tumultuous event during these years was the outbreak of King Philip's War. Winslow played an active role in the conflict, especially after his selection late in 1675 as Commander-in-Chief of the troops mustered by the United Colonies. Although he won a major victory over the Narragansett Indians in December of 1675, his insistence on an immediate return march by the weary army resulted in the loss of more lives. Several months later Winslow was forced by illness to retire from his command, and he resumed his gubernatorial duties after appointing Captain Benjamin Church as head of the colonial forces. Winslow's final years as governor were largely spent in an attempt to further the interests of Plymouth Colony by cultivating the friendship of Edward Randolph, the indefatigable Crown representative and customs collector. Winslow died in Marshfield, Plymouth Colony on December 18, 1680, while still in office.

Bibliography: John H. Sheppard, "Genealogy of the Winslow Family," *New England Historical and Genealogical Register*, XVII (April 1863), 159-62; D. P. and F. K. Holton, *Winslow Memorial*, 2 vols. (New York, 1877-88); George Ernest Bowman, ed., "Governor Josiah Winslow's Will and Inventory," *Mayflower Descendant*, V (April 1903), 82-86; Maria Whitman Bryant, *Genealogy of Edward Winslow of the 'Mayflower' and His Descendants from 1620 to 1865* [New Bedford, Mass., 1915]. *DAB*.

HINCKLEY, Thomas, 1680-1686, 1689-1692

Born *circa* 1618 in England, the son of Samuel and Sarah Hinckley. An Independent. Brother of Samuel, John, Susannah, Sarah, Mary and Elizabeth. Married in December 1641 to Mary Richards, by whom he was the father of Mary, Sarah, Melatiah, Hannah, Samuel, Thomas, Bathshuba and Mehitable; after the death of his first wife in June 1659, remarried in March 1660 to Mary (Smith) Glover, by whom he had Mercy, Experience, John, Abigail, Thankful, Ebenezer, Reliance, and Admire and Ebenezer, both of whom died in infancy.

Immigrated with his parents to New England in March of 1634, and eventually settled with them in Barnstable in 1639. Selected as a Deputy from Barnstable by 1645; served as a Magistrate and an Assistant of Plymouth Colony from 1658 to 1680, when he was chosen Deputy Governor. Named Governor of Plymouth Colony in June 1681, and served in that capacity until 1692, except for the interlude during which Sir Edmund Andros presided over the Dominion of New England. Also served as a Commissioner of the United Colonies during King Philip's War in the 1670's, and as a Commissioner for the General Board of the Colonies of Plymouth and Massachusetts Bay for a number of years.

The choice of Hinckley as successor to the recently deceased Governor Josiah Winslow came at a time when Plymouth Colony was under pressure to secure a charter that would recognize its autonomy from Massachusetts Bay.

When Massachusetts lost its own charter in October 1684, however, it became less likely that Plymouth would be able to remain a distinct political entity in any future reorganization of New England. Nevertheless, despite the threat of absorption by its larger neighbor, Plymouth Colony at first continued to function fairly effectively under Hinckley, and in 1685 the colony's General Court even approved an extensive revision of Plymouth's legal code. A year later the implementation of these new laws was interrupted, as Sir Edmund Andros arrived in Boston with Crown orders giving him authority over Plymouth. The deposed Hinckley remained out of power for over two years, although he retained a voice in the colony's affairs by criticizing what he viewed as the illegal acts of the Andros regime. After the overthrow of Andros in 1689, Hinckley returned as governor, but his second period in office was brief. By 1691 the colony was suffering from serious financial distress and an almost complete breakdown of authority, and in October 1691 the Privy Council in London officially made Plymouth Colony part of the province of Massachusetts Bay. By the next spring Hinckley had stepped down as governor, soon after news of the Privy Council's decision reached the colony.

Following his departure as chief executive, Hinckley seems to have taken no further part in politics. He died in Barnstable, Massachusetts on April 25, 1705.

Bibliography: George W. Messinger, "The Hinckley Family," *New England Historical and Genealogical Register*, XIII (July 1859), 208-12; *The Hinckley Papers*, in Massachusetts Historical Society, *Collections*, 4th ser., vol. V (Boston, 1861), 1-308; George Ernest Bowman, ed., "Governor Thomas Hinckley's Will and Inventory," *Mayflower Descendant*, V (October 1903), 237-46.

ANDROS, Sir Edmund, 1686-1689

New York, 1674-1677, 1678-1681; East Jersey, 1680-1681, 1688-1689; Massachusetts, 1686-1689; New Hampshire, 1686-1689; Rhode Island, 1686-1689; Connecticut, 1687-1689; West Jersey, 1688-1689; Virginia, 1692-1698; Maryland, 1693, 1694

Born on December 6, 1637 on the Island of Guernsey, the son of Amice and Elizabeth (Stone) Andros. Married to a woman who was related to the Earl of Craven.

Served as Major of a regiment of foot soldiers which in 1666 sailed from England to defend the West Indies against the Dutch. Named a Landgrave of Carolina in 1672; received a commission from the Duke of York in July 1674 to govern the colony of New York, and acted in that capacity, except for an absence in England between November 1677 and August 1678, until January 1681; also exercised control over East Jersey from 1680 until his recall early in the following year. Knighted in about 1681, became Gentleman of the Privy Chamber to Charles II in 1683, and was appointed Lieutenant Colonel of the Princess of Denmark's regiment of horse soldiers in 1685. Commissioned Royal Governor of the Dominion of New England in June 1686, and established his authority in Massachusetts Bay, Maine, New Hampshire, Plymouth and Rhode Island (including the King's Province) in December of that year; Connecticut in November of 1687; and the Jerseys and New York in August 1688 (although Francis Nicholson presided as Andros' substitute in the latter colony). Arrested and sent to England following the overthrow of the Dominion in the spring of 1689, but later received a commission as Royal Governor of Virginia, and served as that colony's chief executive from September 1692 to December 1698; also acted briefly as Governor of Maryland in 1693 and 1694, in the absence of any other executive authority.

Andros' first tenure in New York was marked by several important achievements, especially the improvement of the colony's defenses and the settlement of some boundary difficulties with Connecticut. Nevertheless, even at this stage he had begun to display an inclination to behave in an arbitrary fashion. Perhaps the clearest illustration of this tendency was the high-handed manner in which Andros superseded the authority of Governor Philip Carteret in the Jerseys, provoking Carteret to complain that Andros aimed at "usurping the government" of his colony. This insensitivity to local politics became even more noticeable after Andros assumed control of the Dominion of New England. Following a troubled tenure of less than two and one-half years, he was deposed in the spring of 1689, shortly after news of the Glorious Revolution in England reached Boston.

Although Andros was exonerated of the charges brought against his Dominion government and took over as Virginia's chief executive in 1692, he soon encountered resistance from local leaders like Commissary James Blair, who bitterly informed one London official that Andros "never did any considerable service to the King, nor the people" during his colonial career. Finally, late in 1698, Andros departed for England. He served as Lieutenant Governor of Guernsey from 1704 to 1706, and died in London in February 1714.

Bibliography: "Commission to Sir Edmund Andros," Massachusetts Historical Society, *Collections*, 3rd ser., vol. VII (Boston, 1838), 138-49; W. H. Whitmore, ed., *Andros Tracts: Being a Collection of Pamphlets and Official Papers . . . of the Andros Government and the Establishment of the Second Charter of Massachusetts*, 3 vols. (New York, 1868-74) (Publications of the Prince Society, vols. V-VII); Robert N. Toppan, ed., "Andros Records," American Antiquarian Society, *Proceedings*, n.s., vol. XIII (1899-1900), 237-68, 463-99; J.H. Tuttle, ed., "Land Warrants under Andros," Colonial Society of Massachusetts, *Publications*, XXI (1919), 292-361; Albert C. Bates,

''Expedition of Sir Edmund Andros to Connecticut in 1687,'' AAS, *Proceedings*, n.s., vol. 48 (October 1938), 276-99; Jeanne G. Bloom, ''Sir Edmund Andros: A Study in Seventeenth-Century Colonial Administration,'' unpub. Ph.D. diss., Yale University, 1962; Robert C. Ritchie, ''London Merchants, the New York Market, and the Recall of Sir Edmund Andros,'' *New York History*, LVII (January 1976), 5-29. *DAB*, *DNB*.

RHODE ISLAND

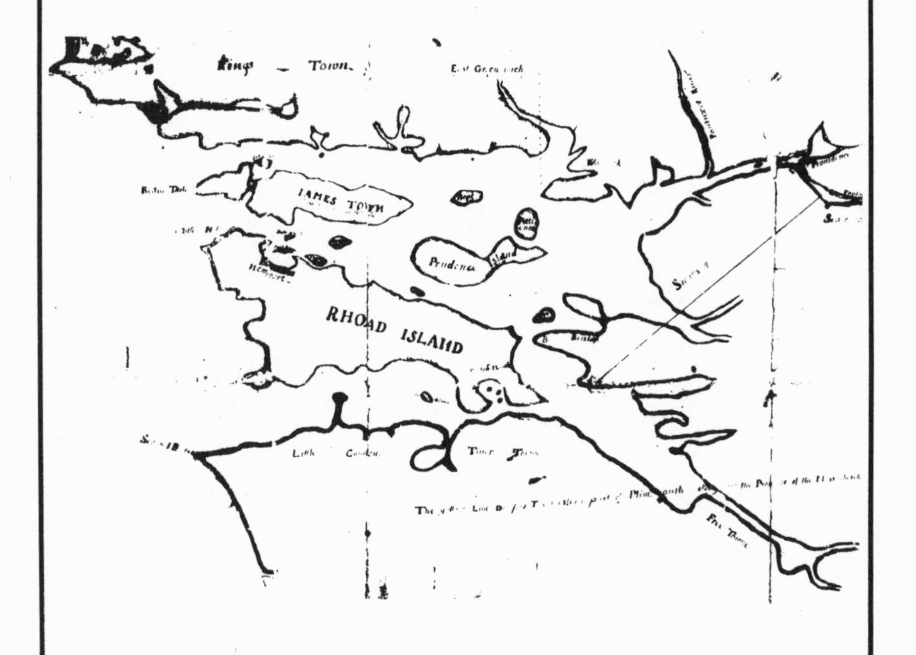

Chronology

1638-1639	William Coddington (as *judge of Portsmouth*)
1639-1640	William Hutchinson (*as judge of Portsmouth*)
1639-1640	William Coddington (*as judge of Newport*)
1640-1647	William Coddington (*as governor of Portsmouth and Newport*)
1644-1647	Roger Williams (*as chief officer of Providence*)
1647	John Coggeshall
1648-1649	Jeremiah (or Jeremy) Clarke
1649-1650	John Smith
1650-1651	Nicholas Easton
1651-1652	Samuel Gorton (*as president of Providence and Warwick*)
1651-1653	William Coddington (*as president of Portsmouth and Newport*)
1652-1653	John Smith (*as president of Providence and Warwick*)
1653	John Sanford (*as president of Portsmouth and Newport*)
1653-1654	Gregory Dexter (*as president of Providence and Warwick*)
1654	Nicholas Easton (as *president of Portsmouth and Newport*)
1654-1657	Roger Williams
1657-1660	Benedict Arnold
1660-1662	William Brenton
1662-1666	Benedict Arnold
1666-1669	William Brenton
1669-1672	Benedict Arnold
1672-1674	Nicholas Easton
1674-1676	William Coddington
1676-1677	Walter Clarke
1677-1678	Benedict Arnold
1678	William Coddington
1678-1680	John Cranston
1680-1683	Peleg Sanford
1683-1685	William Coddington, Jr.
1685-1686	Henry Bull
1686	Walter Clarke
1686	Joseph Dudley
1686-1689	Sir Edmund Andros
1689-1690	John Coggeshall, Jr.
1690	Henry Bull
1690-1695	John Easton
1695	Caleb Carr
1696-1698	Walter Clarke

1698-1727	Samuel Cranston
1727-1732	Joseph Jenckes
1732-1733	William Wanton
1733-1740	John Wanton
1740-1743	Richard Ward
1743-1745	William Greene
1745-1746	Gideon Wanton
1746-1747	William Greene
1747-1748	Gideon Wanton
1748-1755	William Greene
1755-1757	Stephen Hopkins
1757-1758	William Greene
1758-1762	Stephen Hopkins
1762-1763	Samuel Ward
1763-1765	Stephen Hopkins
1765-1767	Samuel Ward
1767-1768	Stephen Hopkins
1768-1769	Josias Lyndon
1769-1775	Joseph Wanton
1775-1778	Nicholas Cooke
1778-1786	William Greene, Jr.
1786-1790	John Collins

BIBLIOGRAPHY

Austin, John Osborne, *The Genealogical Dictionary of Rhode Island; Comprising Three Generations of Settlers who Came Before 1690 . . .*, rev. ed. (Baltimore, 1969).

Bartlett, John Russell, ed., *Records of the Colony of Rhode Island and Providence Plantations in New England [1636-1776]*, I-VII (Providence, 1856-62: reprinted New York, 1968).

———. ed., *Records of the State of Rhode Island and Providence Plantations [1776-1792]*, VIII-X (Providence, 1863-65: reprinted New York, 1968).

Bridenbaugh, Carl, *Fat Mutton and Liberty of Conscience: Society in Rhode Island, 1636-1690* (Providence, 1974).

James, Sydney V., *Colonial Rhode Island: A History* (New York, 1975).

Kimball, Gertrude S., ed., *Correspondence of the Colonial Governors of Rhode Island, 1723-1775*, 2 vols. (Cambridge, Mass., 1902-03).

Lovejoy, David S., *Rhode Island Politics and the American Revolution, 1760-1776* (Providence, 1958).

Mohr, Ralph S., *Governors for Three Hundred Years, 1638-1959: Rhode Island and Providence Plantations* (Providence, 1959).

RHODE ISLAND

CODDINGTON, William, 1638-1639 *(as Judge of Portsmouth), 1639-1640 (as Judge of Newport), 1640-1647, 1651-1653 (as Governor of Portsmouth and Newport), 1674-1676, 1678 (as Governor of Rhode Island)*

Born in 1601 in Boston, Lincolnshire, England; names of parents unknown. A Puritan at the time of his immigration to America, but converted to Quakerism late in life. Married to Mary Moseley, by whom he was the father of Michael and Samuel, both of whom died in infancy; after the death of his first wife in 1630, remarried to a second woman named Mary, by whom he had at least three children, including Mary and Benajah; following his second wife's death in 1647, remarried several years later to Anne Brinley; father of William (who was governor of Rhode Island from 1683 to 1685), Nathaniel, Mary, Thomas, John, Noah (died young), Anne (died young) and Anne by his third wife.

Became one of the leaders of the Massachusetts Bay Company, and immigrated to America in 1630. Chosen as Assistant of Massachusetts Bay in May 1632, a position he held until 1637. Also served as Treasurer from 1634 to 1636, and as a Deputy to the Massachusetts General Court in 1637. Became an adherent of Anne Hutchinson during the Antinomian controversy of the 1630's, a stance which forced him to leave Massachusetts in 1638 for the island of Aquidneck (later part of Rhode Island). Served as Judge, or chief executive officer, of the town of Portsmouth from March 1638 to the spring of 1639, when he became Judge of Newport. Presided as judge in Newport until its merger with Portsmouth in March 1640. Acted as Governor of both towns from March 1640 to May 1647, although his authority was disputed during the last few years of this period by Roger Williams, who had received in 1644 a patent naming him chief executive of a territory which included Aquidneck. Received his own patent establishing Aquidneck as a separate colony in 1651, and attempted to govern that island until May 1653, despite the contention by some of its residents that his administration was illegitimate. Held office as Commissioner from Newport to the Rhode Island General Court (Assembly) in 1656. Served in 1666 as a Deputy, and from 1666 to 1667 as an Assistant, in the Rhode Island General Assembly. Returned to act as chief executive of Rhode Island from May 1674 to May 1676, and from August 1678 until his death.

Most of Coddington's political career was marred by allegations that he employed questionable means to keep himself in power. In October 1652, for example, Roger Williams gained a judgment revoking Coddington's 1651 commission to govern Aquidneck for life, apparently by emphasizing to English officials how Coddington had sought to win support for his administration from the Dutch in New Amsterdam. In 1674, however, Coddington's religious predilections again made him a popular leader in a colony which by then had become a Quaker stronghold. During his last years in office, Coddington was chiefly concerned with the impact of King Philip's War on Rhode Island, although his pacifist beliefs and a reluctant Assembly barred him from endorsing vigorous action to repel the Indian threat. Coddington died on November 1, 1678, scarcely more than a month after he had been named by the Assembly to succeed the deceased governor, Benedict Arnold.

Bibliography: William Coddington, *A Demonstration of True Love unto You the Rulers of the Colony of Massachusetts* . . . (n.p., 1674); David King, "William Coddington and Richard Bellingham," *New England Historical and Genealogical Register*, XXVIII (January 1874), 13-16; Henry E. Turner, *William Coddington in Rhode Island Colonial Affairs: An Historical Inquiry* (Providence, 1878); David King, ed., "William Coddington: Resistance by Him and Others in Lincolnshire to the Royal Loan, 1626-7," *New England Historical and Genealogical Register*, XXXVI (April 1882), 138-43; William Babcock Weeden, "William Coddington," Massachusetts Historical Society, *Proceedings*, XLIV (April 1911), 583-92; David King, "Governor William Coddington," Newport Historical Society, *Bulletin*, no. 5 (Newport, 1913), 1-22; Olive (Cole) Smith, comp., *Ancestral Charts of George Addison Throop* . . . (East St. Louis, Ill., 1934); Emily Coddington Williams, *William Coddington of Rhode Island: A Sketch* (Newport, 1941). *DAB, DNB*.

HUTCHINSON, William, 1639-1640 *(as Judge of Portsmouth)*

Born in 1586 in Lincolnshire, England, the eldest son of Edward and Susan Hutchinson. Brother of Theophilus (died in infancy?), Samuel, Hester [or Esther], John, Richard, Susanna (died young), Susanna, Anne, Mary and Edward. Married on August 9, 1612 to Anne Marbury, who became the leader of the Antinomian movement in Massachusetts during the 1630's; father of Edward, Susanna (died young), Richard, Faith, Bridget, Francis, Elizabeth (died young), William (died young), Samuel, Anne, Mary, Katherine, William and Susanna.

Employed as a mercer in England before he immigrated to Massachusetts Bay in 1634, arriving in the colony in September of that year. Admitted as a Freeman in March 1635, and served as Deputy to the Massachusetts General Court in 1635 and 1636. After it became apparent that his wife would be expelled for her part in the Antinomian controversy, set out early in 1638 for the island of Aquidneck, where he helped to found the town of Portsmouth. Named Treasurer of the settlement several months later, along with John Coggeshall. Chosen as Judge of Portsmouth in the spring of 1639, a position which he held until that town and Newport fell under the jurisdiction of William Coddington in March 1640.

Hutchinson's election as judge, or chief executive officer, of Portsmouth was made necessary by the decision of Coddington and his supporters to leave the community in order to establish the new town of Newport. Behind this separation lay conflicts over both land and the teachings of Samuel Gorton, whose contention that Portsmouth should govern itself according to divine law was rejected by Hutchinson in favor of a community founded on English precedent. By March of 1640, however, Coddington had broken with Gorton and decided to accept English law, a concession which set the stage for the organization of a single government uniting the two towns under his leadership. Meanwhile, Hutchinson and his family remained on Aquidneck, where he served as an Assistant for one year, until his death in 1642.

Bibliography: George E. Ellis, *Life of Anne Hutchinson; with a Sketch of the Antinomian Controversy in Massachusetts*, in Jared Sparks, ed., *The Library of American Biography*, 2nd ser., vol. VI (Boston, 1845), 167-376; Joseph Lemuel Chester, "The Hutchinson Family of England and New England, and Its Connection with the Marburys and Drydens," *New England Historical and Genealogical Register*, XX (October 1866), 355-67; Edith R. Curtis, *Anne Hutchinson* (Cambridge, 1930); Winnifred King Rugg, *Unafraid: A Life of Anne Hutchinson* (Boston and New York, 1930).

WILLIAMS, Roger, 1644-1647 *(as Chief Officer of Providence), 1654-1657 (as President of Rhode Island)*

Born *circa* 1603 in London, England, the son of James and Alice (Pemberton) Williams. Brother of Sydrach, Katherine and Robert. Married on December 15, 1629 to Mary Barnard, by whom he was the father of Mary, Freeborn, Providence, Mercy, Daniel and Joseph.

Entered the Charterhouse school in 1621, a *protégé* of Sir Edward Coke; matriculated at Pembroke College, Cambridge in July 1624, and received a B.A. from that institution in January 1627. Apparently took holy orders sometime before February 1629, becoming Chaplain in that year to Sir

William Masham of Otes, Essex. Took an interest in the activities of the Massachusetts Bay Company, and in December of 1630 embarked for New England. Rejected a call as Teacher of the church at Boston and, after a brief period as Teacher of the Salem church, left for Plymouth. Returned to Salem in 1633, and in 1634 again became teacher of that congregation, despite the General Court's opposition to his religious and political views. Banished from Massachusetts Bay by the General Court in October 1635; founded the town of Providence in 1636. Returned to England, where he received a patent in March 1644 giving him authority over the "Providence Plantations in Narragansett Bay"; served as "Chief Officer" of Providence, probably from September 1644 to 1647, and struggled for several years to uphold his right to govern elsewhere in Rhode Island, according to the terms of his patent. Elected an Assistant of Rhode Island in May 1647, and held that office until May 1649. After another voyage to England in the early 1650's, returned to a divided Rhode Island and in August 1654 persuaded the feuding towns to resume their union. Chosen President of Rhode Island in September 1654, a position he held until May of 1657.

Although Williams had immediately tried to create a unified Rhode Island under his patent of 1644, territorial disputes with both William Coddington of Newport and the neighboring colonies of Plymouth, Connecticut and Massachusetts Bay delayed the accomplishment of his plan until May of 1647. Four years later that fragile alliance collapsed, and while his diplomatic efforts in 1654 convinced the towns of Portsmouth and Newport on the island of Aquidneck to reunite with the mainland communities of Providence and Warwick, Williams was once again faced with the need to strengthen that union. In 1656 his goal of restoring political tranquility to Rhode Island was greatly facilitated by Coddington's decision to abandon his claim of jurisdiction over the settlers on Aquidneck. This concession, combined with Williams' firm treatment of attempts by Massachusetts Bay to interfere with his colony's internal affairs, indicates that by 1657 Rhode Island had started to emerge as a cohesive political unit.

Following his tenure as president, Williams continued to play an active role in Rhode Island politics. In November 1659 he was chosen as a Commissioner from Providence to the Rhode Island General Court, an office he also held in August 1659 and August 1661. Williams again served as an Assistant of the colony in 1658, and intermittently from March 1664 to 1672. During King Philip's War the aged ex-president commanded a troop of soldiers from Providence who fought against the Narragansett Indians. Williams died sometime between January 16 and March 15, 1683.

Bibliography: James D. Knowles, *Memoir of Roger Williams, the Founder of the State of Rhode-Island* (Boston, 1834); Edmund J. Carpenter, *Roger Williams: A Study of the Life, Times and Character of a Political Pioneer* (New York, 1909); James E. Ernst, *The Political Thought of Roger Williams* (Seattle, 1929); James Ernst, *Roger Williams, New England Firebrand* (New

York, 1932); Samuel H. Brockunier, *The Irrepressible Democrat, Roger Williams* (New York, 1940); Perry Miller, *Roger Williams: His Contribution to the American Tradition* (Indianapolis, 1953); Ola E. Winslow, *Master Roger Williams* (New York, 1957); *The Complete Writings of Roger Williams*, 7 vols. (New York, 1963); Theodore P. Greene, ed., *Roger Williams and the Massachusetts Magistrates* (Boston, 1964); Cyclone Covey, *The Gentle Radical: A Biography of Roger Williams* (New York, 1966); Edmund S. Morgan, *Roger Williams, The Church and the State* (New York, 1967); Henry Chupack, *Roger Williams* (New York, 1969); John Garrett, *Roger Williams: Witness Beyond Christendom, 1603-1683* (New York, 1970); W. Clark Gilpin, *The Millenarian Piety of Roger Williams* (Chicago, 1979). *DAB, DNB*.

COGGESHALL, John, 1647

Born in 1601 and baptized in Halstead, Essex County, England, the son of John and Anne (Butter) Coggeshall. Brother of Anne and Katherine. Married to a woman named Mary; father of John, Jr. (who was deputy governor of Rhode Island in 1689-90), Ann, Mary, Joshua, James, Hananiel (died young), Wait and Bedaiah (died young).

Employed for a time as a silk merchant in England. Immigrated to New England in 1632, arriving in Boston in September of that year. Became a Boston Selectman in 1634, and served as a Deputy in the General Court from 1634 to 1637; lost his seat as a deputy in November 1637, after asserting his belief in the innocence of the Reverend John Wheelwright, a supporter of Anne Hutchinson. Left Massachusetts Bay in 1638, and became one of the founders of Portsmouth in March of that year; moved to Newport in 1639. Acted as an Assistant for Newport from 1640 to 1644, and as the town's Corporal in 1644. Elected President of Rhode Island in the spring of 1647, and served in that capacity until his death.

Coggeshall's election marked the first attempt to form a central Rhode Island government with jurisdiction over the four towns of Providence, Warwick, Portsmouth and Newport, and the new president's chief objective was to establish that union on a sound footing. Unfortunately, Coggeshall had little opportunity to organize his administration properly before he died in Newport on November 27, 1647. In the years immediately following his death, the colony was wracked by political divisions, divisions which culminated in 1651 with the separation of the mainland communities of Providence and Warwick from the island towns of Portsmouth and Newport.

Bibliography: Charles Pierce Coggeshall and Thellwell Russell Coggeshall, comps., *The Coggeshalls in America: Genealogy of the Descendants of John Coggeshall of Newport, with a Brief Notice of Their English Antecedents* (Boston, 1930).

CLARKE, Jeremiah [or Jeremy], 1648-1649

Born in 1605 in England, the son of William and Mary (Weston) Clarke. Married in about 1637 to Frances (Latham) Dungan; father of Walter (who was governor of Rhode Island, 1676-77, 1686, 1689, 1696-98), Mary, Jeremiah, Latham, Weston, James and Sarah.

Immigrated to New England in about 1637, and became one of the first settlers of Newport in 1639. Acted as Town Constable in 1639 and 1640. Served as Treasurer for the town of Newport in 1640 and again from 1644 to 1647. Named Lieutenant of the Newport militia in 1642 and Captain in 1644. Served as General Treasurer of Rhode Island from 1647 to 1649, following the union of 1647. Became an Assistant of the colony in 1648, and from May 1648 to May 1649 acted as President of Rhode Island.

Clarke assumed the presidency of Rhode Island at a time when the recent union of the four towns of Providence, Warwick, Portsmouth and Newport was already beginning to disintegrate. Quarrels among the communities were becoming more troublesome, and the central government complicated matters by yielding more authority to the individual towns without insisting upon their allegiance in return. By the time that Clarke turned over the administration of the colony to John Smith of Warwick in May 1649, factionalism in Rhode Island had made it virtually impossible for the president to govern effectively.

After his period as chief executive, Clarke seems to have engaged in commerce. In 1649, for example, he is recorded as having been the main owner of "the good barque called the *Sea flowre*," which sailed out of Newport. Clarke died in Newport in January 1652, and was buried in that town.

Bibliography: George Austin Morrison, Jr., *The "Clarke" Families of Rhode Island* (New York, 1902); Louise Tracy, "Historic Strain of Blood in America . . . Progeny of Jeremiah Clarke and His Wife, Frances Latham, 'The Mother of Governors' . . .," *Journal of American History*, II (1908), 501-13; "Genealogical Research in England: Clarke," *New England Historical and Genealogical Register*, LXXIV (January-April 1920), 68-76, 130-40; Alfred Rudulph Justice, comp., *Ancestry of Jeremy Clarke of Rhode Island and Dungan Genealogy* (Philadelphia, 1923?).

SMITH, John, 1649-1650 *(as President of Rhode Island), 1652-1653 (as President of Providence and Warwick)*

Date and place of birth, and names of parents unknown. Married to a widow named Ann Collins; no children. Employed as a shopkeeper in Boston before moving to Rhode Island. Had become an inhabitant of Warwick by June 1648, and in that same year was named an Assistant of the colony. Chosen President of the four towns which comprised Rhode Island in the spring of 1649, and served until May 1650; also acted as President of Providence and Warwick from May 1652 to May 1653, following the separation of those two mainland communities from the island towns of Portsmouth and Newport.

Smith's two terms as president were plagued by political turmoil. By 1650 quarreling among the towns of Providence, Warwick, Portsmouth and Newport had become so commonplace that their union, established only a few years earlier, was put in serious jeopardy. In 1651 the long-threatened break finally occurred, with Providence and Warwick choosing Samuel Gorton as their president. Consequently, when Smith resumed office in May of 1652 he, as a resident of Warwick, was only able to exercise jurisdiction on the mainland. During Smith's second term, proponents of reunification held a meeting at Portsmouth in March 1653, in order to discuss ways of resolving the dispute. They accomplished little, however, and the mainland and island governments remained independent of each other until 1654.

After his service as chief executive, Smith continued to take an interest in the colony's political affairs. Between 1658 and 1663, for example, he acted as a Commissioner in the Rhode Island General Court. Smith died in July of 1663.

EASTON, Nicholas, 1650-1651 *(as President of Rhode Island), 1654 (as President of Portsmouth and Newport), 1672-1674 (as Governor of Rhode Island)*

Born in 1593 in Wales; names of parents unknown. A Quaker. Married first to a woman whose name is unknown, and who died before Easton's immigration to New England; remarried in 1638 to Christian, the widow of Thomas Beecher; after the death of his second wife in February 1665, remarried on March 2, 1671 to Ann Clayton; father by his first wife of Peter and John (who was governor of Rhode Island from 1690 to 1695).

Employed for a time as a tanner. Immigrated to New England in 1634, settling first in Massachusetts Bay. Supported the religious ideas of Anne Hutchinson, and in 1638 left Massachusetts to found a town in what is now Hampton, New Hampshire; forced to abandon his Hampton settlement, but soon became, with other followers of Mrs. Hutchinson, one of the founders of the town of Portsmouth, Rhode Island. Removed to Newport in 1639, and in 1640 was elected an Assistant for that town; also served as an assistant from 1642 to 1644, and again in 1653. Acted as President of Rhode Island from May 1650 to August 1651, and of Portsmouth and Newport from May to September of 1654. Named a Newport Commissioner to the General Court (Assembly) in 1660, and served as Deputy from 1665 to 1666, after the implementation of the

Charter of 1663. Also served as Deputy Governor of Rhode Island from May 1666 to May 1669, and from May 1670 to May 1671; elected Governor of the colony in the spring of 1672, a position which he held until May 1674.

Easton's terms as president and governor occurred during three separate phases of Rhode Island history. From 1650 to 1651 he acted as head of the united towns of Providence, Warwick, Portsmouth and Newport, a union that was already in serious jeopardy. By May of 1654, when Easton resumed the post of president, the long-threatened disruption of this political alliance had taken place. Despite a General Assembly which convened at the time of his election and which theoretically represented all four communities, Easton was unable to exercise effective jurisdiction over the residents of Providence and Warwick. Late in August of 1654, however, Roger Williams managed to persuade the four feuding towns to re-establish their earlier connection, and Easton soon stepped down in Williams' favor. Almost two decades later Easton returned as chief executive, but this time he served as governor of a more cohesive colony which was under the firm political control of men who were also members of the Society of Friends.

The aged Easton died on August 15, 1675, little more than a year after he left the governor's office for the final time. He was interred in the Friends' Burial Ground in Newport.

Bibliography: George C. Mason, "Nicholas Easton *vs.* the City of Newport," Rhode Island Historical Society, *Collections*, VII (1885), 327-44. *DAB*.

GORTON, Samuel, 1651-1652 *(as President of Providence and Warwick)*

Born *circa* 1592 in Gorton, near Manchester, England, the son of Thomas and Anne Gorton. Brother of Thomas (died young), Katherine, William (died young), Thomas, Francis (died in infancy), Mary, Edward and one other who died in infancy. Married before January 11, 1630 to Mary Maplett, by whom he was the father of Samuel, John, Benjamin, Mahershalalhashbaz, Mary, Sarah, Ann, Elizabeth and Susanna.

Worked in London as a cloth finisher while a young man. Immigrated to New England in 1637 and settled first in Boston and later in Plymouth, but was banished from both of those communities for his radical religious beliefs. Travelled to Aquidneck (later part of Rhode Island), where in April 1639 he helped to establish a government at Portsmouth. Encountered new opposition from authorities on Aquidneck, and eventually moved to Shawomet (now Warwick, Rhode Island). Charged with being an enemy "of all civil authority" by officials in Boston, who imprisoned him in November of 1643;

banished from Massachusetts Bay in March 1644, and for four years sought satisfaction for the harassment which he had endured. After a trip to England, returned to Warwick in May 1648 and quickly became a prominent political figure. Chosen as an Assistant from Warwick to the Rhode Island General Court in 1649. Became President of the towns of Providence and Warwick in the autumn of 1651, a position he held until May 1652.

Although his major significance was in his activities as a religious controversialist, Gorton also displayed a fondness for politics, especially after 1648. During his brief period as president of the towns of Providence and Warwick, Gorton firmly opposed the claims of Nicholas Easton, who branded as illegal Gorton's administration of those two mainland settlements apart from the island towns of Portsmouth and Newport. By May of 1652, when Gorton turned over the presidency of the mainland to John Smith, the four squabbling communities had still done little to resolve their politically chaotic situation.

Subsequent to his term as chief executive, Gorton became an Assistant to the General Court governing Providence and Warwick. Except for a brief interval, he was also a member of Rhode Island's General Court of Commissioners from 1656 to 1663, after Roger Williams had succeeded in reuniting the four towns. Later, following the implementation of the Charter of 1663, Gorton served intermittently from 1664 to 1670 as a Deputy from Warwick in the Rhode Island General Assembly. Gorton died in Warwick, Rhode Island sometime between November 27 and December 10, 1677.

Bibliography: Samuel Gorton, *Simplicities Defense Against Seven-Headed Policy. Or Innocency Vindicated* . . . (London, 1646); Samuel Gorton, *Saltmarsh Returned from the Dead* . . . (London, 1655); Samuel Gorton, *An Antidote Against the Common Plague of the World* (London, 1657); John M. Mackie, *Life of Samuel Gorton*, in Jared Sparks, ed., *Library of American Biography*, n.s., vol. V (Boston, 1845); George A. Brayton, *A Defence of Samuel Gorton and the Settlers of Shawomet* (Providence, 1883); L. G. Janes, *Samuel Gorton* (Providence, 1896); Adelos Gorton, *The Life and Times of Samuel Gorton* . . . (Philadelphia, 1907); Kenneth W. Porter, "Samuell Gorton, New England Firebrand," *New England Quarterly*, VII (September 1934), 405-44; William Greene Roelker, *Massachusetts' War with Samuell Gorton* . . . (Warwick, R.I., 1942); William Greene Roelker, "Samuel Gorton's Master Stroke," *Rhode Island History*, II (January 1943), 1-10. Genealogical information about Gorton and the Gorton family appears in the *New England Historical and Genealogical Register*, LXXXII (April-July 1928), 185-93, 333-42, and CV (October 1951), 258-60. *DAB, DNB*.

SANFORD, John, 1653 *(as President of Portsmouth and Newport)*

Probably born between 1606 and 1608 in England; parents unknown, although he seems to have belonged to a family of prominence, falling somewhere between the gentry and the highest rank of the yeomanry. Appears to have had at least two brothers. Married in about 1631-32 to Elizabeth Webb, by whom he was the father of John and Samuel; after the death of his first wife, remarried in or about 1636 to Bridget Hutchinson; father by this marriage of Eliphal, Peleg (who was governor of Rhode Island from 1680 to 1683), Endcome (died young), Restcome, William, Esbon, Francis (died in infancy), Elisha and Anne.

Worked for a time as a servant in the household of John Winthrop. Immigrated to Massachusetts Bay in 1631, and became a Freeman of Boston in April 1632. Appointed to various town committees in the 1630's; from 1636 to early 1638, served as a Boston Selectman. Lost favor with the Winthrop faction because of his support for Anne Hutchinson, and left Boston in about mid-March 1638; present at the first Portsmouth town meeting in 1638, and two years later took part in the union of Portsmouth with Newport. Chosen as a Constable for Portsmouth at about the same time. Performed various other public functions during the 1640's, and from 1647 to 1649 served as an Assistant for Portsmouth. Became Head Magistrate of the town of Portsmouth in June 1651; less than two years later, in the spring of 1653, was elected President of Portsmouth and Newport.

Sanford died soon after his selection as president. His will was dated June 22, 1653, and on November 20 of that year Sanford's widow received receipts from his two eldest sons for their legacies. Consequently, his period in office could have lasted no more than six months. One of the colony's major concerns in 1653 was the recent declaration of war between England and the Dutch, and it is reasonable to assume that Sanford may have begun to make defensive preparations before his death. In April 1653, for example, one month before his election as president, Sanford had been appointed a Conservator of the Peace for Portsmouth, charged with the protection of the community from foreign attack. Political dissension among Rhode Island's towns was another source of uneasiness during the brief Sanford administration, as Providence and Warwick on the mainland continued their separation from the island towns of Portsmouth and Newport.

Bibliography: G. Andrews Moriarty, "President John Sanford of Portsmouth, R.I., and His Family," *New England Historical and Genealogical Register*, CIII (July-October 1949), 208-16, 271-77; Edwin G. Sanford, "The Early Years of President John Sanford of Boston, Mass., and Portsmouth, R.I.," *New England Historical and Genealogical Register*, CXIV (April 1960), 84-95; Jack M. Sanford, *President John Sanford of. . .Portsmouth, Rhode Island* (Rutland, Vt., 1966).

DEXTER, Gregory, 1653-1654 *(as President of Providence and Warwick)*

Thought to have been born in 1610 in Old, Northamptonshire, England; names of parents unknown. A Baptist. Married to Abigail Fullerton; father of Stephen, James, John and Abigail.

Apprenticed to a stationer (printer) in England, and in December 1639 was admitted as a Master Printer at Stationers' Hall in London; worked for several years in a London printing house. Immigrated to New England in about 1644, probably accompanying Roger Williams. Represented Providence as a Commissioner in the General Court (Assembly) from 1647 to 1648 and from 1650 to 1654; acted as Moderator of a number of Court sessions held between 1652 and 1654. Also served in other public capacities, including Clerk of the Peace (1649), Surveyor of Highways (1652), and Town Clerk of Providence (probably 1648-55). Elected President of Providence and Warwick in the spring of 1653, serving until May 1654.

Dexter's year as president of Providence and Warwick was marked by considerable political turmoil, as the mainland communities over which he exercised jurisdiction remained separate from the island towns of Portsmouth and Newport. Nevertheless, despite the secession which complicated his administration, Dexter was still convinced that he enjoyed a more tranquil environment than that of England. When Sir Henry Vane wrote to ask why Rhode Island and Providence Plantations were torn by so much divisiveness, Dexter pointedly replied that at least they were free from the "overzealous fire of the Godly and Christian magistrates" who plagued his native country.

Following his term as chief executive, Dexter was ordained in 1655 as Pastor of the First Baptist Church in Providence. He also served as a Deputy in the Rhode Island General Assembly in 1664 and 1666. For the remainder of his long life, Dexter took little part in politics, although he was occasionally honored with positions of public trust. In April 1676, for example, he was named to a committee of sixteen which advised the Assembly on means of defending the colony during King Philip's War. Dexter probably died in Providence in 1700, and was buried in his private burying ground.

Bibliography: S. C. Newman, *Dexter Genealogy: Being a Record of the Families Descended from Rev. Gregory Dexter . . .* (Providence, 1859); Howard M. Chapin, "Gregory Dexter, Master Printer," Rhode Island Historical Society, *Collections*, XII (October 1919), 105-21; Bradford Fuller Swan, *Gregory Dexter of London and New England, 1610-1700* (Rochester, N.Y., 1949); Bradford F. Swan, "A Note on Gregory Dexter," *Rhode Island History*, 20 (October 1961), 125-26.

ARNOLD, Benedict, 1657-1660, 1662-1666, 1669-1672, 1677-1678

Born on December 21, 1615 at (or near) Leamington, Warwickshire, England, the son of William and Christian (Peak) Arnold. Brother of Elizabeth, Joanna and Stephen. Married on December 17, 1640 to Damaris Westcott; father of Benedict, Josiah, Oliver, Caleb, Godsgift, Freelove, Damaris, Penelope and another who died young.

Arrived in New England with his family in June 1635. With his father, became one of the first settlers of Providence in the late 1630's, and in 1651 moved to Newport. Served from 1654 to 1663 as a member of the General Court (Assembly) of Commissioners which, until the implementation of the Charter of 1663, acted as a legislative body for the colony; also served as an Assistant for Newport at various times between 1654 and 1661. Named President of the colony in the spring of 1657, filling that office until 1660, and again from 1662 to 1663. Became the first Governor of Rhode Island (after the Charter of 1663 was received in November of that year); served as governor, with two intervals, until his death in 1678.

Arnold's tenure as chief executive spanned over two decades of Rhode Island history. Perhaps this period's most significant political development was the granting of a royal charter to the colony in 1663, a charter which replaced the patent that had been issued by authority of Parliament during the English Civil Wars. Partly because of a confusion over jurisdiction which this charter had failed to resolve, Rhode Island and Connecticut were soon involved in a bitter quarrel over the Narragansett Country. In 1664 a royal commission arrived in the colony and, in an effort to settle the issue, proclaimed the Narragansett Country to be the "King's Province" and placed it temporarily under Rhode Island. Nevertheless, the dispute, which was further complicated by a group of proprietors who claimed to hold a mortgage on the territory, continued to be a fertile source of dissension throughout Arnold's administration. With the Narragansett question still unsettled, Arnold died in office on June 19, 1678.

Bibliography: Hamilton Bullock Tompkins, "Benedict Arnold, First Governor of Rhode Island," Newport Historical Society, *Bulletin*, no. 30 (October 1919), 1-18; Elisha Stephen Arnold, comp., *The Arnold Memorial: William Arnold of Providence and Pawtuxet, 1587-1675, and a Genealogy of His Descendants* (Rutland, Vt., 1935); Ethan L. Arnold, *An Arnold Family Record: 323 Years in America. A Record of Some of the Descendants of William Arnold and His Son, Governor Benedict Arnold of Rhode Island and His Grandson, Benedict Arnold, Junior, 1635 to 1958* [Elkhart, Ind., 1958].

BRENTON, William, 1660-1662, 1666-1669

Born, probably early in the seventeenth century, in Hammersmith, Middlesex County, England, a member of a family of some prominence. Married to Martha Burton; father of Mary, Martha, Elizabeth, Sarah, Mehitable, Jahleel, Abigail, William and Ebenezer.

Became a prominent trader and stockbreeder in the years following his immigration to America in 1633. First elected as a Selectman of Boston in 1634, and became a Deputy in the Massachusetts General Court in 1635. Fell into disfavor with the Winthrop faction during the Hutchinson controversy, and left the colony to take part in the founding of Newport in 1639; served as Deputy Governor of Portsmouth and Newport from 1640 to 1647. Returned to Massachusetts Bay in the early 1650's, and again served as a Boston selectman from 1652 to 1657. Eventually returned to Newport, where from May 1660 to May 1662, he acted as President of the four towns which comprised Rhode Island. After leaving the presidency, became Deputy Governor of the newly-chartered colony of Rhode Island in 1663, as office which he held until shortly before his election as Governor in the spring of 1666; served as chief executive until May 1669.

Like that of his predecessor in office, Brenton's period as governor of Rhode Island was troubled by land disputes, especially over the Narragansett Country. Still, these years witnessed the steady growth of Rhode Island's trading community, a growth spurred in part by the decision taken in the late 1650's to permit Quakers to settle in the colony. By the end of Brenton's administration, a group of "Quaker Grandees" had begun to establish commercial connections with other Quaker and non-Quaker merchants in American outposts, such as Barbados and Virginia.

Following his service as governor, Brenton moved to Taunton, Massachusetts. Although he was again elected governor of Rhode Island in May 1672, he refused to accept the office. Brenton died in Taunton two years later, in 1674.

CLARKE, Walter, 1676-1677, 1686, [1689]*, 1696-1698

Born *circa* 1638 in Newport, Rhode Island, the son of Governor Jeremiah (or Jeremy) and Frances (Latham) Dungan Clarke. A Quaker. Brother of Mary, Jeremiah, Latham, Weston, James and Sarah. Married in about 1660 to Content Greenman, by whom he was the father of Mary, Content and a son whose name is unknown; after the death of his first wife in March 1666, remarried in February 1667 to Hannah Scott, by whom he had Hannah, Catharine, Frances, Jeremiah and Deliverance; following the death of his second wife in July 1681, married a third time on March 6, 1683 to Freeborn

(Williams) Hart, who died in December 1709; married a fourth time on August 31, 1711 to Sarah (Prior) Gould; no children by his third or fourth wives.

Served as a Deputy in the Rhode Island General Assembly in 1667, 1670, 1672 and 1673; elected as an Assistant of the colony in 1673, a position he filled until 1675; also acted as an assistant in 1699. Became Deputy Governor in the spring of 1679, and served until May 1686; again held office as deputy governor from May 1700 until his death. Chosen as Governor of Rhode Island in the spring of 1676, and served until May 1677; also acted in that capacity from May to June of 1686, and from January 1696 to March 1698. Elected but declined to serve as governor in the spring of 1689.

While Clarke actually occupied the office of governor for less than four years in all, his terms encompassed more than two decades of Rhode Island history. During Clarke's first administration the colony was troubled by the still unresolved question of ownership of the Narragansett Country, but the colony was at least enjoying the firm guidance of its powerful Quaker leadership. By the spring of 1686 this political picture had changed dramatically, as Rhode Island learned that its charter had been suspended and that the colony was to be considered part of the Dominion of New England in the future. Because of this development, Clarke's term as governor ended abruptly on June 29, 1686, less than two months after his election, although he continued to keep the whereabouts of the Rhode Island charter hidden from Dominion officials. Clarke refused to served as chief executive in the spring of 1689, probably because his Quaker beliefs precluded any involvement in military preparation for England's war against France. Almost seven years later, however, in January 1696, he agreed to replace the deceased Governor Caleb Carr. Clarke's final administration was marked by considerable controversy over Rhode Island's alleged role as a refuge for pirates. Threatened by impeachment because of his refusal to swear to uphold the Acts of Trade, Clarke resigned in March 1698 in favor of his nephew, Samuel Cranston.

Following his resignation as governor, Clarke remained in public service, holding office as an assistant in 1699 and as deputy governor from May 1700 until his death on May 23, 1714. He was interred in the Clifton Burial Ground in Newport, Rhode Island.

Bibliography: George Austin Morrison, Jr., *The "Clarke" Families of Rhode Island* (New York, 1902); Louise Tracy, "Historic Strain of Blood in America . . . Progeny of Jeremiah Clarke and His Wife, Frances Latham, 'Mother of Governors' . . .," *Journal of American History*, II (1908), 501-13; "Genealogical Research in England: Clarke," *New England Historical and Genealogical Register*, LXXIV (January-April 1920), 68-76, 130-40; Alfred Rudulph Justice, comp., *Ancestry of Jeremy Clarke of Rhode Island and Dungan Genealogy* (Philadelphia, 1923?). *DAB*.

*Elected Governor, but declined to serve in that year.

CRANSTON, John, 1678-1680

Born *circa* 1626 in either England or Scotland, the son of the Reverend James Cranstoun, a chaplain to King Charles I; as a child, became the ward of Jeremiah (or Jeremy) Clarke, a prominent London merchant who later served as governor of Rhode Island from 1648 to 1649. Brother of Samuel, Caleb and perhaps others. Married on June 3, 1658 to Mary Clarke; father of Samuel (who was governor of Rhode Island from 1698 to 1727), Caleb, James (died young), Jeremiah, Mary (died young), Benjamin, William, John, Elizabeth and Peleg.

Immigrated to New England in about 1637, and worked as a physician for a number of years. Served as Attorney General for Providence and Warwick in 1654, and continued to act as attorney general from 1654, after the union of the four towns was re-established, until 1656. Also appointed as a Newport Commissioner in the General Court (Assembly) in 1655, and held that office, apart from two brief intervals, until 1663; following the implementation of the Rhode Island Charter of 1663, served the colony as a Deputy from 1664 to 1668. Became an Assistant in 1668, and filled that position until his election as Deputy Governor in 1672; served as deputy governor until 1673 and again from 1676 to the autumn of 1678, when he replaced the recently deceased governor, William Coddington. Also named "Major and chief Captain of all the colony forces" in April 1676, during King Philip's War.

Cranston's brief administration was largely occupied by the continuing dispute over ownership of the Narragansett Country. The end of King Philip's War had encouraged new settlers from Rhode Island to push into the controversial territory, a development which for the moment gave the colony a strategic advantage over the claims of Connecticut and the Narragansett Proprietors. Still, the legalities of the case remained clouded by a complex and contradictory set of agreements, and at the time of Cranston's death in office on March 12, 1680, the issue seemed further from resolution than ever. Cranston was buried in Newport's Common Burial Ground.

Bibliography: Henry E. Turner, *The Two Governors Cranston* (Newport, R.I., 1889); William Jones, "The Ancestry of Governors John and Samuel Cranston of Rhode Island," *New England Historical and Genealogical Register*, LXXIX (January 1925), 57-66; Charles Albert DuBosq and William Jones, "Descendants of Gov. John Cranston of Rhode Island," *New England Historical and Genealogical Register*, LXXIX (July 1925), 247-68; Bertha W. Clark, "Notes on Two Early Rhode Island Governors," *Rhode Island History*, XII (July 1953), 72-75. *DAB*.

SANFORD, Peleg, 1680-1683

Born on May 10, 1639 in Portsmouth, Rhode Island, the son of President John and Bridget (Hutchinson) Sanford. Brother of Eliphal, Endcome (died young), Restcome, William, Esbon, Francis (died in infancy), Elisha and Anne. Married to Mary Brenton, the daughter of Rhode Island Governor William Brenton; father by his first wife of several children, all of whom died young; remarried on December 1, 1674 to Mary Coddington, the daughter of Rhode Island Governor William Coddington, Sr.; father by his second wife of Anne, Bridget, Elizabeth, Peleg, Jr., William, and a son and daughter, both of whom died young.

Lived in Barbados for several years, where he was involved in commerce; returned to Newport, Rhode Island in 1666, and became a prominent trader and land owner. Appointed Captain of a troop of horse soldiers in July 1667. Served as an Assistant from 1667 to 1670 and again from 1677 to 1679; also acted as a Deputy for Newport from 1670 to 1677. Served as General Treasurer of the colony from 1678 to 1681, and was named Major of the Rhode Island military force in 1679. Elected Governor of Rhode Island in March of 1680, replacing the deceased John Cranston; filled that office until May 1683.

Sanford's administration, like that of his predecessors, was troubled by disputes stemming from the controversy over the Narragansett Country. At the same time, Rhode Island faced a potentially even greater problem during these years, as Edward Randolph, the zealous Crown agent, continued his investigations into colonial violations of English trade laws. By the end of Sanford's period in office, Massachusetts was already in danger of losing its charter, and Rhode Island had likewise become more vulnerable, particularly since Randolph's criticism of the smuggling which he saw in Boston could also be applied to Rhode Island's small commercial community.

Following his tenure as governor, Sanford continued to hold various military and political positions. In 1687 he was named Lieutenant Colonel of the colony's military, and in the late 1680's he became a member of the Council of Governor General Sir Edmund Andros. When the deposed Andros sought refuge in Newport in 1689, however, Sanford had him arrested and sent back to Boston. Toward the end of the seventeenth century, Sanford was made a Vice-Admiralty Court Judge, an office in which he devoted much attention to the problem of piracy. Sanford died shortly before September 1, 1701.

Bibliography: *The Letter Book of Peleg Sanford of Newport, Merchant . . . 1666-1668* (Providence, 1928); G. Andrews Moriarty, "President John Sanford of Portsmouth, R.I., and His Family," *New England Historical and Genealogical Register*, CIII (July-October 1949), 208-16, 271-77; Jack M. Sanford, *President John Sanford of . . . Portsmouth, Rhode Island* (Rutland, Vt., 1966).

CODDINGTON, William, Jr., 1683-1685

Born on January 18, 1651 in Newport, Rhode Island, the eldest son of Governor William Coddington and his third wife, Anne (Brinley) Coddington. Brother of Nathaniel, Mary, Thomas, John, Noah (died young), Anne (died young) and Anne. Never married.

Named a Freeman of Newport in May 1675. Served as a Deputy in the Rhode Island General Assembly from 1679 to 1680, and as an Assistant from 1681 to 1683. Elected Governor of Rhode Island in the spring of 1683, and served in that capacity until May 1685.

During the administration of the younger Coddington, the longstanding controversy over the Narragansett Country flared up again when a commission appointed by Charles II attempted to resolve the issue. Led by Lieutenant Governor Edward Cranfield of New Hampshire, the commissioners decided that jurisdiction over the Narragansett Country should be given to Connecticut, while land ownership rightfully belonged to the company of speculators who had earlier purchased the land from the Indians. Upset by these proceedings, the Rhode Island government denied the legality of the Cranfield commission. In response, the commissioner's report to the King criticized the "riotous manner" displayed by the Rhode Islanders during their deliberations. Towards the end of Coddington's term, news arrived of the revocation of the Rhode Island charter. Despite urging by the Assembly that he accept re-election during this period of political uncertainty, Coddington declined the offer, and Henry Bull was selected as his replacement.

Coddington appears to have taken no further part in politics after leaving the governor's office. He died on February 5, 1689, and was interred in the Coddington Burial Ground.

BULL, Henry, 1685-1686, 1690

Born in 1610 in England; names of parents unknown. A Puritan, but became a Quaker in later life. Married in (or before) 1636 to a woman named Elizabeth; after his first wife's death in October 1665, remarried *circa* 1666 to Esther Allen; following the death of his second wife in March 1676, married a third time on March 28, 1677 to Ann (Clayton) Easton, the widow of Rhode Island Governor Nicholas Easton; father by his first wife of Jireh, Amey, and a daughter whose name may have been Elizabeth.

Emigrated from England in July 1635, and joined the Congregational church at Roxbury, Massachusetts a year later. Became a supporter of the religious ideas of Anne Hutchinson; eventually forced to leave Massachusetts because of his support for Mrs. Hutchinson's "opinions and revelations." Moved to Portsmouth, where he became one of the founders of that community. Named Corporal of the Portsmouth Train Band in 1638, and a year later was appointed Sergeant, a position which had among its duties the keeping of the town prison. Participated in the settlement of Newport in 1639, and served as that town's Sergeant from 1640 to 1642. Named a Commissioner of the Rhode Island General Assembly in 1655, an office which he held until 1657. Served as a Deputy from Newport in 1666, 1672-74, 1679-81, and 1690; acted as an Assistant of the colony from 1674 to 1675. Became Governor of Rhode Island in May 1685, and filled that position until May of 1686; also served as governor from February to May of 1690.

During Bull's first period as chief executive, plans were already underway in England to make Rhode Island part of a vast Dominion of New England. Indeed, by the beginning of 1686 the "King's Province" in the Narragansett Country had already been included in the new governmental scheme, forecasting the fate of the rest of Rhode Island less than a year later. By early 1690, however, the Dominion had collapsed and its Governor General, Sir Edmund Andros, deposed. Under these circumstances Rhode Island was anxious to restore its charter government, but many of the colony's leading men were not yet convinced that the Dominion had been permanently destroyed. Consequently, few were prepared to risk serving as chief executive, and it was left to Bull, now about eighty years old, to take up the reins of administration until the election of John Easton in May of 1690.

After his second period as governor, the aged Bull appears to have taken no further part in the colony's politics. He died in Newport, Rhode Island on January 22, 1694, and was interred in the Coddington Burial Ground.

Bibliography: Henry Bull, 4th, "The Bull Family of Newport," Newport Historical Society, *Bulletin*, no. 81 (October 1931), 1-30.

DUDLEY, Joseph, 1686

also Massachusetts and New Hampshire, 1686, 1702-1715

Born on September 23, 1647 in Roxbury, Massachusetts, the son of Governor Thomas and Catherine (Dighton) Hackburn Dudley. A Congregationalist, but converted to Anglicanism in the 1690's. Brother of Deborah and Paul; half-brother of Samuel, Anne (the poet, who married Governor Simon Bradstreet), Patience, Sarah and Mercy. Married in 1668 to Rebecca Tyng, by whom he was the father of Thomas, Edward, Joseph, Paul, Samuel, John, Rebecca, Catherine (died in infancy), Ann, William, Daniel, Catherine and Mary.

Attended Harvard College, graduating from that institution in 1665. Served as a member of the Massachusetts General Court, representing Roxbury, from

1673 to 1676. Participated in King Philip's War, after which he was chosen as an Assistant of the colony in almost every year until 1685; also acted as one of the Massachusetts commissioners to the United Colonies from 1677 to 1681. Sailed for England in May 1682, in an unsuccessful attempt to save the Massachusetts charter. Returned to Boston in October 1683, and two years later, in October of 1685, received a royal commission making him President of the Council and chief executive of Massachusetts Bay, New Hampshire and the King's Province (later part of Rhode Island); assumed office in Massachusetts in May 1686, establishing his authority in New Hampshire and the King's Province a short time later; relinquished the governorship to Sir Edmund Andros in December 1686, but remained in office under the Dominion of New England as a member of Andros' Council. Also served for a time as Chief Justice of the Massachusetts Superior Court during the Andros regime. Jailed for ten months following the demise of Andros in the spring of 1689, and eventually transported to England, where he successfully defended his behavior during the Dominion period. Returned to America in 1691 and acted briefly as head of the Council in New York and Chief Justice of that province, although he soon gave up those offices and returned to Massachusetts in 1692. Sailed for England a short time later, remained from 1693 to 1702, and became Deputy Governor of the Isle of Wight during his stay. Awarded a commission as Royal Governor of Massachusetts Bay and New Hampshire in February of 1702, and arrived in America to begin his administration in June of that year.

Although Dudley's first tenure as governor had lasted for only about seven months in 1686, his subsequent support of Sir Edmund Andros during the Dominion period made him especially unpopular in New England, a feeling which was still strong when he appeared in Boston sixteen years later with a new commission to govern. Forced to begin his administration under these inauspicious circumstances, Dudley did little to make himself more acceptable in either Massachusetts or New Hampshire. In Massachusetts, for example, he began by purging old political enemies like Elisha Cooke, who was removed from his position as judge of the Superior Court. Although he apparently modified his arbitrary behavior after 1708, Dudley left a legacy of mistrust and suspicion which plagued the administration of Samuel Shute, his successor as royal governor.

Following his departure from office in 1715, Dudley retired to private life until his death on April 2, 1720. He was buried in Roxbury, Massachusetts.

Bibliography: [D. D.], "Governor Thomas Dudley and His Descendants," *New England Historical and Genealogical Register*, X (April, October 1856), 133-42, 337-44; George Adlard, *The Sutton-Dudleys of England and the Dudleys of Massachusetts in New England*... (New York, 1862); Dean Dudley, *History of the Dudley Family* (Wakefield, Mass., 1886-94); Everett Kimball, *The Public Life of Joseph Dudley* (New York, 1911); Augustine Jones, *Joseph Dudley, Ninth Governor of Massachusetts* (Boston, 1916);

Arthur H. Buffinton, "Governor Dudley and the Proposed Treaty of Neutrality, 1705," *Publications of the Colonial Society of Massachusetts*, XXVI (1927), 211-29; William A. Polf, "Puritan Gentlemen: The Dudleys of Massachusetts, 1576-1686," unpub. Ph.D. diss., Syracuse University, 1973. *DAB*.

ANDROS, Sir Edmund, 1686-1689

New York, 1674-1677, 1678-1681; East Jersey, 1680-1681, 1688-1689; Massachusetts, 1686-1689; New Hampshire, 1686-1689; Plymouth Colony, 1686-1689; Connecticut, 1687-1689; West Jersey, 1688-1689; Virginia, 1692-1698; Maryland, 1693, 1694

Born on December 6, 1637 on the Island of Guernsey, the son of Amice and Elizabeth (Stone) Andros. Married to a woman who was related to the Earl of Craven.

Served as Major of a regiment of foot soldiers which in 1666 sailed from England to defend the West Indies against the Dutch. Named a Landgrave of Carolina in 1672; received a commission from the Duke of York in July 1674 to govern the colony of New York, and acted in that capacity, except for an absence in England between November 1677 and August 1678, until January 1681; also exercised control over East Jersey from 1680 until his recall early in the following year. Knighted in about 1681, became Gentleman of the Privy Chamber to Charles II in 1683, and was appointed Lieutenant Colonel of the Princess of Denmark's regiment of horse soldiers in 1685. Commissioned Royal Governor of the Dominion of New England in June 1686, and established his authority in Massachusetts Bay, Maine, New Hampshire, Plymouth and Rhode Island (including the King's Province) in December of that year; Connecticut in November of 1687; and the Jerseys and New York in August 1688 (although Francis Nicholson presided as Andros' substitute in the latter colony). Arrested and sent to England following the overthrow of the Dominion in the spring of 1689, but later received a commission as Royal Governor of Virginia, and served as that colony's chief executive from September 1692 to December 1698; also acted briefly as Governor of Maryland in 1693 and 1694, in the absence of any other executive authority.

Andros' first tenure in New York was marked by several important achievements, especially the improvement of the colony's defenses and the settlement of some boundary difficulties with Connecticut. Nevertheless, even at this stage he had begun to display an inclination to behave in an arbitrary fashion. Perhaps the clearest illustration of this tendency was the high-handed manner in which Andros superseded the authority of Governor Philip Carteret in the Jerseys, provoking Carteret to complain that Andros aimed at "usurping the government" of his colony. This insensitivity to local politics became even more noticeable after Andros assumed control of the Dominion of New England. Following a troubled tenure of less than two and one-half years, he was deposed in the spring of 1689, shortly after news of the Glorious Revolution in England reached Boston.

Although Andros was exonerated of the charges brought against his Dominion government and took over as Virginia's chief executive in 1692, he soon encountered resistance from local leaders like Commissary James Blair, who bitterly informed one London official that Andros "never did any considerable service to the King, nor the people" during his colonial career. Finally, late in 1698, Andros departed for England. He served as Lieutenant Governor of Guernsey from 1704 to 1706, and died in London in February 1714.

Bibliography: "Commission to Sir Edmund Andros," Massachusetts Historical Society, *Collections*, 3rd ser., vol. VII (Boston, 1838), 138-49; W. H. Whitmore, ed., *Andros Tracts: Being a Collection of Pamphlets and Official Papers ... of the Andros Government and the Establishment of the Second Charter of Massachusetts*, 3 vols. (New York, 1868-74) (Publications of the Prince Society, vols. V-VII); Robert N. Toppan, ed., "Andros Records," American Antiquarian Society, *Proceedings*, n.s., vol. XIII (1899-1900), 237-68, 463-99; J.H. Tuttle, ed., "Land Warrants under Andros," Colonial Society of Massachusetts, *Publications*, XXI (1919), 292-361; Albert C. Bates, "Expedition of Sir Edmund Andros to Connecticut in 1687," AAS, *Proceedings*, n.s., vol. 48 (October 1938), 276-99; Jeanne G. Bloom, "Sir Edmund Andros: A Study in Seventeenth-Century Colonial Administration," unpub. Ph.D. diss., Yale University, 1962; Robert C. Ritchie, "London Merchants, the New York Market, and the Recall of Sir Edmund Andros," *New York History*, LVII (January 1976), 5-29. *DAB, DNB*.

COGGESHALL, John, Jr., 1689-1690

Born *circa* 1620 in Essex County, England, the son of President John and Mary Coggeshall. A Quaker. Brother of Ann, Mary, Joshua, James, Hananiel (died young), Wait and Bedaiah (died young). Married on June 17, 1647 to Elizabeth Baulstone, by whom he was the father of John, Elizabeth and William; after receiving a divorce from his first wife, remarried in December 1655 to Patience Throckmorton; father by his second wife of Freegift, James, Mary, Joseph, Rebecca, Patience, Benjamin, Content (died young) and Content; following the death of his second wife in September 1676, married a third time on October 1, 1679 to Mary (Hedge) Sturgis, by whom he was the father of Joseph, Abraham, Samuel and Elisha.

Served as General Treasurer for Portsmouth and Newport in 1653-54, and in the latter year also became General Treasurer for Providence and Warwick.

Acted as a Commissioner in the General Court (Assembly) from 1654 to 1663; after the implementation of the Rhode Island Charter of 1663, served the colony as an Assistant (1663-65, 1672, 1674, 1676, 1683-86), Deputy (1665, 1667-71, 1675, 1683), General Treasurer (1664-72), General Recorder (1676-77, 1691-92), and Major for the Island (1683-84). Elected Deputy Governor in 1686, an office which he again filled in 1689-90 following the overthrow of the Dominion of New England; during his second term as deputy governor, presided as the colony's chief executive when Governor Walter Clarke declined to serve soon after his election in the spring of 1689.

A Quaker with strong pacifist beliefs, Clarke's decision to step down as governor was probably due to his reluctance to prepare the colony for war after the outbreak of hostilities between England and France. Whatever Clarke's motives, the colony was left without a governor at a critical time, and Coggeshall assumed control until the aged Henry Bull accepted the governorship in February 1690. During Coggeshall's brief administration, Rhode Island began to seek royal approval for its resumption of government under the Charter of 1663, a charter which had been supplanted in 1686 by the Dominion of New England under Sir Edmund Andros. Andros was out of power by the spring of 1689, however, and Coggeshall eventually decided to send a petition to William and Mary which proclaimed his colony's loyalty and asked that its charter be confirmed.

Except for his service as general recorder in 1691 and 1692, Coggeshall appears to have taken little part in Rhode Island politics following his tenure as deputy governor. He died on October 1, 1708.

Bibliography: Charles Pierce Coggeshall and Thellwell Russell Coggeshall, comps., *The Coggeshalls in America: Genealogy of the Descendants of John Coggeshall of Newport, with a Brief Notice of Their English Antecedents* (Boston, 1930).

EASTON, John, 1690-1695

Born in 1624 in Wales, the son of Governor Nicholas Easton and his first wife, whose name is unknown. A Quaker. Brother of Peter. Married on January 4, 1661 to Mehitable Gaunt, by whom he was the father of James, Peter, Mary, John and Paul; after the death of his first wife in November 1673, remarried to a woman named Alice; no children by his second wife.

Immigrated with his father to New England in 1634, and later became one of the first settlers of Newport. Served as Attorney General for Portsmouth and Newport from 1653 to 1654; also acted as Rhode Island's attorney general from 1656 to 1674, with several brief intervals. Elected in 1654 as a Newport Commissioner to the General Court (Assembly), filling that office until 1660 and again in 1663; after the implementation of the Rhode Island Charter of

1663, served as a Deputy in the General Assembly from 1665 to 1666 and from 1671 to 1672. First elected as an Assistant of the colony in 1666, a position he held, apart from three brief intervals, until 1690; also served as Deputy Governor from 1674 to 1676. Elected Governor of Rhode Island in the spring of 1690, and continued in that capacity until May 1695.

Easton's administration was plagued by confusion over the status of Rhode Island's charter, a confusion which resulted in large part from the sudden demise of the Dominion of New England. Although Rhode Islanders attempted to clarify their legal position, the recent revolution in England, combined with the colony's relative insignificance in the imperial scheme, made the restoration of regular government a long and laborious process. Rhode Island also provoked officials in London during Easton's period as chief executive, when reports reached England in 1694 that the colony's deputy governor had granted commissions to privateers.

Easton appears to have retired from public life after leaving the governor's office. He died on December 12, 1705, and was buried in the Coddington Burial Ground. Easton was the author of a *Narrative of the Causes which Led to Philip's War*..., a work which remains an important source of information on that conflict.

Bibliography: John Easton, *A Narrative of the Causes which Led to Philip's Indian War*... (Albany, N.Y., 1858). *DAB*.

CARR, Caleb, 1695

Born on December 9, 1616 in London, England, the son of Benjamin and Martha (Hardington) Carr. Brother of Robert and perhaps others. Married to Mercy Vaughn, by whom he was the father of Nicholas, Mercy (died young), Caleb, Samuel, Mercy (or Mary), John and Edward; after the death of his first wife in 1675, remarried to Sarah (Clarke) Pinner; father by his second wife of Francis, James, Sarah and Elizabeth.

Sailed for America with his brother Robert in 1635. Served as a Commissioner of the Rhode Island General Assembly in 1654 and again from 1658 to 1662. Acted as General Treasurer of Rhode Island in 1661 and 1662. Represented Newport as a Deputy in the colony's Assembly, with several intervals, from 1664 to 1690; also served as an Assistant at various times between 1679 and 1691. Presided as a Justice of the General Quarter Sessions and Inferior Court of Common Pleas in 1687 and 1688, during the regime of Governor General Sir Edmund Andros. Chosen Governor of Rhode Island in the spring of 1695, but drowned seven months later.

Although Carr's administration was cut short by his accidental death on December 17, 1695, his brief period in office was marked by a dramatic meeting in Jamestown, Rhode Island, where the governor, acting as moderator, helped to reinstitute that town's government. This election of local officials in Jamestown symbolized the progress made toward restoring Rhode Island's regular political system, a system which had fallen into disarray following the confusion that attended the demise of the Dominion government.

Bibliography: Arthur Adkins Carr, *The Carr Book: Sketches of the Lives of Many of the Descendants of Robert and Caleb Carr* . . . (Ticonderoga, N.Y., 1947); Bertha W. Clark, "Notes on Two Early Rhode Island Governors," *Rhode Island History*, XII (July 1953), 72-75.

CRANSTON, Samuel, 1698-1727

Born on August 7, 1659 in Newport, Rhode Island, the son of John and Mary (Clarke) Cranston. Brother of Caleb, James (died young), Jeremiah, Mary (died young), Benjamin, William, John, Elizabeth and Peleg. Married in 1680 to Mary Hart, by whom he was the father of John, Samuel, Thomas, Frances, Mary, Hart and James; after the death of his first wife in September 1710, remarried to Judith (Parrott) Cranston, the widow of his brother Caleb; no children by his second wife.

Became a sea captain as a young man; later worked for a time as a merchant. Elected as a Rhode Island Assistant in 1696, and named Major of the colony's forces in 1698. Succeeded Walter Clarke in March 1698 as Governor of Rhode Island, an office which he held until his death in 1727.

Samuel Cranston's tenure as Rhode Island's chief executive was the longest in the history of the colony. Indeed, his twenty-nine years of service were unsurpassed by any governor of the original thirteen colonies. At the outset of his long administration, Rhode Island was threatened by the revocation of its charter because of what the Board of Trade in London called "disorders and irregularities"—a reference in part to the benign attitude which the colony took toward privateering, and the alleged favoritism displayed by its courts. Cranston, an astute politician, successfully confronted this and later crises, and by 1707 the campaign against Rhode Island's chartered privileges had crumbled. In subsequent years Cranston was able to devote more attention to the political and legal structure of the colony. By the 1720's, for example, his policies had greatly enhanced the powers of the colony's central government. This development in turn fostered the growth of the Rhode Island economy, with Newport emerging as a significant commercial center. Another major achievement of Cranston's governorship was the settlement of the longstanding dispute over the Narragansett Country, a settlement which was of great benefit to Rhode Island at the expense of neighboring Connecticut.

The long Cranston era of Rhode Island history finally ended in Newport on April 26, 1727, when the governor died while still in office.

Bibliography: Henry E. Turner, *The Two Governors Cranston* (Newport, R.I., 1889); William Jones, "The Ancestry of Governors John and Samuel Cranston of Rhode Island," *New England Historical and Genealogical Register*, LXXIX (January 1925), 57-66; Charles Albert Du Bosq and William Jones, "Descendants of Gov. John Cranston of Rhode Island," *New England Historical and Genealogical Register*, LXXIX (July 1925), 247-68; "Some Correspondence of Samuel Cranston, Esq., Governor of Rhode Island, 1698-1727," *New England Historical and Genealogical Register*, LXXX (October 1926), 370-78. *DAB*.

JENCKES, Joseph, 1727-1732

Born in 1656, probably in Providence, Rhode Island, the son of Joseph, an iron manufacturer, and Esther (Ballard) Jenckes. A Baptist. Brother of Elizabeth, Sarah, Nathaniel, Esther, Ebenezer, Joanna, Abigail and William. Married first to Martha Brown, by whom he was the father of Joseph (died young), Obadiah, Nathaniel, Martha, Lydia, Mary, Catherine, Esther and John; after the death of his first wife, remarried on February 3, 1727 to Alice (Smith) Dexter; no children by his second wife.

Employed for a number of years as a land surveyor, and on several occasions represented Rhode Island during its boundary negotiations with neighboring colonies. Elected as a Deputy to the Rhode Island General Assembly in 1691; again served as a deputy from 1698 to 1708, and acted as Speaker of that body from 1698 to 1699 and from 1707 to 1708. Appointed Major for the Main in 1707, an office which he held until 1711. First chosen as an Assistant of the colony in 1708, and served until 1712. Named Deputy Governor of Rhode Island in 1715, retaining that position until his election as Governor in the spring of 1727.

During the Jenckes administration Rhode Island was divided by disputes between supporters and opponents of paper money, with the governor eventually becoming involved in the controversy. After the Rhode Island Assembly passed a bill providing for a new emission of £60,000 in paper notes, Jenckes voiced his opposition, but his decision was overruled by the legislators. As the next gubernatorial election approached, Jenckes judiciously decided to retire from public life. Because his unpopular monetary views had cost him so much of his earlier popularity, the governor realized that his chances of retaining office were slim anyway. His appraisal of the political situation was confirmed in the spring of 1732, when the proponents of paper money in Rhode Island elected William Wanton, a strong advocate of their position.

Jenckes died eight years later, on June 15, 1740. Blind and apparently not in full possession of his mental faculties at the end of his life, he died intestate "by reason of his insanity of mind." Jenckes was of an exceptional size and stature, and is reputed to have measured seven feet two inches in height.

Bibliography: Thomas Scott, comp., "Ancestry of Camden Crosby Dike . . . and the Jenks or Jenckes Families of Rhode Island" (1909), typescript volume in Local History and Genealogy Division, New York Public Library; William B. Browne, comp., *Genealogy of the Jenks Family of America* (Concord, N.H., 1952); Meredith B. Colket, Jr., "The Jenks Family of England," *New England Historical and Genealogical Register*, CX (January-October 1956), 9-20, 81-93, 161-72, 244-56. *DAB*.

WANTON, William, 1732-1733

Born on September 15, 1670 in Scituate, Massachusetts, the son of Edward, a shipbuilder, and Elizabeth Wanton. A Quaker in early life, but abandoned that faith at the time of his first marriage, when he became a member of the Church of England. Brother of Joseph, George, Elizabeth, John (who was governor of Rhode Island from 1733 to 1740), Sarah (died young) and Margaret (died young). Married on June 1, 1691 to Ruth Bryant, by whom he was the father of Margaret, George, William, Peter, Ruth, Edward, Joseph (who was governor of Rhode Island from 1769 to 1775), Benjamin and Elizabeth; after his first wife's death, remarried on April 10, 1717 to Mary Godfrey.

Employed as a merchant for a number of years. Engaged in various naval activities, and acquired the title of Captain by 1703; promoted to Major for the Island in 1705, a rank which he also held from 1707 to 1709; named Colonel of the militia regiment on the island in 1719 and 1720. Served as a Deputy in the Rhode Island General Assembly in 1705-06, 1708-11, 1713 and 1715-24; chosen as Speaker of the House of Deputies in each of those years (except 1713). Also acted as an Assistant in 1706-07, 1713 and 1725-32. Occupied other positions of public trust, including that of Commissioner for Rhode Island during the negotiations in 1726 over the colony's boundary with Connecticut. Elected Governor of Rhode Island in the spring of 1732.

Wanton's career as governor was cut short by his death in December 1733, less than two years after he entered office. Nevertheless, his administration witnessed the growing importance of an issue which for most of the eighteenth century would have a major impact on Rhode Island politics—the issue of paper money. Unlike Joseph Jenckes, his predecessor as governor, Wanton was an advocate of paper currency, and his election in the spring of 1732 had been in large part the result of backing by supporters who shared his monetary views. Soon after his inauguration, these interests secured legislation which authorized a land bank, funded to the sum of £104,000. Although this was Rhode Island's fifth land bank, the emission of currency was by far the largest yet, and in London the Board of Trade began to investigate the colony's financial practices.

Bibliography: John Russell Bartlett, *History of the Wanton Family of Newport, Rhode Island*, in *Rhode Island Historical Tracts*, nos. 3-4 (Providence, 1878).

WANTON, John, 1733-1740

Born on December 24, 1672 in Scituate, Massachusetts, the son of Edward, a shipbuilder, and Elizabeth Wanton. A Quaker. Brother of Joseph, George, Elizabeth, William (who was governor of Rhode Island from 1732 to 1733), Sarah (died young) and Margaret (died young). Married to Mary Stafford; father of John, Elizabeth, Susanna, Mary and James.

Employed as a merchant for many years. Engaged in various naval exploits with his brother William, and by 1707 had apparently risen to the rank of Colonel. Served as a Newport Deputy in the Rhode Island General Assembly from 1706 to 1710, and again in 1713; acted as Speaker of the House of Deputies in 1707, 1710 and 1713. Became Deputy Governor in 1721, and served until 1722; also occupied that office from 1729 to 1734. As deputy governor, succeeded his deceased brother William in December 1733; elected Governor in his own right in the spring of 1734, and served in that capacity until his death.

Like his brother, John Wanton was a supporter of paper money, and in 1738 his administration won approval for a sixth land (old tenor) bank, this time with an emission totalling £100,000. Despite vigorous protests from opponents of paper currency, this monetary policy seems to have benefited Rhode Island's economy, especially after the colony became involved in England's war with Spain. Newport merchants in particular were anxious in the autumn of 1739 to take up privateering, and many of the town's leading citizens, including the governor's nephew, sailed the Caribbean in search of Spanish prizes. Wanton himself did not live to witness the war's conclusion, however. He died in office on July 5, 1740, and was buried in the Coddington Burial Ground.

Bibliography: John Russell Bartlett, *History of the Wanton Family of Newport, Rhode Island*, in *Rhode Island Historical Tracts*, nos. 3-4 (Providence, 1878).

WARD, Richard, 1740-1743

Born on April 15, 1689 in Newport, Rhode Island, the son of Thomas, a merchant, and Amey (Billings) Ward. Brother of Mary and Thomas. Married on November 2, 1709 to Mary Tillinghast; father of Thomas, Mary, Amey, Isabel, Hannah, Samuel (who was governor of Rhode Island from 1762 to 1763 and again from 1765 to 1767), Margaret, Henry and Elizabeth; also the father of Amey, Elizabeth, John, Mercy and Richard, all of whom died young.

Became a prominent Newport merchant and the owner of a considerable body of land, including a large tract in the Narragansett Country. Served as Attorney General of Rhode Island from 1712 to 1713. Named Deputy and Clerk of the Rhode Island Assembly in 1714, and from 1714 to 1730 acted as the colony's General Recorder. Became one of the four commissioners who represented Rhode Island in 1726, during boundary negotiations with Connecticut. Served as Rhode Island's Secretary of State from 1730 to 1733. Elected Deputy Governor of Rhode Island in the spring of 1740, and in July of that year replaced the deceased governor, John Wanton; elected Governor in his own right in 1741, and remained in that position until May of 1743.

Ward assumed the governorship of Rhode Island at a time when the colony was being subjected to heavy criticism for its reliance on paper currency. Ward himself defended the emission of bills of credit, and in a 1741 letter to the Board of Trade in London, he claimed that both Rhode Island's trade and defense were dependent on the "right application" of paper money. Ward's years in office were also marked by the continuation of Britain's war against Spain. During the first months of the conflict Rhode Island privateers had looked forward to the capture of Spanish vessels, but the prizes that were taken rarely yielded the revenue necessary to operate at a profit. Consequently, privateering remained at a low ebb until a year after Ward's departure from office, when France's entry into the war provided sea raiders with new and more lucrative targets.

Following his period as governor, Ward seems to have taken little part in public affairs. He died on August 21, 1763, and was buried in Newport Cemetery.

Bibliography: William Gammell, *A Life of Samuel Ward*, in Jared Sparks, ed., *The Library of American Biography*, 2nd ser., vol. IX (Boston, 1846); John Ward, *A Memoir of Lieut.-Colonel Samuel Ward* . . .(New York, 1875); Bernhard Knollenberg, ed., *Correspondence of Governor Samuel Ward, May 1775-March 1776, with a . . . Genealogy of the Ward Family . . . compiled by Clifford P. Monahon* (Providence, 1952). *DAB*.

GREENE, William, 1743-1745, 1746-1747, 1748-1755, 1757-1758

Born on March 16, 1696 in Warwick, Rhode Island, the son of Samuel and Mary (Gorton) Greene. Brother of Mary, Samuel and Benjamin. Married on December 30, 1719 to a second cousin, Catharine Greene, by whom he was the father of six children, including William (who was governor of Rhode Island from 1778 to 1786).

Named a Freeman of the colony of Rhode Island in 1718. First served as a Deputy to the Rhode Island General Assembly in May 1727, representing Warwick; also acted in that capacity in 1732, 1736, 1738 and 1740. Worked for a number of years as a surveyor, and in 1728, 1736 and 1741 assisted in determining the boundary between Rhode Island and Connecticut. Chosen Deputy Governor of Rhode Island in July 1740, following the death of Governor John Wanton and the elevation of Deputy Governor Richard Ward to the post of chief executive. Served as deputy governor until the spring of 1743, when he defeated Ward in that year's gubernatorial race, and remained in office until May 1745; also served as chief executive from May 1746 to May 1747, May 1748 to May 1755, and May 1757 to February 1758.

During Greene's early years as governor, authorities in London accused Rhode Island of trading with the enemy while England was at war with France. Meanwhile, the war and its financial implications contributed to the emergence of a well-organized political opposition within the colony, led by Gideon Wanton. This faction, which advocated greater military expenditures and a liberal policy toward paper money emissions, won a brief victory when it soundly defeated Greene in 1745.

Although political partisanship had temporarily subsided by 1748, it resurfaced in 1754, as a new international war and the old internal disputes over paper currency encouraged Stephen Hopkins to desert Greene's camp and establish himself at the head of another cohesive opposition group. Greene himself continued to fight this Providence-based faction until his death in office in February 1758.

Bibliography: Henry E. Turner, *Greenes of Warwick, in Colonial History* . . . (Newport, R.I., 1877); George Sears Greene and Louise Brownell Clarke, *The Greenes of Rhode Island* (New York, 1903); G. Andrews Moriarty, "Documents Relating to the Ray, Greene, and Turner Families," *Rhode Island History*, VI (July 1947), 65-85. *DAB*.

WANTON, Gideon, 1745-1746, 1747-1748

Born on October 20, 1693 in Tiverton, Rhode Island, the son of Joseph, a shipbuilder, and Sarah (Freeborn) Wanton. A Quaker. Brother of Elizabeth, Edward, Sarah, Joseph and Mary. Married on February 6, 1718 to a widow named Mary Codman; father of Gideon, Jr., John G., Joseph and Edward.

Served as General Treasurer of Rhode Island from 1733 to 1743. Elected Governor of Rhode Island in the spring of 1745, a position which he filled until May 1746; again served as chief executive from May 1747 to May 1748.

Along with his uncles William and John, both of whom had preceded him as governor of Rhode Island, Gideon Wanton favored paper currency. Consequently, after upsetting the incumbent William Greene in the gubernatorial election of 1745, Wanton and his supporters approved new paper money emissions, largely to finance Rhode Island's expenditures during the war between England and France. Wanton was especially concerned with the projected English invasion of French Canada, and he cooperated with other colonial governors in providing troops for the expedition against Louisbourg. Although Greene, his long-time political rival, defeated him in May of 1746, Wanton returned to win the general election of 1747. Military reverses during that year, however, caused him once again to lose to Greene in 1748, and Wanton never regained the governorship nor his earlier political stature. Wanton died on September 12, 1767.

Bibliography: John Russell Bartlett, *History of the Wanton Family of Newport, Rhode Island*, in *Rhode Island Historical Tracts*, nos. 3-4 (Providence, 1878).

HOPKINS, Stephen, 1755-1757, 1758-1762, 1763-1765, 1767-1768

Born on March 7, 1707 in Providence, Rhode Island, the son of William and Ruth (Wickenden) Wilkinson Hopkins. Became a Quaker in 1755, but was expelled by that religious body in 1773. Married in 1726 to Sarah Scott, by whom he had five sons and two daughters; after the death of his first wife in 1753, remarried in 1755 to Mrs. Anne (Smith) Smith; no children by his second wife.

Worked as a farmer and surveyor as a young man. Named Town Clerk of Scituate in 1732, soon after that community separated from Providence; became President of the Scituate Town Council in 1735. Represented Scituate in the Rhode Island General Assembly between 1732 and 1738 (except for one year), and again from 1741 to 1742; chosen Speaker of the Assembly's House of Deputies in 1741. Following his move to Providence in 1742, served as a member of the Assembly from that town in 1744-45, 1746-47, 1749-50 and 1751-53, acting as Speaker for two of those years. Held a variety of judicial offices during his public career, including Justice of the Court of Common Pleas for Providence County (1736-40), Assistant Justice of the Rhode Island Superior Court (1747-49), and Chief Justice of the Superior Court (May 1751-May 1755, August 1755-May 1756). Played a major role in efforts to encourage greater intercolonial cooperation, and attended congresses on that subject in 1746, 1754, 1755, and 1757. Defeated William Greene in the spring of 1755 to become Governor of Rhode Island, a position he held until May 1757; also served as chief executive from March 1758 to May 1762, May 1763 to May 1765, and May 1767 to May 1768.

Between the late 1750's and 1768, the heated rivalry between Hopkins and Samuel Ward became the focal point of Rhode Island politics. Ward, who had succeeded the deceased William Greene as Hopkins' chief opponent early in 1758, defended the interests of Newport, while Hopkins became the standard bearer for those residents of Providence who envied Newport's commercial power. Although this outburst of partisan politics was certainly real enough to the antagonists, the issues over which they quarreled were often trivial in nature. In dealing with the question of financing the French and Indian War, for example, Ward and Hopkins espoused almost identical measures. By the time of Josias Lyndon's election as a compromise gubernatorial candidate in 1768, it was becoming clear that in the future Rhode Island's real quarrel would be with British colonial policy.

Following his final term as chief executive, Hopkins continued to take an active part in politics. From 1770 to 1775 he sat in the Rhode Island General Assembly, and in the five years preceding independence he again presided as Chief Justice of the colony's Superior Court. Hopkins also represented Rhode Island at the continental congresses held between 1774 and 1776. He signed the Declaration of Independence, but in September of 1776 ill health forced him to return to his native state, where during most of the Revolution he sat on the Rhode Island Council of War and attended various conventions of the New England states.

Throughout his life Hopkins maintained a strong interest in areas outside of politics, especially education. Rhode Island College (now Brown University), which was founded in 1764, named him its first Chancellor, and until his death on July 13, 1785, Hopkins remained an active supporter of that institution.

Bibliography: Stephen Hopkins, *The Grievances of the American Colonies Candidly Examined*... (London, 1766: reprint, New York, 1970); Charles Cotesworth Beaman, "The Hopkins Family in Rhode Island, to which Stephen Hopkins, One of the Signers of the Declaration of Independence ... Belonged," *Essex Institute Historical Collections*, II (1860), 115-23; Stephen Hopkins, "A True Representation of the Plan Formed at Albany in 1754...," *Rhode Island Historical Tracts*, no. IX (Providence, 1880); Moses Brown, "Some Account of Stephen Hopkins, Esq., in the Letters of Stephen Hopkins, Collected from Various Sources," Sidney S. Rider, ed., MS copies (Providence, 1881) in Brown University Library; Albert Holbrook, *Genealogy of One Line of the Hopkins Family* (Providence, 1881); William E. Foster, *Stephen Hopkins, A Rhode Island Statesman: A Study in the Political History of the Eighteenth Century* (Providence, 1884); Mack E. Thompson, "The Ward-Hopkins Controversy and the American Revolution in Rhode Island: An Interpretation," *William and Mary Quarterly*, 3rd ser., vol. XVI (July 1959), 363-75; Paul Campbell, ed., *The Rights of Colonies Examined/Stephen Hopkins* (Providence, 1974). *DAB*.

WARD, Samuel, 1762-1763, 1765-1767

Born on May 27, 1725 in Newport, Rhode Island, the son of Governor Richard and Mary (Tillinghast) Ward. Brother of Thomas, Mary, Amey, Isabel, Hannah, Margaret, Henry and Elizabeth; also the brother of Amey, Elizabeth, John, Mercy and Richard, all of whom died young. Married on December 20, 1745 to Anna Ray; father of Charles, Hannah, Anna, Catharine, Mary, Samuel, Deborah, Simon Ray, John, Richard and Elizabeth.

Elected in 1756 as a Deputy to the Rhode Island General Assembly, representing Westerly, and served in that capacity until May of 1758. Also elected Chief Justice of the Rhode Island Superior Court in 1761. Became a member of the political faction which supported Governor William Greene, the elder; ran unsuccessfully for Governor against Stephen Hopkins on four occasions between 1758 and 1761, finally defeating him in the spring of 1762; again served as chief executive between 1765 and 1767.

During the years leading up to the Revolution, Ward and Hopkins engaged in a bitter political dispute, a dispute which defined the nature of Rhode Island politics throughout the period. Originating in the late 1750's, when Ward accused Hopkins of profiting from the French and Indian War while governor, the controversy between the two men quickly affected other aspects of Rhode Island's development. Sectionalism, for example, became a more marked feature of Rhode Island politics, as freemen in the north supported Hopkins, a native of Providence, while the southern counties supported the Newport-based Ward. Ward's first term as chief executive occurred during the period immediately after the French and Indian War, when the colony attempted to secure funds which Parliament had voted to help Rhode Island pay its wartime expenses. Between 1765 and 1767 Ward again sat in the governor's chair, but in these years the focus changed from Parliamentary reimbursement to what many Rhode Islanders referred to as "Parliamentary oppression." In August 1765 John Robinson, the collector of customs at Newport, provoked so many residents by attempting to seize a sloop which had allegedly evaded the Molasses Act, that he was forced to seek refuge aboard a ship in the harbor afterwards. Discontent over the Stamp Act also erupted during Ward's second period in office, and the governor allied himself with popular sentiment by refusing to swear that he would enforce the offensive legislation.

Following his period as governor, Ward continued to take an active part in the revolutionary movement. In 1774 he and his longtime foe, Stephen Hopkins, both represented Rhode Island at the First Continental Congress, and from 1775 to 1776 Ward was a member of the Second Continental Congress. Ward died of smallpox in Philadelphia, Pennsylvania on March 26, 1776, about three months before the colonies declared their independence from Great Britain.

Bibliography: William Gammell, *A Life of Samuel Ward*, in Jared Sparks, ed., *The Library of American Biography*, 2nd ser., vol. IX (Boston, 1846); John Ward, *The Life and Services of Gov. Samuel Ward, of Rhode Island, a Member of the Continental Congress in 1774, 1775 and 1776* (Providence, 1877); William Greene Roelker, "Governor Samuel Ward, Farmer and Merchant," *Rhode Island History*, VI (April 1947), 54-58; Bernhard Knollenberg, ed., *Correspondence of Governor Samuel Ward, May 1775-March 1776* (Providence, 1952); Mack E. Thompson, "The Ward-Hopkins Controversy and the American Revolution in Rhode Island: An Interpretation," *William and Mary Quarterly*, 3rd ser., vol. XVI (July 1959), 363-75. *DAB*.

LYNDON, Josias, 1768-1769

Born on March 10, 1704 in Newport, Rhode Island, the eldest son of Samuel and Priscilla (Tompkins) Lyndon. A Baptist. Brother of Samuel, Mary, John, Elizabeth, Priscilla and Augustus, although all but Samuel died young. Married on October 5, 1727 to Mary Carr; no children.

Named Clerk of the Rhode Island General Assembly in 1728, and served in that capacity continuously until 1767; also acted as clerk from 1770 to 1777. Became one of the founders in 1730 of a literary and philosophical society which was eventually known as the Redwood Library; served as one of the incorporators of Rhode Island College (later Brown University) in 1764. Joined the Newport Sons of Liberty by 1766. Elected Governor of Rhode Island in the spring of 1768.

Since Lyndon was at first acceptable to both of Rhode Island's political factions, his election in 1768 became part of an effort to end the long-standing feud between supporters of Stephen Hopkins and Samuel Ward. Lyndon, however, was unable to prevent the more numerous Ward faction in the House of Deputies from taking over, and the Hopkins group retaliated in 1769 by backing Joseph Wanton's successful candidacy for governor. During Lyndon's brief administration, Rhode Islanders attempted to formulate an effective non-importation policy, in order to oppose the Townshend duties which the British Parliament had recently enacted. Nevertheless, despite the patriotic exhortations which filled the newspapers, most Rhode Island merchants eventually decided to do business with their English counterparts. Indeed, by the end of Lyndon's term in office, Newport was beginning to attract ships whose cargo could not be sold in other ports.

Following his period as governor, Lyndon returned to his former position as clerk of the Rhode Island Assembly. Lyndon remained clerk until one year before he died from smallpox in Warren, Rhode Island on March 30, 1778. He was buried in Warren.

WANTON, Joseph, 1769-1775

Born on August 15, 1705 in Newport, Rhode Island, the son of Governor William and Ruth (Bryant) Wanton. An Anglican. Brother of Margaret, George, William, Peter, Ruth, Edward, Benjamin and Elizabeth. Married on August 21, 1729 to Mary Winthrop, by whom he was the father of Joseph, William, John (died young), Catherine, Mary, Elizabeth, Ruth and Ann.

Became a Freeman of Newport, Rhode Island in April 1728. First served as Newport's Deputy Collector of Customs in 1738, and held that position for more than a decade. Also played a major part in the mercantile activities of the Wanton family; from about 1759 until its collapse in 1780, acted as a partner, with two of his sons, in the firm of Joseph and William Wanton, a business which specialized in trade with the West Indies. Elected Governor of Rhode Island in the spring of 1769, an office he retained until 1775.

A near relation of three earlier governors of Rhode Island, Wanton entered his period as chief executive with both the political backing of the powerful Stephen Hopkins and a family tradition of public service which made him seem ideally suited to administer the colony. Nevertheless, the growing unrest in Rhode Island over Britain's colonial policy soon placed Wanton in a difficult position. While he was sympathetic to many of the grievances voiced by the colony's radical leaders, as evidenced by his reluctance to prosecute the men who had burned the British ship *Gaspée* in 1772, Wanton was unwilling to advocate complete political separation from Great Britain. In the spring of 1775, shortly after the battles of Lexington and Concord, Wanton objected to an Assembly plan which would have raised a military force of 1,500 from Rhode Island to counter British aggression. Provoked by this stance, the Assembly stripped Wanton of virtually all of his gubernatorial powers, and by the autumn of that year he had been replaced as chief executive by Nicholas Cooke. Until his death on July 19, 1780, Wanton remained an outside observer of the Revolution's progress, although he appears not to have been abused personally by the Patriot faction because of his Tory views.

Bibliography: John Russell Bartlett, *History of the Wanton Family of Newport, Rhode Island*, in *Rhode Island Historical Tracts*, nos. 3-4 (Providence, 1878); Charles Albert DuBosq and William Jones, "Joseph Wanton Cranston and His Descendants," *New England Historical and Genealogical Register*, LXXX (July 1926), 251-57; Jarvis M. Morse, "The Wanton Family and Rhode Island Loyalism," Rhode Island Historical Society, *Collections*, XXXI (April 1938), 33-45. *DAB*.

COOKE, Nicholas, 1775-1778

Born on February 3, 1717 in Providence, Rhode Island, the third child of Daniel and Mary (Power) Cooke. Married on September 23, 1740 to Hannah Sabin; father of twelve children.

Became a ship's master in Rhode Island, and later started a mercantile business in Newport; also acquired large land holdings in Rhode Island, Connecticut and Massachusetts. Served for a time in the 1750's as an Assistant in Rhode Island's upper house. Elected Deputy Governor of Rhode Island in the spring of 1768, an office which he filled until May 1769; again chosen as deputy governor in the spring of 1775, and in the autumn of that year succeeded the deposed Joseph Wanton as Governor; served as chief executive until May of 1778.

Cooke appears to have been acting as governor even before he officially replaced Wanton, since the ex-governor, who supported the mother country's position during the Revolution, had been stripped of most of his power in the spring of 1775 by the Rhode Island General Assembly. In any case, Cooke was clearly exercising his gubernatorial powers by November of 1775, powers which he retained until he chose not to stand for reelection in the spring of 1778. His administration was marked by the decision of the General Assembly in May 1776 to repudiate its allegiance to the British king, anticipating by two months the new nation's Declaration of Independence. Militarily, Rhode Island was not a major theater of war during Cooke's tenure in office. Nevertheless, Rhode Island seamen confronted the Royal Navy on a number of occasions, and in December 1776 the state suffered its first occupation, when troops under the command of Sir Henry Clinton seized Newport.

Although Cooke retired from politics following his service as governor, he did continue to perform his duties as Trustee of Rhode Island College (later Brown University), an appointment which he had accepted in 1776. Cooke died on November 14, 1782.

Bibliography: "Revolutionary Correspondence from 1775 to 1782, Comprising Letters Written by Governor Nicholas Cooke, William Greene, John Collins, Jonathan Trumbull, . . .and Others," Rhode Island Historical Society, *Collections*, VI (1867), 105-300; "Revolutionary Correspondence of Governor Nicholas Cooke, 1775-1781," American Antiquarian Society, *Proceedings*, n.s., vol. XXXVI (1926), 231-353.

GREENE, William, Jr., 1778-1786

Born on August 16, 1731 in Warwick, Rhode Island, the son of Governor William and Catharine (Greene) Greene. Brother of five. Married in 1758 to

Catharine Ray, by whom he had four children, including Ray (who was United States senator from Rhode Island between 1797 and 1801).

Elected as a Deputy from Warwick to the Rhode Island General Assembly in 1773, 1774, 1776 and 1777; chosen as Speaker of the House of Deputies in May 1777. Named First Associate Justice of Rhode Island's Superior Court in 1776, and became Chief Justice of that court in February 1777. Appointed to the Rhode Island Council of War in 1776 and 1777; also represented his state on several commissions during the early years of the Revolution. Elected Governor of Rhode Island in the spring of 1778, succeeding Nicholas Cooke, and served in that capacity until May 1786.

During Greene's long tenure Rhode Island endured three years of war with Great Britain, followed by five more years of political warfare over the question of a federal impost. While Rhode Island was usually not of tactical importance, Newport was occupied by the British for almost three years, an occupation which finally ended when Admiral Arbuthnot chose to evacuate the town in October 1779. After the conclusion of the war, Rhode Island began to consider the proposed impost, which, by levying a five percent *ad valorem* tariff on trade, was designed to provide the Continental Congress with a reliable source of income. In 1782 Rhode Island rejected this plan, largely because it offered the state few meaningful benefits to its commerce, but early in 1786 a revised impost finally won the state's approval.

Following his period as governor, Greene was an unsuccessful candidate for Congress in 1796 and for governor in 1802. He died in Warwick, Rhode Island on November 29, 1809.

Bibliography: "Revolutionary Correspondence from 1775 to 1782, Comprising Letters Written by Governors Nicholas Cooke, William Greene, John Collins, Jonathan Trumbull, . . . and Others," Rhode Island Historical Society, *Collections*, VI (1867), 105-300; Henry E. Turner, *Greenes of Warwick, in Colonial History* . . . (Newport, R.I., 1877); George Sears Greene and Louise Brownell Clarke, *The Greenes of Rhode Island* (New York, 1903); G. Andrews Moriarty, "Documents Relating to the Ray, Greene, and Turner Families," *Rhode Island History*, VI (July 1947), 65-85. *DAB*.

COLLINS, John, 1786-1790

Born in 1717 in Newport, Rhode Island, the son of Samuel and Elizabeth Collins. Married to Mary Avery.

Became a prominent Newport merchant, and by 1774 was acting as a member of Newport's Committee of Correspondence. Served as an Assistant in the Rhode Island General Assembly from May 1774 to May 1778. Apart from a twelve-month period between 1781 and 1782, represented Rhode Island in the Continental Congress from 1778 to 1783. Defeated William Greene, Jr. in the gubernatorial election of April 1786, and took the chief executive's oath of office in May of that year; served as governor until May of 1790, after winning reelection in 1787, 1788 and 1789.

During Collins' tenure as chief executive, the issues of paper money and the proposed Federal Constitution were hotly debated in Rhode Island. In 1786 Collins and the state's "Country Party," which had endorsed the idea of a land bank as a means of emitting paper currency, managed to unseat incumbent Governor William Greene, Jr. By the end of 1789 the state had succeeded in liquidating its debt and reducing taxation, suggesting that the fiscal policies adopted by Collins and his allies had been effective.

Although Collins had at first opposed the new Federal Constitution, arguing that ratification would jeopardize Rhode Island's freedom to control its own commerce and finance, he changed his mind when his party's land bank scheme was virtually completed by 1789. In January of 1790 Collins cast a tie-breaking vote in the Senate, insuring that Rhode Island would call a state ratifying convention. This action virtually ended his political career, since anti-ratification sentiment was still strong enough to force his party to replace him with the more circumspect Arthur Fenner as its gubernatorial candidate in 1790.

While Collins was later elected to represent Rhode Island in the United States Congress, he never took his seat in that body. He died in Newport, Rhode Island on March 4, 1795, and was buried at "Brenton Neck," his farm near Newport.

Bibliography: "Revolutionary Correspondence from 1775 to 1782, Comprising Letters Written by Governors Nicholas Cooke, William Greene, John Collins, Jonathan Trumbull, . . . and Others," Rhode Island Historical Society, *Collections*, VI (1867), 105-300; Irwin H. Polishook, "The Collins-Richardson Fracas of 1787," *Rhode Island History*, XXII (October 1963), 117-21; John P. Kaminski, "Political Sacrifice and Demise—John Collins and Jonathan J. Hazard, 1786-1790," *Rhode Island History*, 35 (August 1976), 91-98. *DAB*.

SOUTH CAROLINA

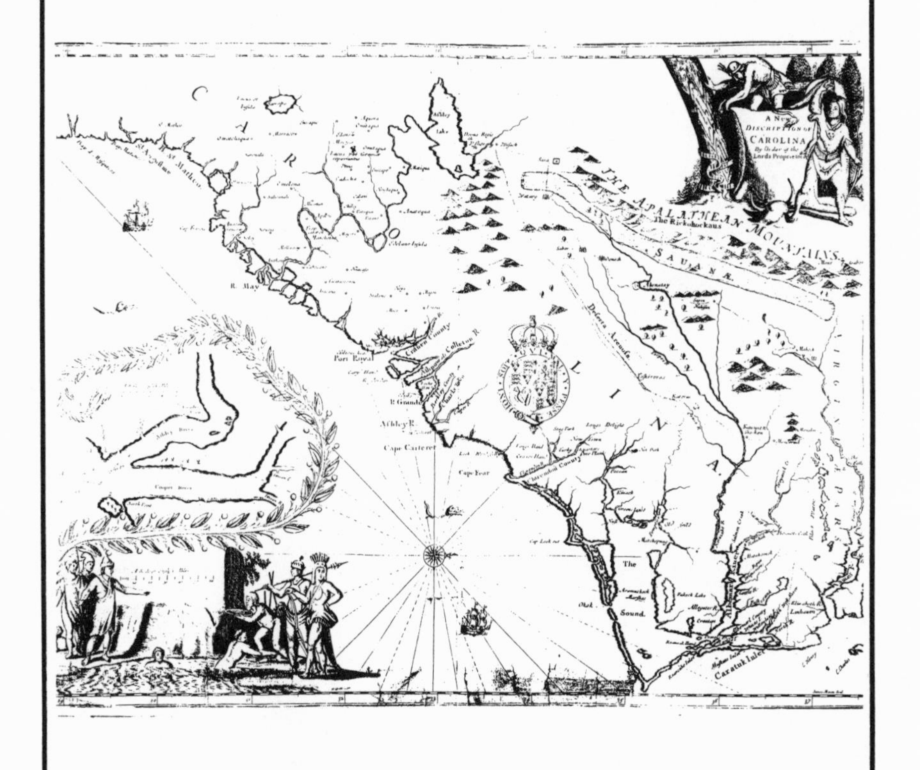

Chronology

South Carolina was known as southern Carolina before 1712.

Carolina "south and west of the Cape Fear River"

1670-1671	William Sayle
1671-1672	Joseph West
1672-1674	Sir John Yeamans
1674-1682	Joseph West
1682-1684	Joseph Morton
1684	Sir Richard Kyrle
1684	Robert Quary
1684-1685	Joseph West
1685-1686	Joseph Morton
1686-1690	James Colleton
1690-1692	Seth Sothel
1692-1693	Philip Ludwell
1693-1694	Thomas Smith
1694-1695	Joseph Blake
1695-1696	John Archdale
1696-1700	Joseph Blake
1700-1703	James Moore, Sr.
1703-1709	Sir Nathaniel Johnson
1709-1710	Edward Tynte
1710-1712	Robert Gibbes

South Carolina

1712-1716	Charles Craven
1716-1717	Robert Daniel
1717-1719	Robert Johnson
1719-1721	James Moore, Jr.
1721-1725	Francis Nicholson
1725-1730	Arthur Middleton
1730-1735	Robert Johnson
1735-1737	Thomas Broughton
1737-1743	William Bull, Sr.
1743-1756	James Glen
1756-1760	William Henry Lyttelton
1760-1761	William Bull, Jr.

1761-1764	Thomas Boone
1764-1766	William Bull, Jr.
1766-1768	Lord Charles Greville Montagu
1768	William Bull, Jr.
1768-1769	Lord Charles Greville Montagu
1769-1771	William Bull, Jr.
1771-1773	Lord Charles Greville Montagu
1773-1775	William Bull, Jr.
1775	Lord William Campbell
1775-1776	Henry Laurens
1776-1778	John Rutledge
1778-1779	Rawlins Lowndes
1779-1782	John Rutledge
1782-1783	John Mathewes
1783-1785	Benjamin Guerard
1785-1787	William Moultrie
1787-1789	Thomas Pinckney

Non-resident Royal Governors of South Carolina

Appointee	*Year of Commission*	*Reason for Absence*
Samuel Horsey	1738	Died before assuming office
Thomas Pownall	1760	Did not go to the colony

BIBLIOGRAPHY

Easterby, J. H., and Ruth S. Green, eds., *Colonial Records of South Carolina: Journals of the Commons House of Assembly [1736/1750-]*, 9 vols. to date (Columbia, 1951/1962-).

Edgar, Walter B., and N. Louise Bailey, *Biographical Directory of the South Carolina House of Representatives: Volume II, The Commons House of Assembly, 1692-1775* (Columbia, 1977).

McCrady, Edward, *The History of South Carolina in the Revolution, 1775-1780* (New York, 1901).

———. *The History of South Carolina in the Revolution, 1780-1783* (New York, 1902).

———. *The History of South Carolina Under the Proprietary Government, 1670-1719* (New York, 1897).

———. *The History of South Carolina Under the Royal Government, 1719-1776* (New York, 1899).

Phillips, Ulrich B., "The South Carolina Federalists," *American Historical Review*, XIV (April-July 1909), 529-43, 731-43.

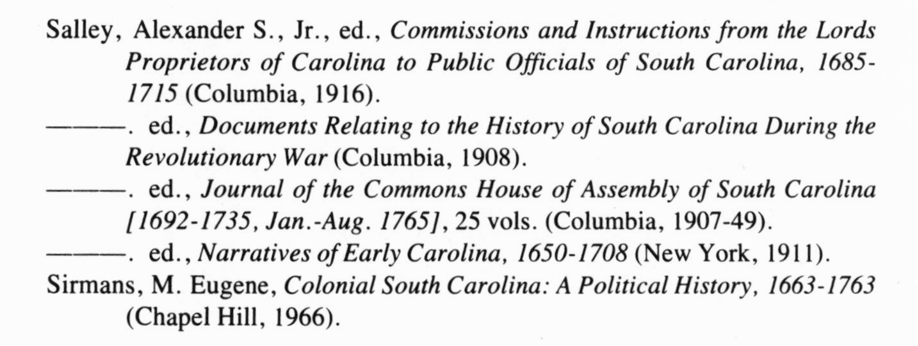

Salley, Alexander S., Jr., ed., *Commissions and Instructions from the Lords Proprietors of Carolina to Public Officials of South Carolina, 1685-1715* (Columbia, 1916).

———. ed., *Documents Relating to the History of South Carolina During the Revolutionary War* (Columbia, 1908).

———. ed., *Journal of the Commons House of Assembly of South Carolina [1692-1735, Jan.-Aug. 1765]*, 25 vols. (Columbia, 1907-49).

———. ed., *Narratives of Early Carolina, 1650-1708* (New York, 1911).

Sirmans, M. Eugene, *Colonial South Carolina: A Political History, 1663-1763* (Chapel Hill, 1966).

SOUTH CAROLINA

SAYLE, William, 1670-1671

Born *circa* 1591; place of birth and names of parents unknown. A Puritan. Married, and the father of Nathaniel and James.

Became a prominent political figure in Bermuda, serving as Lieutenant Governor of that island from September 1641 to 1642, September 1643 to February 1645, and June 1658 to January 1662. Named Governor of southern Carolina by Sir John Yeamans, who decided not to accompany a colonizing venture which sailed from Bermuda. Arrived at Port Royal in March of 1670, and eventually helped to establish a settlement on Albemarle Point (later Charles Town).*

Along with the need to devise an adequate means of feeding the colonists under his command, Sayle was confronted by a serious challenge from Spanish troops based at St. Augustine, Florida. In the summer of 1670 the governor of that military outpost organized an expedition designed to destroy the new English settlement and, although the attempt failed, the experience convinced Carolina's leaders of the need for strong measures to protect their colony from invasion. Sayle's administration was further complicated by political dissension stemming largely from his efforts to eliminate "violations of the Sabbath" and "other grand abuses" which he detected among some of Carolina's less pious residents. Under the guidance of William Owen, a faction opposed to the chief executive quickly attracted considerable sympathy. Nevertheless, an abortive effort by Owen to schedule an illegal election, followed by the death of Sayle on March 4, 1671 and his replacement by the more pragmatic Joseph West, soon deprived this protest movement of most of its influence. *DNB*.

*The spelling of Charles Town was altered to Charlestown in 1719, and assumed its present form (Charleston) after its incorporation in 1783.

WEST, Joseph, 1671-1672, 1674-1682, 1684-1685

Born in England; date of birth and names of parents unknown. A Dissenter, and possibly a Quaker. Married; apparently left his wife in England when he immigrated to America. Connected with the London mercantile community, and by 1667 was serving as a Lieutenant in the Navy.

Appointed Agent and Storekeeper by Carolina's Lords Proprietors in 1669, who instructed him to set up an experimental farm, which was to be used to discover a marketable staple crop. Commanded a group of colonists which sailed for the colony and, following several layovers and misadventures, arrived off Carolina in the spring of 1670. Chosen by the dying Governor William Sayle as his successor in March 1671.

West's selection by Sayle as Governor of Carolina was intended to be a temporary appointment, until the wishes of the Proprietors in England could be determined. After Sir John Yeamans arrived in the colony in June of 1671, he became the leader of a political faction consisting largely of Barbadian immigrants, and in the spring of 1672 he succeeded West on orders from the Proprietors. About two years later, however, Yeamans died and was replaced by West, who was named a Landgrave by the Proprietors and served as governor until his dismissal in 1682. The durable West once again returned to power in 1684, but he acted as chief executive for less than one year before leaving Carolina in 1685.

West's ten years in office were especially significant for the young colony. His leadership from 1671 to 1672 helped the settlers cope with a serious shortage of provisions, while his later activities contributed to a temporary decline in the factionalism which periodically disrupted Carolina's internal politics. On the other hand, the colonists' tactic of ignoring the instructions of the Lords Proprietors in England first became evident during West's administration, especially over the issues of debts to the Proprietors, land grants and the Indian trade.

West's activities following his departure from Carolina are uncertain, although there is reason to believe that he travelled to New York, where he died sometime between May and July of 1691.

Bibliography: Henry A. M. Smith, "Joseph West: Landgrave and Governor," *South Carolina Historical and Genealogical Magazine*, XIX (October 1918), 189-93; "Governors [*sic*] West's Terms as Governor," *South Carolina Historical and Genealogical Magazine*, XX (April 1919), 147-49; Bryle J. Osborn, "Governor Joseph West: A Seventeenth Century Forgotten Man Rediscovered," *New York Genealogical and Biographical Record*, LXV (July 1934), 202-05; Mabel L. Webber, "Joseph West, Landgrave and Governor," *South Carolina Historical Magazine*, XL (July 1939), 79-80; St. Julien R. Childs, "The Naval Career of Joseph West," *South Carolina Historical Magazine*, 71 (April 1970), 109-16. *DAB, DNB*.

YEAMANS, Sir John, 1672-1674

Born *circa* 1610 in the vicinity of Bristol, England, the eldest son of John Yeamans of Bristol, a brewer, and his wife Blanche (Germain) Yeamans. Brother of Deborah, Joseph, Robert, Elizabeth, George, Mary, Anne, Richard, William, Sarah, Martha and Johana. Married first to the daughter of a Mr. Limp; remarried on April 11, 1661 to Margaret (Foster) Berringer; father of William, Frances, Robert, George, Edward, Willoughby, Anne and one other son.

Advanced to the rank of Colonel in the Royalist Army during the English Civil Wars. Immigrated to Barbados in 1650, became a planter, and served on the Barbados Council from 1660 to 1664. In the 1660's began negotiations with Carolina's Lords Proprietors for permission to establish a colony there; made a Baronet and commissioned Governor of Carolina in January 1665, sailing from Barbados with a group of settlers the following October. Resided in Carolina for a short time but soon left, and by 1667 this settlement had been abandoned. Because of his governor's commission, Yeamans was empowered to appoint William Sayle as governor of a new colonizing venture, which arrived in Carolina in March 1670. Came to Carolina himself in June 1671 and, as head of a Barbadian political faction, elected Speaker of the Carolina "Parliament" shortly after his arrival. By the spring of 1672, he had replaced Joseph West, who served as governor following the death of Sayle in March 1671.

Yeamans' actions as governor were the source of much controversy, as his enemies accused him of mismanaging the colony's provisions, and of sending essential food supplies back to Barbados. Although some of these allegations may not be completely accurate, it is clear that Yeamans was a rather unimaginative administrator. By April 1674 the Proprietors, complaining that "since he [Yeamans] came in we cann hear of nothing but wants and suplys," decided to revoke the governor's commission. However, before news of his removal from office reached the colony, Yeamans had died, and the Carolina Council selected former Governor Joseph West as the new chief executive in August 1674.

Bibliography: M. Alston Read, "Notes on Some Colonial Governors of South Carolina and Their Families," *South Carolina Historical and Genealogical Magazine*, XI (April 1910), 107-22; Henry A. M. Smith, "Sir John Yeamans, An Historical Error," *South Carolina Historical and Genealogical Magazine*, XIX (July 1918), 152-56; Grant S. Youmans, comp., *The Yeamans-Yeomans-Youmans Genealogy* (Rutland, Vt., 1946). *DAB, DNB*.

MORTON, Joseph, 1682-1684, 1685-1686

Born *circa* 1630 in England, the son of Ambrose Mourton, a hosier of Wells, Somerset. A Dissenter. Brother of Rebecca, and one other who died in infancy. Married to a woman named Elinor, by whom he was the father of Joseph, John, Deborah and Florence.

Arrived in Carolina about 1681, when he became a Landgrave of that province as a reward for his efforts in encouraging Dissenters to settle in the colony. Commissioned in May 1682 as "Governor and Commander-in-Chief of that part of Carolina lying south and west of Cape Fear," and replaced Joseph West in October of 1682; served as chief executive until the summer of 1684, when he was succeeded by Sir Richard Kyrle. As President of the Carolina Council, returned to power in 1685, and remained in office until the arrival of James Colleton in November 1686.

The decision by Carolina's Proprietors to appoint Morton governor of southern Carolina was part of a broad attempt to reform the administration of the colony. For a number of years the Proprietors had been concerned with the widespread traffic in Indian slaves and the collusion with pirates practiced by many of Carolina's leaders. When Morton and his proprietary party sought to end these abuses, however, they met with strong opposition from an anti-proprietary group which became known as the "Goose Creek men." In 1684 the Proprietors attempted to break the political *impasse* that had resulted by appointing Sir Richard Kyrle as governor, but following Kyrle's death only a few weeks after arriving in the colony and the brief terms of Robert Quary and Joseph West, Morton returned to power. His second term in office was marked by a Spanish invasion of southern Carolina in August 1686 which caused widespread damage, including the destruction of Morton's home on the Edisto River. As Morton was in the midst of preparing a retaliatory attack against Florida that November, he was replaced by James Colleton, the new proprietary appointee, who cancelled the expedition. Morton appears to have died sometime around January of 1688; his will was proved in November of that year.

Bibliography: A. S. Salley, Jr., "Governor Joseph Morton and Some of His Descendants," *South Carolina Historical and Genealogical Magazine*, V (April 1904), 108-16; Seabrook Wilkinson Valley, "The Parentage of Governor Morton," *South Carolina Historical Magazine*, 74 (July 1973), 164-69.

KYRLE, Sir Richard, 1684

Apparently born in Ireland, the son of James and Anne (Waller) Kyrle; date of birth unknown. Brother of ten, including Robert, James, John, William,

Edward and Thomas. According to one source, married twice, once to a woman named Mary, and the father of children by both wives.

Named a Landgrave of Carolina in 1684, a title in the order of nobility devised for the colony by the philosopher John Locke. Commissioned Governor of southern Carolina in April 1684, and arrived in America to begin his administration between July 28 and August 30 of that year.

The selection of Kyrle as chief executive was based partly on the assumption that an administrator from outside the politically-troubled colony would have greater success in controlling such abuses as the Indian slave trade and the collusion with pirates practiced by some Carolina merchants. Unfortunately, the Proprietors in England were never able to measure the impact of this strategy, since Kyrle died soon after his arrival. By September 11, 1684, the date on which Kyrle's will was recorded, the government of southern Carolina had passed into the hands of Robert Quary, a man who sympathized with the anti-proprietary ''Goose Creek'' faction.

QUARY, Robert, 1684

Date and place of birth, and names of parents unknown. An Anglican. Became a Lords Proprietors' Deputy for Carolina, and served for a time as Secretary of the Carolina Council. Chosen by the Council as Acting Governor of southern Carolina in September of 1684, after the death of Governor Sir Richard Kyrle.

Quary's administration ended soon after he took office, when he was accused of trading with pirates who patrolled the waters off Carolina. His political career in America, however, did not come to a close with his replacement as chief executive by Joseph West in the autumn of 1684. In July 1698 Quary arrived in Philadelphia, bringing with him a commission as Judge of the Vice-Admiralty Court for Maryland, Pennsylvania and West Jersey. Despite a quarrel with William Penn in 1702 which caused Quary's dismissal, he quickly regained his judicial office. In 1702 Quary was named to New Jersey's first royal Council, although the appointment was intended merely to enhance the authority of his position as admiralty judge, and he never took a significant role in the Council's deliberations. Quary also acted briefly as a member of the Maryland Council in 1709 and 1710. He died in 1714, while serving as Surveyor General of Customs in America.

Bibliography: James P. Ronda, ''Robert Quary in America: A Study of Colonial and Imperial Factional Politics, 1684-1712,'' unpub. Ph.D. diss., University of Nebraska, 1970.

COLLETON, James, 1686-1690

Born in England, the son of John and Katherine (Amy) Colleton; date of birth unknown. Brother of Peter, Thomas, John and one other. Married to Ann Kendall, by whom he was the father of John and possibly others.

Served for a time as a member of the Assembly in Barbados before settling in Carolina. Granted, mostly in joint tenancy with his brothers Peter and Thomas, extensive property in the southern part of Carolina; also named a Landgrave of that colony. Commissioned Governor of southern Carolina in August 1686, a position he assumed that November and held until his overthrow by Seth Sothel in the summer of 1690.

Although Colleton was a vigorous enforcer of proprietary policy, he was never very astute politically, and by 1687 the "Goose Creek" faction in Carolina was even attempting to discredit the legal basis of his administration. Colleton responded by refusing to call the colony's Parliament into session, a step which lent credence to the claim of his opponents that he and the Carolina Proprietors were arbitrary rulers. In 1689 the threat of a possible French attack on Carolina further weakened Colleton's already perilous position, leading him to commission a tract early in 1690 which responded to attacks on his behavior and defended proprietary government. While this move appears to have won over to his side at least some of his opposition, Colleton made other errors in political judgment in February and March of 1690, when he declared martial law, imposed major restrictions on the Indian trade, and insisted that all landowners pay the quitrents due on their property. In the summer of 1690, outrage over these policies ended in rebellion, as Seth Sothel, who had recently been banished from the Albemarle settlement to the north, led a movement which overthrew Colleton and eventually expelled him from the colony.

Some time after his departure from Carolina, Colleton appears to have returned to Barbados, where he died in about 1706.

Bibliography: Henry A. M. Smith, "The Colleton Family in South Carolina," *South Carolina Historical and Genealogical Magazine*, I (October 1900), 325-41.

SOTHEL, Seth, 1690-1692

North Carolina, 1682-1689

Date and place of birth, and names of parents unknown. Married to Anna Willix; no surviving children. Purchased the Earl of Clarendon's proprietary share in Carolina in 1677, thereby becoming a Proprietor of that colony in his own right. Appointed Governor of Albemarle County late in 1678, but captured by Turkish pirates while *en route* to America. Released in July 1681, and by 1682 had arrived in Albemarle.

Selected as chief executive because of his "discreet" and "sober" character, Sothel eventually showed evidence of the damage which over two years in slavery had done to his personality. His first few years in office won the approval of John Archdale, a Quaker and future governor of Carolina; however, Sothel's actions appear to have become increasingly arbitrary. As a result, late in 1689 he was overthrown, after being accused of seizing property and inflicting imprisonment on his enemies without benefit of trial. Sothel finally left Albemarle when the General Assembly banished him for twelve months and barred him from holding public office for life, but by 1690 he had managed to secure the governorship of the southern part of Carolina. There he soon advocated legislation which would improve his own financial position, such as an act regulating the Indian trade which permitted the governor to receive one-third of the export duties and fines collected on furs and skins.

Within a short time, however, news of Sothel's behavior reached the Proprietors, and in the spring of 1692 Philip Ludwell, who had been appointed governor the previous November, arrived in Charles Town. Following a brief and unsuccessful attempt to resist Ludwell's commission, Sothel seems to have left the colony in the autumn of 1692. He died a short time later, possibly in late 1693 or early 1694. *DNB*.

LUDWELL, Philip, 1692-1693
North Carolina, 1690

Born *circa* 1640 in Bruton, Somersetshire, England, the son of Thomas and Jane (Cottington) Ludwell. Brother of Thomas, Mary, Margaret, Sarah and Jane. Married before October 1667 to Lucy (Higginson) Burwell Bernard; after his first wife's death in 1675, remarried in the spring of 1680 to Frances (Culpeper) Stephens Berkeley, the widow of previous governors of Albemarle County and of Virginia; father of Philip and Jane, both by his first wife.

After his immigration to Virginia in about 1660, acquired "Rich Neck" and "Green Spring," two estates in James City County. Became deputy to his brother, Thomas Ludwell, who served as secretary of the colony. Appointed to the Virginia Council in March 1675, and soon afterwards acted as Secretary; lost his seat on the Council in 1678, but was later reinstated. Also served as Deputy Surveyor of Customs in the 1680's. Played a major role in the resistance to Francis, Lord Howard of Effingham, who governed Virginia from 1684 to 1689; as a result of his opposition to Howard, was suspended and eventually dismissed from the Council. Elected to the Virginia House of

Burgesses in 1688, but forbidden to take his seat. Sent to England that year to present the appeal of the Burgesses against Lord Howard, and while there chosen by Carolina's Lords Proprietors as "Governor of that part of our province . . . that lyes North and East of Cape Fear." Qualified as Governor in May of 1690. Received an expanded commission from the Proprietors in November 1691 which included the southern part of Carolina, and presented his credentials in Charles Town in the spring of 1692.

Since his right to administer the northern section of Carolina was quickly challenged by John Gibbs, Ludwell appointed Thomas Jarvis as acting governor and left for London to defend his claim late in 1690. Following his return to America in 1692, Ludwell encountered other problems in southern Carolina, chiefly over the collection of quitrents and the methods of granting land, and in May 1693 the Proprietors revoked his southern appointment. A short time later Ludwell's northern commission was also recalled by his superiors. He then returned to England, probably in 1695, and died there sometime after 1704 (1723?).

Bibliography: Cassius F. Lee., Jr., "Ludwell Genealogy," *New England Historical and Genealogical Register*, XXXIII (April 1879), 220-22; "Philip Ludwell's Account [of Bacon's Rebellion]," *Virginia Magazine of History and Biography*, I (October 1893), 174-86; "Ludwell Family," *William and Mary Quarterly*, 1st ser., vol. XIX (January 1911), 199-214; "The Ludwells and Other Families," in Cazenove Gardner Lee, Jr., *Lee Chronicle: Studies of the Early Generations of the Lees of Virginia . . .*, comp. and ed. by Dorothy Mills Parker (New York, 1957). *DAB*.

SMITH, Thomas, 1693-1694

Born *circa* 1648 in England, probably the son of Thomas and Joan (Atkins) Smith. A Dissenter. Married in England to Barbara Atkins; following the death of his first wife, remarried on March 22, 1688 to Sabina de Vignon, dowager Van Wernhout, the widow of John D'Arsens; father of Thomas and George, both by his first marriage.

Practiced medicine before his arrival in Carolina in 1684; held office in the colony as Lord Proprietors' Deputy, Justice of the Peace, and member of the Council. Awarded the rank of Cacique in 1690 and that of Landgrave in 1691, two titles in the order of nobility devised for Carolina by John Locke, the philosopher. Served as Governor of southern Carolina from May 1693 until his death.

Although early in his administration Smith complained to the Proprietors that factionalism was hindering his efforts to govern, the sudden departure of several of his chief antagonists soon reduced the level of political tension in the colony. The Assembly responded to this more tranquil climate in 1694 by passing a rent collection law, a piece of legislation which officially acknowledged the right of Carolina's Proprietors to require the payment of quitrents. In large part, the more conciliatory mood of the Assembly was due to an important concession made the previous year, in which the Proprietors had confirmed the authority of the Lower House to initiate legislation. Smith's tenure was also marked by sustained attempts to eliminate the Indian slave trade and to end the complicity of some Carolinians with pirates, but he died on November 16, 1694, before the completion of his reform program.

Bibliography: Arthur M. Smith, *Some Account of the Smiths of Exeter and Their Descendants* . . . (Exeter, 1896); Edward Leodore Smith, "Landgrave Thomas Smith's Visit to Boston," *South Carolina Historical and Genealogical Magazine*, XXII (April 1921), 60-64; A.S. Salley, Jr., "The Family of the First Landgrave Thomas Smith," *South Carolina Historical and Genealogical Magazine*, XXVIII (July 1927), 169-75; A. S. Salley, Jr., "More on Landgrave Smith's Family," *South Carolina Historical and Genealogical Magazine*, XXX (October 1929), 255-56; Annie Elizabeth Miller, comp., *Our Family Circle* (Macon, Ga., 1931); Laurens Tenney Mills, *A South Carolina Family: Mills-Smith and Related Lines* (n.p., 1960).

BLAKE, Joseph, 1694-1695, 1696-1700

Born in England, the son of Captain Benjamin Blake; date of birth unknown. A Presbyterian. Brother of Elizabeth and perhaps others. Married to Deborah Morton, the daughter of Governor Joseph Morton; following the death of his first wife, remarried in December 1698 to Elizabeth (Axtell) Turgis, by whom he was the father of Joseph and Rebecca.

Immigrated to Carolina, where *circa* 1689 he was named Lords Proprietors' Deputy, succeeding his deceased father in that post; removed as Deputy by Governor Seth Sothel in October 1690, but appointed to the Council of Governor Philip Ludwell in November 1691. Continued as a member of the Council under Ludwell's successor, Thomas Smith; replaced Smith as Governor in November 1694, and served in that capacity until the arrival of John Archdale in the fall of 1695. In autumn 1696, following Archdale's departure for England, again took office as chief executive. Also named a Landgrave of Carolina in 1694.

Related by marriage to several of Carolina's most prominent families, Blake used his connections to enhance his political and economic position. Although he generally refrained from persecuting his enemies, Blake was occasionally capable of such behavior. In 1699, for example, he suspended Nicholas Trott from his appointments as attorney general and naval officer, after Trott had criticized the younger Joseph Morton, a judge of the court of vice-admiralty and a prominent member of the governor's ruling clique. Blake's relations with the English Crown and Parliament, however, were somewhat less easy to control. When Parliament in 1696 passed a more stringent Navigation Act, the legislation was defined to include proprietary colonies like Carolina. Henceforth, Carolina would be watched more closely by the new English Board of Trade, an accountability which zealous royal officials like Edward Randolph were eager to enforce. Nevertheless, southern Carolina's economy continued to grow during Blake's tenure, and when he died in office on September 7, 1700 the colony's production of naval stores had become a major source of revenue.

Bibliography: Langdon Cheves, "Blake of South Carolina," *South Carolina Historical and Genealogical Magazine*, I (April 1900), 153-66; G. Blake Palmer, "Blake of South Carolina: A Note on the English Ancestry of Governor Blake," *South Carolina Historical and Genealogical Magazine*, XXXIX (July 1938), 103-09.

ARCHDALE, John, 1695-1696

Born in 1642 in England, the son of Thomas and Mary (Nevill) Archdale. A Quaker. Brother of Thomas, Judith, Mary, Susan, Anne and Elizabeth. Married in December 1673 to Anne (Dobson) Cary, by whom he was the father of Thomas, Mary, Anne and one other daughter.

Attempted in 1664-65 to further the proprietary interests of Sir Ferdinando Gorges' heirs to Maine, by persuading Massachusetts Bay to give up its claim to that area; in 1681 purchased, in trust for his son, the Carolina proprietorship of Lord John Berkeley, and in 1682-83 served as a collector of quitrents for Carolina's Proprietors. Presided as Acting Governor of Albemarle County at various times between 1683 and 1686, when Seth Sothel was absent from the colony. Appointed by the Proprietors as Governor (and Landgrave) of Carolina in 1694, assuming office in the fall of the following year.

Soon after Archdale's arrival in southern Carolina, he was required to deal with the hostility of many of the English settlers to the colony's French Huguenots, who were accused of holding an unfair representation in the Assembly. Archdale ultimately yielded to this Francophobia, and his acquiescence helped him and the Assembly to settle differences between the Proprietors and the colonists over land grants, quitrents and debts owed to the Proprietors. Known as "Archdale's Laws," the code which they devised formed the foundation of South Carolina's legal system for the next twenty years. The Assembly under Archdale also passed a comprehensive slave law which defined slavery, albeit in equivocal terms, and which established a criminal code for the colony's bondsmen.

Archdale returned to London in the autumn of 1696. In 1698 he was elected to Parliament from High Wycombe in Buckinghamshire, but was denied his seat when he refused, based on his Quaker principles, to take the oath of office. He was the author of *A New Description of that Fertile and Pleasant Province of Carolina*..., published in London in 1707. Archdale was buried in the chancel of High Wycombe Church on July 4, 1717.

Bibliography: John Archdale, *A New Description of Carolina*... (London, 1707: reprinted, Charleston, 1822); Stephen B. Weeks, "John Archdale, and Some of His Descendants," *Magazine of American History*, XXIX (February 1893), 157-62; Henry Blackwood Archdale, *Memoirs of the Archdales, with the Descents of Some Allied Families* (Enniskillen, 1925). *DAB, DNB*.

MOORE, James, Sr., 1700-1703

Born *circa* 1650, and believed to have been a descendant of Roger Moore, one of the leaders of the Irish Rebellion of 1641. An Anglican. Married in about 1675 to Margaret Berringer, the step-daughter of Governor Sir John Yeamans; father of James (who served as governor of South Carolina from 1719 to 1721), Jehu, Roger, Maurice, John, Nathaniel, Anne, Mary, Rebecca and Margaret.

Immigrated to America from Barbados and settled in southern Carolina about 1675, where he later became a prominent trader with the Indians. Participated in several protests against the established political order, serving as one of the leaders of the anti-proprietary "Goose Creek men" in the 1680's and 1690's, contributing to the overthrow of Governor James Colleton in 1690, and attacking the policy of collecting quitrents in 1693 and 1694. Member of the Council during the administrations of governors Morton, Archdale and Blake, and representative from Berkeley County in the southern Carolina Commons House of Assembly in 1692-94. Named Secretary of the province by the Lords Proprietors in 1698; also served as Receiver General and Chief Justice in 1699-1700. As President of the Council, succeeded to the governorship in September 1700, after the death of Governor Blake.

Although he took office at a time when southern Carolina's politicians were still deeply divided into Anglican and "Dissenter" factions, Governor Moore was more concerned with using the perquisites of his office than he was with imposing on others his own religious beliefs. Apart from advancing the fortunes of his relations, Moore's major goals were to reform the Indian trade and to further Britain's colonial interests by protecting and extending its southern frontier in America. His efforts to regulate the Indian trade failed, largely because he and the Assembly were unable to agree on a code of conduct, but Moore's military aspirations met with greater success. In August 1702, shortly after official news of Britain's declaration of war against Spain and France reached Charles Town, the Commons House approved Moore's plan for an expedition against St. Augustine. Under the governor's own command, southern Carolina troops invaded Florida in October; they were forced to leave in December, however, when Spanish reinforcements arrived to lift their siege of St. Augustine's fort, the Castillo de San Maria.

Within several months Moore became the colony's Attorney General and was replaced as governor by Sir Nathaniel Johnson. In 1704 Moore organized a raid against the Apalache Indians, ostensibly to weaken Spanish influence among the natives, and he nearly exterminated the tribe. Several years later, in 1706, Moore died of yellow fever in Charles Town.

Bibliography: M. Alston Read, "Notes on Some Colonial Governors of South Carolina and Their Families," *South Carolina Historical and Genealogical Magazine*, XI (April 1910), 107-22; Janie Revill, *Abstract of Moore Records of South Carolina, 1694-1865* (Columbia, S.C., 1931); Mabel L. Webber, "The First Governor Moore and His Children," *South Carolina Historical and Genealogical Magazine*, XXXVII (January 1936), 1-23. *DAB*.

JOHNSON, Sir Nathaniel, 1703-1709

Born on April 7, 1644 near Kibblesworth, Durham, England, the son of William and Margaret (Sherwood) Johnson. A High Church Anglican. Married; father of Robert (who served as governor of South Carolina from 1717 to 1719 and again from 1730 to 1735), William and Anne.

As a young man served as a soldier, a "farmer" of chimney taxes in England's four northern counties, and a member of Parliament for Newcastle-on-Tyne. Knighted in December 1680. Chosen Governor of the Leeward Islands in 1686, resigning the position after the succession of William and Mary to the English throne. Named in 1686 as a "Cacique," a rank in the order of nobility used by Carolina's Lords Proprietors, and settled in southern Carolina in 1689. Became a leading politician, a large slaveholder and a successful cultivator of silk in the 1690's, establishing a plantation called "Silk Hope"; also developed an interest in botany. Appointed Governor of Carolina in June 1702, but because of illness did not take up his appointment until March of the following year; also awarded the hereditary title of Landgrave in 1703.

Johnson's tenure was dominated by a controversy between the colony's Anglicans and Dissenters, resulting from the governor's desire to exclude religious non-conformists from political office. At Johnson's urging, in 1704 the southern Carolina Assembly, which had managed to exclude Dissenters from its deliberations, passed legislation aimed at the establishment of the Anglican Church. After the colony's Dissenters had sent an agent to London with news of the Assembly's restrictive laws, the Crown in 1706 directed the Proprietors to disallow the legislation, but the passage of a modified act of establishment a short time later kept the issue smoldering throughout Johnson's period as governor. Johnson and the southern Carolina legislators confronted each other over several other points, particularly regarding authority to regulate the Indian trade and to nominate several officers who received a public salary. The Assembly eventually asserted its power over the governor in both of these areas, although as a concession Johnson did receive a ''gift'' of £400 and a yearly stipend of £100 in lieu of presents from the Indians.

While Johnson retired as governor after the arrival of Edward Tynte in November of 1709, he continued to reside in South Carolina, where he died in 1712.

Bibliography: Mabel L. Webber, ''Sir Nathaniel Johnson and His Son Robert, Governors of South Carolina,'' *South Carolina Historical and Genealogical Magazine*, XXXVIII (October 1937), 109-15. *DAB*.

TYNTE, Edward, 1709-1710

Date and place of birth unknown; no mention of relations in will, dated July 19, 1709, but may have been a member of the Tynte family of Somersetshire, England. Apparently served in the British Army, rising to the rank of Colonel. Appointed Governor of Carolina by the Lords Proprietors in December 1708, but did not arrive in the colony to begin his administration until November of the following year.

Although the poet William King extolled Tynte as ''the man who first from British shore, Palladian arts to Carolina bore,'' the new proprietary governor had little impact, cultural or otherwise, on the colony. The only General Assembly which met during Tynte's brief tenure passed relatively insignificant legislation, with the exception of an act ''for the founding and erecting of a free school for the use of the Inhabitants of South Carolina.'' On June 26, 1710, seven months after he assumed office, Tynte suddenly died, a development which sparked a resurgence of political factionalism. Before the supporters of Robert Gibbes could establish their candidate's claim to succeed Tynte, the adherents of Thomas Broughton challenged the means by which Gibbes had been elected, bringing the colony close to civil war.

GIBBES, Robert, 1710-1712

Born on January 9, 1644 in Sandwich, Kent, England, the son of Robert and Mary (Coventry) Gibbes. Brother of nine. First married on October 24, 1678 to Jane Davis, by whom he was the father of Thomas (died young) and Mary; remarried to Mary Davis, by whom he had William, Elizabeth and John.

Immigrated to Barbados as a young man. Named a Lords Proprietors' Deputy in Carolina, represented Colleton in the southern Carolina Commons House of Assembly from 1692 to 1694, and acted as a member of the Council after 1698. Served as Chief Justice in southern Carolina, an office he was occupying in 1709. Despite the bitter opposition of Thomas Broughton, became Acting Governor of southern Carolina in 1710, following the death of Edward Tynte, and held that position until his replacement by Charles Craven in March 1712.

Even before Gibbes' administration began, the spirit of factionalism had created a tumultuous political atmosphere. Gibbes managed to win the election held to find a successor to the deceased Tynte only by bribing a member of the Council, and his unscrupulous behavior so antagonized the supporters of Thomas Broughton that they were willing to fight in order to prevent Gibbes from governing the colony. In July of 1710 Broughton finally decided to withdraw his candidacy to avoid bloodshed, but Gibbes, although free to take over as chief executive, had lost the respect of a major segment of Carolina's population. As Anglican Commissary Gideon Johnston noted in a report to the Society for the Propagation of the Gospel in November 1711, Gibbes was "scarce owned or regarded" in either Carolina or England.

After the arrival of newly-appointed Governor Craven in March of 1712, Gibbes left office. He died about three years later, on January 24, 1715.

Bibliography: Rev. Robert Wilson, *Genealogy of the Gibbes Family of South Carolina* (Charleston, 1899); Henry S. Holmes, comp., "Robert Gibbes, Governor of South Carolina, and Some of His Descendants," *South Carolina Historical and Genealogical Magazine*, XII (April 1911), 78-105.

CRAVEN, Charles, 1712-1716

Born on May 6, 1682 in England, the son of Sir William and Lady Mary (Clapham) Craven. An Anglican. Brother of William (who was one of Carolina's Lords Proprietors), Thomas (died young), John, Robert, Christopher, Anthony (died in infancy), Henry (died young), Margaret, Mary, Martha, Elizabeth and Anne. Married to Elizabeth Staples, by whom he was the father of Charles, John, Robert and Elizabeth. Commissioned Deputy Governor of South Carolina in February 1711, and arrived in March of the following year to assume that position.

Craven's tenure was one of the most successful in South Carolina history, as his scrupulous regard for religious toleration helped to end the bickering between Anglicans and Dissenters which had disrupted previous administrations. During his first year as governor, he put to good use the resulting political harmony by encouraging the Assembly to enact laws which affected nearly every aspect of the colony's life. Nevertheless, while this close cooperation between Craven and the Legislature improved South Carolina's political condition, the danger of armed confrontation between white settlers and neighboring Indians grew significantly. Finally, in April of 1715, ill feeling over white violations of an act passed in 1707 to regulate the Indian trade culminated in the Yamasee War. Despite vigorous efforts by the governor to protect the colony, attacks on remote settlements persisted until well after Craven left office. Indeed, local anger over alleged proprietary indifference to South Carolina's Indian problem was a major factor contributing to a rebellion in 1719 which sought the establishment of royal government.

After appointing the elderly Robert Daniel as his deputy, Craven departed for home in April of 1716. He died in Berkshire, England on December 26, 1754.

Bibliography: "Craven Family of England" [a manuscript containing also two leaves of printed family data], in Local History and Genealogy Division, New York Public Library.

DANIEL, Robert, 1716-1717

North Carolina, 1703-1705

Date and place of birth, and names of parents unknown. An Anglican. Emigrated in 1679 from Barbados to Carolina, where he became one of the leaders of the "Goose Creek" political faction. Later named a Landgrave of Carolina. Acquired the military rank of Colonel, and at one time commanded the provincial militia in southern Carolina; played a prominent role in that colony's attack on St. Augustine during the autumn of 1702. Named Deputy Governor of northern Carolina in 1703, when Governor Sir Nathaniel Johnson decided to administer the southern section of Carolina himself and appoint a substitute to preside in the north.

Daniel's tenure as chief executive of Carolina north and east of the Cape Fear River was disrupted by the bitter controversy over the Vestry Act of 1703. That legislation, which denied the colony's large Quaker community the right of affirmation by insisting that all Assembly members take an oath of allegiance to the Queen, became the catalyst which finally resulted in the removal of Daniel from office early in 1705. The former deputy governor appears to have been reluctant to participate in northern Carolina politics after this incident. In October 1708, for example, he was named to the Council under Thomas Cary, but he asked "to be excused from sitting in this House."

Nevertheless, Daniel did not abandon politics completely. He represented Berkeley and Craven counties in the South Carolina Commons House of Assembly in 1706-07, 1708-09 and 1713-15, and in April 1716 he took over as Deputy Governor of that colony, replacing the departing Charles Craven. Daniel's administration in South Carolina, however, was no more tranquil than had been his previous experience in the governor's chair. Along with periodic squabbles with the Lower House, he engaged in a procedural dispute with William Rhett, a surveyor general of customs, who allegedly threatened to "kill the old Rogue" when Daniel interfered with his attempt to seize the Crown's share of cargo from a ship accused of trading with pirates.

Daniel's brief but tumultuous service in South Carolina ended with the arrival of Governor Robert Johnson (*circa* June-October) in 1717. The date of Daniel's death is unknown.

JOHNSON, Robert, 1717-1719, 1730-1735

Born in 1677 in England, the son of Sir Nathaniel Johnson, who served as governor of Carolina from 1703 to 1709. Brother of William and Anne. Married to a woman named Margaret; father of Robert, William, Nathaniel, Thomas, Margaret and Mary.

Became a prominent South Carolina planter. Mentioned by the Lords Proprietors in 1713 as a possible successor to South Carolina Governor Charles Craven; represented Carolina before the Board of Trade in 1715, requesting the Crown's assistance in the defense of the colony from the Yamasee Indians. Appointed Governor of South Carolina by the Proprietors in 1717, and arrived to begin his administration between June and October of that year.

Shortly after his selection as governor, Johnson entered into a dispute with the South Carolina Commons House over collection of quitrents and a proposal by the Proprietors which would have raised the price of land in the colony. Although he would have preferred to practice the art of political compromise, Johnson's hands over the next two years were usually tied by proprietary intransigence. Consequently, when rumors of a Spanish invasion in November of 1719 served as a catalyst for a revolt against proprietary rule, he turned down an offer to head the new revolutionary government, and was replaced by the Commons-appointed James Moore, Jr. Following an unsuccessful attempt to resume his role as chief executive in 1721, Johnson returned to England in 1724 and began to work towards winning a royal commission as governor. Finally, after the Crown's purchase of Carolina from the Proprietors in 1729, Johnson was approved by the Privy Council as South Carolina's second royal governor. Johnson's return to power led to a period of greater political stability, as he pursued a conciliatory policy towards the Commons House of Assembly. One of the most conspicuous achievements of his second administration was his "township scheme" which, by establishing new townships in the colony's back-country, provided an impetus for waves of Swiss, German, Irish and Welsh Protestant immigration. Johnson died on May 3, 1735, while still in office.

Bibliography: Mabel L. Webber, "Sir Nathaniel Johnson and His Son Robert, Governors of South Carolina," *South Carolina Historical and Genealogical Magazine*, XXXVIII (October 1937), 109-15; Richard P. Sherman, *Robert Johnson, Proprietary and Royal Governor of South Carolina* (Columbia, S.C., 1966). *DAB*.

MOORE, James, Jr., 1719-1721

Born *circa* 1680 in South Carolina, the son of James and Margaret (Berringer) Moore. An Anglican. Brother of Jehu, Roger, Maurice, John, Nathaniel, Anne, Mary, Rebecca and Margaret. Married to Elizabeth Beresford, by whom he was the father of James, Jehu, John, Margaret, Mary and Elizabeth.

Became a prominent planter in South Carolina, and represented Berkeley and Craven counties in the Commons House of Assembly from 1706 to 1708. Commanded South Carolina troops during their campaign against the Tuscarora Indians in 1713. Acted as *de facto* chief executive between the overthrow of proprietary rule in South Carolina late in 1719 and the arrival of Francis Nicholson, the colony's first Crown-appointed governor, in May 1721.

The culmination of several decades of opposition to proprietary power in South Carolina occurred in December of 1719, when the Commons House formed itself into a convention "delegated by the People." After Governor Robert Johnson refused to serve under a regime which admitted allegiance only to the Crown, the convention chose Moore as a provisional chief executive, and for the next eighteen months South Carolina experienced a period of transitional rule. Although Moore and his supporters quickly arranged for the election of a new Assembly and Council, they were still forced to contend with the machinations of such men as William Rhett, who sought the restoration of proprietary government. In the spring of 1721 Rhett and the deposed Johnson attempted to topple the rebel administration, but Moore refused to yield his authority until Francis Nicholson arrived late in May with a royal commission to govern the province.

Moore then returned to the Commons House of Assembly, where he served as Speaker from 1721 to 1724. While on February 15, 1724 he was empowered to act as sole Commissioner of Indian Affairs for South Carolina, he died on March 3 of that year, less than three weeks after his appointment.

Bibliography: Janie Revill, *Abstract of Moore Records of South Carolina, 1694-1865* (Columbia, S.C., 1931); Mabel L. Webber, "The First Governor Moore and His Children," *South Carolina Historical and Genealogical Magazine*, XXXVII (January 1936), 1-23.

NICHOLSON, Francis, 1721-1725

New York, 1688-1689; Virginia, 1690-1692, 1698-1705; Maryland 1694-1698

Born on November 12, 1655 at "Downholme Park," near Richmond, in Yorkshire, England, probably the son of Thomas Nicholson. Never married.

Became a protegé of Lord St. John of Basing, acting for a time as page to his wife. Entered the English Army in January 1678, and in 1686 was appointed Captain of a company of foot soldiers accompanying Sir Edmund Andros to New England. Named to the Council organized under the Dominion of New England, and eventually commissioned Lieutenant Governor; served as Andros' deputy in New York from 1688 to 1689. Sailed for England after the fall of the Dominion, but soon received a commission as Lieutenant Governor of Virginia, a position which he held from June of 1690 to September 1692; again served as Virginia's chief executive, with the rank of Royal Governor, from December 1698 to August 1705. Also presided as Governor of Maryland from July 1694 to December 1698, of Nova Scotia for several weeks in 1713, and of South Carolina from May 1721 to the spring of 1725.

Nicholson's remarkable instinct for political survival enabled him to serve as resident chief executive of five different colonies during a period encompassing some thirty-seven years. Throughout his long professional career, he often experienced opposition from local officials, opposition which became especially virulent during his second tenure in Virginia. In that colony a bitter quarrel with Commissary James Blair and other members of the Virginia Council finally brought about his recall in 1705. Nevertheless, despite the hostility which he sometimes provoked, Nicholson's record as a colonial administrator was not without a number of significant achievements. In Maryland, for example, his strong interest in education led him to aid in the establishment of King William's School (later St. John's College), while several years earlier he had supported Commissary Blair's efforts in Virginia to found the College of William and Mary.

By the 1720's ill health and concern in London over his policy regarding paper currency in South Carolina had reduced Nicholson's political effectiveness, and in the spring of 1725 he sailed for England on a leave of absence. He died in London on March 5, 1728, leaving the bulk of his estate to the Society for the Propagation of the Gospel in Foreign Parts, an organization in which, as a staunch Anglican, he had always taken an active role.

Bibliography: [Unsigned], "Instructions to Francis Nicholson," *Virginia Magazine of History and Biography*, IV (1896), 49-54; [unsigned], "Papers Relating to the Administration of Governor Nicholson . . .," *Virginia Magazine of History and Biography*, VII (1899-1900), 153-72, 275-86, 386-401, vol. VIII (1900-01), 46-58, 126-46, 260-73, 366-85, vol. IX (1901-02),

18-33, 152-62, 251-62; Charles William Sommerville, "Early Career of Governor Francis Nicholson," *Maryland Historical Magazine*, IV (June-September 1909), 101-14, 201-20; Louis B. Wright, "William Byrd's Opposition to Governor Francis Nicholson," *Journal of Southern History*, XI (February 1945), 68-79; Samuel Clyde McCullough, "The Fight to Depose Governor Nicholson," *Journal of Southern History*, XII (August 1946), 403-22; Fairfax Downey, "The Governor Goes A-Wooing: The Swashbuckling Courtship of Nicholson of Virginia, 1699-1705," *Virginia Magazine of History and Biography*, LV (January 1947), 6-19; Ruth M. Winton, "Governor Francis Nicholson's Relations with the Society for the Propagation of the Gospel in Foreign Parts, 1701-1727," *Historical Magazine of the Protestant Episcopal Church*, XVII (September 1948), 274-96; Bruce T. McCully, "From the North Riding to Morocco: The Early Years of Governor Francis Nicholson, 1655-1686," *William and Mary Quarterly*, 3rd ser., vol. XIX (October 1962), 534-56; Gary B. Nash, "Governor Francis Nicholson and the New Castle Expedition of 1696," *Delaware History*, XI (April 1965), 229-39; Stephen S. Webb, "The Strange Career of Francis Nicholson," *William and Mary Quarterly*, 3rd ser., vol. XXIII (October 1966), 513-48. *DAB*, *DNB*.

MIDDLETON, Arthur, 1725-1730

Born in 1681 in Charles Town, South Carolina, the son of Edward Middleton and his wife Sarah, the widow of Richard Fowell of Barbados. Married in 1707 to Sarah Amory; after his first wife's death in 1722, remarried on August 3, 1723 to Sarah (Wilkinson) Morton; father by his first wife of William, Henry, Thomas and, among other infants who died young, Hester. Possibly educated in England. A planter, and heir to several estates in Carolina, Barbados and England.

Served in the South Carolina Commons House of Assembly, representing Berkeley and Craven counties in 1706-09 and 1716-17, and St. James Goose Creek Parish in 1717-21. Between his two periods of service in the Commons House, appointed as the Deputy of Lord Carteret, one of Carolina's Proprietors. As the leader of an anti-proprietary movement, served as President of a convention which chose James Moore, Jr. to be provisional governor, in place of Robert Johnson, the last proprietary governor; elected President of the Governor's Council upon the establishment of royal control in 1721. Assumed the executive leadership of South Carolina when Governor Francis Nicholson departed for England in the spring of 1725.

Middleton's five years as Acting Governor were characterized by several crises, the most significant of which involved a major dispute between the Governor's Council and the South Carolina Commons House over the colony's paper money supply. The Council's repeated refusal to approve bills providing for an increase in paper currency finally led to an almost total disruption of government in 1728, when the Commons House stopped meeting in order to demonstrate its opposition to the Council's position. Middleton's administration also felt the effects of a serious depression in 1727. The colony's market for naval stores, formerly subsidized by a royal bounty, lost that subsidy in 1724, and within three years the naval stores market had collapsed. As a result South Carolina's small farmers, who had been particularly affected by this economic setback, organized an anti-tax movement which sponsored protest meetings and drew up petitions to the Commons House. On the other hand, there were occasional instances of effective co-operation under Middleton, especially during a retaliatory attack on the Yamasee Indians in February 1728.

Middleton resumed his seat on the Council when Robert Johnson, this time in the capacity of royal governor, took control of South Carolina's affairs in December 1730. Middleton also served once again as President of the Council, a position which he held when he died on September 7, 1737.

Bibliography: Charlotte Manigault Taylor Akerly, "The Middletons of Twickenham, Co. Middlesex, England, and of the Province of Carolina, America," *New York Genealogical and Biographical Record*, XXVIII (July-October 1897), 167-68, 239-41; Langdon Cheves, "Middleton of South Carolina," *South Carolina Historical and Genealogical Magazine*, I (July 1900), 228-62. *DAB*.

BROUGHTON, Thomas, 1735-1737

Born in England, the son of Andrew and Anne (Overton) Broughton; date of birth unknown. Brother of Constantia, Christiana, Lydia, Mary and Althea. Married *circa* 1683 to Anne, the daughter of Sir Nathaniel Johnson (governor of Carolina from 1703 to 1709); father of Joanna, Nathaniel, Andrew, Robert, Anne, Christiana and Constantia.

Settled near Charles Town in Carolina by the mid-1690's, and in 1702 was acting as a Proprietors' Deputy. Represented Berkeley and Craven counties in the South Carolina Commons House of Assembly from 1696 to 1703, and again from 1716 to 1717; also sat in the Lower House as a representative of St. Thomas and St. Dennis from 1725 to 1727; presided as Speaker of the Commons House in 1716-17 and 1725-27. Served in various other public capacities, including Councillor, Collector of Customs and Surveyor General. Commissioned Lieutenant Governor of South Carolina in October 1730, and became Acting Governor of that province in May 1735, following the death of Robert Johnson.

After the largely harmonious administration of Robert Johnson, Broughton's tenure represented a return to the political divisiveness which had frequently plagued South Carolina in the past. Quarrels over money matters between the chief executive and the Commons House were especially troublesome, with the legislators in the Commons accusing Broughton and the Council of interfering with their authority in that area. Broughton also involved South Carolina in a bitter dispute with Georgia over control of the Indian trade, a dispute which was finally referred to the Board of Trade in London for resolution. Broughton died on November 22, 1737, while still serving as acting governor.

Bibliography: Henry E. Waite, "The Name and Family of Broughton," *New England Historical and Genealogical Register*, XXXVII (July 1883), 298-304; Henry A. M. Smith, "The Baronies of South Carolina: The Fairlawn Barony," *South Carolina Historical and Genealogical Magazine*, XI (October 1910), 193-202; D. E. Huger Smith, ed., "Broughton Letters," *South Carolina Historical and Genealogical Magazine*, XV (October 1914), 171-96; M. Leon Broughton, comp. and ed., *Broughton Memoirs*, 2nd ed. (Tyler, Texas, 1964).

BULL, William, Sr., 1737-1743

Born in April 1683 at "Ashley Hall," near Charles Town, South Carolina, the son of Stephen Bull, one of South Carolina's leading political figures. Brother of John, Catherine and perhaps Burnaby. Married to Mary Quintyne; father of Stephen, William, Jr. (later to become an acting governor of South Carolina as well), Elizabeth, Charlotta and Mary Henrietta. Became a wealthy rice planter and the owner of several large estates; also developed interests as an amateur historian, musician, gardener and botanist.

Member of the South Carolina Commons House of Assembly, representing Berkeley and Craven counties from 1706 to 1708 and again from 1716 to 1717. Served as Captain of militia during the Tuscarora and Yamasee wars; in 1721 appointed one of three commissioners responsible for managing the colony's Indian trade. Member of the Proprietors' Council in 1719 and, despite his alliance with the defeated proprietary faction, appointed to the South Carolina Royal Council in 1720, serving in that role until 1737. In his capacity as President of the Council, became Acting Governor after the death of Governor Thomas Broughton in November 1737, and confirmed as Lieutenant Governor the following year.

Although Bull as lieutenant governor was supposed to serve only until the arrival of South Carolina's royal governor, several developments enabled him to retain effective power for over five years. Colonel Samuel Horsey, who was commissioned royal governor of South Carolina in August 1738, died in England only a few weeks after taking his oath of office, and James Glen, his replacement, remained in England bickering over salary questions and the precise meaning of his instructions until 1743. Consequently, Bull was permitted to exert a stronger influence on South Carolina's development than he might have under different circumstances. Bull's major success was in establishing a large measure of political harmony within the colony, a harmony which in many ways resembled that achieved by Governor Robert Johnson in the early 1730's. This atmosphere of co-operation became especially crucial in 1739, when England and Spain went to war and the southern frontier of England's American colonies became vulnerable to Spanish attack. While no battles during the war were actually fought on South Carolina soil, Bull's administration provided troops for military operations in Georgia and the Floridas. Also during Bull's governorship, the South Carolina Assembly passed a more precise slave code (1740), partly in response to several slave uprisings in the colony during the previous year.

Following the arrival of Royal Governor James Glen in December 1743, Bull stepped down as South Carolina's chief executive, but he held the office of lieutenant governor until his death on March 21, 1755.

Bibliography: Langdon Cheves, "The Bull Family of South Carolina," *South Carolina Historical and Genealogical Magazine*, I (January 1900), 76-90; Thomas Gamble, "Col. William Bull—His Part in the Founding of Savannah," *Georgia Historical Quarterly*, XVII (June 1933), 111-26; M. Eugene Sirmans, Jr., "Masters of Ashley Hall: A Biographical Study of the Bull Family of Colonial South Carolina, 1670-1737," unpub. Ph.D. diss., Princeton University, 1959; Henry D. Bull, *The Family of Stephen Bull . . . 1600-1960* (Georgetown, S.C., 1961); M. Eugene Sirmans, "Politicians and Planters: The Bull Family of Colonial South Carolina," South Carolina Historical Association, *Proceedings for 1962* (1963), 32-41. *DAB*.

GLEN, James, 1743-1756

Born in 1701 in Linlithgow, Scotland, the eldest son of Alexander Glen of Longcroft and his wife, Marion (Graham) Glen. Brother of seven, including John, Thomas, Andrew and Agnes. Married to the illegitimate daughter of the Earl of Wilmington, according to a report spread by the Earl of Egmont; no children.

Studied at Leyden, and later practiced law. Held various public offices in Scotland, among which was that of High Sheriff, a position he used to compel Scottish liquor dealers to pay their license fees. Appointed Royal Governor of

South Carolina in 1738, but did not arrive in the province to assume that office until December of 1743.

Glen presided as chief executive of colonial South Carolina longer than any other governor in its history. Despite periodic arguments with the Commons House over what he perceived to be its encroachment on the royal prerogative, Glen was usually willing to make concessions rather than provoke outright hostility. Indeed, during the first four years of his administration he enjoyed a better relationship with the Commons House than he did with his own Council. Although this harmony between Glen and the Lower House was interrupted in 1748, when the Commons objected to the governor's measures for handling problems stemming from King George's War, Glen was in a strong political position by the beginning of 1750. From 1750 until his departure from office, however, he encountered increased opposition from the Board of Trade in London, which complained of his often loose interpretation of royal instructions. Glen then attempted to please his superiors in England by adopting a sterner manner in his relations with the Commons House, but in doing so he lost much of his legislative support, especially after he sought to take a more independent role in the shaping of Indian policy.

By March 1755 the still dissatisfied Board of Trade had arranged for Glen to be succeeded by William Henry Lyttelton, who arrived in the colony in June of the following year. Glen retired for a time to his plantation outside Charlestown, and later returned to England. He died in London on July 18, 1777.

Bibliography: Charles Rogers, *Memorials of the Scottish Family of Glen* (Edinburgh, 1888); J. G. B. Bullock, *A History of the Glen Family of South Carolina and Georgia* (n.p., 1923); James M. Glen, "Glen: The Genesis of a Scots Family" (1944) typescript volume in Local History and Genealogy Division, New York Public Library; Chapman J. Milling, ed., *Colonial South Carolina: Two Contemporary Descriptions by Governor James Glen and Doctor George Milligen-Johnston* (Columbia, S.C., 1951); Mary F. Carter, "Governor James Glen of Colonial South Carolina: A Study in British Administrative Policies," unpub. Ph.D. diss., University of California, Los Angeles, 1951.

LYTTELTON, William Henry, 1756-1760

Born on December 24, 1724 in England, the sixth son of Sir Thomas and Lady Christian (Temple) Lyttelton. Married to Mary Macartney on June 2, 1761, and remarried to Carolina Bristow in February 1774; father of George Fulke by his first wife and of William Henry by his second. Studied at Eton College and St. Mary Hall, Oxford, receiving an honorary degree from the latter institution in 1781; called to the bar by London's Middle Temple in 1748.

As a Member of Parliament, represented Bewdley in Worcestershire from December 1748 until February 1755; again an M.P. for Bewdley beginning in October 1774. Commissioned Royal Governor of South Carolina in March 1755, and arrived in June of 1756.

Lyttelton's arrival in South Carolina preceded by only one month the news that England had gone to war with France, and this development had the effect of making the colony's Commons House of Assembly more amenable to the governor's wishes than it might have been otherwise. However, while Lyttelton managed to persuade the Commons House to relinquish some of its minor powers, the decline in internal political unrest during his administration was due more to wartime necessity and Lyttelton's conciliatory spirit than it was to any basic agreement in principle between the governor and the legislature. Furthermore, the relative success which Lyttelton enjoyed in his dealings with the Commons House stands in sharp contrast to the clumsy manner with which he handled Cherokee grievances in the late 1750's. In April 1760 Lyttelton, having learned of his selection as Governor of Jamaica, sailed from South Carolina while the colony was still embroiled in a vicious Indian war.

Following his Jamaica governorship, Lyttelton was appointed Ambassador to Portugal in October of 1766. After his return to England in 1771, he was awarded numerous honors, including an Irish peerage in 1776 and a British peerage as Lord Lyttelton, Baron of Frankley, in 1794. Lyttelton also became one of the commissioners of the British Treasury in June 1776, but resigned that post in March 1782. He was the author of "An Historical Account of the Constitution of Jamaica," first published as part of *The Laws of America* (1792), and the privately issued *Trifles in Verse* (1803). Lyttelton died at "Hagley Hall" in Stourbridge, Worcestershire on September 14, 1808.

Bibliography: Maud Wyndham, *Chronicles of the Eighteenth Century, Founded on the Correspondence of Sir Thomas Lyttelton and His Family*, 2 vols. (London, 1924); Lewis M. Wiggin, *The Faction of Cousins: A Political Account of the Grenvilles, 1733-1763* (New Haven, 1958); Clarence John Attig, "William Henry Lyttelton: A Study in Colonial Administration," unpub. Ph.D. diss., University of Nebraska, 1958. *DAB, DNB*.

BULL, William, Jr., 1760-1761, 1764-1766, 1768, 1769-1771, 1773-1775

Born on September 24, 1710 at "Ashley Hall," near Charles Town, South Carolina, the second son of William Bull, Sr., who served as acting and lieutenant governor of South Carolina from 1737 to 1743, and Mary (Quintyne) Bull. Brother of Stephen, Elizabeth, Charlotta and Mary Henrietta. Married on August 17, 1746 to Hannah Beale; no children. Studied medicine in Europe, receiving the degree of Doctor of Medicine from Leyden in 1734. Returned to South Carolina, and became a prominent planter and politician.

Member of the South Carolina Commons House of Assembly, representing St. Andrew's Parish (1736-42, 1746-47), St. John's Berkeley Parish (1742-45), Prince William's Parish (1745-46, 1749), and St. Bartholomew Parish (1748); served as Speaker of the Commons House, 1740-42, 1744-47 and 1748-49. Also became Captain of South Carolina troops during the "War of Jenkins' Ear" between England and Spain from 1739 to 1742. Appointed to the South Carolina Council in December 1748, and remained a member of that body until his selection as Lieutenant Governor in November 1759. In his capacity as lieutenant governor, served as South Carolina's acting chief executive in the absence of the colony's royal governors during 1760-61, 1764-66, 1768, 1769-71 and 1773-75.

William Bull, Jr.'s service as Acting Governor covered eight years of the critical period which began with South Carolina's war with the Cherokee Indians and ended with the colonial rebellion from English rule. Bull demonstrated his adeptness at handling Indian affairs in late 1761, when his policies helped bring an end to the Cherokee War, but he was less successful when confronted by grievances over objectionable British legislation. Although he was sympathetic to colonial complaints, Bull was also required to enforce Crown policy. Consequently, while he endeavored to soften the impact of offensive measures such as the Stamp Act and the Tea Act, he defended the British position on these and other issues, and by the summer of 1774 his effective power in the colony had diminished considerably.

Bull's political career came to an end following the arrival in June 1775 of Lord William Campbell, South Carolina's last royal governor. However, his services to South Carolina did not go unrecognized, and his estates were made exempt from the confiscatory acts directed at Loyalists. He left South Carolina in December 1782 and travelled to London, where he died on July 4, 1791.

Bibliography: Langdon Cheves, "The Bull Family of South Carolina," *South Carolina Historical and Genealogical Magazine*, I (January 1900), 76-90; Eleanor Winthrop Townsend, "William Bull, M.D. (1710-1791), Lieutenant-Governor of South Carolina under the Royal Government," *Annals of Medical History*, n.s., vol. VII (1935), 311-22; M. Eugene Sirmans, Jr., "Masters of Ashley Hall: A Biographical Study of the Bull Family of Colonial South Carolina, 1670-1737," unpub. Ph.D. diss., Princeton University, 1959; Henry D. Bull, *The Family of Stephen Bull . . . 1600-1960* (Georgetown, S.C., 1961); M. Eugene Sirmans, "Politicians and Planters: The Bull Family of Colonial South Carolina," South Carolina Historical Association, *Proceedings for 1962* (1963), 32-41. *DAB*.

BOONE, Thomas, 1761-1764

New Jersey, 1760-1761

Born *circa* 1730 in England, the son of Charles Boone, at one time a member of Parliament, and his wife Elizabeth, the sister of John Garth. Brother of Charles. Married to Sarah Ann (Tattnall) Peronneau; apparently had no children.

Educated at Eton and at Trinity College, Cambridge. Travelled to South Carolina in 1752, where he established his claim to the extensive estate once owned by his uncle Joseph Boone, a leader of the colony's anti-proprietary faction during the early eighteenth century. Returned to England several years later, but in 1758 again sailed for South Carolina. Commissioned Captain General and Governor-in-Chief of New Jersey in January 1760, arriving in that province the following July; left New Jersey in October 1761 in order to accept the governorship of South Carolina, a position he occupied from December 1761 to May 1764.

Boone's brief tenure in New Jersey was rather uneventful, as the Assembly concerned itself chiefly with routine matters, such as the raising of troops needed for the latter stages of the French and Indian War. However, in South Carolina the political harmony which Boone had experienced in New Jersey was replaced by bitter controversy. Despite a warm reception from the Commons House of Assembly, Boone soon became embroiled in a conflict over the naming of Christopher Gadsden to that body, an election whose validity the governor contested in retaliation for the Commons' refusal to consider his proposed amendments to an election act. The *impasse* which resulted eventually disrupted Boone's administration, and in the spring of 1764 the frustrated chief executive decided to return home on a leave of absence.

Once in England Boone defended his actions in South Carolina before the Board of Trade, which nevertheless concluded that he had "been actuated by a degree of passion and resentment inconsistent with good policy." In December 1769 Boone received an appointment as a Commissioner of Customs, an office which he finally resigned in 1805. Boone died at "Lee Place," his paternal home in Kent, on September 25, 1812.

Bibliography: L. B. Namier, "Charles Garth and His Connexions," *English Historical Review*, LIV (July 1939), 443-70; Felix Gilbert, ed., "Letters of Francis Kinloch to Thomas Boone, 1782-1788," *Journal of Southern History*, VIII (February 1942), 87-105.

MONTAGU, Lord Charles Greville, 1766-1768, 1768-1769, 1771-1773

Born on May 29, 1741 in England, the second son of Robert Montagu, 3rd Duke of Manchester, and his wife, the former Harriet Dunch. Brother of George (later 4th Duke of Manchester), Caroline and Louisa. Married on September 20, 1765 to Elizabeth Bulmer, by whom he had George Charles and Elizabeth Harriet (died young).

Commissioned Royal Governor of South Carolina in February 1766, and arrived in the province the following June to assume office; except for absences from May to October of 1768 and July 1769 to September 1771, continued to serve as chief executive until his departure for England in March 1773.

Only twenty-five years old and politically inexperienced at the beginning of his administration, Montagu was unprepared for the turmoil which he soon encountered in South Carolina. Although he had let Lieutenant Governor William Bull, Jr. deal with some of the problems stemming from the Regulator movement of the late 1760's, Montagu had less success in avoiding popular opposition in the province to British imperial policy. After his return to South Carolina in 1771 from a trip to England, Montagu dissolved the Commons in response to a jurisdictional dispute over a money bill, a technique which he employed three more times before he relinquished the governor's chair to Bull in 1773 for the third and final time. By early 1773 the *South-Carolina Gazette* had become severely critical of Montagu's pre-emptory behavior, pointing out that the governor's "unparalleled Succession of Prorogations and Dissolutions" had in effect deprived the province of a representative Assembly for several years.

Montagu later fought on the British side during the final stages of the Revolution. He died in Halifax, Nova Scotia on February 4, 1784.

Bibliography: "Letter from Lord Charles Greville Montagu to Barnard Elliott," *South Carolina Historical and Genealogical Magazine*, XXXIII (October 1932), 259-61.

CAMPBELL, Lord William, 1775

Born in Scotland, the fourth son of John Campbell, the fourth Duke of Argyll, and Mary (Bellenden) Campbell, Duchess of Argyll. Brother of John (later fifth Duke of Argyll), Henry, Frederick and Mary. Married on April 7, 1763 to Sarah Izard of South Carolina; father of William, Louisa and Caroline.

Achieved the rank of Captain in the Royal Navy in 1762, and commanded the *Nightingale*, which visited South Carolina in 1763. Elected to the House of

Commons in 1764, representing Argyllshire, but resigned in 1766 when he was chosen as Governor of Nova Scotia. Although commissioned Governor of South Carolina in August 1773, permitted Lieutenant Governor William Bull, Jr. to serve in his place until June of 1775, when he took over personal supervision of the colony's affairs.

Campbell's arrival was greeted with little of the enthusiasm usually reserved for new royal governors. News of clashes between British and colonial troops had already reached South Carolina, and revolutionary fervor within the colony was on the increase. Indeed, Campbell soon found that most of his executive power had been usurped by a Patriot "Council of Safety." While he tried at first to win support among Loyalists living on South Carolina's frontier, particularly in the Camden and Ninety-Six districts, Campbell's position deteriorated rapidly, and in August 1775 the colonial Assembly convened for the last time. The next month Campbell fled Charlestown, seeking refuge on the British sloop-of-war *Tamar*.

After his departure from Charlestown, Campbell participated in the naval Battle of Sullivan's Island, which was fought in Charlestown harbor on June 28, 1776, and was seriously wounded. He died from the effects of the injury in Southampton, England two years later, on September 5, 1778.

Bibliography: [anonymous], *The House of Argyll and the Collateral Branches of the Clan Campbell, from the Year 420 to the Present Time* (Glasgow, 1871); Rev. Hely Smith, *The MacCallum More: A History of the Argyll Family from the Earliest Times* (London, 1871). *DAB*.

LAURENS, Henry, 1775-1776

Born on February 24, 1724 in Charlestown, South Carolina, the eldest son of John and Hester [or Esther] (Grasset) Laurens. Brother of five. Married on June 25, 1750 to Eleanor Ball; father of at least twelve children, though only Martha, Mary Eleanor, John and Henry reached their maturity. Received early education in South Carolina, and sent to London in 1744 for training in commerce. Partner in a Charlestown general commission firm from the late 1740's until 1762, when he took over the business after the dissolution of the partnership. By the mid-1760's, began to acquire large estates in South Carolina and Georgia, including "Mepkin," "Mt. Tacitus" and "Wambaw," and raised indigo and rice. Travelled to England on business in the early 1770's, returning to Charlestown in December 1774.

Member of the South Carolina Commons House of Assembly as a representative from St. Philip's Parish (1757-61, 1765-72) and St. Michael's Parish (1762-65). Served as Lieutenant Colonel of South Carolina militia in 1761, during the Cherokee War. Elected to South Carolina's First Provincial Congress in early 1775, chosen President of the executive General Committee, and in June 1775 became the Congress' President. Later that month selected as President of the Council of Safety, and in that capacity became the chief executive of South Carolina's Patriot faction.

Laurens' elevation to the presidency of the Council of Safety came at a time when royal authority in South Carolina had begun to deteriorate rapidly, and by September 1775 Lord William Campbell, the royal governor, found it necessary to flee the colony and seek refuge on a British ship off the coast. Taking advantage of Campbell's departure, Laurens quickly consolidated his power. In November of 1775 he played a major part in South Carolina's Second Provincial Congress, and in February 1776 he participated in the deliberations which produced a temporary constitution. He then turned over his administration to President John Rutledge, who was chosen as the new chief executive under the constitution. In recognition of his past services, Laurens was named South Carolina's Vice-President.

From 1777 to 1780 Laurens served in the Continental Congress as a delegate from South Carolina, and from November 1777 to December 1778 he acted as President of that body. In August 1780 he left America on a diplomatic mission to Holland, but he was captured by the British, brought to England, and imprisoned in the Tower of London from October 1780 to December 1781. Laurens spent the two and one-half years following his release from the Tower as an official participant in the Paris peace negotiations and as an unofficial "minister" to Great Britain. He returned to America in August 1784, his health broken, and spent the last years of his life in retirement, dying on December 8, 1792. Laurens carried on an extensive correspondence, and was the author of several political tracts, including the posthumously-published *A South Carolina Protest against Slavery* (1861).

Bibliography: David Ramsay, *Memoirs of the Life of Martha Laurens Ramsay* . . . (Philadelphia, 1811); Martha J. Lamb, "Henry Laurens in the London Tower," *Magazine of American History*, XVIII (July 1887), 1-12; David Duncan Wallace, *The Life of Henry Laurens* . . . (New York, 1915); David R. Chesnutt, "South Carolina's Penetration of Georgia in the 1760's: Henry Laurens as a Case Study," *South Carolina Historical Magazine*, 73 (October 1972), 194-208; Philip M. Hamer *et al.*, eds., *The Papers of Henry Laurens*, 6 vols. to date (Columbia, S.C., 1968-78). *DAB*.

RUTLEDGE, John, 1776-1778, 1779-1782

Born in September 1739 in the vicinity of Charlestown, South Carolina, the eldest son of Dr. John and Sarah (Hext) Rutledge. Brother of Andrew, Thomas, Sarah, Hugh, Mary and Edward. Married on May 1, 1763 to Elizabeth Grimké, by whom he was the father of Martha, Sarah (died young), John, Edward, Frederick, Charles, William, Thomas (died young), Elizabeth and States.

Studied with his father, with an Anglican minister in Christ Church Parish, and with a classics tutor in Charlestown; attended Middle Temple in London, England, and called to the English bar in February 1760. Shortly thereafter returned to Charlestown to practice law and engage in politics. Member of the South Carolina Commons House of Assembly, representing Christ Church Parish from 1761 to 1775. Served as Attorney General *pro tempore* of South Carolina from 1764 to 1765. Represented South Carolina in 1765 at the Stamp Act Congress in New York. Also attended the First and Second Continental Congresses in 1774 and 1775. After returning to South Carolina late in 1775, chosen to the Council of Safety; as a member of the Second Provincial Congress, participated in the drafting of the South Carolina Constitution of 1776, and under that instrument elected President of South Carolina early in 1776. Re-elected to a two-year term as president in December 1776, but resigned early in 1778; elected Governor in January 1779, serving until January 1782.

As president (and later governor) of South Carolina, Rutledge served as the state's chief executive throughout virtually the entire Revolutionary War. Consequently, his chief function was to protect South Carolina from British invasion, and his success in that area was at first remarkable. After the British attack on Charlestown in June 1776 had been repulsed at the Battle of Sullivan's Island, the state remained relatively untouched by the war for over two years. Shortly following Rutledge's return as chief executive in January 1779, however, Charlestown was again placed under British assault, and in May 1780 its defenders finally capitulated to the enemy. For the next year and a half Rutledge conducted what government business he could from several temporary headquarters, and it was not until November of 1781 that conditions had improved enough so that he could call for the election of a legislature. When the "Jacksonborough" Legislature met, it chose John Mathewes to replace Rutledge, who was ineligible to succeed himself.

Subsequent to his service as president and governor, Rutledge became a member of the South Carolina House, representing St. Andrew's Parish, but he soon left the state to attend the Continental Congress in 1782 and 1783. In 1784 he was elected to the South Carolina Court of Chancery, and from late 1784 to 1790 he was again a member of the State House of Representatives. Rutledge also attended the Federal Constitutional Convention in 1787 as a delegate from South Carolina, chairing that convention's Committee of Detail. In 1789 he was appointed Senior Associate Justice of the United States Supreme Court, but gave up that appointment after his election as Chief Justice of South Carolina in February 1791. Although Rutledge was nominated to be chief justice of the United States Supreme Court in 1795, he did not receive the confirmation of the Senate. Even while he was serving as Acting Chief Justice before his Senate defeat, Rutledge had begun to show growing signs of mental illness, and his public career soon ended. He died in Charleston, South Carolina on July 18, 1800.

Bibliography: "Letters of John Rutledge," *South Carolina Historical and Genealogical Magazine*, XVII (October 1916), 131-46, vol. XVIII (January-October 1917), 42-49, 59-69, 131-42, 155-67; Mabel L. Webber, "Dr. John Rutledge and His Descendants," *South Carolina Historical and Genealogical Magazine*, XXXI (January-April 1930), 7-25, 93-106; Robert W. Barnwell, Jr., "Rutledge, 'The Dictator'," *Journal of Southern History*, VII (May 1941), 215-24; Richard H. Barry, *Mr. Rutledge of South Carolina* (New York, 1942); George McCowan, Jr., "Chief Justice John Rutledge and the Jay Treaty," *South Carolina Historical Magazine*, LXII (January 1961), 10-23. *DAB*.

LOWNDES, Rawlins, 1778-1779

Born in January 1721 in St. Kitts, British West Indies, the son of Charles and Ruth (Rawlins) Lowndes. Brother of William and Charles. Married on August 15, 1748 to Amarinthia Elliott, who died in January 1750; remarried on December 23, 1751 to Mary Cartwright, by whom he had Amarinthia, Mary, Rawlins, Harriet, Sarah-Ruth, Thomas and James; after his second wife's death in 1770, remarried in January 1773 to Sarah Jones, by whom he had three children, including William. Immigrated with his family to South Carolina in the 1730's, and studied law under the supervision of Robert Hall, provost marshal of the colony.

Appointed temporary and later permanent Provost Marshal of South Carolina after Hall's death in 1740, a post which he filled until 1754. Became a planter and a member of the South Carolina Commons House of Assembly, representing St. Paul's Parish (1749-51) and St. Bartholomew Parish (1751-54, 1757-60, 1761-68, 1769-75); also served as Speaker of the Commons House from 1763 to 1765 and again from 1772 to 1775. Acted as Assistant Judge of the Court of Common Pleas from 1766 to April 1772, when he was removed from office. Represented St. Bartholomew Parish in 1775 at both of South Carolina's provincial congresses, and became a member of the Council of Safety; also named to the Legislative Council under the new state government in 1776 and participated that year in the framing of South Carolina's first constitution. Chosen by the State Legislature as President of South Carolina in 1778, replacing John Rutledge, who had resigned.

Rutledge's resignation and Lowndes' election to the South Carolina presidency were the result of Rutledge's unwillingness to approve a revised state constitution passed by the Legislature in early 1778, and one of the first acts performed by Lowndes as chief executive was to sign that document into law. Although Lowndes' period of service was not long, his conservative policies led to rioting and aroused the open hostility of many of the state's more radical leaders, who referred to him as "the great procrastinator." Also during Lowndes' administration South Carolina was repeatedly threatened by British invasion, but the anticipated attack did not come until after he had left office.

Lowndes was elected to the South Carolina Senate following his period as president, and a few years later he entered the Lower House of the State Legislature, representing Charleston. He objected to the proposed Federal Constitution, and was chosen to attend South Carolina's constitutional convention called to consider ratification; however, he did not participate in that body's deliberations. Lowndes then retired from public life and died in Charleston, South Carolina on August 24, 1800. He was buried in St. Philip's Church in Charleston.

Bibliography: George B. Chase, *Lowndes of South Carolina* (Boston, 1876); George B. Chase, "The Lowndes Family of South Carolina: A Genealogical Sketch," *New England Historical and Genealogical Register*, XXX (April 1876), 141-64[1]; Mrs. St. Julien Ravenel, *Life and Times of William Lowndes of South Carolina, 1782-1822* (Boston and New York, 1901); Carl J. Vipperman, *The Rise of Rawlins Lowndes, 1721-1800* (Columbia, S.C., 1978). *DAB*.

MATHEWES, John, 1782-1783

Born in 1744 in Charlestown, South Carolina, the son of John and Sarah (Gibbes) Mathewes. Brother of Lois, Ann and Elizabeth. Married to Mary Wragg on December 3, 1766; after his first wife's death, remarried to Sarah Rutledge on May 5, 1799; no surviving children. Accepted in October 1764 by London's Middle Temple to study law, and admitted to the South Carolina bar in 1765. Later settled at "Uxbridge," his plantation on the Ashley River.

Participated in the Cherokee War in 1760, serving as an Ensign and later as a Lieutenant. Served as a member of the South Carolina Commons House of Assembly, representing St. Helena Parish (1767-68) and St. John Colleton Parish (1772); also represented St. George Dorchester Parish in 1775-76 as a delegate to the First and Second Provincial Congresses. Elected Associate Justice of the Court of General Sessions in 1776. Served as Speaker of the South Carolina General Assembly under the Constitution of 1776, and chosen as the first Speaker of the House of Representatives under the revised Constitution of 1778. Member of the Continental Congress, representing South Carolina from 1778 to 1782, and signer of the Articles of Confederation. Elected by the "Jacksonborough" Legislature and succeeded John Rutledge as Governor of South Carolina in January 1782.

Although the continuation of the war forced Mathewes to establish temporary seats of government during his first months in office, he was able to enter Charlestown in December 1782, when the British evacuated the city. Mathewes then began negotiations with the British over such matters as property confiscation, including the question of whether slaves should be restored to their former owners. On that issue Mathewes was able to persuade the departing British Lieutenant-General, Alexander Leslie, to return all slaves, except those who had been promised their freedom or who "may have rendered themselves particularly obnoxious on account of their attachment and services to the British troops."

Following his brief period as chief executive, Mathewes was appointed Chancellor of the Court of Chancery in 1784, and represented St. Philip and St. Michael parishes in the legislature from 1785 to 1790. In 1791 he became Judge of the Court of Equity, a position which he resigned in 1797. He served as an original Trustee of the College of Charleston, and was one of the founders of the St. George's Club, a society in St. George Dorchester Parish which concerned itself with improved methods of horse-breeding. Mathewes died in Charleston, South Carolina on October 26, 1802. *DAB*.

GUERARD, Benjamin, 1783-1785

Born *circa* 1740 in Charlestown, South Carolina, the son of John and Elizabeth (Hill) Guerard. Brother of David, Charles Hill (died young), Martha (died young) and Richard. Married on November 30, 1766 to Sarah Middleton, by whom he was the father of no surviving issue; remarried on April 7, 1786 to Marianne Kennan; no children by his second marriage.

Admitted to the South Carolina bar in January 1761, after studying law at Lincoln's Inn in London. Represented St. Michael's Parish in the South Carolina Commons House of Assembly from 1765 to 1768; also served as Justice of the Peace for Berkeley County at various times during the 1760's. Participated in South Carolina's protest against British colonial policy, serving as a member of the Charlestown Committee of Correspondence in 1766. Became one of South Carolina's leading Whig financiers during the Revolution. Eventually established his legal residence in St. Helena's Parish, and frequently acted as its representative in the General Assembly from 1779 until he became Governor of South Carolina in February 1783; served as chief executive until February 1785.

Although victory over the British was assured when Guerard assumed office, the bitterness which the long war had produced continued to disrupt

South Carolina politics. In July 1783, for example, a group of men gathered in Charleston to harass those individuals whom they denounced as enemies of the state, and Guerard was forced to issue a proclamation which threatened legal action against anyone who broke the peace. Nevertheless, the desire of South Carolina radicals to seek retribution from British "sympathizers" persisted, causing Ralph Izard to complain to Thomas Jefferson in April 1784 that "dissensions and factions" were making it impossible to restore tranquility to the troubled state. By the end of Guerard's tenure a severe economic slump had further complicated South Carolina politics, leading to what Judge Henry Pendleton termed a "rage for running into debt."

Following his gubernatorial service, Guerard represented St. Helena's Parish from 1785 until 1786, when he retired to "Fountainbleu," his plantation on Goose Creek. Guerard died on December 21, 1788.

Bibliography: George C. Guerard, *A History and Genealogy of the Guerard Family of South Carolina, from 1679-1900* . . . [Savannah, 1900].

MOULTRIE, William, 1785-1787, 1792-1794

Born on November 23, 1730 in Charlestown, South Carolina, the son of Dr. John and Lucretia (Cooper) Moultrie. Brother of John, James, Thomas and Alexander (died in infancy). Married on December 10, 1749 to Damaris Elizabeth de St. Julien, by whom he was the father of Lucretia, William and an unnamed infant; remarried on October 10, 1779 to Hannah (Motte) Lynch; no children by his second marriage. Acquired extensive property in St. John's Berkeley Parish.

Member of the South Carolina Commons House of Assembly, representing Prince Frederick Parish (1761-62, 1765-68), St. Helena Parish (1764-65), and St. John's Berkeley Parish (1752-60, 1768-73). Served as Captain of provincial troops in 1761 during the Cherokee War. From 1775 to 1780 acted as a member of South Carolina's two provincial congresses, the Legislative Council, the House, and the State Senate; also elected to the "Jacksonborough" Legislature in late 1781. Chosen Colonel of the Second Regiment of the Continental Army in June 1775, and in June of the following year played a major role in the Battle of Sullivan's Island in Charlestown harbor. Promoted to Brigadier General in the Continental Army in September 1776 and, despite his capture in the spring of 1780 and a subsequent period on parole, took part in a number of significant military engagements. Promoted to Major General in October of 1782. Served in the South Carolina House of Representatives from 1783 until he was chosen Lieutenant Governor of the state in 1784. Elected by the State Legislature to the first of two one-year terms as Governor of South Carolina in February 1785; elected again to a two-year term in 1792.

Moultrie first became chief executive when the state was still in the process of adjusting to peacetime conditions, and he devoted much attention to strengthening South Carolina's credit and to persuading Tories under penalty of banishment to leave the state before they became a source of social unrest. Improvement of South Carolina's inland waterways and its militia were also matters of major concern to Moultrie. During his second term diplomatic affairs became a controversial topic in the state, when Edmond Genet's recruitment of United States citizens for French military intrigues was viewed differently by Moultrie and the South Carolina Legislature. Finally, in December 1793 the State Legislature instructed Moultrie to prohibit such activities. While he complied, Moultrie made no attempt to enforce this edict.

Between his two terms as governor, Moultrie represented St. John's Berkeley Parish in the State Senate until 1791, and was also that area's representative to a state constitutional convention which ratified the Federal Constitution in 1788. After his second gubernatorial term he retired from political life, although he did serve as President of the South Carolina Society of the Cincinnati from its founding until his death in Charleston on September 27, 1805.

Bibliography: William Moultrie, *Memoirs of the American Revolution, so far as it related to the States of North and South Carolina, and Georgia*, 2 vols. (New York, 1802); William Hollinshead, *A Discourse Commemorative of the Late Major-General William Moultrie* . . . (Charleston, 1805); [Dr. James Moultrie], "The Moultries of South Carolina," *South Carolina Historical and Genealogical Magazine*, V (October 1904), 247-60; Charles S. Davis, ed., "The Journal of William Moultrie while a Commissioner on the North and South Carolina Boundary Survey, 1772," *Journal of Southern History*, VIII (November 1942), 549-55. *DAB*.

PINCKNEY, Thomas, 1787-1789

Born on October 23, 1750 in Charlestown, South Carolina, the son of Charles and Elizabeth (Lucas) Pinckney. Brother of Charles Cotesworth, George Lucas (died in infancy) and Harriott. Married on July 22, 1779 to Elizabeth Motte, by whom he had Thomas, Elizabeth Brewton, Harriott Lucas and Rebecca Motte (died young); after his first wife's death, remarried to Frances (Motte) Middleton on October 19, 1797, by whom he was the father of Edward Rutledge and Mary. Brought to England in 1753 and admitted to Westminster School in 1765; matriculated at Christ Church College, Oxford in November 1768, and the next month began legal studies at the Inner Temple* in London; also studied at the royal military academy in Caen, France, and travelled throughout Europe. Admitted to the South Carolina bar shortly after his return to America in the early 1770's, and eventually settled at "Auckland," his estate on the Ashepoo River; owned other estates in later life, including "Fairfield" and "Eldorado."

Served as Lieutenant of a company of South Carolina rangers in early 1775, and soon became Captain of the newly-organized First South Carolina Regiment of the Continental Army; promoted to Major in May 1778, and during the Revolution participated in several important campaigns; wounded and captured at the Battle of Camden in August 1780. Also served in the South Carolina Legislature in 1778. After the war practiced law in Charleston, and in February 1787 elected to the first of two one-year terms as Governor of South Carolina.

Pinckney's period in office was especially noteworthy for the political struggle within the state over ratification of the proposed Federal Constitution. Although anti-ratification sentiment was strong in the South Carolina backcountry, the Constitution's proponents managed to achieve an impressive victory in May 1788, when a state constitutional convention, at which Pinckney presided, gave its approval to the document. During Pinckney's tenure there was also a lingering hostility towards former Loyalists who had supported Great Britain in the recent war, and the governor attempted to avert any possible civil disorder which might have resulted from this animosity.

Following his years as governor, Pinckney sat in the Lower House of the South Carolina Legislature in 1791, and early in 1792 he was confirmed as United States Minister to Great Britain. He served there until the spring of 1795, when he was appointed Special Commissioner and Envoy Extraordinary to Spain; in that capacity he negotiated the Treaty of San Lorenzo el Real, or "Pinckney's Treaty." He returned home in September 1796, and ran unsuccessfully that year as the Federalist Party's candidate for vice-president. As a Federalist, Pinckney became a member of the United States House of Representatives in 1797, serving until he retired in 1801. He emerged from retirement as a Major General during the War of 1812, and although he saw no active service in that war, he did play a role in the peace negotiations which concluded the Creek War in 1814. In his private life Pinckney was an avid agriculturalist and stock breeder. In 1806 he was elected President of South Carolina's Society of the Cincinnati, a position which he held until he became that military organization's President General in 1826. He was also the author of several articles and pamphlets, including *Reflections Occasioned by the late Disturbances in Charleston* (1822), a commentary on the Denmark Vesey slave insurrection. Pinckney died in Charleston, South Carolina on November 2, 1828.

Bibliography: Charles C. Pinckney, *Life of General Thomas Pinckney* (Boston, 1895); Samuel Flagg Bemis, "The London Mission of Thomas Pinckney, 1792-1796," *American Historical Review*, XXVIII (January 1923), 228-47; Mabel L. Webber, "The Thomas Pinckney Family of South

Carolina,'' *South Carolina Historical and Genealogical Magazine*, XXXIX (January 1938), 15-35; Jack L. Cross, ''Thomas Pinckney's London Mission,'' unpub. Ph.D. diss., University of Chicago, 1957; Jack L. Cross, ed., ''Letters of Thomas Pinckney, 1775-1780,'' *South Carolina Historical Magazine*, LVIII (January-October 1957), 19-33, 67-83, 145-62, 224-42; Samuel Flagg Bemis, *Pinckney's Treaty: America's Advantage from Europe's Distress, 1783-1800*, rev. ed. (New Haven and London, 1960); Arthur Scherr, ''The Significance of Thomas Pinckney's Candidacy in the Election of 1796,'' *South Carolina Historical Magazine*, 76 (April 1975), 51-59; Frances Leigh Williams, *A Founding Family: The Pinckneys of South Carolina* (New York and London, 1978). *DAB*.

*S.F. Bemis, in *Pinckney's Treaty*, gives the Inner Temple as the institution where Pinckney studied law, while the *DAB* names the Middle Temple.

VIRGINIA

Chronology

1607	Edward Maria Wingfield
1607-1608	John Sicklemore (*alias* Ratcliffe)
1608	Matthew Scrivener
1608-1609	John Smith
1609	Francis West
1609-1610	George Percy
1610	Sir Thomas Gates
1610-1611	Thomas West, Lord De La Warr
1611	George Percy
1611	Sir Thomas Dale
1611-1614	Sir Thomas Gates
1614-1616	Sir Thomas Dale
1616-1617	Sir George Yeardley
1617-1619	Sir Samuel Argall
1619	Nathaniel Powell
1619-1621	Sir George Yeardley
1621-1626	Sir Francis Wyatt
1626-1627	Sir George Yeardley
1627-1629	Francis West
1629-1630	John Pott
1630-1635	Sir John Harvey
1635-1637	John West
1637-1639	Sir John Harvey
1639-1642	Sir Francis Wyatt
1642-1644	Sir William Berkeley
1644-1645	Richard Kempe
1645-1652	Sir William Berkeley
1652-1655	Richard Bennett
1655-1657	Edward Digges
1657-1660	Samuel Mathews, Jr.
1660-1661	Sir William Berkeley
1661-1662	Francis Moryson
1662-1677	Sir William Berkeley
1677-1678	Herbert Jeffreys
1678-1680	Sir Henry Chicheley
1680	Thomas, Lord Culpeper
1680-1682	Sir Henry Chicheley
1682-1683	Thomas, Lord Culpeper
1683-1684	Nicholas Spencer
1684-1689	Francis, Lord Howard of Effingham

1689-1690	Nathaniel Bacon
1690-1692	Francis Nicholson
1692-1698	Sir Edmund Andros
1698-1705	Francis Nicholson
1705-1706	Edward Nott
1706-1710	Edmund Jenings
1710-1722	Alexander Spotswood
1722-1726	Hugh Drysdale
1726-1727	Robert Carter
1727-1740	William Gooch
1740-1741	James Blair
1741-1749	William Gooch
1749-1750	Thomas Lee
1750-1751	Lewis Burwell
1751-1758	Robert Dinwiddie
1758	John Blair
1758-1768	Francis Fauquier
1768	John Blair
1768-1770	Norborne Berkeley, Baron de Botetourt
1770-1771	William Nelson
1771-1775	John Murray, 4th Earl of Dunmore
1775-1776	Edmund Pendleton
1776-1779	Patrick Henry
1779-1781	Thomas Jefferson
1781	William Fleming
1781	Thomas Nelson, Jr.
1781	David Jameson
1781-1784	Benjamin Harrison
1784-1786	Patrick Henry
1786-1788	Edmund Randolph
1788-1791	Beverley Randolph

Non-resident Royal Governors of Virginia

Appointee	*Year of Commission*	*Reason for Absence*
Robert Hunter	1707	Captured by French
George Hamilton Douglas, Earl of Orkney	1709	Remained in England—served by a deputy
William Anne Keppel, Earl of Albemarle	1737	Remained in England—served by a deputy
John Campbell, Earl of Loudoun	1756	Served by a deputy
Sir Jeffrey Amherst	1759	Served by a deputy

BIBLIOGRAPHY

Barbour, Philip L., ed., *The Jamestown Voyages Under the First Charter, 1606-1609*, 2 vols. (Cambridge, 1969).

Bruce, Philip Alexander, *The Virginia Plutarch*, 2 vols. (Chapel Hill, 1929).

Flippin, Percy S., *The Royal Government in Virginia, 1624-1775* (New York, 1919).

Kibler, J. Luther, "Early Colonial Governors of Virginia," *Tyler's Quarterly Historical and Genealogical Magazine*, XXXII (July 1950-April 1951), 1-12, 153-62, 262-74.

McAnear, Beverley, "The Income of the Royal Governors of Virginia," *Journal of Southern History*, XVI (May 1950), 196-211.

McIlwaine, H. R., ed., *Journal of the Council of the State of Virginia, 1776-1781*, 2 vols. (Richmond, 1931-32).

———. ed., *Minutes of the Council and General Court of Colonial Virginia, 1622-1632, 1670-1676* (Richmond, 1924).

———. and W. L. Hall, eds., *Executive Journals of the Council of Colonial Virginia, 1680-1754*, 5 vols. (Richmond, 1925-45).

———. and J. P. Kennedy, eds., *Journal of the House of Burgesses of Virginia [1619-1776]*, 13 vols. (Richmond, 1905-15).

Meade, William, *Old Churches, Ministers and Families of Virginia*, 2 vols. (Philadelphia, 1857).

Morgan, Edmund S., *American Slavery, American Freedom: The Ordeal of Colonial Virginia* (New York, 1975).

Morton, Richard L., *Colonial Virginia*, 2 vols. (Chapel Hill, 1960).

Neill, E. D., *Virginia Governors Under the London Company*, in *Macalester College Contributions, Department of History, Literature, and Political Science*, 1st ser., no. 1 (1889).

Smith, Margaret V., *Virginia, 1492-1892 . . . With a History of the Executives of the Colony and of the Commonwealth of Virginia* (Washington, D.C., 1893).

Squires, W. H. T., *Through Centuries Three: A Short History of the People of Virginia* (Portsmouth, Va., 1929).

Tyler, Lyon Gardiner, ed., *Narratives of Early Virginia, 1606-1625* (New York, 1907).

Waddell, Joseph A., *Annals of Augusta County, Virginia, from 1726 to 1871* (reprint: Bridgewater, Va., 1958).

Wertenbaker, Thomas J., *The Planters of Colonial Virginia* (Princeton, 1922).

———. *Virginia Under the Stuarts, 1607-1688* (Princeton, 1914).

Wright, Louis B., *The First Gentlemen of Virginia: Intellectual Qualities of the Early Colonial Ruling Class* (San Marino, Calif., 1940).

VIRGINIA

WINGFIELD, Edward Maria, 1607

Date and place of birth unknown; the eldest son of Thomas Maria Wingfield, a Member of Parliament for Huntingdon, and his wife, who was a member of a Yorkshire family named Kerrye or Kaye.

Served as a soldier in Ireland and the Netherlands during the reign of Queen Elizabeth. Became involved in the project to establish a colony in Virginia, and named as one of the grantees of the Virginia charter of April 1606. Sailed with the first group of settlers in December 1606, and helped in the founding of Jamestown in May 1607. Selected as a member of the Council of Seven which was appointed to govern the colony; chosen as President by his fellow councillors.

As president of the Council, Wingfield was the infant colony's first chief executive, but his position was soon made more difficult by an outbreak of epidemics and a decline in the settlement's food supply. Disregarding these danger signals, many of the colonists prospected for gold and ignored the need to conserve for the winter what provisions they did have. In September 1607 Wingfield, whose leadership was further damaged by the suspicion that his family's Roman Catholicism might make him sympathetic to Spain, was removed from office and imprisoned. He was eventually released and sent back to England, where he arrived in May 1608.

Following his return home, Wingfield wrote a defense of his activities, entitled "A Discourse of Virginia." Despite his unhappy experience as Virginia's president, he retained an interest in the London Company's colonization scheme, and in 1609 became a grantee of the second Virginia charter. He is known to have been living in Stoneley, Huntingdonshire in 1613, although it is probable that he died soon after that date.

Bibliography: Edward Maria Wingfield, *A Discourse of Virginia . . .*, in American Antiquarian Society, *Archaeologia Americana*, vol. IV (1860), 67-103, ed. with an introduction and notes by Charles Deane; Mervyn Edward Wingfield, 7th Viscount Powerscourt, comp., *Muniments of the Ancient Saxon Family of Wingfield* (London, 1894); Edward J. McGuire, "Edward Maria Wingfield," in U.S. Catholic Historical Society, *Records and Studies*, X (1917), 164-71. *DAB, DNB*.

SICKLEMORE, John [*alias* RATCLIFFE], 1607-1608

Date and place of birth, and names of parents unknown, but possibly a member of the Sicklemore family of Suffolk, England. Assumed the *alias* ''Ratcliffe'' sometime before his immigration to Virginia. Married to a woman named Dorothy.

Became a member of the Virginia Company and, as Captain of the *Discovery*, sailed for America in December of 1606. Named to the first Virginia Council in 1607; elected President of the young colony in September of that year, replacing the deposed Edward Maria Wingfield.

While Wingfield's removal from office eliminated one source of discord in Virginia, Ratcliffe's accession brought little relief from the constant bickering which characterized the colony's early years. Within a few months the new chief executive managed to alienate a number of Virginia's leaders, including his former ally, John Smith. Indeed, Smith narrowly escaped a death sentence ordered by Ratcliffe, who had blamed Smith for the lives lost during an expedition under his command. By mid-1608, however, Ratcliffe's arbitrary rule and prodigal use of the colony's supplies had given impetus to a movement aimed at his own removal, and in July of that year he was deposed, apparently in favor of an interim government headed by Matthew Scrivener.

Ratcliffe was then arrested for mutiny, but he was soon released and subsequently served briefly on the Virginia Council under Smith. Although he sailed for England with Captain Christopher Newport in December of 1608, Ratcliffe reappeared in the colony in the summer of 1609, where he engaged in a successful campaign to oust Smith from office. Several months later Ratcliffe was dead, one of the victims of an Indian ambush engineered by Powhatan during the winter of 1609-10.

Bibliography: Ratcliffe's will is printed in the *Virginia Magazine of History and Biography*, XXVI (July 1918), 282. *DNB*.

SCRIVENER, Matthew, 1608

Born circa 1582; place of birth and names of parents unknown. Left for Virginia in October of 1607. Served as a member of the Virginia Council from his arrival in January 1608 until July of that year, when he probably became Acting President of the colony in place of the deposed John Ratcliffe.

Soon after his appearance in Virginia, Scrivener joined forces on the Council with John Smith, in opposition to a clique consisting of Captain Christopher Newport, John Ratcliffe and Captain John Martin. However, with the departure of Newport in spring 1608 and of Martin in June of the same year, only Ratcliffe remained as a major political threat to the Smith-Scrivener alliance.

Although his position as president entitled Ratcliffe to two votes rather than one during Council deliberations, Smith and Scrivener still managed to gain control of the colony's affairs, when his imprudent use of supplies led to Ratcliffe's overthrow in July 1608. For the next two months Scrivener apparently carried out many of the functions of the presidency, despite an illness which prevented him from serving at full capacity. In September 1608 Smith's election as president required Scrivener to relinquish that office, but he remained a member of the Council, and on one occasion opposed a proposal by Smith to launch a surprise attack on the Indian chief Powhatan. Scrivener died early in 1609, after a skiff in which he was sailing sank in the James River.

SMITH, John, 1608-1609

Born *circa* late 1579/early 1580 in Willoughby, Lincolnshire, England, the son of George and Alice Smith. Brother of Francis. Never married.

Attended schools in the nearby villages of Alford and Louth. Left school at the age of fifteen and apprenticed to Thomas Sendall of King's Lynn, a prominent merchant. Fought in the Low Countries for several years in the late 1590's. Later travelled in Europe and, after brief visits to Scotland and Lincolnshire, again became a warrior, eventually enlisting in the army of Archduke Ferdinand of Austria engaged against the Turks on the frontiers of Hungary and Transylvania. Finally captured and made a slave before returning to England in 1604 or 1605. Became involved in the project to colonize Virginia, embarked for America in December 1606, and helped in the founding of Jamestown in May of 1607. Named to the Council of Seven which was appointed to govern the colony during its first year. Became embroiled in a controversy with the settlement's other leaders and at one point was sentenced to be hanged, but later released and restored to the Council in June 1608. Engaged in extensive exploration of the area; chosen President of the colony's Council in September 1608, and in that capacity served as Virginia's chief executive.

Smith's tenure as head of Virginia's government was a period of almost dictatorial rule, as the strong-willed leader tried to avert widespread starvation among settlers who were often tempted to search for gold rather than obtain food for the winter. Smith did manage to get some corn from the Indians for the winter of 1608-09, and through a policy of intimidation, succeeded in making the countryside around Jamestown relatively safe from Indian depredations. By the spring of 1609 the colony had made considerable progress, but the infestation of the settlers' corn casks by rats soon reduced their food supply to an alarming level. Despite Smith's endeavors to compel the colonists to make provision for the winter, the growth of resentment over his military rule, combined with the arrival of new and inexperienced colonists in August 1609, placed Virginia in a perilous position. The next month Smith was ousted from office by a cabal which replaced him with Francis West, who quickly gave way to George Percy.

Smith never returned to Virginia after his departure in October 1609. However, he did play a major role in the founding of New England, and took part in numerous other adventures before his death. Smith was the author of many works on exploration and seamanship, including *A True Relation* (1608); *A Map of Virginia, with a Description of the Countrey* (1612); *A Description of New England* (1616); *New Englands Trials* (1620); *The Generall Historie of Virginia, New-England, and the Summer Isles* (1624); *An Accidence, or the Path-way to Experience* (1626); *A Sea Grammar* (1627); and *The True Travels, Adventures, and Observations of Captaine John Smith, in Europe, Asia, Affrica, and America* (1630). Smith died on June 21, 1631, and was buried in St. Sepulchre's Church, London, England.

Bibliography: Edward Arber, ed., *Captain John Smith . . . Works, 1608-1631* (Birmingham, Eng., 1884); A. G. Bradley, *Captain John Smith* (London, 1905); E. Keble Chatterton, *Captain John Smith* (New York, 1927); Wilberforce Eames, *A Bibliography of Captain John Smith* (New York, 1927); John Gould Fletcher, *John Smith—Also Pocahontas* (New York, 1928); Jarvis M. Morse, "John Smith and His Critics: A Chapter in Colonial Historiography," *Journal of Southern History*, I (May 1935), 123-37; Bradford Smith, *Captain John Smith* (Philadelphia, 1953); Laura P. Striker and Bradford Smith, "The Rehabilitation of Captain John Smith," *Journal of Southern History*, XXVIII (November 1962), 474-81; Philip L. Barbour, *The Three Worlds of Captain John Smith* (Boston, 1964); David Freeman Hawke, ed., *Captain John Smith's History of Virginia* (Indianapolis, 1970); Everett H. Emerson, *Captain John Smith* (New York, 1971); Alden T. Vaughan, *American Genesis: Captain John Smith and the Founding of Virginia* (Boston, 1975). *DAB, DNB*.

WEST, Francis, 1609, 1627-1629

Born on October 28, 1586 in England, probably in Hampshire, the fourth son of Thomas West, second or eleventh Baron De La Warr, and his wife, the former Anne Knollys. Brother of Elizabeth, Robert, Thomas, Walsingham (died young), Lettis, Anne (died young), Penelope, Katherine, Helena, Anne, John and Nathaniel. Married to Margaret, the widow of Edward Blayney; remarried to Temperance (Flowerdieu) Yeardley, who died shortly after the wedding; married a third time to Jane Davye; father of one surviving son, Francis. Acquired large estates at Westover and Sherley on the James River in Virginia.

Arrived in Virginia with Captain Christopher Newport in 1608, and named a grantee of the second charter of the London Company in 1609. As President of the colony's Council, assumed the role of chief executive after the overthrow of Captain John Smith in September of 1609, but was soon replaced by George Percy. Between voyages to England and elsewhere, continued to serve as a member of the Virginia Council; also appointed to other offices in Virginia, including Commander at Jamestown in 1612 and Master of the Ordnance in 1617. Commissioned Admiral of New England in November 1622, but quickly returned to Virginia after encountering resistance from the fishermen in that area. As President of the Council, became Acting Governor of Virginia in November 1627, following the death of Governor George Yeardley, and served in that capacity until March 1629.

West's first period as chief executive lasted only about two weeks, but his second term was both longer and more significant. By the late 1620's Virginia has passed through its earliest growing pains and, despite a persistently high death rate, the colony's population was beginning to increase dramatically. In February 1628, for example, it was reported that 1,000 immigrants to Virginia had been "lately receaved." West's tenure was also marked by an increasing awareness of the importance of tobacco to Virginia's economy, and in March 1628 a colonial Assembly, meeting on an *ad hoc* basis and at the Crown's suggestion, considered the question of a royal proclamation which forbade the importation of tobacco into England without the king's license.

Although he sailed for England in 1629, West returned to Virginia by 1631. He appears to have resumed his seat on the colony's Council, since in February 1633 he is noted as being present at one of that body's sessions. He died in Virginia, probably early in 1634.

Bibliography: Alexander Brown, ed., "Extract from the 'Register of Severall of the Ancestors of Samuel Bennet and His Wife Katherine . . . Anno Dom: 1693'," *Magazine of American History*, IX (June 1883), 462-64; Ann Woodard Fox, *The Noble Lineage of the Delaware-West Family of Virginia through Col. John West . . .*, ed. by Margaret McNeill Ayres (Memphis?, 1958). *DAB, DNB*.

PERCY, George, 1609-1610, 1611

Born on September 4, 1580 in England, the youngest son of Henry Percy, eighth Earl of Northumberland, and his wife Catherine, the daughter of John Neville, Lord Latimer. Brother of Henry, Lucy, Eleanor, William, Charles, Richard, Alan and Josceline. Never married.

Served for a time in the Dutch wars, and in December 1606 embarked with Captain Christopher Newport on his voyage to Virginia. As President of the colony's Council, became chief executive in September 1609, and served in that capacity until the arrival of Sir Thomas Gates in May 1610. Also served as Deputy Governor of Virginia from the departure of Lord De La Warr in March 1611 until the arrival of Sir Thomas Dale in May of that year.

Percy's emergence as chief executive came shortly after a factional struggle within Virginia, which ended with the overthrow of Captain John Smith as the colony's leader. When Percy took over the government from Francis West, another member of the anti-Smith party, the settlement at Jamestown was ill prepared for the winter, and Percy sought unsuccessfully to procure food from the Indians in the vicinity. As winter approached the hungry colonists were forced to eat whatever animals they could find, including cats and dogs. Ultimately, conditions became so bad that several settlers resorted to cannibalism, and Percy responded by inflicting severe punishments. By the spring of 1610, this "starving time" had claimed so many victims that only sixty colonists survived of the 500 who were living in Virginia six months earlier. During Percy's second stint as the colony's leader, there was no repetition of the gruesome scenes of his previous term but, despite the efforts of propagandists to portray the colonial venture in an optimistic light, Virginia remained on the edge of disaster.

Percy left the colony in April 1612, and seems never to have returned. He was the author of "Observations gathered out of a Discourse of the Plantation of the Southerne Colonie in Virginia," later abridged and printed by Samuel Purchas in 1625; he also wrote "A Trewe Relacyon of the Procedeinges and Occurrentes of Momente which have happened in Virginie . . .," a defense of his activities in the colony (which remained unpublished in its entirety until 1922). Percy fought in the Netherlands in the 1620's, and in 1627 he was commanding a company there. He died in England, probably around March of 1632.

Bibliography: W. W. Henry, "Did (George) Percy Denounce Smith's History of Virginia?," *Virginia Magazine of History and Biography*, I (April 1894), 473-76; George Percy, "A Trewe Relacyon of the Procedeinges and Occurrentes of Momente . . .," *Tyler's Quarterly Historical and Genealogical Magazine*, III (1922), 260-82; John W. Shirley, "George Percy at Jamestown, 1607-1612," *Virginia Magazine of History and Biography*, 57 (July 1949), 227-43; Philip L. Barbour, "The Honorable George Percy: Premier Chronicler of the First Virginia Voyage," *Early American Literature*, VI (Spring 1971), 7-17. *DAB, DNB*.

GATES, Sir Thomas, 1610, 1611-1614

Birth date and names of parents unknown, although he appears to have been born in Colyford, Colyton Parish, Devonshire, England. Married and the father of Anthony, Thomas, Margaret, Elizabeth and possibly others.

Served as a Lieutenant under Sir Francis Drake in the 1580's, and participated in the capture of Cartagena, the burning of St. Augustine, Florida, and the rescue of the Roanoke colonists. Commanded English troops in Normandy in 1591; took part in the expedition against Cadiz in 1596, and knighted that year for his efforts. Continued to serve in the military in various places, including the Azores, Ireland and the Low Countries. In March 1598 admitted to Gray's Inn in London.

Became involved in the efforts to colonize Virginia, and named a grantee in the charter of April 1606 issued to the Virginia Companies of London and Plymouth. Left England for Virginia in June 1609 but, due to a storm which drove his ship to Bermuda, did not reach his destination until May 1610, when he assumed control of the government from George Percy. The next month prepared to abandon the failing colony, but was turned back by the arriving governor, Lord De La Warr, and sent to England for supplies and aid. Returned to Virginia in August of 1611, and took over as the colony's Lieutenant Governor, a position which he held until he departed for England in March of 1614.

Gates' years as Virginia's chief executive were marked by an effort to bring a greater sense of discipline to the colonial venture. In 1610 Gates drafted a set of rigorous laws which, as later enlarged by Sir Thomas Dale, at last provided the colony with a clear code of behavior. Gates also encouraged Dale in the construction of the new town of Henrico, named in honor of Henry, Prince of Wales. Still, despite these instances of progress, Virginia continued to suffer serious economic problems, and when he returned to England in 1614 Gates warned his superiors in London that the "plantation will fall to the ground, if it be not presently supplied."

After his return Gates continued to promote the interests of the Company, but he eventually seems to have become disillusioned, and in 1619 and 1620 he sold some of his shares in the enterprise. Gates became a member of the Council of New England in 1620, and died in the Low Countries in 1621, probably before April of that year.

Bibliography: William Strachey, "A True Repertory of the Wreck and Redemption of Sir Thomas Gates, Knight," in Louis B. Wright, ed., *A Voyage to Virginia in 1609* (Charlottesville, 1964). *DAB, DNB*.

WEST, Thomas (Lord De La Warr), 1610-1611

Born on July 9, 1577, probably in Wherwell, Hampshire, England, the second but eldest surviving son of Thomas West, second or eleventh Baron De La Warr, and his wife, the former Anne Knollys. Brother of Elizabeth, Robert, Walsingham (died young), Lettis, Anne (died young), Penelope, Katherine, Francis, Helena, Anne, John and Nathaniel. Married on November 25, 1596 to

Cecelia Shirley; father of Henry, Jane, Elizabeth, Anne, Cecily, Lucy and Catherine. Matriculated at Queen's College, Oxford in March 1592 and, although he did not receive a degree at that time, was created M.A. of Oxford in 1605; also travelled in Italy as a young man.

Elected to Parliament in October 1597, representing Lymington. Served in the military for several years, and was knighted in July 1599; succeeded to his father's peerage in March 1602, and became a member of the Privy Council. Appointed one of the grantees in the 1609 charter of the London Company, and chosen as a member of the Company's Council. Named Governor and Captain General for life of Virginia in February 1610; arrived in the colony in June 1610 to take over personal supervision of the enterprise.

De La Warr's arrival in Virginia came at a time when the settlers were on the point of disbanding and returning to England. Following the disastrous "starving time" of the winter of 1609-10, the colony's resident leaders had decided that it would be fruitless to try to continue, but De La Warr was not yet prepared to abandon the venture. He immediately organized the government, sent to Bermuda for supplies, and arranged for the construction of several forts. However, the strain of the Virginia winter and his efforts to keep the colony together eventually had an effect on De La Warr's health, and in March 1611 he embarked for the West Indies in order to recuperate, leaving George Percy, the president of the colony's Council, to act as his deputy.

De La Warr returned to England in June 1611 and continued to promote Virginia by various means, including the publication of *The Relation of the Right Honourable the Lord De-la-Warre, Lord Governour and Captaine Generall of the Colonie, planted in Virginea* . . . (London, 1611). Although De La Warr planned to return to Virginia and actually set sail in March 1618, he became ill while on a stopover in the Azores and died on June 7, 1618.

Bibliography: Alexander Brown, "Sir Thomas West, Third Lord De La Warr," *Magazine of American History*, IX (January 1883), 18-30; Alexander Brown, ed., "Extract from the 'Register of Severall of the Ancestors of Samuel Bennet and His Wife Katherine . . .Anno Dom: 1693'," *Magazine of American History*, IX (June 1883), 462-64; Ann Woodard Fox, *The Noble Lineage of the Delaware-West Family of Virginia through Col. John West* . . ., ed. by Margaret McNeill Ayres (Memphis?, 1958). *DAB, DNB*.

DALE, Sir Thomas, 1611, 1614-1616

Date, place of birth and names of parents unknown. Brother of at least one sister. Married, probably in 1611, to Elizabeth, the daughter of Sir Thomas Throckmorton.

Enlisted in the military service *circa* 1588 as a common soldier in the Netherlands; also fought against the Irish rebels at the end of the sixteenth century, under the Earl of Essex. Returned to the Netherlands *circa* 1603, and made a Captain after winning the favor of King James I of England. Knighted in 1606, and later appointed High Marshal of Virginia, in an effort to bring some discipline to that colonial enterprise. Arrived in Virginia in May 1611 and served as Acting Governor until August of that year. Again became acting governor in March of 1614 when Governor Sir Thomas Gates left the colony, and remained chief executive until the spring of 1616.

Dale's tenure was notable for the strict code of conduct which he enforced in order to keep the colony alive. In June of 1611 Dale "exemplified and enlarged" a set of stern regulations which had been drafted by Gates a year earlier, and throughout his period as acting governor he sought, in accordance with his views as a military man, to foster a greater respect for law among the colony's often unruly inhabitants. Dale also attempted as early as 1614 to use allotments of private property as a means of gaining the co-operation of Virginia's settlers. In spite of these measures, however, the colony does not appear to have been much more prosperous when Dale departed for England in 1616 than it had been when he first arrived.

A year after his return to England, Dale assumed command of a London East India Company fleet, and in February 1618 he sailed for the East Indies. In December 1618 he joined battle with a Dutch fleet, but neither side scored a clear victory. Seven months later, in July 1619, Dale arrived in Masulipatam, India, where he became ill and died on August 9, 1619. His body was returned to England for burial.

Bibliography: Willam Harris Gaines, Jr., "The Discipline of Sir Thomas Dale," *Virginia Cavalcade*, III (Spring 1954), 14-17; Darrett B. Rutman, "The Historian and the Marshal: A Note on the Background of Sir Thomas Dale," *Virginia Magazine of History and Biography*, LXVIII (July 1960), 284-94. *DAB*, *DNB*.

YEARDLEY, Sir George, 1616-1617, 1619-1621, 1626-1627

Born in 1588 in Southwark, England, the second son of Ralph, a member of London's Guild of Merchant Taylors, and Rhoda (Marston) Yeardley. Brother of Ralph and perhaps others. Married to Temperance Flowerdieu, and the father of Argall, Francis and Elizabeth.

As a young man established connections with Sir Thomas Gates, and sailed with Gates for Virginia in 1609, where he served the new colony in a military capacity for several years. Became Acting Governor of Virginia after the departure of Sir Thomas Dale in the spring of 1616, and filled that office until the arrival of Samuel Argall in May 1617. Commissioned Governor and Captain General of Virginia in November 1618, and assumed office in April

1619, shortly after being knighted by King James I. Retired as governor in November 1621, but accepted a third term in 1626, this time as Virginia's Crown-appointed Royal Governor; served as chief executive of the colony until his death in 1627.

Yeardley's three terms at the head of Virginia's government encompassed about five years of what was a critical decade in the evolution of the colony. Perhaps the high point of his service occurred in August 1619, when Yeardley presided at the first meeting of the Virginia General Assembly. Nevertheless, the young settlement was also experiencing some economic and administrative problems from 1619 to 1621, due largely to the ill-advised policies of the parent Company in London. Yeardley himself appealed to England for more provisions, arguing that if the Company continued to encourage more settlers to come to Virginia, the colony would be unable "to feed them owt of others labors." These problems eventually resulted in the dissolution of the London Company in 1623, and the assumption of the colony's charter by the Crown in 1624.

After his second term Yeardley sat on the Virginia Council and filled other political offices, including Governor and Captain of Southampton Hundred, an 80,000 acre land grant owned by about thirty "knights, gentlemen and merchants of the best account in London." When Yeardley went to England in 1625 carrying petitions from the colonists in Virginia, his behavior so impressed Crown officials that they recommended him to replace the retiring Sir Francis Wyatt as Virginia's royal governor. Yeardley's final year as governor was relatively uneventful. He died while in office in November 1627, and was buried on November 13 of that year.

Bibliography: Thomas Teackle Upshur, *Sir George Yeardley, or Yardley, Governor and Captain General of Virginia* . . . [Nashville, 1896]; "Flowerdew Hundred and Sir George Yardley," *Tyler's Quarterly Historical and Genealogical Magazine*, II (October 1920), 115-29; James P. C. Southall, "Concerning George Yardley and Temperance Flowerdew: A Synopsis and Review," *Virginia Magazine of History and Biography*, LV (July 1947), 259-66; Nora Miller Turman, *George Yeardley, Governor of Virginia and Organizer of the General Assembly in 1619* (Richmond, 1959). *DAB, DNB*.

ARGALL, Sir Samuel, 1617-1619

Born *circa* 1580 in England, the son of Richard Argall of East Sutton, Kent, and Mary (Scott) Argall. Brother of Reginald, John, Thomas, Richard, Elizabeth, Jane and Sarah. Probably never married.

Apparently involved in the transatlantic fishing trade before he first became associated with Virginia in 1609, when he was chosen to discover a more expeditious route to the new colony. Accompanied Thomas West, Lord De La Warr, in the spring of 1610, during De La Warr's trip to Virginia to assume the post of governor. Played a major role in the preservation of the colony by procuring food supplies from Cape Cod and elsewhere; also engaged in activities against French settlements in North America. Lured Pocahontas from her village and brought her to Jamestown; in the spring of 1616 travelled with Pocahontas, her husband, John Rolfe, and the departing Virginia governor, Sir Thomas Dale, to England. Appointed Deputy Governor of Virginia in 1617, arriving in the colony in May of that year.

Argall's governorship has been a subject of some controversy among historians, who have either commended him for his promotion of stern measures designed to increase Virginia's food supply and to improve its defense, or have criticized his willingness to profit personally at the colony's expense. In fact, Argall's behavior differed little from that of some of his successors, who saw little inconsistency in attempting to improve the position of the colony while indulging their own self-interest. Still, before he was relieved by Acting Governor Nathaniel Powell on April 9, 1619, Argall was charged with maladministration and piracy. While these charges may have been in part politically motivated, Argall was forced to return to England to defend his actions.

After he had regained the trust of his superiors in London, Argall resumed his earlier career as a seafarer. In 1620 he took command of the *Golden Phoenix*, a ship stationed in the Mediterranean. He was knighted in June 1622 by King James I, and about the same time became a member of the Council of New England. In September 1625 Argall sailed as the Admiral of a naval squadron in search of a fleet of Dunkirkers. Although he succeeded in capturing some prizes while on this mission, Argall's participation a short time later in the English expedition against Cadiz was a failure. Argall died in March 1626.

Bibliography: William Otis Sawtelle, *Sir Samuel Argall, the First Englishman at Mt. Desert*... (Portland?, 1923?); Seymour Connor, "Sir Samuel Argall: A Biographical Sketch," *Virginia Magazine of History and Biography*, LIX (April 1951), 162-75; Philip L. Barbour, "A Possible Clue to Samuel Argall's Pre-Jamestown Activities," *William and Mary Quarterly*, 3rd ser., vol. XXIX (April 1972), 301-06. *DAB, DNB*.

POWELL, Nathaniel, 1619

Born in the vicinity of London, England; date of birth and names of parents unknown. Brother of Thomas, among others. Married to Joyce Tracy *circa* 1620.

Took an active interest in exploration and cartography, and by the early seventeenth century had become associated with the Virginia Company. Immigrated to Virginia in 1607, where he was commissioned Sergeant-Major General in 1617. Appointed Acting Governor of the colony by the departing Governor Samuel Argall, serving in that capacity between April 9 and April 19, 1619.

Argall's sudden desertion of Virginia was motivated in part by the furor which had disrupted his administration. Thus, when he finally decided to leave the colony in order to defend himself against accusations (which included a charge of piracy), Argall was careful to select an interim chief executive who was both popular and uncontroversial. Powell suited these requirements perfectly, a fact recognized by his immediate appointment to the Virginia Council by Governor Sir George Yeardley, Argall's replacement.

Following his brief tenure as chief executive, Powell remained a Council member until he died on March 22, 1622, a victim of the Indian massacre which decimated the Jamestown settlement in that year.

Bibliography: (Mrs. Philip W.) M. W. Hiden, "The Antecedents of Richard Powell, of Amherst County, Virginia," *Tyler's Quarterly Historical and Genealogical Magazine*, XXX (July 1948), 49-67; Helen Reed Powell, "The Early Powell Group of 'Gentlemen Adventurers' to the Colony of Virginia," *Tyler's Quarterly Historical and Genealogical Magazine*, XXXI (July 1949), 53-56; "Captain Nathaniel Powell: His Letter to Ralph Buffkin" [with a note by Martha Woodroof Hiden], *Virginia Magazine of History and Biography*, LX (October 1952), 515-21. *DNB*.

WYATT, Sir Francis, 1621-1626, 1639-1642

Born in 1588 in England, the eldest son of George and Jane (Finch) Wyatt. Brother of Eleanora, Haute and George. Married in 1618 to Margaret Sandys, by whom he had Henry, Francis and Edwin. Knighted in 1618, and in 1623 inherited "Boxley Abbey," the Wyatt family seat. Named by the Virginia Company to succeed George Yeardley as Governor and Captain General of Virginia, and assumed that office in November 1621.

Wyatt's first period of service as Virginia's chief executive was marked by several incidents of great significance to the colony's future development. In March of 1622 the Indians in Virginia went to war with the white settlers, and before peace was restored, the English suffered heavy losses and faced the real prospect of their colony's demise. A year later an important stage in the political evolution of Virginia occurred, as the London Company was dissolved; by 1624, the colony had come under royal control. Wyatt, who remained popular both within the colony and with officials in London, continued for a time as the Crown-appointed royal governor, but in 1626 he left Virginia in order to attend to his family's estates in England. Wyatt returned as royal governor in November 1639, succeeding Sir John Harvey, and served until 1642, when Sir William Berkeley arrived to take over the government. Wyatt's second term was troubled by political factionalism, a problem which diminished the governor's popularity. Still, the royal instructions entrusted to Wyatt did include a major concession to local political interests, since in those instructions Crown authorities had officially recognized the role of the Virginia Assembly by stipulating that that body should be convened "once a year or oftener."

Wyatt returned to England shortly after his replacement by Berkeley, and died there in 1644. He was buried at "Boxley Abbey" on August 24, 1644.

Bibliography: Stanley Charles Wyatt, *Cheneys and Wyatts: A Brief History in Two Parts* [London, 1960]. Documents pertaining to Wyatt's administration are printed in the *William and Mary Quarterly*, 2nd ser., vol. VI (April 1926), 114-21; vol. VII (January-October 1927), 42-47, 125-31, 204-14, 246-54; vol. VIII (January, July 1928), 48-57, 157-67. Relevant notes on the Wyatt family appear in the *William and Mary Quarterly*, 1st ser., vol. III (July 1894), 35-38. *DAB, DNB*.

POTT, John, 1629-1630

Born in England, date of birth unknown; probably the son of Henry and Grace Pott of Harrop, Cheshire. Brother of Francis and perhaps others. Married to a woman named Elizabeth; no surviving children at his death. Received university education at either Oxford or Cambridge, and able to read Latin, Greek and Hebrew. Arrived in Virginia with Governor Wyatt in the fall of 1621 as Physician General of the colony.

Member of the Virginia Council until 1624, when a scandal resulted in his dismissal; reinstated to the Council in March 1626 by Charles I. As President of the Council, became Acting Governor in March 1629, following the departure for England of Acting Governor Francis West, and served until the spring of 1630.

While he was only an interim governor, Pott took an active interest in Virginia's political and military development, as he twice convened the Assembly and worked for regulations which would strengthen the colony's defense. The defensive measures endorsed by Pott were thought to be especially important, since the devastating Indian massacre of 1622 was still fresh in the minds of many Virginians. Pott also gave the newly-arrived Lord Baltimore an intentionally lukewarm welcome, hoping thereby to deter Baltimore's Catholic colonists from settling on Virginia soil.

Soon after his replacement as governor by Sir John Harvey, Pott was charged with and convicted of several crimes, including what appears to have been a seventeenth-century case of cattle rustling ("cuting out the markes of other mens neate cattell and markinge them for himselfe"). Pott lost his seat on the Council and was confined to his plantation; however, following an appeal to England, his conviction was reversed and he received a royal pardon in July 1631. Pott then practiced medicine near what is now Williamsburg, although he maintained his interest in politics and in 1635 joined a protest movement which ended with the deposing of Governor Harvey. After Harvey was restored to power in 1637, Pott and other participants in the anti-Harvey campaign were called before the English Star Chamber on charges of treason, but their case was never tried. Pott died *circa* 1642, probably in Virginia. *DAB*.

HARVEY, Sir John, 1630-1635, 1637-1639

A native of Lyme Regis, Dorset, England; date of birth and names of parents unknown. Brother of Simon and perhaps others. Married *circa* 1639 to Elizabeth (Peirsey) Stephens; father of Ursula and Anne.

Served as Captain of a ship in the East Indies from 1617 to 1619. Arrived in Virginia early in 1624 as part of a commission appointed by the King to inquire into the condition of the colony. Named to the Virginia Council in August 1624, but returned to England a short time later. Continued his career in the English Navy for a few years, until his knighthood and his appointment as Royal Governor of Virginia in March 1628; arrived in the colony in April 1630 to begin his tenure as chief executive.

Although Harvey's administration in Virginia was marked by several impressive achievements, including a significant improvement in the colony's relations with neighboring Indians, his dealings with the Council were turbulent almost from the beginning. Complaining that the Council consisted of "factions seeking to carrie all matters . . . for their owne endes," Harvey was never able to establish a satisfactory working relationship with Virginia's political hierarchy, despite a shaky truce which lasted for about two years. Ultimately, resentment over Harvey's actions, especially his failure to issue a large number of land patents, caused the Council to incite a revolt which expelled him from Virginia in the spring of 1635. By January 1637, however, Harvey had returned to the colony, after persuading English authorities that the rebellion against his rule had been motivated by the Council's self-interest. Harvey's second period as chief executive began with an attempt to seek revenge against those councillors who had been most responsible for his ouster. Eventually, numerous complaints against the retaliatory measures employed by the governor led the Privy Council in London to order his removal, and to replace him with Sir Francis Wyatt, who assumed control in November 1639.

Following his final gubernatorial tenure, Harvey was detained in Virginia for some time, and arraigned for the crimes which he had allegedly committed. He was later allowed to embark for England, where he died *circa* 1650, since his will was proved in July of that year.

Bibliography: "Declaration of Sir John Harvey," *Virginia Magazine of History and Biography*, I (April 1894), 425-30; W. N. Sainsbury, comp., "Harvey's Second Administration," *Virginia Magazine of History and Biography*, X (April 1903), 423-28, XI (July 1903-January 1904), 46-57, 169-82, 284-88, XII (April 1905), 385-96; J. Mills Thornton, III, "The Thrusting Out of Governor Harvey: A Seventeenth-Century Rebellion," *Virginia Magazine of History and Biography*, LXXVI (January 1968), 11-26. Harvey's will is printed in the *Virginia Magazine of History and Biography*, XVIII (July 1910), 305-06.

WEST, John, 1635-1637

Born on December 14, 1590 in England, the fifth son of Thomas West, second or eleventh Baron De La Warr, and his wife, the former Anne Knollys. Brother of Elizabeth, Robert, Thomas, Walsingham (died young), Lettis, Anne (died young), Penelope, Katherine, Francis, Helena, Anne and Nathaniel. Married to a woman named Anne, by whom he was the father of John.

Became a member of the Virginia Company in 1609. Received an A.B. from Magdalen College, Oxford in December 1613. Elected to the Virginia House of Burgesses in 1629, a position he held for several years. Served on the colony's Council almost continuously from 1631 until his death. Acted as Governor of Virginia from the spring of 1635, following the overthrow of Sir John Harvey, to January 1637.

John West's selection by the Council as successor to the ousted Governor Harvey was based largely on his family's prominence in Virginia politics. As the younger brother of Thomas West, Lord De La Warr, and of Francis West, two previous chief executives of the colony, West seemed a logical choice to those Council members who were anxious to legitimize as much as possible their "thrusting out" of Harvey. When he returned to England, however, Harvey successfully defended his administration, and in January 1637 proclaimed his new commission in Virginia, thereby superseding West as governor.

Several months later West was arrested and sent to England, along with other leaders of the group which had deposed Harvey in 1635. After acquitting himself of charges brought by Harvey, West sailed for Virginia, where his confiscated property was restored on orders from the Privy Council. He then resumed his interest in Virginia's public affairs, especially as a member of the Council. West died in Virginia *circa* 1659.

Bibliography: Alexander Brown, ed., "Extract from the 'Register of Severall of the Ancestors of Samuel Bennet and His Wife Katherine . . .Anno Dom: 1693'," *Magazine of American History*, IX (June 1883), 462-64; Ann Woodard Fox, *The Noble Lineage of the Delaware-West Family of Virginia through Col. John West*. . ., ed. by Margaret McNeill Ayres (Memphis?, 1958).

BERKELEY, Sir William, 1642-1644, 1645-1652, 1660-1661, 1662-1677

Born in 1606 in the vicinity of London, England, the son of Maurice Berkeley of Bruton in Somersetshire, England. Brother of John, first Baron Berkeley of Stratton. Married *circa* 1670 to Frances (Culpeper) Stephens; no children.

Matriculated at Queen's College, Oxford in February 1623; received a B.A. from St. Edmund Hall, Oxford in July 1624, and an M.A. from Merton College, Oxford in July 1629. As a young man was a gentleman of the Privy Chamber and the author of a number of plays and other writings, including *The Lost Lady*, a tragedy published in 1638. Appointed a Commissioner of Canadian Affairs in 1632, and knighted by King Charles I in July 1639. Commissioned Governor and Captain General of Virginia in August 1641, and arrived in the colony the following year.

Berkeley's arrival in Virginia represented the commencement of what was to become the longest tenure of any governor of the colony. With the exception of several visits to England, when acting governors presided in his place, and the Cromwellian Interregnum, when he was removed from office by the English Parliament, Berkeley served as governor from 1642 until shortly before his death in 1677. During the course of his governorship, Berkeley developed a complex political alliance consisting mostly of men born in England but loyal to Virginia as a place of permanent residence. After the English Civil Wars ended with the victory of Cromwell, this coterie, which was strongly Royalist, was removed from power. Nevertheless, the restoration of Charles II in 1660 came hard on the heels of the political resurgence of the Berkeley group, which continued to govern effectively until the outbreak of a rebellion led by Nathaniel Bacon in 1676. The origins of Bacon's Rebellion have been the source of much controversy among historians. Recent scholarship suggests that while the immediate cause was clearly a dispute over Indian policy, various economic and non-economic factors contributed to the outbreak, including encroachment by white frontiersmen on Indian lands, the depressed Virginia tobacco market, and the restraints on trade imposed by the Navigation Acts. In any event, Berkeley's final year in office was a tempestuous one, and it was not until after Bacon's death in 1677 that the governor could restore some order to the troubled colony. When Berkeley's reprisals in the aftermath of the rebellion created additional dissension, a commission from England was sent to investigate and the governor was recalled. Berkeley then returned to England to defend his actions, but died there on July 9, 1677, before he could present his case to the King. He was buried in Twickenham.

Bibliography: William Berkeley, *A Discourse and View of Virginia* (London, 1663); Marcia Brownell Bready, "A Cavalier in Virginia—The Right Hon. Sir William Berkeley, His Majesty's Governor," *William and Mary Quarterly*, 1st ser., vol. XVIII (October 1909), 115-29; Jane D. Carson, "Sir William Berkeley, Governor of Virginia: A Study in Colonial Policy," unpub. Ph.D. diss., University of Virginia, 1951; Wilcomb E. Washburn, *The Governor and the Rebel: A History of Bacon's Rebellion in Virginia* (Chapel Hill, 1957); Wilcomb E. Washburn, "Governor Berkeley and King Philip's War," *New England Quarterly*, XXX (September 1957), 363-77. *DAB, DNB*.

KEMPE, Richard, 1644-1645

Born *circa* 1600 in Norfolk, England, the third son of Robert and Dorothy (Harris) Kempe. Brother of Robert (later Sir Robert), John, Arthur, Edmund, Thomas, Edward, Matthew, Dorothy and Elizabeth. Married to Elizabeth Thomas, by whom he was the father of Elizabeth.

Immigrated to Virginia in 1637, where he became Secretary and Council member during the late 1630's. Served as Acting Governor of Virginia from June 1644 to June 1645, while Governor Sir William Berkeley was absent from the colony on a trip to England.

In April 1644, two months before Berkeley left, Virginia endured an Indian massacre reminiscent of the attack twenty-two years earlier which had nearly destroyed the colony. When Berkeley sailed for England in June, Kempe assumed leadership of a campaign intended to retaliate for the approximately five hundred lives lost in these surprise raids led by Chief Opechancanough. By the autumn of 1644 a series of white military successes had convinced the Virginia Assembly to permit the return of settlers to the endangered areas of the colony, and early in 1645 the legislators provided for the protection of the frontier by authorizing the building of four new forts.

Following his brief administration, Kempe appears to have resumed his position as secretary, since he was serving in that capacity in 1648. The date of Kempe's death is unknown, although his will was proved in London in 1656.

Bibliography: "Will of Richard Kemp, 1656," *Virginia Magazine of History and Biography*, II (October 1894), 174-76; Frederick Hitchin-Kemp, *A General History of the Kemp and Kempe Families of Great Britain and Her Colonies* . . . (London, 1902).

BENNETT, Richard, 1652-1655

Born *circà* 1607 in England, the son of Captain Robert Bennet. A Puritan, although he became a Quaker late in life. Married to Mary Ann Utie, and the father of Richard, Anne and Elizabeth.

First arrived in America in about 1623; employed as supervisor in charge of the plantations owned by Edward Bennett, his uncle, who was a member of the Virginia Company. Served as a member of the Virginia House of Burgesses from 1629 to 1631. Named to the Governor's Council in 1642, and acted in that capacity almost continuously until 1648. Joined Maryland's Puritan colony in 1649, but returned to Virginia after a short time. Appointed Governor of Virginia by unanimous vote of the English commissioners and the Virginia House of Burgesses, and filled that office from April 1652 until March 1655; also served as one of the three commissioners who administered the province of Maryland between March and June 1652.

As governor of a colony which had recently transferred its allegiance to the Commonwealth then in power in England, Bennett was faced with several outbreaks of opposition among those who for various reasons were dissatisfied with their condition. In June of 1653, for example, some inhabitants of Northampton County submitted a protest against paying taxes while they remained without representation in the House of Burgesses. When they threatened to separate from Virginia's government unless their demands were met, Bennett himself visited the county, a demonstration of authority which seems to have settled the matter. Bennett's term was also marked by several clashes between the governor and his Assembly. Unlike William Berkeley, who had administered the province by virtue of his royal commission, Bennett owed his appointment at least in part to the Virginia Assembly, and the members of that body tried to insure that they would define the extent of his powers.

After his period as chief executive, Bennett sailed for England, employed as an Agent for Virginia. He returned to the colony several years later and continued to hold public office, including positions as Major General of the train band and member of the Governor's Council. Bennett died prior to April 12, 1675, the date his will was proved.

Bibliography: Mary Nicholson Browne, "Governor Richard Bennet," *Maryland Historical Magazine*, IX (December 1914), 307-15; John Bennett Boddie, "Edward Bennett of London and Virginia," *William and Mary Quarterly*, 2nd ser., vol. XIII (April 1933), 117-31. Richard Bennett's will is printed in the *New England Historical and Genealogical Register*, XLVIII (January 1894), 114-16.

DIGGES, Edward, 1655-1657

Born *circa* 1620 in England, the son of Sir Dudley Digges of Chilham, Kent, a judge and diplomat, and Lady Mary (Kempe) Digges. Married to Elizabeth Page, by whom he was the father of Thomas, William, Mary, Anne, Dudley, Edward and seven others.

Entered Gray's Inn in London in May of 1637, where he studied law. Immigrated to Virginia in about 1650, and eventually established a large plantation on the York River. Appointed to the Virginia Council in November 1654; elected Governor by the General Assembly in March 1655, a position which he held until early 1657.

With the massacre of 1644 still a painful memory for most Virginians, the issue of Indian relations remained a prominent topic of discussion during Digges' administration. In order to avoid further bloodshed, the Assembly devised a system of Indian reservations for the colony, a policy which was intended to placate those tribes who feared further inroads by white settlers seeking new land. Nevertheless, in 1656 misunderstanding between the two groups resulted in a battle near the present site of Richmond, in which a force under Colonel Edward Hill, who had acted briefly in 1646 as governor of Maryland, suffered a major defeat at the hands of an Indian tribe (apparently of Siouan origin).

In December 1656 Digges was named by the Assembly to act as the colony's English Agent, and several months later he relinquished the governorship to Samuel Mathews, Jr. When he returned to America, Digges resumed his seat on the Council, although he seems to have again visited England on an agency mission in about 1663. Digges also served for a time as Virginia's Auditor General before his death on March 15, 1675.

Bibliography: Lyon G. Tyler, "Pedigree of a Representative Virginia Planter," *William and Mary Quarterly*, 1st ser., vol. I (October 1892-April 1893), 80-88, 140-54, 208-13; Edith Roberts Ramsburgh, "Sir Dudley Digges, His English Ancestry and the Digges Line in America," *Daughters of the American Revolution Magazine*, LVII (March 1923), 125-39.

MATHEWS, Samuel, Jr., 1657-1660

Born *circa* 1630 in Virginia, the son of Samuel* and Frances (Grevill) West Peirsey Mathews. Brother of Francis. Married, and the father of a son named John.

Attained the military rank of Lieutenant Colonel by 1652. Named as a representative of Warwick to the Virginia House of Burgesses which met in April 1652. Appointed to the Council in 1655, a position he held until 1657.

Elected to succeed Edward Digges as Governor of Virginia in December 1656, but did not assume office until early 1657.

Mathews' tenure as governor was marked by periodic clashes between the young chief executive and the Virginia House of Burgesses. When in 1658 Mathews and his Council attempted to dissolve the Assembly, the Burgesses, claiming that the governor did not possess that authority, decided to ignore the dissolution order. Mathews and the Council were unable to resist this show of strength, and they eventually yielded when the Assembly called for a new election. Despite his attempt to test the Assembly's power, Mathews was re-elected, probably because he indicated his willingness to co-operate with the effort of the Lower House to seek "confirmation of their present priviledges." Shortly before Mathews' death in January 1660, however, Richard Cromwell resigned as Lord Protector of England, a development which cast into confusion the political status of the Assembly in particular and the colony of Virginia in general.

Bibliography: Minnie G. Cook, "Governor Samuel Mathews, Junior," *William and Mary Quarterly*, 2nd ser., vol. XIV (April 1934), 105-13, vol. XV (July 1935), 299-303; John Frederick Dorman, "Governor Samuel Mathews, Jr.," *Virginia Magazine of History and Biography*, 74 (October 1966), 429-32.

*Samuel Mathews, Jr. has often, as in the biography given in the *DAB*, been confused with Samuel Mathews, Sr., his father and a prominent member of the Virginia Council. For evidence that Samuel Mathews, Jr. was actually the Virginia governor, see the articles cited.

MORYSON, Francis, 1661-1662

Born in England, the son of Sir Richard and Lady Elizabeth (Harington) Moryson; date of birth unknown. Brother of Henry, Richard, Robert, Fynes and Letitia. Married, and the father of Henry, among others.

Apparently fought as an officer in the Royalist Army during the English Civil Wars. Immigrated to Virginia in 1649, bringing with him a commission to command the fort located at Point Comfort; also was acting as a member of the Virginia Council by September 1650. Served as Speaker of the House of Burgesses on several occasions in the 1650's. Presided as Deputy Governor of Virginia from April 1661 to the autumn of 1662, during Governor Berkeley's absence in England.

While Berkeley worked in London to persuade Crown officials to adopt policies consistent with Virginia's economic well-being, Moryson governed the colony with considerable skill. During his administration, however, tobacco prices began to decline appreciably, producing widespread discontent.

Indeed, less than a year after he relinquished the governorship to Berkeley, Moryson was in London defending Virginia's demand that Maryland cease tobacco planting, in order to help reduce the glut on the market and force prices up.

In 1674 Moryson again travelled to London as Virginia's agent, this time to protest a grant to Lords Arlington and Culpeper which allowed them considerable proprietary power over the Northern Neck. Moryson returned to Virginia in January 1677 as one of the commissioners sent to suppress Bacon's Rebellion and investigate the reasons behind that incident. Later that year he sailed for England, where he probably remained until his death *circa* 1678.

JEFFREYS, Herbert, 1677-1678

Date and place of birth unknown, but of Welsh or Cornish descent, and apparently related to Alderman John Jeffreys of London. Married to a woman named Susan, and the father of John.

Served in the English Army, attaining the rank of Colonel. Commissioned Lieutenant Governor of Virginia in November of 1676. Commanded the English troops who arrived in Virginia early in 1677, and succeeded the recalled Governor Sir William Berkeley in the spring of that year; presided in place of the absent Governor Thomas, Lord Culpeper until December 1678.

After replacing Berkeley as chief executive, Jeffreys lent his support to those commissioners from England who were instructed to inquire into the causes of Bacon's Rebellion. By October 1677, however, the Virginia House of Burgesses had decided to address a protest to Jeffreys, in which they contended that the commission's demand for custody of certain records constituted a violation of their privileges. Jeffreys' political position was further eroded by hostility from certain members of his Council, including Philip Ludwell, who referred to the lieutenant governor as "a pitiful little Fellow with a perriwig." Although Jeffreys responded to this challenge by suspending a number of his most outspoken critics, recurrent illness prevented him from effectively defending his authority. Finally, on December 17, 1678, Jeffreys died while still in office, leaving the colony's administration in the hands of Sir Henry Chicheley.

Bibliography: W. N. Sainsbury, comp., "Virginia in 1677-1678" [contains some abstracts of documents to and from Jeffreys], *Virginia Magazine of History and Biography*, XXI (October 1913), 359-71; XXII (January-October 1914), 44-56, 140-49, 232-43, 355-67; XXIII (January-October 1915), 24-33, 146-55, 297-302, 395-403; XXIV (January 1916), 77-80.

CHICHELEY, Sir Henry, 1678-1680, 1680-1682

Born *circa* 1615 in England, the son of Sir Thomas and Lady Dorothy Chicheley of Wimpole, Cambridgeshire. Brother of John, Thomas, Sarah and Elizabeth. Married *circa* 1652 to Agatha (Eltonhead) Wormeley; number of children, if any, unknown.

Matriculated at University College, Oxford, graduating from that institution in February 1635. Fought as an officer in the King's army during the English Civil Wars; immigrated to Virginia in 1649. Served as a member of the House of Burgesses for Lancaster in 1656; appointed to the Virginia Council in 1670, a position which he held until his death. Also received a commission as Deputy Governor of the colony in February 1674. Served as Acting Governor of Virginia from December 1678 to May 1680, in place of the absent Governor Thomas, Lord Culpeper; again presided as Culpeper's substitute from August 1680 to December 1682.

Following the death of Lieutenant Governor Herbert Jeffreys in December 1678, Chicheley, by virtue of the commission as deputy governor which he had received in 1674, assumed control of Virginia's affairs. What was expected to be a short tenure, however, dragged on for eighteen months, as Lord Culpeper, the new royal governor, used every opportunity he could to delay sailing for America. When Culpeper finally arrived in May 1680, he quickly decided that the sophisticated pleasures of London were preferable to the often harsh life of a frontier administrator. Consequently, in August 1680 he again left the colony in the hands of Chicheley and departed for England, where he sought to acquire a greater financial stake in Virginia.

During Chicheley's second period in office, he was confronted by an insurrection which began in the spring of 1682 in Gloucester County and eventually spread elsewhere. Disturbed by the surplus of tobacco which had caused a serious decline in the price of that commodity, groups of "cutters" set out to destroy tobacco plants growing in the fields. Although Chicheley deplored the disregard for law shown by the rioters, he displayed an awareness of their economic plight by granting a general pardon shortly before the return of Culpeper in December of 1682. On February 5, 1683, less than two months after turning over the government to Culpeper, Chicheley died; he was buried in the chancel of Christ Church, Middlesex County, Virginia.

Bibliography: [Benjamin Buckler], *Stemmata Chicheleana: or, a Genealogical Account of Some of the Families Derived from Thomas Chichele . . .* (Oxford, 1765); G. Melvin Herndon, "Sir Henry Chicheley, Virginia Cavalier," *Virginia Cavalcade*, XVI (Summer 1966), 10-16.

CULPEPER, Thomas (2nd Lord), 1680, 1682-1683

Born in 1635 in England, the son of John, first Lord Culpeper and his second wife, Judith. Brother of Elizabeth (died in infancy), Thomas (died in infancy), Elizabeth, Judith, John (later third Lord Culpeper), Cheney (later fourth Lord Culpeper), Philippa and Francis (died young). Married on August 3, 1659 to Margaretta van Hesse, by whom he had Catherine; also fathered two daughters, Susanna and Charlotte, by Susanna Willis, his mistress.

Upon his father's death, assumed the title of second Lord Culpeper and the family estate, which included Leeds Castle in Kent. Appointed Captain, and later Governor, of the Isle of Wight by Charles II. Named to the Council for Foreign Plantations in 1671. Commissioned Governor of Virginia in July 1675, on the understanding that the appointment would begin only after the death or removal of Governor Sir William Berkeley; following Berkeley's death in 1677, administered the colony through two deputies, Colonel Herbert Jeffreys and Sir Henry Chicheley, until Charles II demanded that Culpeper take over the Virginia government in person. Arrived in the colony in May 1680.

As a nobleman accustomed to the worldly pleasures of London, Culpeper soon found his enforced residence in Virginia to be unendurable. He departed for England after only a few months, again leaving the colony in the hands of Chicheley. Nevertheless, when in 1682 news reached England of civil disturbances in Virginia caused by bands of men who were destroying tobacco plants to protest over-production, Culpeper was ordered to return. Following his arrival in December 1682, the governor abandoned the mask of amiability which he had assumed during his previous stay. Culpeper was annoyed by the failure of settlers in the Northern Neck to pay the quitrents to which he believed himself entitled and, partly in retaliation, he carried out a series of unpopular actions which culminated in his dissolution of the House of Burgesses. Culpeper was finally removed from office by Charles II in 1683 for having repeatedly violated his instructions, and for furthering his self-interest at the colony's expense.

Shortly before his death, Culpeper lent his support to the claim of William and Mary to the English throne. He died in London on January 27, 1689.

Bibliography: "Culpeper's Report on Virginia in 1683," *Virginia Magazine of History and Biography*, III (January 1896), 225-38; Fairfax Harrison, *The Proprietors of the Northern Neck: Chapters of Culpeper Genealogy* (Richmond, 1926). *DAB, DNB*.

SPENCER, Nicholas, 1683-1684

Born in Bedfordshire, England, the second son of Nicholas and Mary (Gostwick) Spencer; date of birth unknown. Brother of William, Michael, Robert, Edward and Mary. Married before July 8, 1666 to Frances Mottram, by whom he had William, Mottram, Nicholas, John and Francis.

Probably employed for a time as a London merchant. Immigrated to Virginia in about 1659, and settled in Westmoreland. Served as a member of the Virginia House of Burgesses from 1666 to 1676. Appointed Secretary of State for the colony in 1678, an appointment which was renewed on several occasions. As President of the Virginia Council, served as Acting Governor between May 1683 and February 1684.

Spencer took over the administration of Virginia at the request of Governor Thomas, Lord Culpeper, who in the spring of 1683 decided to return to England without first seeking the permission of the King. In August 1683 Culpeper was deprived of his office for this act of disobedience, and while Francis, Lord Howard of Effingham, was named as his replacement a short time later, the new governor was unable to reach the colony for some months. During the interim Spencer performed the role of a caretaker, despite the fact that Nathaniel Bacon, as senior councillor, was technically entitled to replace Culpeper. Spencer's brief tenure was relatively uneventful, apart from some conflict with a band of Seneca Indians which descended on Virginia from the northwest. During these months the colony also began to emerge from the long economic depression that had resulted from a weak tobacco market. In May of 1683 Spencer notified the Board of Trade that a successful winter had encouraged the planters in Virginia to persevere in their efforts to grow the commodity.

Following the arrival of Lord Howard in February 1684, Spencer stepped down as chief executive and returned to his place on the Council, a position he retained until his death on September 23, 1689.

Bibliography: "Some English Descents of Virginia Families—The Spencers, of Cople, Westmoreland County," *Virginia Magazine of History and Biography*, XVII (April 1909), 215.

HOWARD, Francis (Baron of Effingham), 1684-1689

Born in September 1643 in Surrey, England, the son of Sir Charles and Lady Frances (Courthope) Howard. A Roman Catholic. Married on July 8, 1673 to Philadelphia Pelham, by whom he was the father of Charles, Thomas, Francis and three daughters; after the death of his first wife during the summer of 1686, remarried on January 20, 1690 to Susan (Felton) Harbord; no children by his second wife.

Succeeded to his father's title in March 1673, and in April 1681 became the fifth Baron Howard, following the death of his uncle. Commissioned Royal Governor of Virginia in September 1683 and arrived in the colony some months later, taking his oath of office before the Council in February 1684.

Lord Howard's first meeting with Virginia's General Assembly in April of 1684 resulted in immediate controversy, when the new governor attempted to rescind a law which permitted an individual to appeal to the Assembly a decision made by the General Court. This action was accompanied by other executive recommendations aimed at reducing the power of the Virginia House of Burgesses, and within a few months it was apparent that Lord Howard was chiefly concerned with enhancing his authority and that of the King at the expense of the legislature. The fact that he was a devout Catholic in a predominantly Protestant colony also estranged him from the people whom he had been sent to govern, especially after the succession of the Catholic James II to the English throne became an additional source of mistrust and fear for Virginia's settlers. In 1688, however, rumors of an English revolution began to spread in America, and while Lord Howard was unaware of what had occurred when he left the colony in February 1689, the overthrow of James II several months earlier by the Protestant William of Orange had fatally undermined his authority.

Following his return to England, Lord Howard managed to retain his title as governor, although Francis Nicholson was appointed to succeed him as the colony's resident chief executive. Lord Howard then took his seat in the English House of Lords. He died on March 30, 1695, and was buried nine days later in Lingfield, Sussex.

BACON, Nathaniel, 1689-1690

Born on August 29, 1620 in Bury St. Edmunds, Suffolk, England, the son of Reverend James and Martha (Honeywood) Bacon. Brother of Elizabeth, Martha and Anne, and cousin of Nathaniel Bacon, the rebel. Married to Elizabeth (Kingsmill) Tayloe; no children.

Well educated as a young man, and probably graduated from Cambridge University. Travelled to France, where he was residing in 1647, but immigrated to Virginia in about 1650. Chosen as a member of the Virginia Council in 1657, a position which he filled, apart from a brief interval when he represented York in the House of Burgesses, for more than forty years. Also acted as Auditor General of the colony from March 1675 to December 1687. As President of the Council, served as Acting Governor of Virginia from February 1689 to June 1690, between the administrations of Francis, Lord Howard of Effingham, and Francis Nicholson.

Although the departure of the unpopular Lord Howard eliminated one source of unrest in Virginia, the colony was still disturbed by rumors stemming from incomplete information regarding the recent revolution in England. In March 1689, for example, reports circulated that "foreign Indians" had been enlisted by Catholic supporters of James II to slaughter Virginia's Protestants. Bacon tried to allay such fears a month later, when he and the Council officially proclaimed the accession of William and Mary. Largely as a result of this action, the balance of Bacon's administration was considerably more tranquil, despite a brief recurrence of the "Catholic conspiracy" rumor in Stafford County in June 1689.

After the swearing in of Lieutenant Governor Nicholson in June 1690, Bacon stepped down as chief executive. He died less than two years later, on March 16, 1692, in Hampton, York County, Virginia.

Bibliography: Charles Hervey Townshend, "The Bacons of Virginia and Their English Ancestry," *New England Historical and Genealogical Register*, XXXVII (April 1883), 189-98; "Bacon Family," *William and Mary Quarterly*, 1st ser., vol. X (April 1902), 267-71.

NICHOLSON, Francis, 1690-1692, 1698-1705

New York, 1688-1689; Maryland, 1694-1698; South Carolina, 1721-1725

Born on November 12, 1655 at "Downholme Park," near Richmond, in Yorkshire, England, probably the son of Thomas Nicholson. Never married.

Became a protegé of Lord St. John of Basing, acting for a time as page to his wife. Entered the English Army in January 1678, and in 1686 was appointed Captain of a company of foot soldiers accompanying Sir Edmund Andros to New England. Named to the Council organized under the Dominion of New England, and eventually commissioned Lieutenant Governor; served as Andros' deputy in New York from 1688 to 1689. Sailed for England after the fall of the Dominion, but soon received a commission as Lieutenant Governor of Virginia, a position which he held from June of 1690 to September 1692; again served as Virginia's chief executive, with the rank of Royal Governor, from December 1698 to August 1705. Also presided as Governor of Maryland from July 1694 to December 1698, of Nova Scotia for several weeks in 1713, and of South Carolina from May 1721 to the spring of 1725.

Nicholson's remarkable instinct for political survival enabled him to serve as resident chief executive of five different colonies during a period encompassing some thirty-seven years. Throughout his long professional career, he often experienced opposition from local officials, opposition which became especially virulent during his second tenure in Virginia. In that colony a bitter quarrel with Commissary James Blair and other members of the Virginia Council finally brought about his recall in 1705. Nevertheless, despite the hostility which he sometimes provoked, Nicholson's record as a colonial administrator was not without a number of significant achievements. In Maryland, for example, his strong interest in education led him to aid in the establishment of King William's School (later St. John's College), while several years earlier he had supported Commissary Blair's efforts in Virginia to found the College of William and Mary.

By the 1720's ill health and concern in London over his policy regarding paper currency in South Carolina had reduced Nicholson's political effectiveness, and in the spring of 1725 he sailed for England on a leave of absence. He died in London on March 5, 1728, leaving the bulk of his estate to the Society for the Propagation of the Gospel in Foreign Parts, an organization in which, as a staunch Anglican, he had always taken an active role.

Bibliography: [Unsigned], "Instructions to Francis Nicholson," *Virginia Magazine of History and Biography*, IV (1896), 49-54; [unsigned], "Papers Relating to the Administration of Governor Nicholson . . .," *Virginia Magazine of History and Biography*, VII (1899-1900), 153-72, 275-86, 386-401, vol. VIII (1900-01), 46-58, 126-46, 260-73, 366-85, vol. IX (1901-02), 18-33, 152-62, 251-62; Charles William Sommerville, "Early Career of Governor Francis Nicholson," *Maryland Historical Magazine*, IV (June-September 1909), 101-14, 201-20; Louis B. Wright, "William Byrd's Opposition to Governor Francis Nicholson," *Journal of Southern History*, XI (February 1945), 68-79; Samuel Clyde McCullough, "The Fight to Depose Governor Nicholson," *Journal of Southern History*, XII (August 1946), 403-22; Fairfax Downey, "The Governor Goes A-Wooing: The Swashbuckling Courtship of Nicholson of Virginia, 1699-1705," *Virginia Magazine of History and Biography*, LV (January 1947), 6-19; Ruth M. Winton, "Governor Francis Nicholson's Relations with the Society for the Propagation of the Gospel in Foreign Parts, 1701-1727," *Historical Magazine of the Protestant Episcopal Church*, XVII (September 1948), 274-96; Bruce T. McCully, "From the North Riding to Morocco: The Early Years of Governor Francis Nicholson, 1655-1686," *William and Mary Quarterly*, 3rd ser., vol. XIX (October 1962), 534-56; Gary B. Nash, "Governor Francis Nicholson and the New Castle Expedition of 1696," *Delaware History*, XI (April 1965), 229-39; Stephen S. Webb, "The Strange Career of Francis Nicholson," *William and Mary Quarterly*, 3rd ser., vol. XXIII (October 1966), 513-48. *DAB, DNB*.

ANDROS, Sir Edmund, 1692-1698

New York, 1674-1677, 1678-1681; East Jersey, 1680-1681, 1688-1689; Massachusetts, 1686-1689; New Hampshire, 1686-1689; Plymouth Colony, 1686-1689; Rhode Island, 1686-1689; Connecticut, 1687-1689; West Jersey, 1688-1689; Maryland, 1693, 1694

Born on December 6, 1637 on the Island of Guernsey, the son of Amice and Elizabeth (Stone) Andros. Married to a woman who was related to the Earl of Craven.

Served as Major of a regiment of foot soldiers which in 1666 sailed from England to defend the West Indies against the Dutch. Named a Landgrave of Carolina in 1672; received a commission from the Duke of York in July 1674 to govern the colony of New York, and acted in that capacity, except for an absence in England between November 1677 and August 1678, until January 1681; also exercised control over East Jersey from 1680 until his recall early in the following year. Knighted in about 1681, became Gentleman of the Privy Chamber to Charles II in 1683, and was appointed Lieutenant Colonel of the Princess of Denmark's regiment of horse soldiers in 1685. Commissioned Royal Governor of the Dominion of New England in June 1686, and established his authority in Massachusetts Bay, Maine, New Hampshire, Plymouth and Rhode Island (including the King's Province) in December of that year; Connecticut in November of 1687; and the Jerseys and New York in August 1688 (although Francis Nicholson presided as Andros' substitute in the latter colony). Arrested and sent to England following the overthrow of the Dominion in the spring of 1689, but later received a commission as Royal Governor of Virginia, and served as that colony's chief executive from September 1692 to December 1698; also acted briefly as Governor of Maryland in 1693 and 1694, in the absence of any other executive authority.

Andros' first tenure in New York was marked by several important achievements, especially the improvement of the colony's defenses and the settlement of some boundary difficulties with Connecticut. Nevertheless, even at this stage he had begun to display an inclination to behave in an arbitrary fashion. Perhaps the clearest illustration of this tendency was the high-handed manner in which Andros superseded the authority of Governor Philip Carteret in the Jerseys, provoking Carteret to complain that Andros aimed at "usurping the government" of his colony. This insensitivity to local politics became even more noticeable after Andros assumed control of the Dominion of New England. Following a troubled tenure of less than two and one-half years, he was deposed in the spring of 1689, shortly after news of the Glorious Revolution in England reached Boston.

Although Andros was exonerated of the charges brought against his Dominion government and took over as Virginia's chief executive in 1692, he soon encountered resistance from local leaders like Commissary James Blair, who bitterly informed one London official that Andros "never did any considerable service to the King, nor the people" during his colonial career. Finally, late in 1698, Andros departed for England. He served as Lieutenant Governor of Guernsey from 1704 to 1706, and died in London in February 1714.

Bibliography: "Commission to Sir Edmund Andros," Massachusetts Historical Society, *Collections*, 3rd ser., vol. VII (Boston, 1838), 138-49; W. H. Whitmore, ed., *Andros Tracts: Being a Collection of Pamphlets and Official Papers ... of the Andros Government and the Establishment of the Second Charter of Massachusetts*, 3 vols. (New York, 1868-74) (Publications of the Prince Society, vols. V-VII); Robert N. Toppan, ed., "Andros Records," American Antiquarian Society, *Proceedings*, n.s., vol. XIII (1899-1900), 237-68, 463-99; J.H. Tuttle, ed., "Land Warrants under Andros," Colonial Society of Massachusetts, *Publications*, XXI (1919), 292-361; Albert C. Bates, "Expedition of Sir Edmund Andros to Connecticut in 1687," AAS, *Proceedings*, n.s., vol. 48 (October 1938), 276-99; Jeanne G. Bloom, "Sir Edmund Andros: A Study in Seventeenth-Century Colonial Administration," unpub. Ph.D. diss., Yale University, 1962; Robert C. Ritchie, "London Merchants, the New York Market, and the Recall of Sir Edmund Andros," *New York History*, LVII (January 1976), 5-29. *DAB, DNB*.

NOTT, Edward, 1705-1706

Born *circa* 1657 in England; names of parents unknown. Brother of Susanna and perhaps others. Married to Margaret, the sister of Nathaniel Blakiston, Maryland's governor from 1698 to 1702.

Entered the English Army, and by 1689, when his regiment was sent to Barbados, had risen to the rank of Major. Served as Deputy Governor of Berwick before receiving a commission as Lieutenant Governor of Virginia in April 1705; arrived in the colony to assume that position the following August.

Despite its brevity, Nott's administration was marked by a significant revision of the colony's laws. This revision included provisions for the establishment of new ports, which would have permitted ships from England to load and unload their cargo more efficiently. Although this port act was popular with English tobacco merchants trading with Virginia, it was disallowed in 1710 by royal officials, in response to protests from manufacturers in England who feared that the creation of new towns in the colony would act as a stimulus for domestic manufacturing. In October of 1705, shortly after Nott's arrival, Virginia also experienced a fire which seriously damaged the College of William and Mary. Rebuilding began almost immediately, but it was several years before the institution had completed the restoration made necessary by the conflagration.

Throughout his tenure Nott exhibited a capacity for appeasing different factions in the colony, and his death in office on August 23, 1706 deprived Virginia of a leader whose political tact had even won the praise of the taciturn Commissary James Blair. Nott was buried in the cemetery of Bruton Parish Church in Williamsburg, where a monument was erected in his honor.

JENINGS, Edmund, 1706-1710

Born in 1659 in England, the son of Sir Edmund Jenings of Ripon, Yorkshire and his wife Lady Margaret (Barkham) Jenings. Brother of at least one. Married to Frances Corbin, by whom he was the father of Edmund, Frances and Elizabeth.

Named Clerk of Courts of York County shortly after his immigration to Virginia in about 1680, a position he retained for ten years. Also acted as Collector and Naval Officer, and as Colonel of the militia in his district. Served as either Attorney General or Deputy Attorney General for a number of years between 1680 and 1700. Became a member of the Virginia Council in June 1691. Appointed as Virginia's Deputy Secretary of State in 1696; sworn in as Secretary of State in June 1702, following the death of Christopher Wormeley, and apparently held that office until 1722, apart from several intervals. As senior member of the Council, became Acting Governor of Virginia after the death of Governor Edward Nott in August 1706, and served in that capacity until June of 1710.

Although he was meant to preside as chief executive only until the arrival of Robert Hunter, the newly-appointed royal governor, Jenings remained in office for almost four years when Hunter was captured at sea by the French while *en route* to the province. Nevertheless, Jenings' unexpectedly prolonged administration appears to have been acceptable both to his fellow colonists and to English authorities. Robert Quary, reporting to the Board of Trade in December 1709, noted that "all things are very quiet in Virginia" and that "no Assembly has sat since the death of Colonel [Governor] Nott," an indication that Virginians were content with Jenings' handling of affairs.

Following his tenure as acting governor, Jenings returned to his seat on the Council, a position he held until his suspension by Lieutenant Governor Hugh Drysdale in June 1726. Jenings died on July 5, 1727.

Bibliography: Maurer Maurer, "Notes on the Honorable Edmund Jenings," *Virginia Magazine of History and Biography*, LII (October 1944), 249-61; Maurer Maurer, "Edmund Jenings and Robert Carter," *Virginia Magazine of History and Biography*, LV (January 1947), 20-30.

SPOTSWOOD, Alexander, 1710-1722

Born in 1676 in Tangier, Africa, the son of Robert, a physician, and Catherine (Mercer) Elliott Spotswood. An Anglican. Married in 1724 to Anne Butler Brayne; father of John, Robert and two daughters. Named in 1693 as Ensign in a regiment of foot soldiers under the command of the Earl of Bath; also saw military service as Lieutenant Quartermaster General under Lord Cadogan during the War of the Spanish Succession, and later advanced to the rank of Lieutenant Colonel. Wounded in 1704 at the Battle of Blenheim and captured, but soon exchanged. Appointed Lieutenant Governor of Virginia, taking office in June 1710 in place of the nominal governor, George Hamilton, Earl of Orkney, with whom he shared the governor's salary.

Spotswood's twelve-year tenure as lieutenant governor was a politically turbulent period in Virginia, as the House of Burgesses made its first sustained effort to wield greater authority. At the same time Spotswood and the Virginia Council, a body which had traditionally exercised extensive power, clashed over a number of issues. Much of the political squabbling between Spotswood and the legislature, however, meant little in terms of actual policy formation, since the final decision was often made by the imperial authorities—as when the Crown disallowed two controversial acts for systematizing the Indian and tobacco trades.

Spotswood was removed from office in 1722, after the Crown decided that his series of disputes with the Virginia Legislature called for a change of governors. Spotswood then retired to Spotsylvania County, where about seven years earlier he had founded the town of Germanna, made up mostly of German immigrants who formed a defensive buffer on Virginia's western frontier and engaged in iron mining and smelting. Spotswood returned to England in 1724 in order to resolve some legal questions concerning his large land holdings in Spotsylvania County, but he returned to Virginia six years later as Deputy Postmaster General for the American colonies. In that capacity he helped to improve the rudimentary colonial postal system. Spotswood died in Annapolis, Maryland on June 7, 1740 while, as Major General and second in command, he was in the process of raising a regiment to be employed in Lord Cathcart's Cartagena expedition during the War of Jenkins' Ear.

Bibliography: Charles Campbell, *Genealogy of the Spotswood Family* (Albany, New York, 1868); R. A. Brock, ed., *The Official Letters of Alexander Spotswood, Lieutenant Governor of the Colony, 1710-1722*, in Virginia Historical Society, *Collections*, n.s., vols. I and II (Richmond, 1882-85); Edward Ingle, "Governor Spotswood's Horseshoe Campaign, 1716, as Related to the Romance of Cathay," *Magazine of American History*, XVII (April 1887), 295-306; [unsigned], "Charges against Spotswood," *Virginia Magazine of History and Biography*, IV (1896), 349-63; Leonidas Dodson, *Alex-*

ander Spotswood: Governor of Colonial Virginia, 1710-1722 (Philadelphia, 1932); Lester J. Cappon, ed., "Correspondence of Alexander Spotswood with John Spotswood of Edinburgh," *Virginia Magazine of History and Biography*, LX (April 1952), 211-40; Jack P. Greene, "The Opposition to Lieutenant Governor Alexander Spotswood, 1718," *Virginia Magazine of History and Biography*, LXX (January 1962), 35-48; Walter Havighurst, *Alexander Spotswood: Portrait of a Governor* (Williamsburg, 1967). *DAB*, *DNB*.

DRYSDALE, Hugh, 1722-1726

Date and place of birth, and names of parents unknown. Married to a woman who survived him; father of Ann and perhaps others.

Apparently served in the British Army, where he rose to the rank of Colonel. Commissioned in April 1722 as Lieutenant Governor of Virginia, largely due to his friendship with Prime Minister Sir Robert Walpole, and arrived in the province to begin his administration in September of that year.

Drysdale's tenure was characterized by a generally harmonious relationship between the chief executive and the Virginia General Assembly. Realizing that frequent exercise of the royal prerogative would only alienate Virginia's leading families, Drysdale attempted instead to win the support of key members of the legislature. In 1724, for example, John Carter, the eldest son of the powerful Robert Carter, became a member of the Virginia Council on Drysdale's recommendation, despite the fact that his father was already serving on that body. Personal security was also a major consideration during Drysdale's years in office, especially following the revelation of an intended slave insurrection in 1722. The General Assembly responded to this threat in 1723 by passing additional laws "for the better government of Negroes, mulattoes, and Indians," although the Crown eventually rejected those provisions in the legislation which were intended to curtail the slave trade.

Governor Drysdale's health had deteriorated seriously by May 1726, causing him to consider a recuperative visit to England. However, in a letter to the Board of Trade dated July 10, he announced that he had changed his mind, chiefly because of an anticipated war between England and Spain. Less than two weeks later, on July 22, 1726, Drysdale died in Williamsburg, Virginia.

Bibliography: "P. S. F.," "Hugh Drysdale," typescript biography in files of American Council of Learned Societies, Manuscript Division, Library of Congress, Washington, D.C.

CARTER, Robert, 1726-1727

Born in 1663 at "Corotoman" in Lancaster County, Virginia, the son of John and Sarah (Ludlow) Carter. Brother of Sarah, and half-brother of John II, George, Elizabeth and Charles. Married in 1688 to Judith Armistead, by whom he had John, Elizabeth, Judith and Anne; after his first wife's death in 1699, remarried in 1702 to Elizabeth (Landon) Willis, by whom he had Robert, Charles, George, Landon, Lucy and Mary. Privately educated in England, spending six years in London with the family of a "Mr. Baily." One of the largest landowners among the settlers of Virginia's Northern Neck; holder of numerous local offices, including Colonel and Commander-in-Chief of Lancaster and Northumberland counties, and Justice of the Lancaster County Court.

Member of the Virginia House of Burgesses, representing Lancaster County from 1691 to 1692 and again from 1695 to 1699; elected Speaker of the House in 1696 and in 1699. Served as Treasurer of the colony from 1699 to 1705, and as a member of the Virginia Council from 1700 until 1732. Acted as agent for the Fairfax family, who were proprietors of the Northern Neck, from 1702 to 1712 and again from 1721 to 1732. Appointed President of the Council in 1726, and served as Acting Governor between the death of Governor Hugh Drysdale in the summer of that year and the arrival of Drysdale's replacement, William Gooch, in September 1727.

Known as "King Robin" or "King Carter" because of his wealth and power, Carter did not greatly alter the course of Virginia politics during the rather uneventful year in which he performed the duties of acting governor. However, his cumulative impact in a public career that spanned more than three decades was enormous. As a leader of the colony's House of Burgesses and later a prominent member of the Council, Carter locked horns with a succession of Virginia governors, especially Alexander Spotswood, in an effort to defend the powers of the legislature. Carter continued as president of the Council after the arrival of Lieutenant Governor Gooch, and his prestige in the colony was perhaps unparalleled during his final years. He died on August 4, 1732, and was buried in the cemetery of Christ Church in Lancaster County.

Bibliography: "Carter Papers," *Virginia Magazine of History and Biography*, V (April 1898), 408-28; VI (July 1898-April 1899), 1-22, 145-52, 260-68, 365-70; VII (July 1899), 64-68; "Robert Carter and the Wormeley Estate," *William and Mary Quarterly*, 1st ser., vol. XVII (April 1909), 252-64; Louis B. Wright, ed., *Letters of Robert Carter, 1720-1727: The Commercial Interests of a Virginia Gentleman* (San Marino, California, 1940); Maurer Maurer, "Edmund Jenings and Robert Carter," *Virginia Magazine of History and Biography*, LV (January 1947), 20-30; Robert Randolph Carter and Robert Isham Randolph, *The Carter Tree* (Santa Barbara, California, 1951); Clifford Dowdey, *The Virginia Dynasties: The Emergence of "King Carter" and the Golden Age* (Boston and Toronto, 1969). *DAB*.

GOOCH, Sir William, 1727-1740, 1741-1749

Born on October 21, 1681 in Yarmouth, England, the eldest son of Thomas and Frances (Love) Gooch. An Anglican. Brother of Sir Thomas Gooch, who became bishop of Ely in 1748, and perhaps others. Married to Rebecca Staunton, and the father of William and probably others.

Served in the English Army as a young man, and was present at the Battle of Blenheim in 1704. Appointed Lieutenant Governor of Virginia, arriving in the colony to assume that office in September of 1727.

With the exception of a seven-month period during which Commissary James Blair was the acting governor of Virginia, Gooch remained the colony's chief executive from 1727 to 1749, a period of service surpassed in length only by that of Sir William Berkeley. Gooch's long period in office was marked by the steady development of self-rule in Virginia, as the governor established an informal political alliance with the colony's gentry, and the House of Burgesses made use of Gooch's co-operative attitude by expanding its own powers. So effective was the collaboration between Gooch and Virginia's leaders that towards the end of his tenure he was able to report to his brother, with only a trace of exaggeration, that he had "ruled without so much as a murmur of discontent." While serving as governor Gooch also retained his interest in military affairs, and after the death of Alexander Spotswood, who had recruited troops for an assault on the Spanish stronghold of Cartagena, Gooch assumed Spotswood's command himself.

In reward for his efforts, Gooch was made a Baronet in 1746; the next year he was promoted to the rank of Major General in the British Army. He finally resigned his commission as lieutenant governor in the summer of 1749 for reasons of health, and returned to England. Gooch died in Bath on December 17, 1751, and was buried in Yarmouth. Goochland County, Virginia, formed in 1728, was named in his honor.

Bibliography: Percy Scott Flippin, "William Gooch: Successful Royal Governor of Virginia," *William and Mary Quarterly*, 2nd ser., vol. V (October 1925), 225-58, vol. VI (January 1926), 1-38; Andrew K. Prinz, "Sir William Gooch in Virginia: The King's Good Servant," unpub. Ph.D. diss., Northwestern University, 1963; Frank W. Porter, III, "Expanding the Domain: William Gooch and the Northern Neck Boundary Dispute," *Maryland Historian*, V (Spring 1974), 1-13; typescript collection of Gooch's correspondence to England in the Research Library, Colonial Williamsburg, Inc., Williamsburg, Va. *See also* David Alan Williams, "The Phantom Governorship of John Robinson, Sr., 1749," *Virginia Magazine of History and Biography*, LXVIII (January 1960), 104-06. *DAB, DNB*.

BLAIR, James, 1740-1741

Born in 1655 or 1656 in Scotland, the son of Robert Blair, a Scots clergyman. Brother of William, John, Marjory and Archibald. Married on June 2, 1687 to Sarah Harrison; apparently had no children. Attended the University of Edinburgh, receiving an M.A. in 1673.

Ordained by a bishop of the Church of Scotland, and served for several years as rector of Cranston parish in the diocese of Edinburgh. Deprived of his ministerial position in 1681 for refusing to take an oath required by the future James II, and left Scotland for London, where he worked as a clerk in the office of the Master of Rolls until 1684 or 1685. Immigrated to Virginia, arrived in 1685, and chosen as rector of the parish of Varina in Henrico County. Named in December 1689 as Commissary, and in that capacity served as the Bishop of London's Deputy in Virginia. Played a major role in the founding of the College of William and Mary, travelling to London in 1691 to carry a memorial concerning the proposed institution to the King and Queen; named as the college's first President in the charter granted in 1693; also a member of the college Board of Visitors during its first year. Resigned in 1694 as rector of the parish of Varina and served as minister of the Anglican church in Jamestown from 1694 to 1710; became rector of the parish of Bruton in Williamsburg, a post which he held from 1710 until his death. Appointed to the Virginia Council in 1694 and, with the exception of a brief interval from April 1695 to August 1696, remained a member of that body until his death. As President of the Council, served as Acting Governor of Virginia from December 1740 to July 1741, while Governor William Gooch participated in the Cartagena expedition against the Spanish.

Advanced in age and hard of hearing, Blair had no significant effect on Virginia politics during his brief tenure as acting governor. His major activities were all in the past, including his great effort on behalf of the colony's college. Throughout his long career Blair also acquired a reputation as a man to be treated with caution, since his political machinations were thought to have contributed to the recall of Virginia Governors Andros, Nicholson and Spotswood.

Commissary Blair died on April 18, 1743, less than two years after Governor Gooch returned to resume his duties as chief executive. Blair was the author of several works, including *Our Savior's Divine Sermon on the Mount*, published in five volumes (London, 1722). He also collaborated with Henry Hartwell and Edward Chilton on *The Present State of Virginia and the College . . .to Which is Added the Charter* (London, 1727).

Bibliography: Frederick Horner, *The History of the Blair, Banister and Braxton Families* (Philadelphia, 1898); D. E. Motley, "Life of Commissary James Blair," in *Johns Hopkins University Studies in History and Political*

Science, vol. XIX, no. 10 (1901), 455-503; Samuel R. Mohler, "Commissary James Blair, Churchman, Educator, and Politician of Colonial Virginia," unpub. Ph.D. diss., University of Chicago, 1940; G. MacLaren Brydon, "James Blair, Commissary," *Historical Magazine of the Protestant Episcopal Church*, XIV (June 1945), 85-118; Samuel Clyde McCulloch, "James Blair's Plan of 1699 to Reform the Clergy of Virginia," *William and Mary Quarterly*, 3rd ser., vol. IV (January 1947), 70-86; Bradford Spangenberg, "Vestrymen in the House of Burgesses: Protection of Local Vestry Autonomy during James Blair's Term as Commissary (1690-1743)," *Historical Magazine of the Protestant Episcopal Church*, XXXII (June 1963), 77-99; Parke Rouse, Jr., *James Blair of Virginia* (Chapel Hill, 1971); John C. Van Horne, ed., "The Correspondence of James Blair as Acting Governor of Virginia, 1740-1741," *Virginia Magazine of History and Biography*, LXXXIV (January 1976), 19-48; P. G. Scott, "James Blair and the Scottish Church: A New Source," *William and Mary Quarterly*, 3rd ser., vol. XXXIII (April 1976), 300-08. *DAB, DNB*.

LEE, Thomas, 1749-1750

Born in 1690 in Virginia, the son of Richard and Laetitia (Corbin) Lee. Brother of John (died in infancy), Richard, Philip, Francis, Henry and Ann. Married in 1722 to Hannah Ludwell, by whom he was the father of Philip Ludwell, Hannah, Thomas Ludwell, Richard Henry, Francis Lightfoot, Alice, William and Arthur.

Privately educated. Served as Resident Agent for the extensive Culpeper-Fairfax proprietary in Virginia's Northern Neck, acting as deputy for his absent uncle, Edmund Jenings, from 1713 to 1716. Elected to the Virginia House of Burgesses in 1726, representing Westmoreland, and continued in that capacity until his elevation to the Virginia Council in 1732. Remained a member of the Council for the next eighteen years, eventually becoming its President. As president of the Council, succeeded Sir William Gooch as chief executive of Virginia in September 1749.

Although he did not survive long after his accession as Acting Governor, Lee did take some ambitious steps in the face of what he perceived to be a serious threat from the French in North America. In an extensive report to London, written shortly after he replaced Gooch, Lee suggested several means of countering French influence in the Virginia back-country, including a proposal to encourage settlement of the area by German immigrants. Just before his death in office on November 14, 1750, Lee sent the frontiersman Christopher Gist on an exploratory mission, asking him to make careful note of the most likely locations for colonization. While Lee's appointment as President of the newly-organized Ohio Company in 1748 certainly suggests that such efforts were not wholly disinterested, he was also aware of the strategic and economic benefits which would result from establishing British hegemony over the trans-Alleghany region.

Bibliography: J. Henry Lea, "Lee of Virginia," *New England Historical and Genealogical Register*, XLIV (January 1890), 103-11; vol. XLVI (January-April 1892), 64-78, 161-66; Burton J. Hendrick, *The Lees of Virginia: Biography of a Family* (Boston, 1935); William M. E. Rachal, "President Thomas Lee of Virginia," *Virginia Cavalcade*, III (Summer 1953), 12-19; Cazenove Gardner Lee, Jr., *Lee Chronicle: Studies of the Early Generations of the Lees of Virginia . . .*, comp. and ed. by Dorothy Mills Parker (New York, 1957).

BURWELL, Lewis, 1750-1751

Born in 1710 in Gloucester County, Virginia, the son of Nathaniel and Elizabeth (Carter) Burwell. Brother of Carter. Married in September 1736 to Mary Willis, by whom he was the father of Lewis, Rebecca, and probably two other daughters.

Educated in England, attending Eton from 1722 to 1729; admitted as a fellow commoner at Gonville and Caius College, Cambridge in June 1729, where he studied until 1733, although he apparently never received a degree from that institution. Returned to Virginia in 1733, and served in the Virginia House of Burgesses from 1742 to 1743, representing Gloucester County. Became a member of the Virginia Council in August 1743 and, as President of that body, served as Acting Governor of the province between the death of Thomas Lee in November 1750 and the arrival of Lieutenant Governor Robert Dinwiddie in November 1751.

Burwell's interim governorship was rather uneventful politically, since no Assembly met during his tenure. Nevertheless, in the early 1750's Virginia was undergoing rapid territorial expansion, and Burwell continued his predecessor's attempts to make peace with the Ohio Indians, in order to encourage settlement of the Virginia back-country. Burwell was also closely involved with the work of Joshua Fry and Peter Jefferson, two men who had been hired to prepare a new map of Virginia. After seeing the result of their efforts, Burwell observed that the map's precision was especially remarkable, "considering . . . we are yet a country of woods."

Following Dinwiddie's inauguration as chief executive, Burwell returned to his seat on the Virginia Council, a position he held until his death in May 1756.

Bibliography: George Harrison Burwell, *Sketch of Carter Burwell (1716-1756)* (Millwood, Va., 1961?); William Hamilton Bryson, ed., "A Letter of Lewis Burwell to James Burrough, July 8, 1734," *Virginia Magazine of History and Biography*, LXXXI (October 1973), 405-14.

DINWIDDIE, Robert, 1751-1758

Born on October 3, 1692 at "Germiston," near Glasgow, Scotland, the son of Robert and Elizabeth (Cumming) Dinwiddie. Brother of Matthew, John, Lawrence and at least five others. Married sometime before 1738 to Rebecca Auchinleck, by whom he was the father of Elizabeth and Rebecca. Employed as a young man in his father's countinghouse, and eventually became a merchant.

Named Collector of Customs for Bermuda in December 1727; received a regular customs appointment in 1730. Promoted in 1738 to the post of Surveyor General for the Southern District of America, and uncovered a number of fraudulent practices in the collection of revenues. Entitled as surveyor general to a place on the councils of America's southern colonies, and took a seat on the Virginia Council in October 1741. Almost ten years later, in July 1751, appointed Lieutenant Governor of Virginia; in November of that year, arrived in New York and set out for Virginia to assume his new position.

Dinwiddie's tenure was marked by several clashes between the governor and the Virginia House of Burgesses, the most significant of which was the "pistole fee" controversy. Traditionally the Virginia Lower House had assumed the power of establishing fees, and although the colony's governors were from 1679 legally authorized to set fees with the Council's consent, previous chief executives had in general not attempted to exercise that right. Consequently, when Dinwiddie, with the Board of Trade's consent, attempted to charge a "pistole" (approximately three and one half Spanish dollars) for sealing land patents, he encountered a hostile reaction in the House of Burgesses. After much political maneuvering, the English Privy Council settled the matter in June of 1754 by upholding Dinwiddie's right to collect the fee, while at the same time appeasing the Burgesses by exempting certain patents from payment. Apart from this and other internal political convulsions, Dinwiddie's service as governor was troubled by the external danger of French and Indian attacks on Virginia's western frontier during the Seven Years' War. This threat did not subside until late in his administration.

Dinwiddie left Virginia in January 1758, after requesting a leave of absence to recover his health. However, he never returned to the colony, and died in England at Clifton, Bristol on July 27, 1770. Dinwiddie County, Virginia, founded in 1752, was named in his honor.

Bibliography: R. A. Brock, ed., *The Official Records of Robert Dinwiddie*, in Virginia Historical Society, *Collections*, n.s., vols. III and IV (Richmond, 1883-84); Louis K. Koontz, "Robert Dinwiddie: A Chapter in the American Colonial Frontier," *Pacific Historical Review*, V (December 1936), 359-67; Louis K. Koontz, *Robert Dinwiddie: His Career in American Colonial Government and Westward Expansion* (Glendale, Calif., 1941); Elizabeth

Dinwiddie Holladay, comp. and ed., *Dinwiddie Family Records* (Charlottesville, 1957); John Richard Alden, *Robert Dinwiddie: Servant of the Crown* (Charlottesville, 1973). Dinwiddie's will appears in the *Virginia Magazine of History and Biography*, XIX (July 1911), 282-83. *DAB*.

BLAIR, John, 1758, 1768

Born in 1687, probably in Virginia, the son of Dr. Archibald Blair and his first wife, whose name is unknown. Brother of Harrison and Elizabeth. Nephew of Commissary James Blair, the acting governor of Virginia from 1740 to 1741. Married to Mary Monro, and the father of John, James, Sarah, Ann, Christian, Elizabeth and four others. Educated at the College of William and Mary, graduating *circa* 1707. Accumulated extensive land holdings in western Virginia.

By 1713 was holding office as Virginia's Deputy Auditor General *pro tempore*; also served as deputy auditor general from August 1728, when he assumed the position on a regular basis, until his death. Became Naval Officer for the upper district of the James River in February 1727. Acted as a member of the Virginia House of Burgesses from Jamestown in 1734, and as a representative of Williamsburg from 1736 to 1740. Appointed to the Virginia Council in 1745 and named to various committees, such as the one chosen in 1746 to revise the colony's legal code. As Council President, served as Acting Governor from January to June 1758, between the administrations of Governors Dinwiddie and Fauquier, and from March to October 1768, between the administrations of Governors Fauquier and Botetourt.

Blair's brief service as acting governor was fairly tranquil. Nevertheless, there were several significant political developments while he held office, particularly in April of 1758, when the Virginia Council rejected a proposal which would have given the House of Burgesses authority over the colony's agent in London. That same month a controversial bill permitting the issuing of £32,000 in paper money was approved by Blair, a decision which, although popular within the colony, was strenuously opposed by British merchants.

After Governor Botetourt's death in 1770, Blair was in line to serve as acting governor for a third time, but because of his advanced age he instead resigned from the Council. Blair died on November 5, 1771.

Bibliography: Frederick Horner, *The History of the Blair, Banister and Braxton Families* (Philadelphia, 1898); Lyon G. Tyler, ed., "Diary of John Blair," *William and Mary Quarterly*, 1st ser., vol. VII (January 1899), 133-53, vol. VIII (July 1899), 1-17. *DAB*.

FAUQUIER, Francis, 1758-1768

Born *circa* 1704 in London, England, the eldest son of Dr. John Francis Fauquier, a physician and director of the Bank of England, and Elizabeth (Chamberlayne) Fauquier. Brother of William and perhaps others. Married to Catharine Dalston.

Pursued a military career until his marriage, when he apparently retired for a time to a country estate in Hertfordshire. Became a Director of the South Sea Company in 1751, and elected a Fellow of the Royal Society in February 1753. Maintained a lifelong interest in science and economics, and wrote *An Essay on Ways and Means of Raising Money for the Support of the Present War without Increasing the Public Debts* (1756), a treatise first published during the early part of the Seven Years' War. Named Lieutenant Governor of Virginia in January 1758, and arrived in the colony to take up his new appointment in June of that year.

The ten years during which Fauquier served as lieutenant governor were characterized by a general spirit of co-operation between the chief executive and the Virginia House of Burgesses. Fauquier's relationship with John Robinson II, who held office as both speaker of the House and treasurer of the colony, is an instance of the collaboration which contributed to this political harmony. Although Fauquier was instructed by the Board of Trade in London to separate the offices of Speaker and Treasurer, a move that would have diminished Robinson's power, the governor ignored the Board's directive thereby placing Robinson in his debt. Robinson responded by supporting proposals favored by Fauquier for defense against French and Indian attacks during the Seven Years' War. To be sure, there were occasional outbreaks of hostility between Fauquier and the Burgesses, most notably in 1765, when the governor dissolved that body for passing four resolutions which implied disapproval of the Stamp Act. Nevertheless, Fauquier was an extremely skillful political tactician, and appears to merit Thomas Jefferson's later estimate of him as Virginia's ablest governor.

Fauquier died in Williamsburg, Virginia on March 3, 1768, while still in office. Fauquier County, Virginia, founded in 1759, was named in his honor.

Bibliography: *The Speech of the Honorable Francis Fauquier, esq.; His Majesty's lieutenant governor . . .to the General assembly . . .*(Williamsburg, 1758); Fairfax Harrison, ''A Portrait of Governor Fauquier,'' Fairfax County Historical Society, *Bulletin*, no. 4 (1924), 323-40; Nellie Norkus, ''Francis Fauquier, Lieutenant Governor of Virginia, 1758-1768: A Study in Colonial Problems,'' unpub. Ph.D. diss., University of Pittsburgh, 1954; George H. Reese, ''Portraits of Governor Francis Fauquier,'' *Virginia Magazine of History and Biography*, LXXVI (January 1968), 3-10. *DAB*, *DNB*.

BERKELEY, Norborne (Baron de Botetourt), 1768-1770

Born *circa* 1718 in London, England, the son of John Symes and Elizabeth (Norborne) Devereux Berkeley. Brother of Elizabeth. Never married.

While resident in England, engaged in unsuccessful business practices that almost caused bankruptcy. Became a Member of Parliament for Gloucestershire in 1741, a position which he held for many years. Named Colonel of the South Gloucestershire militia in 1758; also assumed the colonelcy of the North Gloucestershire militia in 1762, the same year in which he was appointed Lord Lieutenant of Gloucestershire. Received the title of Baron de Botetourt in 1764. Commissioned Royal Governor of Virginia in August 1768, and arrived in the colony to assume office in October of that year.

Botetourt's arrival in Virginia was an unusual event, since the colony's chief executive was normally a lieutenant governor appointed by the royal governor resident in England, rather than the royal governor himself. The rare distinction of receiving a direct emissary of the Crown, combined with Botetourt's engaging manner, made him personally very popular with the Virginians, although the growing dispute over the extent of Parliament's authority did damage his relationship with the Virginia House of Burgesses. In May 1769, for example, Botetourt was forced to dissolve the Burgesses when that body continued to question the legitimacy of both the Townshend duties and a parliamentary proposal that some Americans be tried in England under a treason statute passed during the reign of Henry VIII. The legislators responded to this dissolution by meeting illegally and forming the Virginia Association, which pledged to use the tactic of non-importation of a wide variety of English goods until the Townshend duties were repealed.

Botetourt died while in office on October 15, 1770. Botetourt County, Virginia, established in 1770, was named in his honor.

Bibliography: Charles Washington Coleman, "Norborne, Baron de Botetourt, Governor-General of Virginia, 1768-1770," *William and Mary Quarterly*, 1st ser., vol. V (January 1897), 165-70; Lyon Gardiner Tyler, ed., "Correspondence Relating to Lord Botetourt," *Tyler's Quarterly Historical and Genealogical Magazine*, III (October 1921), 106-26; Bryan D. G. Little, "Norborne Berkeley: Gloucestershire Magnate," *Virginia Magazine of History and Biography*, LXII (October 1955), 379-409. *DAB*.

NELSON, William, 1770-1771

Born in 1711 in the vicinity of Yorktown, Virginia, the son of Thomas, a prosperous merchant and landowner, and Margaret (Reade) Nelson. An Anglican. Brother of Thomas and Mary. Married in February 1738 to Elizabeth Burwell; father of six children who reached maturity: Thomas (who served as governor of Virginia in 1781), Nathaniel, Hugh, Robert, William and Elizabeth. Inherited a large estate and, like his father, became a merchant and a member of the landed aristocracy.

Named Sheriff of York County as early as 1738, and represented that county in the Virginia House of Burgesses from 1742 to 1745. Member for many years of the Board of Visitors for the College of William and Mary. Chosen to the Virginia Council in 1745, a position which he held until his death in 1772. As President of the Council, served as Acting Governor of Virginia between the death of Governor Botetourt in October 1770 and the arrival of Botetourt's replacement, John Murray, fourth Earl of Dunmore, in late 1771.

Nelson's period as interim governor occurred at a time when the revolutionary movement in Virginia was losing much of its previous momentum. Perhaps the best indication of this trend was the colonists' failure to enforce their threat to refrain from importing most English goods until the British government repealed the Townshend Acts. By late 1770 Virginia's merchants had become disenchanted with the policy of non-importation, and the colony's planters, who had become accustomed to English-made luxury products, were beginning to agree. Finally, in July 1771, a committee in Fairfax County consisting of both merchants and planters recommended that, with the exception of the tea still taxed by Parliament, non-importation should be abandoned as a means of protest. Along with the decision by the British in the spring of 1770 to repeal all of the Townshend duties except for the impost on tea, an economic slump which plagued the colony during Nelson's administration might have affected the Virginians' will to resist. This depressed Virginia economy was further damaged by a devastating flood in the spring of 1771, which destroyed crops and caused heavy property loss in the tidewater region.

Following his gubernatorial service, Nelson returned to his seat on the Council. He died on November 19, 1772, and was buried in the churchyard in Yorktown.

Bibliography: R. A. Brock, "The Nelson House, Yorktown, Virginia," *Magazine of American History*, VII (July 1881), 47-58; Samuel Davis Page, "William Nelson, Acting Governor of Virginia, 1770-71," Pennsylvania Society of Colonial Governors, *Publications*, I (1916), 271-78; Emory Gibbons Evans, "The Nelsons: A Biographical Study of a Virginia Family in the Eighteenth Century," unpub. Ph.D. diss., University of Virginia, 1957; Emory G. Evans, "The Rise and Decline of the Virginia Aristocracy in the Eighteenth Century: The Nelsons," in Darrett B. Rutman, ed., *The Old Dominion: Essays for Thomas Perkins Abernethy* (Charlottesville, 1964), 62-78; Charles E. Hatch, Jr., *The Nelson House and the Nelsons* (Washington, D.C., 1969); John C. Van Horne, ed., *The Correspondence of William Nelson as Acting Governor of Virginia, 1770-1771* (Charlottesville, 1975). *DAB*.

MURRAY, John (4th Earl of Dunmore), 1771-1775
New York, 1770-1771

Born in 1732, the eldest son of William Murray, third Earl of Dunmore, and his wife, Catherine Nairne. Married on February 21, 1759 to Lady Charlotte Stewart, the daughter of the Earl of Galloway; father of five sons and four daughters, including Virginia. Inherited his father's title and estate in 1756; also held the titles of Viscount Fincastle, and Baron of Blair, of Moulin, and of Tillymont.

Chosen in 1761 as a Peer representing Scotland in the British Parliament; again elected to Parliament in 1768. Commissioned Royal Governor of New York in January 1770 and arrived in the colony in October of that year.

Dunmore's tenure as governor of New York was brief and uneventful. His arrival in the colony coincided with the beginning of a three-year interlude between the protests of the 1760's and the resurgence of opposition in 1773 (which would eventually culminate in revolution). Within a year Dunmore was replaced in New York by William Tryon and sent to Virginia as that colony's Royal Governor. In this new setting he at first enjoyed a period of tranquility, but by 1773 the revolutionary movement in Virginia had gained momentum, and Dunmore faced a House of Burgesses which was becoming more intractable. The governor responded by dissolving the Burgesses in March 1773 and again in May 1774, when that body expressed sympathy with colonial complaints. By the summer of 1774 the already troubled colony found itself at war with the Shawnee and Ottawa Indians who lived along the frontier. Taking an active role in the military operations against the Indians, Dunmore helped to suppress the outbreak, though some critics contended that the war had been due to the governor's aggressive land policy and had been used by him as a means of drawing attention from the colonists' grievances. By the spring of 1775 these grievances had reached such a point that Dunmore no longer felt safe, and in June 1775 he left Virginia and retreated to the British man-of-war *Fowey*, off Yorktown, from which he directed efforts to subdue the rebellion. In July of 1776 he left Virginia for England, where he once again represented Scotland in Parliament.

Dunmore also served as Governor of the Bahamas from 1787 to 1796. He died in Ramsgate, England on March 5, 1809.

Bibliography: Randolph C. Downes, "Dunmore's War: An Interpretation," *Mississippi Valley Historical Review*, XXI (December 1934), 311-30; Percy B. Caley, "Lord Dunmore and the Pennsylvania-Virginia Boundary Dispute," *Western Pennsylvania Historical Magazine*, XXII (1939), 87-100; Percy B. Caley, "Dunmore: Colonial Governor of New York and Virginia, 1770-1782," unpub. Ph.D. diss., University of Pittsburgh, 1939; Benjamin Quarles, "Lord Dunmore as Liberator," *William and Mary Quarterly*, 3rd ser., vol. XV (October 1958), 494-507; Richard O. Curry, "Lord Dunmore—Tool of Land Jobbers or Realistic Champion of Colonial 'Rights'?: An Inquiry," *West Virginia History*, XXIV (April 1963), 289-95; J. Leitch Wright, Jr., "Lord Dunmore's Loyalist Asylum in the Floridas," *Florida Historical Quarterly*, XLIX (April 1971), 370-79. *DAB, DNB*.

PENDLETON, Edmund, 1775-1776

Born on September 9, 1721 in Caroline County, Virginia, the youngest son of Henry and Mary (Taylor) Pendleton. An Anglican. Brother of James, Philip, Isabella, Nathaniel, Mary and John. Married on January 21, 1742 to Elizabeth Roy, who died in childbirth on November 17 of that year; remarried on June 20, 1743 to Sarah Pollard; no children by his second wife.

Apprenticed at the age of fourteen to Colonel Benjamin Robinson, clerk of the court in Caroline County. Admitted in 1741 to the practice of law in Virginia's county courts; qualified as a lawyer before the Virginia General Court in 1745. Named Justice of the Peace of Caroline County in late 1751, an office he held until 1777. Represented Caroline County in the Virginia House of Burgesses from 1752 until the Revolution. Took a leading role in the revolutionary movement during the 1770's, and became a member of Virginia's Committee of Correspondence in 1773; also represented his home state at the First and Second Continental Congresses in 1774 and 1775. Attended the various revolutionary conventions which met in Virginia before the state declared its independence. Named President of the Virginia Committee of Safety in August 1775, thereby becoming the *de facto* chief executive of the province; served in that capacity, and as President of Virginia's Provincial Convention, until the accession of Governor Patrick Henry in July 1776.

Pendleton's tenure as head of the Committee of Safety lasted less than a year, but during this brief period Virginia was transformed from a colony into an independent commonwealth. Even after the Revolution had begun, Pendleton usually advocated a moderate policy, an approach which often put him at odds with the more impetuous Patrick Henry. Nevertheless, when a state convention met in May 1776 under his presidency to consider separation from Great Britain, Pendleton was firmly on the side of independence, and he personally drafted the resolves which instructed Virginia's delegates in Congress to suggest that course of action.

Pendleton was named Speaker of Virginia's House of Delegates in October 1776, following his period as chief executive. In 1777 he became Presiding Judge of the new commonwealth's Court of Chancery, and in 1779 he was made President of the Virginia Supreme Court of Appeals, a position he held until his death. Pendleton also acted as President of the state convention which in 1788 considered the proposed Federal Constitution, where his staunch defense of that document was a major factor in Virginia's eventual decision to ratify. Pendleton died in Richmond, Virginia on October 26, 1803.

Bibliography: Katherine Cox Gottschalk and John Bailey Calvert Nicklin, "The Pendleton Family," *Virginia Magazine of History and Biography*, XXXIX-XLIV (July 1931-October 1936); Robert Leroy Hillrup, *The Life and Times of Edmund Pendleton* (Chapel Hill,1939); David J. Mays, *Edmund Pendleton, 1721-1803: A Biography* (Cambridge, 1952); David J. Mays, *The Letters and Papers of Edmund Pendleton, 1734-1803*, 2 vols. (Charlottesville, 1967). *DAB*.

HENRY, Patrick, 1776-1779, 1784-1786

Born on May 29, 1736 near Hanover, Virginia, the son of John and Sarah (Winston) Syme Henry. Brother of William, Jane, Sarah, Susannah, Mary, Anne, Elizabeth, Lucy and two others. Married in 1754 to Sarah Shelton, by whom he was the father of Martha, John, William, Edward, Anne and Elizabeth; following his first wife's death early in 1775, remarried on October 9, 1777 to Dorothea Dandridge; father of Dorothea Spotswood, Martha Catharina, Sarah Butler, Patrick, Fayette, Alexander Spotswood, Nathaniel, Edward Winston, John and two others by his second wife.

Privately educated as a young man. Became a storekeeper and, after failing both at that occupation and in a brief attempt at farming, began to study law; admitted to the bar in 1760, a profession which enabled him to achieve widespread fame when he argued the case for the defense in the "Parson's Cause" of 1763-64. Admitted to the Virginia House of Burgesses in May 1765, and represented Louisa County until 1768; acted as a member of the Burgesses from Hanover County between 1769 and 1775. Emerged as one of the colony's most prominent opponents of British policy during the 1760's and 1770's, especially after he introduced his Stamp Act resolutions late in May of 1765. Attended the First Continental Congress in 1774; delivered his famous "Give Me Liberty" speech in March 1775; elected to the Second Continental Congress in March 1775, but postponed his trip to Philadelphia in order to lead a group of volunteers from Hanover County, who sought the restoration of gunpowder seized by Virginia's governor. Attended the Second Continental Congress from mid-May to early August of 1775. Served as Colonel of the First Regiment and Commander of Virginia's regular forces from August 1775 to February 1776. Acted as a delegate to the Virginia convention which met from May to July of 1776, and passed a resolution instructing its congressional representatives to propose the adoption of a declaration of independence. Elected Governor of Virginia in June 1776 and took office, under the state's first constitution, in July of that year; re-elected in May 1777 and May 1778, each time without opposition; again named chief executive in November 1784, winning re-election in November 1785. Also served as a member of the Virginia Legislature from May 1780 to November 1784.

Henry's first period in the governor's chair was dominated by military considerations, as his administration endeavored to support the efforts of Washington's Continental Army. Based on the quotas of men and supplies required from Virginia by Congress, Henry appears to have enjoyed considerable success as a wartime leader. During his post-war tenure Henry presided over a state which, besides suffering from widespread economic distress, had become the scene of a heated dispute over the role of religion in public life. This controversy was finally resolved in 1786 with the passage of Jefferson's bill of religious freedom.

Following his gubernatorial career, Henry served in the State Legislature from 1787 to 1791, where he became an outspoken opponent of the proposed Federal Constitution. Toward the end of his life, however, he adopted a more conciliatory view, especially when the Bill of Rights was ratified in December 1791. Henry died at "Red Hill," his estate in Charlotte County, Virginia, on June 6, 1799, after declining appointments as secretary of state in 1795 and chief justice in 1796.

Bibliography: William Wirt, *Sketches of the Life and Character of Patrick Henry* (Philadelphia, 1817); Moses Coit Tyler, *Patrick Henry* (Boston, 1887); William W. Henry, *Patrick Henry: Life, Correspondence and Speeches*, 3 vols. (New York, 1891); George Morgan, *The True Patrick Henry* (Philadelphia and London, 1907); H. R. McIlwaine, gen. ed., *Official Letters of the Governors of the State of Virginia,* vol. I: *The Letters of Patrick Henry* (Richmond, 1926); Charles Leroy Anger, "Patrick Henry: Practical Politician," unpub. Ph.D. diss., University of Virginia, 1940; Robert D. Meade, *Patrick Henry*, 2 vols. (Philadelphia and New York, 1957-69); Eldon Glasco Bowman, "Patrick Henry's Political Philosophy," unpub. Ph.D. diss., Claremont, California Graduate School, 1961; George F. Willison, *Patrick Henry and His World* (Garden City, N.Y., 1969); Harrison M. Ethridge, "Governor Patrick Henry and the Reorganization of the Virginia Militia, 1784-1786," *Virginia Magazine of History and Biography*, 85 (October 1977), 427-39. *DAB*.

JEFFERSON, Thomas, 1779-1781

Born on April 2, 1743 at "Shadwell" in present-day Albemarle County, Virginia, the eldest son of Peter and Jane (Randolph) Jefferson. Brother of Jane, Mary, Elizabeth, Martha, Peter Field (died in infancy), Lucy, Anna Scott, Randolph and an unnamed male who died in infancy. Married on January 1, 1772 to Martha (Wayles) Skelton, by whom he was the father of Martha, Jane Randolph (died in infancy), Mary, Lucy Elizabeth (died in infancy), Lucy Elizabeth (died young) and an unnamed son who died in infancy.

Attended a school run by the Reverend James Maury, and entered the College of William and Mary in 1760, where he remained for two years. Also studied law under George Wythe for five years; admitted to the Virginia bar in 1767. Elected to the Virginia House of Burgesses late in 1768, and served in that capacity, representing Albemarle County, from May 1769 to 1775. Became a leader in the opposition to British policy during the 1770's; acted as a delegate from Albemarle at two of the provincial conventions which met in Virginia in 1775. Represented Virginia at the Continental Congress from 1775 to 1776, where he wrote the draft of the document which eventually became the Declaration of Independence. Served in the Virginia House of Delegates from October 1776 until June of 1779,when he became Governor of the commonwealth; re-elected as chief executive in 1780.

By comparison with Jefferson's spectacular political career prior to 1779, his tenure as governor of Virginia proved to be frustrating and disappointing. Restricted by a constitution which gave him little authority, Jefferson could do little besides implement the decisions of the Assembly. Early in 1781 the problems he faced in attempting to raise men and supplies for the war effort were exacerbated by a British invasion of Virginia, which forced the commonwealth to transfer its capital from Richmond to Charlottesville. Within several months Virginia's government was in shambles, and on June 1, 1781 Jefferson turned over his shattered administration to William Fleming who, as the only available member of the Council, presided as acting governor until the accession of Thomas Nelson, Jr. later that month.

Jefferson's unhappy experience as a wartime governor caused him to shun politics for several years, but in June of 1783 he agreed to resume his seat in the Continental Congress. In 1784 he sailed for France as part of a commission charged with negotiating treaties of commerce and friendship with various European nations, and in 1785 he replaced Benjamin Franklin as Minister to France. For the next twenty-five years Jefferson continued to hold high public office, serving as Secretary of State (1790-1793), Vice President (1797-1801) and President (1801-1809). Following his retirement from public life, Jefferson founded the University of Virginia in 1819. He died at "Monticello," his Virginia estate, on July 4, 1826.

Bibliography: G. Lichtenstein, *Thomas Jefferson as War Governor* (Richmond, 1925); H. R. McIlwaine, gen. ed., *Official Letters of the Governors of the State of Virginia*, vol. II: *The Letters of Thomas Jefferson* (Richmond, 1928); Adolf F. Meisen, "Thomas Jefferson, War Governor of Virginia," unpub. Ph.D. diss., University of North Carolina, 1943; Dumas Malone, *Jefferson and His Time*, 5 vols. (Boston, 1948-74); Nathan Schachner, *Thomas Jefferson, A Biography* (New York, 1957); Frances L. Harrold, "Thomas Jefferson and the Commonwealth of Virginia: A Study in Constitutional Thought," unpub. Ph.D. diss., Bryn Mawr College, 1960; Fawn M. Brodie, *Thomas Jefferson: An Intimate History* (New York, 1974). *DAB*.

FLEMING, William, 1781

Born on February 18, 1729 in Jedburgh, Scotland; names of parents unknown. An Anglican. Married in 1763 to Anne Christian, by whom he was the father of John, William, Leonard Israel, Priscilla, Dorothy, Eliza and Anne.

Studied medicine at the University of Edinburgh, and served for a time as a surgeon in the Royal Navy. Immigrated to Virginia in 1755, arriving in Norfolk in August of that year. Participated in a number of military engagements during the French and Indian War, and rose to the rank of Captain in 1760. Chosen Vestryman of his parish in Augusta County, Virginia in November 1764, held that office until June 1769, and became Justice of the Peace for Botetourt County shortly after moving there in the autumn of 1769. Pursued a combined medical and military career during the 1770's, achieving the rank of Colonel. Represented Virginia in the Continental Congress in 1779. Later elected to the Virginia Council, and as President of that body served as Acting Governor of the state from June 1 to June 12, 1781.

Obviously, Fleming's period as interim chief executive was too brief to have any enduring impact on Virginia's political development. Indeed, with the state government in considerable disarray as a result of the British invasion of 1781, Fleming was chiefly occupied by the need to avert complete chaos. Although he managed to hold his "court" at the parish church in Staunton on June 7, some of the state's legislators fled several days later, in reaction to a false rumor that the British Colonel Banastre Tarleton was *en route* to the town. Nevertheless, by June 12 the legislators had recovered from this scare and returned to Staunton, where they chose General Thomas Nelson as Virginia's new governor.

Following his brief gubernatorial career, Fleming continued to take part in public affairs, especially by serving as an arbiter of conflicting land claims in Kentucky. He died at "Bellmont," his estate near Roanoke, Virginia, on August 5, 1795.

Bibliography: William Dana Hoyt, Jr., "Colonel William Fleming on the Virginia Frontier, 1755-1783," unpub. Ph.D. diss., Johns Hopkins University, 1940.

NELSON, Thomas, Jr., 1781

Born on December 26, 1738 in York County, Virginia, the eldest son of Acting Governor William and Elizabeth (Burwell) Nelson. Brother of five who reached maturity: Nathaniel, Hugh, Robert, William and Elizabeth. Married on July 29, 1762 to Lucy Grymes, by whom he was the father of William, Thomas, Philip, Francis, Hugh, Elizabeth, Mary, Lucy, Robert, Susanna, Judith and two others who died young.

Sent to England for his education in the summer of 1753; studied at Christ's College, Cambridge during his residence abroad, but did not take a degree. Returned to Virginia in 1761, and began to work for his father's mercantile firm. Represented York County in the Virginia House of Burgesses from 1761 to 1775, where he gradually took a more prominent role in his colony's opposition to British policy. Elected to represent Virginia at the Continental Congress in 1775, and served in that capacity almost continuously until the spring of 1777; signed the Declaration of Independence in July 1776; also attended Congress briefly in 1779. Acted as a member of the Virginia House of Delegates from June 1777 to June 1780, participating in that body's discussions whenever he was in the state. Awarded the military rank of Brigadier General in 1777, and commanded his state's militia in 1777, 1779 and 1780-81. Elected Governor of Virginia in June 1781, a position he held until his resignation in November of that year.

Although ill health forced him to resign after only five months, Nelson presided as his state's chief executive during an especially critical phase of the Revolution. When the Virginia Legislature decided to give him and the Council authority far surpassing the powers granted to his predecessors, Nelson used this expanded commission to prosecute the war more vigorously. He quickly introduced a policy of impressment as a means of obtaining supplies needed by the army, and implemented stern measures to counter Loyalist activities. By late summer of 1781, largely as a result of his controversial efforts, Continental troops in Virginia had embarked on a campaign which culminated in the surrender of Cornwallis at Yorktown that October.

While Nelson was elected to the Virginia House of Delegates on several occasions after his gubernatorial career, the combination of illness and preoccupation with his growing business losses kept him from taking a very active role in politics. Nelson died at "Montair," his plantation in Hanover County, Virginia, on January 4, 1789.

Bibliography: "Letters of Thomas Nelson, Jr.," Virginia Historical Society, *Publications*, n.s., no. 1 (1874); R. A. Brock, "The Nelson House, Yorktown, Virginia," *Magazine of American History*, VII (July 1881), 47-58; H. R. McIlwaine, gen. ed., *Official Letters of the Governors of the State of Virginia*, vol. III: *The Letters of Thomas Nelson and Benjamin Harrison* (Richmond, 1929); William H. Gaines, Jr., "Thomas Nelson, Jr.—Governor-at-Arms," *Virginia Cavalcade*, I (Autumn 1951), 40-43; Emory Gibbons Evans, "The Nelsons: A Biographical Study of a Virginia Family in the Eighteenth Century," unpub. Ph.D. diss., University of Virginia, 1957; Emory G. Evans, "The Rise and Decline of the Virginia Aristocracy in the Eighteenth Century: The Nelsons," in Darrett B. Rutman, ed., *The Old Dominion: Essays for Thomas Perkins Abernethy* (Charlottesville, 1964), 62-78; Charles E. Hatch, Jr., *The Nelson House and the Nelsons* (Washington, D.C., 1969); Emory G. Evans, *Thomas Nelson of Yorktown: Revolutionary Virginian* (Charlottesville, 1975). *DAB*.

JAMESON, David, 1781

Born in 1732 in St. Anne's Parish, Essex County, Virginia, the son of James and Margaret Jameson. Brother of Thomas and James. Married to Mildred Smith; apparently had no children.

Became a prominent merchant in Yorktown, Virginia; also acquired a reputation as a scientist and inventor, and in 1773 was acting as Treasurer of the Society for the Advancement of Useful Knowledge. Named to the Virginia Council in 1777, and served as Lieutenant Governor of the commonwealth between 1780 and 1781. In his capacity as lieutenant governor, presided as Acting Governor of Virginia from November 22 to November 30 of 1781, following the resignation of Governor Thomas Nelson, Jr.

Jameson's nine-day administration was simply that of a caretaker who conducted the ordinary business of government until the accession of Benjamin Harrison on December 1, 1781. A year after his brief tenure as Virginia's chief executive, Jameson left politics altogether, stepping down from his position on the Council. Nevertheless, he continued to take an interest in public affairs. In July of 1783, for example, he wrote a letter to a member of Virginia's delegation to the Continental Congress, requesting funds from that body to level the Yorktown earthworks, which had originally been constructed to repel invading troops during the Revolution.

Jameson died between May 21 and July 22 of 1793, probably in Yorktown. In a codicil to his will he emancipated two of his slaves, although he bequeathed another to Mrs. Mary Mennis.

Bibliography: E. O. Jameson, *The Jamesons in America* (Boston, 1901); Donald O. Dewey, ed., "...To Level the Works at York...: A Letter of David Jameson," *Virginia Magazine of History and Biography*, LXXI (April 1963), 150-52; K. B. Lawrence, "History of the Lawrence Family in England, Virginia and North Carolina..." (1964), typescript volume in Local History and Genealogy Division, New York Public Library.

HARRISON, Benjamin, 1781-1784

Born on April 5, 1726 at "Berkeley," Charles City County, Virginia, the son of Benjamin and Anne (Carter) Harrison. Brother of Carter Henry, Henry, Robert, Nathaniel, Charles, Elizabeth, Anne, Lucy and Hannah. Married to Elizabeth Bassett, by whom he was the father of Benjamin, Carter B., William Henry (who served as president of the United States in 1841), Elizabeth, Anna, Lucy and Sarah.

Studied at William and Mary College, but left without receiving a degree from that institution. Elected to the Virginia House of Burgesses in 1748, a position he held until 1775; also served as Speaker of that body on a number of occasions. Despite his early caution in opposing parliamentary measures during the 1760's, eventually became a leader of the resistance to British colonial policy. Named as a delegate to the First Continental Congress which met in September 1774, and continued to represent Virginia in Congress, except for a brief period, until 1778; signed the Declaration of Independence in 1776. Also chosen as a member of Virginia's newly-organized House of Delegates in 1776, an office he retained until his election as Governor of Virginia late in 1781; re-elected governor in 1782 and 1783.

Harrison's tenure as chief executive was marked by an easing of the legal restrictions which had been imposed on Loyalists during the Revolution. In the autumn of 1783, for example, the Assembly declared that all British sympathizers, except those who had actually fought against American troops, were free to return to their former homes in Virginia. Harrison also presided over the Virginia government when the commonwealth agreed to relinquish her claim to lands north and west of the Ohio River, a decision which paved the way for the organization of that extensive territory.

Following his gubernatorial service Harrison returned to the Virginia House of Delegates, where he remained until his death on April 24, 1791. Despite his opposition to certain provisions in the proposed Federal Constitution, Harrison later endorsed that document when his state voted in favor of ratification.

Bibliography: Ella B. Washington, "The Harrisons in History," *Magazine of American History*, XXI (May 1889), 403-09; Charles P. Keith, *The Ancestry of Benjamin Harrison, President of the United States of America, 1889-1893* (Philadelphia, 1893); W. G. Stanard, "Harrison of James River," *Virginia Magazine of History and Biography*, XXX-XLI (October 1922-April 1933), especially vol. XXXII (July 1924), 299-304; R. C. Ballard Thruston, "Birth of Benjamin Harrison, the Signer," *Virginia Magazine of History and Biography*, XXXVII (January 1929), 74-77; H. R. McIlwaine, gen. ed., *Official Letters of the Governors of the State of Virginia*, vol. III: *The Letters of Thomas Nelson and Benjamin Harrison* (Richmond, 1929); Clifford Dowdey, *The Great Plantation: A Profile of Berkeley Hundred and Plantation Virginia from Jamestown to Appomattox* (New York and Toronto, 1957). *DAB*.

RANDOLPH, Edmund, 1786-1788

Born on August 10, 1953 at "Tazewell Hall" near Williamsburg, Virginia, the son of John and Ariana (Jenings) Randolph. Brother of Ariana and Susanna Beverley. Married on August 29, 1776 to Elizabeth Nicholas, by whom he was the father of Peyton (acting governor of Virginia from 1811 to 1812), Susan, John (died young), Edmonia and Lucy.

Attended the College of William and Mary from 1770 to 1771, but left that institution without receiving a degree; also studied law with his father. Appointed Aide-de-Camp to General Washington in August 1775. Returned to Virginia a short time later, where he served as a member of the convention which adopted the state's first constitution. Named Attorney General of Virginia in May 1776, and Mayor of Williamsburg in November of the same year. Elected to the Continental Congress in June 1779, a position which he held, except for an interval from December 1779 to June 1781, until 1782. Chosen Governor of Virginia early in November 1786, and took the oath of office about three weeks later; continued to serve as chief executive until December of 1788.

The proposed Federal Constitution was the dominant political issue during Randolph's tenure as governor, and from the beginning he took a strong interest in the debate. Indeed, despite his burden of state business, Randolph attended the Philadelphia Constitutional Convention from May to September of 1787, where he put forth his home state's "Virginia Plan." Although he at first refused to endorse the finished Constitution, Randolph had changed his mind when the Virginia ratifying convention met in June 1788, and during that body's deliberations, he joined forces with James Madison and other state leaders who urged acceptance of the document.

Randolph relinquished his position as governor in December 1788, taking a seat in the Virginia Assembly. Late in 1789 President Washington offered him a Cabinet post as Attorney General, an office which he held from early 1790 until his appointment as Secretary of State in January 1794. Stepping down from the position of secretary of state in August 1795, Randolph soon returned to Virginia, and spent the rest of his life as a lawyer, author and political observer. Randolph died while visiting at the home of Nathaniel Burwell in Frederick County, Virginia on September 12, 1813.

Bibliography: M. D. Conway, *Omitted Chapters of History, Disclosed in the Life and Papers of Edmund Randolph* (New York, 1888); D. R. Anderson, "Edmund Randolph," in S. F. Bemis, *The American Secretaries of State and Their Diplomacy*, vol. II (1927); "Edmund Randolph's Essay on the Revolutionary History of Virginia (1774-1782)," *Virginia Magazine of History and Biography*, XLIII (1935), 113-38, 209-32, 294-315; XLIV (1936), 35-50, 105-15, 223-31, 312-22; XLV (1937), 46-47; Hamilton J. Eckenrode, *The Randolphs: The Story of a Virginia Family* (New York, 1946); Irving Brant, "Edmund Randolph, 'Not Guilty'," *William and Mary Quarterly*, 3rd ser., vol. VII (1950), 179-98; Emory M. Thomas, "Edmund Randolph," *Virginia Cavalcade*, XVIII (Spring 1969), 5-12; Charles F. Hobson, "The Early Career of Edmund Randolph, 1753-1789," unpub. Ph.D. diss., Emory University, 1971; Jonathan Daniels, *The Randolphs of Virginia* (Garden City, N.Y., 1972); John J. Reardon, *Edmund Randolph: A Biography* (New York and London, 1975). *See also* W. P. Palmer, ed., *Calendar of Virginia State Papers*, vol. IV (1884) for source material on Randolph's governorship. *DAB*.

RANDOLPH, Beverley, 1788-1791

Born in 1754 at "Chatsworth" in Henrico County, Virginia, the son of Peter, a surveyor general of customs, and Lucy (Bolling) Randolph. Brother of William, Robert and Anne. Married in 1775 to Martha Cocke, by whom he was the father of Lucy.

Studied at the College of William and Mary, graduating from that institution in 1771. Played a prominent military role in the Revolution, serving as a Colonel of the Virginia militia from 1776 to 1779, and as Commander of a regiment in General Robert Lawson's Brigade. Acted as a member of the Virginia House of Delegates from 1777 to 1781; also served as President of the Virginia Council and Lieutenant Governor in 1787. First elected Governor of Virginia by the State Legislature in 1788, a position to which he was re-elected in 1789 and 1790; served as chief executive from December 1788 to December 1791.

Although Virginia had ratified the Constitution before Randolph took office, the question of a permanent site for the new federal capital remained unsettled. During Randolph's administration, however, the Virginia Legislature matched Maryland's gift to the nation by ceding that part of its territory which later would become the District of Columbia. In December of 1789 the Virginia Assembly reached a legislative decision of perhaps even greater significance, when it authorized residents of the District of Kentucky, who had formerly been under Virginia's jurisdiction, to call a convention which would consider whether the District should seek separate admission to the federal union. Speculation in western lands also became a major concern of many investors during these years, with men such as David Ross seeking to win Randolph's endorsement of the Virginia Yazoo Company.

Since he had served the limit of three successive terms as provided by the State Constitution of 1776, Randolph was ineligible to compete for the governor's chair in 1791. While he did act for a time during the 1790's as an Indian Commissioner, Randolph eventually retired to "Green Creek," his estate in Cumberland County, Virginia, where he died in February 1797. Randolph was buried on his estate.

Bibliography: Hamilton J. Eckenrode, *The Randolphs: The Story of a Virginia Family* (New York, 1946); Jonathan Daniels, *The Randolphs of Virginia* (Garden City, N.Y., 1972).

INDEX

C

E

F

G

H

M

N

O

P

Q

R

S

T

U

V

W

Y